Interconnection Networks

An Engineering Approach

IEEE Computer Society Press
Mohamed E. Fayad
Editor-in-Chief, Practices for Computer Science and Engineering

SELECTED TITLES

Distributed Objects: Methodologies for Customizing Operating Systems
Nayeem Islam

Software Engineering Risk Management
Dale Karolak

Digital Design and Modeling with VHDL and Synthesis
K.C. Chang

Industrial Strength Software: Effective Management Using Measurement
Lawrence Putnam and Ware Myers

Unified Objects: Object-Oriented Programming Using C++
Babak Sadr

Interconnection Networks: An Engineering Approach
José Duato, Sudhakar Yalamanchili, and Lionel Ni

Meeting Deadlines in Real-Time Systems: The Rate Monotonic Analysis
Daniel Roy and Loic Briand

Executive Briefings

Controlling Software Development
Lawrence Putnam and Ware Myers

Interconnection Networks

An Engineering Approach

José Duato
Sudhakar Yalamanchili
Lionel Ni

IEEE
COMPUTER SOCIETY

Los Alamitos, California

Washington • Brussels • Tokyo

Library of Congress Cataloging-in-Publication Data

Duato, José
    Interconnection networks: an engineering approach / José Duato, Sudhakar
Yalamanchili, Lionel Ni.
       p.   cm.
    Includes bibliographical references.
    ISBN 0-8186-7800-3
    1. Computer networks.   2. Multiprocessors.   I. Yalamanchili.
II. Ni, Lionel M. III. Title.
TK5105.5.D88   1997
004.6—dc21

                                    97-20502
                                        CIP

IEEE Computer Society Press Order Number BP07800
Library of Congress Number 97-20502
ISBN 0-8186-7800-3

Additional copies may be ordered from:

IEEE Computer Society Press	IEEE Service Center	IEEE Computer Society	IEEE Computer Society
Customer Service Center	445 Hoes Lane	13, Avenue de l'Aquilon	Ooshima Building
10662 Los Vaqueros Circle	P.O. Box 1331	B-1200 Brussels	2-19-1 Minami-Aoyama
P.O. Box 3014	Piscataway, NJ 08855-1331	BELGIUM	Minato-ku, Tokyo 107
Los Alamitos, CA 90720-1314	Tel: +1-908-981-1393	Tel: +32-2-770-2198	JAPAN
Tel: +1-714-821-8380	Fax: +1-908-981-9667	Fax: +32-2-770-8505	Tel: +81-3-3408-3118
Fax: +1-714-821-4641	mis.custserv@computer.org	euro.ofc@computer.org	Fax: +81-3-3408-3553
Email: cs.books@computer.org			tokyo.ofc@computer.org

Editor-in-Chief: Mohamed Fayad
Publisher: Matt Loeb
Acquisitions Editor: Bill Sanders
Developmental Editor: Cheryl Baltes
Advertising/Promotions: Tom Fink
Production Editor: Lisa O'Conner
Cover Artist: John Marshall

About the cover: *Interconnection Networks* by John Marshall, oil on canvass, 1997, is based on a concept by José Duato. The painting includes symbols representing important elements in the field. To find out more about the symbols in the painting, visit the book's website at http://computer.org/books.

Printed in the United States of America

To Josep, Albert, and Joana

To Sunil, Chitra and Padma

To Ching, Wayland, and Elaine

Peace comes within the source of the men, when they realize the wonders of the Universe, when they realize that it is really everywhere, and it is within each of us.

— In the beginning (Swahili song), Beautiful World

Foreword

The performance of most digital systems today is limited by their communication or interconnection, not by their logic or memory. In a high-end system today, most of the power is used to drive wires and most of the clock cycle is spent on wire delay, not gate delay. As technology improves, memories and processors become small, fast, and inexpensive. The speed of light, however, remains unchanged. The pin density and wiring density that govern interconnections between system components are scaling at a slower rate than the components themselves. Also, the frequency of communication between components is lagging far beyond the clock rates of modern processors. These factors combine to make interconnection the key factor in the success of future digital systems.

As designers strive to make more efficient use of scarce interconnection bandwidth, interconnection networks are emerging as a nearly universal solution to the system-level communication problems for modern digital systems. Originally developed for the demanding communication requirements of multicomputers, interconnection networks are beginning to replace buses as the standard system-level interconnection. They are also replacing dedicated wiring in special-purpose systems as designers discover that routing packets is both faster and more economical than routing wires.

Interconnection networks have a long history. Circuit switched networks have long been used in telephony. The 1950s saw many proposals for interconnecting computers and cellular automata, but few prototypes. These came in the 1960s. Solomon in 1962 was the first of a long line of mesh-connected, bit-serial multicomputers. Staran with its flip network, C.mmp with a crossbar, and Illiac-IV with a wider 2-D mesh followed in the early 1970s. This period also saw several indirect networks used in vector and array processors to connect multiple processors to multiple memory banks. To address this problem the academic community developed several variants of multistage interconnection networks. The BBN Butterfly in 1982 was one of the first multiprocessors to use an indirect network. The binary n-cube or hypercube network was proposed in 1978 and first implemented in the Caltech Cosmic Cube in 1981. In the early 1980s, the academic community focused on mathematical properties of these networks and became increasingly separated from the practical problems of interconnecting real systems.

The last decade has been a golden-age for interconnection network research. Driven by the demanding communication problems of multicomputers and enabled by the ability to construct single-chip VLSI routers, the research community has made a series of breakthroughs that have revolutionized communication in digital systems. The Torus Routing Chip, in 1985, was one of the first steps along this path. The first of a series of single-chip routing components, it introduced wormhole routing and the use of virtual channels for deadlock avoidance. This chip, and others like it, laid the framework for analysis of routing, flow-control, deadlock, and livelock issues in modern direct networks. A flurry of research followed with new theories of deadlock and livelock, new adaptive routing algorithms, new methods for performance analysis, new approaches to collective communication, and new network architectures arriving on a regular basis. By the early 1990s, low-dimensional direct networks based on these concepts had largely replaced the indirect networks of the 1970s and the hypercubes of the 1980s and could be found in machines from Cray, Intel, Mercury, and others.

The applicability of interconnection networks to the general communication problem in digital systems was clear by 1995 with the appearance of Myrinet. These point-to-point networks were the technology of choice to replace buses which were running into a performance ceiling due to electrical limits. As evidenced by their use in the barrier network in the Cray T3E, they also represented an economical alternative to dedicated wiring. However, one barrier remained to the widespread use of interconnection network technology. The information on the design and analysis of these networks was not readily available to practicing engineers and designers. Descriptions of the technology were scattered across hundreds of conference papers and journal articles with overlapping treatment and often inconsistent notation.

This book, for the first time, makes the technology of interconnection networks accessible to the engineering student and the practicing engineer. It gives a comprehensive treatment of interconnection networks from topology, through routing and flow control, to a discussion of the software layer. The authors of the book are three key members of the research community and are responsible for developing much of the technology described. Their unique knowledge and rare insight into the material make for a technically rich treatment of the material that brings together the best of many research papers and fills in the gaps by putting the work in context.

This book improves upon the original research papers in several ways. It presents the material in a logical order, as opposed to the chronological order of the original papers. The text eliminates overlap between related papers, introduces a consistent notation, and fills in gaps. Perhaps most importantly, the book places each piece of work in context painting a "big picture" of interconnection network technology throughout the text. Finally, unlike many research papers, the presentation is at a level appropriate for a first-year engineering graduate student or a practicing engineer. By demystifying interconnection networks and making the technology accessible and available for wide application, this book will empower a generation of digital designers.

I trust that you will find this book as enjoyable and insightful as I have.

William J. Dally
Cambridge, MA
June 1997

Preface

Interconnection networks are becoming increasingly pervasive in many different applications, with the operational costs and characteristics of these networks considerably depending on the application. For some applications, interconnection networks have been studied in depth for decades. This is the case for telephone networks, computer networks (telecommunications), and backplane buses. The design and operation of these networks are covered in many excellent books. However, in the last 10 years we have seen a rapid evolution of the interconnection network technology that is currently being infused into a new generation of multiprocessor systems. The technology is mature enough to find its way into commercial products, while constantly presenting new avenues for growth and application. This is the case for the interconnection networks used in multicomputers and distributed shared-memory multiprocessors. At the current time, the basic design issues governing this new generation of multiprocessor network technology are diffused over a large number of technical papers. This book is an attempt to present a coherent description of this technology in a form that emphasizes the engineering aspects of their construction and use.

The lack of standards and the need for very high performance and reliability have been primarily responsible for pushing the development of interconnection networks for multicomputers. This technology was transferred to distributed shared-memory multiprocessors. More recently, this network technology began to be transferred to local area networks (LANs). Also, it has been proposed as a replacement for backplane buses, creating the concept of system area networks. Hence, the advances in interconnection networks for multicomputers are becoming the basis for the development of interconnection networks for other architectures and environments. Therefore, there is a need for formally stating the basic concepts, the alternative design choices, and the design tradeoffs for most of those networks. In this book, we address this challenge and present in an structured way the basic underlying concepts of most interconnection networks, and representative solutions that have currently been implemented or proposed in the literature.

Style of the Book

The literature on routing algorithms and architectures for multiprocessors is extensive. It is not our intent to serve as a resource for a comprehensive review of this area, although we hope that the bibliography will serve as a good starting point for the interested reader. With the fast pace of development in this area, any such attempt would have a rather short lifetime. Rather we hope to bring together the basic issues and results, and present them from a practical perspective. We hope such a presentation will have a more lasting value. As a result, selections from the literature for inclusion have more been guided by the nature of the problems they address, and the authors' familiarity with the work. We hope to be as comprehensive as possible in the treatment of fundamental issues rather than extent.

This book follows an engineering approach. It only considers those issues that should be taken into account by the designer. However, for each of those issues, we present a broad set of solutions proposed in the literature. Most of these solutions have been proposed very recently (1991–1996). These solutions are described and compared in an informal but rigorous way. We explicitly avoided including complex mathematical descriptions, making the text clear and easier to understand. The reader can certainly find the detailed mathematical treatment in the associated journal and conference papers. We have striven to ensure that the vast majority of material is from refereed journal and conference proceedings, presented from an engineering perspective. However, descriptions are precise. Moreover, we define some new concepts and structure the knowledge on interconnection networks. A considerable effort has been made to establish new and more accurate classifications for different issues (topologies, switching techniques, routing algorithms, problems that prevent message delivery, etc). Also, we introduce new views that make concepts easier to understand, like the unified view of direct and indirect networks, the unified theory of deadlock avoidance and recovery, etc. In addition to structuring the knowledge on interconnection networks, this book also describes several recently proposed routers. Also, it presents very detailed performance evaluation results.

Intended Audience

This book is intended to be used by engineers, network designers, faculty, and students. A considerable effort was made to select the material in this book and structure the organization and presentation in a manner that would be useful to all of these very different communities. For engineers, this book provides an overall view of what we feel are the most important issues concerning interconnection networks. Descriptions rely on concepts rather than detailed design specifications and as a result are easy to understand even for people who have had relatively little prior exposure to computer architecture and multiprocessor interconnection networks. For network designers, this book addresses the main issues facing the design of interconnection networks. All the chapters have been written with an engineering approach in mind. Moreover, a section on engineering issues at the end of most chapters focuses on the practical aspects of the issues described in the chapter. Designers will find the description of routers in Chapter 7 and the performance results in Chapter 9 particularly useful. Those issues have been grouped into separate chapters for easier access.

For students, this book provides thorough classifications, clear descriptions, accurate definitions and unified views, thus structuring the knowledge on interconnection networks. Most of those classifications, definitions, and unified views are new and have not been previously published. The frequent figures contribute to improved understanding of concepts while detailed descriptions of many routing algorithms provide more accurate descriptions. The book also provides numerous examples throughout the text, helping students to understand the concepts, mechanisms, and algorithms explained in the book. A set of solved and unsolved exercises complement most chapters. Finally, a section on commented references provides pointers to more than 300 papers for further reading. For faculty, this book arranges material on interconnection networks in several well-defined chapters, making it easy to design quarter or semester system courses. Liberal use of examples and figures provides a convenient way to explain the main issues. We plan to make our view graphs and network simulators available via the web site whose address is indicated in the back cover, thus considerably simplifying the task of teaching courses on interconnection networks and organizing laboratory classes. Contributions from people using the book will also be made available. The web site will also serve as a forum for discussion and exchange of ideas for interconnection networks.

Organization of the Book

The book is organized to serve as a reference as well as a source of learning. Therefore each chapter is self-contained in many respects.

Chapter 1: Introduction. The introductory chapter provides a presentation of the various classes of interconnection networks and seeks to present them in the context of recent advances in engineering high-performance interconnection networks.

Chapter 2: Message Switching Layer. This chapter describes the components that comprise the switching layer, including flow-control protocols and buffering mechanisms that have been proposed in recent years. The major mechanisms employed in all currently available routers are covered.

Chapter 3: Deadlock, Livelock, and Starvation. This chapter is the heart of the basic issues covered in this book. Descriptions are provided for developing deadlock-free routing protocols and ensuring livelock-free routing. The emphasis is on constructive principles rather than formal proofs.

Chapter 4: Routing Algorithms. This chapter presents a taxonomy of routing protocols and descriptions of representative routing algorithms in each class. Methodologies are presented for constructing deadlock-free routing algorithms for different switching techniques.

Chapter 5: Collective Communication Support. Modern algorithms for collective communication are described that exploit the properties of pipelined networks. Hardware and software support for broadcast, multicast, barrier synchronization, and other collective communication operations is described.

Chapter 6: Fault-Tolerant Routing. As parallel computing architectures grow in size and find their way into mission critical applications, the need for robust and reliable communication grows. Chapter 6 covers the current generation of fault-tolerant routing algorithms. Particular attention is paid to paradigms, fault models, and network features in support of such routing algorithms.

Chapter 7: Network Architectures. Optimizing the design of networks is a process of optimizing performance in the presence of physical constraints such as wiring density, pin-out, and chip area. This chapter covers models for optimizing the network topology as well as the design of router architectures to date.

Chapter 8: Messaging Layer Software. As "time on the wire" continues to drop, the software overheads start becoming an increasingly large portion of the overall message latency. This chapter covers the issues facing the design of the software messaging layer, and the implementation of two current lightweight message layers: active messages and fast messages. A brief introduction and pointers to the Message Passing Interface (MPI) standard are also provided as an example of a user-level application programming interface.

Chapter 9: Performance Evaluation. Accurate and reliable estimates of the network performance are crucial in developing and assessing design approaches. This chapter takes a detailed walk through evaluation of routing algorithms, network design parameters, and switching techniques. Network interfaces and support for collective communication and fault tolerance are evaluated as well. Emphasis is placed in evaluation techniques and interpretation of simulation results.

Two appendices and a list of references complete the book. The first appendix contains a formal version of the theory of deadlock avoidance described in Chapter 3. The second appendix lists the acronyms used in this book.

Course Organization and Instructional Materials

This text has been used in an advanced graduate course on Multiprocessor Interconnection Networks taught in a 10-week quarter. For such quarter-long courses recommended coverage is Chapters 1, 2, 3, 4, 7, 8, and the corresponding part of Chapter 9. Chapters 5 and 6 represent specialized areas that build on the remaining material. These two chapters can easily be covered in a traditional semester course, possibly augmented with recent papers in the last week or two to further the engineering aspect of the book.

A variety of course related material is available for instructors via web page for the text from the IEEE Computer Society Press web site at the address indicated in the back cover. This available material includes the following.

- A complete set of class notes that can be used as view graphs for class lectures.

- Solutions to the exercises in the text. This is available for instructors only.

- Java-based network simulator that can be used by students and instructors to generate an intuition about the behavior of the networks. The simulator can be invoked from this site.

Acknowledgments

Trying to selectively integrate as much material as we have attempted to do would not have been feasible without the generous support of many of our colleagues. We would like to thank all those people who contributed to this effort. First of all, we thank Dr. P. López, who contributed most of the performance plots in Chapter 9. He ran the simulations and plotted the performance results presented in Sections 9.3 through 9.10. Some of those plots were prepared for his Ph.D. dissertation [218] but many other were specially developed for this book. We gratefully acknowledge Dr. T. M. Pinkston for reviewing several chapters, rewriting some sections and providing two new sections, including figures and performance plots. We also thank Dr. D. K. Panda for reviewing Chapter 5 and supplying some figures in Chapters 5 and 7 as well as the performance plots in Sections 9.11.3 through 9.11.6. Also, we thank Dr. J. Miguel, Dr. R. Beivide, Dr. A. Arruabarrena, and Dr. J. A. Gregorio for supplying some of the performance results in Section 9.12. We gratefully acknowledge the time taken by Dr. K. Bolding and Dr. C. Stunkel in discussing details of their work, and Dr. S. Scott, Dr. M. Galles, and Dr. J. Carbonaro for providing advance copies of papers describing state of the art advances so that the material could be included in this text. We hope we have accurately described their excellent work. We are also grateful to the Ohio State Supercomputing Center for allowing us to use their MPI example. We would also like to thank Dr. W. J. Dally for writing an excellent foreword for this book. And last but not least, we would like to thank Mr. V. Garg, Mr. J. M. Martínez and Mr. J. Martínez for reading early drafts of some chapters and provide useful suggestions.

This book would not have been possible without the indulgence and infinite patience of our families during what often appeared to be an overwhelming task. They graciously accommodated the lost time during evenings, weekends, and vacations. As a small measure of our appreciation, we dedicate this book to them.

Contents

Chapter 1

Introduction

Interconnection networks are currently being used for many different applications, ranging from internal buses in very large-scale integration (VLSI) circuits to wide area computer networks. Among others, these applications include backplane buses and system area networks, telephone switches, internal networks for asynchronous transfer mode (ATM) switches, processor/memory interconnects for vector supercomputers, interconnection networks for multicomputers and distributed shared-memory multiprocessors, clusters of workstations, local area networks, metropolitan area networks, wide area computer networks, and networks for industrial applications. Additionally, the number of applications requiring interconnection networks is continuously growing. For example, an integral control system for a car requires a network connecting several microprocessors and devices.

The characteristics and cost of these networks considerably depend on the application. There are no general solutions. For some applications, interconnection networks have been studied in depth for decades. This is the case for telephone networks, computer networks, and backplane buses. These networks are covered in many books. However, there are some other applications that have not been fully covered in the existing literature. This is the case for the interconnection networks used in multicomputers and distributed shared-memory multiprocessors.

The lack of standards and the need for very high performance and reliability pushed the development of interconnection networks for multicomputers. This technology was transferred to distributed shared-memory multiprocessors, improving the scalability of those machines. However, distributed shared-memory multiprocessors require an even higher network performance than multicomputers, pushing the development of interconnection networks even more. More recently, this network technology began to be transferred to local area networks (LANs). Also, it has been proposed as a replacement for backplane buses, creating the concept of system area network. Hence, the advances in interconnection networks for multicomputers are the basis for the development of interconnection networks for other architectures and environments. Therefore, there is a need for structuring the concepts and solutions for this kind of interconnection networks. Obviously, when this technology is transferred to another environment, new issues arise that have to be addressed.

Moreover, several of these networks are evolving very quickly, and the solutions proposed for different kinds of networks are overlapping. Thus, there is a need for formally stating the basic concepts, the alternative design choices, and the design trade-offs for most of those networks. In this book, we take that challenge and present in a structured way the basic underlying concepts of most interconnection networks, as well as the most interesting solutions currently implemented or proposed in the literature. As indicated above, the network technology developed for multicomputers has been transferred to other environments. Therefore, in this book we will mainly describe techniques

1

developed for multicomputer networks. Most of these techniques can also be applied to distributed shared-memory multiprocessors, and to local and system area networks. However, we will also describe techniques specifically developed for these environments.

1.1 Parallel Computing and Networks

The demand for even more computing power has never stopped. Although the performance of processors has doubled in approximately every three-year span from 1980 to 1996, the complexity of the software as well as the scale and solution quality of applications have continuously driven the development of even faster processors. A number of important problems have been identified in the areas of defense, aerospace, automotive applications, and science, whose solution requires tremendous amount of computational power. In order to solve these grand challenge problems, the goal has been to obtain computer systems capable of computing at the teraflops (10^{12} floating-point operations per second) level. Even the smallest of these problems requires gigaflops (10^9 floating-point operations per second) of performance for hours at a time. The largest problems require teraflops performance for more than a thousand hours at a time.

Parallel computers with multiple processors are opening the door to teraflops computing performance to meet the increasing demand of computational power. The demand includes more computing power, higher network and input/output (I/O) bandwidths, and more memory and storage capacity. Even for applications requiring a lower computing power, parallel computers can be a cost-effective solution. Processors are becoming very complex. As a consequence, processor design cost is growing so fast that only a few companies all over the world can afford to design a new processor. Moreover, design cost should be amortized by selling a very high number of units. Currently, personal computers and workstations dominate the computing market. Therefore, designing custom processors that boost the performance one order of magnitude is not cost-effective. Similarly, designing and manufacturing high-speed memories and disks is not cost-effective. The alternative choice consists of designing parallel computers from commodity components (processors, memories, disks, interconnects, etc.). In these parallel computers, several processors cooperate to solve a large problem. Memory bandwidth can be scaled with processor computing power by physically distributing memory components among processors. Also, redundant arrays of inexpensive disks (RAID) allow the implementation of high-capacity reliable parallel file systems meeting the performance requirements of parallel computers.

However, a parallel computer requires some kind of communication subsystems to interconnect processors, memories, disks and other peripherals. The specific requirements of these communication subsystems depend on the architecture of the parallel computer. The simplest solution consists of connecting processors to memories and disks as if there were a single processor, using system buses and I/O buses. Then, processors can be interconnected using the interfaces to local area networks. Unfortunately, commodity communication subsystems have been designed to meet a different set of requirements, i.e., those arising in computer networks. Although networks of workstations have been proposed as an inexpensive approach to build parallel computers, the communication subsystem becomes the bottleneck in most applications.

Therefore, designing high-performance interconnection networks becomes a critical issue to exploit the performance of parallel computers. Moreover, as the interconnection network is the only subsystem that cannot be efficiently implemented by using commodity components, its design becomes very critical. This issue motivated the writing of this book. Up to now, most manufacturers designed custom interconnection networks (nCUBE-2, nCUBE-3, Intel Paragon, Cray T3D, Cray T3E, Thinking Machines Corp. CM-5, NEC Cenju-3, IBM SP2). More recently, several high-

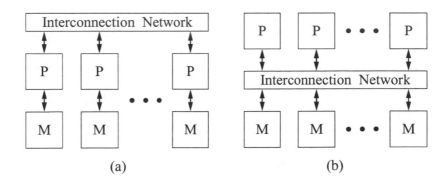

Figure 1.1. Schematic representation of parallel computers: (a) A multicomputer. (b) A UMA shared-memory multiprocessor. (M = memory; P = processor.)

performance switches have been developed (Autonet, Myrinet, ServerNet) and are being marketed. These switches are targeted to workstations and personal computers, offering the customer the possibility of building an inexpensive parallel computer by connecting cost-effective computers through high-performance switches. The main issues arising in the design of networks for both approaches are covered in this book.

1.2 Parallel Computer Architectures

In this section, we briefly introduce the most popular parallel computer architectures. This description will focus on the role of the interconnection network. A more detailed description is beyond the scope of this book.

The idea of using commodity components for the design of parallel computers led to the development of *distributed-memory multiprocessors*, or *multicomputers* in early 1980s. These parallel computers consist of a set of processors, each one connected to its own local memory. Processors communicate between them by passing messages through an interconnection network. Figure 1.1a shows a simple scheme for this architecture. The first commercial multicomputers utilized commodity components, including Ethernet controllers to implement communication between processors. Unfortunately, commodity communication subsystems were too slow, and the interconnection network became the bottleneck of those parallel computers. Several research efforts led to the development of interconnection networks that are several orders of magnitude faster than Ethernet networks. Most of the performance gain is due to architectural rather than technological improvements.

Programming multicomputers is not an easy task. The programmer has to take care of distributing code and data among the processors in an efficient way, invoking message-passing calls whenever some data are needed by other processors. On the other hand, *shared-memory multiprocessors* provide a single memory space to all the processors, simplifying the task of exchanging data among processors. Access to shared memory has been traditionally implemented by using an interconnection network between processors and memory (Figure 1.1b). This architecture is referred to as *uniform memory access* (UMA) architecture. It is not scalable because memory access time includes the latency of the interconnection network, and this latency increases with system size.

More recently, shared-memory multiprocessors followed some trends previously established for multicomputers. In particular, memory has been physically distributed among processors, therefore reducing the memory access time for local accesses and increasing scalability. These parallel computers are referred to as *distributed shared-memory multiprocessors* (DSM). Accesses to remote memory are performed through an interconnection network, very much like in multicomputers. The main difference between DSMs and multicomputers is that messages are initiated by memory accesses rather than by calling a system function. In order to reduce memory latency, each processor has several levels of cache memory, thus matching the speed of processors and memories. This architecture provides *nonuniform memory access* (NUMA) time. Indeed, most of the nonuniformity is due to the different access time between caches and main memories, rather than the different access time between local and remote memories. The main problem arising in DSMs is cache coherence. Several hardware and software cache coherence protocols have been proposed. These protocols produce additional traffic through the interconnection network.

The use of custom interconnects makes multicomputers and DSMs quite expensive. So, *networks of workstations* (NOW) have been proposed as an inexpensive approach to build parallel computers. NOWs take advantage of recent developments in LANs. In particular, the use of ATM switches has been proposed to implement NOWs. However, ATM switches are still expensive, which has motivated the development of high-performance switches, specifically designed to provide a cost-effective interconnect for workstations and personal computers.

Although there are many similarities between interconnection networks for multicomputers and DSMs, it is important to keep in mind that performance requirements may be very different. Messages are usually very short when DSMs are used. Additionally, network latency is important because memory access time depends on that latency. However, messages are typically longer and less frequent when using multicomputers. Usually the programmer is able to adjust the granularity of message communication in a multicomputer. On the other hand, interconnection networks for multicomputers and NOWs are mainly used for message passing. However, the geographical distribution of workstations usually imposes constraints on the way processors are connected. Also, individual processors may be connected to or disconnected from the network at any time, thus imposing additional design constraints.

1.3   Network Design Considerations

Interconnection networks play a major role in the performance of modern parallel computers. There are many factors that may affect the choice of an appropriate interconnection network for the underlying parallel computing platform. These factors include:

1. *Performance requirements.* Processes executing in different processors synchronize and communicate through the interconnection network. These operations are usually performed by explicit message passing or by accessing shared variables. Message *latency* is the time elapsed between the time a message is generated at its source node and the time the message is delivered at its destination node. Message latency directly affects processor idle time and memory access time to remote memory locations. Also, the network may *saturate* — it may be unable to deliver the flow of messages injected by the nodes, limiting the effective computing power of a parallel computer. The maximum amount of information delivered by the network per time unit defines the *throughput* of that network.

2. *Scalability.* A scalable architecture implies that as more processors are added, their memory bandwidth, I/O bandwidth, and network bandwidth should increase proportionally. Otherwise the components whose bandwidth does not scale may become a bottleneck for the rest of the system, decreasing the overall efficiency accordingly.

3. *Incremental expandability.* Customers are unlikely to purchase a parallel computer with a full set of processors and memories. As the budget permits, more processors and memories may be

added until a system's maximum configuration is reached. In some interconnection networks, the number of processors must be a power of 2, which makes them difficult to expand. In other cases, expandability is provided at the cost of wasting resources. For example, a network designed for a maximum size of 1,024 nodes may contain many unused communication links when the network is implemented with a smaller size. Interconnection networks should provide incremental expandability, allowing the addition of a small number of nodes while minimizing resource wasting.

4. *Partitionability.* Parallel computers are usually shared by several users at a time. In this case, it is desirable that the network traffic produced by each user does not affect the performance of other applications. This can be ensured if the network can be partitioned into smaller functional subsystems. Partitionability may also be required for security reasons.

5. *Simplicity.* Simple designs often lead to higher clock frequencies and may achieve higher performance. Additionally, customers appreciate networks that are easy to understand because it is easier to exploit their performance.

6. *Distance span.* This factor may lead to very different implementations. In multicomputers and DSMs, the network is assembled inside a few cabinets. The maximum distance between nodes is small. As a consequence, signals are usually transmitted using copper wires. These wires can be arranged regularly, reducing the computer size and wire length. In NOWs, links have very different lengths and some links may be very long, producing problems such as coupling, electromagnetic noise, and heavy link cables. The use of optical links solves these problems, equalizing the bandwidth of short and long links up to a much greater distance than when copper wire is used. Also, geographical constraints may impose the use of irregular connection patterns between nodes, making distributed control more difficult to implement.

7. *Physical constraints.* An interconnection network connects processors, memories, and/or I/O devices. It is desirable for a network to accommodate a large number of components while maintaining a low communication latency. As the number of components increases, the number of wires needed to interconnect them also increases. Packaging these components together usually requires meeting certain physical constraints, such as operating temperature control, wiring length limitation, and space limitation. Two major implementation problems in large networks are the arrangement of wires in a limited area, and the number of pins per chip (or board) dedicated to communication channels. In other words, the complexity of the connection is limited by the maximum wire density possible, and by the maximum pin count. The speed at which a machine can run is limited by the wire lengths, and the majority of the power consumed by the system is used to drive the wires. This is an important and challenging issue to be considered. Different engineering technologies for packaging, wiring, and maintenance should be considered.

8. *Reliability and repairability.* An interconnection network should be able to deliver information reliably. Interconnection networks can be designed for continuous operation in the presence of a limited number of faults. These networks are able to send messages through alternative paths when some faults are detected. In addition to reliability, interconnection networks should have a modular design, allowing hot upgrades and repairs. Nodes can also fail or be removed from the network. In particular, a node can be powered off in a network of workstations. Thus, NOWs usually require some reconfiguration algorithm for the automatic reconfiguration of the network when a node is powered on or off.

9. *Expected workloads.* Users of a general-purpose machine may have very different requirements. If the kind of applications that will be executed in the parallel computer are known in advance, it may be possible to extract some information on usual communication patterns, message sizes, network load, etc. That information can be used for the optimization of some design parameters. When it is not possible to get information on expected workloads, network design should be robust, i.e., design parameters should be selected in such a way that performance is good over a wide range of traffic conditions.

10. *Cost constraints.* Finally, it is obvious that the "best" network may be too expensive. Design decisions very often are trade-offs between cost and other design factors. Fortunately, cost is not always directly proportional to performance. Using commodity components whenever possible may considerably reduce the overall cost.

1.4   Classification of Interconnection Networks

Among other criteria, interconnection networks have been traditionally classified according to the operating mode (synchronous or asynchronous), and network control (centralized, decentralized, or distributed). Nowadays, multicomputers, multiprocessors, and NOWs dominate the parallel computing market. All of these architectures implement asynchronous networks with distributed control. Therefore, we will focus on other criteria that are currently more significant.

A classification scheme is shown in Figure 1.2 which categorizes the known interconnection networks into four major classes based primarily on network topology: shared-medium networks, direct networks, indirect networks, and hybrid networks. For each class, the figure shows a hierarchy of subclasses, also indicating some real implementations for most of them. This classification scheme is based on the classification proposed in [252], and it mainly focuses on networks that have been implemented. It is by no means complete as other new and innovative interconnection networks may emerge as technology further advances, such as mobile communication and optical interconnections.

In *shared-medium networks*, the transmission medium is shared by all communicating devices. An alternative to this approach consists of having point-to-point links directly connecting each communicating device to a (usually small) subset of other communicating devices in the network. In this case, any communication between nonneighboring devices requires transmitting the information through several intermediate devices. These networks are known as *direct networks*. Instead of directly connecting the communicating devices between them, *indirect networks* connect those devices by means of one or more switches. If several switches exist, they are connected between them using point-to-point links. In this case, any communication between communicating devices requires transmitting the information through one or more switches. Finally, *hybrid* approaches are possible. These network classes and the corresponding subclasses will be described in the following sections.

1.5   Shared-Medium Networks

The least complex interconnect structure is one in which the transmission medium is shared by all communicating devices. In such *shared-medium networks*, only one device is allowed to use the network at a time. Every device attached to the network has requester, driver, and receiver circuits to handle the passing of address and data. The network itself is usually passive, since the network itself does not generate messages.

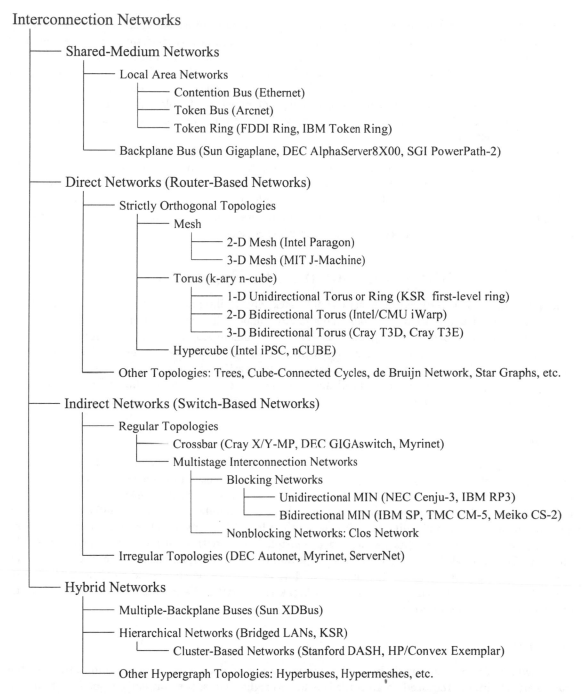

Interconnection Networks

Shared-Medium Networks

Local Area Networks

Contention Bus (Ethernet)

Token Bus (Arcnet)

Token Ring (FDDI Ring, IBM Token Ring)

Backplane Bus (Sun Gigaplane, DEC AlphaServer8X00, SGI PowerPath-2)

Direct Networks (Router-Based Networks)

Strictly Orthogonal Topologies

Mesh

2-D Mesh (Intel Paragon)

3-D Mesh (MIT J-Machine)

Torus (k-ary n-cube)

1-D Unidirectional Torus or Ring (KSR first-level ring)

2-D Bidirectional Torus (Intel/CMU iWarp)

3-D Bidirectional Torus (Cray T3D, Cray T3E)

Hypercube (Intel iPSC, nCUBE)

Other Topologies: Trees, Cube-Connected Cycles, de Bruijn Network, Star Graphs, etc.

Indirect Networks (Switch-Based Networks)

Regular Topologies

Crossbar (Cray X/Y-MP, DEC GIGAswitch, Myrinet)

Multistage Interconnection Networks

Blocking Networks

Unidirectional MIN (NEC Cenju-3, IBM RP3)

Bidirectional MIN (IBM SP, TMC CM-5, Meiko CS-2)

Nonblocking Networks: Clos Network

Irregular Topologies (DEC Autonet, Myrinet, ServerNet)

Hybrid Networks

Multiple-Backplane Buses (Sun XDBus)

Hierarchical Networks (Bridged LANs, KSR)

Cluster-Based Networks (Stanford DASH, HP/Convex Exemplar)

Other Hypergraph Topologies: Hyperbuses, Hypermeshes, etc.

Figure 1.2. Classification of interconnection networks. (1-D = one-dimensional; 2-D = two-dimensional; 3-D = three-dimensional; CMU = Carnegie Mellon University; DASH = Directory Architecture for Shared-Memory; DEC = Digital Equipment Corp.; FDDI = Fiber Distributed Data Interface; HP = Hewlett-Packard; KSR = Kendall Square Research; MIN = Multistage Interconnection Network; MIT = Massachusetts Institute of Technology; SGI = Silicon Graphics Inc.; TMC = Thinking Machines Corp.)

An important issue here is the *arbitration strategy* that determines the mastership of the shared-medium network to resolve network access conflicts. A unique characteristic of a shared medium is its ability to support atomic *broadcast* in which all devices on the medium can monitor network activities and receive the information transmitted on the shared medium. This property is important to efficiently support many applications requiring one-to-all or one-to-many communication services, such as barrier synchronization and snoopy cache coherence protocols. Due to limited network bandwidth, a single shared medium can only support limited number of devices before the medium becomes a bottleneck.

Shared-medium networks constitute a well established technology. Additionally, their limited bandwidth restricts their use in multiprocessors. So, these networks will not be covered in this book, but we will present a short introduction in the following sections. There are two major classes of shared-medium networks: local area networks, mainly used to construct computer networks that span physical distances no longer than a few kilometers, and backplane buses, mainly used for internal communication in uniprocessors and multiprocessors.

1.5.1   Shared-Medium Local Area Networks

High-speed LANs can be used as a networking backbone to interconnect computers to provide an integrated parallel and distributed computing environment. Physically, a shared-medium LAN uses copper wires or fiber optics in a bit-serial fashion as the transmission medium. The network topology is either a bus or a ring. Depending on the arbitration mechanism used, different LANs have been commercially available. For performance and implementation reasons, it is impractical to have a centralized control or to have some fixed access assignment to determine the bus master who can access the bus. Three major classes of LANs based on distributed control are described below.

Contention Bus

The most popular bus arbitration mechanism is to have all devices to compete for the exclusive access right of the bus. Due to the broadcast nature of the bus, all devices can monitor the state of the bus, such as idle, busy, and collision. Here the term "collision" means that two or more devices are using the bus at the same time and their data collided. When the collision is detected, the competing devices will quit transmission and try later. The most well-known contention-based LAN is Ethernet which adopts carrier-sense multiple access with collision detection (CSMA/CD) protocol. The bandwidth of Ethernet is 10 Mbps and the distance span is 250 meters (coaxial cable). As processors are getting faster, the number of devices that can be connected to Ethernet is limited to avoid the network bottleneck. In order to break the 10 Mbps bandwidth barrier, Fast Ethernet can provide 100 Mbps bandwidth.

Token Bus

One drawback of the contention bus is its nondeterministic nature as there is no guarantee of how much waiting time is required to gain the bus access right. Thus, the contention bus is not suitable to support real-time applications. To remove the nondeterministic behavior, an alternate approach involves passing a token among the network devices. The owner of the token has the right to access the bus. Upon completion of the transmission, the token is passed to the next device based on some scheduling discipline. By restricting the maximum token holding time, the upper bound that a device has to wait for the token can be guaranteed. Arcnet supports token bus with a bandwidth of 2.5 Mbps.

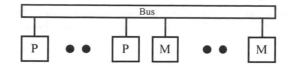

Figure 1.3. A single-bus network. (M = memory; P = processor.)

Token Ring

The idea of token ring is a natural extension of token bus as the passing of the token forms a ring structure. IBM token ring supports bandwidths of both 4 and 16 Mbps based on coaxial cable. Fiber Distributed Data Interface (FDDI) provides a bandwidth of 100 Mbps using fiber optics.

1.5.2   Shared-Medium Backplane Bus

A *backplane bus* is the simplest interconnection structure for bus-based parallel computers. It is commonly used to interconnect processor(s) and memory modules to provide UMA architecture. Figure 1.3 shows a single-bus network. A typical backplane bus usually has 50 − 300 wires and is physically realized by printed lines on a circuit board or by discrete (backplane) wiring. Additional costs are incurred by interface electronics, such as line drivers, receivers, and connectors.

There are three kinds of information in the backplane bus: data, address, and control signals. Control signals include bus request signal and request grant signal, among many others. In addition of the width of data lines, the maximum bus bandwidth that can be provided is dependent on the technology. The number of processors that can be put on a bus depends on many factors, such as processor speed, bus bandwidth, cache architecture, and program behavior.

Methods of Information Transfer

Both data and address information must be carried in the bus. In order to increase the bus bandwidth and provide a large address space, both data width and address bits have to be increased. Such an increase implies another increase in the bus complexity and cost. Some designs try to share address and data lines. For *multiplexed transfer*, address and data are sent alternatively. Hence, they can share the same physical lines and require less power and fewer chips. For *nonmultiplexed transfer*, address and data lines are separated. Thus, data transfer can be done faster.

In *synchronous bus* design, all devices are synchronized with a common clock. It requires less complicated logic and has been used in most existing buses. However, a synchronous bus is not easily upgradable. New faster processors are difficult to fit into a slow bus.

In *asynchronous buses*, all devices connected to the bus may have different speeds and their own clocks. They use a handshaking protocol to synchronize with each other. This provides independence for different technologies and allows slower and faster devices with different clock rates to operate together. This also implies buffering is needed, since slower devices cannot handle messages as fast as faster devices.

Bus Arbitration

In a single-bus network, several processors may attempt to use the bus simultaneously. To deal with this, a policy must be implemented that allocates the bus to the processors making such requests. For performance reasons, bus allocation must be carried out by hardware arbiters. Thus, in order to perform a memory access request, the processor has to exclusively own the bus and become the *bus master*. To become the bus master, each processor implements a *bus requester*, which is a collection of logic to request control of the data transfer bus. On gaining control, the requester notifies the requesting master.

Two alternative strategies are used to release the bus:

- Release-when-done: release the bus when data transfer is done

- Release-on-request: hold the bus until another processor requests it

Several different *bus arbitration algorithms* have been proposed, which can be classified into *centralized* or *distributed*. A centralized method has a central *bus arbiter*. When a processor wants to become the bus master, it sends out a bus request to the bus arbiter which then sends out a request grant signal to the requesting processor. A bus arbiter can be an encoder-decoder pair in hardware design. In distributed method, such as daisy chain method, there is no central bus arbiter. The bus request signals form a daisy chain. The mastership is released to the next device when data transfer is done.

Split Transaction Protocol

Most bus transactions involve request and response. This is the case for memory read operations. After a request is issued, it is desirable to have a fast response. If a fast response time is expected, the bus mastership is not released after sending the request, and data can be received soon. However, due to memory latency, the bus bandwidth is wasted while waiting for a response. In order to minimize the waste of bus bandwidth, the *split transaction protocol* has been used in many bus networks.

In this protocol, the bus mastership is released immediately after the request, and the memory has to gain mastership before it can send the data. Split transaction protocol has a better bus utilization but its control unit is much more complicated. *Buffering* is needed in order to save messages before the device can gain the bus mastership.

To support shared-variable communication, some atomic read/modify/write operations to memories are needed. With the split transaction protocol, the atomic read/modify/write can no longer be indivisible. One approach to solve this problem is to disallow bus release for those atomic operations.

Bus Examples

Several examples of buses and the main characteristics are listed below.

- Gigaplane used in Sun Ultra Enterprise X000 Server (ca. 1996): 2.6 Gbyte/s peak, 256 bits data, 42 bits address, split-transaction protocol, 83.8 MHz clock.

- DEC AlphaServer8X00, i.e., 8200 and 8400 (ca. 1995): 2.1 Gbyte/s, 256 bits data, 40 bits address, split-transaction protocol, 100 MHz clock (1 foot length).

- SGI PowerPath-2 (ca. 1993): 1.2 Gbyte/s, 256 bits data, 40 bits address, 6 bits control, split-transaction protocol, 47.5 MHz clock (1 foot length).

- HP9000 Multiprocessor Processor Memory Bus (ca. 1993): one Gbyte/s, 128 bits data, 64 bits address, 13 inches, pipelined-bus, 60 MHz clock.

1.6 Direct Networks

Scalability is an important issue in designing multiprocessor systems. Bus-based systems are not scalable as the bus becomes the bottleneck when more processors are added. The *direct network* or *point-to-point network* is a popular network architecture that scales well to a large number of processors. A direct network consists of a set of *nodes*, each one being directly connected to a (usually small) subset of other nodes in the network. Figures 1.5 through 1.7 show several direct networks. The corresponding interconnection patterns between nodes will be studied below. Each node is a programmable computer with its own processor, local memory, and other supporting devices. These nodes may have different functional capabilities. For example, the set of nodes may contain vector processors, graphics processors, and I/O processors. Figure 1.4 shows the architecture of a generic node. A common component of these nodes is a *router*, which handles message communication among nodes. For this reason, direct networks are also known as router-based networks. Each router has direct connections to the router of its neighbors. Usually, two neighboring nodes are connected by a pair of unidirectional channels in opposite directions. A bidirectional channel may also be used to connect two neighboring nodes. Although the function of a router can be performed by the local processor, dedicated routers have been used in high-performance multicomputers, allowing overlapped computation and communication within each node. As the number of nodes in the system increases, the total communication bandwidth, memory bandwidth, and processing capability of the system also increase. Thus, direct networks have been a popular interconnection architecture for constructing large-scale parallel computers.

Each router supports some number of input and output channels. *Internal* channels or *ports* connect the local processor/memory to the router. Although it is common to provide only one pair of internal channels, some systems use more internal channels in order to avoid a communication bottleneck between the local processor/memory and the router [39]. *External* channels are used for communication between routers. By connecting input channels of one node to the output channels of other nodes, the direct network is defined. Unless otherwise specified, the term "channel" will refer to an external channel. Two directly connected nodes are called *neighboring* or *adjacent* nodes. Usually, each node has a fixed number of input and output channels, and every input channel is paired with a corresponding output channel. Through the connections among these channels, there are many ways to interconnect these nodes. Obviously, every node in the network should be able to reach every other node.

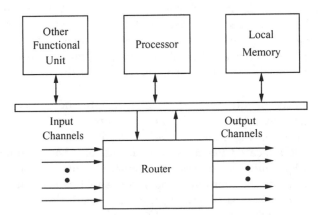

Figure 1.4. A generic node architecture.

1.6.1   Characterization of Direct Networks

Direct networks have been traditionally modeled by a graph $G(N, C)$, where the vertices of the graph N represent the set of processing nodes, and the edges of the graph C represent the set of communication channels. This is a very simple model that does not consider implementation issues. However, it allows the study of many interesting network properties. Depending on the properties under study, a bidirectional channel may be modeled either as an edge or as two arcs in opposite directions (two unidirectional channels). The latter is the case for deadlock avoidance in Chapter 3. Let us assume that a bidirectional channel is modeled as an edge. Some basic network properties can be defined from the graph representation:

- *Node degree:* Number of channels connecting that node to its neighbors.

- *Diameter:* The maximum distance between two nodes in the network.

- *Regularity:* A network is *regular* when all the nodes have the same degree.

- *Symmetry:* A network is *symmetric* when it looks alike from every node.

A direct network is mainly characterized by three factors: topology, routing, and switching. The *topology* defines how the nodes are interconnected by channels, and is usually modeled by a graph as indicated above. For direct networks, the ideal topology would connect every node to every other node. No message would even have to pass through an intermediate node before reaching its destination. This fully connected topology requires a router with N links (including the internal one) at each node for a network with N nodes. Therefore, the cost is prohibitive for networks of moderate to large size. Additionally, the number of physical connections of a node is limited by hardware constraints such as the number of available pins and the available wiring area. These engineering and scaling difficulties preclude the use of such fully connected networks even for small network sizes. As a consequence, many topologies have been proposed, trying to balance performance and some cost parameters. In these topologies, messages may have to traverse some intermediate nodes before reaching the destination node.

From the programmer's perspective, the unit of information exchange is the *message*. The size of messages may vary depending on the application. For efficient and fair use of network resources, a message is often divided into packets prior to transmission. A *packet* is the smallest unit of communication that contains the destination address and sequencing information, which are carried in the packet *header*. For topologies in which packets may have to traverse some intermediate nodes, the *routing* algorithm determines the path selected by a packet to reach its destination. At each intermediate node, the routing algorithm indicates the next channel to be used. That channel may be selected among a set of possible choices. If all the candidate channels are busy, the packet is blocked and cannot advance. Obviously, efficient routing is critical to the performance of interconnection networks.

When a message or packet header reaches an intermediate node, a *switching* mechanism determines how and when the router switch is set, i.e., the input channel is connected to the output channel selected by the routing algorithm. In other words, the switching mechanism determines how network resources are allocated for message transmission. For example, in circuit switching, all the channels required by a message are reserved before starting message transmission. In packet switching, however, a packet is transmitted through a channel as soon as that channel is reserved but the next channel is not reserved (assuming that it is available) until the packet releases the channel it is currently using. Obviously, some buffer space is required to store the packet until the next channel is reserved. That buffer should be allocated before starting packet transmission. So, *buffer allocation* is closely related to the switching mechanism. Flow control is also closely related to the switching and buffer allocation mechanisms. The *flow control* mechanism establishes a dialog between sender and receiver nodes, allowing and stopping the advance of information. If a packet is blocked, it requires some buffer space to be stored. When there is no more available buffer space, the flow control mechanism stops information transmission. When the packet advances and buffer space is available, transmission is started again. If there is no flow control and no more buffer space is available, the packet may be dropped, or derouted through another channel.

The above factors affect the network performance. They are not independent of each other but are closely related. For example, if a switching mechanism reserves resources in an aggressive way (as soon as a packet header is received), packet latency can be reduced. However, each packet may be holding several channels at the same time. So, such a switching mechanism may cause severe network congestion and, consequently, make the design of efficient routing and flow control policies difficult. The network topology also affects performance, as well as how the network traffic can be distributed over available channels. In most cases, the choice of a suitable network topology is restricted by wiring and packaging constraints.

1.6.2   Popular Network Topologies

Many network topologies have been proposed in terms of their graph theoretic properties. However, very few of them have ever been implemented. Most of the implemented networks have an orthogonal topology. A network topology is *orthogonal* if and only if nodes can be arranged in an orthogonal n-dimensional space, and every link can be arranged in such a way that it produces a displacement in a single dimension. Orthogonal topologies can be further classified as strictly orthogonal and weakly orthogonal. In a *strictly orthogonal* topology, every node has at least one link crossing each dimension. In a *weakly orthogonal* topology, some nodes may not have any link in some dimensions. Hence, it is not possible to cross every dimension from every node. Crossing a given dimension from a given node may require moving in another dimension first.

Strictly Orthogonal Topologies

The most interesting property of strictly orthogonal topologies is that routing is very simple. Thus, the routing algorithm can be efficiently implemented in hardware. Effectively, in a strictly orthogonal topology nodes can be numbered by using their coordinates in the n-dimensional space. As each link traverses a single dimension and every node has at least one link crossing each dimension, the distance between two nodes can be computed as the sum of dimension offsets. Also, the displacement along a given link only modifies the offset in the corresponding dimension. Taking into account that it is possible to cross any dimension from any node in the network, routing can be easily implemented by selecting a link that decrements the absolute value of the offset in some dimension. The set of dimension offsets can be stored in the packet header, and updated (by adding or subtracting one unit) every time the packet is successfully routed at some intermediate node. If the topology is not strictly orthogonal, however, routing may become much more complex.

The most popular direct networks are the *n-dimensional mesh*, the *k-ary n-cube* or *torus*, and the *hypercube*. All of them are strictly orthogonal. Formally, an n-dimensional mesh has $k_0 \times k_1 \times \cdots \times k_{n-2} \times k_{n-1}$ nodes, k_i nodes along each dimension i, where $k_i \geq 2$ and $0 \leq i \leq n-1$. Each node X is identified by n coordinates, $(x_{n-1}, x_{n-2}, \ldots, x_1, x_0)$, where $0 \leq x_i \leq k_i - 1$ for $0 \leq i \leq n-1$. Two nodes X and Y are neighbors if and only if $y_i = x_i$ for all i, $0 \leq i \leq n-1$, except one, j, where $y_j = x_j \pm 1$. Thus, nodes have from n to $2n$ neighbors, depending on their location in the mesh. Therefore, this topology is not regular.

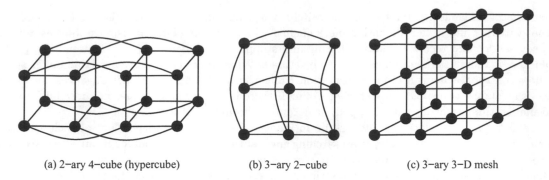

(a) 2–ary 4–cube (hypercube)   (b) 3–ary 2–cube   (c) 3–ary 3–D mesh

Figure 1.5. Strictly orthogonal direct network topologies.

In a bidirectional k-ary n-cube [71], all nodes have the same number of neighbors. The definition of a k-ary n-cube differs from that of an n-dimensional mesh in that all of the k_i are equal to k and two nodes X and Y are neighbors if and only if $y_i = x_i$ for all i, $0 \le i \le n - 1$, except one, j, where $y_j = (x_j \pm 1)$ mod k. The change to modular arithmetic in the definition adds wraparound channels to the k-ary n-cube, giving it regularity and symmetry. Every node has n neighbors if $k = 2$ and $2n$ neighbors if $k > 2$. When $n = 1$, the k-ary n-cube collapses to a bidirectional *ring* with k nodes.

Another topology with regularity and symmetry is the hypercube, which is a special case of both n-dimensional meshes and k-ary n-cubes. A hypercube is an n-dimensional mesh in which $k_i = 2$ for $0 \le i \le n - 1$, or a 2-ary n-cube, also referred to as a binary n-cube.

Figure 1.5a depicts a binary 4-cube or 16-node hypercube. Figure 1.5b illustrates a 3-ary 2-cube or two-dimensional (2-D) torus. Figure 1.5c shows a 3-ary three-dimensional (3-D) mesh, resulting by removing the wraparound channels from a 3-ary 3-cube.

Two conflicting requirements of a direct network are that it must accommodate a large number of nodes while maintaining a low network latency. This issue will be addressed in Chapter 7.

Other Direct Network Topologies

In addition to the topologies defined above, many other topologies have been proposed in the literature. Most of them were proposed with the goal of minimizing the network diameter for a given number of nodes and node degree. As will be seen in Chapter 2, for pipelined switching techniques network latency is almost insensitive to network diameter, especially when messages are long. So it is unlikely that those topologies are implemented. In the following paragraphs, we present an informal description of some relevant direct network topologies.

A popular topology is the *tree*. This topology has a *root* node connected to a certain number of descendant nodes. Each of these nodes is in turn connected to a disjoint set (possibly empty) of descendants. A node with no descendants is a *leaf* node. A characteristic property of trees is that every node but the root has a single parent node. Therefore, trees contain no cycles. A tree in which every node but the leaves has a fixed number k of descendants is a k-ary tree. When the distance from every leaf node to the root is the same, i.e., all the branches of the tree have the same length, the tree is *balanced*. Figures 1.6a and 1.6b show an unbalanced and a balanced binary tree, respectively.

The most important drawback of trees as general-purpose interconnection networks is that the root node and the nodes close to it become a bottleneck. Additionally, there are no alternative paths between any pair of nodes. The bottleneck can be removed by allocating a higher channel

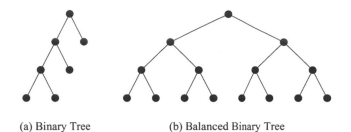

(a) Binary Tree   (b) Balanced Binary Tree

Figure 1.6. Some tree topologies.

bandwidth to channels located close to the root node. The shorter the distance to the root node, the higher the channel bandwidth. However, using channels with different bandwidth is not practical, specially when message transmission is pipelined. A practical way to implement trees with higher channel bandwidth in the vicinity of the root node (fat trees) will be described in Section 1.7.5.

One of the most interesting properties of trees is that, for any connected graph, it is possible to define a tree that spans the complete graph. As a consequence, for any connected network, it is possible to build an acyclic network connecting all the nodes by removing some links. This property can be used to define a routing algorithm for any irregular topology. However, that routing algorithm may be inefficient due to the concentration of traffic across the root node. A possible way to circumvent that limitation will be presented in Section 4.9.

Some topologies have been proposed with the purpose of reducing node degree while keeping the diameter small. Most of these topologies can be viewed as a hierarchy of topologies. This is the case for the cube-connected cycles [283]. This topology can be considered as an n-dimensional hypercube of virtual nodes, where each virtual node is a ring with n nodes, for a total of $n2^n$ nodes. Each node in the ring is connected to a single dimension of the hypercube. Therefore, node degree is fixed and equal to three: two links connecting to neighbors in the ring, and one link connecting to a node in another ring through one of the dimensions of the hypercube. However, the diameter is of the same order of magnitude as that of a hypercube of similar size. Figure 1.7a shows a 24-node cube-connected cycles network. It is worth to note that cube-connected cycles are weakly orthogonal because the ring is a one-dimensional network, and displacement inside the ring does not change the position in the other dimensions. Similarly, a displacement along a hypercube dimension does not affect the position in the ring. However, it is not possible to cross every dimension from each node.

Many topologies have been proposed with the purpose of minimizing the network diameter for a given number of nodes and node degree. Two well-known topologies proposed with this purpose are the de Bruijn network and the star graphs. In the *de Bruijn* network [300] there are d^n nodes, and each node is represented by a set of n digits in base d. A node $(x_{n-1}, x_{n-2}, \ldots, x_1, x_0)$, where $0 \leq x_i \leq d-1$ for $0 \leq i \leq n-1$ is connected to nodes $(x_{n-2}, \ldots, x_1, x_0, p)$ and $(p, x_{n-1}, x_{n-2}, \ldots, x_1)$, for all p such that $0 \leq p \leq d-1$. In other words, two nodes are connected if the representation of one node is a right or left shift of the representation of the other. Figure 1.7b shows an eight-node de Bruijn network. When networks are very large, this network topology achieves a very low diameter for a given number of nodes and node degree. However, routing is complex. Additionally, the average distance between nodes is high, close to the network diameter. Finally, some nodes have links connecting to themselves. All of these issues make the practical application of these networks very difficult.

A *star graph* [6] can be informally described as follows. The vertices of the graph are labeled by permutations of n different symbols, usually denoted as 1 to n. A permutation is connected to every other permutation that can be obtained from it by interchanging the first symbol with any

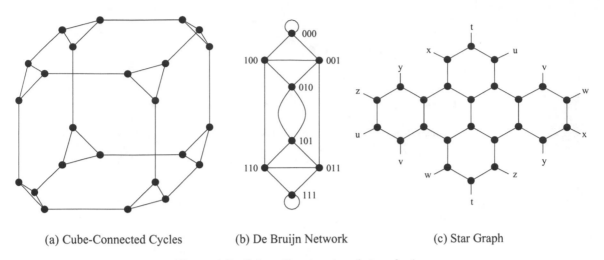

(a) Cube-Connected Cycles   (b) De Bruijn Network   (c) Star Graph

Figure 1.7. Other direct network topologies.

of the other symbols. A star graph has $n!$ nodes and node degree is equal to $n - 1$. Figure 1.7c shows a star graph obtained by permutations of four symbols. Although a star graph has a lower diameter than a hypercube of similar size, routing is more complex. Star graphs were proposed as a particular case of Cayley graphs [6]. Other topologies like hypercubes and cube-connected cycles are also particular cases of Cayley graphs.

1.6.3   Examples

Several examples of parallel computers with direct networks and the main characteristics are listed below.

- Cray T3E: Bidirectional 3-D torus, 14-bit data in each direction, 375 MHz link speed, 600 Mbytes/s per link.

- Cray T3D: Bidirectional 3-D torus, up to 1,024 nodes ($8 \times 16 \times 8$), 24-bit links (16-bit data, 8-bit control), 150 MHz, 300 Mbytes/s per link.

- Intel Cavallino: Bidirectional 3-D topology, 16-bit-wide channels operating at 200 MHz, 400 Mbytes/s in each direction.

- SGI SPIDER: Router with 20-bit bidirectional channels operating on both edges, 200 MHz clock, aggregate raw data rate of 1 Gbyte/s. Support for regular and irregular topologies.

- MIT M-Machine: 3-D mesh, 800 Mbytes/s for each network channel.

- MIT Reliable Router: 2-D mesh, 23-bit links (16-bit data), 200 MHz, 400 Mbytes/s per link per direction, bidirectional signaling, reliable transmission.

- Chaos Router: 2-D torus topology, bidirectional 8-bit links, 180 MHz, 360 Mbytes/s in each direction.

- Intel iPSC-2 Hypercube: Binary hypercube topology, bit-serial channels at 2.8 Mbytes/s.

1.7   Indirect Networks

Indirect or *switch-based networks* are another major class of interconnection networks. Instead of providing a direct connection among some nodes, the communication between any two nodes has to be carried through some *switches*. Each node has a network adapter that connects to a network switch. Each switch can have a set of *ports*. Each port consists of one input and one output link. A (possibly empty) set of ports in each switch are either connected to processors or left open, whereas the remaining ports are connected to ports of other switches to provide connectivity between the processors. The interconnection of those switches defines various network topologies.

Switch-based networks considerably evolved over time. A wide range of topologies have been proposed, ranging from regular topologies used in array processors and shared-memory UMA multi-processors to the irregular topologies currently used in NOWs. Both network classes will be covered in this book. Regular topologies have regular connection patterns between switches while irregular topologies do not follow any predefined pattern. Figures 1.19 and 1.21 show several switch-based networks with regular topology. The corresponding connection patterns will be studied below. Figure 1.8 shows a typical switch-based network with irregular topology. Both network classes can be further classified according to the number of switches a message has to traverse before reaching its destination. Although this classification is not important in the case of irregular topologies, it makes a big difference in the case of regular networks because some specific properties can be derived for each network class.

1.7.1   Characterization of Indirect Networks

Indirect networks can also be modeled by a graph $G(N, C)$, where N is the set of switches, and C is the set of unidirectional or bidirectional links between the switches. For the analysis of most properties, it is not necessary to explicitly include processing nodes in the graph. Although a similar model can be used for direct and indirect networks, a few differences exist between them. Each switch in an indirect network may be connected to zero, one, or more processors. Obviously, only the switches connected to some processor can be the source or the destination of a message. Additionally, transmitting a message from a node to another node requires crossing the link between

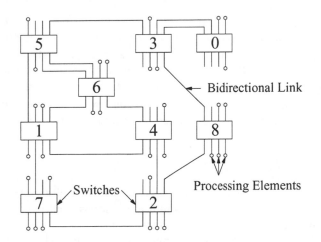

Figure 1.8. A switch-based network with irregular topology.

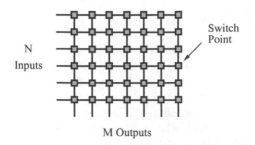

Figure 1.9. An $N \times M$ crossbar.

the source node and the switch connected to it, and the link between the last switch in the path and the destination node. Therefore, the distance between two nodes is the distance between the switches directly connected to those nodes plus two units. Similarly, the diameter is the maximum distance between two switches connected to some node plus two units. It may be argued that it is not necessary to add two units because direct networks also have internal links between routers and processing nodes. However, those links are external in the case of indirect networks. This gives a consistent view of the diameter as the maximum number of external links between two processing nodes. In particular, the distance between two nodes connected through a single switch is two instead of zero.

Similar to direct networks, an indirect network is mainly characterized by three factors: topology, routing, and switching. The topology defines how the switches are interconnected by channels, and can be modeled by a graph as indicated above. For indirect networks with N nodes, the ideal topology would connect those nodes through a single $N \times N$ switch. Such a switch is known as a *crossbar*. Although using a single $N \times N$ crossbar is much cheaper than using a fully connected direct network topology (requiring N routers, each one having an internal $N \times N$ crossbar), the cost is still prohibitive for large networks. Similar to direct networks, the number of physical connections of a switch is limited by hardware constraints such as the number of available pins and the available wiring area. These engineering and scaling difficulties preclude the use of crossbar networks for large network sizes. As a consequence, many alternative topologies have been proposed. In these topologies, messages may have to traverse several switches before reaching the destination node. In regular networks, these switches are usually identical and have been traditionally organized as a set of *stages*. Each stage (but the input/output stages) is only connected to the previous and next stages using regular connection patterns. Input/output stages are connected to the nodes as well as to another stage in the network. These networks are referred to as *multistage* networks, and have different properties depending on the number of stages, and how those stages are arranged.

The remaining issues discussed in Section 1.6.1 (routing, switching, flow control, buffer allocation, and their impact on performance) are also applicable to indirect networks.

1.7.2   Crossbar Networks

Crossbar networks allow any processor in the system to connect to any other processor or memory unit so that many processors can communicate simultaneously without contention. A new connection can be established at any time as long as the requested input and output ports are free. Crossbar networks are used in the design of high-performance small-scale multiprocessors, in the design of routers for direct networks, and as basic components in the design of large-scale indirect networks. A crossbar can be defined as a switching network with N inputs and M outputs, which allows up to

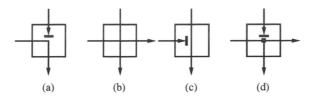

Figure 1.10. States of a switch point in a crossbar network.

$\min\{N, M\}$ one-to-one interconnections without contention. Figure 1.9 shows an $N \times M$ crossbar network. Usually, $M = N$ except for crossbars connecting processors and memory modules.

The cost of such a network is $O(NM)$, which is prohibitively high with large N and M. Crossbar networks have been traditionally used in small-scale shared-memory multiprocessors, where all processors are allowed to access memories simultaneously as long as each processor reads from, or writes to, a different memory. When two or more processors contend for the same memory module, arbitration lets one processor proceed while the others wait. The arbiter in a crossbar is distributed among all the switch points connected to the same output. However, the arbitration scheme can be less complex than the one for a bus because conflicts in crossbar are the exception rather than the rule, and therefore easier to resolve.

For a crossbar network with distributed control, each switch point may have four states as shown in Figure 1.10. In Figure 1.10a, the input from the row containing the switch point has been granted access to the corresponding output while inputs from upper rows requesting the same output are blocked. In Figure 1.10b, an input from an upper row has been granted access to the output. The input from the row containing the switch point does not request that output, and can be propagated to other switches. In Figure 1.10c, an input from an upper row has also been granted access to the output. However, the input from the row containing the switch point also requests that output and is blocked. The configuration in Figure 1.10d is only required if the crossbar has to support multicasting (one-to-many communication).

The advent of VLSI permitted the integration of hardware for thousands of switches into a single chip. However, the number of pins on a VLSI chip cannot exceed a few hundreds, which restricts the size of the largest crossbar that can be integrated into a single VLSI chip. Large crossbars can be realized by partitioning them into smaller crossbars, each one implemented using a single chip. Thus, a full crossbar of size $N \times N$ can be implemented with $(N/n)(N/n)$ $n \times n$ crossbars.

1.7.3   Multistage Interconnection Networks

Multistage interconnection networks (MINs) connect input devices to output devices through a number of switch stages, where each switch is a crossbar network. The number of stages and the connection patterns between stages determine the routing capability of the networks.

MINs were initially proposed for telephone networks and later for array processors. In these cases, a central controller establishes the path from input to output. In cases where the number of inputs equals the number of outputs, each input synchronously transmits a message to one output, and each output receives a message from exactly one input. Such unicast communication patterns can be represented as a permutation of the input addresses. For this application, MINs have been popular as alignment networks for storing and accessing arrays in parallel from memory banks. Array storage is typically skewed to permit conflict-free access, and the network is used to unscramble the arrays during access. These networks can also be configured with the number of inputs greater than the number of outputs (concentrators) and vice versa (expanders). On the other hand, in asynchronous

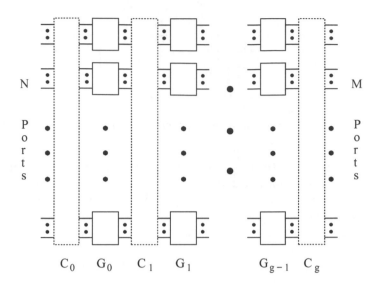

Figure 1.11. A generalized MIN with N inputs, M outputs, and g stages.

multiprocessors, centralized control and permutation routing are infeasible. In this case, a routing algorithm is required to establish the path across the stages of a MIN.

Depending on the interconnection scheme employed between two adjacent stages and the number of stages, various MINs have been proposed. MINs are good for constructing parallel computers with hundreds of processors and have been used in some commercial machines.

1.7.4 A Generalized MIN Model

There are many ways to interconnect adjacent stages. Figure 1.11 shows a generalized multistage interconnection network with N inputs and M outputs. It has g *stages*, G_0 to G_{g-1}. As shown in Figure 1.12, each stage, say G_i, has w_i switches of size $a_{i,j} \times b_{i,j}$, where $1 \leq j \leq w_i$. Thus, stage G_i has p_i inputs and q_i outputs, where

$$p_i = \sum_{j=1}^{w_i} a_{i,j} \quad \text{and} \quad q_i = \sum_{j=1}^{w_i} b_{i,j}$$

The connection between two adjacent stages, G_{i-1} and G_i, denoted C_i, defines the *connection pattern* for $p_i = q_{i-1}$ links, where $p_0 = N$ and $q_{g-1} = M$. A MIN thus can be represented as

$$C_0(N)G_0(w_0)C_1(p_1)G_1(w_1)\ldots G_{g-1}(w_{g-1})C_g(M)$$

A connection pattern $C_i(p_i)$ defines how those p_i links should be connected between the $q_{i-1} = p_i$ outputs from stage G_{i-1} and the p_i inputs to stage G_i. Different connection patterns give different characteristics and topological properties of MINs. The links are labeled from 0 to $p_i - 1$ at C_i.

From a practical point of view, it is interesting that all the switches are identical, thus amortizing the design cost. Banyan networks are a class of MINs with the property that there is a unique path between any pair of source and destination [133]. An N-node ($N = k^n$) Delta network is a subclass of banyan networks, which is constructed from identical $k \times k$ switches in n stages, where each stage contains $\frac{N}{k}$ switches. Many of the known MINs, such as Omega, flip, cube, butterfly, and baseline,

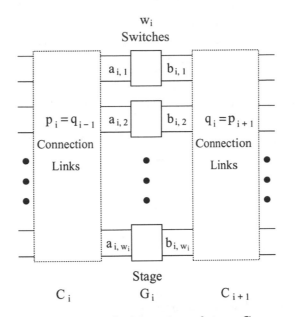

Figure 1.12. A closer view of stage G_i.

belong to the class of Delta networks [272] and have been shown to be topologically and functionally equivalent [351]. A good survey of those MINs can be found in [317]. Some of those MINs are defined below.

When switches have the same number of input and output ports, MINs also have the same number of input and output ports. Since there is a one-to-one correspondence between inputs and outputs, these connections are also called *permutations*. Five basic permutations are defined below. Although these permutations were originally defined for networks with 2×2 switches, for most definitions we assume that the network is built by using $k \times k$ switches, and that there are $N = k^n$ inputs and outputs, where n is an integer. However, some of these permutations are only defined for the case where N is a power of 2. With $N = k^n$ ports, let $X = x_{n-1}x_{n-2}\ldots x_0$ be an arbitrary port number, $0 \leq X \leq N-1$, where $0 \leq x_i \leq k-1$, $0 \leq i \leq n-1$.

Perfect Shuffle Connection

The *perfect k-shuffle* connection σ^k is defined by

$$\sigma^k(X) = (kX + \left\lfloor \frac{kX}{N} \right\rfloor) \bmod N$$

A more cogent way to describe the perfect k-shuffle connection σ^k is

$$\sigma^k(x_{n-1}x_{n-2}\ldots x_1x_0) = x_{n-2}\ldots x_1x_0x_{n-1}$$

The perfect k-shuffle connection performs a cyclic shifting of the digits in X to the left for one position. For $k = 2$, this action corresponds to perfectly shuffling a deck of N cards, as demonstrated in Figure 1.13a for the case of $N = 8$. The perfect shuffle cuts the deck into two halves from the center and intermixes them evenly. The *inverse perfect shuffle* does the opposite as defined below:

$$\sigma^{k^{-1}}(x_{n-1}x_{n-2}\ldots x_1x_0) = x_0x_{n-1}\ldots x_2x_1$$

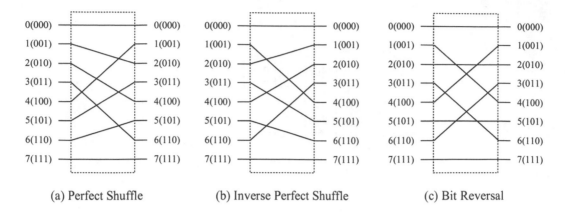

(a) Perfect Shuffle   (b) Inverse Perfect Shuffle   (c) Bit Reversal

Figure 1.13. The perfect shuffle, inverse perfect shuffle, and bit reversal connections for $N = 8$.

Digit Reversal Connection

The *digit reversal* permutation ρ^k is defined by

$$\rho^k(x_{n-1}x_{n-2}\ldots x_1x_0) = x_0x_1\ldots x_{n-2}x_{n-1}$$

This permutation is usually referred to as *bit reversal*, clearly indicating that it was proposed for $k = 2$. However, its definition is also valid for $k > 2$. Figure 1.13c demonstrates a bit reversal connection for the case of $k = 2$ and $N = 8$.

Butterfly Connection

The *i*th *k*-ary *butterfly* permutation β_i^k, for $0 \le i \le n - 1$, is defined by

$$\beta_i^k(x_{n-1}\ldots x_{i+1}x_ix_{i-1}\ldots x_1x_0) = x_{n-1}\ldots x_{i+1}x_0x_{i-1}\ldots x_1x_i$$

The *i*th butterfly connection interchanges the zeroth and *i*th digits of the index. Figure 1.14 shows the butterfly connection for $k = 2$, and $i = 0$, 1, and 2 with $N = 8$. Note that β_0^k defines a straight one-to-one connection and is also called *identity connection, I*.

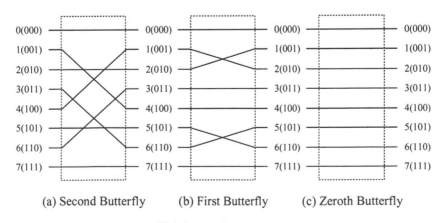

(a) Second Butterfly   (b) First Butterfly   (c) Zeroth Butterfly

Figure 1.14. The butterfly connection for $N = 8$.

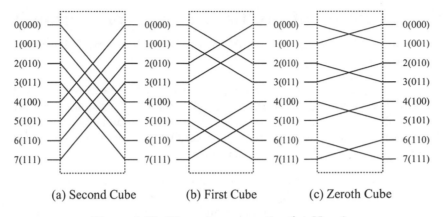

Figure 1.15. The cube connection for $N = 8$.

Cube Connection

The ith *cube* connection E_i, for $0 \leq i \leq n - 1$, is defined only for $k = 2$ by

$$E_i(x_{n-1} \ldots x_{i+1} x_i x_{i-1} \ldots x_0) = x_{n-1} \ldots x_{i+1} \overline{x}_i x_{i-1} \ldots x_0$$

The ith cube connection complements the ith bit of the index. Figure 1.15 shows the cube connection for $i = 0$, 1, and 2 with $N = 8$. E_0 is also called the *exchange* connection.

Baseline Connection

The ith k-ary *baseline* permutation δ_i^k, for $0 \leq i \leq n - 1$, is defined by

$$\delta_i^k(x_{n-1} \ldots x_{i+1} x_i x_{i-1} \ldots x_1 x_0) = x_{n-1} \ldots x_{i+1} x_0 x_i x_{i-1} \ldots x_1$$

The ith baseline connection performs a cyclic shifting of the $i + 1$ least significant digits in the index to the right for one position. Figure 1.16 shows the baseline connection for $k = 2$, and $i = 0$, 1, and 2 with $N = 8$. Note that δ_0^k also defines the identity connection I.

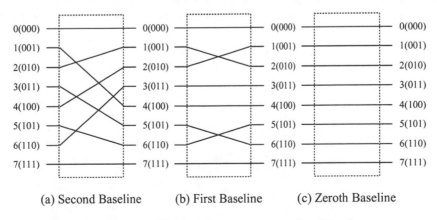

Figure 1.16. The baseline connection for $N = 8$.

1.7.5 Classification of Multistage Interconnection Networks

Depending on the availability of paths to establish new connections, MINs have been traditionally divided into three classes:

1. *Blocking.* A connection between a free input/output pair is not always possible because of conflicts with the existing connections. Typically, there is a unique path between every input/output pair, thus minimizing the number of switches and stages. However, it is also possible to provide multiple paths to reduce conflicts and increase fault tolerance. These blocking networks are also known as *multipath*.

2. *Nonblocking.* Any input port can be connected to any free output port without affecting the existing connections. Nonblocking networks have the same functionality as a crossbar. They require multiple paths between every input and output, which in turn leads to extra stages.

3. *Rearrangeable.* Any input port can be connected to any free output port. However, the existing connections may require rearrangement of paths. These networks also require multiple paths between every input and output but the number of paths and the cost is smaller than in the case of nonblocking networks.

Nonblocking networks are expensive. Although they are cheaper than a crossbar of the same size, their cost is prohibitive for large sizes. The best known example of nonblocking multistage network is the Clos network, initially proposed for telephone networks. Rearrangeable networks require less stages or simpler switches than a nonblocking network. The best known example of rearrangeable network is the Beneš network. Figure 1.17 shows an 8×8 Beneš network. For 2^n inputs, this network requires $2n - 1$ stages, and provides 2^{n-1} alternative paths. Rearrangeable networks require a central controller to rearrange connections, and were proposed for array processors. However, connections cannot be easily rearranged on multiprocessors because processors access the network asynchronously. So, rearrangeable networks behave like blocking networks when accesses are asynchronous. Thus, this class has not been included in Figure 1.2. We will mainly focus on blocking networks.

Depending on the kind of channels and switches, MINs can be split into two classes [253]:

1. *Unidirectional MINs.* Channels and switches are unidirectional.

2. *Bidirectional MINs.* Channels and switches are bidirectional. This implies that information can be transmitted simultaneously in opposite directions between neighboring switches.

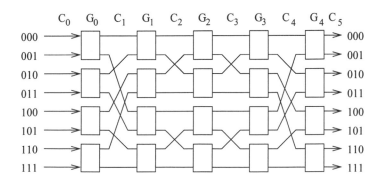

Figure 1.17. An 8×8 Beneš network.

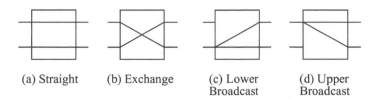

(a) Straight   (b) Exchange   (c) Lower Broadcast   (d) Upper Broadcast

Figure 1.18. Four possible states of a 2×2 switch.

Additionally, each channel may be either multiplexed or replaced by two or more channels. In the latter case, the network is referred to as *dilated MIN*. Obviously, the number of ports of each switch must increase accordingly.

Unidirectional Multistage Interconnection Networks

The basic building blocks of unidirectional MINs are unidirectional switches. An $a \times b$ switch is a crossbar network with a inputs and b outputs. If each input port is allowed to connect to exactly one output port, at most $\min\{a, b\}$ connections can be supported simultaneously. If each input port is allowed to connect to many output ports, a more complicated design is needed to support the so-called *one-to-many* or *multicast* communication. In the *broadcast* mode or *one-to-all* communication, each input port is allowed to connect to all output ports. Figure 1.18 shows four possible states of a 2×2 switch. The last two states are used to support one-to-many and one-to-all communications.

In MINs with $N = M$, it is common to use switches with the same number of input and output ports, i.e., $a = b$. If $N > M$, switches with $a > b$ will be used. Such switches are also called *concentration switches*. In the case of $N < M$, *distribution switches* with $a < b$ will be used.

It can be shown that with N input and output ports, a unidirectional MIN with $k \times k$ switches requires at least $\lceil \log_k N \rceil$ stages to allow a connection path between any input port and any output port. By having additional stages, more connection paths may be used to deliver a message between an input port and an output port at the expense of extra hardware cost. Every path through the MIN crosses all the stages. Therefore, all the paths have the same length.

Four topologically equivalent unidirectional MINs are considered below. These MINs are a class of Delta networks.

Baseline MINs. In a baseline MIN, connection pattern C_i is described by the $(n - i)$th baseline permutation δ_{n-i}^k for $1 \leq i \leq n$. Connection pattern C_0 is selected to be σ^k.

Butterfly MINs. In a butterfly MIN, connection pattern C_i is described by the ith butterfly permutation β_i^k for $0 \leq i \leq n - 1$. Connection pattern C_n is selected to be β_0^k.

Cube MINs. In a cube MIN (or multistage cube network [317]), connection pattern C_i is described by the $(n - i)$th butterfly permutation β_{n-i}^k for $1 \leq i \leq n$. Connection pattern C_0 is selected to be σ^k.

Omega network. In an Omega network, connection pattern C_i is described by the perfect k-shuffle permutation σ^k for $0 \leq i \leq n - 1$. Connection pattern C_n is selected to be β_0^k. Thus, all the connection patterns but the last one are identical. The last connection pattern produces no permutation.

The topological equivalence of these MINs can be viewed as follows: Consider that each input link to the first stage is numbered using a string of n digits $s_{n-1}s_{n-2} \ldots s_1 s_0$, where $0 \leq s_i \leq k - 1$, for $0 \leq i \leq n - 1$. The least significant digit s_0 gives the address of the input port at the corresponding switch and the address of the switch is given by $s_{n-1}s_{n-2} \ldots s_1$. At each stage, a given switch is able to connect any input port with any output port. This can be viewed as changing the value of

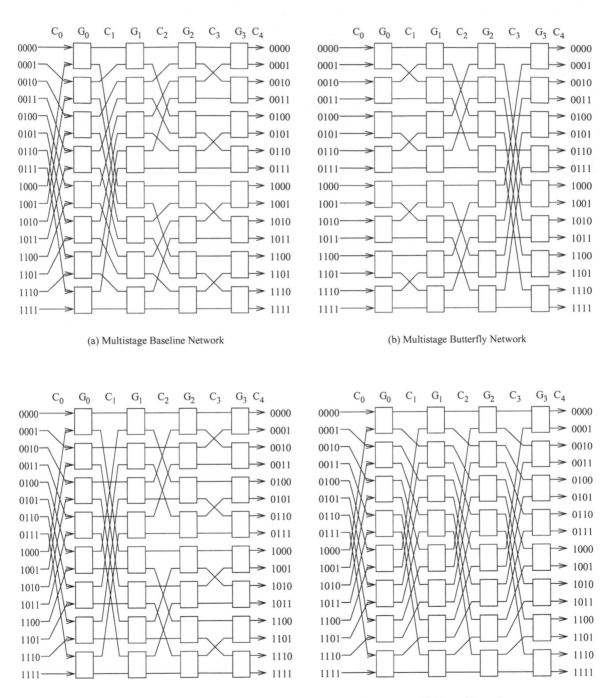

Figure 1.19. Four 16×16 unidirectional multistage interconnection networks.

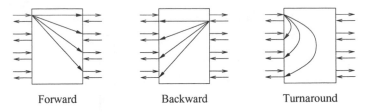

Figure 1.20. Connections in a bidirectional switch.

the least significant digit of the address. In order to be able to connect any input to any output of the network, it should be possible to change the value of all the digits. As each switch is only able to change the value of the least significant digit of the address, connection patterns between stages are defined in such a way that the position of digits is permuted, and after n stages all the digits have occupied the least significant position. Therefore, the above defined MINs differ in the order in which address digits occupy the least significant position.

Figure 1.19 shows the topology of four 16×16 unidirectional multistage interconnection networks: (a) baseline network, (b) butterfly network, (c) cube network, and (d) omega network.

Bidirectional Multistage Interconnection Networks

Figure 1.20 illustrates a bidirectional switch in which each port is associated with a pair of unidirectional channels in opposite directions. This implies that information can be transmitted simultaneously in opposite directions between neighboring switches. For ease of explanation, it is assumed that processor nodes are on the left-hand side of the network, as shown in Figure 1.21. A bidirectional switch supports three types of connections: *forward*, *backward*, and *turnaround* (see Figure 1.20). As turnaround connections between ports at the same side of a switch are possible, paths have different lengths. An eight-node butterfly bidirectional MIN (BMIN) is illustrated in Figure 1.21.

Paths are established in BMINs by crossing stages in forward direction, then establishing a turnaround connection, and finally crossing stages in backward direction. This is usually referred to as *turnaround routing*. Figure 1.22 shows two alternative paths from node S to node D in an eight-node butterfly BMIN. When crossing stages in forward direction, several paths are possible. Each switch can select any of its output ports. However, once the turnaround connection is crossed,

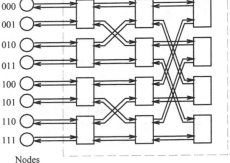

Figure 1.21. An eight-node butterfly bidirectional MIN.

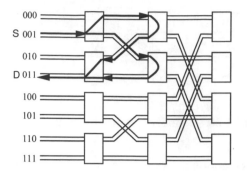

Figure 1.22. Alternative paths in an eight-node butterfly bidirectional MIN.

a single path is available up to the destination node. In the worst case, establishing a path in an n-stage BMIN requires crossing $2n - 1$ stages. This behavior closely resembles that of the Beneš network. Indeed, the baseline BMIN can be considered as a folded Beneš network.

As shown in Figure 1.23, a butterfly BMIN with turnaround routing can be viewed as a *fat tree* [201]. In a fat tree, processors are located at leaves, and internal vertices are switches. Transmission bandwidth between switches is increased by adding more links in parallel as switches become closer to the root switch. When a message is routed from one processor to another, it is sent up (in forward direction) the tree to the least common ancestor of the two processors, and then sent down (in backward direction) to the destination. Such a tree routing well explains the turnaround routing mentioned above.

1.7.6   Examples

Several examples of parallel computers with indirect networks and commercial switches to build indirect networks are listed below.

- Myricom Myrinet: Supports regular and irregular topologies, 8×8 crossbar switch, 9-bit channels, full-duplex, 640 Mbits/s per link.

- Thinking Machines CM-5: Fat tree topology, 4-bit bidirectional channels at 40 MHz, aggregate bandwidth in each direction of 20 Mbytes/s.

- Inmos C104: Supports regular and irregular topologies, 32×32 crossbar switch, serial links, 100 Mbits/s per link.

- IBM SP2: Crossbar switches supporting Omega network topologies with bidirectional, 16-bit channels at 150MHz, 300 Mbytes/s in each direction.

- SGI SPIDER: Router with 20-bit bidirectional channels operating on both edges, 200 MHz clock, aggregate raw data rate of 1 Gbyte/s. Offers support for configurations as nonblocking multistage network topologies as well as irregular topologies.

- Tandem ServerNet: Irregular topologies, 8-bit bidirectional channels at 50 MHz, 50 Mbytes/s per link.

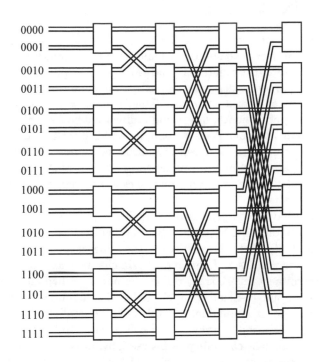

(a) A 16−Node Butterfly BMIN Built with 2 x 2 Switches

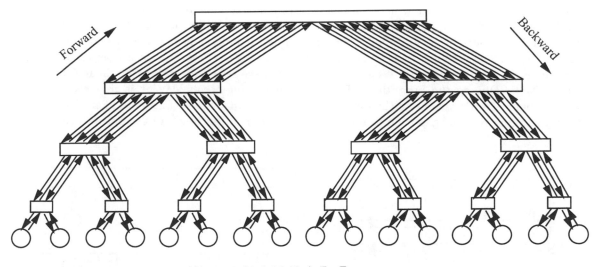

(b) A 16−Node Fat Tree

Figure 1.23. Fat tree and butterfly BMIN.

1.8 Hybrid Networks

In this section, we briefly describe some network topologies that do not fit into the classes described above. In general, hybrid networks combine mechanisms from shared-medium networks and direct or indirect networks. Therefore, they increase bandwidth with respect to shared-medium networks, and reduce the distance between nodes with respect to direct and indirect networks. There exist well-established applications of hybrid networks. This is the case for bridged LANs. However, for systems requiring very high performance, direct and indirect networks achieve better scalability than hybrid networks because point-to-point links are simpler and faster than shared-medium buses. Most high-performance parallel computers use direct or indirect networks. Recently hybrid networks have been gaining acceptance again. The use of optical technology enables the implementation of high-performance buses. Currently, some prototype machines are being implemented based on electrical as well as optical interconnects.

Many hybrid networks have been proposed for different purposes. The classification proposed for these networks is mainly dictated by the application fields. In general, hybrid networks can be modeled by a hypergraph [23], where the vertices of the hypergraph represent the set of processing nodes, and the edges represent the set of communication channels and/or buses. Note that an edge in a hypergraph can interconnect an arbitrary number of nodes. When an edge connects exactly two nodes then it represents a point-to-point channel. Otherwise it represents a bus. In some network designs, each bus has a single driving node. No other device is allowed to drive that bus. In this case, there is no need for arbitration. However, it is still possible to have several receivers at a given time, thus retaining the broadcast capability of buses. Obviously, every node in the network must drive at least one bus, therefore requiring a number of buses not lower than the number of nodes. In this case, the network topology can be modeled by a directed hypergraph.

1.8.1 Multiple Backplane Buses

Due to limited shared-medium network bandwidth, a shared-medium network can only support a small number of devices, has limited distance, and is not scalable to support a large system. Some approaches have been used or studied to remove such bottlenecks. One approach to increase network bandwidth is to have multiple buses as shown in Figure 1.24. However, concern about wiring and interface costs is a major reason why multiple buses have seen little use so far in multiprocessor design [246]. Due to the limitations of electrical packaging technology, it is unlikely to have a multiple-bus network with more than four buses. However, many more buses are likely feasible with other packaging technologies such as wavelength division multiplexing on fiber optics [279].

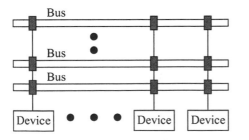

Figure 1.24. A multiple-bus network.   Figure 1.25. Two-level hierarchical buses.

1.8.2 Hierarchical Networks

Another approach to increase the network bandwidth is to have a hierarchical structure as shown in Figure 1.25. Different buses are interconnected by routers or bridges to transfer information from one side of the network to the other side of the network. These routers or bridges can filter the network traffic by examining the destination address of each passing message. The hierarchical network can expand the network area and handle more devices, but it is no longer a simple shared-medium network. This approach is used in bridged LANs. Usually, a higher bandwidth is available at the global bus. Otherwise, it may become a bottleneck. This can be achieved by using a faster technology. This is the case for the backbone LAN in some bridged LANs. Hierarchical networks have also been proposed as the interconnection scheme for shared-memory multiprocessors. Again, the global bus may become a bottleneck. For example, the Encore Gigamax addressed this problem by having an optical fiber bus to increase the bandwidth of the global bus.

1.8.3 Cluster-Based Networks

Cluster-based networks also have a hierarchical structure. Indeed, they can be considered as a subclass of hierarchical networks. Cluster-based networks combine the advantages of two or more kinds of networks at different levels in the hierarchy. For example, it is possible to combine the advantages of buses and point-to-point links by using buses at the lower level in the hierarchy to form clusters, and a direct network topology connecting clusters at the higher level. This is the case for the Stanford Directory Architecture for Shared-Memory (DASH) [203]. Figure 1.26 shows the basic architecture of this parallel computer. At the lower level, each cluster consists of four processors connected by a bus. At the higher level, a 2-D mesh connects the clusters. The broadcast capability of the bus is used at the cluster level to implement a snoopy protocol for cache coherence. The direct network at the higher level overcomes the bandwidth constraints of the bus, considerably increasing the scalability of the machine.

Other combinations are possible. Instead of combining buses and direct networks, the HP/Convex

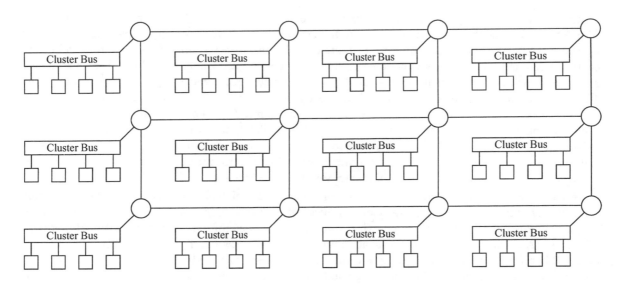

Figure 1.26. Cluster-based 2-D mesh.

Figure 1.27. A two-dimensional hypermesh.

Exemplar multiprocessor combines indirect and direct networks. This multiprocessor has 5×5 nonblocking crossbars at the lower level in the hierarchy, connecting four functional blocks and one I/O interface to form clusters or *hypernodes*. Each functional block consists of two processors, two memory banks and interfaces. These hypernodes are connected by a second level *coherent toroidal interconnect* made out of multiple rings using Scalable Coherent Interface (SCI). Each ring connects one functional block from all the hypernodes. At the lower level of the hierarchy, the crossbars allow all the processors within a hypernode to access the interleaved memory modules in that hypernode. At the higher level, the rings implement a cache coherence protocol.

1.8.4   Other Hypergraph Topologies

Many other hybrid topologies have been proposed [25, 336, 348]. Among them, a particularly interesting class is the *hypermesh* [335]. A hypermesh is a regular topology consisting of a set of nodes arranged into several dimensions. Instead of having direct connections to the neighbors in each dimension, each node is connected to all the nodes in each dimension through a bus. There are several ways to implement a hypermesh. The most straightforward way consists of connecting all the nodes in each dimension through a shared bus. Figure 1.27 shows a 2-D hypermesh. In this network, multiple buses are arranged in two dimensions. Each node is connected to one bus in each dimension. This topology was proposed by Wittie [348], and was referred to as *spanning-bus hypercube*. This topology has a very low diameter, and average distance between nodes scales very well with network size. However, the overall network bandwidth does not scale well. Additionally, the frequent changes of bus mastership incur significant overheads.

An alternative implementation that removes the above mentioned constraints consists of replacing the single shared bus connecting the nodes along a given dimension by a set of as many buses as nodes in that dimension. This is the approach proposed in the Distributed Crossbar Switch Hypermesh (DCSH) [222, 223]. Figure 1.28 shows one dimension of the network. Each bus is driven by a single node. Therefore, there are no changes in mastership. Also, bandwidth scales with the number of nodes. Two major concerns, however, are the high number of buses required in the system and the very high number of input ports required at each node. Although the authors propose an electrical implementation, this topology is also suitable for optical interconnects.

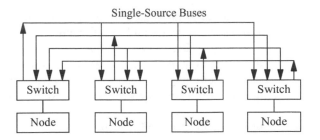

Figure 1.28. A one-dimensional Distributed Crossbar Switch Hypermesh.

1.9 A Unified View of Direct and Indirect Networks

Up to this point, most researchers and manufacturers considered direct and indirect networks as two completely different approaches for the interconnection of a set of nodes. However, the last few years have seen developments in router architecture, algorithms, and switch design evolve to a point that is blurring the distinction between these two classes of networks. For performance driven environments, as networks converge on the use of pipelined message transmission and source based routing algorithms, the major differences between the switch architectures for direct and indirect networks is becoming more a question of topology. Direct networks have typically used routers with routing algorithms implemented in the network. Switch-based designs have had routing performed at the source. Modern routers are being designed to support simple, fast, reprogrammable routing decisions within the network with substantial control of routing at the message source. This expands the base of applications for the (sizeable) investment in router/switch designs. This flexibility is also evidenced by the fact that the traditional high-performance multiprocessor router/switch designs are moving up to implementations involving workstation and personal computer (PC) clusters.

In particular, during the last few years several manufacturers have introduced switches to interconnect a set of processors. These switch-based networks allow the user to define the topology. Let us consider the particular case in which each switch has a single processor directly attached to it, and the remaining ports are used to connect with other switches. This network does not differ substantially from a direct network because each switch can be considered as a router associated with the corresponding node. Indeed, the functionality of current routers and switches is practically identical. Moreover, some manufacturers proposed the use of the same switch to implement either direct or indirect networks. This is the case of the Inmos C104 switch [228] and the SGI SPIDER [118]. For interconnection networks using the former switch, Inmos proposed the use of bidirectional multistage interconnection networks as well as direct topologies like meshes. In the latter case, each switch is connected to a single node through a set of independent ports. Also, two adjacent switches may use several ports in parallel to communicate between them. The SGI SPIDER router implementation was designed to support configurations as nonblocking multistage networks, as irregular topologies, and as routers for conventional multiprocessor topologies. Such flexibility is typically achieved using topology-independent routing algorithms and flexible switching techniques.

Therefore, we can view networks using point-to-point links as a set of interconnected switches, each one being connected to zero, one, or more nodes. Direct networks correspond to the case where every switch is connected to a single node. Crossbar networks correspond to the case where there is a single switch connected to all the nodes. Multistage interconnection networks correspond to the case where switches are arranged into several stages and the switches in intermediate stages are not connected to any processor. However, other choices are possible under this unified view of direct and indirect interconnection networks. Effectively, nothing prevents the designer from interconnecting switches using a typical direct network topology, and connecting several processors to each switch. This is the case for the Cray T3D, which implements a 3-D torus topology, connecting two processors to each router.

The unified view allows the development of generic routing algorithms. In these algorithms, the destination address specifies the destination switch as well as the port number in that switch that is connected to the destination processor. Note that routing algorithms for direct networks are a particular case of these generic algorithms. In this case, there is a single processor connected to each switch. So, the output port in the last switch is not required, assuming that processors are connected to the same port in every switch. This unified view also allows the application of many results developed for direct networks to indirect networks, and vice versa. For example, the theory of deadlock avoidance presented in Chapter 3 was initially developed for direct networks but can also be applied to indirect networks with minor changes, as will be shown in that chapter. Obviously, not all the results can be directly applied to both network classes. Additionally, applying some results to other network classes may require a considerable effort. In the remaining chapters of the book, most techniques will be described for the class of networks for which they were initially proposed. However, it is important to keep in mind that most of those techniques can also be applied to other network topologies by taking into account the unified view proposed in this section.

Chapter 2

Message Switching Layer

Interprocessor communication can be viewed as a hierarchy of services starting from the physical layer that synchronizes the transfer of bit streams to higher-level protocols layers that perform functions such as packetization, data encryption, data compression, etc. Such a layering of communication services is common in the local and wide area network communities. While there currently may not be a consensus on a standard set of layers for multiprocessor systems, we find it useful to distinguish between three layers in the operation of the interconnection network: the *routing layer*, the *switching layer*, and the *physical layer*. The physical layer refers to link-level protocols for transferring messages and otherwise managing the physical channels between adjacent routers. The switching layer utilizes these physical layer protocols to implement mechanisms for forwarding messages through the network. Finally, the routing layer makes routing decisions to determine candidate output channels at intermediate router nodes and thereby establish the path through the network. The design of routing protocols and their properties, e.g., deadlock and livelock freedom, are largely determined by the services provided by the switching layer.

This chapter focuses on the techniques that are implemented within the network routers to realize the switching layer. These techniques differ in several respects. The *switching techniques* determine when and how internal switches are set to connect router inputs to outputs and the time at which message components may be transferred along these paths. These techniques are coupled with *flow control* mechanisms for the synchronized transfer of units of information between routers and through routers in forwarding messages through the network. Flow control is tightly coupled with *buffer management* algorithms that determine how message buffers are requested and released, and as a result determine how messages are handled when blocked in the network. Implementations of the switching layer differ in decisions made in each of these areas, and in their relative timing, i.e., when one operation can be initiated relative to the occurrence of the other. The specific choices interact with the architecture of the routers and traffic patterns imposed by parallel programs in determining the latency and throughput characteristics of the interconnection network.

As we might expect, the switching techniques employed in multiprocessor networks initially followed those techniques employed in local and wide area communication networks, e.g., circuit switching and packet switching. However, as the application of multiprocessor systems spread into increasingly compute-intensive domains, the traditional layered communication designs borrowed from LANs became a limiting performance bottleneck. New switching techniques and implementations evolved that were better suited to the low latency demands of parallel programs. This chapter reviews these switching techniques and their accompanying flow control and buffer management algorithms.

35

2.1   Network and Router Model

In comparing and contrasting alternative implementations of the switching layer we are interested in evaluating their impact on the router implementations. The implementations in turn determine the cycle time of router operation and therefore the resulting message latency and network bandwidth. The architecture of a generic router is shown in Figure 2.1 and is comprised of the following major components.

- *Buffers.* These are first-in first-out (FIFO) buffers for storing messages in transit. In the above model, a buffer is associated with each input physical channel and each output physical channel. In alternative designs, buffers may be associated only with inputs (input buffering) or outputs (output buffering). The buffer size is an integral number of flow control units.

- *Switch.* This component is responsible for connecting router input buffers to router output buffers. High-speed routers will utilize crossbar networks with full connectivity, while lower-speed implementations may utilize networks that do not provide full connectivity between input buffers and output buffers.

- *Routing and arbitration unit.* This component implements the routing algorithms, selects the output link for an incoming message, and accordingly sets the switch. If multiple messages simultaneously request the same output link this component must provide for arbitration between them. If the requested link is busy, the incoming message remains in the input buffer. It will be routed again after the link is freed and if it successfully arbitrates for the link.

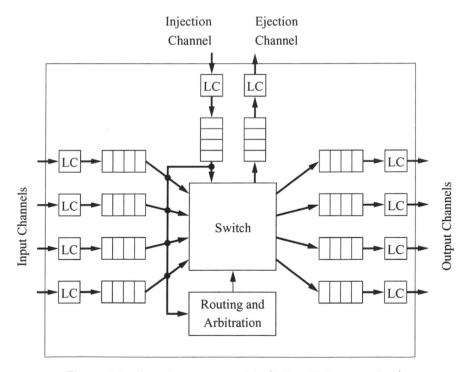

Figure 2.1. Generic router model. (LC = Link controller.)

- *Link controllers (LC)*. The flow of messages across the physical channel between adjacent routers is implemented by the link controller. The link controllers on either side of a channel coordinate to transfer units of flow control.

- *Processor interface*. This component simply implements a physical channel interface to the processor rather than to an adjacent router. It consists of one or more injection channels from the processor and one or more ejection channels to the processor. Ejection channels are also referred to as delivery channels or consumption channels.

From the point of view of router performance we are interested in two parameters [57]. When a message first arrives at a router, it must be examined to determine the output channel over which the message is to be forwarded. This is referred to as the *routing delay*, and typically includes the time to set the switch. Once a path has been established through a router by the switch, we are interested in the rate at which messages can be forwarded through the switch. This rate is determined by the propagation delay through the switch (intrarouter delay), and the signaling rate for synchronizing the transfer of data between the input and output buffers. This delay has been characterized to as the the *internal flow control* latency [57]. Similarly, the delay across the physical links (interrouter delay) is referred to as the *external flow control* latency. The routing delay and flow control delays collectively determine achievable message latency through the switch, and along with contention by messages for links, determines the network throughput.

The following section addresses some basic concepts in the implementation of the switching layer, assuming the generic router model shown in Figure 2.1. The remainder of the chapter focuses on alternative implementations of the switching layer.

2.2   Basic Concepts

Switching layers can be distinguished by the implementation and relative timing of flow control operations and switching techniques. In addition, these operations may be overlapped with the time to make routing decisions.

Flow control is a synchronization protocol for transmitting and receiving a unit of information. The *unit of flow control* refers to that portion of the message whose transfer must be synchronized. This unit is defined as the smallest unit of information whose transfer is requested by the sender and acknowledged by the receiver. The request/acknowledgment signaling is used to ensure successful transfer and the availability of buffer space at the receiver. Note that there is no restriction on when requests or acknowledgments are actually sent or received. Implementation efficiency governs the actual exchange of these control signals, e.g., the use of block acknowledgments. For example, it is easy to think of messages in terms of fixed-length packets. A packet is forwarded across a physical channel or from the input buffers of a router to the output buffers. Note that these transfers are atomic in the sense that sufficient buffering must be provided so that a packet is either transferred in its entirety, or transmission is delayed until sufficient buffer space becomes available. In this example, the *flow* of information is managed and *controlled* at the level of an entire packet.

Flow control occurs at two levels. In the preceding example, *message flow control* occurs at the level of a packet. However, the transfer of a packet across a physical channel between two routers make take several steps or cycles, e.g., the transfer of a 128-byte packet across a 16-bit data channel. The resulting multicycle transfers use *physical channel flow control* to forward a message flow control unit across the physical link connecting routers.

Switching techniques differ in the relationship between the sizes of the physical and message flow control units. In general, each message may be partitioned into fixed-length *packets*. Packets in

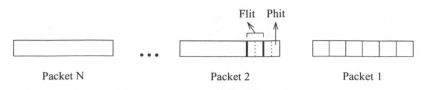

Figure 2.2. Alternative flow control units in a message.

turn may be broken into message flow control units or *flits* [78]. Due to channel width constraints, multiple physical channel cycles may be used to transfer a single flit. A *phit* is the unit of information that can be transferred across a physical channel in a single step or cycle. Flits represent logical units of information as opposed to phits which correspond to physical quantities, i.e., the number of bits that can be transferred in parallel in a single cycle. An example of a message comprised of N packets, 6 flits/packet and 2 phits/flit is shown in Figure 2.2.

The relationships between the sizes of phits, flits, and packets differs across machines. Many machines have the phit size equivalent to the flit size. In the IBM SP2 switch [327], a flit is 1 byte and is equivalent to a phit. Alternatively, the Cray T3D [311] utilizes flit-level message flow control where each flit is comprised of eight 16-bit phits. The specific choices reflect trade-offs in performance, reliability, and implementation complexity.

Example 2.1

There are many candidate synchronization protocols for coordinating phit transfers across a channel, and Figure 2.3 illustrates an example of a simple four-phase asynchronous handshaking protocol. Only one direction of transfer is shown. Router $R1$ asserts the RQ signal when information is to be transferred. Router $R2$ responds by reading the data and asserting the ACK signal. This leads to deasserting RQ by $R1$ which in turn causes $R2$ to deassert ACK. This represents one cycle of operation wherein 1 phit is transferred across the channel.

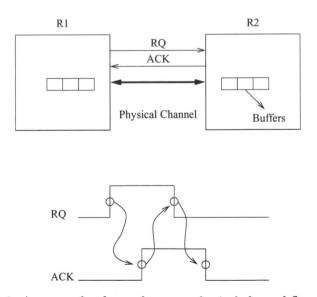

Figure 2.3. An example of asynchronous physical channel flow control.

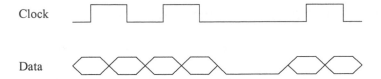

Figure 2.4. An example of synchronous physical channel flow control.

Another transfer may now be initiated. The ACK signal can serve to both acknowledge reception (rising edge) as well as the availability of buffer space (falling edge) for the transmission of the next unit of information. Thus, the flow of phits across the channel is synchronized to prevent buffer overflow in the receiving end of the channel. Note that higher-level message flow control mechanisms can ensure the availability of sufficient buffer space for each flit.

Example 2.2

Physical channel flow control can also be synchronous as shown in Figure 2.4. The clock signal is transmitted across the channel and both the rising and falling edges of the clock line validate the data on the data lines for the receiver. Such physical channel flow control mechanism can be found within the routers of the Intel iPSC/2 and iPSC 860 machines [257]. Figure 2.4 does not show the acknowledgment signals to indicate the availability of buffer space on the receiving node. Acknowledgment signals may be provided for the transfer of each data item, or the channel may utilize block acknowledgments, i.e., each acknowledgment signal indicates the availability of buffer space for some fixed number of data items. Such an approach both reduces the acknowledgment traffic as well as the signaling rate of acknowledgments. It also enables other optimizations for high-speed channel operation that are discussed in Chapter 7.

While interrouter transfers are necessarily constructed in terms of phits, the switching technique deals with flits (which could be defined to be the complete message packet!). The switching techniques set the internal switch to connect input buffers to output buffers, and forward flits along this path. These techniques are distinguished by the time at which they occur relative to the message flow control operation and the routing operation. For example, switching may take place after a flit has been received in its entirety. Alternatively, the transfer of a flit through the switch may begin as soon as the routing operation has been completed, but before the remainder of the flit has been received from the preceding router. In this case switching is overlapped with message-level flow control. In at least one proposed switching technique, switching begins after the first phit is received and even before the routing operation is complete! In general, high-performance switching techniques seek to overlap switching and message flow control as far as possible. While such an approach provides low-latency communication, it does complicate link-level diagnosis and error recovery.

This chapter describes the prevalent switching techniques that have been developed to date for use in current-generation multiprocessors. Switching layers can share the same physical channel flow control mechanism, but differ in the choice of message flow control. Unless otherwise stated, flow control will refer to message flow control.

2.3   Basic Switching Techniques

For the purposes of comparison, for each switching technique we will consider the computation of the base latency of an L-bit message in the absence of any traffic. The phit size and flit size are assumed to be equivalent and equal to the physical data channel width of W bits. The routing header is assumed to be 1 flit, thus the message size is $L + W$ bits. A router can make a routing decision in t_r seconds. The physical channel between two routers operates at B Hz, i.e., the physical channel bandwidth is BW bits per second. The propagation delay across this channel is denoted by $t_w = \frac{1}{B}$. Once a path has been set up through the router, the intrarouter delay or switching delay is denoted by t_s. The router internal data paths are assumed to be matched to the channel width of W bits. Thus, in t_s seconds a W-bit flit can be transferred from the input of the router to the output. The source and destination processors are assumed to be D links apart. The relationship between these components as they are used to compute the no-load message latency is shown in Figure 2.5.

2.3.1   Circuit Switching

In circuit switching, a physical path from the source to the destination is reserved prior to the transmission of the data. This is realized by injecting the routing header flit into the network. This *routing probe* contains the destination address and some additional control information. This routing probe progresses towards the destination reserving physical links as it is transmitted through intermediate routers. When the probe reaches the destination, a complete path has been set up and an acknowledgment is transmitted back to the source. The message contents may now be transmitted at the full bandwidth of the hardware path. The circuit may be released by the destination or by the last few bits of the message. In the Intel iPSC/2 routers [257], the acknowledgments are multiplexed in the reverse direction on the same physical line as the message. Alternatively, implementations may provide separate signal lines to transmit acknowledgment signals. A time-space diagram of the transmission of a message over three links is shown in Figure 2.6. The header probe is forwarded across three links followed by the return of the acknowledgment. The shaded boxes represent the times during which a link is busy. The space between these boxes represents the time to process the routing header, and the intrarouter propagation delays. The clear box represents the duration the links are busy transmitting data through the circuit. Note that the routing and intrarouter delays at the source router are not included and would precede the box corresponding to the first busy link.

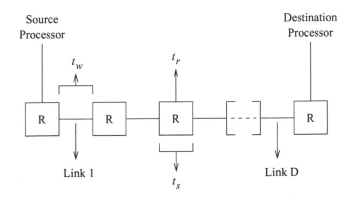

Figure 2.5. View of the network path for computing the no-load latency. (R = Router.)

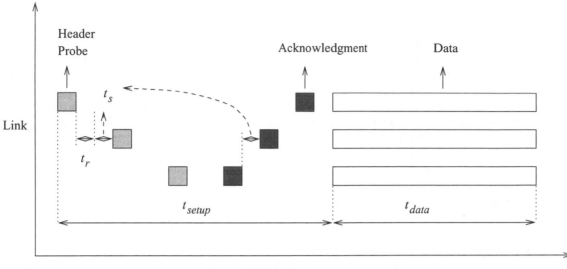

Figure 2.6. Time-space diagram of a circuit-switched message.

An example of a routing probe used in the JPL Mark III binary hypercube is shown in Figure 2.7. The network of the Mark III was quite flexible, supporting several distinct switching mechanisms in configurations up to 2,048 nodes. Bits 0 and 16 of the header define the switching technique being employed. The values shown in Figure 2.7 are for circuit switching. Bits 17–19 are unused while the destination address is provided in bits 1–11. The remaining 4-bit fields are used to address 1 of 11 output links at each individual router. There are 11 such fields supporting a 11-dimensional hypercube and requiring a two-word, 64-bit header. The path is computed at the source node. An alternative could have been to compute the value of the output port at each node rather than storing the addresses of all intermediate ports in the header. This would significantly reduce the size of the routing header probe. However, this scheme would require routing time and buffering logic within the router. In contrast, the format shown in Figure 2.7 enables a fast lookup using the header and simple processing within the router.

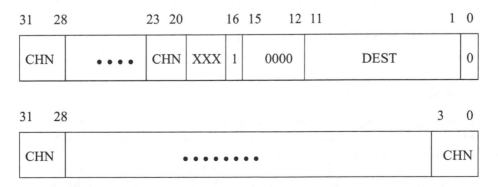

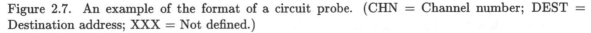

Figure 2.7. An example of the format of a circuit probe. (CHN = Channel number; DEST = Destination address; XXX = Not defined.)

Circuit switching is generally advantageous when messages are infrequent and long, i.e., the message transmission time is long compared to the path setup time. The disadvantage is that the physical path is reserved for the duration of the message and may block other messages. For example, consider the case where the probe is blocked waiting for a physical link to become free. All of the links reserved by the probe up to that point remain reserved, cannot be used by other circuits, and may be blocking other circuits preventing them from being set up. Thus, if the size of the message is not that much greater than the size of the probe, it would be advantageous to transmit the message along with the header and buffer the message within the routers while waiting for a free link. This alternative technique is referred to as *packet switching*, and will be studied in Section 2.3.2.

The base latency of a circuit-switched message is determined by the time to set up a path, and the subsequent time the path is busy transmitting data. The router operation differs a bit from that shown in Figure 2.1. While the routing probe is buffered at each router, data bits are not. There are no intervening data buffers in the circuit which operates effectively as a single wire from source to destination. This physical circuit may use asynchronous or synchronous flow control as shown in Figures 2.3 or 2.4. In this case the time for the transfer of each flit from source to destination is determined by the clock speed of the synchronous circuit or signaling speed of the asynchronous handshake lines. The signaling period or clock period must be greater than the propagation delay through this circuit. This places a practical limit on the speed of circuit switching as a function of system size. More recent techniques have begun to investigate the use of this delay as a form of storage. At very high signal speeds, multiple bits may be present on a wire concurrently, proceeding as *waves* of data. Such techniques have been referred to as *wave pipelining* [112]. Using such techniques the technological limits of router and network designs have been reexamined [102, 310] and it has been found that substantial improvements in wire bandwidth is possible. The challenges to widespread use remain the design of circuits that can employ wave pipelining with stable and predictable delays, while in large designs the signal skew remains particularly challenging.

Without wave pipelining, from Figure 2.6 we can write an expression for the base latency of a message as follows:

$$
\begin{aligned}
t_{circuit} &= t_{setup} + t_{data} \\
t_{setup} &= D[t_r + 2(t_s + t_w)] \\
t_{data} &= \frac{1}{B}\left\lceil \frac{L}{W} \right\rceil
\end{aligned}
\tag{2.1}
$$

Actual latencies clearly depend on a myriad of implementation details. Figure 2.6 represents some simplifying assumptions about the time necessary for various events such as processing an acknowledgment, or initiating the transmission of the first data flit. The factor of 2 in the setup cost represents the time for the forward progress of the header and the return of the acknowledgment. The use of B Hz as the channel speed represents the transmission across hardwired path from source to destination.

2.3.2   Packet Switching

In circuit switching, the complete message is transmitted after the circuit has been set up. Alternatively, the message can be partitioned and transmitted as fixed-length packets, e.g., 128 bytes. The first few bytes of a packet contain routing and control information and are referred to as the *packet header*. Each packet is individually routed from source to destination. A packet is completely buffered at each intermediate node before it is forwarded to the next node. This is the reason why this switching technique is also referred to as *store-and-forward* (SAF) switching. The header information is extracted by the intermediate router and used to determine the output link over which

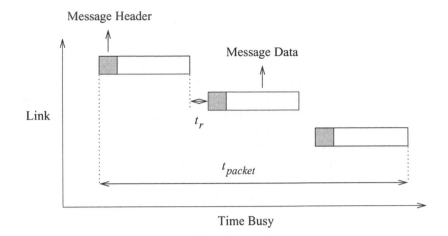

Figure 2.8. Time-space diagram of a packet-switched message.

the header is to be forwarded. A time-space diagram of the progress of a packet across three links is shown in Figure 2.8. From the figure we can see that the latency experienced by a packet is proportional to the distance between the source and destination nodes. Note that the figure has omitted the packet latency through the router.

Packet switching is advantageous when messages are short and frequent. Unlike circuit switching, where a segment of a reserved path may be idle for a significant period of time, a communication link is fully utilized when there are data to be transmitted. Many packets belonging to a message can be in the network simultaneously even if the first packet has not yet arrived at the destination. However, splitting a message into packets produces some overhead. In addition to the time required at source and destination nodes, every packet must be routed at each intermediate node. An example of the format of a data packet header is shown in Figure 2.9. This is the header format used in the JPL Hyperswitch. Since the hyperswitch can operate in one of many modes, bit field 12–16 and bit 0 collectively identify the switching technique being used: in this case it is packet switching using a fixed-path routing algorithm. Bits 1–11 identify the destination address, limiting the format to systems of 2,048 processors or less. The LEN field identifies the packet size in units of 192 bytes. For the current implementation packet size is limited to 384 bytes. If packets are routed adaptively through the network, packets from the same message may arrive at the destination out of order. In this case the packet headers must also contain sequencing information so that the messages can be reconstructed at the destination.

In multidimensional, point-to-point networks it is evident that the storage requirements at the individual router nodes can become extensive if packets can become large and multiple packets must be buffered at a node. In the JPL implementation, packets are not stored in the router,

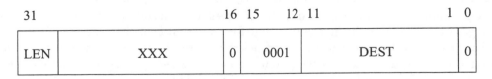

Figure 2.9. An example packet header format. (DEST = Destination address; LEN = Packet length in units of 192 bytes; XXX = Not defined.)

but are rather stored in the memory of the local node and a special-purpose message coprocessor is used to process the message, i.e., compute the address of an output channel and forward the message. Other multicomputers using packet switching also buffer packets in the memory of the local node (Cosmic Cube [313], Intel iPSC/1 [164]). This implementation is no doubt a carryover from implementations in local and wide area networks where packets are buffered in memory and special-purpose coprocessors and network interfaces have been dedicated to processing messages. In modern multiprocessors, the overhead and impact on message latency render such message processing impractical. To be viable, messages must be buffered and processed within the routers. Storage requirements can be reduced by using central queues in the router that are shared by all input channels rather than providing buffering at each input channel, output channel, or both. In this case, internal and external flow control delays will typically take many cycles.

The base latency of a packet-switched message can be computed as follows:

$$t_{packet} = D \left\{ t_r + (t_s + t_w) \left\lceil \frac{L + W}{W} \right\rceil \right\} \tag{2.2}$$

This expression follows the router model in Figure 2.1, and as a result includes factors to represent the time for the transfer of packet of length $L + W$ bits across the channel (t_w) as well as from the input buffer of the router to the output buffer (t_s). However, in practice, the router could be only input-buffered, output-buffered, or use central queues. The above expression would be modified accordingly. The important point to note is that the latency is directly proportional to the distance between the source and destination nodes.

2.3.3   Virtual Cut-Through (VCT) Switching

Packet switching is based on the assumption that a packet must be received in its entirety before any routing decision can be made and the packet forwarded to the destination. This is not generally true. Consider a 128-byte packet and the router model shown in Figure 2.1. In the absence of 128-byte-wide physical channels, the transfer of the packet across the physical channel will take multiple cycles. However, the first few bytes will contain routing information that is typically available after the first few cycles. Rather than waiting for the entire packet to be received, the packet header can be examined as soon as it is received. The router can start forwarding the header and following data bytes as soon as routing decisions have been made and the output buffer is free. In fact, the message does not even have to be buffered at the output and can *cut through* to the input of the next router before the complete packet has been received at the current router. This switching technique is referred to as *virtual cut-through* (VCT) switching. In the absence of blocking, the latency experienced by the header at each node is the routing latency and propagation delay through the router and along the physical channels. The message is effectively pipelined through successive switches. If the header is blocked on a busy output channel, the complete message is buffered at the node. Thus, at high network loads, VCT switching behaves like packet switching.

Figure 2.10 illustrates a time-space diagram of a message transferred using VCT switching where the message is blocked after the first link waiting for an output channel to become free. In this case we see that the complete packet has to be transferred to the first router where it remains blocked waiting for a free output port. However, from the figure we can see that the message is successful in cutting through the second router and across the third link.

The base latency of a message that successfully cuts through each intermediate router can be computed as follows:

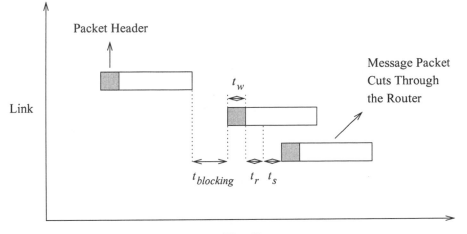

Figure 2.10. Time-space diagram of a virtual cut-through switched message. ($t_{blocking}$ = Waiting time for a free output link.)

$$t_{vct} = D(t_r + t_s + t_w) + \max(t_s, t_w) \left\lceil \frac{L}{W} \right\rceil \tag{2.3}$$

Cut-through routing is assumed to occur at the flit level with the routing information contained in 1 flit. This model assumes that there is no time penalty for cutting through a router if the output buffer and output channel are free. Depending on the speed of operation of the routers this may not be realistic. Note that only the header experiences routing delay, as well as the switching delay and wire delay at each router. This is because the transmission is pipelined and the switch is buffered at the input and output. Once the header flit reaches the destination, the cycle time of this message pipeline is determined by the maximum of the switch delay and wire delay between routers. If the switch had been buffered only at the input, then in one cycle of operation, a flit traverses the switch and channel between the routers. In this case the coefficient of the second term and the pipeline cycle time would be $(t_s + t_w)$. Note that the unit of message flow control is a packet. Therefore even though the message may cut through the router, sufficient buffer space must be allocated for a complete packet in case the header is blocked.

2.3.4   Wormhole Switching

The need to buffer complete packets within a router can make it difficult to construct small, compact, and fast routers. In wormhole switching, message packets are also pipelined through the network. However the buffer requirements within the routers are substantially reduced over the requirements for VCT switching. A message packet is broken up into flits. The flit is the unit of message flow control, and input and output buffers at a router are typically large enough to store a few flits. For example, the message buffers in the Cray T3D are 1 flit deep and each flit is comprised of eight 16-bit phits. The message is pipelined through the network at the flit level and is typically too large to be completely buffered within a router. Thus, at any instant in time a blocked message occupies buffers in several routers. The time-space diagram of a wormhole-switched message is shown in Figure 2.11. The clear rectangles illustrate the propagation of flits across the physical channel. The

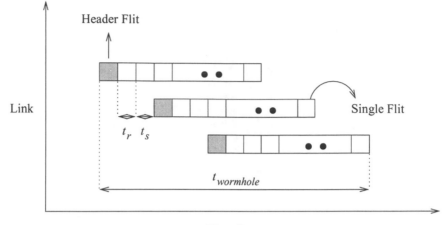

Figure 2.11. Time-space diagram of a wormhole-switched message.

shaded rectangles illustrate the propagation of header flits across the physical channels. Routing delays and intrarouter propagation of the header flits are also captured in this figure. The primary difference between wormhole switching and VCT switching is that the unit of message flow control is a single flit and, as a consequence, the use of small buffers. An entire message cannot be buffered at a router.

In the absence of blocking the message packet is pipelined through the network. However, the blocking characteristics are very different from that of VCT. If the required output channel is busy, the message is blocked "in place." For example, Figure 2.12 illustrates a snapshot of a message being transmitted through routers $R1$, $R2$, and $R3$. Input and output buffers are 2 flits deep and the routing header is 2 flits. At router $R3$, message A requires an output channel that is being used by message B. Therefore message A blocks in place. The small buffer sizes at each node ($<$ message size) causes the message to occupy buffers in multiple routers, similarly blocking other messages. In effect dependencies between buffers span multiple routers. This property complicates the issue of deadlock freedom. However, it is no longer necessary to use the local processor memory to buffer messages, significantly reducing average message latency. The small buffer requirements and message pipelining enable the construction of routers that are small, compact, and fast.

Examples of the format of wormhole-switched packets in the Cray T3D are shown in Figure 2.13. In this machine, a phit is 16 bits wide — the width of a T3D physical channel — and a flit is comprised of 8 phits. A word is 64 bits and thus 4 phits. A message is comprised of header phits and possibly data phits. The header phits contain the routing tag, destination node address, and control information. The routing tag identifies a fixed path through the network. The control information is interpreted by the receiving node to determine any local operations that may have to be performed, e.g., read and return a local datum. Depending on the type of packet, additional header information may include the source node address, and memory address at the receiving node. For example, in the figure, a read-request packet is comprised of only header phits while the read response packet contains four 64-bit words. Each word has an additional phit that contains 14 check bits for error correction and detection.

From the example in Figure 2.13 we note that routing information is associated *only* with the header phits (flits) and not with the data flits. As a result, each incoming data flit of a message packet is simply forwarded along the same output channel as the preceding data flit. As a result, the

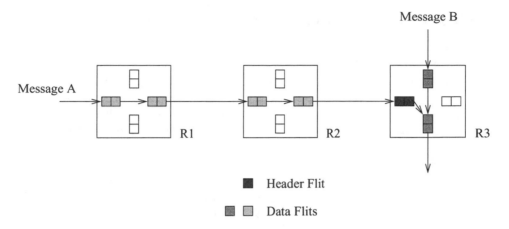

Figure 2.12. An example of a blocked wormhole-switched message.

transmission of distinct messages cannot be interleaved or multiplexed over a physical channel. The message must cross the channel in its entirety before the channel can be used by another message. This is why messages A and B in Figure 2.12 cannot be multiplexed over the physical channel without some additional architectural support.

The base latency of a wormhole-switched message can be computed as follows:

$$t_{wormhole} = D(t_r + t_s + t_w) + \max(t_s, t_w) \left\lceil \frac{L}{W} \right\rceil \tag{2.4}$$

This expression assumes flit buffers at the router inputs and outputs. Note that in the absence of contention, VCT and wormhole switching have the same latency. Once the header flit arrives at the destination, the message pipeline cycle time is determined by the maximum of the switch delay and wire delay. For an input-only, or output-only buffered switch this cycle time would be given by the sum of the switch and wire delays.

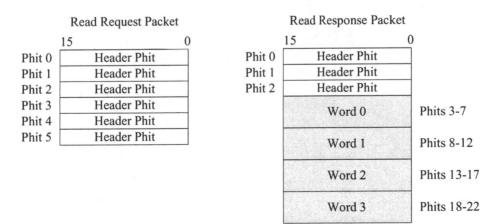

Figure 2.13. Format of wormhole-switched packets in the Cray T3D.

2.3.5 Mad Postman Switching

VCT switching improved the performance of packet switching by enabling pipelined message flow while retaining the ability to buffer complete message packets. Wormhole switching provided further reductions in latency by permitting small buffer VCT so that routing could be completely handled within single-chip routers, therefore providing low latency necessary for tightly coupled parallel processing. This trend toward increased message pipelining is continued with the development of the *mad postman switching* mechanism in an attempt to realize the minimal possible routing latency per node.

The technique is best understood in the context of bit-serial physical channels. Consider a 2-D mesh network with message packets that have a 2-flit header. Routing is dimension-order: messages are first routed completely along dimension 0 and then along dimension 1. The leading header flit contains the destination address of a node in dimension 0. When the message reaches this node, the message is forwarded along dimension 1. The second header flit contains the destination in dimension 1. In VCT and wormhole switching flits cannot be forwarded until the header flits have been received in their entirety at the router. If we had 8-bit flits, transmission of the header flits across a bit-serial physical channel will take 16 cycles. Assuming a 1-cycle delay to select the output channel at each intermediate router, the minimum latency for the header to reach a destination router three links away is 51 cycles. The mad postman attempts to reduce the per-node latency further by pipelining at the bit level. When a header flit starts arriving at a router, it is assumed that the message will be continuing along the same dimension. Therefore header bits are forwarded to the output link in the same dimension as soon as they are received (assuming that the output channel is free). Each bit of the header is also buffered locally. Once the last bit of the first flit of the header has been received, the router can examine this flit and determine if the message should indeed proceed further along this dimension. If it is to proceed along the second dimension, the remainder of the message starting with the second flit of the header is transmitted to the output along the second dimension. If the message has arrived at its destination, it is delivered to the local processor. In essence, the message is first delivered to an output channel and the address is checked later, hence the name of this switching technique. This strategy can work very well in 2-D networks

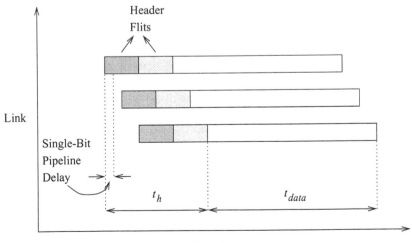

Figure 2.14. Time-space diagram for message transmission using mad postman switching.

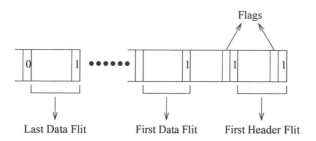

Figure 2.15. An example message format for the mad postman switching technique.

since a message will make at most one turn from one dimension to another and we can encode each dimension offset in 1 header flit. The common case of messages continuing along the same dimension is made very fast. A time-space diagram of a message transmitted over three links using the mad postman switching technique is illustrated in Figure 2.14.

Some constraints must be placed on the organization of the header. An example is shown in Figure 2.15, wherein each dimension offset is encoded in a header flit, and these flits are ordered according to the order of traversal. For example, when the message packet has completely traversed the first dimension the router can start transmitting in the second dimension with the start of the first bit of the second header flit. The first flit has effectively been stripped off the message, but continues to traverse the first dimension. Such a flit is referred to as a *dead address flit*. In a multidimensional network, each time a message changes to a new dimension, a dead flit is generated and the message becomes smaller. At any point if a dead flit is buffered, i.e., blocked by another message packet, it can be detected in the local router and removed.

Let us consider an example of routing in a 4×4, 2-D mesh. In this example the routing header is comprised of 2 flits. Each flit is 3 bits long: a special start bit and 2 bits to identify the destination node in each dimension. The message is pipelined through the network at the bit level. Each input and output buffer is 2 bits deep. Consider the case where a message is being transmitted from node 20 to node 32. Figure 2.16 illustrates the progress and location of the header flits. The message

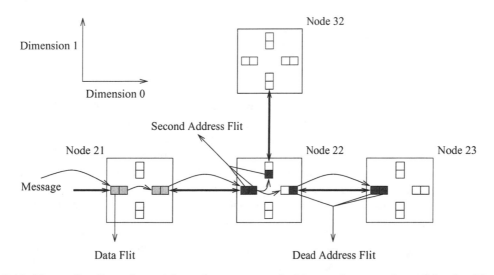

Figure 2.16. Example of routing with mad postman switching and generation of dead address flits.

is transmitted along dimension 0 to node 22 where it is transmitted along dimension 1 to node 32. At node 22, the first flit is pipelined through to the output as it is received. After receiving the third bit, it is determined the message must continue along dimension 1. The first bit of the second header flit is forwarded to the output in dimension 1 as shown in the figure. Note that header flits are stripped off as the message changes dimensions and the message becomes smaller. The dead address flit proceeds along dimension 0 until it can be detected and removed.

For a given number of processors the size of the dead address flit is determined by the number of processors in a dimension. Therefore it follows that for a given number of processors, low-dimension networks will introduce a smaller number of larger dead address flits while higher-dimension networks will introduce a larger number of smaller dead address flits. Initially it would appear that the dead address flits would adversely affect performance until they are removed from the network since they consume physical channel bandwidth. Since message packets will generally be larger than a dead address flit, the probability of a packet being blocked by a dead address flit is very small. It is more likely that a dead address flit will be blocked by a message packet. In this case the local router has an opportunity to detect the dead address flit and remove it from the network. At high loads, we are concerned with dead address flits consuming precious network bandwidth. It is interesting to note that increased blocking in the network will provide more opportunities for routers to remove dead address flits. The greater the congestion, the less likely that a packet will encounter a dead address flit!

By optimistically forwarding the message bit stream to an output channel the routing latency at a node is minimized and full bit-level pipelining can be achieved. Considering again a 2-D mesh with bit-serial physical channels and packets that have two 8-bit header flits, traversing three links, the minimum latency for the header to reach the destination is 18 rather than 51 cycles. In general, the mad postman strategy is useful when it takes multiple cycles for a header to cross a physical channel. In this case latency can be reduced by optimistically forwarding portions of the header onward before the correct output link is actually determined. However, the pin-out constraints of modern routers permit wider flits to be transmitted across a channel in a single cycle. If the header can be transmitted in one cycle, there is little if any advantage to be gained.

The base latency of a message routed using the mad postman switching technique can be computed as follows:

$$
\begin{aligned}
t_{madpostman} &= t_h + t_{data} \\
t_h &= (t_s + t_w)D + \max(t_s, t_w)W \\
t_{data} &= \max(t_s, t_w)L
\end{aligned}
\tag{2.5}
$$

The above expression makes several assumptions. The first is the use of bit-serial channels which is the most favorable for the mad postman strategy. The routing time t_r is assumed to be equivalent to the switch delay and occurs concurrently with bit transmission, and therefore does not appear in the expression. The term t_h corresponds to the time taken to completely deliver the header.

Let us consider the general case where we do not have bit-serial channels, but rather C bit channels, where $1 < C < W$. Multiple cycles would be required to transfer the header flit across the physical channel. In this case the mad postman switching strategy would realize a base latency of

$$
t_{madpostman} = D(t_s + t_w) + \max(t_s, t_w)\left\lceil \frac{W}{C} \right\rceil + \max(t_s, t_w)\left\lceil \frac{L}{C} \right\rceil
\tag{2.6}
$$

For comparison purposes, in this case the expression for wormhole switching would have been

$$t_{wormhole} = D \left\{ t_r + (t_s + t_w) \left\lceil \frac{W}{C} \right\rceil \right\} + \max(t_s, t_w) \left\lceil \frac{L}{C} \right\rceil \qquad (2.7)$$

Assuming that the internal and external channel widths are C bits, a header flit (of width W bits) requires $\left\lceil \frac{W}{C} \right\rceil$ cycles to cross the channel and the router. This cost is incurred at each intermediate router. When $C = W$, the above expression reduces to the previous expression for wormhole switching with single-flit headers. As larger physical channel widths become feasible in practice, the advantage of the mad postman switching over wormhole switching will diminish.

2.4 Virtual Channels

The preceding switching techniques were described assuming that messages or parts of messages were buffered at the input and output of each physical channel. Buffers are commonly operated as FIFO queues. Therefore once a message occupies a buffer for a channel, no other message can access the physical channel, even if the message is blocked. Alternatively, a physical channel may support several *logical* or *virtual channels* multiplexed across the physical channel. Each unidirectional virtual channel is realized by an independently managed pair of message buffers as illustrated in Figure 2.17. This figure shows two unidirectional virtual channels in each direction across the physical channel. Consider wormhole switching with a message in each virtual channel. Each message can share the physical channel on a flit-by-flit basis. The physical channel protocol must be able to distinguish between the virtual channels using the physical channel. Logically, each virtual channel operates as if each were using a distinct physical channel operating at half the speed. Virtual channels were originally introduced to solve the problem of deadlock in wormhole-switched networks. Deadlock is a network state where no messages can advance because each message requires a channel occupied by another message. This issue is discussed in detail in Chapter 3.

Virtual channels can also be used to improve message latency and network throughput. By allowing messages to share a physical channel, messages can make progress rather than remain blocked. For example, Figure 2.18 shows two messages crossing the physical channel between routers $R1$ and $R2$. With no virtual channels message A will prevent message B from advancing until the transmission of message A has been completed. However, in the figure, there are two single-flit virtual channels multiplexed over each physical channel. By multiplexing the two messages on a flit-by-flit basis, both messages continue to make progress. The rate at which each message is forwarded

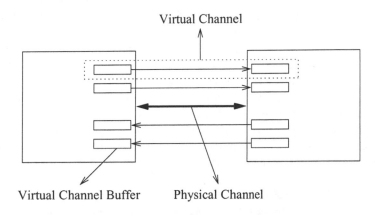

Figure 2.17. Virtual channels.

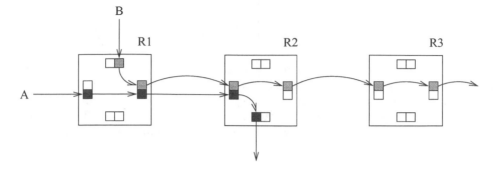

Figure 2.18. An example of the reduction in header blocking delay by using two virtual channels for each physical channel.

is nominally one half the rate achievable when the channel is not shared. In effect, the use of virtual channels decouples the physical channels from message buffers allowing multiple messages to share a physical channel in the same manner that multiple programs may share a central processing unit (CPU). The overall time a message spends blocked at a router waiting for a free channel is reduced leading to an overall reduction in individual message latency. There are two specific cases where such sharing of the physical link bandwidth is particularly beneficial. Consider the case where message A is temporarily blocked downstream from the current node. With an appropriate physical channel flow control protocol, message B can be make use of the full bandwidth of physical channel between the routers. Without virtual channels, both messages would be blocked. Alternatively, consider the case where message A is a very long message relative to message B. Message B can still make progress at half the link speed, and then message A can resume transmission at the full link speed. Studies have shown that message traffic in parallel programs is often bimodal comprised of short (cache lines, control messages) and long messages (data structures) [176].

The approach described in the preceding paragraph does not place any restrictions on the use of the virtual channels. Therefore, when used in this manner these buffers are referred to as *virtual lanes*. Virtual channels were originally introduced as a mechanism for deadlock avoidance in networks with physical cycles, and as such routing restrictions are placed on their use. For example, packets may be prohibited from being transferred between certain classes of virtual channels to prevent cyclic waiting dependencies for buffer space. Thus, in general we have virtual channels that may in turn be comprised of multiple lanes. While the choice of virtual channels at a router may be restricted, it does not matter which lane within a virtual channel is used by a message, although all of the flits within a message will use the same lane within a channel.

We have seen from Section 2.2 that acknowledgment traffic is necessary to regulate the flow of data and to ensure the availability of buffer space on the receiver. Acknowledgments are necessary for each virtual channel or lane, increasing the volume of such traffic across the physical channel. Furthermore, for a fixed amount of buffer space within a router, the size of each virtual channel or lane buffer is now smaller. Therefore the effect of optimizations such as the use of acknowledgments for a block of flits or phits is limited. If physical channel bandwidth is allocated in a demand-driven fashion, the operation of the physical channel now includes the transmission of the virtual channel address to correctly identify the receiving virtual channel, or to indicate which virtual channel has available message buffers.

We can envision continuing to add virtual channels to further reduce the blocking experienced by each message. The result is increased network throughput measured in flits/s, due to increased physical channel utilization. However, each additional virtual channel improves performance by a smaller amount, and the increased channel multiplexing reduces the data rate of individual messages, increasing the message latency. This increase in latency due to data multiplexing will eventually overshadow the reduction in latency due to blocking leading to overall increasing average message latency. An analysis of this phenomena can be found in Chapter 9 which provides detailed performance data to quantify various aspects of network performance.

Increasing the number of virtual channels has a direct impact on router performance through their effect on the achievable hardware cycle time of the router. The link controllers now become more complex since they must support arbitration between multiple virtual channels/lanes for the physical channel, and this arbitration function can be on the critical path for internode delay. The number of inputs and outputs that must be switched at each node is increased, substantially increasing the switch complexity. For a fixed amount of buffer space in a node, how is this buffer space to be allocated among channels, and lanes within a channel? Further, the flow of messages through the router must be coordinated with the allocation of physical channel bandwidth. The increasing complexity of these functions can lead to net increases in internal and external flow control latencies. This increase affects all messages through the routers. Such trade-offs and related issues affecting the design of routers are discussed in detail in Chapter 7 and evaluated in Chapter 9.

2.5 Hybrid Switching Techniques

The availability and flexibility of virtual channels have led to the development of several hybrid switching techniques. These techniques have been motivated by a desire to combine the advantages of several basic approaches, or have been motivated by the need to optimize performance metrics other than traditional latency and throughput, e.g., fault tolerance and reliability. Some common hybrid switching techniques are presented in this section.

2.5.1 Buffered Wormhole Switching

A switching technique that combines aspects of wormhole switching and packet switching is *buffered wormhole switching* (BWS), proposed and utilized in IBM's Power Parallel SP systems. The switching technique and message formats have been motivated by the interconnection network utilized in the SP systems. This network is a multistage, generalized Omega network using 4×4 crossbar switches with bidirectional links. The system building block is a 16-processor system configured around the two-stage switch with eight crossbar switches as shown in Figure 2.19a. This module is referred to as a frame. Each 4×4 switch uses bidirectional links, and therefore can be viewed as an 8×8 implementation of the router organization shown in Figure 2.1 with the functionality described below.

The basic switching mechanism is wormhole switching. Message packets can be of variable length and up to 255 flits in length. Each flit is 1 byte and is equal to the physical channel width. The first flit of a message contains the length of the message while the following flits contain routing information. Routing is source-based where each routing flit contains the address of the output ports in intermediate switches. There is 1 routing flit for each frame, i.e., for each group of 16 processors. The format of the routing flit is shown in Figure 2.19b. Note that these 4×4 crossbar switches have bidirectional links, and therefore eight input ports and eight output ports. Bits 4–6 are used to select the output port of the first switch in the frame. Bits 0–2 are used to select the output port of the second switch in the frame. Bit 7 is used to determine which field is to be used. It is initially cleared and set by the first switch in the frame. Larger systems are built up as groups of frames. Every frame requires 1 routing flit.

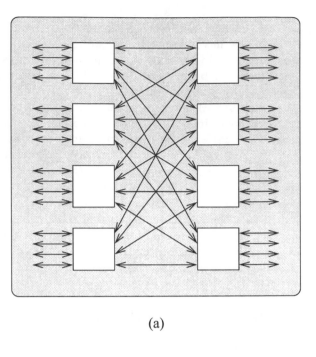

(a)

7	6		4	2		0
	Port No.			Port No.		

(b)

Figure 2.19. (a) Organization of the switch used in the IBM Power Series parallel machines. (b) Routing flit format.

As the message is routed through the switches, the corresponding routing flit is discarded, shortening the message. This is similar to the mad postman switching strategy. As long as the path is conflict-free, the message progresses as in wormhole switching with interswitch flow control operating at the flit level. When output channels are available, data flow through the switch is through byte-wide paths through the internal crossbar and to the output port. When messages block, flow control within the switch is organized into 8-flit units referred to as *chunks*. When messages block, chunks are constructed at the input port of a switch, transmitted through 64-bit-wide paths to the a local memory. Subsequently, buffered chunks are transferred to an output port where they are converted to a flit stream for transmission across the physical channel.

When there is a conflict at the output of a routing node, flits are buffered within the switch as chunks. These chunks are buffered in a dynamically allocated central storage. The storage is organized as a linked list for each output, where each element of the list is a message to be transmitted on that output port. Since only the first chunk of a message contains routing information, each message is in turn organized as a list of chunks. Thus, ordering of flits within a message packet is preserved. This type of organization is depicted in Figure 2.20 where two messages are shown queued at an output port. The first message is comprised of 24 flits and the second message is 16 flits long. Messages waiting on each of the other output ports are similarly organized. When an

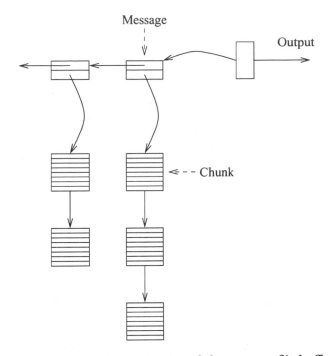

Figure 2.20. Logical organization of the message flit buffers.

output port becomes free, messages are transmitted to the output channel as 64-bit chunks in a single cycle: since the internal datapath and flow control to/from central memory is based on 8-flit chunks. The central storage is dual-ported and can support 128 chunks. A minimum of one chunk is made available for each output port. The remaining chunks are dynamically allocated as necessary. In a single cycle, one input port or one output port can be serviced from the central storage. Thus we see that short messages can be completely buffered.

BWS differs from wormhole switching in that flits are not buffered in place. Rather flits are aggregated and buffered in a local memory within the switch. If the message is small and space is available in the central queue, the input port is released for use by another message even though this message packet remains blocked. In this respect, BWS appears similar to packet switching. BWS differs from packet switching and VCT switching in that flow control is largely at the flit level and when messages are blocked, flow control (within the switch) is at the level of 8-flit chunks. If the central queue were made large enough to ensure that complete messages could always be buffered, the behavior of BWS would approach that of VCT switching.

The base latency of a message routed using BWS is identical to that of wormhole-switched messages.

2.5.2 Pipelined Circuit Switching

In many environments rather than minimizing message latency or maximizing network throughput, the overriding issue is the ability to tolerate the failure of network components such as routers and links. In wormhole switching, header flits containing routing information establish a path through the network from source to destination. Data flits are pipelined through the path immediately following the header flits. If the header cannot progress due to a faulty component, the message is

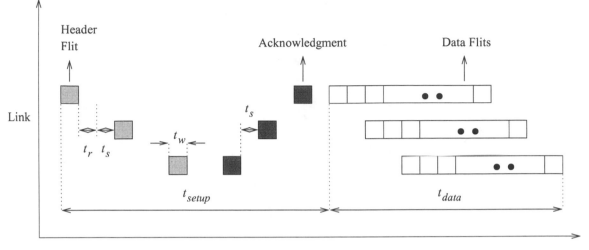

Figure 2.21. Time-space diagram of a message transmitted using PCS.

blocked in place indefinitely, holding buffer resources and blocking other messages. This situation can eventually result in a deadlocked configuration of messages. While techniques such as adaptive routing can alleviate the problem, it cannot by itself solve the problem. This has motivated the development of different switching techniques.

Pipelined circuit switching (PCS) combines aspects of circuit switching and wormhole switching. PCS sets up a path before starting data transmission as in circuit switching. Basically, PCS differs from circuit switching in that paths are formed by virtual channels instead of physical channels. In pipelined circuit switching, data flits do not immediately follow the header flits into the network as in wormhole switching. Consequently, increased flexibility is available in routing the header flit. For example, rather than blocking on a faulty output channel at an intermediate router, the header may backtrack to the preceding router and release the previously reserved channel. A new output channel may now be attempted at the preceding router in finding an alternative path to the destination. When the header finally reaches the destination node, an *acknowledgment flit* is transmitted back to the source node. Now data flits can be pipelined over the path just as in wormhole switching. The resilience to component failures is obtained at the expense of larger path setup times. This approach is flexible in that headers can perform a backtracking search of the network, reserving and releasing virtual channels in an attempt to establish a fault-free path to the destination. This technique combines message pipelining from wormhole switching with a more conservative path setup algorithm based on circuit switching techniques. A time-space diagram of a PCS message transmission over three links in the absence of any traffic or failures is shown in Figure 2.21.

Since headers do not block holding channel or buffer resources, routing restrictions are not necessary to avoid deadlock. This increases the probability of finding a path while still avoiding deadlocked configurations of messages. Moreover, reservation of virtual channels by the header does not by itself lead to use of physical channel bandwidth. Therefore, unlike circuit switching, path setup does not lead to excessive blocking of other messages. As a result, multipath networks in conjunction with the flexibility of PCS are good candidates for providing low-latency fault-tolerant performance. For purely performance-driven applications where fault tolerance is not a primary concern, the added overhead of PCS makes wormhole switching the mechanism of choice.

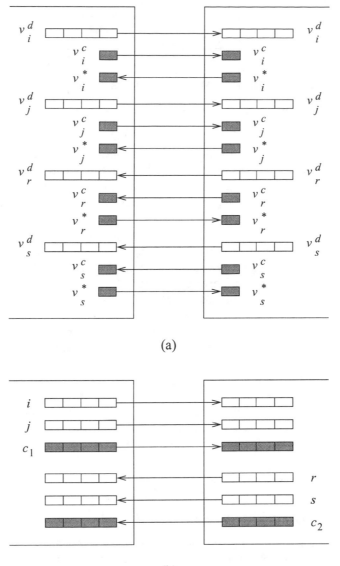

(a)

(b)

Figure 2.22. Virtual channel model for PCS.

In PCS, we distinguish between flits that carry control information, e.g., header flits and acknowledgment flits, and those that carry data. This distinction is supported in the virtual channel model that separates control flit traffic and data flit traffic. A unidirectional virtual channel v_i is composed of a *data channel*, a *corresponding channel*, and a *complementary channel* (v_i^d, v_i^c, v_i^*) and is referred to as a *virtual channel trio*. The router header will traverse v_i^c while subsequent data flits will traverse v_i^d. The complementary channel v_i^* is reserved for use by acknowledgment flits and backtracking header flits. The complementary channel of a trio traverses the physical channel in the direction opposite to that of its associated data channel. The channel model is illustrated in Figure 2.22. There are two virtual channels $v_i(v_r)$ and $v_j(v_s)$ from $R1$ $(R2)$ to $R2$ $(R1)$. Only

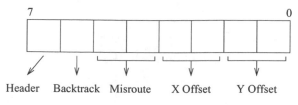

Figure 2.23. Example format of a PCS header.

one message can be in progress over a given data channel. Therefore, compared to existing channel models, this model requires exactly two extra flit buffers for each data channel — one each for the corresponding channel and the complementary channel, respectively. Since control flit traffic is a small percentage of the overall flit traffic, in practice all control channels across a physical link are multiplexed through a single virtual control channel as shown in Figure 2.22a. Thus, compared to the more common use of virtual channels, this model requires one extra virtual channel in each direction between a pair of adjacent routers. For example, channel c_1 in Figure 2.22b corresponds to flit buffers $v_i^c, v_j^c, v_r^*, v_s^*$. The implementation of PCS in the Ariadne router [7] utilized two data channels and one virtual control channel over each physical link.

This separation of control traffic and data traffic is useful in developing fault tolerant routing and distributed fault recovery mechanisms. Such mechanisms are discussed in greater detail in Chapter 6. The Ariadne router [7] is a single-chip PCS router with two virtual channel trios per physical channel. The prototype router had byte-wide physical channels and 8-bit flits. The format of the header flit is shown in Figure 2.23. In this design a single bit distinguished a control flit from a data flit (this only left 7-bit data flits!). A single bit distinguishes between backtracking flits and flits making forward progress. The misroute field keeps track of the number of misrouting steps the header has taken. The maximum number of misroutes that the header can take in this design is 3. Finally, two fields provide X and Y offsets for routing in a 2-D mesh.

The base latency of a pipelined circuit switched message can be computed as follows:

$$
\begin{aligned}
t_{pcs} &= t_{setup} + t_{data} \\
t_{setup} &= D(t_r + t_s + t_w) + D(t_s + t_w) \\
t_{data} &= D(t_s + t_w) + \max(t_s, t_w)\left(\left\lceil \frac{L}{W} \right\rceil - 1\right)
\end{aligned}
\tag{2.8}
$$

The first term in t_{setup} is the time taken for the header flit to reach the destination. The second term is the time taken for the acknowledgment flit to reach the source node. We then have t_{data} as the time for pipelining the data flits into the destination network interface. The first term is the time for the first data flit to reach the destination. The second term is the time required to receive the remaining flits. The message pipeline cycle time is determined by the maximum of the switch delay and wire delay.

2.5.3 Scouting Switching

Scouting switching is a hybrid message flow control mechanism that can be dynamically configured to provide specific trade-offs between fault tolerance and performance. In PCS the first data flit is injected into the network only after the complete path has been set up. In an attempt to reduce PCS path setup time overhead, in scouting switching the first data flit is constrained to remain at least K links behind the routing header. When $K = 0$, the flow control is equivalent to wormhole switching, while large values can ensure path setup prior to data transmission (if a path exists).

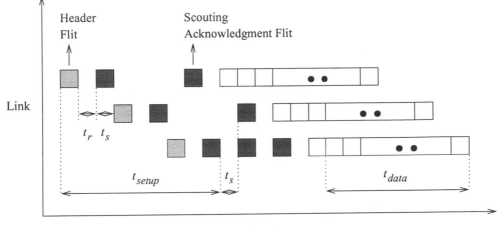

Figure 2.24. Time-space diagram of a message transmitted using scouting switching.

Intermediate values of K permit the data flits to follow the header at distance, while still allowing the header to backtrack if the need arises. Therefore when the header reaches the destination, the first data flit arrives shortly thereafter rather than immediately (as in wormhole switching). Figure 2.24 illustrates a time-space diagram for messages being pipelined over three links using scouting switching ($K = 2$). The parameter, K, is referred to as the *scouting distance* or *probe lead*. Every time a channel is successfully reserved by the routing header, a positive acknowledgment is returned in the opposite direction. As a particular case, positive acknowledgments are continuously transmitted when the routing header has reached the destination node. Associated with each virtual channel is a programmable counter. The counter associated with the virtual channel reserved by a header is incremented when a positive acknowledgment is received, and is decremented when a negative acknowledgment is received. When the value of the counter is equal to K, data flits are allowed to advance. As acknowledgments flow in the direction opposite to the routing header, the gap between the header and the first data flit can grow up to a maximum of $2K - 1$ links while the header is advancing. If the routing header backtracks, a negative acknowledgment is transmitted. For performance reasons, when $K = 0$ no acknowledgments are sent across the channels. In this case, data flits immediately follow the header flit and flow control is equivalent to wormhole switching.

For example, in Figure 2.25 a message is being transmitted between nodes A and G and $K = 2$. The initial path attempted by the header is row first. Data flits remain at least two links behind the header. On encountering faulty output link at node B, the header can backtrack over the previous link. Encountering another faulty link the header can still backtrack one more link to node C. During this time the first data flit remains blocked at node C. From node C it is possible to make progress towards the destination via node D. When the header reaches node F, it is $2K - 1 = 3$ links from the first data flit at node C, and data flits can begin to flow again.

By statically fixing the value of K, we fix the trade-off between network performance (overhead of positive and negative acknowledgment) and fault tolerance (the number of faults that must be tolerated). By dynamically modifying K, we can gain further improvement via run-time trade-offs between fault tolerance and performance. Such configurable flow control protocols are discussed in the context of fault tolerant and reliable routing in Chapter 6.

The base latency of scouting switching can be computed as follows:

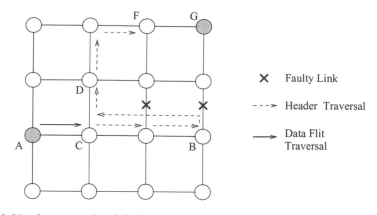

Figure 2.25. An example of fault-tolerant routing enabled by scouting switching.

$$t_{scouting} = t_{setup} + (t_s + t_w)(2K - 1) + t_{data}$$
$$t_{setup} = D(t_r + t_s + t_w) \qquad (2.9)$$
$$t_{data} = \max(t_s, t_w)\left(\left\lceil \tfrac{L}{W} \right\rceil - 1\right)$$

The first term is the time taken for the header flit to reach the destination. The first data flit can be at a maximum of $(2K - 1)$ links behind the header. The second term is the time taken for the first data flit to reach the destination. The last term is the time for pipelining the remaining data flits into the destination network interface.

2.6   Optimizing Switching Techniques

The switching techniques described in this chapter are subject to application-specific optimizations to further improve performance and/or reliability. Such optimizations do not fundamentally alter the nature of these techniques but can lead to considerable improvements in performance in specific application domains. For example, consider the overheads experienced in transmitting and receiving a message. The programming interface may be a message-passing library comprised of various send and receive procedures. The concern at this level has been to provide consistent semantics for sending and receiving messages. The source program builds a message in local buffers and transfers control to the operating system via system calls. Data are copied into operating system space where protected device drivers construct message headers, packetize the data, and interact with special-purpose network interfaces to inject data into the network. This overhead is experienced with every message. When message sizes are small, the overhead on a per-message basis can be substantial. There have been several successful efforts to reduce this overhead. Often, hardware support is provided for packetization and network interfaces are becoming tightly coupled with memory and in some cases even the processor registers through memory-mapped techniques and existence on the processor memory bus rather than on the slower I/O buses. Copying to and from system buffers is also being eliminated through the use of message handlers that operate within the user address spaces. Modern machines are now beginning to focus on the design of the interface between the network and memory. These techniques are beneficial regardless of the switching techniques.

Similarly, optimizations within the low-level physical channel flow control protocols benefit most switching techniques. High-speed signaling mechanisms for physical channel flow control affect the interrouter latency. As higher-dimensional networks and wider channels are employed the number of inputs and outputs at a router can become very large. Current packaging technology provides chip carriers with 300–400 pins. These pins can begin to become a scarce resource. One innovative technique to addressing this problem is the use of bidirectional signaling [75, 193]. This technique allows simultaneous signaling between two routers across a single signal line. Thus, full-duplex, bidirectional communication of a single bit between two routers can be realized with one pin (signal) rather than two signals. A logic 1 (0) is transmitted as positive (negative) current. The transmitted signal is the superposition of these two signals. Each transmitter generates a reference signal which is subtracted from the superimposed signal to generate the received signal. The result is a considerable savings over the number of input/output pins required, and consequent reduction in the packaging cost. Such optimizations at the physical level are also clearly independent of and benefit all switching techniques.

Application environments that exhibit locality in interprocessor communication are particularly good candidates for application-specific optimizations. For example, systolic computation makes use of fine-grained, pipelined, parallel transmission of multiple data streams through a fixed communication topology such as multidimensional mesh or hexagonal interconnection topologies. In such cases, it is beneficial to set up interprocessor communication paths once to be shared by many successive data elements (i.e., messages). The Intel iWarp chip was designed to support such systolic communication through *message pathways*: long-lived communication paths [39]. Rather than set up and remove network paths each time data are to be communicated, paths through the network persist for long periods of time. Special messages called *pathway begin markers* are used to reserve virtual channels (referred to as *logical channels* in iWarp) and set up interprocessor communication paths. Messages are periodically injected into the network to use these existing paths utilizing wormhole switching. On completion of the computation, the paths are explicitly removed by other control messages. Unlike conventional wormhole switching, the last flit of the message does not cause the routers to tear down the path. The overhead of preparing a node for message transmission is incurred once, and amortized over all messages that use the path. Such optimizations are possible due to the regular, predictable nature of systolic communication. The basic switching technique is wormhole, but it is applied in a manner to optimize the characteristics of the applications.

Not only fine-grained parallel algorithms exhibit communication locality that can be exploited by switching techniques. Studies of VLSI CAD programs and programs from linear algebra have shown that coarse-grained message-passing applications can also exhibit sufficient communication locality to benefit from long-lived communication paths and justify the design of an enhanced wormhole router [159]. As in the iWarp chip, paths are set up and shared by multiple messages until they are explicitly removed. The basic wormhole switching technique is modified to prevent the path from being removed when the first message has been successfully received at the destination. In this case interprocessor paths can even be shared between applications in a multiprogrammed parallel architecture. Message flow control must avoid deadlock as well as ensuring that reserved paths do not preclude new messages from being injected into the network.

The need for reliable message transmission has also led to proposals for enhancing switching techniques. For example, one way to ensure message delivery is to buffer the message at the source until it can be asserted that the message has been received at the destination. Receipt at the destination can be determined through the use of message acknowledgments. In this case, paths are removed by explicit control signals/messages generated by the source/destination rather than by a part of the message. Alternatively, consider the use of wormhole switching when the number of flits in the message exceeds the number of links, D, between the source and destination nodes. If each router only buffers a single flit, receipt of the header at the destination can be asserted at the source when flit $D + 1$ is injected into the network. If messages are short, they can be padded with empty flits so that the number of flits in the message exceeds the distance between the source and destination (padding must also account for buffer space within each router). By keeping track of the number of flits that have been injected into the network, the source router can determine if the header has been received at the destination. Moreover, the source node can determine if the whole message has been received at the destination by injecting $D + 1$ padding flits after the last data flit of the message. Such reliable switching techniques modify the basic wormhole switching mechanisms to include additional flits or control signals, e.g., acknowledgments or padding flits. This particular technique was proposed as *compressionless routing* by its developers [179].

The need to support distinct traffic types also leads to new optimizations of switching techniques [293]. Real-time communication traffic places distinct demands on the performance and behavior of network routers. Such traffic requires guaranteed bounds on latency and throughput. The manner in which messages are buffered and scheduled across physical channels must be able to provide such guarantees on a per-router basis. Such guarantees would be used by higher-level, real-time scheduling algorithms. Packet switching is attractive from this point of view since predictable demands are made on buffer requirements and channel bandwidth at each intermediate router. In contrast, the demands that will be placed on router resources by a message using VCT will vary depending on the load and communication pattern (i.e., is the output link free). Buffering of packets permits the application of priority-based scheduling algorithms and thus provide some control over packet latencies. Wormhole-switched messages use demand-driven scheduling disciplines for accessing physical channel bandwidth and may be blocked across multiple nodes. Demand-driven scheduling and very low buffer requirements work to provide low average latency but high variability and thus poor predictability. Priority-based scheduling of virtual channels is infeasible since a channel may have messages of multiple priorities, and messages may be blocked over multiple links. These properties make it difficult to utilize wormhole switching to support real-time traffic. Rexford and Shin [293] observed that packet switching and wormhole switching made demands on distinct router resources while sharing physical channel bandwidth. Thus, the authors proposed a scheme where virtual channels were partitioned to realize two distinct virtual networks: one packet-switched, and the other wormhole-switched. The two networks share the physical link bandwidth in a controlled manner, thus enabling the network to provide latency and throughput guarantees for real-time traffic, while standard traffic realized low average latency. The switching technique experienced by a message is determined at the source node, based on the traffic type.

We can envision other optimizations that deal with issues such as allocation/deallocation of buffer space within routers, allocation/deallocation of virtual channels, scheduling of virtual channels (equivalently messages) over the physical channel, etc. Some of these optimizations are examined in greater detail in the Exercises section at the end of this chapter.

2.7   A Comparison of Switching Techniques

The evolution of switching techniques was naturally influenced by the need for better performance. VCT switching introduced pipelined message transmission, and wormhole switching further contributed reduced buffer requirements in conjunction with fine-grained pipelining. The mad postman switching technique carried pipelining to the bit level to maximize performance. In packet switching and VCT messages are completely buffered at a node. As a result, the messages consume network bandwidth proportional to the network load. On the other hand, wormhole-switched messages may block occupying buffers and channels across multiple routers, precluding access to the network bandwidth by other messages. Thus, while average message latency can be low, the network saturates at a fraction of the maximum available bandwidth and the variance of message latency can be high.

The use of virtual channels decouples the physical channel from blocked messages, thus reducing the blocking delays experienced by messages and enabling a larger fraction of the available bandwidth to be utilized. However, the increasing multiplexing of multiple messages increases the delay experienced by data flits. Furthermore, multiple virtual channels can increase the flow control latency through the router and across the physical channel, producing upward pressure on average message latency.

The effects of wormhole switching on individual messages can be highly unpredictable. Since buffer requirements are low, contention in the network can substantially increase the latency of a message in parts of the network. Packet switching tends to have more predictable latency characteristics, particularly at low loads since messages are buffered at each node. VCT will operate like wormhole switching at low loads and approximate packet switching at high loads where link contention will force packets to be buffered at each node. Thus, at low loads we expect to see wormhole switching techniques providing superior latency/throughput relative to packet-switched networks, while at high loads we expect to see packet-switched schemes perform better. As expected, the performance of VCT approaches that of wormhole switching at low loads and that of packet switching at high loads. More detailed performance comparisons can be found in Chapter 9.

These switching techniques can be characterized as *optimistic* in the sense that buffer resources and links are allocated as soon as they become available, regardless of the state of progress of the remainder of the message. In contrast, pipelined circuit switching and scouting switching may be characterized as *conservative*. Data flits are transmitted only after it is clear that flits can make forward progress. These flow control protocols are motivated by fault tolerance concerns. BWS seeks to improve the fraction of available bandwidth that can be exploited by wormhole switching by buffering groups of flits.

In packet switching, error detection and retransmission can be performed on a link-by-link basis. Packets may be adaptively routed around faulty regions of the network. When messages are pipelined over several links, error recovery and control becomes complicated. Error detection and retransmission (if feasible) must be performed by higher-level protocols operating between the source and destination, rather than at the level of the physical link. If network routers or links have failed, message progress can be indefinitely halted, with messages occupying buffer and channel resources. This can lead to deadlocked configurations of messages and eventually failure of the network.

2.8   Engineering Issues

Switching techniques have a very strong impact on the performance and behavior of the interconnection network. Performance is more heavily influenced by the switching technique than by the topology or the routing algorithm. Furthermore, true tolerance to faulty network components can only be obtained by using a suitable switching technique. The use of topologies with multiple alternative paths between every source destination pair, and the availability of adaptive routing protocols simply reduces the probability of a message encountering a faulty component. The switching technique determines how messages may recover from faulty components.

Switching techniques also have a considerable influence on the architecture of the router, and as a result, the network performance. For example, consider the magnitude of the improvement in performance that wormhole switching provides over packet switching. First-generation multicomputers such as the Intel iPSC/1 utilized packet switching. The iPSC/1 network had routing times on the order of several milliseconds. In addition, message latency was proportional to the distance traveled by the message. In contrast, modern multicomputers such as the Intel Paragon and the Cray T3D have routing and switch delays on the order of several nanoseconds. Message latency has decreased from a few tens of milliseconds to a few hundreds of nanoseconds. In one decade, latency improved by five orders of magnitude! Obviously, this improvement benefits from advances in VLSI technology. However, VLSI technology only improved performance by one order of magnitude. Network devices were clocked at 10 MHz in the Intel iPSC/1 while the Cray T3D is clocked at 150 MHz.

Pipelined message transfer alone cannot be responsible for this magnitude of performance improvement. What then is the source? An important difference between first-generation multicomputers and current multicomputers is that the routing algorithm is computed in hardware. However, packet switching would still be much slower than wormhole switching even if the routing algorithm were computed in hardware in both cases. Wormhole switching performs flow control at the flit level. This apparently unimportant change considerably reduces the need for buffering space. Small hardware buffers are enough to handle flit propagation across intermediate routers. As a consequence, wormhole routers are small, compact, and fast. Moreover, wormhole routers are able to handle messages of any length. However, packet-switched routers must provide buffering space for full packets, either limiting packet size or necessitating the use of local processor memory for storing packets. Access to local node memory is very expensive in terms of time. Storing packets in node memory not only consumes memory bandwidth, but also the network bandwidth of a node is reduced to a fraction of the memory bandwidth. However, wormhole routers do not store packets in memory. Memory is only accessed for injecting and delivering packets. As a consequence, channel bandwidth can be much higher than in packet-switched routers. Depending on the design of the network interface, channel bandwidth may even exceed memory bandwidth. This is the case for the iWarp chip, in which the processor directly accesses the network through special registers.

Even if the router is able to buffer full packets, the larger packet buffers are slower than flit buffers, increasing the flow control latency through the router and slowing down clock frequency. Furthermore, the use of hardware packet buffers implies a fixed packet size. Variable-sized messages must be partitioned into fixed-size packets. This increases message latency and percentage of network bandwidth devoted to overhead, e.g., processing and transmitting packet headers. The unit of flow control in VCT switching is also a packet. Thus, many of these design considerations are applicable to VCT switching. However, wormhole switching does not require messages to be split into packets. This is one of the reasons why VCT routers have not replaced wormhole routers.

We might expect that the mad postman switching technique may considerably increase performance over wormhole switching. However, mad postman switching can only improve performance if the default output channel selected at an intermediate router has a high probability of being the correct output channel. The highest probabilities occur in low-dimensional networks, e.g., 2-D meshes because messages turn only once. However, for a fixed pin-out on the router chips, low-dimensional networks allow the use of wider data channels. Consequently, a header can be transmitted across a physical channel in a single clock cycle, rendering finer-grained pipelining unnecessary and nullifying any advantage of using the mad postman switching.

In summary, we observe that wormhole switching owes its popularity in part to the fact that it performs flow control at the flit level, requiring only small flit buffers. Messages are not stored in memory when they block, but rather span multiple routers. However, the small buffers produce a short delay, and wormhole routers can be clocked at a very high frequency. The result is very high channel bandwidth, potentially higher than the bandwidth to local memory. Given the current state of the technology, we believe that the most promising approach to increase performance considerably with respect to current interconnection networks consists of defining new switching techniques that take advantage of communication locality, and optimize performance for groups of messages rather than individual messages. Similarly, we believe that the most effective way to offer an architectural support for collective communication, and for fault-tolerant communication, is by designing specific switching techniques. These issues will be explored in Chapters 5 and 6.

2.9 Commented references

Circuit switching has its origin in telephone networks. Packet switching has its origin in data networks for intercomputer communication. The first parallel machines were generally packet- or circuit-switched. The Intel iPSC/1 was packet-switched with message latencies on the order of milliseconds. The Direct Connect Module (DCM) introduced in the later-generation Intel iPSC/2 and iPSC/860 machines [257] employed circuit-switched communication with short messages being transmitted in a manner akin to wormhole switching. The GP 1000 from BBN employed a circuit-switched multistage network. The original Denelcor HEP [190], the MIT Tagged Token Dataflow Machine [12], and the Manchester Dynamic Dataflow Machine [144, 145], were all early machines that utilized a packet-switched interprocessor communication network.

Wormhole switching was introduced in the Torus Routing Chip [77, 78] and the performance for wormhole-switched multidimensional tori was examined in [71]. The latest in the line of machines from Intel, the Paragon [165], utilizes wormhole-switched communication. Other machines that utilize wormhole switching include the Cray T3D [258], the IBM Power Parallel SP series [326, 327], and the Meiko Computing Surface [22]. At the time of this writing, interconnection networks in current generation machines appear to be adopting wormhole switching as the mechanism of choice. While the introduction of VCT switching [172] predates wormhole switching, it is not yet in use in commercially available parallel architectures. The best known implementation of VCT is the Chaos router [188]. The use of virtual channel flow control was introduced in [73]. The Cray T3D [258] and the Cray T3E [312] utilize multiple virtual channels per physical channel.

Mad postman switching was introduced in [167] and has found its way into the implementation of low-cost asynchronous routers. However, with the increasing pin-out and channel width in modern routers, wormhole switching still appears to hold an advantage over the mad postman switching technique. More recently, pipelined circuit switching was proposed as a robust switching mechanism [127] and was subsequently realized in the Ariadne router [7]. Scouting switching [100] and the use of dynamically configurable switching techniques [80] was designed to improve the performance of pipelined circuit switching on message traffic that did not encounter any faulty channels.

A thorough study of router architectures and the development of a cost/performance model for router architectures can be found in [11, 57]. These models provide definitions of critical measures of router performance and enable assessment of the impact of virtual channels, channel signaling speed, message formats, etc. on the flow control latency and router delays.

EXERCISES

2.1 Modify the router model shown in Figure 2.1 to use input buffering only and no virtual channels. Rewrite the expressions for the base latency of wormhole switching and packet switching for this router model.

Solution Figure 2.26 illustrates an input-buffered version of Figure 2.1. In this case, in a single cycle a flit is routed through the switch across a physical channel, and into the input buffer of the next router. When a message arbitrates for the output of the router switch, it simultaneously acquires the output physical channel. In general, the duration of a cycle in an input-buffered switch will be longer than that of a switch that has both buffered inputs and buffered outputs. Similar observations can be made about output-buffered switches.

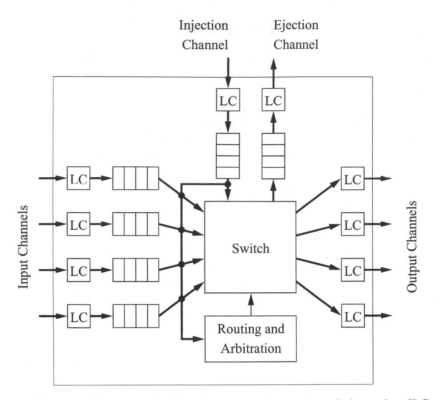

Figure 2.26. Architecture of an input-buffered router with no virtual channels. (LC = Link controller.)

The no-load latency for wormhole switching and packet switching can be rewritten as follows:

$$
\begin{aligned}
t_{wormhole} &= D(t_r + t_s + t_w) + (t_s + t_w)\left\lceil \frac{L}{W} \right\rceil \\
t_{packet} &= D\left\{ t_r + (t_s + t_w)\left\lceil \frac{L+W}{W} \right\rceil \right\}
\end{aligned}
\tag{2.10}
$$

2.2 Assume that the physical channel flow control protocol assigns bandwidth to virtual channels on a strict time-sliced basis rather than a demand-driven basis. Derive a expression for the base latency of a wormhole-switched message in the worst case as a function of the number of virtual channels. Assume that the routers are input-buffered.

Solution   Assume that we have V virtual channels. Regardless of network traffic, each message will receive only $\frac{1}{V}$ of the physical channel bandwidth over every link. Therefore the ideal link speed seen by a message is Vt_w seconds. After routing a header, it takes a random number of cycles until the time slice is assigned to the selected virtual channel. In the worst case, it will take V cycles. Therefore the no-load latency becomes

$$
t_{wormhole} = D[t_r + V(t_s + t_w)] + V(t_s + t_w)\left\lceil \frac{L}{W} \right\rceil
\tag{2.11}
$$

PROBLEMS

2.1 In wormhole switching, the last flit or tail flit causes the intermediate routers to release resources such as buffers or links. The time-space diagram used to describe wormhole switching adopts this view. Consider a modification to wormhole switching where the message path is not removed by the tail flit. Rather an acknowledgment is received from the destination, following which a tail flit is transmitted. Draw a time-space diagram of the transmission of a message over three links and write an expression for the number of cycles a link remains reserved for the transmission of this message. What percentage of this time is the link busy assuming no contention for any physical channel along the path? Assume that the routers are input-buffered only.

2.2 One of the advantages of virtual channels is the reduction of header blocking delay. However, this assumes that the physical channel bandwidth is allocated on a fair basis. Suppose we were to schedule virtual channels over the physical channel on a priority basis. Consider a design with two virtual channels. Show how priority scheduling of a low-priority message and a high-priority message over the same physical channel can result in deadlock.

2.3 Physical channel flow control synchronizes the transmission of phits across a channel. Assuming a synchronous channel, show how phits can be streamed across a channel, i.e., a sequence of K phits are transmitted before any acknowledgment is received from the receiver, so that we need only synchronize the transmission and receipt of K phits at a time. What are the requirements for buffer space on the receiver?

2.4 Consider a wormhole-switched network where virtual circuits persist until they are explicitly torn down by control signals or special messages. Draw a time-space diagram of the transmission of three messages over a path three links in length before it is removed by a special control flit injected into the path at the source node.

2.5 The IBM Power Parallel SP-2 represents a balanced design where the rate at which chunks can be transferred to switch memory is eight times the rate at which flits cross a physical channel. A similar observation can be made about the interface between switch memory and the output channels. The maximum message size is 8 chunks. Write an expression for the size of switch memory in flits in terms of the internal data path width (equal to one chunk), number of flits/chunk, and the number of input/output ports. Assume that one flit can be transmitted across the physical channel in one cycle. Validate this expression by instantiating with parameters from the SP-2.

2.6 The main advantage of packet switching over message switching is that several packets can be simultaneously in transit along the path from source to destination. Assuming that all the packets follow the same path, there is no need to add a sequence number to each packet. Draw a time-space diagram of the transmission of a message consisting of four packets over a path three links in length. Assuming that the routers are input-buffered only, compute the optimal number of packets that minimizes the base latency for the transmission of a message of L bits along D channels.

2.7 In the previous exercise, as all the packets follow the same path, assume that packet headers are stripped from all the packets but the first one. Assuming that the routers are input-buffered only, compute the optimal number of packets and the optimal packet size that minimizes the base latency for the transmission of a message of L bits along D channels. Make the analogy between packets without headers and flits in wormhole switching, and determine the optimal flit size.

2.8 Consider a network using wormhole switching, and a node architecture that is able to send and receive up to four packets simultaneously without interference. The start-up latency to initiate a new packet transmission after initiating the previous one is t_s. Assuming that there are four minimal paths between two nodes that are D links apart, compute the base latency to send a message of L bits when the message is split into four sequences of packets, each sequence following a different path. Assume that routers are input-buffered only.

2.9 A hierarchical network topology has channels of two different widths, W and $\frac{W}{2}$, all of them being clocked at the same frequency B. The network uses wormhole switching, and routers have input buffers and output buffers deep enough to avoid filling the buffers in the absence of contention. Internal data paths are W bits wide. Compute the base latency to send a message of L bits across two channels in two cases: (a) the width of the first and second channels are W and $\frac{W}{2}$, respectively; (b) the width of the first and second channels are $\frac{W}{2}$ and W, respectively. Assume that messages are not split into packets.

Chapter 3

Deadlock, Livelock, and Starvation

The nodes of an interconnection network send and receive messages or packets through the network interface. Both messages and packets carry information about the destination node. Thus, the techniques described in this chapter can be applied to both of them indistinctly. Without loss of generality, in what follows we will only refer to packets.

In direct networks, packets usually travel across several intermediate nodes before reaching the destination. In switch-based networks, packets usually traverse several switches before reaching the destination. However, it may happen that some packets are not able to reach their destinations, even if there exist fault-free paths connecting the source and destination nodes for every packet. Assuming that the routing algorithm is able to use those paths, there are several situations that may prevent packet delivery. This chapter studies those situations and proposes techniques to guarantee packet delivery.

As seen in Chapter 2, some buffers are required to store fragments of each packet, or even the whole packet, at each intermediate node or switch. However, buffer storage is not free. Thus, buffer capacity is finite. As each packet whose header has not already arrived at its destination requests some buffers while keeping the buffers currently storing the packet, a deadlock may arise. A *deadlock* occurs when some packets cannot advance toward their destination because the buffers requested by them are full. All the packets involved in a deadlocked configuration are blocked forever. Note that a packet may be permanently blocked in the network because the destination node does not consume it. This kind of deadlock is produced by the application, and it is beyond the scope of this book. In this chapter, we will assume that packets are always consumed by the destination node in finite time. Therefore, in a deadlocked configuration, a set of packets is blocked forever. Every packet is requesting resources held by other packet(s) while holding resources requested by other packet(s).

A different situation arises when some packets are not able to reach their destination, even if they never block permanently. A packet may be traveling around its destination node, never reaching it because the channels required to do so are occupied by other packets. This situation is known as *livelock*. It can only occur when packets are allowed to follow nonminimal paths.

Finally, a packet may be permanently stopped if traffic is intense and the resources requested by it are always granted to other packets also requesting them. This situation is known as *starvation* and it usually occurs when an incorrect resource assignment scheme is used to arbitrate in case of conflict.

Deadlocks, livelocks, and starvation arise because the number of resources is finite. Additionally, some of these situations may produce the others. For instance, a deadlock permanently blocks some

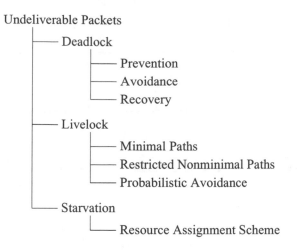

Figure 3.1. A classification of the situations that may prevent packet delivery.

packets. As those packets are occupying some buffers, other packets may require them to reach their destination, being continuously misrouted around their destination node and producing livelock.

It is extremely important to remove deadlocks, livelocks, and starvation when implementing an interconnection network. Otherwise, some packets may never reach their destination. As these situations arise because the storage resources are finite, the probability of reaching them increases with network traffic and decreases with the amount of buffer storage. For instance, a network using wormhole switching is much more deadlock-prone than the same network using SAF switching if the routing algorithm is not deadlock-free.

A classification of the situations that may prevent packet delivery and the techniques to solve these situations are shown in Figure 3.1. Starvation is relatively easy to solve. Simply, a correct resource assignment scheme should be used. A simple demand-slotted round-robin scheme is enough to produce a fair use of resources. When some packets must have a higher priority, some bandwidth must be reserved for low-priority packets in order to prevent starvation. This can be done by limiting the number of high-priority packets, or by reserving some virtual channels or buffers for low-priority packets.

Livelock is also relatively easy to avoid. The simplest way consists of using only minimal paths. This restriction usually increases performance in networks using wormhole switching because packets do not occupy more channels than the ones strictly necessary to reach their destination. The main motivation for the use of nonminimal paths is fault tolerance. Even when nonminimal paths are used, livelock can be prevented by limiting the number of misrouting operations. Another motivation for using nonminimal paths is deadlock avoidance when deflection routing is used. In this case, routing is probabilistically livelock-free. This issue will be analyzed in Section 3.7.

Deadlock is by far the most difficult problem to solve. This chapter is almost completely dedicated to this subject. There are three strategies for deadlock handling: deadlock *prevention*, deadlock *avoidance*, and deadlock *recovery*[1] [320]. In deadlock prevention, resources (channels or buffers) are granted to a packet in such a way that a request never leads to a deadlock. It can be achieved by reserving all the required resources before starting packet transmission. This is the case for all the variants of circuit switching when backtracking is allowed. In deadlock avoidance, resources

---

[1]Deadlock recovery was referred to as deadlock detection in [320].

are requested as a packet advances through the network. However, a resource is granted to a packet only if the resulting global state is safe. This strategy should avoid sending additional packets to update the global state, because these packets consume network bandwidth and they may contribute to produce deadlock. Achieving this in a distributed manner is not an easy task. A common technique consists of establishing an ordering between resources and granting resources to each packet in decreasing order. In deadlock recovery strategies, resources are granted to a packet without any check. Therefore, deadlock is possible and some detection mechanism must be provided. If a deadlock is detected, some resources are deallocated and granted to other packets. In order to deallocate resources, packets holding those resources are usually aborted.

Deadlock prevention strategies are very conservative. However, reserving all the required resources before starting packet transmission may lead to a low resource utilization. Deadlock avoidance strategies are less conservative, requesting resources when they are really needed to forward a packet. Finally, deadlock recovery strategies are optimistic. They can only be used if deadlocks are rare and the result of a deadlock can be tolerated. Deadlock avoidance and recovery techniques considerably evolved during the last few years, making obsolete most of the previous proposals. In this chapter we present a unified approach to deadlock avoidance for the most important flow control techniques proposed up to now. With a simple trick, this technique is also valid for deadlock recovery. Also, we will survey the most interesting deadlock handling strategies proposed up to now. The techniques studied in this chapter are restricted to unicast routing in fault-free networks. Deadlock handling in multicast routing and fault-tolerant routing will be studied in Chapters 5 and 6, respectively.

This chapter is organized as follows. Section 3.1 proposes a necessary and sufficient condition for deadlock-free routing in direct networks, giving application examples for SAF, VCT, and wormhole switching. This theory is extended in Section 3.2 by grouping channels into classes, extending the domain of the routing function, and considering central queues instead of edge buffers. Alternative approaches for deadlock avoidance are considered in Section 3.3. Switch-based networks are considered in Section 3.4. Deadlock prevention and recovery are covered in Sections 3.5 and 3.6, respectively. Finally, livelock avoidance is studied in Section 3.7. The chapter ends with a discussion of some engineering issues and commented references.

3.1   A Theory of Deadlock Avoidance

This section proposes a necessary and sufficient condition for deadlock-free routing in direct networks using SAF, VCT or wormhole switching. For the sake of clarity, this theory is presented in an informal way. A formal version of this theory, restricted to wormhole switching, can be found in Appendix A. Section 3.4 shows the application of this condition to switch-based networks. The results for wormhole switching can also be applied to mad postman switching, assuming that dead flits are removed from the network as soon as they are blocked. Necessary and sufficient conditions for wormhole switching become sufficient conditions when applied to scouting switching.

3.1.1   Network and Router Models

Direct networks consist of a set of nodes interconnected by point-to-point links or channels. No restriction is imposed on the topology of the interconnection network. Each node has a router. The architecture of a generic router was described in Section 2.1. In this section, we highlight the aspects that affect deadlock avoidance.

We assume that the switch is a crossbar, therefore allowing multiple packets to traverse a node simultaneously without interference. The routing and arbitration unit configures the switch, determining the output channel for each packet as a function of the destination node, the current node, and the output channel status. The routing and arbitration unit can only process one packet header at a time. If there is contention for this unit, access is round-robin. When a packet gets the routing and arbitration unit but cannot be routed because all the valid output channels are busy, it waits in the corresponding input buffer until its next turn. By doing so, the packet gets the first valid channel that becomes available when it is routed again. This strategy achieves a higher routing flexibility than strategies in which blocked packets wait on a single predetermined channel.

Physical channels are bidirectional full-duplex. Physical channels may be split into virtual channels. Virtual channels are assigned the physical channel cyclically, only if they are ready to transfer a flit (demand-slotted round robin). In wormhole switching, each virtual channel may have buffers at both ends, although configurations without output buffers are also supported. In both cases, we will refer to the total buffer storage associated with a virtual channel as the channel queue.

For SAF and VCT switching with edge buffers (buffers associated with input channels), we assume the same model except that the buffers associated with the input channels must be large enough to store one or more packets. These buffers are required to remove packets from the network whenever no output channel is available. A channel will only accept a new packet if there is enough buffer space to store the whole packet. The message flow control protocol is responsible for ensuring the availability of buffer space.

The above-described model uses edge buffers. However, most routing functions proposed up to now for SAF switching use central queues. The theory presented in the next sections is also valid for SAF and VCT switching with central queues after introducing some changes in notation. Those changes will be summarized in Section 3.2.3. In this case, a few central buffers deep enough to store one or more packets are used. As above, a channel will only accept a new packet if there is enough buffer space to store the whole packet. Buffer space must be reserved before starting packet transmission, thus preventing other channels from reserving the same buffer space. The message flow control protocol is responsible for ensuring the availability of buffer space and arbitrating between concurrent requests for space in the central queues.

As we will see in Section 3.2.3, it is also possible to consider models that mix both kinds of resources, edge buffers and central queues. It will be useful in Section 3.6. In this case, each node has edge buffers and central queues. The routing function determines the resource to be used in each case. This mixed model may consider either flit buffers or packet buffers, depending on the switching technique. For the sake of clarity, we will restrict definitions and examples to use only edge buffers. Results can be easily generalized by introducing the changes in notation indicated in Section 3.2.3.

3.1.2 Basic Definitions

The interconnection network I is modeled by using a strongly connected directed graph with multiple arcs, $I = G(N, C)$. The vertices of the graph N represent the set of processing nodes. The arcs of the graph C represent the set of communication channels. More than a single channel is allowed to connect a given pair of nodes. Bidirectional channels are considered as two unidirectional channels. We will refer to a channel and its associated edge buffer indistinctly. The source and destination nodes of a channel c_i are denoted s_i and d_i, respectively.

A routing algorithm is modeled by means of two functions: routing and selection. The *routing function* supplies a set of output channels based on the current and destination nodes. A selection from this set is made by the *selection function* based on the status of output channels at the current node. This selection is performed in such a way that a free channel (if any) is supplied. If all the output channels are busy, the packet will be routed again until it is able to reserve a channel, thus getting the first channel that becomes available. As we will see, the routing function determines whether the routing algorithm is deadlock-free or not. The selection function only affects performance.

Note that, in our model, the domain of the routing function is $N \times N$ because it only takes into account the current and destination nodes. Thus, we do not consider the path followed by the packet while computing the next channel to be used. We do not even consider the input channel on which the packet arrived at the current node. The reason for this choice is that it enables the design of practical routing protocols for which specific properties can be proven. These results may not be valid for other routing functions. Furthermore, this approach enables the development of methodologies for the design of fully adaptive routing protocols (covered in Chapter 4). These methodologies are invalid for other routing functions. Thus, this choice is motivated by engineering practice that is developed without sacrifice in rigor. Other definitions of the routing function will be considered in Section 3.2.

In order to make the theoretical results as general as possible, we assume no restriction about packet generation rate, packet destinations, and packet length. Also, we assume no restriction on the paths supplied by the routing algorithm. Both minimal and nonminimal paths are allowed. However, for performance reasons, a routing algorithm should supply at least one channel belonging to a minimal path at each intermediate node. Additionally, we are going to focus on deadlocks produced by the interconnection network. Thus, we assume that packets will be consumed at their destination nodes in finite time.

Several switching techniques can be used. Each of them will be considered as a particular case of the general theory. However, a few specific assumptions are required for some switching techniques. For SAF and VCT switching, we assume that edge buffers are used. Central queues will be considered in Section 3.2.3. For wormhole switching, we assume that a queue cannot contain flits belonging to different packets. After accepting a tail flit, a queue must be emptied before accepting another header flit. When a virtual channel has queues at both ends, both queues must be emptied before accepting another header flit. Thus, when a packet is blocked, its header flit will always occupy the head of a queue. Also, for every path P that can be established by a routing function R, all subpaths of P are also paths of R. The routing functions satisfying the latter property will be referred to as *coherent*. For mad postman switching, we assume the same restrictions as for wormhole switching. Additionally, dead flits are removed from the network as soon as they are blocked.

A *configuration* is an assignment of a set of packets or flits to each queue. Before analyzing how to avoid deadlocks, we are going to present a *deadlocked configuration* by using an example.

Example 3.1

Consider a 2-D mesh with bidirectional channels. The routing function R forwards packets following any minimal path. This routing function is not deadlock-free. Figure 3.2 shows a deadlocked configuration. Dotted incomplete boxes represent nodes of a 3×3 mesh. Dashed boxes represent switches. Solid boxes represent packet buffers or flit buffers, depending on the switching technique used. The number inside each buffer indicates the destination node. Solid arrows indicate the channel requested by the packet or the header at the queue head. As packets are allowed to follow all the minimal paths, packets wait for each other in a cyclic way. Additionally, there is no alternative path for the packets in the figure because packets are only allowed to follow minimal paths. As all the buffers are full, no packet can advance.

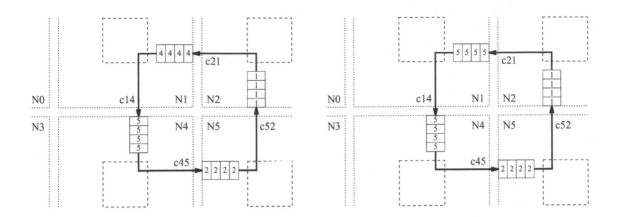

Figure 3.2. Deadlocked configuration for R.   Figure 3.3. Illegal configuration for R.

So, a deadlocked configuration is a configuration in which some packets are blocked forever, waiting for resources that will never be granted because they are held by other packets. The configuration described in Example 3.1 would also be deadlocked if there were some additional packets traveling across the network that are not blocked. A deadlocked configuration in which all the packets are blocked is referred to as *canonical*. Given a deadlocked configuration, the corresponding canonical configuration can be obtained by stopping packet injection at all the nodes, and waiting for the delivery of all the packets that are not blocked. From a practical point of view, we only need to consider canonical deadlocked configurations.

Note that a configuration describes the state of an interconnection network at a given time. Thus, we do not need to consider configurations describing impossible situations. A configuration is *legal* if it describes a possible situation. In particular, we should not consider configurations in which buffer capacity is exceeded. Also, a packet cannot occupy a given channel unless the routing function supplies it for the packet destination. Figure 3.3 shows an illegal configuration for the above-defined routing function R because a packet followed a nonminimal path, and R only forwards packets following minimal paths.

In summary, a *canonical deadlocked configuration* is a legal configuration in which no packet can advance. If SAF or VCT switching is used:

- No packet has already arrived at its destination node.

- Packets cannot advance because the queues for all the alternative output channels supplied by the routing function are full.

If wormhole switching is used:

- There is no packet whose header flit has already arrived at its destination.

- Header flits cannot advance because the queues for all the alternative output channels supplied by the routing function are not empty (remember we make the assumption that a queue cannot contain flits belonging to different packets).

- Data flits cannot advance because the next channel reserved by their packet header has a full queue. Note that a data flit can be blocked at a node even if there are free output channels to reach its destination because data flits must follow the path reserved by their header.

In some cases, a configuration cannot be reached by routing packets starting from an empty network. This situation arises when two or more packets require the use of the same channel at the same time to reach the configuration. A configuration that can be reached by routing packets starting from an empty network is *reachable* or *routable* [64]. It should be noted that by defining the domain of the routing function as $N \times N$, every legal configuration is also reachable. Effectively, as the routing function has no memory of the path followed by each packet, we can consider that, for any legal configuration, a packet stored in a channel queue was generated by the source node of that channel. In wormhole switching, we can consider that the packet was generated by the source node of the channel containing the last flit of the packet. This is important because when all the legal configurations are reachable, we do not need to consider the dynamic evolution of the network leading to those configurations. We can simply consider legal configurations, regardless of the packet injection sequence required to reach them. When all the legal configurations are reachable, a routing function is deadlock-free if and only if there is not any deadlocked configuration for that routing function.

A routing function R is *connected* if it is able to establish a *path* between every pair of nodes x and y using channels belonging to the sets supplied by R. It is obvious that a routing function must be connected, and most authors implicitly assume this property. However, we mention it explicitly because we will use a restricted routing function to prove deadlock freedom, and restricting a routing function may disconnect it.

3.1.3 Necessary and Sufficient Condition

The theoretical model of deadlock avoidance we are going to present relies on the concept of *channel dependency* [78]. Other approaches are possible. They will be briefly described in Section 3.3. When a packet is holding a channel, and then it requests the use of another channel, there is a dependency between those channels. Both channels are in one of the paths that may be followed by the packet. If wormhole switching is used, those channels are not necessarily adjacent because a packet may hold several channels simultaneously. Also, at a given node, a packet may request the use of several channels, then selecting one of them (adaptive routing). All the requested channels are candidates for selection. Thus, every requested channel will be selected if all the remaining channels are busy. Also, in our router model, when all the alternative output channels are busy, the packet will get the first requested channel that becomes available. So, all the requested channels produce dependencies, even if they are not selected in a given routing operation.

The behavior of packets regarding deadlock is different depending on whether there is a single or several routing choices at each node. With deterministic routing, packets have a single routing option at each node. Consider a set of packets such that every packet in the set has reserved a channel and it requests a channel held by another packet in the set. Obviously, that channel cannot be granted, and that situation will last forever. Thus, it is necessary to remove all the cyclic dependencies between channels to prevent deadlocks [78], as shown in the next example. This example will be revisited in Chapter 4.

Example 3.2

Consider a unidirectional ring with four nodes denoted $n_i, i = \{0, 1, 2, 3\}$ and a unidirectional channel connecting each pair of adjacent nodes. Let $c_i, i = \{0, 1, 2, 3\}$ be the outgoing channel from node n_i. In this case, it is easy to define a connected routing function. It can be stated as follows: If the current node n_i is equal to the destination node n_j, store the packet. Otherwise, use $c_i, \ \forall j \neq i$. Figure 3.4a shows the network. There is a cyclic dependency

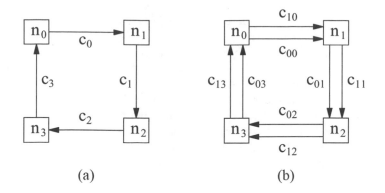

Figure 3.4. Networks for Example 3.2.

between c_i channels. Effectively, a packet at node n_0 destined for n_2 can reserve c_0 and then request c_1. A packet at node n_1 destined for n_3 can reserve c_1 and then request c_2. A packet at node n_2 destined for n_0 can reserve c_2 and then request c_3. Finally, a packet at node n_3 destined for n_1 can reserve c_3 and then request c_0. It is easy to see that a configuration containing the above-mentioned packets is deadlocked because every packet has reserved one channel and is waiting for a channel occupied by another packet.

Now consider that every physical channel c_i is split into two virtual channels, c_{0i} and c_{1i}, as shown in Figure 3.4b. The new routing function can be stated as follows: If the current node n_i is equal to the destination node n_j, store the packet. Otherwise, use c_{0i}, if $j < i$ or c_{1i}, if $j > i$. As can be seen, the cyclic dependency has been removed because after using channel c_{03}, node n_0 is reached. Thus, all the destinations have a higher index than n_0, and it is not possible to request c_{00}. Note that channels c_{00} and c_{13} are never used. Also, the new routing function is deadlock-free. Let us show that there is not any deadlocked configuration by trying to build one. If there were a packet stored in the queue of channel c_{12}, it would be destined for n_3 and flits could advance. So c_{12} must be empty. Also, if there were a packet stored in the queue of c_{11}, it would be destined for n_2 or n_3. As c_{12} is empty, flits could also advance and c_{11} must be empty. If there were a packet stored in the queue of c_{10}, it would be destined for n_1, n_2, or n_3. As c_{11} and c_{12} are empty, flits could advance and c_{10} must be empty. Similarly, it can be shown that the remaining channels can be emptied.

When adaptive routing is considered, packets usually have several choices at each node. Even if one of those choices is a channel held by another packet, other routing choices may be available. Thus, it is not necessary to eliminate all the cyclic dependencies, provided that every packet can always find a path toward its destination whose channels are not involved in cyclic dependencies. This is shown in the next example.

Example 3.3

Consider a unidirectional ring with four nodes denoted $n_i, i = \{0, 1, 2, 3\}$ and two channels connecting each pair of adjacent nodes, except nodes n_3 and n_0 that are linked by a single channel. Let $c_{Ai}, i = \{0, 1, 2, 3\}$ and $c_{Hi}, i = \{0, 1, 2\}$ be the outgoing channels from node n_i. The routing function can be stated as follows: If the current node n_i is equal to the

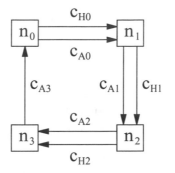

Figure 3.5. Network for Example 3.3.

destination node n_j, store the packet. Otherwise, use either c_{Ai}, $\forall j \neq i$ or c_{Hi}, $\forall j > i$. Figure 3.5 shows the network.

There are cyclic dependencies between c_{Ai} channels. Effectively, a packet at node n_0 destined for n_2 can reserve c_{A0} and then request c_{A1} and c_{H1}. A packet at node n_1 destined for n_3 can reserve c_{A1} and then request c_{A2} and c_{H2}. A packet at node n_2 destined for n_0 can reserve c_{A2} and then request c_{A3}. Finally, a packet at node n_3 destined for n_1 can reserve c_{A3} and then request c_{A0} and c_{H0}.

However, the routing function is deadlock-free. Although we focus on wormhole switching, the following analysis is also valid for other switching techniques. Let us show that there is not any deadlocked configuration by trying to build one. If there were a packet stored in the queue of channel c_{H2}, it would be destined for n_3 and flits could advance. So, c_{H2} must be empty. Also, if there were a packet stored in the queue of c_{H1}, it would be destined for n_2 or n_3. As c_{H2} is empty, flits could also advance and c_{H1} must be empty. If there were flits stored in the queue of c_{H0}, they would be destined for n_1, n_2 or n_3. Even if their header were stored in c_{A1} or c_{A2}, as c_{H1} and c_{H2} are empty, flits could advance and c_{H0} must be empty.

Thus, any deadlocked configuration can only use channels c_{Ai}. Although there is a cyclic dependency between them, c_{A0} cannot contain flits destined for n_0. That configuration would not be legal because n_0 cannot forward packets for itself through the network. For any other destination, those flits can advance because c_{H1} and c_{H2} are empty. Again, c_{A0} can be emptied, thus breaking the cyclic dependency. Thus, the routing function is deadlock-free.

Example 3.3 shows that deadlocks can be avoided even if there are cyclic dependencies between some channels. Obviously, if there were cyclic dependencies between all the channels in the network, there would be no path to escape from cycles. Thus, the key idea consists of providing a path free of cyclic dependencies to escape from cycles. That path can be considered as an escape path. Note that at least one packet from each cycle should be able to select the escape path at the current node, whichever its destination is. In Example 3.3, for every legal configuration, a packet whose header flit is stored in channel c_{A0} must be destined for either n_1, n_2, or n_3. In the first case, it can be immediately delivered. In the other cases, it can use channel c_{H1}.

It seems that we could focus only on the escape paths and forget about the other channels to prove deadlock freedom. In order to do so, we can restrict a routing function in such a way that it only supplies channels belonging to the escape paths as routing choices. In other words, if a routing function supplies a given set of channels to route a packet from the current node toward its destination, the restricted routing function will supply a subset of those channels. The restricted routing function will be referred to as *routing subfunction*. Formally, if R is a routing function and R_1 is a routing subfunction of R, we have

$$R_1(x,y) \subseteq R(x,y) \quad \forall x,y \in N \tag{3.1}$$

Channels supplied by R_1 for a given packet destination will be referred to as *escape channels* for that packet. Note that the routing subfunction is only a mathematical tool to prove deadlock freedom. Packets can be routed by using all the channels supplied by the routing function R. Simply, the concept of routing subfunction will allow us to focus on the set of escape channels. This set is $C_1 = \bigcup_{\forall x,y \in N} R_1(x,y)$.

When we restrict our attention to escape channels, it is important to give an accurate definition of channel dependency because there are some subtle cases. There is a channel dependency from an escape channel c_i to another escape channel c_k if there exists a packet that is holding c_i and it requests c_k as an escape channel for itself. It does not matter whether c_i is an escape channel for this packet, as far as it is an escape channel for some other packets. Also, it does not matter whether c_i and c_k are adjacent or not. These cases will be analyzed in Sections 3.1.4 and 3.1.5.

Channel dependencies can be grouped together to simplify the analysis of deadlocks. A convenient form is the *channel dependency graph* [78]. It is a directed graph, $D = G(C,E)$. The vertices of D are the channels of the interconnection network I. The arcs of D are the pairs of channels (c_i, c_j) such that there is a channel dependency from c_i to c_j. As indicated above, we can restrict our attention to a subset of channels $C_1 \subset C$, thus defining a channel dependency graph in which all the vertices belong to C_1. That graph has been defined as the *extended channel dependency graph* of R_1 [93, 98]. The word "extended" means that although we are focusing on a channel subset, packets are allowed to use all the channels in the network.

The extended channel dependency graph is a powerful tool to analyze whether a routing function is deadlock-free or not. The following theorem formalizes the ideas presented in Example 3.3 by proposing a necessary and sufficient condition for a routing function to be deadlock-free [93, 98]. This theorem is only valid under the previously mentioned assumptions.

Theorem 3.1 *A connected routing function R for an interconnection network I is deadlock-free if and only if there exists a routing subfunction R_1 that is connected and has no cycles in its extended channel dependency graph.*

This theorem is mostly used for deadlock avoidance. However, it is valid even if packets wait for a finite period of time before using a channel supplied by R_1, as shown in [89, 95]. Thus, Theorem 3.1 can also be applied to prove deadlock freedom when deadlock recovery techniques are used, as will be seen in Section 3.6.

The theorem is valid for both deterministic and adaptive routing. However, for deterministic routing, restricting the routing function will disconnect it because a single path is supplied for each packet. The only connected routing subfunction is $R_1 = R$. In this case, the channel dependency graph and the extended channel dependency graph of R_1 are identical. The resulting condition for deadlock-free routing is stated in the following corollary. It was proposed as a theorem in [78].

Corollary 3.1 *A (deterministic) routing function R for an interconnection network I is deadlock-free if and only if there are no cycles in the channel dependency graph D.*

For adaptive routing functions, the application of Theorem 3.1 requires the definition of a suitable routing subfunction. This is not an easy task. Intuition and experience considerably help. A rule of thumb that usually works consists of looking at deterministic deadlock-free routing functions previously proposed for the same topology. If one of those routing functions is a restriction of the routing function we are analyzing, we can try it. As we will see in Chapter 4, a simple way to propose adaptive routing algorithms follows this rule in the opposite way. It starts from a deterministic deadlock-free routing function, adding channels in a regular way. The additional channels can be used for fully adaptive routing.

Theorem 3.1 is valid for SAF, VCT, and wormhole switching under the previously mentioned assumptions. The application to each switching technique will be presented in Sections 3.1.4 and 3.1.5. For wormhole switching, the condition proposed by Theorem 3.1 becomes a sufficient one if the routing function is not coherent. Thus, it is still possible to use this theorem to prove deadlock freedom on incoherent routing functions, as can be seen in Exercise 3.3.

Finally, when a packet uses an escape channel at a given node, it can freely use any of the available channels supplied by the routing function at the next node. It is not necessary to restrict that packet to use only channels belonging to the escape paths. Also, when a packet is blocked because all the alternative output channels are busy, the header is not required to wait on any predetermined channel. Instead, it waits in the input channel queue. It is repeatedly routed until any of the channels supplied by the routing function becomes free. Both issues are important, because they considerably increase routing flexibility, especially when the network is heavily loaded.

3.1.4   Deadlock Avoidance in SAF and VCT Switching

In this section, we restrict our attention to SAF and VCT switching. Note that dependencies arise because a packet is holding a resource while requesting another one. Although VCT pipelines packet transmission, it behaves in the same way as SAF regarding deadlock because packets are buffered when they are blocked. A blocked packet is buffered into a single channel. Thus, dependencies only exist between adjacent channels.

According to expression (3.1), it is possible to restrict a routing function in such a way that a channel c_i supplied by R for destination nodes x and y is only supplied by the routing subfunction R_1 for destination node x. In this case, c_i is an escape channel for packets destined for x but not for packets destined for y.

As indicated in Section 3.1.3, there is a channel dependency from an escape channel c_i to another escape channel c_k if there exists a packet that is holding c_i and it requests c_k as an escape channel for itself. If c_i is also an escape channel for the packet destination, we refer to this kind of channel dependency as *direct dependency* [87, 92]. If c_i is not an escape channel for the packet destination, the dependency is referred to as *direct cross-dependency* [93, 98]. Direct cross-dependencies must be considered because a packet may be holding a channel needed by another packet to escape from cycles. The following example shows both kinds of dependency.

Example 3.4

Let us consider again the routing function R defined in Example 3.3, in order to show how the general theory can be applied to SAF and VCT switching.

A well-known deterministic deadlock-free routing function for the ring was proposed in [78]. It requires two virtual channels per physical channel. One of those channels is used when the destination node has a higher label than the current node. The other channel is used when the destination has a lower label. This routing function is a restriction of the routing function proposed in Example 3.3. Instead of allowing c_{Ai} channels to be used for all the destinations, they are only used when the destination is lower than the current node. Let us define the

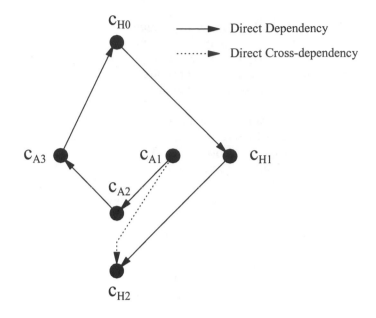

Figure 3.6. Extended channel dependency graph for R_1 using SAF switching.

routing subfunction R_1 more formally: If the current node n_i is equal to the destination node n_j, store the packet. Otherwise, use c_{Ai}, if $j < i$ or c_{Hi}, if $j > i$.

Figure 3.6 shows the extended channel dependency graph for R_1 when SAF switching is used. As will be seen, the graph for wormhole switching is different. Black circles represent the unidirectional channels supplied by R_1. Arrows represent channel dependencies. This notation will be used in all the drawings of channel dependency graphs. Note that the graph only considers the channels supplied by R_1. In particular, c_{A0} is not a node of the graph.

A packet destined for n_2 that is currently stored at n_0 can use c_{H0} to reach n_1, and then c_{H1} to reach n_2. After reaching n_1, it is holding a buffer from c_{H0} and it requests c_{H1}. Thus, there is a direct dependency from c_{H0} to c_{H1}, because both channels are supplied by the routing subfunction for the packet destination. Similarly, there is a direct dependency from c_{H1} to c_{H2}.

A packet destined for n_0 that is currently stored at n_1 can use c_{A1} to reach n_2, then c_{A2} to reach n_3, and then c_{A3} to reach n_0. Thus, there are direct dependencies from c_{A1} to c_{A2} and from c_{A2} to c_{A3}. Finally, a packet destined for n_1 that is currently stored at n_3 can use c_{A3} to reach n_0, and then c_{H0} to reach n_1. Once again, both channels are supplied by the routing subfunction for the packet destination, and there is a direct dependency from c_{A3} to c_{H0}.

Now consider a packet destined for n_3 that is currently stored at n_1. It can use c_{A1} and c_{H2} to reach node n_3 because both channels are supplied by R. Although c_{A1} is not supplied by R_1 for the packet destination, it is supplied by R_1 for other destinations. Thus, there is a direct cross-dependency from c_{A1} to c_{H2}.

The routing subfunction R_1 is obviously connected. Packets use either c_{Ai} or c_{Hi} channels depending on whether the destination node is lower or higher than the current node. As there are no cycles in the graph, we can conclude that R is deadlock-free.

In Example 3.4, direct cross-dependencies do not produce any cycle. In some cases, if direct cross-dependencies were not considered, one could erroneously conclude that the routing function is deadlock-free. See Exercise 3.1 for an example. The channel dependency graph and the extended channel dependency graph of a routing subfunction would be identical if direct cross-dependencies were not considered. There are some cases in which direct cross-dependencies do not exist. Remember that direct cross-dependencies exist because some channels are used as escape channels or not depending on packet destination. We can define a routing subfunction R_1 by using a channel subset C_1, according to the following expression:

$$R_1(x, y) = R(x, y) \cap C_1 \quad \forall x, y \in N \tag{3.2}$$

In this case, a channel belonging to C_1 is used as escape channel for all the destinations for which it can be supplied by R. Thus, there is not any direct cross-dependency between channels in C_1. As a consequence, the channel dependency graph and the extended channel dependency graph of a routing subfunction are identical, supplying a simple condition to check whether a routing function is deadlock-free. This condition is proposed by the following corollary [87]. Note that it only supplies a sufficient condition.

Corollary 3.2 *A connected routing function R for an interconnection network I is deadlock-free if there exists a channel subset $C_1 \subseteq C$ such that the routing subfunction $R_1(x, y) = R(x, y) \cap C_1$ $\forall x, y \in N$ is connected and has no cycles in its channel dependency graph D_1.*

Another interesting property of routing subfunctions defined by channel subsets according to expression 3.2 is proposed by the following theorem:

Theorem 3.2 *A connected routing function R for an interconnection network I is deadlock-free if there exists a channel subset $C_1 \subseteq C$ such that the routing subfunction $R_1(x, y) = R(x, y) \cap C_1$ $\forall x, y \in N$ is connected and deadlock-free.*

This theorem indicates that we can start from a connected deadlock-free routing function R_1, adding as many channels as we wish. The additional channels can be used in any way, either following minimal or nonminimal paths. The resulting routing function will be deadlock-free. The only restriction is that we cannot add routing options to the channels initially used by R_1.[2] Corollary 3.2 and Theorem 3.2 are valid for SAF and VCT switching, but not for wormhole switching. The following example shows the application of Theorem 3.2.

Example 3.5

Let us consider a 2-D mesh with bidirectional channels. The routing function uses the north-last routing algorithm[3] [130]. For the sake of simplicity, consider that only minimal paths are allowed. This routing function allows the use of every minimal path with one exception: North channels can only be used when the destination node is located north from the current node. As a consequence, packets are not allowed to turn after using north channels. Channels corresponding to north, east, south, and west directions will be denoted as N, E, S, and W. The north-last routing function is not fully adaptive. As shown in Figure 3.2, fully adaptive

---

[2]Note that in Exercise 3.1, R uses the same channels used by R_1 by adding more routing choices.
[3]See the turn model in Chapter 4.

routing without virtual channels may produce deadlocks. We are going to add the minimum number of virtual channels to obtain a fully adaptive deadlock-free routing function.

Consider that N channels are split into two virtual channels, namely, N_1 and N_2. After using N_1 channels, no turns are allowed. However, 90-degree turns are allowed after using N_2 channels. In other words, it is possible to use E or W channels after using N_2 channels. The new routing function R is fully adaptive. N_2 channels can be used when the destination is located north-east or north-west from the current node. R is also deadlock-free. Effectively, consider that C_1 is the subset containing N_1, E, S, and W channels. According to expression 3.2, C_1 defines a routing subfunction R_1 identical to the north-last routing function. As shown in [130], R_1 is connected and deadlock-free. Thus, according to Theorem 3.2, R is deadlock-free for VCT and SAF switching.

3.1.5 Deadlock Avoidance in Wormhole Switching

Wormhole switching pipelines packet transmission. The main difference with respect to VCT regarding deadlock avoidance is that when a packet is blocked, flits remain in the channel buffers. Remember that when a packet is holding a channel and it requests another channel, there is a dependency between them. As we assume no restrictions for packet length, packets will usually occupy several channels when blocked. Thus, there will exist channel dependencies between nonadjacent channels. Of course, the two kinds of channel dependency defined for SAF and VCT switching are also valid for wormhole switching.

Dependencies between nonadjacent channels are not important when all the channels of the network are considered because they cannot produce cycles. Effectively, a packet holding a channel and requesting a nonadjacent channel is also holding all the channels in the path it followed from the first channel up to the channel containing its header. Thus, there is also a sequence of dependencies between the adjacent channels belonging to the path reserved by the packet. The information offered by the dependency between nonadjacent channels is redundant.

However, the application of Theorem 3.1 requires the definition of a routing subfunction in such a way that the channels supplied by it could be used as escape channels from cyclic dependencies. When we restrict our attention to the escape channels, it may happen that a packet reserved a set of adjacent channels $c_i, c_{i+1}, \ldots, c_{k-1}, c_k$ in such a way that c_i and c_k are escape channels but $c_{i+1}, \ldots, c_{k-1}$ are not. In this case, the dependency from c_i to c_k is important because the information offered by it is not redundant. If c_i is an escape channel for the packet destination, we will refer to this kind of channel dependency as *indirect dependency* [87]. If c_i is not an escape channel for the packet destination but it is an escape channel for some other destinations, the dependency is referred to as *indirect cross-dependency* [93, 98]. In both cases, the channel c_k requested by the packet must be an escape channel for it. Indirect cross-dependencies are the indirect counterpart of direct cross-dependencies. To illustrate these dependencies, we present another example.

Example 3.6

Consider a unidirectional ring using wormhole switching with six nodes denoted $n_i, i = \{0, 1, 2, 3, 4, 5\}$ and three channels connecting each pair of adjacent nodes. Let c_{Ai}, c_{Bi}, and $c_{Hi}, i = \{0, 1, 2, 3, 4, 5\}$ be the outgoing channels from node n_i. The routing function can be stated as follows: If the current node n_i is equal to the destination node n_j, store the packet. Otherwise, use either c_{Ai} or c_{Bi}, $\forall j \neq i$, or c_{Hi}, $\forall j > i$. This routing function is identical

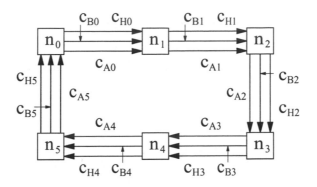

Figure 3.7. Network for Example 3.6.

to the one for Example 3.4, except that c_{Bi} channels have been added. Figure 3.7 shows the network.

Suppose that we define a routing subfunction in the same way as in Example 3.4: c_{Ai} channels are supplied by the routing subfunction when the packet destination is lower than the current node. c_{Hi} channels are always supplied by the routing subfunction. Consider a packet destined for n_4 whose header is at n_1. It can use channels c_{H1}, c_{B2}, and c_{H3} to reach n_4. Thus, while the packet is holding c_{H1} and c_{B2}, it requests c_{H3}. As c_{B2} is not an escape channel, there is an indirect dependency from c_{H1} to c_{H3}. Again, consider the packet destined for n_4 whose header is at n_1. It can use channels c_{A1}, c_{B2}, and c_{H3} to reach n_4. As c_{A1} is not an escape channel for the packet destination but it is an escape channel for some other destinations, it produces an indirect cross-dependency from c_{A1} to c_{H3}. The same packet can also use channels c_{A1}, c_{A2}, and c_{H3}, again producing an indirect cross-dependency from c_{A1} to c_{H3}. But in this case, it also produces a direct cross-dependency from c_{A2} to c_{H3}.

We have defined several kinds of channel dependency, showing examples for all of them. Except for direct dependencies, all kinds of channel dependency arise because we restrict our attention to a routing subfunction (the escape channels). Defining several kinds of channel dependency allowed us to highlight the differences between SAF and wormhole switching. However, it is important to note that all kinds of channel dependency are particular cases of the definition given in Section 3.1.3. Now let us revisit Example 3.3 to show how Theorem 3.1 is applied to networks using wormhole switching.

Example 3.7

Consider once again the unidirectional ring and the routing function R defined in Example 3.3. We are going to use the same routing subfunction R_1 defined in Example 3.4. It can be stated as follows: If the current node n_i is equal to the destination node n_j, store the packet. Otherwise, use c_{Ai}, if $j < i$ or c_{Hi}, if $j > i$.

Figure 3.8 shows the extended channel dependency graph for R_1 when wormhole switching is used. Direct dependencies and direct cross-dependencies are the same as in Example 3.4. Let us analyze indirect dependencies. Consider a packet destined for n_2 whose header is at n_3. It can use c_{A3}, c_{A0}, and c_{H1} to reach n_2. There is an indirect dependency from c_{A3} to c_{H1}, because c_{A3} and c_{H1} are supplied by the routing subfunction for the packet destination. However, c_{A0} is not supplied by the routing subfunction for the packet destination. No

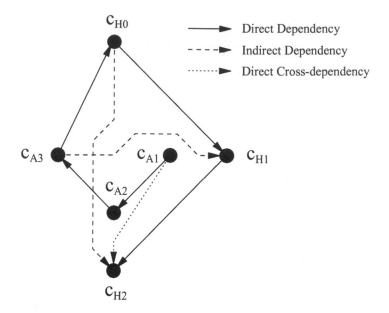

Figure 3.8. Extended channel dependency graph for R_1 using wormhole switching.

consider a packet destined for n_3 whose header is at n_0. It can use c_{H0}, c_{A1}, and c_{H2} to reach n_3. Thus, there is an indirect dependency from c_{H0} to c_{H2}. In this example, there is not any indirect cross-dependency between channels. As there are no cycles in the graph, the routing function R is also deadlock-free under wormhole switching.

In wormhole switching, a packet usually occupies several channels when blocked. As a consequence, there are many routing functions that are deadlock-free under SAF, but they are not when wormhole switching is used. See Exercise 3.2 for an example.

Note that Theorem 3.1 does not require that all the connected routing subfunctions have an acyclic extended channel dependency graph to guarantee deadlock freedom. So the existence of cycles in the extended channel dependency graph for a given connected routing subfunction does not imply the existence of deadlocked configurations. It would be necessary to try all the connected

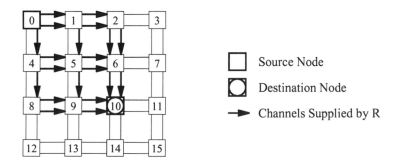

Figure 3.9. Routing example for R (defined in Example 3.8).

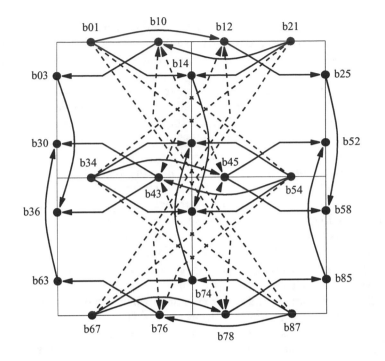

Figure 3.10. Extended channel dependency graph for R_1 (defined in Example 3.8).

routing subfunctions. If the graphs for all of them have cycles, then we can conclude that there are deadlocked configurations. Usually it is not necessary to try all the routing subfunctions. If a reasonably chosen routing subfunction has cycles in its extended channel dependency graph, we can try to form a deadlocked configuration by filling one of the cycles, as shown in Exercise 3.2.

The next example presents a fully adaptive minimal routing algorithm for 2-D meshes. It can be easily extended to n-dimensional meshes. This algorithm is simple and efficient. It is the basic algorithm currently implemented in the Reliable Router [75] to route packets in the absence of faults.

Example 3.8

Consider a 2-D mesh using wormhole switching. Each physical channel c_i has been split into two virtual channels, namely, a_i and b_i. The routing function R supplies all the a channels belonging to a minimal path. It also supplies one b channel according to dimension-order routing (XY routing algorithm).[4] Figure 3.9 shows a routing example. Arrows show all the alternative paths that can be followed by a packet traveling from node 0 to node 10. Note that both a and b channels can be used to go from node 0 to node 1. However, only the a channel can be used if the packet is sent across the Y dimension at node 0.

Let C_1 be the set of b channels. Consider the routing subfunction R_1 defined by C_1 according to expression 3.2. It is the XY routing algorithm. It is connected because every destination can be reached using dimension-order routing. Figure 3.10 shows part of the extended channel dependency graph for R_1 on a 3×3 mesh. Black circles represent the

---

[4]The Reliable Router uses two virtual channels for fully adaptive minimal routing and two virtual channels for dimension-order routing in the absence of faults.

unidirectional channels belonging to C_1. They are labeled as bij, where i and j are the source and destination nodes, respectively. As a reference, channels are also represented by thin lines. Arrows represent channel dependencies, dashed arrows corresponding to indirect dependencies. For the sake of clarity, we have removed all the indirect dependencies that do not add information to the graph. In particular, the indirect dependencies that can be obtained by composing two or more direct or indirect dependencies have been removed. As R_1 has been defined according to expression 3.2, there is not any cross-dependency. It can be seen that the graph is acyclic. Thus, R is deadlock-free.

Some nonminimal routing functions may not be coherent. As mentioned in Section 3.1.3, Theorem 3.1 can also be applied to prove deadlock freedom on incoherent routing functions (see Exercise 3.3). However, Theorem 3.1 only supplies a sufficient condition if the routing function is not coherent. Thus, if there is no routing subfunction satisfying the conditions proposed by Theorem 3.1, we cannot conclude that it is not deadlock-free (see Exercise 3.4). Fortunately, incoherent routing functions that cannot be proved to be deadlock-free by using Theorem 3.1 are very rare.

The reason why Theorem 3.1 becomes a sufficient condition is that incoherent routing functions allow packets to cross several times through the same node. If a packet is long enough, it may happen that it is still using an output channel from a node when it requests again an output channel from the same node. Consider again the definition of channel dependency. The packet is holding an output channel and it requests several output channels, including the one it is occupying. Thus, there is a dependency from the output channel occupied by the packet to itself, producing a cycle in the channel dependency graph. However, the selection function will never select that channel because it is busy.

A theoretical solution consists of combining routing and selection functions into a single function in the definition of channel dependency. Effectively, when a packet long enough using wormhole switching crosses a node twice, it cannot select the output channel it reserved the first time because it is busy. The dependency from that channel to itself no longer exists. With this new definition of channel dependency, Theorem 3.1 would also be a necessary and sufficient condition for deadlock-free routing in wormhole switching. However, the practical interest of this extension is very small. As mentioned above, incoherent routing functions that cannot be proved to be deadlock-free by using Theorem 3.1 are very rare. Additionally, including the selection function in the definition of channel dependency implies a dynamic analysis of the network because the selection function considers channel status. We will present alternative approaches to consider incoherent routing functions in Section 3.3.

3.2   Extensions

In this section we extend the theory presented in Section 3.1 by proposing methods to simplify its application as well as by considering alternative definitions of the routing function.

3.2.1   Channel Classes

Theorem 3.1 proposes the existence of an acyclic graph as a condition to verify deadlock freedom. As the graph indicates relations between some channels, the existence of an acyclic graph implies that an ordering can be defined between those channels. It is possible to define a total ordering between channels in most topologies [78]. However, the relations in the graph only supply information to establish a partial ordering in all but a few simple cases, like unidirectional rings.

Consider two unrelated channels c_i, c_j that have some common predecessors and successors in the ordering. We can say that they are at the same level in the ordering or that they are *equivalent*. This equivalence relation groups equivalent channels so that they form an *equivalence class* [90]. Note that there is no dependency between channels belonging to the same class. Now, it is possible to define the concept of *class dependency*. There is a dependency from class K_i to class K_j if there exist two channels $c_i \in K_i$ and $c_j \in K_j$ such that there is a dependency from c_i to c_j. We can represent class dependencies by means of a graph. If the classes contain all the channels, we define the *class dependency graph*. If we restrict our attention to classes formed by the set of channels C_1 supplied by a routing subfunction R_1, we define the *extended class dependency graph* [90].

Theorem 3.1 can be restated by using the extended class dependency graph instead of the extended channel dependency graph.

Theorem 3.3 *A connected routing function R for an interconnection network I is deadlock-free if there exist a connected routing subfunction R_1 and an equivalence relation $\mathcal{R}_1$ defined on $C_1 = \bigcup_{\forall x,y \in N} R_1(x,y)$, such that the extended class dependency graph for R_1 is acyclic.*

Note that the existence of a dependency between two classes does not imply the existence of a dependency between every pair of channels in those classes. Thus, the existence of cycles in the extended class dependency graph does not imply that the extended channel dependency graph has cycles. As a consequence, Theorem 3.3 only supplies a sufficient condition. However, this is enough to prove deadlock freedom.

It is not always possible to establish an equivalence relation between channels. However, when possible, it considerably simplifies the analysis of deadlock freedom. The channels that can be grouped into the same class usually have some common topological properties. For instance, channels crossing the same dimension of a hypercube in the same direction. Classes are not a property of the topology alone. They also depend on the routing function. The next example shows the definition of equivalence classes in a 2-D mesh.

Example 3.9

Consider the extended channel dependency graph drawn in Figure 3.10. There is not any dependency between channels $b01$, $b34$, and $b67$. However, there are dependencies from $b01$, $b34$, and $b67$ to $b12$, $b45$, and $b78$. Channels $b01$, $b34$, and $b67$ can be grouped into the same class. The same can be done with channels $b12$, $b45$, and $b78$. Suppose that we define classes such that all the horizontal (vertical) channels in the same column (row) and direction are in the same class. It is easy to see that there is not any dependency between channels belonging to the same class. Let us denote the classes containing east (X-positive) channels as $X0+, X1+$, starting from the left. For instance, $X0+ = \{b01, b34, b67\}$. Similarly, classes containing west channels are denoted as $X0-, X1-$, starting from the right. Also, classes containing north channels are denoted as $Y0+, Y1+$, starting from bottom, and classes containing south channels are denoted as $Y0-, Y1-$, starting from top. Figure 3.11 shows the extended class dependency graph corresponding to the extended channel dependency graph shown in Figure 3.10.

Note that there are class dependencies from each X class to each Y class. This is because there is at least one horizontal channel from which it is possible to request the corresponding vertical channel. As can be seen, the extended class dependency graph is much simpler than the extended channel dependency graph. However, it supplies the same information about the absence of cyclic dependencies.

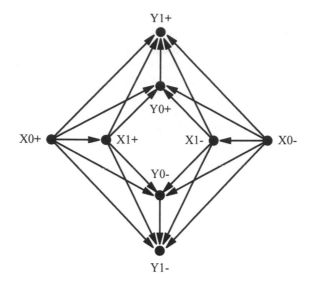

Figure 3.11. Extended class dependency graph for R_1 (defined in Example 3.8).

As mentioned above, classes depend on the routing function. Exercise 3.5 shows a routing function for the 2-D mesh for which classes are formed by channels in the same diagonal.

3.2.2 Extending the Domain of the Routing Function

In Section 3.1.2 we defined the domain of the routing function as $N \times N$. Thus, routing functions only considered the current and destination nodes to compute the routing options available to a given packet. It is possible to extend the domain of the routing function by considering more information. For instance, a packet can carry the address of its source node in its header. Also, packets can record some history information in the header, like number of misrouting operations performed. Carrying additional information usually produces some overhead, unless header flits have enough bits to accommodate the additional information.

It is also possible to use additional local information to compute the routing function. The most interesting one is the input channel queue in which the packet header (or the whole packet) is stored. The use of this information does not produce a noticeable overhead. However, it allows a higher flexibility in the definition of routing functions. Their domain is now defined as $C \times N$, i.e., the routing function takes into account the input channel and the destination node.

Including the input channel in the domain of the routing function implies that some deadlocked configurations may be unreachable [308]. So, the existence of a deadlocked configuration does not imply that deadlock can occur because all the deadlocked configurations may be unreachable. However, up to now, nobody proposed unreachable deadlocked configurations for the most common topologies. So, for practical applications, we can assume that all the configurations are reachable. As a consequence, Theorem 3.1 remains valid for routing functions defined on $C \times N$. Moreover, even if some deadlocked configurations are not reachable, the sufficient condition of Theorem 3.1 is valid. So, for practical applications, this theorem can be used to prove deadlock freedom on routing functions defined on $C \times N$, regardless of the existence of unreachable deadlocked configurations. On the other hand, Theorem 3.2 is only valid for routing functions defined on $N \times N$.

3.2.3 Central Queues

For the sake of clarity, in Section 3.1 we only considered routing functions using edge buffers. However, most routing functions proposed up to now for SAF switching use central queues. In this case, a few central buffers deep enough to store one or more packets are used. The router model was described in Section 3.1.1.

Let Q be the set of all the queues in the system. The node containing a queue q_i is denoted n_i. When routing a packet at queue q_i, instead of supplying a set of channels, the routing function supplies a set of queues belonging to nodes adjacent to n_i. It may take into account the current and destination nodes of the packet. In this case, the domain of the routing function is $N \times N$. Alternatively, the routing function may consider the current queue and the destination node. In this case, its domain is $Q \times N$. Note that this routing function is distinct as there may be multiple queues per node.

Now, central queues are the shared resources. We used channel dependencies to analyze the use of edge buffers. Similarly, we can use queue dependencies to analyze deadlocks arising from the use of central queues. There is a queue dependency between two central queues when a packet is totally or partially stored in one of them, and it requests the other one. All the definitions given for edge buffers have their counterpart for central queues. In particular, queue dependency graphs replace channel dependency graphs. Also, instead of restricting the use of channels, a routing subfunction restricts the use of queues. With these changes in notation, the results presented in Section 3.1 for routing functions defined on $N \times N$ are also valid for routing functions defined on $N \times N$ that use central queues. Also, those results can be applied to routing functions defined on $Q \times N$, supplying only a sufficient condition for deadlock freedom as mentioned in Section 3.2.2.

We can generalize the results for edge buffers and central queues by mixing both kinds of resources [10]. It will be useful in Section 3.6. A resource is either a channel or a central queue. Note that we only consider the resources that can be held by a packet when it is blocked. Thus, there is a resource dependency between two resources when a packet is holding one of them, and it requests the other one. Once again, the definitions and theoretical results proposed for edge buffers have their counterpart for resources. All the issues, including coherency and reachability can be considered in the same way as for edge buffers. In particular, Theorem 3.1 can be restated simply by replacing the extended channel dependency graph by the extended resource dependency graph. Note that the edge buffer or central queue containing the packet header is usually required in the domain of the routing function to determine the kind of resource being used by the packet. So, strictly speaking, the resulting theorem would only be a sufficient condition for deadlock freedom, as mentioned in Section 3.2.2. Note that this generalized result is valid for all the switching techniques considered in Section 3.1.

3.3 Alternative Approaches

There are alternative approaches to avoid deadlocks. Some of them are theoretical approaches based on other models. Other approaches are simple and effective tricks to avoid deadlocks. These tricks do not work for all switching techniques.

3.3.1 Theoretical Approaches

The theory presented in Section 3.1 relies on the concept of channel dependency or resource dependency. However, some authors used different tools to analyze deadlocks. The most interesting one is the concept of *waiting channel* [207]. The basic idea is the same as for channel dependency: a packet is holding some channel(s) while waiting for other channel(s). The main difference with respect to channel dependency is that waiting channels are not necessarily the same channels offered by the routing function to that packet. More precisely, if the routing function supplies a set of channels C_i to route a packet in the absence of contention, the packet only waits for a channel belonging to $C_j \subseteq C_i$ when it is blocked. The subset C_j may contain a single channel. In other words, if a packet is blocked, the number of routing options available to that packet may be reduced. This is equivalent to dynamically changing the routing function depending on packet status.

By reducing the number of routing options when a packet is blocked, it is possible to allow more routing flexibility in the absence of contention [74]. In fact, some routing options that may produce deadlock are forbidden when the packet is blocked. Remember that deadlocks arise because some packets are holding resources while waiting for other resources in a cyclic way. If we prevent packets from waiting on some resources when blocked, we can prevent deadlocks. However, the additional routing flexibility offered by this model is usually small.

Models based on waiting channels are more general than the ones based on channel dependencies. In fact, the latter are particular cases of the former when a packet is allowed to wait on all the channels supplied by the routing function. Another particular case of interest arises when a blocked packet always waits on a single channel. In this case, this model matches the behavior of routers that buffer blocked packets in queues associated with output channels. Note that those routers do not use wormhole switching, because they buffer whole packets.

Although models based on waiting channels are more general than the ones based on channel dependencies, note that adaptive routing is useful because it offers alternative paths when the network is congested. In order to maximize performance, a blocked packet should be able to reserve the first valid channel that becomes available. Thus, restricting the set of routing options when a packet is blocked does not seem to be an attractive choice from the performance point of view.

A model that increases routing flexibility in the absence of contention is based on the *wait-for graph* [74]. This graph indicates the resources that blocked packets are waiting for. Packets are even allowed to use nonminimal paths as long as they are not blocked. However, blocked packets are not allowed to wait for channels held by other packets in a cyclic way. Thus, some blocked packets are obliged to use deterministic routing until delivered if they produce a cycle in the wait-for graph.

An interesting model based on waiting channels is the *message flow model* [207, 209]. In this model, a routing function is deadlock-free if and only if all the channels are deadlock-immune. A channel is deadlock-immune if every packet that reserves that channel is guaranteed to be delivered. The model starts by analyzing the channels for which a packet reserving them is immediately delivered. Those channels are deadlock-immune. Then the model analyzes the remaining channels step by step. In each step, the channels adjacent to the ones considered in the previous step are analyzed. A channel is deadlock-immune if for all the alternative paths a packet can follow, the next channel to be reserved is also deadlock-immune. Waiting channels play a role similar to routing subfunctions, serving as escape paths when a packet is blocked.

Another model uses a *channel waiting graph* [308]. This graph captures the relationship between channels in the same way as the channel dependency graph. However, this model does not distinguish between routing and selection functions. Thus, it considers the dynamic evolution of the network because the selection function takes into account channel status. Two theorems are proposed. The first one considers that every packet has a single waiting channel. It states that a routing algorithm is deadlock-free if it is wait-connected and there are no cycles in the channel waiting graph. The routing algorithm is wait-connected if it is connected by using only waiting channels.

But the most important result is a necessary and sufficient condition for deadlock-free routing. This condition assumes that a packet can wait on any channel supplied by the routing algorithm.

It uses the concept of *true cycles*. A cycle is a true cycle if it is reachable, starting from an empty network. The theorem states that a routing algorithm is deadlock-free if and only if there exists a restricted channel waiting graph that is wait-connected and has no true cycles [308]. This condition is valid for incoherent routing functions and for routing functions defined on $C \times N$. However, it proposes a dynamic condition for deadlock avoidance, thus requiring the analysis of all the packet injection sequences to determine whether a cycle is reachable (true cycle). True cycles can be identified by using the algorithm proposed in [308]. This algorithm has nonpolynomial complexity. When all the cycles are true cycles, this theorem is equivalent to Theorem 3.1. The theory proposed in [308] has been generalized in [306], supporting SAF, VCT, and wormhole switching. Basically, the theory proposed in [306] replaces the channel waiting graph by a buffer waiting graph.

Up to now, nobody proposed static necessary and sufficient conditions for deadlock-free routing for incoherent routing functions and for routing functions defined on $C \times N$. This is a theoretical open problem. However, as mentioned in previous sections, it is of very little practical interest because the cases where Theorem 3.1 cannot be applied are very rare. Remember that this theorem can be used to prove deadlock freedom for incoherent routing functions and for routing functions defined on $C \times N$. In these cases it becomes a sufficient condition.

3.3.2 Deflection Routing

Unlike wormhole switching, SAF and VCT switching provide more buffer resources when packets are blocked. A single central or edge buffer is enough to store a whole packet. As a consequence, it is much simpler to avoid deadlock.

A simple technique, known as *deflection routing* [138] or *hot potato* routing is based on the following idea: The number of input channels is equal to the number of output channels. Thus, an incoming packet will always find a free output channel.

The set of input and output channels includes memory ports. If a node is not injecting any packet into the network, then every incoming packet will find a free output channel. If several options are available, a channel belonging to a minimal path is selected. Otherwise, the packet is misrouted. If a node is injecting a packet into the network, it may happen that all the output channels connecting to other nodes are busy. The only free output channel is the memory port. In this case, if another packet arrives at the node, it is buffered. Buffered packets are reinjected into the network before injecting any new packet at that node.

Deflection routing has two limitations. First, it requires storing the packet into the current node when all the output channels connecting to other nodes are busy. Thus, it cannot be applied to wormhole switching. Second, when all the output channels belonging to minimal paths are busy, the packet is misrouted. This increases packet latency and bandwidth consumption, and may produce livelock. The main advantages are its simplicity and flexibility. Deflection routing can be used in any topology, provided that the number of input and output channels per node is the same.

Deflection routing was initially proposed for communication networks. It has been shown to be a viable alternative for networks using VCT switching. Misrouting has a small impact on performance [188]. Livelock will be analyzed in Section 3.7.

3.3.3 Injection Limitation

Another simple technique to avoid deadlock consists of restricting packet injection. Again, it is only valid for SAF and VCT switching. This technique was proposed for rings [297]. Recently it has been extended for tori [166].

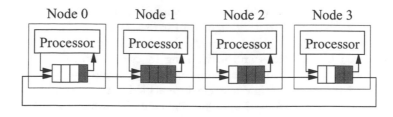

Figure 3.12. Deadlock avoidance by limiting packet injection.

The basic idea for the unidirectional ring is the following: In a deadlocked configuration no packet is able to advance. Thus, if there is at least one empty packet buffer in the ring, there is no deadlock. A packet from the previous node is able to advance, and sooner or later, all the packets will advance. To keep at least one empty packet buffer in the ring, a node is not allowed to inject a new packet if it fills the local queue. Two or more empty buffers in the local queue are required to inject a new packet. Note that each node only uses local information. Figure 3.12 shows a unidirectional ring with four nodes. Node 1 cannot inject packets because its local queue is full. Note that this queue was not filled by node 1, but by transmission from node 0. Node 2 cannot inject packets because it would fill its local queue. In this case, injecting a packet at node 2 would not produce deadlock but each node only knows its own state. Nodes 0 and 3 are allowed to inject packets.

This mechanism can be easily extended for tori with central queues and dimension-order routing. Assuming bidirectional channels, every dimension requires two queues, one for each direction. A given queue can receive packets from the local node and from lower dimensions. As above, a node is not allowed to inject a new packet if it fills the corresponding queue. Additionally, a packet cannot move to the next dimension if it fills the queue corresponding to that dimension (in the appropriate direction). When two or more empty buffers are available in some queue, preference is given to packets changing dimension over newly injected packets. This mechanism can also be extended to other topologies like meshes.

Although this deadlock avoidance mechanism is very simple, it cannot be used for wormhole switching. Also, modifying it so that it supports adaptive routing is not trivial.

3.4 Deadlock Avoidance in Switch-Based Networks

Deadlocks arise because network resources (buffers or channels) are limited. If we compare a router in a direct network with a switch in a switch-based network (either a buffered multistage network or a switch-based network with regular or irregular topology), they are very similar. Regarding deadlocks, the only difference is that a router has a single processor attached to it while a switch may be connected to zero, one, or more processors. So, we can focus on the topology connecting the switches and model a switch-based network by means of a direct network. Switches that are not connected to any processor can neither send nor receive packets. Switches connected to one or more processors are allowed to send and receive packets. With this simple model, the theoretical results for deadlock avoidance in direct networks can also be applied to switch-based networks.

There is a special case that is worth to mention because it includes most MINs. The behavior of these networks regarding deadlocks is different depending on whether recirculation is allowed. If it is allowed, a packet may cross the network several times, reaching an intermediate node after each circulation but the last one. Assuming that the packet is not ejected from the network at

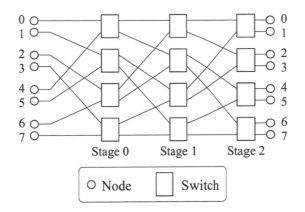

Figure 3.13. A multistage interconnection network.

intermediate nodes, the behavior of MINs regarding deadlocks is similar to that of direct networks. As mentioned above, the theoretical results for the latter are valid for the former.

However, if recirculation is not allowed, there exists a natural ordering in the way resources are reserved, thus avoiding deadlock. Usually, recirculation is not allowed. Consider the unidirectional MIN in Figure 3.13. Packets are only routed from left to right. The critical resources regarding deadlock are the channels connecting stages or the buffers associated with them. Packets are first routed at a switch from the first stage. Then they are routed at the second stage, and so on, until they reach their destination. As there is no recirculation, once a packet has reserved an output channel from the first stage it will not request another output channel from the first stage. Thus, there is no dependency between channels from the same stage. Similarly, a packet that has reserved an output channel from a given stage will not request another output channel from a previous stage. There are only dependencies from channels in a given stage to channels in the next stages. As a consequence, there is not any cyclic dependency between channels, thus avoiding deadlocks.

Using the concept of channel class defined in Section 3.2.1, we can define as many classes as stages, because there is no dependency between channels from the same stage. Dependencies between classes also form an acyclic graph because there is not any dependency from the class corresponding to a given stage to the classes corresponding to previous stages.

For bidirectional MINs the situation is very similar. Bidirectional channels can be considered as two unidirectional channels. Although some stages are crossed twice by each packet (in forward and backward direction), different channels are used for each direction. Thus, there is also a natural ordering of stages.

3.5 Deadlock Prevention in Circuit Switching and PCS

Deadlock prevention techniques request resources in such a way that no deadlock can arise. The simplest deadlock prevention technique consists of reserving all the resources before they are used. This is the way circuit switching and PCS work [125, 127]. In these switching techniques, the source node sends a probe that sets up the whole path. Once the path has been established, data flits are forwarded into the network. No deadlock can arise because all the resources have been reserved before starting packet transmission. If the probe cannot advance, it is allowed to backtrack, releasing some previously reserved resources. If the probe is not able to establish any path (usually due to the existence of faulty channels or nodes), it returns to the source node releasing all the network resources.

It should be noted that if backtracking is not allowed then the probe may block during path setup, keeping all the channels it previously reserved. In this case, the behavior of circuit switching and PCS regarding deadlocks is identical to that of wormhole switching, and deadlock prevention techniques cannot be used.

3.6   Deadlock Recovery

Deadlock recovery techniques do not impose any restriction on routing functions, thereby allowing deadlocks to form. These techniques require a mechanism to detect and resolve potential deadlock situations. When a deadlock is detected, one or more packets are obliged to release the buffer resources they are keeping, allowing other packets to use them, and breaking the deadlock.

Deadlock recovery techniques are useful only if deadlocks are rare. Otherwise the overhead produced by deadlock detection and buffer releasing would degrade performance considerably. Also, deadlock recovery mechanisms should be able to recover from deadlocks faster than they occur.[5] Therefore, it is important for us to know how probable deadlocks might be for certain network configurations and to understand the parameters which most influence deadlock formation. For example, wormhole switching is more prone to deadlock than are other switching techniques [346]. This is because each packet may hold several channel resources spanning multiple nodes in the network while being blocked. We therefore concentrate on wormhole-switched recovery schemes.

3.6.1   Deadlock Probability

Recent work by Pinkston and Warnakulasuriya on characterizing deadlocks in interconnection networks has shown that a number of interrelated factors influence the probability of deadlock formation [282, 346]. Among the more influential of these factors is the routing freedom, the number of blocked packets, and the number of resource dependency cycles. Routing freedom corresponds to the number of routing options available to a packet being routed at a given node within the network and can be increased by adding physical channels, adding virtual channels, and/or increasing the adaptivity of the routing algorithm. It has been quantitatively shown that as the number of network resources (physical and virtual channels) and the routing options allowed on them by the routing function increase (routing freedom), the number of packets that tend to block significantly decreases, the number of resource dependency cycles decreases, and the resulting probability of deadlock also decreases exponentially. This is due to the fact that deadlocks require highly correlated patterns of cycles, the complexity of which increases with routing freedom. A conclusion of Pinkston and War-nakulasuriya's work is that deadlocks in interconnection networks can be highly improbable when sufficient routing freedom is provided by the network and fully exploited by the routing function. In fact, it has been shown that as few as two virtual channels per physical channel are sufficient to virtually eliminate all deadlocks up to and beyond saturation in 2-D toroidal networks when using unrestricted fully adaptive routing [282, 346]. This verifies previous empirical results which estimated

---

[5]Consider a boat with a hole in the hull. If water is not drained faster than it fills the boat, it will sink.

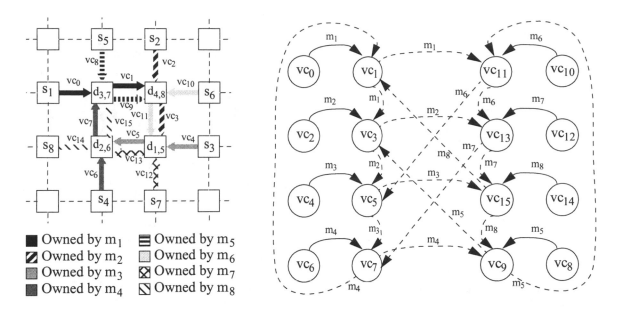

Figure 3.14. A multicycle deadlock formed under minimal adaptive routing with two virtual channels per physical channel. (From [282].)

that deadlocks are infrequent [9, 179]. However, the frequency of deadlock increases considerably when no virtual channels are used.

The network state reflecting resource allocations and requests existing at a particular point in time can be depicted by the *channel wait-for graph* (CWG). The nodes of this graph are the virtual channels reserved and/or requested by some packet(s). The solid arcs point to the next virtual channel reserved by the corresponding packet. The dashed arcs in the CWG point to the alternative virtual channels a blocked packet may acquire in order to continue routing. The highly correlated resource dependency pattern required to form a deadlocked configuration can be analyzed with the help of the CWG. A *knot* is a set of nodes in the graph such that from each node in the knot it is possible to reach every other node in the knot. The existence of a knot is a necessary and sufficient condition for deadlock [282]. Note that checking the existence of knots requires global information and cannot be efficiently done at run-time.

Deadlocks can be characterized by deadlock set, resource set, and knot cycle density attributes. The *deadlock set* is the set of packets that own the virtual channels involved in the knot. The *resource set* is the set of all virtual channels owned by members of the deadlock set. The *knot cycle density* represents the number of unique cycles within the knot. The knot cycle density indicates complexity in correlated resource dependency required for deadlock. Deadlocks with smaller knot cycle densities are likely to affect local regions of the network only whereas those having larger knot cycle densities are likely to affect more global regions of the network and will therefore be more harmful.

Example 3.10

Figure 3.14 shows eight packets (m_1, m_2, m_3, m_4, m_5, m_6, m_7, and m_8) being routed minimal adaptively in a network with two virtual channels per physical channel. The source and

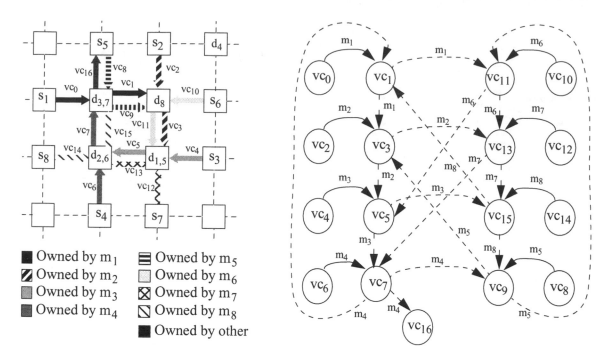

Figure 3.15. A cyclic nondeadlocked network state under minimal adaptive routing with two virtual channels per physical channel. (From [282].)

destination nodes of packet m_i are labeled s_i and d_i, respectively. Packet m_1 has acquired channels vc_0 and vc_1, and requires either vc_3 or vc_{11} to continue. Similarly, all other packets have also acquired two virtual channels each, and are awaiting to acquire one of two possible alternative channels in order to proceed. All of the packets depicted here are waiting for resources held by other packets in the group, and therefore will be blocked indefinitely, thus constituting a deadlock.

The CWG for the packets in this example is also depicted in Figure 3.14. The deadlock set is the set $\{m_0 \ldots m_7\}$. The resource set is $\{vc_0 \ldots vc_{15}\}$. The knot cycle density is 24.

Example 3.11

A cyclic nondeadlocked configuration in which multiple cycles exists but do not form a deadlock is depicted in Figure 3.15. The dependencies are similar to those in Example 3.10 except that the destination of packet m_4 is changed, giving it an additional channel alternative to use to continue routing. While the same resource dependency cycles as in the previous example still exist, this scenario does not constitute a deadlock since packet m_4 may eventually acquire vc_{16} to reach its destination and subsequently release vc_7, which will allow one of the two packets waiting for this channel (m_3 or m_7) to continue. Other packets will then be able to follow in a like manner. Hence, this small increase in routing freedom is sufficient enough to complicate the correlated resource dependencies required for deadlock. It can be observed in the CWG in Figure 3.15 that virtual channels do not form any knot because it is not possible to reach any other node from vc_{16}.

The deadlock in Example 3.10 formed because all of the packets involved had exhausted much of their routing freedom. Increasing routing freedom makes deadlocks highly improbable even beyond network saturation. However, increased routing freedom does not completely eliminate the formation of cyclic nondeadlocks resulting from correlated packet blocking behavior, as illustrated in Example 3.11. Even though they do not lead to deadlock formation, cyclic nondeadlocks can lead to situations where packets block cyclically faster than they can be drained and, therefore, remain blocked for extended periods, causing increased latency and reduced throughput. It has been shown in [282] that networks that maximize routing freedom have the benefit of reducing the probability of cyclic nondeadlocks over those that do not. In general, given sufficient routing freedom provided by the network, deadlock recovery-based routing algorithms designed primarily to maximize routing freedom have a potential performance advantage over deadlock avoidance-based routing algorithms designed primarily to avoid deadlock (and secondarily to maximize routing freedom). This is what makes deadlock recovery-based routing interesting. In Chapter 9, we will confirm this intuitive view.

In addition to increasing routing freedom, another method for reducing the probability of deadlock (and cyclic nondeadlock) is to limit packet injection, thereby limiting the number of packets which enter and block within the network at saturation. One approach is to limit the number of injection ports to one. Other mechanisms can be used to further limit injection. For example, a simple mechanism that uses only local information allows the injection of a new packet if the total number of free output virtual channels in the node is higher than a given threshold. This mechanism was initially proposed to avoid performance degradation in networks using deadlock avoidance techniques [220]. It is also well suited for minimizing the likelihood of deadlock formation in deadlock recovery [226].

3.6.2 Detection of Potential Deadlocks

Deadlock recovery techniques differ in the way deadlocks are detected and in the way packets are obliged to release resources. A deadlocked configuration often involves several packets. Completely accurate deadlock detection mechanisms are not feasible because they require exchanging information between nodes (centralized detection). This is not always possible because channels may be occupied by deadlocked packets. Thus, less accurate heuristic mechanisms that use only local information (distributed detection) are preferred. For instance, if a header flit is blocked for longer than a certain amount of time, it can be assumed that the corresponding packet is potentially deadlocked.

Deadlock detection mechanisms using a timeout heuristic can be implemented either at the source node or at intermediate nodes which contain a packet header. If deadlocks are detected at the source node, a packet can be considered deadlocked when the time since it was injected is longer than a threshold [288] or when the time since the last flit was injected is longer than a threshold [179]. In either case, a packet cannot be purged from the source node until the header reaches the destination. This can be achieved without end-to-end acknowledgments by padding packets with additional dummy flits as necessary to equal the maximum distance allowed by the routing algorithm for the source to destination pair [179]. Detection at the source node requires that each injection port have an associated counter and comparator. On the other hand, if deadlocks are detected at intermediate nodes, each virtual channel requires an associated counter and comparator to measure the time headers block [8].

Heuristic deadlock detection mechanisms may not detect deadlocks immediately. Also, they may indicate that a packet is deadlocked when it is simply waiting for a channel occupied by a long packet (i.e., false deadlock detection). Moreover, when several packets form a deadlocked configuration, it is sufficient to release the buffer occupied by only one of the packets to break the deadlock. However, because heuristic detection mechanisms operate locally and in parallel, several nodes may detect deadlock concurrently and release several buffers in the same deadlocked configuration. In the worst case, it may happen that all the packets involved in a deadlock release the buffers they occupy. These overheads suggest that deadlock recovery-based routing can benefit from highly selective deadlock detection mechanisms. For instance, turn selection criteria could also be enforced to limit a packet's eligibility to use recovery resources [278].

The most important limitation of heuristic deadlock detection mechanisms arises when packets have different lengths. The optimal value of the timeout for deadlock detection heavily depends on packet length unless some type of physical channel monitoring of neighboring nodes is implemented. When a packet is blocked waiting for channels occupied by long packets, the selected value for the timeout should be high in order to minimize false-deadlock detection. As a consequence, deadlocked packets have to wait for long until deadlock is detected. In these situations, latency becomes much less predictable. The poor behavior of current deadlock detection mechanisms considerably limits the practical applicability of deadlock recovery techniques. Some current research efforts aim at improving deadlock detection techniques [226].

3.6.3   Progressive and Regressive Recovery Techniques

Once deadlocks are detected and packets made eligible to recover, there are several alternative actions that can be taken to release the buffer resources occupied by deadlocked packets. Deadlock recovery techniques can be classified as *progressive* or *regressive*. Progressive techniques deallocate resources from other (normal) packets and reassign them to deadlocked packets for quick delivery. Regressive techniques deallocate resources from deadlocked packets, usually killing them (abort-and-retry). The set of possible actions taken depends on where deadlocks are detected.

If deadlocks are detected at the source node, regressive deadlock recovery is usually used. A packet can be killed by sending a control signal that releases buffers and propagates along the path reserved by the header. This is the solution proposed in *compressionless routing* [179]. After a random delay, the packet is injected again into the network. This reinjection requires a packet buffer associated with each injection port. Note that a packet that is not really deadlocked may resume advancement and even start delivering flits at the destination after the source node presumes it is deadlocked. Thus, this situation also requires a packet buffer associated with each delivery port to store fragments of packets that should be killed if a kill signal reaches the destination node. If the entire packet is consumed without receiving a kill signal, it is delivered. Obviously, this use of packet buffers associated with ports restricts packet size.

If deadlocks are detected at an intermediate node containing the header, then both regressive and progressive deadlock recovery are possible. In regressive recovery, a deadlocked packet can be killed by propagating a backward control signal that releases buffers from the node containing the header back to the source by following the path reserved by the packet in the opposite direction. Instead of killing a deadlocked packet, progressive recovery allows resources to be temporarily deallocated from normal packets and assigned to a deadlocked packet so that it can reach its destination. Once the deadlocked packet is delivered, resources are reallocated to the preempted packets. This progressive deadlock recovery technique was first proposed in [8, 9]. This technique is clearly more efficient than regressive deadlock recovery. Hence, we will study it in more detail.

Figure 3.16 shows the router organization for the first progressive recovery technique proposed, referred to as *Disha* [8, 9, 10]. It is identical to the router model proposed in Section 2.1 except that each router is equipped with an additional central buffer or *deadlock buffer*. This resource can be accessed from all neighboring nodes by asserting a control signal (arbitration for it will be discussed below) and is used only in the case of suspected deadlock. Systemwide, these buffers form what is collectively a deadlock-free recovery lane which can be visualized as a floating virtual channel

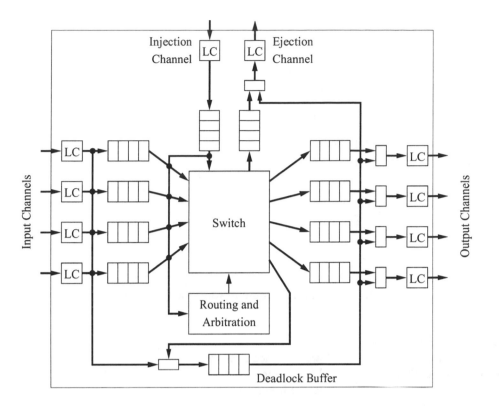

Figure 3.16. Router organization for Disha. (LC = Link controller.)

shared by all physical dimensions of a router. On the event of a suspected deadlock, a packet is switched to the deadlock-free lane and routed adaptively along a path leading to its destination where it is consumed to avert the deadlock. Physical bandwidth is deallocated from normal packets and assigned to the packet being routed over the deadlock-free lane to allow swift recovery. The aforementioned control signal is asserted every time a deadlocked packet flit uses physical channel bandwidth so that the flit is assigned to the deadlock buffer at the next router. The mechanism that makes the recovery lane deadlock-free is specific to how recovery resources are allocated to suspected deadlocked packets. Implementations can be based on restricted access (Disha sequential [8]) or structured access (Disha concurrent [10]) to the deadlock buffers as discussed below.

Example 3.12

To gain an intuitive understanding of how deadlock can be progressively recovered from, consider the deadlocked configuration depicted in Figure 3.17 for a k-ary 2-cube network. For simplicity, we illustrate operation with two virtual channels per physical channel. In this configuration, packets P_2 and P_3 reserved the virtual channels connecting routers R_a and R_b, and are blocked at router R_b waiting for any of the virtual channels occupied by P_4 and P_5 (and, likewise, P_4 and P_5 are waiting for any of the virtual channels occupied by P_6 and P_7, and so on). There may be other cycles in the network. Assume that k cycles exist (one is shown in the figure). We illustrate the formation of Disha recovery paths through routers R_a, R_b, and R_c in Figures 3.18 and 3.19 for this deadlock scenario.

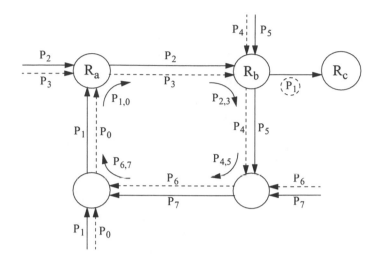

Figure 3.17. Deadlocked configuration for Example 3.12.

In the absence of deadlocks, the router switch is configured as specified by the normal decision and arbitration logic. However, once a potential deadlock situation is detected by router R_a, its crossbar is configured to redirect the deadlocked packet to its deadlock buffer for handling by the deadlock routing logic. Figure 3.18 shows the state of routers R_a and R_b when packet P_1 (which is being minimally routed in the final dimension toward its destination) is blocked by packets P_2 and P_3.

Unable to route P_1's header for the specified timeout threshold, router R_a suspects the packet is involved in a deadlock and checks its eligibility to recover. Router R_a then routes the header of the eligible packet through its crossbar, into its central deadlock buffer (bypassing normal edge output buffers currently occupied by blocked packets P_2 and P_3), and preempts the idle output physical channel from P_2 and P_3 which were already inactive due to deadlock blockage further downstream (see Figure 3.19). The corresponding control line is asserted for

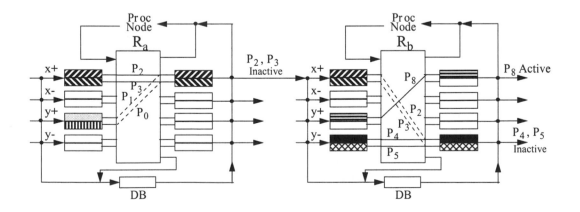

Figure 3.18. Formation of Disha recovery paths — initial state. (DB = Deadlock buffer.)

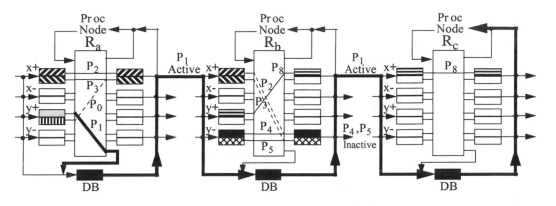

Figure 3.19. Formation of Disha recovery paths — removing packet P_1. (DB = Deadlock buffer.)

the channel, indicating to router R_b to route the incoming header of P_1 through the recovery lane (deadlock buffer) instead of the normal virtual channel lane (edge input buffer) currently occupied by P_2 and P_3.

In like manner at subsequent routers, packet P_1 is routed entirely on deadlock buffer resources until it reaches its destination (R_c), bypassing completely the normal routing section of each router for speedy recovery. These actions are shown in Figure 3.19. This eliminates one cycle, reducing the number of cycles to $k-1$. By induction, it follows that the network safely recovers from all deadlocks. Note that allowing any one of the packets to progressively recover breaks one cycle in the deadlocked configuration. Also, there is no ordering as to which packet should be placed on the deadlock-free recovery lane.

It could happen that a recovering packet in the deadlock buffer requires the same output physical channel at a router as normal unblocked (active) packets currently being routed using edge buffer resources. This case, which is illustrated in Figure 3.19 at router R_b, poses no problem. Here, packet P_8 may be active. However, P_1 takes precedence and preempts the physical channel bandwidth, suspending normal packet transmission until deadlock has cleared. Although this might lead to additional discontinuities in flit reception beyond that suffered from normal virtual channel multiplexing onto physical channels, all flits of packet P_8 are guaranteed to reach their destination safely. Given that suspected deadlock occurrences are infrequent anyway, the occasional commandeering of output channels should not significantly degrade performance. However, router organizations that place the deadlock buffer on the input side of the crossbar would require crossbar reconfiguration and logic to remember the state of the crossbar before it was reconfigured so that the suspended input buffer can be reconnected back to the preempted output buffer once deadlock has cleared [9]. This situation can be avoided simply by connecting the deadlock buffer to the output side of the crossbar as shown in Figure 3.16. This positioning of the deadlock buffer also makes recovering from self-deadlocking situations less complicated (i.e., those situations arising from nonminimal routing where packets are allowed to visit the same node twice).

Although deadlock buffers are dedicated resources, no dedicated channels are required to handle deadlocked packets. Instead, network bandwidth is allocated for deadlock freedom only in the rare instances when probable deadlocks are detected; otherwise, all network bandwidth is devoted to fully adaptive routing of normal packets. Thus, most of the time, all edge virtual channels are used for fully adaptive routing to optimize performance. This is as opposed to deadlock avoidance routing schemes that constantly devote some number of edge virtual channels for avoiding improbable deadlock situations. The number of deadlock buffers per node should be kept minimal. Otherwise, crossbar size would increase, requiring more gates and resulting in increased propagation delay. This is the reason why central buffers are used in Disha. Some alternative approaches use edge buffers instead of central buffers, therefore providing a higher bandwidth to drain blocked packets [95, 273]. However, in these cases more buffers are required, increasing crossbar size and propagation delay.

Deadlock freedom on the deadlock buffers is essential to recovery. This can be achieved by restricting access with a circulating token that enforces mutual exclusion on the deadlock buffers. In this scheme, referred to as Disha sequential [8], only one packet at a time is allowed to use the deadlock buffers. An asynchronous token scheme was proposed in [8] and implemented in [281] to drastically reduce propagation time and hide token capture latency. The major drawback of this scheme, however, is the token logic which presents a single point of failure. Another potential drawback is the fact that recovery from deadlocks is sequential. This could affect performance if deadlocks become frequent or get clustered in time. Simultaneous deadlock recovery avoids these drawbacks, which will be discussed shortly.

An attractive and unique feature of Disha recovery is that it reassigns resources to deadlocked packets instead of killing packets and releasing the resources occupied by them. Based on the extension of Theorem 3.1 as mentioned in Section 3.2.3, Disha ensures deadlock freedom by the existence of a routing subfunction that is connected and has no cyclic dependencies between resources. Disha's routing subfunction is usually defined by the deadlock buffers, but, for concurrent recovery discussed below, it may also make use of some edge virtual channels. An approach similar to Disha was proposed in [89, 95, 273], where the channels supplied by the routing subfunction can only be selected if packets are waiting for longer than a threshold. The circuit required to measure packet waiting time is identical to the circuit for deadlock detection in Disha. However, the routing algorithms proposed in [89, 95, 273] use dedicated virtual channels to route packets waiting for longer than a threshold.

Disha can also be designed so that several deadlocks can be recovered from concurrently (Disha Concurrent [10]). In this case, the token logic is no longer necessary. Instead, an arbiter is required in each node so that simultaneous requests for the use of the deadlock buffer coming from different input channels are handled [280]. For concurrent recovery, more than one deadlock buffer may be required at each node for some network topologies, but even this is still the minimum required by progressive recovery. Exercise 3.6 shows how simultaneous deadlock recovery can be achieved on meshes by using a single deadlock buffer and some edge buffers.

In general, simultaneous deadlock recovery can be achieved on any topology with Hamiltonian paths by using two deadlock buffers per node. Nodes are labeled according to their position in the Hamiltonian path. One set of deadlock buffers is used by deadlocked packets whose destination node has a higher label than the current node. The second set of deadlock buffers is used by deadlocked packets whose destination node has a lower label than the current node. All edge virtual channels can be used for fully adaptive routing. As deadlock buffers form a connected routing subfunction without cyclic dependencies between them, all deadlocked packets are guaranteed to be delivered by using deadlock buffers. Similarly, simultaneous deadlock recovery can be achieved on any topology with an embedded spanning tree by using two deadlock buffers per node.

3.7   Livelock Avoidance

The simplest way to avoid livelock is by limiting misrouting. Minimal routing algorithms are a special case of limited misrouting in which no misrouting is allowed. The number of channels reserved by a packet is upper-bounded by the network diameter. If there is no deadlock, the packet is guaranteed to be delivered in the absence of faults. Minimal routing algorithms usually achieve a higher performance when wormhole switching is used because packets do not consume more channel bandwidth than the minimum amount required.

An important reason to use misrouting is routing around faulty components. If only minimal paths are allowed, and the link connecting the current and destination nodes is faulty, the packet is not able to advance. Given a maximum number of faults that do not disconnect the network, it has been shown that limited misrouting is enough to reach all the destinations [127]. By limiting misrouting, there is also an upper-bound for the number of channels reserved by a packet, thus avoiding livelock. Misrouting can be limited either by designing an appropriate routing algorithm or by adding a field to the packet header to keep the misrouting count.

As far as we know, the only case in which misrouting cannot be limited without inducing deadlock is deflection routing. As indicated in Section 3.3.2, this routing technique avoids deadlock by using any free channel to forward packets. Limiting misrouting may produce deadlock if the only available channel at a given node cannot be used because misrouting is limited.

It has been shown that deflection routing is livelock-free in a probabilistic way [189]. Assuming that channels belonging to minimal paths are given preference over those ones belonging to non-minimal paths, the probability of finding all the minimal paths busy decreases as the number of tries increases. Thus, when a sufficiently long period of time is considered, the probability of not reaching the destination approaches zero for all the packets. In other words, packets will reach their destination sooner or later. In practice, it has been shown that very few misrouting operations are required on average when deflection routing is used.

3.8 Engineering Issues

This chapter is mostly theoretical. However, the ideas presented in this chapter have a direct application to the design of routing algorithms. Thus, the impact on performance is directly related to the impact of routing algorithms on performance. Wormhole routers could not be used in multiprocessors and multicomputers if deadlock handling were not considered in the router design. Moreover, multicast and fault-tolerant routing algorithms also require handling deadlock and livelock. The techniques presented in Chapters 5 and 6 will build upon the techniques presented in this chapter.

As indicated in Chapter 2, the design of hardware routers using wormhole switching increased performance by several orders of magnitude. But designers of wormhole routers had to consider deadlock avoidance seriously. SAF switching provided enough buffering space so that deadlock avoidance was not a serious problem, even if the routing algorithm was not deadlock-free. The probability of deadlock was almost negligible. Additionally, routing algorithms were implemented in software, considerably easing the task of recovering from deadlocks. When wormhole switching was proposed, deadlock avoidance techniques were immediately considered. The probability of deadlock in wormhole networks is high enough to block the whole network in a few seconds if the routing algorithm is not deadlock-free.

The first theory of deadlock avoidance for wormhole switching followed the ideas previously proposed for operating systems: deadlocks are avoided by avoiding cyclic dependencies between resources. Despite its simplicity it had a tremendous impact. It allowed the design of the routers used in almost all current multicomputers.

Adaptive routing algorithms may improve performance over deterministic routing algorithms considerably, especially when traffic is not uniform. However, adaptive routers are more complex, slowing down clock frequency. Thus, there is a trade-off. Designing fully adaptive routing algorithms under the constraint of eliminating cyclic dependencies between resources produces a considerable increase in the complexity of the router.

Except for 2-D networks, fully adaptive routers were not feasible until the proposal of more relaxed conditions for deadlock avoidance (similar to Theorem 3.1). Relaxed conditions allowed minimal fully adaptive routing by adding only one virtual channel per physical channel. Thus, relaxed conditions like the one proposed by Theorem 3.1 are the key for the design of adaptive routers. But even by using those relaxed conditions, adaptive routing algorithms require more resources than deterministic ones. In addition to increasing the number of virtual channels, crossbars become more complex. Also, adaptive routing has to select one routing option, considering channel status. As a consequence, deterministic routers are faster than adaptive routers. But the benefits from using fully adaptive routing may well outweigh the slower clock frequency (see Chapter 9).

Most researchers think that adaptive routing algorithms will be used for future router designs. We agree with this view. Chips are becoming faster but transmission delay across wires remains the same. When routers become so fast that flit transmission across physical channels becomes the slowest stage in the pipeline, adaptive routers will definitely outperform deterministic routers under all traffic conditions.

Meanwhile, in an attempt to eliminate the need for excessive hardware resources and use existing resources more efficiently, some researchers proposed the use of deadlock recovery techniques. Deadlocks are frequent when the network reaches the saturation point if the number of dimensions is small and no virtual channels are used. Because deadlocks in wormhole switching were believed to be frequent regardless of design parameters, deadlock recovery techniques were not rigorously pursued until recently. New empirical studies have shown that deadlocks are generally very infrequent in the presence of sufficient routing freedom, making deadlock recovery an attractive alternative. However, deadlock recovery has some overhead associated with it, particularly if deadlocked packets are killed and injected again into the network as with regressive recovery. Progressive recovery techniques such as Disha minimize overheads as they reassign channel bandwidth so that deadlocked packets are quickly delivered and removed from the network.

Moreover, as Disha does not require dedicated channels for deadlock avoidance, the overhead in the absence of deadlock is small. The advantages of Disha are especially noticeable in tori. At least three virtual channels per physical channel are required for fully adaptive routing using the condition proposed by Theorem 3.1, and only one of them is used for fully adaptive routing. Disha requires only a single virtual channel for fully adaptive routing plus one central buffer (or two, depending on whether sequential or concurrent deadlock recovery is implemented). Therefore, additional virtual channels in Disha serve to increase throughput as all can be used for fully adaptive routing.

However, Disha has some potential drawbacks. The circuit implementing the circulating token is a single point of failure. This drawback can be easily eliminated by using concurrent deadlock recovery, but this may require an additional central buffer. Also, deadlock detection circuitry is required such as a counter and comparator for each virtual input channel. But perhaps the most important drawback arises when some or all packets are long. The small bandwidth offered by a single central buffer is usually enough to deliver short deadlocked packets. However, when long packets become deadlocked, recovering from deadlock may take a while. As a consequence, other deadlocked packets have to wait a considerable amount of time before the central buffer becomes available, increasing latency and reducing throughput. In these situations, latency becomes much less predictable. Additionally, the optimal value of the timeout threshold for deadlock detection heavily depends on packet length unless some type of physical channel monitoring of neighboring nodes is implemented. Therefore, short messages or messages split into fixed-length shorter packets may be preferred. In this case, the increased performance achieved by Disha should be weighed against the overheads associated with packetizing messages.

It is important to note that performance may degrade considerably before reaching a deadlocked configuration. Even if deadlock does not occur, performance may degrade severely when the network reaches the saturation point. This behavior typically arises when cyclic dependencies between channels are allowed. In this case, regardless of whether deadlock avoidance or progressive recovery are used, the bandwidth provided by the resources to escape from deadlock should be high enough to drain packets from cyclic waiting chains as fast as they are formed. For some traffic patterns, providing that bandwidth would require too many resources. Alternatively, packet injection can be limited so that the network cannot reach the saturation point (see Section 9.9). Injection limitation techniques not only eliminate performance degradation beyond the saturation point but also reduce the frequency of deadlock to negligible values.

Finally, as the number of transistors per chip increases, VCT switching becomes more feasible. Although the probability of deadlocks is less than in wormhole switching, VCT switching must still guard against deadlocks. Simple techniques such as deflection routing have proven to be very effective. Nevertheless, the main drawback of VCT is that it requires buffers deep enough to store one or more packets. If these buffers are implemented in hardware, messages must be split into relatively short packets, thus increasing latency. Like Disha, VCT switching is more suitable when messages are short or packetized, like in distributed shared-memory multiprocessors with hardware cache coherence protocols.

3.9 Commented References

The alternative approaches to handle deadlocks were described in [320]. This paper mainly focuses on distributed systems. Thus, the conclusions are not directly applicable to interconnection networks. The theoretical background for deadlock avoidance in packet-switched networks (SAF) can be found in [134, 141, 237]. These results were developed for data communication networks.

Some tricks were developed to avoid deadlock in SAF and VCT switching, like restricting packet injection [166, 297]. The most popular trick is deflection routing [138], also known as "hot potato" routing.

Wormhole switching achieves a higher performance than SAF switching, but it is also more deadlock-prone. A necessary and sufficient condition for deadlock-free routing was proposed in [78]. Although this condition was only proposed for deterministic routing functions, it has been extensively applied to adaptive routing functions. In this case, that condition becomes a sufficient one. An innovative view of the condition for deadlock-free adaptive routing is the turn model [130]. This model analyzes how cyclic dependencies are formed, prohibiting enough turns to break all the cycles. The turn model is based on the theory proposed in [78]. It will be studied in detail in Chapter 4.

With the exception of the tricks, all of the above-mentioned results avoid deadlock by preventing the existence of cyclic dependencies between storage resources. Fully adaptive routing requires a considerable amount of resources if cyclic dependencies are avoided. More flexibility can be achieved by relaxing the condition for deadlock-free routing. Sufficient conditions for deadlock-free adaptive routing in SAF networks were proposed in [87, 276, 277]. A necessary condition was proposed in [64]. The combination of those conditions does not produce a necessary and sufficient condition.

Developing relaxed conditions for wormhole switching is more difficult because packets can hold several channels simultaneously. Sufficient conditions for deadlock-free adaptive routing were independently proposed by several authors [24, 87, 92, 137, 207, 330].

The above-mentioned conditions can be relaxed even more. A necessary and sufficient condition for deadlock-free routing in wormhole switching was proposed in [93, 98]. The necessary condition is only valid for coherent routing functions defined on $N \times N$. This condition can be easily modified for SAF and VCT switching, as shown in [99], where the restriction about coherency is removed. The restrictions about coherency and the domain of the routing function are removed in [111, 306, 308] for wormhole switching. However, these results supply temporal (dynamic) conditions rather than structural (static) ones. Another necessary and sufficient condition for deadlock-free routing is proposed in [209], extending the sufficient condition presented in [207].

An intermediate approach between deadlock avoidance and recovery was proposed in [89, 95] and, more recently, in [273] which use a time-dependent selection function. The use of deadlock recovery techniques for wormhole switching was first proposed in [288] and later in [179]. The recovery techniques proposed were based on regressive abort-and-retry, thus incurring large overheads and increased packet latency. More recently, Disha was proposed in [8, 9]; it is a more efficient progressive deadlock recovery technique. From a logical point of view, it is similar to the time-dependent selection function proposed in [89, 95]. However, the implementation of Disha is more efficient. Deadlock freedom is based on an extension of the conditions proposed in [87, 93]. That extension was proposed in [10]. The frequency of deadlocks was first approximated in [9, 179] and found to be rare. More recent empirical studies by [282, 346] confirm that deadlocks are highly improbable in networks with few virtual channels, small node degree, and relaxed routing restrictions, thus making deadlock recovery routing tenable.

Deadlock prevention in pipelined circuit-switching was analyzed in [125, 127]. The corresponding analysis for scouting and configurable flow control techniques was presented in [80, 100]. These techniques will be studied in Chapter 6.

Finally, probabilistic livelock avoidance was analyzed in [189].

EXERCISES

3.1 Consider a 2-D mesh using VCT switching. The routing function R_1 uses dimension-order routing (XY routing). This routing function forwards a packet across horizontal channels until it reaches the column where its destination node is. Then the packet is forwarded through vertical channels until it reaches its destination. Draw the channel dependency graph for R_1 on a 3×3 mesh. Now consider a minimal fully adaptive routing function R. It forwards packets following any minimal path without adding virtual channels. Draw the extended channel dependency graph for R_1 on a 3×3 mesh, considering R_1 as a subfunction of R.

Solution   It is well-known that R_1 is connected and deadlock-free. Figure 3.20 shows the channel dependency graph for R_1 on a 3×3 mesh. Black circles represent the unidirectional channels supplied by R_1 and are labeled as cij, where i and j are the source and destination nodes of the channel, respectively. As a reference, channels are also represented by thin lines. Arrows represent channel dependencies. The graph has no cycles.

Figure 3.21 shows the extended channel dependency graph for R_1 on a 3×3 mesh when it is considered as a routing subfunction of R. Solid arrows represent direct dependencies. Obviously these dependencies are the same as in Figure 3.20. Dashed arrows represent direct cross-dependencies. It can be seen that there are direct cross-dependencies from Y channels toward X channels that produce cycles. Effectively, a packet traveling southeast may use a Y channel (supplied by R but not by R_1), then requesting a X channel (supplied by R_1). The same Y channel may be requested as an escape channel by a packet traveling south (supplied by R_1). If direct cross-dependencies were not considered, we would erroneously conclude that R is deadlock-free. Figure 3.2 shows a deadlocked configuration for R.

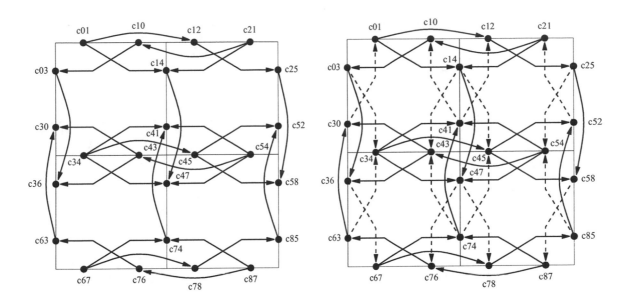

Figure 3.20. Channel dependency graph for R_1 on a 3×3 mesh.

Figure 3.21. Extended channel dependency graph for R_1 on a 3×3 mesh.

3.2 Consider a 2-D mesh using wormhole switching. Each physical channel consists of a single virtual channel in each direction, except north channels that are split into two virtual channels. Channels corresponding to north, east, south, and west directions are denoted as N_1, N_2, E, S, and W. The routing function R allows the use of every minimal path using N_2, E, S, and W channels. N_1 channels can only be used when the destination node is located north from the current node. Draw a deadlocked configuration for R on a 3×3 mesh. If R_1 is defined by the set of channels N_1, E, S, and W, using expression 3.2, draw the extended channel dependency graph for R_1.

Solution   As shown in Example 3.5, R is deadlock-free for VCT and SAF switching. However, R is not deadlock-free when wormhole switching is used. Figure 3.22 shows a deadlocked configuration on a 3×3 mesh. Solid lines represent the channel(s) already reserved by each packet. Dashed arrows represent the next channel requested by each packet. Dashed arrows also point at the destination node for the packet. In this configuration, a single routing option is available to each packet. As can be seen, no packet is able to advance. One of the packets has reserved one E channel and two N_2 channels, then requesting another E channel. Thus, such a deadlocked configuration is only valid for wormhole switching.

Figure 3.23 shows the extended channel dependency graph for R_1 on a 3×3 mesh. Solid arrows represent direct dependencies. Dashed arrows represent indirect dependencies. As the routing subfunction is defined by a channel subset, there is not any cross-dependency. As can be seen, there are cycles in the graph. For instance, channels $c12$, $c25$, $c54$, $c43$, $c36$, and $c67$ form a cycle. This cycle corresponds to the deadlocked configuration presented in Figure 3.22.

3.3 Consider a 2-D mesh using wormhole switching such that each physical channel is split into two virtual channels. Virtual channels are grouped into two sets or virtual networks. The first

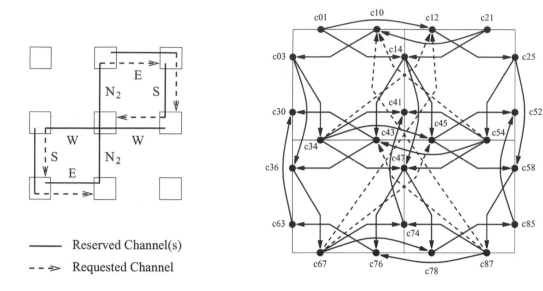

Figure 3.22. Deadlocked configuration for R on a 3×3 mesh using wormhole switching.

Figure 3.23. Extended channel dependency graph for R_1 using wormhole switching.

virtual network consists of one virtual channel in each direction. It is used to send packets toward the east (X-positive). It will be referred to as the *eastward* virtual network. The second virtual network also consists of one virtual channel in each direction. It is used to send packets toward the west (X-negative) and it will be referred to as the *westward* virtual network. When the X coordinates of the source and destination nodes are equal, packets can be introduced in either virtual network. Figure 3.24 shows the virtual networks for a 4×4 mesh. The routing algorithms for eastward and westward virtual networks are based on west-last and east-last, respectively [130]. Once a packet has used a west (east) channel in the eastward (westward) virtual network, it cannot turn again. However, 180-degree turns are allowed in Y channels

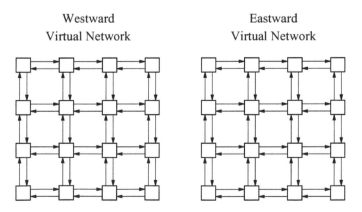

Figure 3.24. Virtual networks for a 4×4 mesh.

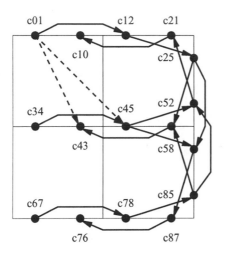 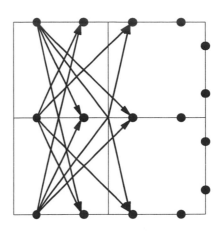

Figure 3.25. Extended channel dependency graph for R_1 (only two indirect dependencies are shown).

Figure 3.26. Indirect dependencies of the extended channel dependency graph for R_1.

except in the east (west) border. Assuming that a node cannot forward a packet destined for itself through the network, show that the routing function is not coherent, and prove that it is deadlock-free.

Solution   As 180-degree turns are allowed, packets may cross a node several times. As a node cannot forward a packet destined for itself through the network, there exist allowed paths with forbidden subpaths. Thus, the routing function is not coherent.

The application of Theorem 3.1 to prove that the routing function is deadlock-free requires the definition of a routing subfunction. We will define it by defining the subset of channels C_1 that can be supplied by the routing subfunction. In the eastward (westward) virtual network we have chosen the east and west channels plus the channels located on the east (west) border. The routing subfunction R_1 defined by C_1 is obviously connected. Also, packets introduced in the eastward (westward) virtual network cannot use channels from the other virtual network. Thus, there is not any channel dependency between channels of C_1 that belong to different virtual networks. So, we only need to prove that the extended channel dependency graph for R_1 in one virtual network has no cycles. We have chosen the eastward virtual network.

Figure 3.25 shows part of the extended channel dependency graph for R_1 on a 3×3 mesh. The channels belonging to C_1 are labeled as cij, where i and j are the source and destination nodes, respectively. Arrows represent channel dependencies; dashed arrows correspond to indirect dependencies. For the sake of clarity, we have only drawn two indirect dependencies. All the indirect dependencies are shown in Figure 3.26. There is not any cross-dependency. It can be seen that the graph is acyclic. Thus, R is deadlock-free.

3.4 Consider a linear array of four nodes denoted $n_i, i = \{0, 1, 2, 3\}$. Each pair of adjacent nodes are linked by two unidirectional channels. Let $c_{Hi}, i = \{0, 1, 2\}$ and $c_{Li}, i = \{1, 2, 3\}$ be the outgoing channels from node n_i, that connect to higher-numbered nodes and lower-numbered nodes, respectively. Additionally, there is a unidirectional channel c_{A1} from n_1 to n_2 and

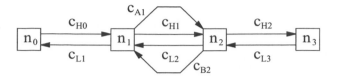

Figure 3.27. Channel labeling for the linear array.

a unidirectional channel c_{B2} from n_2 to n_1. Figure 3.27 shows the channel labeling. The routing function R is as follows: If the current node n_i is equal to the destination node n_j, store the packet. Otherwise, if the destination node n_j is higher than the current node n_i, use c_{Hi}, $\forall j > i$ or c_{A1} if $n_i = n_1$ or c_{B2} if $n_i = n_2$. If the destination node n_j is lower than the current node n_i, use c_{Li}, $\forall j < i$. If the network uses wormhole switching, show that R is not coherent. Prove that R is deadlock-free by showing that there is not any deadlocked configuration. Finally, show that there is not any routing subfunction satisfying the conditions proposed by Theorem 3.1.

Solution   Channel c_{B2} can only be used to send packets destined for higher-numbered nodes across n_1. However, it cannot be used to send packets destined for lower-numbered nodes, like n_1. Thus, R is not coherent.

There are two nested cycles in the channel dependency graph D for R. The first one is formed by channels c_{H1} and c_{B2}. The second one is formed by channels c_{A1} and c_{B2}. However, R is deadlock-free. Effectively, only packets destined for n_3 are allowed to use c_{B2} and c_{H2}. Thus, all the flits stored in the queue for c_{H2} can be delivered. We can try to fill the cycles by storing a single packet destined for n_3 in the queues for channels c_{H1} and c_{B2}; the latter contains the packet header. This packet can be forwarded through c_{A1}. If the queue for c_{A1} contains flits, they must be destined for either n_2 or n_3. If the flits are destined for n_2, the queue can be emptied. If they are destined for n_3, there are two routing options at node n_2: c_{B2} and c_{H2}. c_{B2} is busy. However, c_{H2} is empty or it can be emptied. A similar analysis can be made if we start by storing a single packet destined for n_3 in the queues for channels c_{A1} and c_{B2}. Thus, there is not any deadlocked configuration.

Now, we have to define a connected routing subfunction R_1. Obviously, channels $c_{Hi}, i = \{0, 1, 2\}$ and $c_{Li}, i = \{1, 2, 3\}$ must belong to R_1. Note that c_{H1} and c_{A1} have the same routing capabilities. So, any of them may be selected to belong to R_1. Without loss of generality, we have chosen c_{H1}. c_{B2} can only be used to send packets destined for n_3. Thus, the only way to restrict routing on c_{B2} consists of removing it. If c_{B2} belongs to R_1, then there are cycles in the extended channel dependency graph D_E for R_1, because there are direct dependencies from c_{H1} to c_{B2} and from c_{B2} to c_{H1}. If c_{B2} does not belong to R_1, then there are also cycles in D_E, because there is an indirect dependency from c_{H1} to c_{H1}. It is produced by packets destined for n_3 that cross c_{H1}, then c_{B2} and then c_{H1} again. Even if we split the routing capabilities of c_{H1} among c_{H1} and c_{A1}, the result is the same. Effectively, we can define R_1 in such a way that c_{A1} can only be used by packets destined for n_2 and c_{H1} by packets destined for n_3. However, the indirect dependency from c_{H1} to c_{H1} still exists. Thus, there is not any connected routing subfunction satisfying the conditions proposed by Theorem 3.1.

3.5 Consider a 2-D mesh using the negative-first routing function [130]. This routing function R routes packets in such a way that west and south channels are used first, then switching to

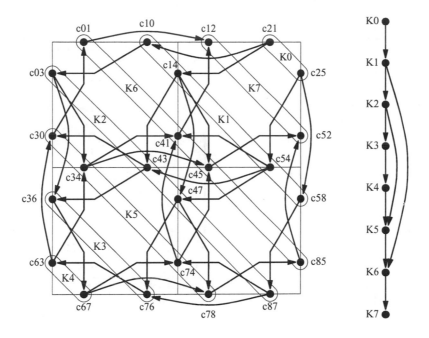

Figure 3.28. Channel dependency graph and class dependency graph for R.

east and north channels. It is not possible to use west or south channels again after using east and/or north channel(s). Draw the channel dependency graph for R, group channels into equivalence classes, and draw the class dependency graph for R.

Solution   Figure 3.28 shows the channel dependency graph for R on a 3×3 mesh. It also shows how channels are grouped into classes $K0, K1, \ldots, K7$ as well as the class dependency graph for R. These graphs are valid for SAF, VCT, and wormhole switching.

3.6 Consider a 2-D mesh using wormhole switching and without channel multiplexing (a single virtual channel per physical channel). The routing function R is minimal and fully adaptive. Design a deadlock recovery strategy based on Disha that allows simultaneous deadlock recovery and uses a single deadlock buffer per node.

Solution   Let us assume that each node has one deadlock buffer. When a packet is waiting for longer than a threshold, it is assumed to be deadlocked. Some deadlocked packets are transferred to the deadlock buffer of a neighboring node. Those packets will continue using deadlock buffers until delivered. As we will see, not all the deadlocked packets can be transferred to a deadlock buffer. Those packets will be able to advance when the remaining deadlocked packets are delivered by using deadlock buffers.

First, we define the routing function for deadlock buffers. Let Q be the set of deadlock buffers. Consider a Hamiltonian path on the 2-D mesh and a node labeling according to that path. Figure 3.29 shows the path and node labeling for a 4×4 mesh. The routing function R_{db} defined on deadlock buffers allows packets to reach nodes with a label greater than the current node label. This routing function is used when routing a packet header stored in a deadlock

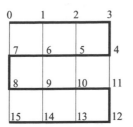

Figure 3.29. Hamiltonian path and node labeling for a 4×4 mesh.

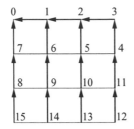

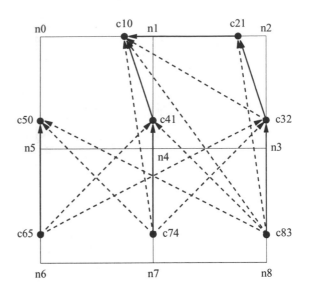

Figure 3.30. Subset of channels C_{edge} that defines R_{edge}.

Figure 3.31. Extended channel dependency graph for R_{edge}.

buffer. However, when a deadlock is detected, the packet header is stored in an edge buffer. In this case, it can be routed to the deadlock buffer of any neighboring node.

Now we have to prove that the deadlock recovery mechanism is able to recover from all dead-locked configurations. We use Theorem 3.1, extended as indicated in Section 3.2.3 to support edge buffers and central buffers. Thus, we need to define a connected routing subfunction R_1, proving that it has no cycles in its extended channel dependency graph. R_{db} is not connected. It only allows packets to reach nodes whose label is greater than the label of a neighboring node. Thus, we define a routing subfunction R_{edge} that allows packets to reach nodes with a lower label. It is a routing subfunction of R and is defined by defining the subset of channels C_{edge} supplied by it. Figure 3.30 shows that subset for a 4×4 mesh. Let $B_1 = Q \cup C_{edge}$. The routing subfunction R_1 defined by B_1 is $R_1 = R_{edge} \cup R_{db}$. It is obviously connected.

To prove that the extended channel dependency graph has no cycles, note that R_{db} can only route packets by using deadlock buffers. Thus, there is not any dependency from deadlock buffers to edge buffers. Additionally, there is not any cyclic dependency between deadlock buffers because R_{db} only uses deadlock buffers in increasing label order. Thus, we only need to prove that the extended channel dependency graph for R_{edge} has no cycles. Figure 3.31 shows that graph for a 3×3 mesh. The channels belonging to C_{edge} are labeled as cij, where i and j are the source and destination nodes, respectively. As a reference, thin lines represent the mesh, also including node labeling. Solid arrows represent direct dependencies. Dashed arrows correspond to indirect dependencies. There is not any cross-dependency because R_{edge} has been defined from a set of channels. The graph is acyclic. Thus, the deadlock recovery mechanism is able to recover from all deadlocked configurations.

PROBLEMS

3.1 Draw the channel dependency graph for R_1 defined in Example 3.5.

3.2 Extend the negative-first routing function defined in Exercise 3.5 for 2-D meshes by splitting each physical channel into two virtual channels. One set of virtual channels is used according to the negative-first routing function. The other set of channels is used for minimal fully adaptive routing. Is the routing function deadlock-free under wormhole switching? Is it deadlock-free when VCT is used?

3.3 Consider a 2-D mesh using the minimal west-first routing function [130]. This routing function routes packets in such a way that a packet traveling north or south cannot turn to the west. All the remaining turns are allowed, as far as the packet follows a minimal path. Extend the minimal west-first routing function by splitting each physical channel into two virtual channels. One set of virtual channels is used according to the minimal west-first routing function. The other set of channels is used for minimal fully adaptive routing. Is the routing function deadlock-free under wormhole switching? Is it deadlock-free when VCT is used?

3.4 Draw the extended class dependency graph for R_1 defined in Exercise 3.3.

3.5 Consider a hypercube using wormhole switching. Each physical channel c_i has been split into two virtual channels, a_i and b_i. The routing function R can be stated as follows: Route over any minimal path using the a channels. Alternatively, route in dimension order using the corresponding b channel. Prove that R is deadlock-free by using Theorem 3.1, and by using Theorem 3.3.

3.6 Consider a 2-D mesh. Physical channels are bidirectional full-duplex. Each physical channel has been split into two virtual channels. North virtual channels are denoted as N_1, N_2, east channels as E_1, E_2, south channels as S_1, S_2, and west channels as W_1, W_2, respectively. Virtual channels are grouped into four virtual networks, according to Table 3.1. Packets introduced into a virtual network are routed using channels in the same virtual network until delivered. The routing function is minimal fully adaptive. Define the routing function on $C \times N$. Define the routing function on $N \times N$.

3.7 Extend the routing function proposed in Exercise 3.6 so that it can be used in 3-D meshes.

3.8 Show that the routing function proposed in Exercise 3.6 for 2-D meshes cannot be used in 2-D tori. Draw a deadlocked configuration that cannot be recovered from.

Table 3.1. Virtual networks and the associated virtual channels.

Virtual Network	Channels
North-west	N_1 and W_2
North-east	N_2 and E_1
South-west	S_2 and W_1
South-east	S_1 and E_2

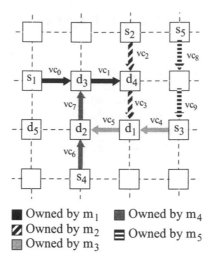

Figure 3.32. Deadlocked configuration for Problem 3.9.

3.9 Consider the 2-D mesh network depicted in Figure 3.32. This figure shows a single-cycle deadlock formed under minimal adaptive routing with one virtual channel per physical channel. The source and destination nodes of packet m_i are labeled s_i and d_i, respectively. Draw the CWG depicting the deadlocked configuration. What is the deadlock set, resource set, and knot cycle density? Is there a packet in the CWG which, if eliminated through recovery resources, still does not result in deadlock recovery?

3.10 What is the minimum number of packets that can result in deadlock assuming one virtual channel per physical channel and wormhole switching in:

- A unidirectional k-ary 1-cube?

- A bidirectional k-ary 1-cube with minimal routing?

- A unidirectional k-ary n-cube with nonminimal routing?

- A bidirectional k-ary n-cube with nonminimal routing?

- A bidirectional k-ary n-cube with minimal routing?

- A bidirectional n-dimensional mesh with minimal routing?

3.11 Consider a 2-D torus using wormhole switching and without channel multiplexing. The routing function R is minimal and fully adaptive. Design a deadlock recovery strategy based on Disha that allows simultaneous deadlock recovery and uses two deadlock buffers per node.

Chapter 4

Routing Algorithms

In this chapter we study routing algorithms. Routing algorithms establish the path followed by each message or packet. The list of routing algorithms proposed in the literature is almost endless. We clearly cannot do justice to all of these algorithms developed to meet many distinct requirements. We will focus on a representative set of approaches, being biased toward those being used or proposed in modern and future multiprocessor interconnects. Thus, we hope to equip the reader with an understanding of the basic principles that can be used to study the spectrum of existing algorithms. Routing algorithms for wormhole switching are also valid for other switching techniques. Thus, unless explicitly stated, the routing algorithms presented in this chapter are valid for all the switching techniques. Specific proposals for some switching techniques will also be presented. Special emphasis is given to design methodologies, because they provide a simple and structured way to design a wide variety of routing algorithms for different topologies.

Many properties of the interconnection network are a direct consequence of the routing algorithm used. Among these properties we can cite the following:

- *Connectivity*. Ability to route packets from any source node to any destination node. This property was introduced in Chapter 3.

- *Adaptivity*. Ability to route packets through alternative paths in presence of contention or faulty components.

- *Deadlock and livelock freedom*. Ability to guarantee that packets will not block or wander across the network forever. This issue was discussed in depth in Chapter 3.

- *Fault tolerance*. Ability to route packets in presence of faulty components. Although it seems that fault tolerance implies adaptivity, this is not necessarily true. Fault tolerance can be achieved without adaptivity by routing a packet in two or more phases, storing it in some intermediate nodes. Fault tolerance also requires some additional hardware mechanisms, as will be detailed in Chapter 6.

The next section presents a taxonomy of routing algorithms. The most interesting classes in the taxonomy are studied in the remaining sections of this chapter.

4.1   Taxonomy of Routing Algorithms

Figure 4.1 presents a taxonomy of routing algorithms that extends an earlier classification scheme
[126]. Routing algorithms can be classified according to several criteria. Those criteria are indicated
in the left column in italics. Each row contains the alternative approaches that can be followed
for each criterion. Arrows indicate the relations between different approaches. An overview of the
taxonomy is presented first, developing it in greater detail later. Routing algorithms can be first
classified according to the number of destinations. Packets may have a single destination (*unicast
routing*) or multiple destinations (*multicast routing*). Multicast routing will be studied in depth in
Chapter 5 and is included here for completeness.

Routing algorithms can also be classified according to the place where routing decisions are taken.
Basically, the path can be either established by a centralized controller (*centralized routing*) at the
source node prior to packet injection (*source routing*) or determined in a distributed manner while
the packet travels across the network (*distributed routing*). Hybrid schemes are also possible. We
call these hybrid schemes *multiphase routing*. In multiphase routing, the source node computes some
destination nodes. The path between them is established in a distributed manner. The packet may
be delivered to all the computed destination nodes (*multicast routing*) or only to the last destination
node (*unicast routing*). In this case, intermediate nodes are used to avoid congestion or faults.

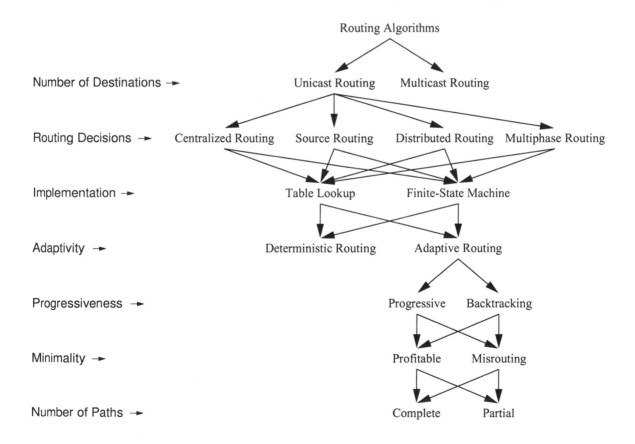

Figure 4.1. A taxonomy for routing protocols.

Routing algorithms can be implemented in different ways. The most interesting ways proposed up to now consist of either looking at a routing table (*table-lookup*) or executing a routing algorithm in software or hardware according to a *finite-state machine*. In both cases, the routing algorithm can be either *deterministic* or *adaptive*. Deterministic routing algorithms always supply the same path between a given source/destination pair. Adaptive routing algorithms use information about network traffic and/or channel status to avoid congested or faulty regions of the network. Routing algorithms designed to tolerate faults will be studied in depth in Chapter 6.

Adaptive routing algorithms can be classified according to their progressiveness as *progressive* or *backtracking*. Progressive routing algorithms move the header forward, reserving a new channel at each routing operation. Backtracking algorithms also allow the header to backtrack, releasing previously reserved channels. Backtracking algorithms are mainly used for fault-tolerant routing.

At a lower level, routing algorithms can be classified according to their minimality as *profitable* or *misrouting*. Profitable routing algorithms only supply channels that bring the packet closer to its destination. They are also referred to as *minimal*. Misrouting algorithms may also supply channels that send the packet away from its destination. They are also referred to as *nonminimal*. At the lowest level, routing algorithms can be classified according to the number of alternative paths as completely adaptive (also known as *fully adaptive*) or *partially adaptive*.

In this chapter we focus on unicast routing algorithms for multiprocessors and multicomputers. Centralized routing requires a central control unit. This is the kind of routing algorithms used in single-instruction multiple-data (SIMD) machines [163]. In source routing, the source node specifies the routing path on the basis of a deadlock-free routing algorithm (either using table-lookup or not). The computed path is stored in the packet header, being used at intermediate nodes to reserve channels. The routing algorithm may use only the addresses of current and destination nodes to compute the path (deterministic routing) or may also use information collected from other nodes about traffic conditions in the network (adaptive routing). Note that collecting information from other nodes may produce a considerable overhead. Additionally, that information may be obsolete. Thus, adaptive source routing is only interesting if traffic conditions change very slowly. Source routing has been mainly used in computer networks with irregular topologies [337]. Myrinet [30], a high-performance LAN supporting irregular topologies, also uses source routing. The first few flits of the packet header contain the address of the switch ports on intermediate switches. See Section 7.2.8 for a description of Myrinet.

Source routing has also been proposed for multicomputer interconnection networks. As traffic conditions may change very quickly in these networks, adaptive source routing is not interesting. Since the header itself must be transmitted through the network, thereby consuming network bandwidth, it is important to minimize header length. One source routing method that achieves this goal is called street-sign routing. The header is analogous to a set of directions given to a driver in a city. Only the names of the streets that the driver must turn on, along with the direction of the turn, are needed. More precisely, packets arriving at an intermediate node have a default output channel in the same dimension and direction as the current channel. For each turn, the header must contain the node address at which the turn will take place and the direction of the turn. Furthermore, this information must be stored in the header according to the order in which nodes are reached. Upon receiving a header flit, the router compares the node address in the flit to the local node address. If they match, the packet either turns or has reached its destination, as specified in the header flit. Otherwise, the packet will be forwarded through the default output channel. Street-sign routing was proposed in iWarp [39]. See Exercise 4.1 for an example of street-sign routing.

For efficiency reasons most hardware routers use distributed routing. Pipelined switching techniques route the header of the packet as soon as it is received at an intermediate node. With distributed routing, the header is very compact. It only requires the destination address and a few

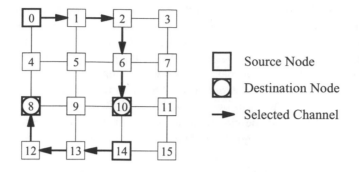

Figure 4.2. Routing example for dimension-order routing on a 2-D mesh.

implementation-dependent control bits. In distributed routing, each intermediate node has to make a routing decision based on the local knowledge of the network. By repeating this process at each intermediate node, the packet should be able to reach its destination. Note that distributed routing algorithms route packets at intermediate nodes without requiring a global knowledge of the network. This can be done because the designer knows the topology of the whole network. Distributed routing algorithms are mainly used in regular topologies so that the same routing algorithm can be used in all the nodes. Almost all commercial topologies can be seen as consisting of several orthogonal dimensions. In these topologies, it is easy to compute the distance between current and destination nodes as the sum of the offsets in all the dimensions. As a consequence, routing decisions are much simpler than in other topologies.

It is also possible to route a packet in two or more phases. In multiphase unicast routing the source node computes an intermediate node. The packet is routed toward this node using distributed routing. On reception of the packet, the intermediate node reinjects the packet into the network, using either another intermediate node or the final destination as the next destination for the packet. An example of multiphase routing algorithm is the random routing algorithm [344]. In this algorithm, the source node computes a random intermediate destination. On reception, the intermediate node forwards the packet toward its final destination. Random routing was proposed to reduce contention by randomizing the paths followed by a set packets transferred between every source-destination pair. However, random routing destroys all the communication locality existing in network traffic. Multiphase routing has also been proposed for fault-tolerant routing [332]. In this case, intermediate destinations are used to break dependencies between channels and avoid deadlocks in the presence of faults. This algorithm will be analyzed in Chapter 6.

Regardless of the place where the routing algorithm is computed, it should be able to deliver the packet to its destination node. In most parallel computers, the designer chooses the topology of the interconnection network. As indicated above, most machines use topologies that can be decomposed into orthogonal dimensions. This is the case for hypercubes, meshes, and tori. In these topologies, it is possible to use simple routing algorithms based on finite-state machines like e-cube (dimension-order routing) [333]. This routing algorithm routes packets by crossing dimensions in increasing order, nullifying the offset in one dimension before routing in the next one. A routing example is shown in Figure 4.2. Note that dimension-order routing can be executed at the source node, storing information about turns (changes of dimension) in the header. This is the street-sign routing algorithm described above. Dimension-order routing can also be executed in a distributed manner. At each intermediate node, the routing algorithm supplies an output channel crossing the lowest dimension for which the offset is not null.

Some manufacturers supply building blocks for parallel computers, so that different topologies can be built by using the same chips [227]. Also, some parallel computers feature reconfigurable topologies, so that the user can change the topology even dynamically at run-time [113]. Finally, some manufacturers allow the final users to build the topology that best fits their needs, allowing the use of irregular topologies [256]. In all these cases, specially for irregular topologies, it is very difficult to derive a routing algorithm based on a finite-state machine. An alternative implementation approach consists of using table-lookup [337]. This is a traditional approach used in computer networks.

An obvious implementation of table-lookup routing is to place a routing table at each node, with the number of entries in the table equal to the number of nodes in the network. Once again, routing can be performed either at the source node or at each intermediate node. In the first case, given a destination node address, the corresponding entry in the table indicates the whole path to reach that node. In the second case, each table entry indicates which outgoing channel should be used to forward the packet toward its destination. However, such an implementation is only practical for very small systems because table size increases linearly with network size. One way to reduce the table size for distributed routing is to define a range of addresses to be associated with each output channel. In this case, each routing table requires only one entry per output channel. Each entry contains an interval of destination addresses, specified by indicating its bounds. This routing technique is called interval routing [199] and has been implemented in the Inmos T9000 transputer and its associated router C104 [227, 228]. An important issue in interval routing is how to assign appropriate labels to nodes so that a single interval per output channel is enough to route all the packets and the resulting routing algorithm is minimal and deadlock-free. See Exercise 4.2 for an example of interval routing.

While establishing a path between source and destination nodes, the routing algorithm may supply a single path (*deterministic routing*). When source routing is used, this path is computed at the source node without considering network traffic. When deterministic routing is implemented in a distributed way, the routing algorithm supplies a single routing choice at each intermediate node, based on current and destination node addresses. In this case, channel status is not considered while computing the output channel to be used. Deterministic routing algorithms for regular topologies are simple. When implemented in hardware using a finite-state machine, routing logic is compact and fast. Most commercially available multicomputers use distributed deterministic routing. Deterministic routing algorithms usually perform well under uniform traffic. However, performance is poor when traffic is not uniform, especially when some pairs of nonneighbor nodes exchange information very frequently.

Alternatively, *adaptive routing* algorithms consider network state while making a decision. As indicated above, it is not interesting to combine source routing and adaptive routing. Thus, in what follows, we only consider distributed routing. Although some authors considered nonlocal information [288], most proposals only use local information for efficiency reasons. As seen in Chapter 3, adaptive routing algorithms can be decomposed into two functions: routing and selection. The *routing function* supplies a set of output channels based on the current node or buffer and the destination node. A selection from this set is made by the *selection function* based on the status of output channels at the current node. This selection is performed in such a way that a free channel (if any) is supplied. As a consequence, adaptive routing algorithms are able to follow alternative paths instead of waiting on busy channels. Thus, these algorithms increase routing flexibility at the expense of a more complex and slower hardware. Several experimental parallel computers use adaptive routing [75]. Also, commercial machines with adaptive routing are being developed [256] or are even available in the market [312]. Example 3.8 describes a distributed adaptive routing algorithm.

Adaptive routing algorithms can be classified as *progressive* or *backtracking*. Progressive routing algorithms move the header forward, reserving a new channel at each routing operation. Backtracking algorithms allow the header to backtrack, releasing previously reserved channels. Backtracking algorithms systematically search the network, backtracking as needed, using history information to ensure that no path is searched more than once. Note that in most switching techniques, data immediately follow the packet header. In these switching techniques, backtracking is not possible without a very complex hardware support. However, limited backtracking (one channel) is possible with some hardware support [181]. On the other hand, pipelined circuit switching is very well suited for backtracking because data flits do not follow the header immediately, giving more freedom to the header to search the network. Backtracking algorithms are mainly used for fault-tolerant routing, as will be seen in Chapter 6.

At a lower level, routing algorithms can be classified as *profitable* or *misrouting*. Profitable routing algorithms only supply channels that bring the packet closer to its destination. Misrouting algorithms may also supply channels that send the packet away from its destination. Misrouting algorithms are based on an optimistic view of the network: taking an unprofitable channel is likely to bring the header to another set of profitable channels that will allow further progress to the destination. Although misrouting algorithms are more flexible, they usually consume more network resources. As a consequence, misrouting algorithms usually exhibit a lower performance when combined with pipelined switching techniques. Also, misrouting algorithms may suffer from livelock, as seen in Chapter 3. Misrouting algorithms are usually proposed for fault-tolerant routing because they are able to find alternative paths when all the minimal paths are faulty. These algorithms will also be studied in Chapter 6.

At the lowest level, routing algorithms can be completely adaptive (also known as *fully adaptive*) or *partially adaptive*. A fully adaptive algorithm can use all the physical paths in its class. For example, a profitable algorithm that is fully adaptive is able to choose among all the minimal paths available in the network. These algorithms are also called *fully adaptive minimal* routing algorithms. It should be noted that although all the physical paths are available, a given routing algorithm may restrict the use of virtual channels in order to avoid deadlock. A routing algorithm that maximizes the number of routing options while avoiding deadlock is referred to as *maximally adaptive*. An even higher flexibility in the use of virtual channels can be achieved by using deadlock recovery techniques. In this case, there is no restriction on the use of virtual channels, and the corresponding routing algorithm is referred to as *true fully adaptive*. A completely adaptive backtracking algorithm is also called *exhaustive*. Partially adaptive algorithms are only able to use a subset of the paths in their class.

Note that deterministic routing algorithms should be progressive and profitable. Backtracking makes no sense because the same path will be reserved again. Also, misrouting is not interesting because some bandwidth is wasted without any benefit.

This chapter is organized as follows. Section 4.2 studies some deterministic routing algorithms as well as a basic design methodology. Section 4.3 presents some partially adaptive routing algorithms and a design methodology. Section 4.4 analyzes fully adaptive routing algorithms and their evolution, also presenting design methodologies. Section 4.5 describes some routing algorithms that maximize adaptivity or minimize the routing resources required for fully adaptive routing. Section 4.6 presents some nonminimal routing algorithms. Section 4.7 describes some backtracking algorithms. As backtracking algorithms have interesting properties for fault-tolerant routing, these algorithms will also be analyzed in Chapter 6. Sections 4.8 and 4.9 study some routing algorithms for switch-based networks, focusing on multistage interconnection networks and irregular topologies, respectively. Finally, Section 4.10 presents several selection functions as well as some resource allocation policies. The chapter ends with some engineering issues and commented references.

4.2 Deterministic Routing Algorithms

Deterministic routing algorithms establish the path as a function of the destination address, always supplying the same path between every pair of nodes. Deterministic routing is distinguished from *oblivious* routing. Although both concepts are sometimes considered to be identical, in the latter the routing decision is independent of (i.e., oblivious to) the state of the network. However, the choice is not necessarily deterministic. For example, a routing table may include several options for an output channel based on the destination address. A specific option may be selected randomly, cyclically or in some other manner that is independent of the state of the network. A deterministic routing algorithm will always provide the same output channel for the same destination. While deterministic algorithms are oblivious, the converse is not necessarily true.

Deterministic routing became very popular when wormhole switching was invented [78]. Wormhole switching requires very small buffers. Wormhole routers are compact and fast. However, pipelining does not work efficiently if one of the stages is much slower than the remaining stages. Thus, wormhole routers have the routing algorithm implemented in hardware. It is not surprising that designers chose the simplest routing algorithms in order to keep routing hardware as compact and fast as possible. Most commercial multicomputers (Intel Paragon [165], Cray T3D [174], nCUBE-2/3 [247]) and experimental multiprocessors (Stanford DASH [203], MIT J-Machine [255]) use deterministic routing.

In this section, we present the most popular deterministic routing algorithms as well as a design methodology. Obviously, the most popular routing algorithms are the simplest ones. Some topologies can be decomposed into several orthogonal dimensions. This is the case for hypercubes, meshes, and tori. In these topologies, it is easy to compute the distance between current and destination nodes as the sum of the offsets in all the dimensions. Progressive routing algorithms will reduce one of those offsets in each routing step. The simplest progressive routing algorithm consists of reducing an offset to zero before considering the offset in the next dimension. This routing algorithm is known as dimension-order routing. This routing algorithm routes packets by crossing dimensions in strictly increasing (or decreasing) order, reducing to zero the offset in one dimension before routing in the next one.

For n-dimensional meshes and hypercubes, dimension-order routing produces deadlock-free routing algorithms. These algorithms are very popular and receive several names, like XY routing (for 2-D mesh) or e-cube (for hypercubes) [333]. These algorithms are described in Figures 4.3 and 4.4, respectively, where $FirstOne()$ is a function that returns the position of the first bit set to one, and *Internal* is the channel connecting to the local node. Although these algorithms assume that the packet header carries the absolute address of the destination node, the first few sentences in each algorithm compute the offset from the current node to the destination node. This offset is the value carried by the header when relative addressing is used. So, the remaining sentences in each algorithm describe the operations for routing using relative addressing. Note that relative addressing would also require updating the header at each intermediate node. Exercises 3.1 and 4.3 show that the channel dependency graphs for dimension-order routing in n-dimensional meshes and hypercubes are acyclic. However, the channel dependency graph for tori has cycles. This topology was analyzed by Dally and Seitz [78], who proposed a design methodology for deadlock-free deterministic routing algorithms.

The methodology starts by considering some connected routing function and its channel dependency graph D. If it is not acyclic, routing is restricted by removing arcs from the channel dependency graph D to make it acyclic. If it is not possible to make D acyclic without disconnecting the routing function, arcs can be added to D by splitting physical channels into a set of virtual channels. As proposed in [78], this methodology establishes a total order among virtual channels,

Algorithm: XY Routing for 2-D Meshes
Inputs: Coordinates of current node $(Xcurrent, Ycurrent)$
        and destination node $(Xdest, Ydest)$
Output: Selected output $Channel$
Procedure:
   $Xoffset := Xdest - Xcurrent;$
   $Yoffset := Ydest - Ycurrent;$
   if $Xoffset < 0$ **then**
     $Channel := X-;$
   endif
   if $Xoffset > 0$ **then**
     $Channel := X+;$
   endif
   if $Xoffset = 0$ **and** $Yoffset < 0$ **then**
     $Channel := Y-;$
   endif
   if $Xoffset = 0$ **and** $Yoffset > 0$ **then**
     $Channel := Y+;$
   endif
   if $Xoffset = 0$ **and** $Yoffset = 0$ **then**
     $Channel := Internal;$
   endif

Figure 4.3. The XY routing algorithm for 2-D meshes.

Algorithm: Dimension-Order Routing for Hypercubes
Inputs: Addresses of current node $Current$
        and destination node $Dest$
Output: Selected output $Channel$
Procedure:
   $offset := Current \oplus Dest;$
   if $offset = 0$ **then**
     $Channel := Internal;$
   else
     $Channel := \text{FirstOne}(offset);$
   endif

Figure 4.4. The dimension-order routing algorithm for hypercubes.

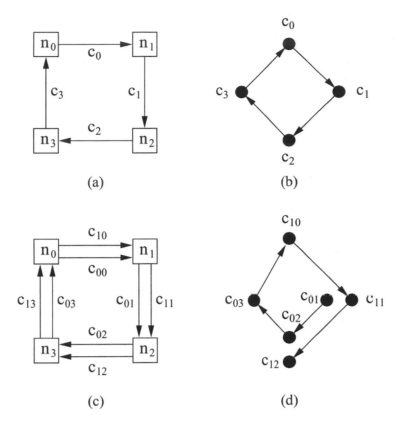

Figure 4.5. Unidirectional rings and their channel dependency graphs.

labeling them accordingly. Every time a cycle is broken by splitting a physical channel into two virtual channels, a new channel index is introduced to establish the ordering between virtual channels. Also, every time a cycle is broken by adding a virtual channel to each physical channel, the new set of virtual channels is assigned a different value for the corresponding index. The next example shows the application of this methodology to unidirectional rings and k-ary n-cubes.

Example 4.1

Consider a unidirectional ring with four nodes denoted $n_i, i = \{0, 1, 2, 3\}$ and a unidirectional channel connecting each pair of adjacent nodes. Let $c_i, i = \{0, 1, 2, 3\}$ be the outgoing channel from node n_i. In this case, it is easy to define a connected routing function. It can be stated as follows: If the current node n_i is equal to the destination node n_j, store the packet. Otherwise, use $c_i, \forall j \neq i$. Figure 4.5a shows the network. Figure 4.5b shows that the channel dependency graph for this routing function contains a cycle. Thus, every physical channel c_i is split into two virtual channels, c_{0i} and c_{1i}, as shown in Figure 4.5c. Virtual channels are ordered according to their indices. The routing function is redefined in such a way that virtual channels are used in strictly increasing order. The new routing function can be stated as follows: If the current node n_i is equal to the destination node n_j, store the packet. Otherwise, use c_{0i}, if $j < i$ or c_{1i}, if $j > i$. Figure 4.5d shows the channel dependency graph

---

Algorithm: Dimension-Order Routing for Unidirectional 2-D Tori

Inputs: Coordinates of current node $(Xcurrent, Ycurrent)$
and destination node $(Xdest, Ydest)$

Output: Selected output $Channel$

Procedure:

  $Xoffset := Xdest - Xcurrent$;
  $Yoffset := Ydest - Ycurrent$;
  if $Xoffset < 0$ **then**
    $Channel := c_{00}$;
  endif
  if $Xoffset > 0$ **then**
    $Channel := c_{01}$;
  endif
  if $Xoffset = 0$ **and** $Yoffset < 0$ **then**
    $Channel := c_{10}$;
  endif
  if $Xoffset = 0$ **and** $Yoffset > 0$ **then**
    $Channel := c_{11}$;
  endif
  if $Xoffset = 0$ **and** $Yoffset = 0$ **then**
    $Channel := Internal$;
  endif

Figure 4.6. The dimension-order routing algorithm for unidirectional 2-D tori.

for this routing function. As can be seen, the cycle has been removed because after using channel c_{03}, node n_0 is reached. Thus, all the destinations have a higher index than n_0, and it is not possible to request c_{00}. Note that channels c_{00} and c_{13} are not in the graph because they are never used.

It is possible to extend the routing function for unidirectional rings so that it can be used for unidirectional k-ary n-cubes. As above, each physical channel is split into two virtual channels. Additionally, a new index is added to each virtual channel. Channels are labeled as c_{dvi}, where $d, d = \{0, \dots, n-1\}$ is the dimension traversed by the channel, $v, v = \{0, 1\}$ indicates the virtual channel, and $i, i = \{0, \dots, k-1\}$ indicates the position inside the corresponding ring. The routing function routes packets in increasing dimension order. Inside each dimension, the routing function for rings is used. It is easy to see that this routing function routes packets in strictly increasing order of channel indices. Figure 4.6 shows the dimension-order routing algorithm for unidirectional k-ary 2-cubes. Note that the third subindex of each channel is not indicated because it is only required to distinguish between channels from different routers. So, there is no ambiguity.

Although dimension-order routing is usually implemented in a distributed way using a finite-state machine, it can also be implemented using source routing and distributed table-lookup. See Exercises 4.1 and 4.2 to see how dimension-order routing can be implemented using source routing (street-sign routing) and table-lookup (interval routing), respectively.

Finally, as will be seen in Chapter 7, dimension-order routing is very simple to implement in hardware. Additionally, switches can be decomposed into smaller and faster switches (one for each dimension), thus increasing the speed.

4.3 Partially Adaptive Algorithms

Several partially adaptive routing algorithms have been proposed. Partially adaptive routing algorithms represent a trade-off between flexibility and cost. They try to approach the flexibility of fully adaptive routing at the expense of a moderate increase in complexity with respect to deterministic routing. Most partially adaptive algorithms proposed up to now rely upon the absence of cyclic dependencies between channels to avoid deadlock. Some proposals aim at maximizing adaptivity without increasing the resources required to avoid deadlocks. Other proposals try to minimize the resources needed to achieve a given level of adaptivity.

4.3.1 Planar-Adaptive Routing

Planar-adaptive routing aims at minimizing the resources needed to achieve a given level of adaptivity. It has been proposed by Chien and Kim for n-dimensional meshes and hypercubes [58]. The idea in planar-adaptive routing is to provide adaptivity in only two dimensions at a time. Thus, a packet is routed adaptively in a series of 2-D planes. Routing dimensions change as the packet advances toward its destination.

Figure 4.7 shows how planar-adaptive routing works. A fully adaptive routing algorithm allows a packet to be routed in the m-dimensional subcube defined by the current and destination nodes, as shown in Figure 4.7a for three dimensions. Planar-adaptive routing restricts packets to be routed in plane A_0, then moving to plane A_1, and so on. This is depicted in Figures 4.7b and 4.7c for three and four dimensions, respectively. All the paths within each plane are allowed. The number of paths in a plane depends on the offsets in the corresponding dimensions.

Each plane A_i is formed by two dimensions, d_i and d_{i+1}. There are a total of $(n-1)$ adaptive planes. The order of dimensions is arbitrary. However, it is important to note that planes A_i and A_{i+1} share dimension d_{i+1}. If the offset in dimension d_i is reduced to zero, then routing can be immediately shifted to plane A_{i+1}. If the offset in dimension d_{i+1} is reduced to zero while routing in plane A_i, no adaptivity will be available while routing in plane A_{i+1}. In this case, plane A_{i+1} can be skipped. Moreover, if in plane A_i, the offset in dimension d_{i+1} is reduced to zero first, routing

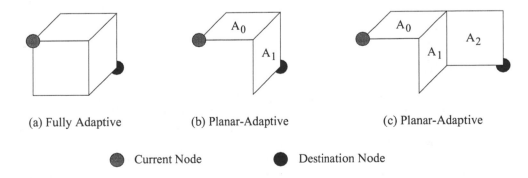

    (a) Fully Adaptive   (b) Planar-Adaptive   (c) Planar-Adaptive

● Current Node   ● Destination Node

Figure 4.7. Allowed paths in fully adaptive and planar-adaptive routing.

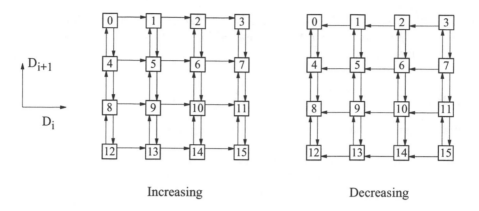

Increasing   Decreasing

Figure 4.8. Increasing and decreasing networks in plane A_i for planar-adaptive routing.

continues in dimension d_i exclusively, until the offset in dimension d_i is reduced to zero. Thus, in order to offer alternative routing choices for as long as possible, a higher priority is given to channels in dimension d_i while routing in plane A_i.

As defined, planar-adaptive routing requires three virtual channels per physical channel to avoid deadlocks in meshes and six virtual channels to avoid deadlocks in tori. In what follows, we analyze meshes in more detail. Channels in the first and last dimension need only one and two virtual channels, respectively. Let $d_{i,j}$ be the set of virtual channels j crossing dimension i of the network. This set can be decomposed into two subsets, one in the positive direction and one in the negative direction. Let $d_{i,j}+$ and $d_{i,j}-$ denote the positive and negative direction channels, respectively.

Each plane A_i is defined as the combination of several sets of virtual channels:

$$A_i = d_{i,2} + d_{i+1,0} + d_{i+1,1}$$

In order to avoid deadlock, the set of virtual channels in A_i is divided into two classes: *increasing* and *decreasing* networks. The increasing network is formed by $d_{i,2}+$ and $d_{i+1,0}$ channels. The decreasing network is formed by $d_{i,2}-$ and $d_{i+1,1}$ channels (Figure 4.8). Packets crossing dimension d_i in the positive direction are routed in the increasing network of plane A_i. Similarly, packets crossing dimension d_i in the negative direction are routed in the decreasing network of A_i. As there is no coupling between increasing and decreasing networks of A_i, and planes are crossed in sequence, it is easy to see that there are no cyclic dependencies between channels. Thus, planar-adaptive routing is deadlock-free.

4.3.2   Turn Model

The turn model proposed by Glass and Ni [130] provides a systematic approach to the development of partially adaptive routing algorithms, both minimal and nonminimal, for a given network. As shown in Figure 3.2, deadlock occurs because the packet routes contain turns that form a cycle. As indicated in Chapter 3, deadlock cannot occur if there is not any cyclic dependency between channels. In many topologies, channels are grouped into dimensions. Moving from one dimension to another one produces a turn in the packet route. Changing direction without moving to another dimension can be considered as a 180-degree turn. Also, when physical channels are split into virtual channels, moving from one virtual channel to another one in the same dimension and direction can be

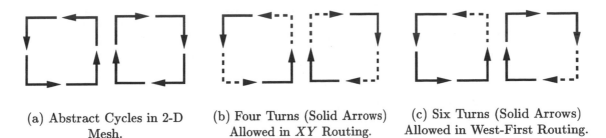

(a) Abstract Cycles in 2-D Mesh. (b) Four Turns (Solid Arrows) Allowed in *XY* Routing. (c) Six Turns (Solid Arrows) Allowed in West-First Routing.

Figure 4.9. An illustration of the turn model in 2-D mesh.

considered as a 0-degree turn. Turns can be combined into cycles. The fundamental concept behind the turn model is to prohibit the smallest number of turns such that cycles are prevented. Thus, deadlock can be avoided by prohibiting just enough turns to break all the cycles. The following six steps can be used to develop maximally adaptive routing algorithms for n-dimensional meshes and k-ary n-cubes:

1. Classify channels according to the directions in which they route packets.

2. Identify the turns that occur between one direction and another.

3. Identify the simple cycles that these turns can form.

4. Prohibit one turn in each cycle.

5. In the case of k-ary n-cubes, incorporate as many turns as possible that involve wraparound channels, without reintroducing cycles.

6. Add 0-degree and 180-degree turns without reintroducing cycles. These turns are needed if there are multiple channels in the same direction and for nonminimal routing algorithms.

In order to illustrate the use of the turn model, we may consider the case of a 2-D mesh. There are eight possible turns and two possible abstract cycles, as shown in Figure 4.9a. The deterministic XY routing algorithm prevents deadlock by prohibiting four of the turns, as shown in Figure 4.9b. The remaining four turns cannot form a cycle, but neither do they allow any adaptiveness.

However, prohibiting fewer than four turns can still prevent cycles. In fact, for a 2-D mesh, only two turns need to be prohibited. Figure 4.9c shows six turns allowed, suggesting the corresponding *west-first routing algorithm*: route a packet first west, if necessary, and then adaptively south, east, and north. The two turns prohibited in Figure 4.9c are the two turns to the west. Therefore, in order to travel west, a packet must begin in that direction. Figure 4.10 shows the minimal west-first routing algorithm for 2-D meshes, where *Select*() is the selection function defined in Section 3.1.2. This function returns a free channel (if any) from the set of channels passed as parameters. See Exercise 4.5 for a nonminimal version of this algorithm. Three example paths for the west-first algorithm are shown in Figure 4.11. The channels marked as unavailable are either faulty or are being used by other packets. One of the paths shown is minimal, while the other two paths are nonminimal, resulting from routing around unavailable channels. Because cycles are avoided, west-first routing is deadlock-free. For minimal routing, the algorithm is fully adaptive if the destination is on the right-hand side (east) of the source; otherwise, it is deterministic. If nonminimal routing is allowed, the algorithm is adaptive in either case. However, it is not fully adaptive.

Algorithm: Minimal West-First Algorithm for 2-D Meshes
Inputs: Coordinates of current node $(Xcurrent, Ycurrent)$
            and destination node $(Xdest, Ydest)$
Output: Selected output *Channel*
Procedure:
     $Xoffset := Xdest - Xcurrent$;
     $Yoffset := Ydest - Ycurrent$;
     if $Xoffset < 0$ **then**
         $Channel := X-$;
     endif
     if $Xoffset > 0$ **and** $Yoffset < 0$ **then**
         $Channel := \text{Select}(X+, Y-)$;
     endif
     if $Xoffset > 0$ **and** $Yoffset > 0$ **then**
         $Channel := \text{Select}(X+, Y+)$;
     endif
     if $Xoffset > 0$ **and** $Yoffset = 0$ **then**
         $Channel := X+$;
     endif
     if $Xoffset = 0$ **and** $Yoffset < 0$ **then**
         $Channel := Y-$;
     endif
     if $Xoffset = 0$ **and** $Yoffset > 0$ **then**
         $Channel := Y+$;
     endif
     if $Xoffset = 0$ **and** $Yoffset = 0$ **then**
         $Channel := Internal$;
     endif

Figure 4.10. The minimal west-first routing algorithm for 2-D meshes.

There are other ways to select six turns so as to prohibit cycles. However, the selection of the two prohibited turns may not be arbitrary [130]. If turns are prohibited as in Figure 4.12, deadlock is still possible. Figure 4.12a shows that the three remaining left turns are equivalent to the prohibited right turn, and Figure 4.12b shows that the three remaining right turns are equivalent to the prohibited left turn. Figure 4.12c illustrates how cycles may still occur. Of the 16 different ways to prohibit two turns, 12 prevent deadlock and only 3 are unique if symmetry is taken into account. These three combinations correspond to the west-first, north-last, and negative-first routing algorithms. The *north-last routing* algorithm does not allow turns from north to east or from north to west. The *negative-first routing* algorithm does not allow turns from north to west and from east to south.

In addition to 2-D mesh networks, the turn model can be used to develop partially adaptive routing algorithms for n-dimensional meshes, for k-ary n-cubes and for hypercubes [130]. By applying the turn model to the hypercube, an adaptive routing algorithm, namely, *P-cube routing*, can be developed. Let $s = s_{n-1}s_{n-2} \ldots s_0$ and $d = d_{n-1}d_{n-2} \ldots d_0$ be the source and destination nodes, respectively, in a binary n-cube. The set E consists of all the dimension numbers in which s and

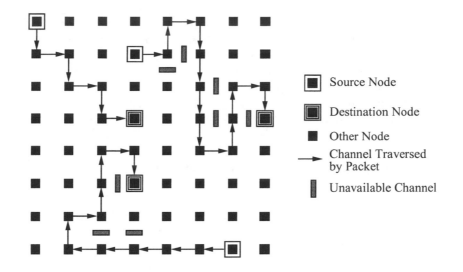

Figure 4.11. Examples of west-first routing in an 8×8 2-D mesh.

d differ. The size of E is the Hamming distance between s and d. Thus, $i \in E$ if $s_i \neq d_i$. E is divided into two disjoint subsets, E_0 and E_1, where $i \in E_0$ if $s_i = 0$ and $d_i = 1$, and $j \in E_1$ if $s_j = 1$ and $d_j = 0$. The fundamental concept of P-cube routing is to divide the routing selection into two *phases*. In the first phase, a packet is routed through the dimensions in E_0 in any order. In the second phase, the packet is routed through the dimensions in E_1 in any order. If E_0 is empty, then the packet can be routed through any dimension in E_1. Figure 4.13 shows the pseudocode for the P-cube routing algorithm. The **for** loop computes the sets E_0 and E_1. This can be done at each intermediate node as shown or at the source node. In the latter case, the selected channel should be removed from the corresponding set. The *digit*() function computes the value of the digit in the given position.

Note that cycles cannot exist only traversing dimensions in E_0 since they represent channels from a node to a higher-numbered node. In a cycle, at least one channel must be from a node to a lower-numbered node. For similar reasons, packets cannot form cycles by only traversing dimensions

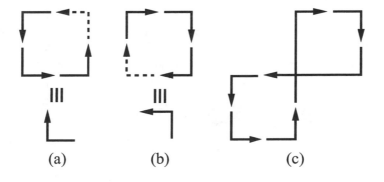

Figure 4.12. Six turns that complete the abstract cycles.

Algorithm: Minimal P-Cube Routing for Hypercubes
Inputs: Addresses of current node $Current$
  and destination node $Dest$
Output: Selected output $Channel$
Procedure:
  $E_0 := \{\ \}$;
  $E_1 := \{\ \}$;
  for $i := 0$ **to** $n - 1$ **do**
    if $\mathrm{digit}(Current, i) = 0$ **and** $\mathrm{digit}(Dest, i) = 1$ **then**
      $E_0 := E_0 + \{i\}$;
    endif
    if $\mathrm{digit}(Current, i) = 1$ **and** $\mathrm{digit}(Dest, i) = 0$ **then**
      $E_1 := E_1 + \{i\}$;
    endif
  end;
  if $E_0 \neq \{\ \}$ **then**
    $Channel := \mathrm{Select}(E_0)$;
  endif
  if $E_0 = \{\ \}$ **and** $E_1 \neq \{\ \}$ **then**
    $Channel := \mathrm{Select}(E_1)$;
  endif
  if $E_0 = \{\ \}$ **and** $E_1 = \{\ \}$ **then**
    $Channel := Internal$;
  endif

Figure 4.13. The minimal P-cube routing algorithm for hypercubes.

in set E_1. Finally, since packets only use dimensions in E_1 after traversing all of the dimensions in E_0, deadlock freedom is preserved. In effect, the algorithm prohibits turns from dimensions in E_1 to dimensions in E_0. This is sufficient to prevent cycles. By partitioning the set of dimensions to be traversed in other ways that preserve the acyclic properties, one can derive other variants of this algorithm.

Let the sizes of E, E_0, and E_1 be k, k_0, and k_1, respectively; $k = k_0 + k_1$. There exist $k!$ shortest paths between s and d. Using P-cube routing, a packet may be routed through any of $(k_0!)(k_1!)$ of those shortest paths. A similar algorithm was proposed in [184], however, the P-cube routing algorithm can be systematically generalized to handle nonminimal routing as well [130].

4.4 Fully Adaptive Algorithms

This section presents several methodologies for the design of fully adaptive routing algorithms as well as some specific routing algorithms. Where possible, the presentation follows a chronological order, showing the evolution of design methodologies. First, we present some algorithms developed for computer networks in Section 4.4.1, as well as a methodology to adapt those algorithms for wormhole switching in Section 4.4.2. Then we present some methodologies based on the concept of virtual network in Section 4.4.3. Both the methodologies presented in Sections 4.4.2 and 4.4.3 are based on Dally and Seitz's theorem [78] (Corollary 3.1), thus requiring the absence of cyclic dependencies between channels. The resulting routing algorithms require a large number of virtual channels. When the restriction on cyclic dependencies is relaxed, the number of resources needed to avoid deadlock is reduced considerably. In Section 4.4.4 we first present a routing algorithm that is not based on Theorem 3.1, showing the transition. It is followed by a design methodology based on Theorem 3.1. Although this design methodology presents a practical way to design efficient fully adaptive routing algorithms for a variety of topologies, some more adaptivity can be obtained by proposing specific routing algorithms for some topologies. This is done in Section 4.5.

4.4.1 Algorithms Based on Structured Buffer Pools

These routing algorithms were designed for SAF networks using central queues. Deadlocks are avoided by splitting buffers into several classes and restricting packets to move from one buffer to another in such a way that buffer class is never decremented. Gopal proposed several fully adaptive minimal routing algorithms based on buffer classes [134]. These algorithms are known as hop algorithms.

The simplest hop algorithm starts by injecting a packet into the buffer of class 0 at the current node. Every time a packet stored in a buffer of class i takes a hop to another node, it moves to a buffer of class $i + 1$. This routing algorithm is known as the positive-hop algorithm. Deadlocks are avoided by using a buffer of a higher class every time a packet requests a new buffer. By doing so, cyclic dependencies between resources are prevented. A packet that has completed i hops will use a buffer of class i. Since the routing algorithm only supplies minimal paths, the maximum number of hops taken by a packet is limited by the diameter of the network. If the network diameter is denoted by D, a minimum of $D + 1$ buffers per node are required to avoid deadlock. The main advantage of the positive-hop algorithm is that it is valid for any topology. However, the number of buffers required for fully adaptive deadlock-free routing is very high and this number depends on network size.

The minimum number of buffers per node can be reduced by allowing packets to move between buffers of the same class. In this case, classes must be defined such that packets moving between buffers of the same class cannot form cycles. In the negative-hop routing algorithm, the network is partitioned into several subsets in such a way that no subset contains two adjacent nodes. If S is the number of subsets, then subsets are labeled $0, 1, \ldots, S - 1$, and nodes in subset i are labeled i. Hops from a node with a higher label to a node with a lower label are negative. Otherwise, hops are nonnegative. When a packet is injected, it is stored into the buffer of class 0 at the current node. Every time a packet stored in a buffer of class i takes a negative hop, it moves to a buffer of class $i + 1$. If a packet stored in a buffer of class i takes a nonnegative hop, then it requests a buffer of the same class. Thus, a packet that has completed i negative hops will use a buffer of class i.

There is not any cyclic dependency between buffers. Effectively, a cycle starting at node A must return to node A and contains at least another node B. If B has a lower label than A, some hop between A and B (possibly through intermediate nodes) is negative, and the buffer class is increased. If B has a higher label than A, some hop between B and A (possibly through intermediate nodes) is negative, and the buffer class is increased. As a consequence, packets cannot wait for buffers cyclically, thus avoiding deadlocks. If D is the network diameter and S is the number of subsets, then the maximum number of negative hops that can be taken by a packet is $H_N = \lceil D(S - 1)/S \rceil$. The minimum number of buffers per node required to avoid deadlock is $H_N + 1$. Figure 4.14 shows a partition scheme for k-ary 2-cubes with even k. Black and white circles correspond to nodes of subsets 0 and 1, respectively.

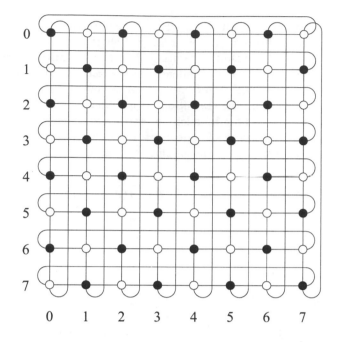

Figure 4.14. Partition scheme for k-ary 2-cubes with even k.

Although the negative-hop routing algorithm requires approximately half the buffers required by the positive-hop algorithm in the best case, this number is still high. It can be improved by partitioning the network into subsets and numbering the partitions, such that there are no cycles in any partition. This partitioning scheme does not require that adjacent nodes belong to different subsets. In this case, a negative hop is a hop that takes a packet from a node in a higher-numbered partition to a node in a lower-numbered partition. The resulting routing algorithm still requires a relatively large number of buffers, and the number of buffers depends on network size. In general, hop routing algorithms require many buffers. However, these algorithms are fully adaptive and can be used in any topology. As a consequence, these routing algorithms are suitable for SAF switching when buffers are allocated in main memory.

4.4.2   Algorithms Derived from SAF Algorithms

Boppana and Chalasani proposed a methodology for the design of fully adaptive minimal routing algorithms for networks using wormhole switching [36]. This methodology starts from a hop algorithm, replacing central buffers by virtual channels. The basic idea consists of splitting each physical channel into as many virtual channels as there were central buffers in the original hop algorithm, and assigning virtual channels in the same way that central buffers were assigned.

More precisely, if the SAF algorithm requires m classes of buffers, the corresponding algorithm for wormhole switching requires m virtual channels per physical channel. Let the virtual channels corresponding to physical channel c_i be denoted as $c_{i,1}, c_{i,2}, \ldots, c_{i,m}$. If a packet occupies a buffer b_k of class k in the SAF algorithm and can use channels $c_i, c_j, \ldots$ to move to the next node, the corresponding wormhole algorithm will be able to use virtual channels $c_{i,k}, c_{j,k}, \ldots$. This situation is depicted in Figure 4.15 where a single physical channel c_i has been drawn.

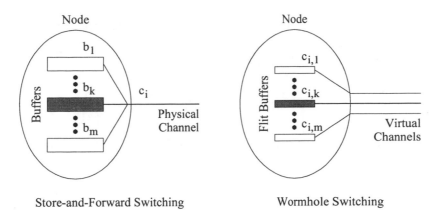

Figure 4.15. Derivation of wormhole routing algorithms from SAF algorithms.

This scheme produces an unbalanced use of virtual channels because all the packets start using virtual channel 0 of some physical channel. However, very few packets take the maximum number of hops. This scheme can be improved by giving each packet a number of bonus cards equal to the maximum number of hops minus the number of hops it is going to take [36]. At each node, the packet has some flexibility in the selection of virtual channels. The range of virtual channels that can be selected for each physical channel is equal to the number of bonus cards available plus one. Thus, when no bonus cards are available, a single virtual channel per physical channel can be selected. If the packet uses virtual channel j after using virtual channel i, it consumes $j - i - 1$ bonus cards.

Using this methodology, the hop algorithms presented in Section 4.4.1 can be redefined for wormhole switching. The routing algorithms resulting from the application of this methodology have the same advantages and disadvantages than the original hop algorithms for SAF networks: They provide fully adaptive minimal routing for any topology at the expense of a high number of virtual channels. Additionally, the number of virtual channels depends on network size, thus limiting scalability.

4.4.3 Virtual Networks

A useful concept to design routing algorithms consists of splitting the network into several virtual networks. A *virtual network* is a subset of channels that are used to route packets toward a particular set of destinations. The channel sets corresponding to different virtual networks are disjoint. Depending on the destination, each packet is injected into a particular virtual network, where it is routed until it arrives at its destination. In some proposals, packets traveling in a given virtual network have some freedom to move to another virtual network. Virtual networks can be implemented by using disjoint sets of virtual channels for each virtual network, and mapping those channels over the same set of physical channels. Of course it is also possible to implement virtual networks by using separate sets of physical channels.

The first design methodologies for fully adaptive routing algorithms were based on the concept of virtual networks [167, 213]. This concept considerably eases the task of defining deadlock-free routing functions. Effectively, deadlocks are only possible if there exist cyclic dependencies between channels. Cycles are formed by sets of turns, as shown in Section 4.3.2. By restricting the set of

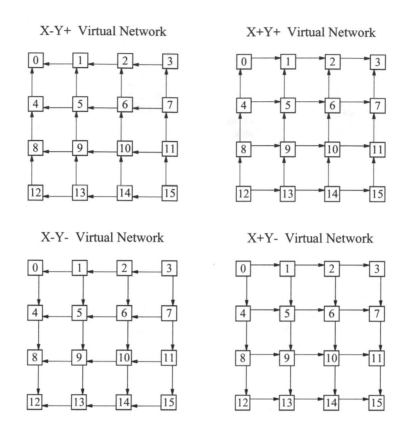

Figure 4.16. Virtual networks for a 2-D mesh.

destinations for each virtual network, it is possible to restrict the set of directions followed by packets. Thus, each virtual network can be defined in such a way that the corresponding routing function has no cyclic dependencies between channels. However, this routing function is not connected because it is only able to deliver packets to some destinations. By providing enough virtual networks so that all the destinations can be reached, the resulting routing function is connected and deadlock-free. Packet transfers between virtual networks are not allowed or restricted in such a way that deadlocks are avoided.

In this section, we present some fully adaptive routing algorithms based on virtual networks. Jesshope, Miller, and Yantchev proposed a simple way to avoid deadlock in n-dimensional meshes. It consists of splitting the network into several virtual networks in such a way that packets injected into a given virtual network can only move in one direction for each dimension [167]. Figure 4.16 shows the four virtual networks corresponding to a 2-D mesh. Packets injected into the $X + Y +$ virtual network can only move along the positive direction of dimensions X and Y. Packets injected into the $X + Y -$ virtual network can only move along the positive direction of dimension X and the negative direction of dimension Y, and so on. Packets are injected into a single virtual network, depending on their destination. Once a packet is being routed in a given virtual network, all the channels belonging to minimal paths can be used for routing. However, the packet cannot be transferred to another virtual network. It is obvious that there are no cyclic dependencies between channels, thus avoiding deadlock.

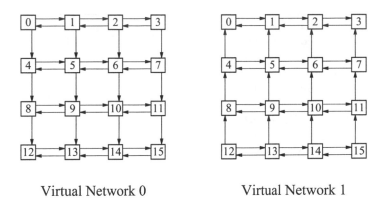

Figure 4.17. Reducing the number of virtual networks for a 2-D mesh.

This strategy can be easily extended for meshes with more than two dimensions. For example, a 3-D mesh requires eight virtual networks, corresponding to the following directions: $X-Y-Z-$, $X-Y-Z+$, $X-Y+Z-$, $X-Y+Z+$, $X+Y-Z-$, $X+Y-Z+$, $X+Y+Z-$, and $X+Y+Z+$. In general, a n-dimensional mesh requires 2^n virtual networks, each one consisting of n unidirectional virtual or physical channels per node (except some nodes in the border of the mesh). Thus, from a practical point of view, this routing algorithm can only be used for a very small number of dimensions (two or three at most). Also, a similar strategy can be applied to torus (k-ary n-cube) networks, as shown in [137] for a 2-D torus.

Linder and Harden showed that the number of virtual networks required for n-dimensional meshes can be reduced to a half [213]. Instead of having a unidirectional channel in each dimension, each virtual network has channels in both directions in the 0th dimension and only one direction in the remaining $n-1$ dimensions. This is shown in Figure 4.17 for a 2-D mesh. With this reduction, an n-dimensional mesh requires 2^{n-1} virtual networks. However, channels in the 0th dimension are bidirectional instead of unidirectional. Therefore, the number of virtual channels per node is equal to $n2^{n-1}$, in addition to an extra virtual channel in dimension 0 for a total of $(n+1)2^{n-1}$ per node. The number of virtual channels across each physical channel is 2^{n-1}, except for dimension 0 which has 2^n virtual channels due to the bidirectional nature. Again, this strategy can only be used for a very small number of dimensions. Note that the virtual networks for a 2-D mesh (see Figure 4.17) are equivalent to the virtual networks for a plane in planar-adaptive routing (see Figure 4.8). Figures 4.18 and 4.19 show the routing algorithm for 2-D meshes.

The reduction in the number of virtual networks does not introduce cyclic dependencies between channels, as far as packets are routed following only minimal paths. Effectively, as shown in Section 4.3.2, cycles are formed by sets of turns. The restriction to minimal paths eliminates all the 180-degree turns. At least two dimensions with channels in both directions are required to form a cycle. Thus, no virtual network has cyclic dependencies between channels.

Linder and Harden also applied the concept of virtual network to k-ary n-cube networks [213]. The basic idea is the same as for meshes: each virtual network has channels in both directions in the 0th dimension and only one direction in the remaining $n-1$ dimensions. However, the existence of wraparound channels makes more difficult to avoid cyclic dependencies. Thus, each virtual network is split into several levels, each level having its own set of virtual channels. Every time a packet crosses a wraparound channel, it moves to the next level. If only minimal paths are allowed, the wraparound channels in each dimension can only be crossed once by each packet. In the worst case,

---

Algorithm: Linder-Harden and PAR for 2-D Meshes (Virtual Network 0)
Inputs: Coordinates of current node $(Xcurrent, Ycurrent)$
            and destination node $(Xdest, Ydest)$
Output: Selected output $Channel$
Procedure:
    $Xoffset := Xdest - Xcurrent$;
    $Yoffset := Ydest - Ycurrent$;
    if $Xoffset < 0$ **and** $Yoffset < 0$ **then**
      $Channel := \text{Select}(X-, Y-)$;
    endif
    if $Xoffset < 0$ **and** $Yoffset = 0$ **then**
      $Channel := X-$;
    endif
    if $Xoffset > 0$ **and** $Yoffset < 0$ **then**
      $Channel := \text{Select}(X+, Y-)$;
    endif
    if $Xoffset > 0$ **and** $Yoffset = 0$ **then**
      $Channel := X+$;
    endif
    if $Xoffset = 0$ **and** $Yoffset < 0$ **then**
      $Channel := Y-$;
    endif
    if $Xoffset = 0$ **and** $Yoffset = 0$ **then**
      $Channel := Internal$;
    endif

Figure 4.18. The Linder-Harden and planar-adaptive routing algorithms for 2-D meshes (virtual network 0). (PAR = Planar-adaptive routing.)

a packet will need to cross wraparound channels in all the dimensions. Thus, one level per dimension is required, in addition to the initial level, for a total of $n + 1$ levels. Figure 4.20 shows the virtual networks and their levels for a 2-D torus. For reference purposes, one of the levels is enclosed in a dashed box. This fully adaptive routing algorithm for k-ary n-cube networks requires 2^{n-1} virtual networks and $n + 1$ levels per virtual network, resulting in $(n + 1)2^{n-1}$ virtual channels per physical channel across each dimension except dimension 0 which has $(n + 1)2^n$ virtual channels. Thus, fully adaptive routing requires many resources if cyclic dependencies between channels are to be avoided. As we will see in Section 4.4.4, the number of resources required for fully adaptive routing can be drastically reduced by relying on Theorem 3.1 for deadlock avoidance.

Some recent proposals allow cyclic dependencies between channels, relying on some version of Theorem 3.1 to guarantee deadlock freedom [96]. In general, virtual networks are defined in such a way that the corresponding routing functions are deadlock-free. Packet transfers between virtual networks are restricted in such a way that deadlocks are avoided. By allowing cyclic dependencies between channels and cyclic transfers between virtual networks, guaranteeing deadlock freedom is much more difficult [96, 217]. However, virtual networks still have proven to be useful to define deadlock-free routing algorithms. See Exercise 3.3 for an example.

Algorithm: Linder-Harden and PAR for 2-D Meshes (Virtual Network 1)
Inputs: Coordinates of current node $(Xcurrent, Ycurrent)$
        and destination node $(Xdest, Ydest)$
Output: Selected output *Channel*
Procedure:
    $Xoffset := Xdest - Xcurrent;$
    $Yoffset := Ydest - Ycurrent;$
    if $Xoffset < 0$ **and** $Yoffset > 0$ **then**
       $Channel := \text{Select}(X-, Y+);$
    endif
    if $Xoffset < 0$ **and** $Yoffset = 0$ **then**
       $Channel := X-;$
    endif
    if $Xoffset > 0$ **and** $Yoffset > 0$ **then**
       $Channel := \text{Select}(X+, Y+);$
    endif
    if $Xoffset > 0$ **and** $Yoffset = 0$ **then**
       $Channel := X+;$
    endif
    if $Xoffset = 0$ **and** $Yoffset > 0$ **then**
       $Channel := Y+;$
    endif
    if $Xoffset = 0$ **and** $Yoffset = 0$ **then**
       $Channel := Internal;$
    endif

Figure 4.19. The Linder-Harden and planar-adaptive routing algorithms for 2-D meshes (virtual network 1). (PAR = Planar-adaptive routing.)

4.4.4 Deterministic and Adaptive Subnetworks

In this section we first present a routing algorithm that is not based on Theorem 3.1, followed by a design methodology based on that theorem.

Dally and Aoki proposed two adaptive routing algorithms based on the concept of *dimension reversal* [74]. The most interesting one is the *dynamic* algorithm. This routing algorithm allows the existence of cyclic dependencies between channels, as far as packets do not wait for channels in a cyclic way. Before describing the dynamic algorithm, let us define the concept of dimension reversal. The dimension reversal (DR) number of a packet is the count of the number of times a packet has been routed from a channel in one dimension, p, to a channel in a lower dimension, $q < p$.

The dynamic algorithm divides the virtual channels of each physical channel into two nonempty classes: adaptive and deterministic. Packets injected into the network are first routed using adaptive channels. While in these channels, packets may be routed in any direction without a maximum limit on the number of dimension reversals a packet may make. Whenever a packet acquires a channel, it labels the channel with its current DR number. To avoid deadlock, a packet with a DR of p cannot wait on a channel labeled with a DR of q if $p \geq q$. A packet that reaches a node where all output

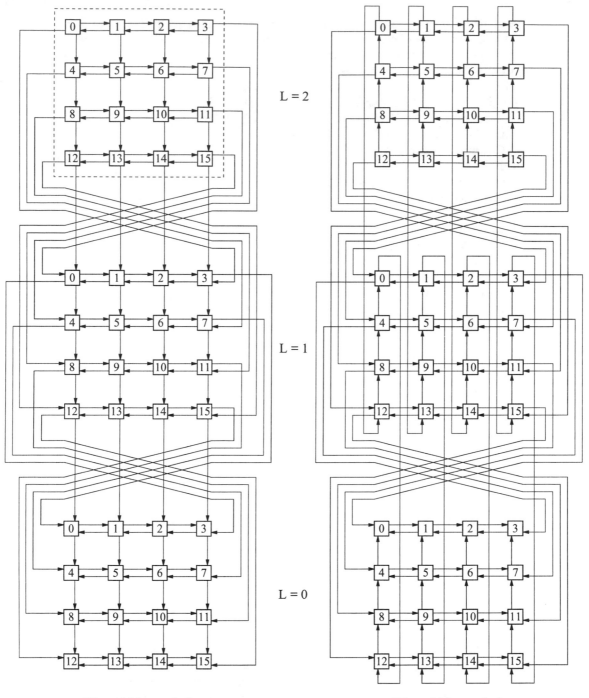

Figure 4.20. Virtual networks for a 2-D torus.

channels are occupied by packets with equal or lower DRs must switch to the deterministic class of virtual channels. Once on the deterministic channels, the packet must be routed in dimension order using only the deterministic channels and cannot reenter the adaptive channels.

The dynamic algorithm represents a first step toward relaxing the restrictions for deadlock avoidance. Instead of requiring the absence of cyclic dependencies between channels as the algorithms presented in Section 4.4.3, it allows those cyclic dependencies as far as packets do not wait for channels in a cyclic way. When a packet may produce a cyclic waiting, it is transferred to the deterministic class of virtual channels where it is routed in dimension order. The dynamic algorithm provides the maximum routing flexibility when packets are routed using adaptive channels. However, that flexibility is lost when packets are transferred to the deterministic channels.

More routing flexibility can be obtained by using Theorem 3.1. Fully adaptive routing algorithms described in Sections 4.4.1, 4.4.2, and 4.4.3 do not allow cyclic dependencies between resources to avoid deadlocks. However, those algorithms require a large set of buffer resources. Using Theorem 3.1, it is possible to avoid deadlocks even when cyclic dependencies between resources are allowed. The resulting routing algorithms require a smaller set of buffers or channels.

Defining routing algorithms and checking if they are deadlock-free is a tedious task. In order to simplify this task, Duato proposed some design methodologies [87, 92, 99]. In general, design methodologies do not supply optimal routing algorithms. However, they usually supply near-optimal routing algorithms with much less effort. In this section, we present a general methodology for the design of deadlock-free fully adaptive routing algorithms that combines the methodologies previously proposed by Duato. For VCT and SAF switching it automatically supplies deadlock-free routing algorithms. For wormhole switching, a verification step is required.

The design methodology presented in this section is based on the use of edge buffers. For SAF switching, a similar methodology can be defined for networks using central queues. This methodology describes a way to add channels to an existing network, also deriving the new routing function from the old one. Channels are added following a regular pattern, using the same number of virtual channels for all the physical channels. This is important from the implementation point of view because bandwidth sharing and propagation delay remains identical for all the output channels.

Methodology 4.1 *This methodology supplies fully adaptive minimal and nonminimal routing algorithms, starting from a deterministic or partially adaptive routing algorithm. When restricted to minimal paths, the resulting routing algorithms have been referred to as* Duato's protocol *(DP) [126]. The steps are the following:*

1. *Given an interconnection network I_1, select one of the existing routing functions for it. Let R_1 be this routing function. It must be deadlock-free and connected. It can be deterministic or adaptive. For wormhole switching, it is recommended that R_1 is minimal. Let C_1 be the set of channels at this point.*

2. *Split each physical channel into a set of additional virtual channels. Let C be the set of all the (virtual) channels in the network. Let C_{xy} be the set of output channels from node x belonging to a path (minimal or not) from node x to node y. Define the new routing function R as follows:*

$$R(x,y) = R_1(x,y) \cup (C_{xy} \cap (C - C_1)) \quad \forall x, y \in N \tag{4.1}$$

That is, the new routing function can use any of the new channels or, alternatively, the channels supplied by R_1. The selection function can be defined in any way. However, it is recommended to give a higher priority to the new channels belonging to minimal paths. For wormhole switching, it is recommended that R is restricted to use only minimal paths.

3. *For wormhole switching, verify that the extended channel dependency graph for R_1 is acyclic. If it is, the routing algorithm is valid. Otherwise, it must be discarded, returning to step 1.*

Step 1 establishes the starting point. We can use either a deterministic or adaptive routing function as the basic one. All the algorithms proposed in previous sections are candidates for selection. However, algorithms proposed in Sections 4.2 and 4.3.2 should be preferred because they require a small amount of resources.

Step 2 indicates how to add more (virtual) channels to the network and how to define a new fully adaptive routing function from the basic one. As defined, this methodology supplies nonminimal routing functions. It is possible to define minimal routing functions by restricting C_{xy} to contain only the output channels belonging to minimal paths from x to y. This methodology can also be applied by adding physical channels instead of virtual ones.

For wormhole switching, step 3 verifies whether the new routing function is deadlock-free or not. If the verification fails, the above proposed methodology may lead to an endless cycle. Thus, it does not supply a fully automatic way to design fully adaptive routing algorithms. Many minimal routing functions pass the verification step. However, very few nonminimal routing functions pass it. This is the reason why we recommend the use of minimal routing functions for wormhole switching.

For VCT and SAF switching, step 3 is not required. The methodology supplies deadlock-free routing functions. Effectively, according to the definition for R given in expression 4.1, $R_1(x, y) = R(x, y) \cap C_1 \quad \forall x, y \in N$. Thus, there exists a subset of channels $C_1 \subset C$ that defines a routing subfunction R_1 that is connected and deadlock-free. Taking into account Theorem 3.2, it is easy to see that R is deadlock-free. This is indicated in the next lemma.

Lemma 4.1 *For VCT and SAF switching, the routing functions supplied by Methodology 4.1 are deadlock-free.*

Methodology 4.1 is not defined for routing functions whose domain includes the current channel or queue containing the packet header. In fact, this methodology cannot be applied to such routing functions because it extends the range of the routing function but not its domain. If the domain is not extended, it is not possible to consider the newly added channels, and the packets stored in them cannot be routed.

Note that if the domain of R were extended by considering the newly added channels, the initial routing function R_1 would be modified. For example, consider the positive hop algorithm described in Section 4.4.1 and adapted to wormhole switching in Section 4.4.2. Routing decisions are taken based on the class of the channel occupied by the packet. Knowledge of the class is necessary to ensure deadlock freedom. If the packet uses a channel supplied by R_1, and subsequently a newly added channel, it is not possible for the receiving router to know the class of the channel previously occupied by the packet.

So, this methodology cannot be directly applied to routing functions that consider the current channel or queue in their domain. However, a closer examination will reveal that in practice this is not as restrictive as it may initially appear because most of those routing functions can be redefined so that they do not require the current channel or queue. For example, the class of the channel occupied by a packet in the positive hop algorithm can be made available by providing a field containing the class in the packet header. If this field is added, the input channel is no longer required in the domain of the routing function.

Examples 4.3 and 4.2 show the application of Methodology 4.1 to a 2-D mesh using SAF switching, and a binary n-cube using wormhole switching, respectively. Exercise 4.4 shows the application of this methodology to k-ary n-cubes as well as some optimizations.

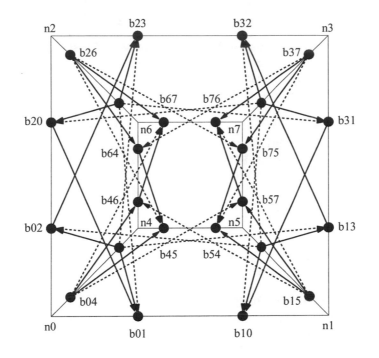

Figure 4.21. Extended channel dependency graph for R_1.

Example 4.2

Consider a binary n-cube using wormhole switching. For the step 1 we can select the e-cube routing algorithm. It forwards packets crossing the channels in order of decreasing dimensions. This routing function is connected and deadlock-free. For the step 2, consider that each physical channel c_i has been split into k virtual channels, namely, $a_{i,1}, a_{i,2}, \ldots, a_{i,k-1}, b_i$. Let C_1 be the set of b channels. The algorithm obtained applying the step 2 can be stated as follows: Route over any useful dimension using any of the a channels. If all of them are busy, route over the highest useful dimension using the corresponding b channel. A useful dimension is one that forwards a packet nearer to its destination.

Figure 4.21 shows the extended channel dependency graph for R_1 on a 3-cube. Black circles represent the unidirectional channels belonging to C_1 and are labeled as bij, where i and j are the source and destination nodes, respectively. As a reference, channels are also represented by thin lines, horizontal and vertical ones corresponding to dimensions 0 and 1, respectively. Also, the nodes of the 3-cube have been labeled as nk, where k is the node number. Thick lines represent channel dependencies, dashed arrows corresponding to indirect dependencies. It can be seen that the graph is acyclic. Then, R is deadlock-free.

Example 4.3

Consider a 2-D mesh using SAF switching. For the step 1 we select dimension-order routing (XY routing). Let R_1 denote this routing function. R_1 is connected and deadlock-free. Split each physical channel c_i into two virtual channels, namely, a_i and b_i. Let C_1 be the set of b_i

Algorithm: Duato's Fully Adaptive Algorithm for 2-D Meshes (Duato's Protocol)
Inputs: Coordinates of current node $(Xcurrent, Ycurrent)$
        and destination node $(Xdest, Ydest)$
Output: Selected output $Channel$
Procedure:
  $Xoffset := Xdest - Xcurrent$;
  $Yoffset := Ydest - Ycurrent$;
  if $Xoffset < 0$ **and** $Yoffset < 0$ **then**
    $Channel := \text{Select}(Xa-, Ya-, Xb-)$;
  endif
  if $Xoffset < 0$ **and** $Yoffset > 0$ **then**
    $Channel := \text{Select}(Xa-, Ya+, Xb-)$;
  endif
  if $Xoffset < 0$ **and** $Yoffset = 0$ **then**
    $Channel := \text{Select}(Xa-, Xb-)$;
  endif
  if $Xoffset > 0$ **and** $Yoffset < 0$ **then**
    $Channel := \text{Select}(Xa+, Ya-, Xb+)$;
  endif
  if $Xoffset > 0$ **and** $Yoffset > 0$ **then**
    $Channel := \text{Select}(Xa+, Ya+, Xb+)$;
  endif
  if $Xoffset > 0$ **and** $Yoffset = 0$ **then**
    $Channel := \text{Select}(Xa+, Xb+)$;
  endif
  if $Xoffset = 0$ **and** $Yoffset < 0$ **then**
    $Channel := \text{Select}(Ya-, Yb-)$;
  endif
  if $Xoffset = 0$ **and** $Yoffset > 0$ **then**
    $Channel := \text{Select}(Ya+, Yb+)$;
  endif
  if $Xoffset = 0$ **and** $Yoffset = 0$ **then**
    $Channel := Internal$;
  endif

Figure 4.22. Duato's fully adaptive minimal routing algorithm for 2-D meshes (Duato's protocol).

channels. Thus, $C - C_1$ is the set of a_i channels. According to expression 4.1, the routing function R supplies all the outgoing a channels from the current node, also supplying one b channel according to dimension-order routing (XY routing). Taking into account Lemma 4.1, R is deadlock-free. When restricted to minimal paths, R is also deadlock-free for wormhole switching, as shown in Example 3.8. The resulting routing algorithm is shown in Figure 4.22. In this figure, $Xa+$ and $Xb+$ denote the a and b channels, respectively, in the positive direction of the X dimension. A similar notation is used for the other direction and dimension.

4.5 Maximally Adaptive Routing Algorithms

In this section, we present some routing algorithms based on deadlock avoidance that either maximize adaptivity for a given set of resources (channels or buffers) or minimize the use of resources for fully adaptive routing. We present below some routing algorithms based on deadlock recovery that accomplish both.

Some authors have proposed metrics to measure adaptivity [130]. However, such metrics are not related to performance. In fact, although maximally adaptive routing algorithms are optimal or near optimal in the use of resources for deadlock avoidance-based routing, they do not necessarily achieve the highest performance. The reason is that the use of resources may be unbalanced. For instance, different physical channels may have a different number of virtual channels or some virtual channels may be more heavily used than other ones. This may produce an uneven traffic distribution, as shown in [343]. This is not the case for true fully adaptive routing based on deadlock recovery. This algorithm maximizes adaptivity for a given set of resources while balancing the use of resources. As a consequence, this algorithm usually achieves the highest performance.

4.5.1 Algorithms with Maximum Adaptivity

The fully adaptive routing algorithm proposed by Linder and Harden requires two and one virtual channels per physical channel for the first and second dimension, respectively, when applied to 2-D meshes (see Section 4.4.3 and Figure 4.17). If dimensions are exchanged the resulting routing algorithm requires one and two virtual channels per physical channel for the X and Y dimension, respectively. This algorithm is called *double-y*. The double-y routing algorithm uses one set of Y channels, namely $Y1$, for packets traveling $X-$, and the second set of Y channels, namely $Y2$, for packets traveling $X+$.

Based on the turn model, Glass and Ni analyzed the double-y routing algorithm, eliminating the unnecessary restrictions [131]. The resulting algorithm is called *maximally adaptive double-y (mad-y)*. It improves adaptivity with respect to the double-y algorithm. Basically, mad-y allows packets using $Y1$ channels to turn to the $X+$ direction and packets using $X-$ channels to turn and use $Y2$ channels. Figures 4.23 and 4.24 show the turns allowed by the double-y and mad-y algorithms, respectively.

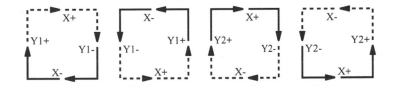

Figure 4.23. Turns allowed (solid lines) by the double-y algorithm.

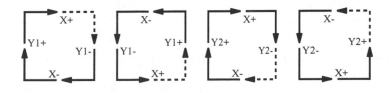

Figure 4.24. Turns allowed (solid lines) by the mad-y algorithm.

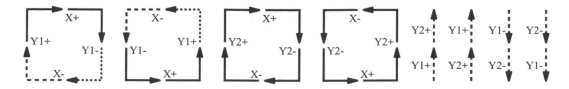

Figure 4.25. Turns allowed (solid lines) by the opt-y algorithm. Dotted lines are prohibited turns. Dashed lines are restricted turns.

The mad-y algorithm has the maximum adaptivity that can be obtained without introducing cyclic dependencies between channels. However, as shown in Theorem 3.1, cycles do not necessarily produce deadlock. Thus, the mad-y algorithm can be improved. It was done by Schwiebert and Jayasimha, who proposed the *opt-y* algorithm [305, 307]. This algorithm is deadlock-free and optimal with respect to the number of routing restrictions on the virtual channels for deadlock avoidance-based routing. Basically, the opt-y algorithm allows all the turns between X and $Y2$ channels as well as turns between $X+$ and $Y1$ channels. Turns from $Y1$ to $X-$ channels are prohibited. Turns from $X-$ to $Y1$ channels as well as 0-degree turns between $Y1$ and $Y2$ channels are restricted. These turns are only allowed when the packet has completed its movement along $X-$ channels (the X-offset is zero or positive). Figure 4.25 shows the turns allowed by the opt-y algorithm.

Defining a routing algorithm by describing the allowed and prohibited turns makes difficult to understand how routing decisions are taken at a given node. The opt-y algorithm is described in Figure 4.26 using pseudocode.

The opt-y algorithm can be generalized to n-dimensional meshes by using the following steps [307]:

- Assign a channel to both directions of each dimension.

- Number the dimensions in some order and add a second virtual channel to both directions of all dimensions except the first dimension.

- Allow packets to route along the second virtual channel at any time.

- For each dimension except the last, select one of the two directions as the chosen direction of that dimension. Prohibit a packet from routing on the first virtual channel of any direction until it has completed routing in the chosen direction of all lower dimensions.

- Allow a packet to make a 0-degree turn between the two virtual channels of a direction only after the packet has completed routing in the chosen direction of all lower dimensions.

Basically, the generalized opt-y algorithm allows fully adaptive minimal routing in one set of virtual channels. If packets have completed their movement along the chosen direction in all the dimensions then fully adaptive routing is also allowed on the second set of virtual channels. Otherwise the second set of virtual channels only allows partially adaptive routing across the dimensions for which packets have completed their movement along the chosen direction in all the lower dimensions.

4.5.2   Algorithms with Minimum Buffer Requirements

Cypher and Gravano [66] proposed two fully adaptive routing algorithms for torus networks using SAF switching. These algorithms have been proven to be optimal with respect to buffer space [64] for deadlock avoidance-based routing. Thus, there is no deadlock avoidance-based fully adaptive

Algorithm: Opt-y Fully Adaptive Algorithm for 2-D Meshes
Inputs: Coordinates of current node $(Xcurrent, Ycurrent)$
and destination node $(Xdest, Ydest)$
Output: Selected output $Channel$
Procedure:
$Xoffset := Xdest - Xcurrent$;
$Yoffset := Ydest - Ycurrent$;
if $Xoffset < 0$ **and** $Yoffset < 0$ **then**
    $Channel := \text{Select}(X-, Y2-)$;
endif
if $Xoffset < 0$ **and** $Yoffset > 0$ **then**
    $Channel := \text{Select}(X-, Y2+)$;
endif
if $Xoffset < 0$ **and** $Yoffset = 0$ **then**
    $Channel := X-$;
endif
if $Xoffset > 0$ **and** $Yoffset < 0$ **then**
    $Channel := \text{Select}(X+, Y2-, Y1-)$;
endif
if $Xoffset > 0$ **and** $Yoffset > 0$ **then**
    $Channel := \text{Select}(X+, Y2+, Y1+)$;
endif
if $Xoffset > 0$ **and** $Yoffset = 0$ **then**
    $Channel := X+$;
endif
if $Xoffset = 0$ **and** $Yoffset < 0$ **then**
    $Channel := \text{Select}(Y2-, Y1-)$;
endif
if $Xoffset = 0$ **and** $Yoffset > 0$ **then**
    $Channel := \text{Select}(Y2+, Y1+)$;
endif
if $Xoffset = 0$ **and** $Yoffset = 0$ **then**
    $Channel := Internal$;
endif

Figure 4.26. The opt-y fully adaptive routing algorithm for 2-D meshes.

routing algorithm for tori that requires less buffer space. Obviously, these routing algorithms have cyclic dependencies between queues or channels. The first algorithm (Algorithm 1) only requires three central buffers or queues to avoid deadlock, regardless of the number of dimensions of the torus. The second algorithm (Algorithm 2) uses edge buffers, requiring only two buffers per input channel to avoid deadlock. These routing algorithms are also valid for VCT switching but not for wormhole switching.

The routing algorithms are based on four node orderings. The first ordering, which is called the *right-increasing* ordering, is simply a standard row-major ordering of the nodes. The second

Table 4.1. The right-increasing ordering for an 8 × 8 torus.

0	1	2	3	4	5	6	7
8	9	10	11	12	13	14	15
16	17	18	19	20	21	22	23
24	25	26	27	28	29	30	31
32	33	34	35	36	37	38	39
40	41	42	43	44	45	46	47
48	49	50	51	52	53	54	55
56	57	58	59	60	61	62	63

Table 4.2. The left-increasing ordering for an 8 × 8 torus.

63	62	61	60	59	58	57	56
55	54	53	52	51	50	49	48
47	46	45	44	43	42	41	40
39	38	37	36	35	34	33	32
31	30	29	28	27	26	25	24
23	22	21	20	19	18	17	16
15	14	13	12	11	10	9	8
7	6	5	4	3	2	1	0

Table 4.3. The inside-increasing ordering for an 8 × 8 torus.

0	1	2	3	7	6	5	4
8	9	10	11	15	14	13	12
16	17	18	19	23	22	21	20
24	25	26	27	31	30	29	28
56	57	58	59	63	62	61	60
48	49	50	51	55	54	53	52
40	41	42	43	47	46	45	44
32	33	34	35	39	38	37	36

Table 4.4. The outside-increasing ordering for an 8 × 8 torus.

63	62	61	60	56	57	58	59
55	54	53	52	48	49	50	51
47	46	45	44	40	41	42	43
39	38	37	36	32	33	34	35
7	6	5	4	0	1	2	3
15	14	13	12	8	9	10	11
23	22	21	20	16	17	18	19
31	30	29	28	24	25	26	27

ordering, which is called the *left-increasing* ordering, is the reverse of the right-increasing ordering. The third ordering, which is called the *inside-increasing* ordering, assigns the smallest values to nodes near the wraparound edges of the torus and the largest values to nodes near the center of the torus. The fourth ordering, which is called the *outside-increasing* ordering, is the reverse of the inside-increasing ordering. Tables 4.1 through 4.4 show the node orderings for an 8 × 8 torus. A transfer of a packet from a node a to an adjacent node b will be said to occur to the *right* (similarly, *left*, *inside*, or *outside*) if and only if node a is smaller than node b when they are numbered in right-increasing (similarly, left-increasing, inside-increasing, or outside-increasing) ordering.

Algorithm 1:   Three queues per node are required, denoted A, B, and C. Additionally, each node has an injection queue and a delivery queue. Each packet moves from its injection queue to the A queue in the source node and it remains using A queues as long as it is possible for it to move to the right along at least one dimension following a minimal path. When a packet cannot move to the right following a minimal path, it moves to the B queue in its current node and it remains using B queues as long as it is possible for it to move to the left along at least one dimension following a

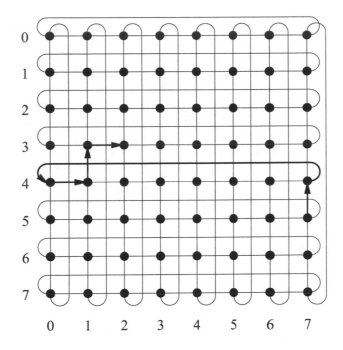

Figure 4.27. Routing example for Algorithms 1 and 2.

minimal path. When a packet cannot move to the left following a minimal path, it moves to the C queue in its current node and it remains moving to the inside using C queues until it arrives at its destination node. It then moves to the delivery queue in its destination node.

Note that a packet in an A queue may move to an A queue in any adjacent node. It may not actually move to the right, but this option must exist on at least one of the minimal paths to the destination. Similarly, a packet in a B queue may move to a B queue in any adjacent node. Also, note that a packet entering a C queue cannot move to an A or B queue. However, the routing algorithm is fully adaptive because a packet in a C queue only needs to move to the inside [66].

Example 4.4

Consider a packet p that is routed from node $(5, 7)$ to node $(3, 2)$ in an 8×8 torus using Algorithm 1 (Figure 4.27). The packet p will first be stored in the injection queue in node $(5, 7)$. Then, it moves to the A queue in node $(5, 7)$. At this point, p cannot move to the right. Thus, it moves to the B queue in node $(5, 7)$. At this point, p is allowed to move to the left (moving to the B queue in node $(5, 0)$ or in node $(4, 7)$). Thus, all the B queues in neighboring nodes along minimal paths can be used. Assume that p moves to the B queue in node $(4, 7)$, and then p moves to the B queue in node $(4, 0)$. At this point, p is still allowed to move to the left (moving to the B queue in node $(3, 0)$). Assume that p moves to the B queue in node $(4, 1)$, and then to the B queue in node $(3, 1)$. At this point, p can no longer move to the left. Thus, it moves to the C queue in node $(3, 1)$. Then, p moves to the C queue in node $(3, 2)$, reaching its destination node, and moving to the delivery queue in node $(3, 2)$. Note that p moved to the inside when moving from node $(3, 1)$ to node $(3, 2)$.

Algorithm 2: Two edge queues per input channel are required, denoted A and C if the channel moves packets to the outside, and denoted B and D if the channel moves packets to the inside. Additionally, each node has an injection queue and a delivery queue. Assuming that a packet has not arrived at its destination, a packet in an injection, A or B queue moves to an A or B queue of an outgoing channel along a minimal path if it is possible for it to move to the inside along at least one dimension. Otherwise, it moves to the C queue of an outgoing channel along a minimal path. A packet in a C queue moves to a B or C queue of an outgoing channel along a minimal path if it is possible for it to move to the outside along at least one dimension. Otherwise, it moves to the D queue of an outgoing channel along a minimal path. A packet in a D queue can only move to the D queue of an outgoing channel along a minimal path. In any of the previous cases, when a packet arrives at its destination node, it moves to the delivery queue in that node.

Note that Algorithm 2 allows packets to move from C queues back to B queues and from B queues back to A queues. However, when a packet enters a D queue, it must remain using D queues until delivered. Once again, a packet entering a D queue can only move to the inside. However, the routing algorithm is fully adaptive because a packet in a D queue only needs to move to the inside [66].

Example 4.5

Consider a packet p that is routed from node $(5,7)$ to node $(3,2)$ in an 8×8 torus using Algorithm 2. Assume that p follows the same path as in Example 4.4 (see Figure 4.27). The packet p will first be stored in the injection queue in node $(5,7)$. At this point, p is allowed to move to the inside (moving to node $(4,7)$). Thus, p can select between the A queue in node $(5,0)$ and the B queue in node $(4,7)$. Assume that p moves to the B queue in node $(4,7)$. At this point, p can no longer move to the inside. Thus, it can move to the C queues in neighboring nodes along minimal paths. Assume that p moves to the C queue in node $(4,0)$. At this point, p is allowed to move to the outside (moving to the C queue in node $(3,0)$). Thus, p can select between the B queue in node $(4,1)$ and the C queue in node $(3,0)$. Assume that p moves to the B queue in node $(4,1)$. At this point, p is allowed to move to the inside (moving to the B queue in node $(4,2)$). Thus, p can select between the A queue in node $(3,1)$ and the B queue in node $(4,2)$. Assume that p moves to the A queue in node $(3,1)$. As p is still allowed to move to the inside, it moves to the B queue in node $(3,2)$, reaching its destination node, and moving to the delivery queue in node $(3,2)$.

4.5.3 True Fully Adaptive Routing Algorithms

All the routing algorithms described in previous sections use avoidance techniques to handle deadlocks, therefore restricting routing. Deadlock recovery techniques do not restrict routing to avoid deadlock. Hence, routing strategies based on deadlock recovery allow maximum routing adaptivity (even beyond that proposed in [305, 307]) as well as minimum resource requirements. In particular, progressive deadlock recovery techniques, like Disha (see Section 3.6), decouple deadlock handling resources from normal routing resources by dedicating minimum hardware to efficient deadlock recovery in order to make the common case (i.e., no deadlocks) fast. As proposed, sequential recovery from deadlocks requires only one central flit-sized buffer applicable to arbitrary network topologies [8, 9] and concurrent recovery requires at most two central buffers for any topology on which a Hamiltonian path or a spanning tree can be defined [10].

When routing is not restricted, no virtual channels are dedicated to avoid deadlocks. Instead, virtual channels are used for the sole purpose of improving channel utilization and adaptivity. Hence, *true fully adaptive* routing is permitted on all virtual channels within each physical channel, regardless of network topology. True fully adaptive routing can be minimal or nonminimal, depending on whether routing is restricted to minimal paths or not. Note that fully adaptive routing used in the context of avoidance-based algorithms connotes full adaptivity across all physical channels but only partial adaptivity across virtual channels within a given physical channel. On the other hand, true fully adaptive routing used in the context of recovery-based algorithms connotes full adaptivity across all physical channel dimensions as well as across all virtual channels within a given physical channel. Routing restrictions on virtual channels are therefore completely relaxed so that no ordering among these resources is enforced.

As an example, Figure 4.28 shows a true fully adaptive minimal routing algorithm for 2-D meshes. Each physical channel is assumed to be split into two virtual channels a and b. In this figure, $Xa+$ and $Xb+$ denote the a and b channels, respectively, in the positive direction of the X dimension. A similar notation is used for the other direction and dimension. As can be seen, no routing restrictions are enforced, except for paths to be minimal.

Figure 4.28 only shows the routing algorithm. It does not include deadlock handling. This issue was covered in Section 3.6. For the sake of completeness, Figure 4.29 shows a flow diagram of the true fully adaptive nonminimal routing algorithm implemented by Disha. The shaded box corresponds to the routing algorithm described in Figure 4.28 (extended to handle nonminimal routing). If after a number of tries a packet cannot access any virtual channel along any minimal path to its destination, it is allowed to access any misrouting channel except those resulting in 180-degree turns. If all minimal and misrouting channels remain busy for longer than the timeout for deadlock detection, the packet is eventually suspected of being deadlocked. Once this determination is made, its eligibility to progressively recover using the central *deadlock buffer* recovery path is checked. As only one of the packets involved in a deadlock needs to be eliminated from the dependency cycle to break the deadlock, a packet either uses the recovery path (is eligible to recover) or will eventually use one of the normal edge virtual channel buffers for routing (i.e., is not eligible to recover, but the deadlock is broken by some other packet that is eligible). Hence, Disha aims at optimizing routing performance in the absence of deadlocks and efficiently dealing with the rare cases when deadlock may be impending. If deadlocks are truly rare, substantial performance benefits can be gleaned (see Section 9.4.1).

4.6 Nonminimal Routing Algorithms

As indicated in the previous section, routing algorithms based on deadlock recovery can be designed to use nonminimal paths. Some methodologies proposed in previous sections can also be used for the design of avoidance-based nonminimal routing algorithms. This is the case for turn model, Dally and Aoki's algorithm and the methodology proposed in Section 4.4.4 for VCT switching. Also, PAR, hop algorithms, most algorithms based on virtual networks and the methodology proposed in Section 4.4.4 for wormhole switching can be extended so as to consider nonminimal routing.

For networks using wormhole switching, nonminimal routing algorithms usually degrade performance because packets consume more network resources. In particular, blocked packets occupy more channels on average, reducing the bandwidth available to the remaining packets. As a consequence, nonminimal routing algorithms are usually proposed for fault-tolerant routing because they are able to find alternative paths when all the minimal paths are faulty. These algorithms will be studied in Chapter 6.

Algorithm: True Fully Adaptive Minimal Algorithm for 2-D Meshes (Disha)
       (not including deadlock recovery)
Inputs: Coordinates of current node $(Xcurrent, Ycurrent)$
       and destination node $(Xdest, Ydest)$
Output: Selected output *Channel*
Procedure:
   $Xoffset := Xdest - Xcurrent;$
   $Yoffset := Ydest - Ycurrent;$
   if $Xoffset < 0$ **and** $Yoffset < 0$ **then**
      $Channel := \text{Select}(Xa-, Ya-, Xb-, Yb-);$
   endif
   if $Xoffset < 0$ **and** $Yoffset > 0$ **then**
      $Channel := \text{Select}(Xa-, Ya+, Xb-, Yb+);$
   endif
   if $Xoffset < 0$ **and** $Yoffset = 0$ **then**
      $Channel := \text{Select}(Xa-, Xb-);$
   endif
   if $Xoffset > 0$ **and** $Yoffset < 0$ **then**
      $Channel := \text{Select}(Xa+, Ya-, Xb+, Yb-);$
   endif
   if $Xoffset > 0$ **and** $Yoffset > 0$ **then**
      $Channel := \text{Select}(Xa+, Ya+, Xb+, Yb+);$
   endif
   if $Xoffset > 0$ **and** $Yoffset = 0$ **then**
      $Channel := \text{Select}(Xa+, Xb+);$
   endif
   if $Xoffset = 0$ **and** $Yoffset < 0$ **then**
      $Channel := \text{Select}(Ya-, Yb-);$
   endif
   if $Xoffset = 0$ **and** $Yoffset > 0$ **then**
      $Channel := \text{Select}(Ya+, Yb+);$
   endif
   if $Xoffset = 0$ **and** $Yoffset = 0$ **then**
      $Channel := Internal;$
   endif

Figure 4.28. True fully adaptive minimal routing algorithm for 2-D meshes (Disha).

However, blocked packets are completely removed from the network when VCT switching is used. In this case, taking an unprofitable channel is likely to bring the packet to another set of profitable channels that will allow further progress to the destination. As indicated in Chapter 3, deadlock can be avoided in VCT switching by using deflection routing. This routing technique uses nonminimal paths to avoid deadlock when all the minimal paths are busy.

The Chaos router [188, 189] implements a fully adaptive nonminimal routing algorithm and uses deflection routing to avoid deadlock. This router uses VCT switching and splits messages into fixed-

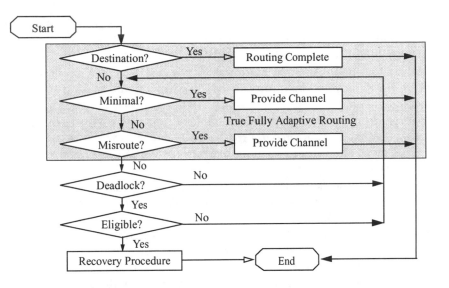

Figure 4.29. Flow diagram of the true fully adaptive nonminimal routing algorithm implemented by Disha.

length packets. It has a central packet queue implemented in hardware to remove packets from the network when they are blocked. The Chaos routing algorithm routes packets following a minimal path whenever possible. If all the minimal paths for a packet are busy, routing is retried for a fixed period of time. When waiting time exceeds a threshold, the packet is stored in the packet queue. To prevent starvation, packets in the queue have the highest priority in accessing a free output channel belonging to a minimal path when it becomes available. Queue overflow is prevented by derouting (misrouting) packets. When a queue slot is requested and the queue is full, a queued packet is randomly selected and forwarded along a nonminimal path.

Derouting packets requires guaranteeing that a nonminimal path is always available. This is equivalent to guaranteeing that some output channel is free. As indicated in Chapter 3, this can be ensured because the number of input channels (including injection channels) is equal to the number of output channels (including delivery channels). However, the Chaos router implements a more elaborate protocol to select the output channel for derouting. The protocol and formal proofs of deadlock freedom can be found in [189].

4.7 Backtracking Protocols

Backtracking protocols work on the premise that it is better to be searching for alternative paths than to be waiting for a channel to become available. This premise is specially true when the channel is faulty because it will not be available until repaired. The application of backtracking protocols to fault-tolerant routing will be studied in Chapter 6. In this section, we only consider the use of backtracking protocols to improve performance.

From a performance point of view, backtracking protocols are suited to circuit switching or some variant of it. Backtracking protocols search the network for a path in a depth-first manner. Potential paths from source to destination are searched by routing a header flit or probe through the network. The header acquires (virtual) channels as it moves toward its destination. When the header cannot continue onward, it backtracks over the last acquired channel, releases it, and continues its search from the previous node. As seen in Chapter 3, deadlock is prevented in circuit switching by reserving all the required resources before starting packet transmission. During the reservation phase, the header backtracks as needed instead of blocking when a channel is not available. Also, livelock is not a problem because backtracking protocols can use history information to avoid searching the same path repeatedly.

Although backtracking protocols can also be implemented with SAF switching, the performance overhead can be substantial compared to the use of deadlock avoidance techniques. From the behavioral point of view, the actual switching technique is unimportant and will not be referenced unless necessary in the remainder of this discussion.

Most backtracking protocols use the routing header to store history information [52, 62]. This significantly increases the size of the header over progressive protocols and, consequently, increases the time required to route the probe through the network. This is particularly a problem for misrouting backtracking protocols, since the number of links traversed during path setup can be very high. To overcome this problem, the history information can be distributed throughout the nodes of the network, reducing the header to a size comparable to that of e-cube [126, 127]. At each node in the network, each input link has a history bit vector h with as many bits as the node has channels. This history vector is associated with the circuit probe that came in on that channel. As each candidate outgoing channel is searched, the corresponding bit is set to "remember" that the channel has been searched. Each node also has a history bit vector h, for the node itself, since the node (not a channel) may be the source of the probe.

In this section, we briefly describe several backtracking protocols. Exhaustive profitable backtracking (EPB) performs a straightforward depth-first search of the network using only profitable links [140]. It is guaranteed to find a minimal path if one exists. This protocol is completely adaptive, profitable, and backtracking. Although the EPB protocol does not repeatedly search the same paths, it can visit a specific node several times (see Example 4.6). This can lead to unnecessary backtracking and longer setup times. The k-family routing paradigm is a family of partially adaptive, profitable, backtracking protocols proposed for binary hypercubes that use a heuristic to help minimize redundancy in the search for a path [62].

k-Family protocols are two-phased, using a heuristic search in the first phase and an exhaustive search in the second. Each protocol is distinguished by a parameter k that determines when the heuristic is used an when exhaustive backtracking is used. When the probe is at a distance from the destination greater than k, the heuristic is used; when the distance is less than or equal to k, an exhaustive profitable search is used. If $k = 1$, the protocol is a strictly heuristic search. As k grows to the distance between the source and destination, the search becomes more and more exhaustive. A k protocol makes use of a history mask contained in the circuit probe. At each level in the search tree, the cumulative history mask of the ancestor nodes determines which links might be explored. The history mask records all the dimensions explored at each link and all dimensions explored at all ancestor nodes. The heuristic limits exploration to dimensions not marked in the history mask. In this manner, the search tree in Example 4.6 is pruned of links that are likely to lead into areas of the network that have been searched already.

The multilink paradigm is a family of profitable backtracking protocols that only make a partial reservation of the path [296]. Instead of sending a probe to setup a path from source to destination, the multilink protocol uses wormhole switching in the absence of contention. When the requested output channel is busy, the router switches to multilink mode. In this mode, it sends a probe to search the network for a path of a given maximum size (multilink). The maximum number of channels that can be reserved at once is a fixed parameter for each protocol (multilink size). Once the path has been established, the router returns to normal mode and data flits advance. If

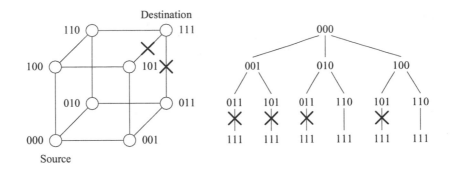

Figure 4.30. Search tree for a profitable backtracking protocol.

another busy channel is found, the router switches to multilink mode again, sending another probe. By limiting the number of channels that can be reserved at once, the search tree is pruned and the setup phase is much faster. However, the resulting routing algorithm is only partially adaptive. Also, deadlock freedom must be ensured by establishing an ordering between channels and multilinks. Additionally, once the data flits advance up to a given node, the probe can only backtrack up to that node. Although this protocol was initially proposed as profitable, it can be easily modified to use misrouting.

The exhaustive misrouting backtracking (EMB) protocol does a depth-first search of the network using both profitable and unprofitable links [126]. It uses the "best first" heuristic, taking profitable links over unprofitable ones. Although, on the average, the established circuits are longer than with a purely profitable protocol, EMB's probability of finding a path is greater. The drawback of this algorithm is that it cannot detect that a packet is undeliverable until it searches every path it can reach in the network. In the worst case, a single probe can tie up large amounts of network resources searching in vain for a nonexistent path. The protocol is just "too optimistic." Also, reserved paths may be too long, unnecessarily wasting channel bandwidth.

Misrouting freedom can be limited by using a partially adaptive two-phase protocol analogous to the k-family protocol where the probe is free to misroute only if it is within a certain distance u of its destination [126]. The first phase of two-phase backtracking (TPB-u) performs an exhaustive profitable search when the probe is at a distance greater than u from the destination. When TPB-u is within u of the destination, it enters the second phase, where it performs an exhaustive misrouting search. A TPB-u probe can switch phases several times during a single route.

The misrouting backtracking protocol with m misroutes (MB-m) is very much like the exhaustive misrouting backtracking protocol, except that it limits to m the maximum number of misroutes allowed at any time [127]. This protocol will be studied in Chapter 6.

In general, backtracking protocols do not improve performance over progressive ones when packets are short because the overhead to set up a path is very high. For very long packets or messages, backtracking protocols may perform better than progressive ones, specially when the number of alternative paths offered by the network is high.

Example 4.6

To illustrate backtracking protocols, we present the network shown in Figure 4.30. We will examine routing from node 000 to node 111 for EPB, k-family with $k = 1$, EMB, TPB-1, MB-1, and multilinks. Figure 4.30 shows the search tree for a profitable backtracking protocol routing a packet from node 000 to node 111 in a binary 3-cube. EPB will perform a depth-first search of the tree (left to right). Each path from the root node to a leaf node corresponds to a path from the source node (000) to the destination node (111) in the network. In Figure 4.30, links $(011, 111)$ and $(101, 111)$ are busy. In routing from 000 to 111, the EPB probe would visit the following nodes in sequence:

$$000 \rightarrow 001 \rightarrow 011 \rightarrow 001 \rightarrow 101 \rightarrow 001 \rightarrow 000 \rightarrow 010 \rightarrow 011 \rightarrow 010 \rightarrow 110 \rightarrow 111$$

The final circuit the probe established would be

$$000 \rightarrow 010 \rightarrow 110 \rightarrow 111$$

Note that the probe had to backtrack all the way back to the source node and visited node 011 twice. The k-family probe would visit the following node sequence:

$$000 \rightarrow 001 \rightarrow 011 \rightarrow 001 \rightarrow 101 \rightarrow 001 \rightarrow 000 \rightarrow 010 \rightarrow 110 \rightarrow 111$$

The resulting circuit would be the same as for EPB. Note that the k-family protocol pruned the second visit to 011 because the history mask passed to 010 from the source indicated that dimension 0 had already been searched. For EMB, TPB-1, and MB-1 the probe's search would proceed as follows:

$$000 \rightarrow 001 \rightarrow 011 \rightarrow 010 \rightarrow 110 \rightarrow 111$$

The final circuit would be

$$000 \rightarrow 001 \rightarrow 011 \rightarrow 010 \rightarrow 110 \rightarrow 111$$

In this case, since misrouting occurs at a node only one hop from the destination, TPB-1 behaves identically to EMB. If it were not possible to route at node 010, EMB would be free to misroute again, but TPB-1 would have to backtrack. MB-1 also behaves identically to EMB because only one misroute is required to search an alternative free path. Again, if it were not possible to route at node 010, MB-1 would have to backtrack. The final circuits established by the profitable protocols will always be the minimal length. The circuits established by the misrouting protocols can be much longer.

The multilinks protocol uses wormhole switching in the absence of contention. Thus, the header would reserve the following path:

$$000 \rightarrow 001 \rightarrow 011$$

As data flits immediately follow the header, it cannot backtrack at node 011. Thus, the header will have to wait for link $(011, 111)$ to become free. The partially optimistic behavior of multilinks protocol prevents it from backtracking. However, if this protocol were modified to support misrouting, a probe would be sent from node 011 instead of waiting for a free channel. This probe would visit the following node sequence:

$$010 \rightarrow 110 \rightarrow 111$$

The resulting circuit would be the same as for MB-1.

4.8 Routing in MINs

In this section, we describe several issues concerning routing in MINs. For array processors, a central controller establishes the path from input to output. In cases where the number of inputs equals the number of outputs, each input synchronously transmits a message to one output, and each output receives a message from exactly one input. Computing the switch settings to realize such a permutation is a complex task. Furthermore, some permutations may not be realizable in one pass through the network. In this case, multiple passes of the data through the network may be required and the goal is to minimize the number of passes. The complexity of the off-line computation of the switch settings is proportional to the number of switches. This section and most multiprocessor applications consider only networks with the same number of inputs and outputs. Contention-free centralized routing will be addressed in Section 4.8.1. Also, see [262] for a brief survey.

On the other hand, in asynchronous multiprocessors, centralized control, and permutation routing are infeasible. So, a routing algorithm is required to establish the path across the stages of a MIN. The simplest solution consists of using source routing. In this case, the source node specifies the complete path. As this solution produces a considerable overhead, we will focus on distributed routing. Routing algorithms for MINs will be described in Section 4.8.2.

There are many ways to interconnect adjacent stages. See Sections 1.7.4 and 1.7.5 for a definition of some connection patterns and MIN topologies, respectively.

4.8.1 Blocking Condition in MINs

The goal of this section is to derive necessary and sufficient conditions for two circuits to block, i.e., require the same intermediate link. In an N processor system, there are exactly N links between every stage of $k \times k$ switches. The network consists of $n = \log_k N$ stages, where each stage is comprised of $\frac{N}{k}$ switches. The intermediate link patterns connect an output of switch stage i to an input of switch stage $i + 1$. Blocking occurs when two packets must traverse the same output at a switch stage $i, i = 0, 1, \ldots n - 1$. At any stage i, we can address all of the outputs of that stage from 0 to $N - 1$. Let us refer to these as the intermediate outputs at stage i. If we take a black box view of the network, we can represent it as shown in Figure 4.31 for an Omega network with 2×2 switches. Each stage of switches and each stage of links can be represented as a function that permutes the inputs. An example is shown in the figure of a path from network input 6, to network output 1. The intermediate outputs on this path are marked as shown. They are 4, 0, and 1 at the output of switch stages 0, 1, and 2, respectively. Our initial goal is the following. Given an input/output pair, generate the addresses of all of the intermediate outputs on this path. Since these networks have a single path from input to output, these addresses will be unique. Two input/output paths conflict if they traverse a common intermediate link or share a common output at any intermediate stage.

In the following, we derive the blocking condition for the Omega network. Equivalent conditions can be derived for other networks in a similar manner. All input/output addresses in the following are represented in base k. For ease of discussion, we will assume a circuit-switched network. Consider establishing a circuit from $s_{n-1}s_{n-2}\ldots s_1 s_0$ to $d_{n-1}d_{n-2}\ldots d_1 d_0$. Consider the first link stage in Figure 4.31. This part of the network functionally establishes the following connection between its input and output.

$$s_{n-1}s_{n-2}\ldots s_1 s_0 \rightarrow s_{n-2}s_{n-3}\ldots s_1 s_0 s_{n-1} \tag{4.2}$$

The right-hand side (RHS) of the above equation is the address of the output of the k-shuffle pattern and the address of the input to the first stage of switches. As mentioned in the previous

Omega Network: Structural View

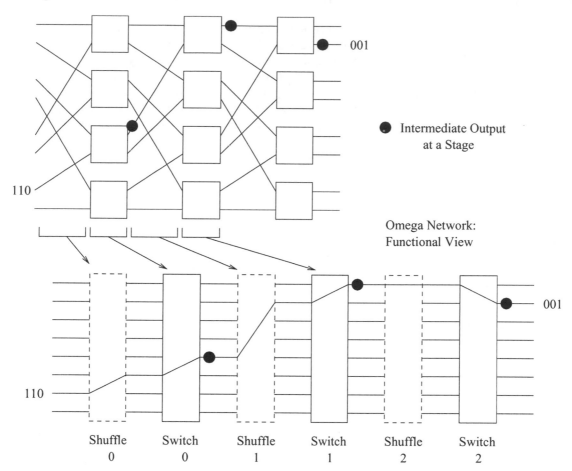

Figure 4.31. Functional view of the structure of a multistage Omega network.

section, each switch is only able to change the least significant digit of the current address. After the shuffle permutation, this is s_{n-1}. So the output of the first stage of switches will be such that the least significant digit of the address be equal to d_{n-1}. Thus, the input/output connection established at the first stage of switches should be such that the input is connected to the output as follows.

$$s_{n-2}s_{n-3}\ldots s_1 s_0 s_{n-1} \rightarrow s_{n-2}s_{n-3}\ldots s_1 s_0 d_{n-1} \qquad (4.3)$$

The RHS of the above expression is the address of the input to the second link stage. It is also the output of the first stage of switches and is therefore the first intermediate output. An example is shown in Figure 4.31 for a path from input 6 to output 1 which has a total of three intermediate outputs. Similarly, we can write the expression for the address of the intermediate output at stage i as

$$s_{n-i-2}s_{n-i-3}\ldots s_0 d_{n-1}d_{n-2}\ldots d_{n-i-1} \qquad (4.4)$$

This is assuming that stages are numbered from 0 to $n - 1$. We can now write the blocking condition. For any two input/output pairs (S, D) and (R, T), the two paths can be set up in a conflict-free manner if and only if, $\forall i, 0 \leq i \leq n - 1$

$$s_{n-i-2}s_{n-i-3} \cdots s_0 d_{n-1}d_{n-2} \cdots d_{n-i-1} \neq r_{n-i-2}r_{n-i-3} \cdots r_0 t_{n-1}t_{n-2} \cdots t_{n-i-1} \qquad (4.5)$$

Testing for blocking between two input/output pairs is not quite as computationally demanding as it may first seem. Looking at the structure of the blocking condition we can see that if it is true and the circuits do block, then $n - i - 1$ least significant digits of the source addresses are equal and $i + 1$ most significant digits of the destination addresses are equal. Let us assume that we have a function $\phi(S, R)$ that returns the largest integer l such that the l least significant digits of S and R are equal. Similarly, let us assume that we have a function $\psi(D, T)$ that returns the largest integer m such that the m most significant digits of D and T are equal. Then two paths (S, D) and (R, T) can be established in a conflict-free manner if and only if

$$\phi(S, R) + \psi(D, T) < n \qquad (4.6)$$

where $N = k^n$. As a practical matter, blocking can be computed by sequences of shift and compare operations, as follows:

$$s_{n-1}s_{n-2} \cdots \boxed{s_2 s_1 s_0 d_{n-1}d_{n-2} \cdots d_3}\ d_2 d_1 d_0$$
$$r_{n-1}r_{n-2} \cdots \boxed{r_2 r_1 r_0\ t_{n-1}t_{n-2} \cdots t_3}\ t_2 t_1 t_0$$

The addresses of the two input/output pairs are concatenated. Figuratively, a window of size n slides over both pairs and the contents of both windows are compared. If they are equal at any point, then there is a conflict at some stage. This will take $O(\log_k N)$ steps to perform. To determine if all paths can be set up in a conflict-free manner, we will have to perform $O(N^2)$ comparisons and each taking $O(\log_k N)$ steps resulting in an $O(N^2 \log_k N)$ algorithm. By comparison, the best known algorithm for centralized control to setup all of the switches in advance takes $O(N \log_k N)$ time. However, when using the above formulation of blocking it is often not necessary to perform the worst-case number of comparisons. Often the structure of the communication pattern can be exploited in off-line determination of whether patterns can be setup in a conflict-free manner.

4.8.2 Self-Routing Algorithms for MINs

A unique property of Delta networks is their self-routing property [272]. The self-routing property of these MINs allows the routing decision to be determined by the destination address, regardless of the source address. Self-routing is performed by using routing tags. For a $k \times k$ switch, there are k output ports. If the value of the corresponding routing tag is i ($0 \leq i \leq k - 1$), the corresponding packet will be forwarded via port i. For an n-stage MIN, the routing tag is $T = t_{n-1} \ldots t_1 t_0$, where t_i controls the switch at stage G_i.

As indicated in Section 1.7.5, each switch is only able to change the least significant digit of the current address. Therefore, routing tags will take into account which digit is the least significant one at each stage, replacing it by the corresponding digit of the destination address. For a given destination $d_{n-1}d_{n-2} \ldots d_0$, in a butterfly MIN the routing tag is formed by having $t_i = d_{i+1}$ for $0 \leq i \leq n - 2$ and $t_{n-1} = d_0$. In a cube MIN, the routing tag is formed by having $t_i = d_{n-i-1}$ for $0 \leq i \leq n - 1$. Finally, in an Omega network, the routing tag is formed by having $t_i = d_{n-i-1}$ for $0 \leq i \leq n - 1$. Example 4.7 shows the paths selected by the tag-based routing algorithm in a 16-node butterfly MIN.

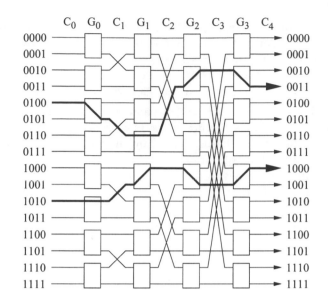

Figure 4.32. Paths selected by the tag-based routing algorithm in a 16-node butterfly MIN.

Example 4.7

Figure 4.32 shows a 16-node butterfly MIN using 2×2 switches, and the paths followed by packets from node 0100 to node 0011 and from node 1010 to node 1000. As indicated above, the routing tag for a given destination $d_{n-1}d_{n-2}\ldots d_0$ is formed by having $t_i = d_{i+1}$ for $0 \le i \le n-2$ and $t_{n-1} = d_0$. Thus, the routing tag for destination 0011 is 1001. This tag indicates that the packet must take the the upper switch output (port 0) at stages G_2 and G_1, and the lower switch output (port 1) at stages G_3 and G_0. The routing tag for destination 1000 is 0100. This tag indicates that the packet must take the upper switch output at stages G_3, G_1, and G_0, and the lower switch output at stage G_2.

One of the nice features of the above traditional MINs (TMINs) is that there is a simple algorithm for finding a path of length $\log_k N$ between any input/output pair. However, if a link becomes congested or fails, the unique path property can easily disrupt the communication between some input and output pairs. The congestion of packets over some channels causes the known *hot spot* problem [274]. Many solutions have been proposed to resolve the hot spot problem. A popular approach is to provide multiple routing paths between any source and destination pair so as to reduce network congestion as well as to achieve fault tolerance. These methods usually require additional hardware, such as extra stages or additional channels.

The use of additional channels gives rise to dilated MINs. In a d-dilated MIN (DMIN), each switch is replaced by a d-dilated switch. In this switch, each port has d channels. By using replicated channels, DMINs offer substantial network throughput improvement [191]. The routing tag of a DMIN can be determined by the destination address as mentioned for TMINs. Within the network switches, packets destined for a particular output port are randomly distributed to one of the free channels of that port. If all channels are busy, the packet is blocked.

Another approach for the design of MINs consists of allowing for bidirectional communication. In this case, each port of the switch has dual channels. In a butterfly bidirectional MIN (BMIN)

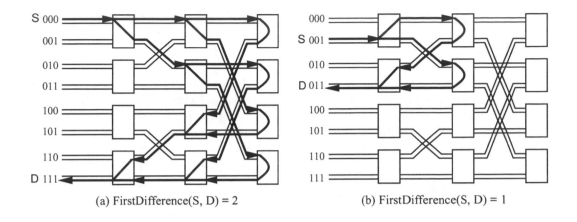

(a) FirstDifference(S, D) = 2   (b) FirstDifference(S, D) = 1

Figure 4.33. Paths available in an eight-node butterfly BMIN.

built with $k \times k$ switches, source address S and destination address D are represented by k-ary numbers $s_{n-1} \dots s_1 s_0$ and $d_{n-1} \dots d_1 d_0$, respectively. The function *FirstDifference(S, D)* returns t, the position where the first (leftmost) different digit appears between $s_{n-1} \dots s_1 s_0$ and $d_{n-1} \dots d_1 d_0$.

A turnaround routing path between any source and destination pair is formally defined as follows. A turnaround path is a route from a source node to a destination node. The path must meet the following conditions:

- The path consists of some forward channel(s), some backward channel(s), and exactly one turnaround connection.

- The number of forward channels is equal to the number of backward channels.

- No forward and backward channels along the path are the channel pair of the same port.

Note that the last condition is to prevent redundant communication from occurring. To route a packet from source to destination, the packet is first sent forward to stage G_t. It does not matter which switch (at stage G_t) the packet reaches. Then, the packet is turned around and sent backward to destination. As it moves forward to stage G_t, a packet may have multiple choices as to which forward output channel to take. The decision can be resolved by randomly selecting from among those forward output channels which are not blocked by other packets. After the packet has attained a switch at stage G_t, it takes the unique path from that switch backward to its destination. The backward routing path can be determined by the tag-based routing algorithm for TMINs.

Note that the routing algorithms described above are distributed routing algorithms, in which each switch determines the output channel based on the address information carried in the packet. Example 4.8 shows the paths available in an eight-node butterfly BMIN.

Example 4.8

Figure 4.33 shows the paths available in an eight-node butterfly BMIN using 2×2 switches. Figure 4.33a shows the case when the source and destination nodes are 000 and 111, respectively. In this case, FirstDifference$(S, D) = 2$. Thus, packets turn at stage G_2 and there are four different shortest paths available. In Figure 4.33b, the source and destination nodes are 001 and 011, respectively. FirstDifference$(S, D) = 1$, and packets turn at stage G_1.

4.9 Routing in Switch-Based Networks with Irregular Topologies

Recently, switch-based interconnects like Autonet [304], Myrinet [30], and ServerNet [157] have been proposed to build NOWs for cost-effective parallel computing. Typically, these switches support networks with irregular topologies. Such irregularity provides the wiring flexibility required in LANs, also allowing the design of scalable systems with incremental expansion capability. The irregularity also makes the routing on such systems quite complicated.

Switch-based networks consist of a set of switches where each switch can have a set of ports. Each port consists of one input and one output link. A set of ports in each switch are either connected to processors or left open, where as the remaining ports are connected to ports of other switches to provide connectivity between the processors. Such connectivity is typically irregular and the only guarantee is that the network is connected. Typically, all links are bidirectional full-duplex and multiple links between two switches are allowed. Such a configuration allows a system with a given number of processors to be built using less number of switches than a direct network while allowing a reasonable number of external communication ports per processor. Figure 4.34a shows a typical NOW using switch-based interconnect with irregular topology. In this figure, it is assumed that switches have eight ports and each processor has a single port.

The switch may implement different switching techniques: wormhole switching, VCT, or ATM. However, wormhole switching is used in most cases. Several deadlock-free routing schemes have been proposed in the literature for irregular networks [30, 157, 284, 304]. Routing in irregular topologies can be performed by using source routing or distributed routing. In the former case, each processor has a routing table that indicates the sequence of ports to be used at intermediate switches to reach

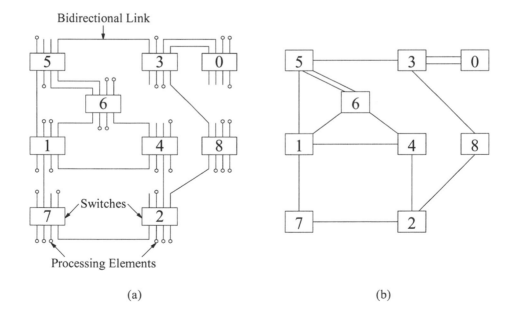

(a)   (b)

Figure 4.34. (a) An example system with switch-based interconnect and irregular topology. (b) The corresponding graph G.

the destination node. That information is stored in the packet header [30]. In the latter case, processors and switches require routing tables. The use of table lookup routing allows the use of the same switch fabric for different topologies. However, some network mapping algorithm must be executed in order to fill those tables before routing can be performed. The details of the mapping algorithm greatly depend on the underlying hardware support. Typically, switches support some broadcasting capability in the absence of routing tables.

In this section, we briefly describe the deadlock-free routing scheme used in DEC AN1 (Autonet) networks [304]. This routing scheme is valid for all the switching techniques. In addition to providing deadlock-freedom, it provides adaptive communication between some nodes in an irregular network. Also, we describe a fully adaptive routing algorithm for irregular topologies [318, 319] that considerably improves performance over the routing scheme proposed in [304].

Once a packet reaches a switch directly connected to its destination processor, it can be delivered as soon as the corresponding link becomes free. Therefore, we are going to focus on routing packets between switches. As indicated in Chapter 3, the interconnection network I between switches can be modeled by a multigraph $I = G(N, C)$, where N is the set of switches and C is the set of bidirectional links between the switches. It should be noted that bidirectional links were considered as two unidirectional channels in Chapter 3 but not in this section. Figure 4.34b shows the graph for the irregular network in Figure 4.34a.

The Autonet routing algorithm is distributed, and implemented using table-lookup. When a packet reaches a switch, the destination address stored in the packet header is concatenated with the incoming port number and the result is used to index the routing table at that switch. The table-lookup returns the outgoing port number that the packet should be routed through. When multiple routes exist from the source to the destination, the routing table entries return alternative outgoing ports. In case multiple outgoing ports are free, the routing scheme selects one port randomly.

In order to fill the routing tables, a breadth-first spanning tree (BFS) on the graph G is computed first using a distributed algorithm. This algorithm has the property that all nodes will eventually agree on a unique spanning tree. Routing is based on an assignment of direction to the operational links. In particular, the up end of each link is defined as: (1) the end whose switch is closer to the root in the spanning tree; (2) the end whose switch has the lower ID, if both ends are at switches at the same tree level. Links looped back to the same switch are omitted from the configuration. The result of this assignment is that each cycle in the network has at least one link in the up direction and one link in the down direction.

To eliminate deadlocks while still allowing all links to be used, this routing uses the following up/down rule: a legal route must traverse zero or more links in the up direction followed by zero or more links in the down direction. Thus, cyclic dependencies between channels are avoided because a packet may never traverse a link along the up direction after having traversed one in the down direction. Such routing not only allows deadlock-freedom but also adaptivity. The lookup tables can be constructed to support both minimal and nonminimal adaptive routing. However, in many cases, up/down routing is not able to supply any minimal path between some pairs of nodes, as shown in the following example.

Example 4.9

Figure 4.35 shows the link direction assignment for the example irregular network shown in Figure 4.34a. Switches are arranged in such a way that all the switches at the same tree level in the BFS spanning tree (rooted at switch 6) are at the same vertical position in the figure. The assignment of up direction to the links in this network is illustrated. The down direction is along the reverse direction of the link. Note that every cycle has at least one link in the

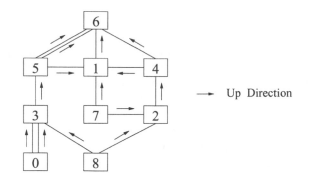

Figure 4.35. Link direction assignment for the irregular network shown in Figure 4.34a.

up direction and one link in the down direction. It can be observed that all the alternative minimal paths are allowed in some cases. For example, a packet transmitted from switch 5 to switch 4 can be either routed through switch 6 or switch 1. In some other cases, however, only some minimal paths are allowed. For example, a packet transmitted from switch 2 to switch 1 can be routed through switch 4 but it cannot be routed through switch 7. In this example, the packet can also be routed through switches 4 and 6, thus following a nonminimal path. It should be noted that any transmission between adjacent switches is always allowed to use the link(s) connecting them, regardless of the direction assigned to that link. However, when two switches are located two or more links away, it may happen that all the minimal paths are forbidden. This is the case for packets transmitted from switch 3 to switch 2. The shortest path (through switch 8) is not allowed. All the allowed paths (through switches 5, 1, 4, through switches 5, 6, 4, through switches 5, 1, 6, 4, and through switches 5, 6, 1, 4) are nonminimal.

The use of nonminimal paths consumes more channel bandwidth than strictly required to transmit packets. This drawback becomes more pronounced as network size increases. Nonminimal paths are imposed by the need to avoid deadlock. However, as indicated in Section 3.1.3, it is not necessary to remove all the cyclic dependencies between channels in order to avoid deadlock.

The design methodology presented in Section 4.4.4 cannot be directly applied to irregular networks implementing wormhole switching. The reason is that most routing functions defined for irregular networks only provide nonminimal paths between some pairs of nodes. As a consequence, the routing functions supplied by that methodology do not pass the verification step (step 3) in most cases.

A general methodology for the design of adaptive routing algorithms for networks with irregular topology was proposed in [319]. It is similar to the design methodology presented in Section 4.4.4 but it provides less routing flexibility. That methodology can be summarized as follows. Given an interconnection network and a deadlock-free routing function defined on it, it is possible to duplicate all the physical channels in the network, or to split them into two virtual channels. In both cases, the graph representation of the new network contains the original and the new channels. Then, the routing function is extended so that newly injected messages can use the new channels without any restriction as long as the original channels can only be used in the same way as in the original routing function. However, once a message reserves one of the original channels, it can no longer reserve any of the new channels again. This constraint is the only difference between this methodology and Methodology 4.1 presented in Section 4.4.4. Indeed, the resulting routing algorithms are very much like the dynamic dimension reversal routing algorithm described in Section 4.4.4, except that packets do not need to carry the dimension reversal number.

It is easy to see that the design methodology described above supplies deadlock-free routing algorithms. Effectively, consider a routing subfunction R_1 identical to the original routing function. The channels supplied by R_1 are used exactly in the same way in the original routing function and in the extended routing function. Hence there are no (direct or indirect) cross-dependencies between channels supplied by R_1. Also, packets using channels supplied by R_1 can no longer use other channels not supplied by R_1. Hence, there are no indirect dependencies between channels supplied by R_1. Therefore, the extended channel dependency graph for R_1 is identical to the channel dependency graph for the original routing function, which is acyclic. Thus, the extended routing function is deadlock-free.

According to the extended routing function defined above, new channels provide more routing flexibility than original channels. Besides they can be used to route messages through minimal paths. However, once a message reserves an original channel, it is routed through the original paths, which, in most cases, are nonminimal. Also, routing through original paths produces a loss of adaptivity.

Following this reasoning, the general methodology proposed in [319] can be refined by restricting the transition from new channels to original channels, since they provide less adaptivity and nonminimal paths in most cases. The extended routing function can be redefined in the following way. Newly injected messages can only leave the source switch using new channels belonging to minimal paths, and never using original channels. When a message arrives at a switch from another switch through a new channel, the routing function gives a higher priority to the new channels belonging to minimal paths. If all of them are busy, then the routing algorithm selects an original channel belonging to a minimal path (if any). To ensure that the new routing function is deadlock-free, if none of the original channels provides minimal routing, then the original channel that provides the shortest path will be used. Once a message reserves an original channel, it will be routed using this kind of channels according to the original routing function until it is delivered.

This enhanced design methodology was proposed in [318] and can be applied to any routing algorithm that avoids deadlock by prohibiting cyclic dependencies between channels. In particular, it can be applied to networks using up/down routing simply by splitting physical channels into two virtual channels (or duplicating each physical channel), and using up/down routing as the original routing function. By restricting the use of original channels as indicated above, most messages are allowed to follow minimal paths, and therefore a more efficient use of resources is made. Also, adaptivity is considerably increased with respect to the original up/down routing algorithm. As a result, latency decreases significantly, and the network is able to deliver a throughput several times higher than the one achieved by the original up/down routing algorithm [318](see Section 9.8).

4.10 Resource Allocation Policies

In this section we briefly describe several policies proposed in the literature for the allocation of network resources. Resource allocation policies can be grouped into two classes: those required to select a resource for a packet when several resources are available, and those required to arbitrate between several packets contending for the same resource. The first class of policies is usually required to select a channel or buffer among the options offered by an adaptive routing function. The function that performs this selection is usually referred to as *selection function*. The second class of policies is usually required to allocate resources like the routing control unit (the circuit that computes the routing algorithm), or the bandwidth of a physical channel when it is multiplexed among several virtual channels. Both classes of policies are studied in the next sections.

4.10.1   Selection Function

Without loss of generality, let us assume that when a packet is routed, the network resources requested by that packet are the output channels at the current node. As indicated in Section 4.1, adaptive routing algorithms can be decomposed into two functions: routing and selection. The routing function supplies a set of output channels based on the current node or buffer and the destination node. The selection function selects an output channel from the set of channels supplied by the routing function. This selection can be random. In this case, network state is not considered (oblivious routing). However, the selection is usually done taking into account the status of output channels at the current node. Obviously, the selection is performed in such a way that a free channel (if any) is supplied. However, when several output channels are available, some policy is required to select one of them. Policies may have different goals, like balancing the use of resources, reserving some bandwidth for high-priority packets, or even delaying the use of resources that are exclusively used for deadlock avoidance. Regardless of the main goal of the policy, the selection function should give preference to channels belonging to minimal paths when the routing function is nonminimal. Otherwise the selection function may produce livelock. In this section we present some selection functions proposed in the literature for several purposes.

In [74], three different selection functions were proposed for n-dimensional meshes using wormhole switching with the goal of maximizing performance: *minimum congestion*, *maximum flexibility*, and *straight lines*. In minimum congestion, a virtual channel is selected in the dimension and direction with the most available virtual channels. This selection function tries to balance the use of virtual channels in different physical channels. The motivation for this selection function is that packet transmission is pipelined. Hence, flit transmission rate is limited by the slowest stage in the pipeline. Balancing the use of virtual channels also balances the bandwidth allocated to different virtual channels. In maximum flexibility, a virtual channel is selected in the dimension with the greatest distance to travel to the destination. This selection function tries to maximize the number of routing choices as a packet approaches its destination. In meshes, this selection function has the side effect of concentrating traffic in the central part of the network bisection, therefore producing an uneven channel utilization and degrading performance. Finally, in straight lines, a virtual channel is selected in the dimension closest to the current dimension. So, the packet will continue traveling in the same dimension whenever possible. This selection function tries to route packets in dimension order unless the requested channels in the corresponding dimension are busy. In meshes, this selection function achieves a good distribution of traffic across the network bisection. These selection functions were evaluated in [74] for 2-D meshes, showing that minimum congestion achieves the lowest latency and highest throughput. Straight lines achieves similar performance. However, maximum flexibility achieves much worse results. These results may change for other topologies and routing functions, but in general minimum congestion is a good choice for the reason mentioned above.

For routing functions that allow cyclic dependencies between channels, the selection function should give preference to adaptive channels over channels used to escape from deadlocks [92]. By doing so, escape channels are only used when all the remaining channels are busy, therefore increasing the probability of escape channels being available when they are required to escape from deadlock. The selection among adaptive channels can be done by using any of the strategies described above. Note that if escape channels are not free when requested, it does not mean that the routing function is not deadlock-free. Escape channels are guaranteed to become free sooner or later. However, performance may degrade if packets take long to escape from deadlock. In order to reduce the utilization of escape channels and increase their availability to escape from deadlock, it is possible to delay the use of escape channels by using a timeout. In this case, the selection function can only select an escape channel if the packet header is waiting for longer than the timeout. The motivation for this kind of selection function is that there is a high probability of an adaptive channel becoming available before the timeout expires. This kind of selection function was referred to as *time-dependent selection function* [89, 95]. In particular, the behavior of progressive deadlock recovery mechanisms (see Section 3.6) can be modeled by using a time-dependent selection function.

The selection function also plays a major role when real-time communication is required. In this case, best-effort packets and guaranteed packets compete for network resources. If the number of priority classes for guaranteed packets is small, each physical channel may be split into as many virtual channels as priority classes. In this case, the selection function will select the appropriate virtual channel for each packet according to its priority class. When the number of priority classes is high, the set of virtual channels may be split into two separate virtual networks, assigning best-effort packets and guaranteed packets to different virtual networks. In this case, scheduling of guaranteed packets corresponding to different priority classes can be achieved by using packet switching [293]. In this switching technique, packets are completely buffered before being routed in intermediate nodes, therefore allowing the scheduling of packets with earliest deadline first. Wormhole switching is used for best-effort packets. Latency of guaranteed packets can be made even more predictable by using an appropriate policy for channel bandwidth allocation, as indicated in the next section.

4.10.2 Policies for Arbitration and Resource Allocation

There exist some situations where several packets contend for the use of resources, therefore requiring some arbitration and allocation policy. These situations are not related to the routing algorithm but are described here for completeness. The most interesting cases of conflict in the use of resources arise when several virtual channels belonging to the same physical channel are ready to transfer a flit, and when several packet headers arrived at a node and need to be routed. In the former case, a virtual channel allocation policy is required while the second case requires a routing control unit allocation policy.

Flit level flow control across a physical channel involves allocating channel bandwidth among virtual channels that have a flit ready to transmit and have space for this flit at the receiving end. Any arbitration algorithm can be used to allocate channel bandwidth including random, round-robin, or priority schemes. For random selection, an arbitrary virtual channel satisfying the above mentioned conditions is selected. For round-robin selection, virtual channels are arranged in a circular list. When a virtual channel transfers a flit, the next virtual channel in the list satisfying the above-mentioned conditions is selected for the next flit transmission. This policy is usually referred to as *demand-slotted round-robin*, and is the most frequently used allocation policy for virtual channels.

Priority schemes require some information to be carried in the packet header. This information should be stored in a status register associated with each virtual channel reserved by the packet. Deadline scheduling can be implemented by allocating channel bandwidth based on a packet's deadline or age (earliest deadline or oldest age first) [73]. Scheduling packets by age reduces the variance of packet latency. For real-time communication, the latency of guaranteed packets can be made more predictable by assigning a higher priority to virtual channels reserved by those packets. By doing so, best-effort packets will not affect the latency of guaranteed packets because flits belonging to best-effort packets will not be transmitted unless no flit belonging to a guaranteed packet is ready to be transmitted. This approach, however, may considerably increase the latency of best-effort packets. A possible solution consists of allowing up to a fixed number of best-effort flits to be transmitted every time a guaranteed packet is transmitted [293].

When traffic consists of messages of very different lengths, a few long messages may reserve all of the virtual channels of a given physical channel. If a short message requests that channel, it will have to wait for long. A simple solution consists of splitting long messages into fixed length packets. This approach reduces waiting time for short messages but introduces some overhead because each packet carries routing information and has to be routed. Channel bandwidth is usually allocated to virtual channels at the granularity of a flit. However, it can also be allocated at the granularity of a block of flits, or even a packet, thus reducing the overhead of channel multiplexing. The latter approach is followed in the T9000 transputer [228]. In this case, buffers must be large enough to store a whole packet.

A different approach to support messages of very different lengths has been proposed in the Segment Router [185, 186]. This router has different buffers (virtual channels) for short and long messages. Additionally, it provides a central queue for short messages. The Segment Router implements VCT switching for short messages and a form of buffered wormhole switching for long messages. Instead of allocating channel bandwidth at the granularity of a flit, the Segment Router allocates channel bandwidth to short messages for the transmission of the whole message. For long messages, however, channel bandwidth is allocated for the transmission of a segment. A *segment* is the longest fragment of a long message that can be stored in the corresponding buffer. Segments do not carry header information and are routed in order following the same path. If a physical channel is assigned to a long message, after the transmission of each segment it checks for the existence of waiting short messages. If such a message exists, it is transmitted over the physical channel followed by the next segment of the long message. In this channel allocation scheme a channel is only multiplexed between one long and (possibly) many short messages. It is never multiplexed between two long messages. However, no priority scheme is used for channel allocation. It should be noted that once the transmission of a short message or segment starts over a channel, it is guaranteed to complete because there is enough buffer space at the receiving end.

A router is usually equipped with a routing control unit that computes the routing algorithm when a new packet header is received, eventually assigning an output channel to that packet. In this case, the routing control unit is a unique resource, requiring arbitration when several packets contend for it. Alternatively, the circuit computing the routing function can be replicated at each input virtual channel, allowing the concurrent computation of the sets of candidate output channels when several packet headers need to be routed at the same time. This is the approach followed in the Reliable Router [75]. However, the selection function cannot be fully replicated because the execution of this function requires updating the channel status register. This register is a centralized resource. Otherwise, several packets may simultaneously reserve the same output channel. So when two or more packets compete for the same output channel, some arbitration is required.

The traditional scheduling policy for the allocation of the routing control unit (or for granting access to the channel status register) is round-robin among input channels. In this scheduling policy, input channel buffers form a logical circular list. After routing the header stored in a buffer, the pointer to the current buffer is advanced to the next input buffer where a packet header is ready to be routed. The routing function is computed for that header, supplying a set of candidate output channels. Then, one of these channels is selected, if available, and the packet is routed to that channel. This scheduling policy is referred to as *input driven* [117]. It is simple but when the network is heavily loaded a high percentage of routing operations may fail because all of the requested output channels are busy.

An alternative scheduling policy consists of selecting a packet for which there is a free output channel. In this strategy, output channels form a logical circular list. After routing a packet, the pointer to the current output channel is advanced to the next free output channel. The router tries to find a packet in an input buffer that needs to be routed to the current output channel. If packets are found, it selects one to be routed to the current output channel. If no packet is found, the pointer to the current output channel is advanced to the next free output channel. This scheduling policy is referred to as *output-driven* [117]. Output-driven strategies may be more complex than input-driven ones. However, performance is usually higher when the network is heavily loaded [117]. Output-driven scheduling can be implemented by replicating the circuit computing the routing function at each input channel, and adding a register to each output channel to store information about the set of input channels requesting that output channel. Although output-driven scheduling usually improves performance over input-driven scheduling, the difference between them is much smaller when channels are randomly selected [117]. Indeed, a random selection usually performs better than round-robin when input-driven scheduling is used. Finally, it should be noted that most selection functions described in the previous section cannot be implemented with output-driven scheduling.

4.11 Engineering Issues

From an engineering point of view, the "best" routing algorithm is either the one that maximizes performance or the one that maximizes the performance/cost ratio, depending on the design goals. A detailed quantitative analysis must consider the impact of the routing algorithm on node design. Even if we do not consider the cost, a more complex routing algorithm may increase channel utilization at the expense of a higher propagation delay and a lower clock frequency. A slower clock also implies a proportional reduction in channel bandwidth if channels are driven synchronously. Thus, router design must be considered to make performance evaluation more realistic. This is the reason why we postpone performance evaluation until a detailed study of the routing hardware is presented.

In this section, we present a brief qualitative performance study. It would be nice if we could conclude that some routing algorithm is the "best" one. However, even if we do not consider the cost, the optimal routing algorithm may vary depending on network traffic conditions. For wormhole switching, fully adaptive routing algorithms that require many virtual channels are not interesting in general because they drastically slow down clock frequency. This is the case for the algorithms presented in Sections 4.4.2 and 4.4.3.

For low-dimensional meshes and a uniform distribution of packet destinations, the performance of deterministic routing algorithms is similar to or even higher than that of partially or fully adaptive algorithms. This is because meshes are not symmetric and adaptive algorithms concentrate traffic in the central part of the network bisection. However, deterministic algorithms distribute traffic across the bisection more evenly. For symmetric networks, like tori and hypercubes, fully adaptive algorithms that require few resources to avoid deadlock (like the ones presented in Section 4.4.4) usually outperform deterministic routers, even for uniform traffic. For switch-based networks with irregular topology, adaptive routing algorithms that allow cyclic dependencies between channels (like the ones presented in Section 4.9) also increase performance over deterministic or partially adaptive routing. This increment is usually much higher than in symmetric networks. The reason is that deterministic or partially adaptive routing algorithms for irregular networks usually route many messages across nonminimal paths, thus offering more chances for improvement.

When traffic is not uniformly distributed, the behavior may differ completely. On one hand, when there are hot spots, partially and fully adaptive algorithms usually outperform deterministic algorithms considerably. This is the case for some synthetic loads like bit-reversal, perfect shuffle, and butterfly [101]. On the other hand, when traffic locality is very high, adaptive algorithms do not help and the lower clock frequency affects performance negatively [101].

Some optimizations like the ones presented in Sections 4.5.1 and 4.5.2 have a small impact on performance. They may actually reduce performance because the use of resources is less balanced than in routing algorithms like the ones designed with Methodology 4.1. On the other hand, the true fully adaptive routing algorithm presented in Section 4.5.3 provides full adaptivity and allows a better balanced use of resources, usually achieving the highest performance. However, this routing algorithm must be combined with deadlock detection and recovery techniques. Currently available detection techniques only work efficiently when all the packets are short and have a similar length.

Traffic pattern is not the only parameter that influences performance. Packet size affects performance considerably. If messages or packets are very short, as is the case in distributed shared-memory multiprocessors, adaptive minimal and even nonminimal routing algorithms usually increase performance but the additional complexity introduced by the arrival of packets out of order may not be worth the additional performance. Additionally, as indicated above, if traffic locality is high, adaptive algorithms are not interesting at all.

For long messages that are not split into small packets, nonminimal routing algorithms are not interesting because bandwidth is wasted every time a long message reserves a nonminimal path. Note that this is not the case for short packets because misrouting is an alternative to waiting for a free minimal path and channels are reserved for a short period of time. However, profitable backtracking algorithms may outperform progressive algorithms when messages are long because they look for alternative minimal paths instead of waiting for a free channel. The main drawback of backtracking algorithms is the overhead produced by the circuits required to keep track of the header history, thus avoiding to search a path twice. Also, note that backtracking algorithms cannot be easily combined with wormhole or VCT switching. They are usually used on networks using some variant of circuit switching. As data does not follow the header immediately, some additional performance degradation is produced.

In summary, the optimal routing algorithm depends on traffic conditions. For uniform or local traffic, deterministic routing algorithms are the best choice. For irregular traffic or hot spots, adaptive routers usually outperform deterministic ones. However, as we will see in Chapter 9, the impact of the routing algorithm on performance is small when compared with other parameters like traffic characteristics.

4.12 Commented References

This chapter aims at describing the most interesting routing algorithms and design methodologies proposed up to now. References to the original work have been included along with the descriptions. Also, some proposals were presented in Chapter 3 while describing deadlock handling mechanisms. Although the number of routing algorithms proposed in the literature is very high, most of them have some points in common with other proposals. For example, several algorithms proposed in the literature [137, 330] are equivalent or very similar to those obtained by using Methodology 4.1. Other proposals tried to maximize adaptivity, very much like the algorithms proposed in Section 4.5.1. This is the case for the *mesh-route* algorithm proposed in [42]. Also, some proposals combine previously proposed methodologies in an interesting way. The *positive-first, negative-first* routing algorithm for 2-D meshes proposed in [343] combines two algorithms from the turn model in a balanced way, trying to distribute traffic more evenly.

A detailed description of every proposed routing algorithm is beyond the scope of this book. The interested reader can refer to [317] for a survey on multistage interconnection networks and to [262] for a brief survey on switch-based networks. Routing algorithms for direct interconnection networks are surveyed in [126, 241, 254]. These surveys mainly focus on distributed routing using wormhole switching. However, source routing and table-lookup routing are also covered in [254]. Additionally, backtracking protocols are covered in [126]. Nevertheless this chapter covers several proposals that have not been surveyed elsewhere.

EXERCISES

4.1 Indicate the information stored in the packet header for the paths shown in Figure 4.36 when the routing algorithm is implemented using street-sign routing.

Solution To implement the routing algorithm using street-sign routing, the packet header must encode the information indicated in Table 4.5 for the packet destined for node 10. Table 4.6 contains the corresponding information for the packet destined for node 8.

Table 4.5. Routing actions for the packet destined for node 10.

Node	Action
2	Turn right
10	Deliver

Table 4.6. Routing actions for the packet destined for node 8.

Node	Action
12	Turn right
8	Deliver

4.2 Indicate the destination interval for each channel in each node to implement XY routing using interval routing on a 4×4 mesh.

Solution It is possible to implement XY routing using interval routing. However, the implementation is somewhat tricky, and requires labeling the nodes in a different way. Figure 4.37 shows a different node labeling as well as the paths followed by two packets using XY routing. Table 4.7 shows the destination intervals for all the output channels in the network. The output channel has been indicated in the first column for all the nodes in each row. Empty boxes indicate that packets cannot use that channel (the channel does not exist). Note that intervals do not overlap. Also, the union of the intervals for all the output channels of each node is the whole set of nodes, excluding the current one.

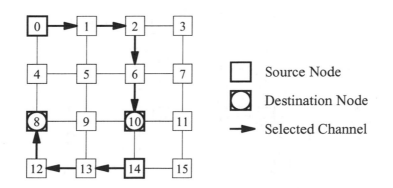

Figure 4.36. Node labeling and routing example for street-sign routing on a 2-D mesh.

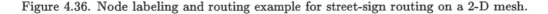

Table 4.7. Routing tables for the output channels in a 4 × 4 mesh.

Channel	Node	Interval	Node	Interval	Node	Interval	Node	Interval
$X+$	0	4–15	4	8–15	8	12–15	12	
$X-$	0		4	0–3	8	0–7	12	0–11
$Y-$	0	1–3	4	5–7	8	9–11	12	13–15
$X+$	1	4–15	5	8–15	9	12–15	13	
$X-$	1		5	0–3	9	0–7	13	0–11
$Y+$	1	0–0	5	4–4	9	8–8	13	12–12
$Y-$	1	2–3	5	6–7	9	10–11	13	14–15
$X+$	2	4–15	6	8–15	10	12–15	14	
$X-$	2		6	0–3	10	0–7	14	0–11
$Y+$	2	0–1	6	4–5	10	8–9	14	12–13
$Y-$	2	3–3	6	7–7	10	11–11	14	15–15
$X+$	3	4–15	7	8–15	11	12–15	15	
$X-$	3		7	0–3	11	0–7	15	0–11
$Y+$	3	0–2	7	4–6	11	8–10	15	12–14

4.3 Draw the channel dependency graph for dimension-order routing on a binary 3-cube.

Solution   Figure 4.38 shows the channel dependency graph for dimension-order routing on a 3-cube. This graph assumes that dimensions are crossed in decreasing order. Black circles represent the unidirectional channels and are labeled as cij, where i and j are the source and destination nodes, respectively. As a reference, channels are also represented by thin lines, horizontal and vertical ones corresponding to dimensions 0 and 1, respectively. Also, the nodes of the 3-cube have been labeled as nk, where k is the node number. Thick arrows represent channel dependencies. It can be seen that the graph is acyclic.

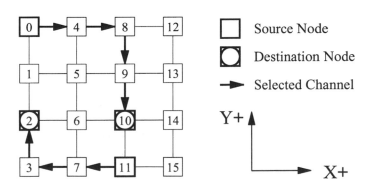

Figure 4.37. Node labeling and routing example for interval routing on a 2-D mesh.

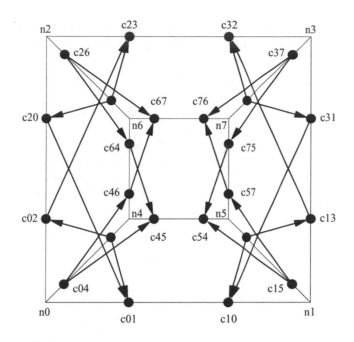

Figure 4.38. Channel dependency graph for dimension-order routing on a 3-cube.

4.4 Define a fully adaptive minimal routing algorithm for bidirectional k-ary n-cubes using Methodology 4.1.

Solution   For step 1, it is possible to use the deterministic routing algorithm proposed in Example 4.1. Although this algorithm was proposed for unidirectional k-ary n-cubes, extending it for bidirectional channels is straightforward. Simply, a similar routing algorithm is used for both directions of each ring. As packets only follow minimal paths, there is not any dependency between channels in one direction and channels in the opposite direction. Thus, the routing algorithm is deadlock-free.

Step 2 adds a new virtual channel to each physical channel (one in each direction). The new virtual channels can be used for fully adaptive minimal routing. The resulting routing algorithm is deadlock-free because the extended channel dependency graph has no cycles (drawing this graph is left as an exercise).

As a consequence of extending the routing algorithm for bidirectional rings, some virtual channels are never used and can be removed. This optimization was proposed in [24, 137]. However, this optimization requires the use of different routers depending on the position in the network. A more efficient optimization was proposed in [101]. Instead of using the routing algorithm described in Example 4.1 for step 1, it uses the routing algorithm proposed in Example 3.3 for unidirectional rings, extended for bidirectional k-ary n-cubes by using dimension-order routing. Again, step 2 adds a new virtual channel to each physical channel (one in each direction) that can be used for fully adaptive minimal routing. In this case, no optimization is required after applying Methodology 4.1 because the resulting routing algorithm uses all the virtual channels.

4.5 Consider the minimal-path west-first routing algorithm. Using the turn model, include as many 180-degree turns as possible and describe the resulting algorithm using pseudocode.

Solution   For each dimension, it is possible to include a single 180-degree turn. In dimension X, the only possible turn is from west to east. In dimension Y, there is a choice. Let us assume that the turn from north to south is allowed. Figure 4.39 shows the pseudocode for the resulting nonminimal west-first routing algorithm. It is assumed that the $Select()$ function uses a static priority to select channels. For the list of parameters of this function, priority decreases from left to right. By doing so, a higher priority is assigned to the channels belonging to minimal paths. Also, note that the routing function requires the use of the current input channel buffer $InChannel$ to select the output channel. This is necessary because a given packet may traverse a node twice.

PROBLEMS

4.1 The cube-connected cycle [283] can be defined as a binary hypercube of rings. It is an interconnection network based on the binary n-cube. Each node of a binary n-cube is replaced by an n-cycle, and the cube connection in the nth dimension is attached to the nth node in the cycle. Define a deterministic routing algorithm for the cube-connected cycle using the methodology proposed in Section 4.2.

4.2 The shuffle-exchange interconnection network [325] has two outgoing channels per node: a shuffle channel and an exchange channel. The shuffle channel from node n_i is connected to node n_j where the binary representation of j is the left rotation of the binary representation of i. The exchange channel from node n_i is connected to node n_k where the binary representations of i and k differ in the least significant bit. Define a deterministic routing algorithm for the shuffle-exchange network using the methodology proposed in Section 4.2.

4.3 Using the turn model, propose minimal-path partially adaptive routing algorithms for 3-D meshes that have as few routing restrictions as possible.

4.4 Apply Methodology 4.1 to design fully adaptive minimal routing algorithms for 2-D meshes, using the north-last, west-first and negative-first algorithms as the starting point (step 1). Verify whether the resulting algorithms are deadlock-free if wormhole switching is used.

4.5 Prove that the opt-y routing algorithm described in Section 4.5.1 is deadlock-free by drawing the extended channel dependency graph for a suitable routing subfunction and showing the absence of cycles.

Hint   The routing subfunction can be defined by restricting R to use channels X and $Y1$.

4.6 Show that Algorithm 1 in Section 4.5.2 is deadlock-free by using Theorem 3.1.

Hint   The routing subfunction R_1 can be defined as follows: When a packet is in an A queue and it is possible for it to move to the right along at least one dimension, R_1 supplies A queues that move the packet to the right. When a packet is in an A queue and it cannot move

Algorithm: Nonminimal West-First Algorithm for 2-D Meshes

Inputs: Coordinates of current node $(Xcurrent, Ycurrent)$
and destination node $(Xdest, Ydest)$,
and current input channel buffer $InChannel$

Output: Selected output $Channel$

Procedure:
$Xoffset := Xdest - Xcurrent; Yoffset := Ydest - Ycurrent;$
if $Xoffset < 0$ **then** $Channel := X-;$ **endif**
if $Xoffset > 0$ **and** $Yoffset < 0$ **then**
    if $InChannel = X-$ **then** $Channel := \text{Select}(Y-, X+, Y+, X-);$
    else if $InChannel = Y-$ **then** $Channel := \text{Select}(Y-, X+);$
    else if $InChannel = Y+$ **then** $Channel := \text{Select}(Y-, X+, Y+);$
    else $Channel := \text{Select}(Y-, X+, Y+);$
    endif
endif
if $Xoffset > 0$ **and** $Yoffset > 0$ **then**
    if $InChannel = X-$ **then** $Channel := \text{Select}(Y+, X+, Y-, X-);$
    else if $InChannel = Y-$ **then** $Channel := \text{Select}(X+, Y-);$
    else if $InChannel = Y+$ **then** $Channel := \text{Select}(Y+, X+, Y-);$
    else $Channel := \text{Select}(Y+, X+, Y-);$
    endif
endif
if $Xoffset > 0$ **and** $Yoffset = 0$ **then**
    if $InChannel = X-$ **then** $Channel := \text{Select}(X+, Y-, Y+, X-);$
    else if $InChannel = Y-$ **then** $Channel := \text{Select}(X+, Y-);$
    else if $InChannel = Y+$ **then** $Channel := \text{Select}(X+, Y+, Y-);$
    else $Channel := \text{Select}(X+, Y-, Y+);$
    endif
endif
if $Xoffset = 0$ **and** $Yoffset < 0$ **then**
    if $InChannel = X-$ **then** $Channel := \text{Select}(Y-, X-, Y+);$
    else if $InChannel = Y-$ **then** $Channel := Y-;$
    else if $InChannel = Y+$ **then** $Channel := \text{Select}(Y-, Y+);$
    else $Channel := \text{Select}(Y-, Y+);$
    endif
endif
if $Xoffset = 0$ **and** $Yoffset > 0$ **then**
    if $InChannel = X-$ **then** $Channel := \text{Select}(Y+, X-);$
    else $Channel := Y+;$
    endif
endif
if $Xoffset = 0$ **and** $Yoffset = 0$ **then** $Channel := Internal;$ **endif**

Figure 4.39. The nonminimal west-first routing algorithm for 2-D meshes.

to the right, R_1 supplies the B queue at current node. When a packet is in a B queue and it is possible for it to move to the left along at least one dimension, R_1 supplies B queues that move the packet to the left. When a packet is in a B queue and it cannot move to the left, R_1 supplies the C queue at current node. When a packet is in a C queue and it has not arrived at its destination, R_1 supplies C queues that move the packet to the inside. Obviously, when a packet has arrived at its destination, R_1 supplies no external channel.

4.7 Show that Algorithm 2 in Section 4.5.2 is deadlock-free by using Theorem 3.1.

Hint   The routing subfunction R_1 can be defined as follows: When a packet is in an injection, A or B queue and it is possible for it to move to the inside along at least one dimension, R_1 supplies channels containing B queues. When a packet is in an injection, A or B queue and it can only move to the outside, R_1 supplies channels containing C queues. When a packet is in a C queue and it is possible for it to move to the outside along at least one dimension, R_1 supplies channels containing C queues. When a packet is in a C queue and it can only move to the inside, R_1 supplies channels containing D queues. When a packet is in a D queue and it has not arrived at its destination, R_1 supplies channels containing D queues. Obviously, when a packet is in any queue and it has arrived at its destination, R_1 supplies no external channel.

Chapter 5

Collective Communication Support

Historically, the programmer of a distributed-memory multiprocessor has invoked various system primitives to send messages among processes executing on different nodes, resulting in a *message-passing* program. In order to simplify the programmer's task and improve code portability, an alternative approach has been pursued whereby a sophisticated compiler generates data movement operations from shared-memory parallel programs. In order to support a portable and scalable software design across different platforms, the *data parallel programming* model, which is characterized by executing the same program on different processors with different data, is considered the most promising programming model for multicomputers. Several data parallel languages have been proposed, including Fortran D [114], Vienna Fortran [356], Distributed Fortran 90 [236], Cray MPP Fortran [271], CM Fortran [339], and High Performance Fortran (HPF) [152].

These languages support a variety of global data movement and process control operations. Such operations include replication, reduction, segmented scan, and permutation. Data movement operations are often applied to different dimensions of data arrays. *Replication* is needed in sending a single datum to many other processors for use in a computation. For example, in Gaussian elimination, a copy of pivot element must be sent to all the processors to which the pivot row is distributed. *Reduction* is the opposite of replication and may be used to implement such functions as array summation and to determine the maximum and minimum values of an array. *Segmented scan* operations are useful for solving linear algebra problems using representations of sparse matrices, such as banded and tridiagonal matrices. Parallel prefix is a special case of segmented scan, which is useful for solving dense linear algebra problems. *Permutation* involves rearrangement of data for different purposes, such as transposing a matrix, rotating data blocks, and exchanging data in certain dimensions [271]. In addition to data manipulation operations, control operations, such as barrier synchronization and global conditionals, are an essential part of data parallel programming [340, 354].

Example 5.1

The following Gaussian elimination example illustrates the use of several data parallel operations. The algorithm is used in solving the equation $Ax = b$, where A is an $n \times n$ matrix and x and b are n-element vectors. For efficient data manipulation, in addition to storing the matrix A in `A[1:N,1:N]`, the vector b is stored in `A[1:N,N+1]`, and the vector x is stored in `A[0,1:N]`. The following code segment, based on a pseudo-high-level data parallel language, demonstrates one approach to solving the problem.

```
S1:  DO I=1,N
S2:     MAX(A[I,I:N], VAL, LOC)
S3:     EXCHANGE(A[O:N,I],A[O:N,LOC])
S4:     A[I,I:N+1]=A[I,I:N+1]/A[I,I]
S5:     DO J=I+1,N
S6:       DO K=I+1,N+1
S7:         A[J,K]=A[J,K]-A[J,I]*A[I,K]
S8:       ENDDO
S9:     ENDDO
S10: ENDDO
```

Although the above code is by no means optimal parallel code, it serves to show how the data parallel operations mentioned above are fundamental to parallel programming. The function MAX in statement S2 is a reduction operation, which finds the location of the pivot element. The function EXCHANGE in S3 is a permutation operation, which exchanges the i-th column and the column with the pivot element. S4 performs row-wise normalization with respect to the pivot element. Since one operand has a higher dimension than the other operand, a replication operation of the lower dimension data is implied. Using data dependence analysis, both loops in S5 and S6 can be parallelized. Furthermore, in S7 the replication of A[J,I] and A[I,K] across multiple processors is implied because one of the dimensions is not a function of the loop indices. The ENDDO statements in S8 and S9 imply barrier synchronization when the corresponding DO is parallelized.

The above operations which involve global data movement and global control are known as *collective communication* as many processes are collectively involved in performing such operations. As indicated in [115], many scientific applications exhibit the need of such communication patterns, and providing collective communication services can simplify the programming of multicomputers. Details of those frequently used collective communication operations will be described in the next section. This chapter will emphasize on efficient support, both hardware and software, for implementing multicast communication, which is essential to the efficient implementation of collective communication operations.

5.1 Collective Communication Services

Collective communication involves a group of processes. In order to simplify the programming and allow for efficient implementation, these communicating processes are usually defined within a context called *process group*. A unique group ID is associated with each distinct process group. Members of a process group may not be fixed. During different phases of a computation, new members may be added to the process group and old members may be removed from the process group.

Various collective communication services have been identified for processes within a process group. Providing such services can simplify the programming effort and facilitate efficient implementation. Consider a process group, G, with n processes, $P_1, P_2, \ldots, P_n$. We assume that all processes will involve in collective communication although it is possible that some processes are disabled or masked off from participation. Four basic types of collective communication services within the context of a process group are described below.

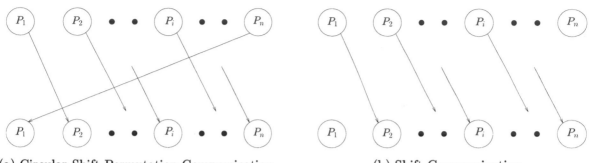

(a) Circular Shift Permutation Communication.　　(b) Shift Communication.

Figure 5.1. Two multiple one-to-one communication patterns.

5.1.1　Multiple One-to-One Communication

In this category, each process can send at most one message and receive at most one message. If each process has to send exactly one message and receive exactly one message, there are $n!$ different permutation or communication patterns. Figure 5.1a shows a circular shift communication pattern in which P_i sends a message to P_{i+1} for $1 \leq i \leq n-1$ and P_n delivers its message to P_1. In some applications, with no need of wraparound, a shift communication pattern can be supported in which P_1 only sends a message, and P_n only receives a message as shown in Figure 5.1b.

5.1.2　One-to-All Communication

In one-to-all communication, one process is identified as the sender (or called *root*) and all processes in the group are receivers. There are some variations. In some design, the sender may or may not be a member of the process group. Also, if the sender is a member of the process group, it may or may not be a receiver. Here we assume that the sender is a member of the process group and itself is also a receiver. There are two distinct services in this category.

- *Broadcast.* The same message is delivered from the sender to all receivers.

- *Scatter.* The sender delivers different messages to different receivers. This is also referred to as *personalized broadcast.*

Figure 5.2 shows the communication patterns of these two services.

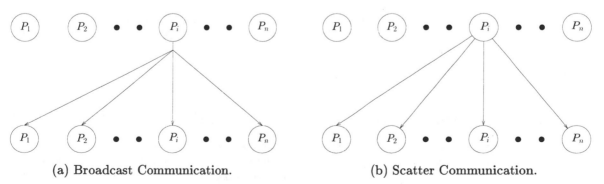

(a) Broadcast Communication.　　(b) Scatter Communication.

Figure 5.2. Two one-to-all communication patterns.

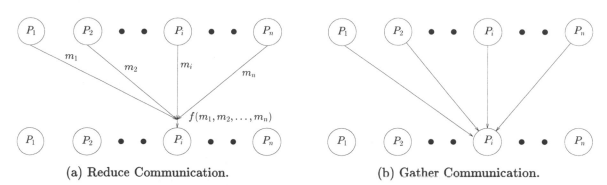

(a) Reduce Communication.   (b) Gather Communication.

Figure 5.3. Two all-to-one communication patterns.

5.1.3   All-to-One Communication

In all-to-one communication, all processes in a process group are senders and one process (or called *root*) is identified as the sole receiver. Again, there are two distinct services.

- *Reduce.* Different messages from different senders are combined together to form a single message for the receiver. The combining operator is usually commutative and associative, such as addition, multiplication, maximum, minimum, and logical OR, AND, exclusive OR operators. This service is also referred to as *personalized combining* or *global combining*.

- *Gather.* Different messages from different senders are concatenated together for the receiver. The order of concatenation is usually dependent on the ID of the senders.

Figure 5.3 shows the communication patterns of these two services.

5.1.4   All-to-All Communication

In all-to-all communication, all processes in a process group perform their own one-to-all communication. Thus, each process will receive n messages from n different senders in the process group. Again, there are two distinct services.

- *All_Broadcast.* All processes perform their own broadcast. Usually, the received n messages are concatenated together based on the ID of the senders. Thus, all processes have the same set of received messages. This service is also referred to as *gossiping* or *total-exchange*.

- *All_Scatter.* All processes perform their own scatter. The n concatenated messages are different for different processes. This service is also referred to as *personalized all-to-all broadcast*, *index*, or *complete-exchange*.

Figure 5.4 shows the communication patterns of these two services.

5.1.5   Convenient Collective Communication Services

In addition to the four basic types of collective communication services, some collective communication services require the combination of these basic services. Some of these frequently used collective communication services, referred to as *convenient* or *composite* collective communication services, are listed below.

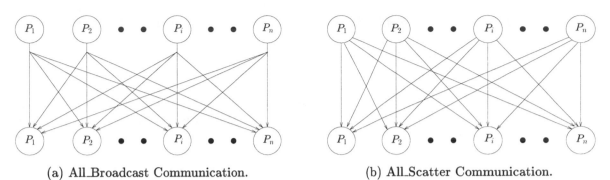

(a) All_Broadcast Communication.   (b) All_Scatter Communication.

Figure 5.4. Two all-to-all communication patterns.

- *All combining.* The result of a *reduce* operation is available to all processes. This is also referred to as *reduce and spread* operation. The result may be broadcast to all processes after the reduce operation, or multiple reduce operations are performed with each process as a root.

- *Barrier synchronization.* A synchronization barrier is a logical point in the control flow of an algorithm at which all processes in a process group must arrive before any of the processes in the group are allowed to proceed further. Obviously, barrier synchronization involves a reduce operation followed by a broadcast operation.

- *Scan.* A scan operation performs a *parallel prefix* with respect to a commutative and associative combining operator on messages in a process group. Figure 5.5a shows a parallel prefix operation in a four-member process group with respect to the associative combining operator f. Apparently, a scan operation involves many reduce operations. The reverse (or downward) of parallel prefix is called *parallel suffix* as shown in Figure 5.5b.

Collective communication services are demanded in many scientific applications. Such services have been supported by several communication packages for multicomputers. However, efficient implementation of various collective communication services is machine-dependent. The next section will describe system support for collective communication.

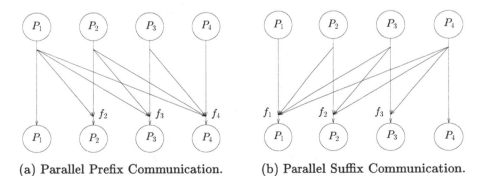

(a) Parallel Prefix Communication.   (b) Parallel Suffix Communication.

Figure 5.5. Scan communication patterns.

5.2   System Support for Collective Communication

From the programmer's perspective, collective communication services are provided in the context of a process group. In a multicomputer, each individual application is usually allocated with a subset of processors, called a *processor cluster*, in order to achieve the best performance (the performance may be degraded when more processors are allocated due to increased penalty from communication overhead) and to increase the system throughput. The scheduling of processors in a multicomputer should carefully consider the trade-off between space sharing and time sharing, which is beyond the scope of this book.

From the viewpoint of system or processors, a process group only involves a subset of processors as shown in Figure 5.6 with two process groups. The four processes of process group 1 are assigned to four different processors, so are the three processes in process group 2. Process 2 from group 1 and process 0 from group 2 share the same processor.

Obviously, as indicated in Figure 5.6, the "*all*" communication in a process group becomes the "*many*" communication, which involves an arbitrary subset of processors, from the system's point of view. In order to efficiently support collective communication, it is desirable that at the processor level the system can support "one-to-one" (unicast), "one-to-many," "many-to-one," and "many-to-many" communication primitives in hardware. All multiprocessors directly support various forms of unicast communication, such as blocking versus nonblocking, synchronous versus asynchronous, and direct remote memory access. One-to-many communication, mainly in the form of *multicast* in which the same message is delivered to those destinations, has received attention. Some vendors are aware of the importance of collective communication and have facilitated it by implementing broadcast and multicast support in hardware, such as nCUBE-2, or by implementing barrier synchronization in hardware, such as Cray T3D. However, in many-to-one and many-to-many communication, the

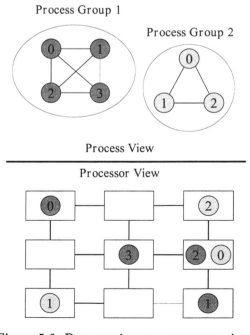

Figure 5.6. Process view vs. processor view.

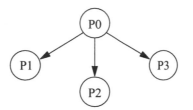

Figure 5.7. A multicast communication pattern with three destinations.

multiple senders may start at a different time. Thus, certain combining and buffering mechanisms are required to efficiently support such service. This may be expensive in hardware design.

In the remainder of this chapter we will mainly focus on the efficient implementation of multicast, both hardware and software, in parallel computers. We will also describe some hardware approaches designed to support barrier synchronization, reduction, and global combining.

5.3 Preliminary Considerations

5.3.1 The Need for Multicast Communication

Figure 5.7 shows a multicast communication pattern with three destinations, where process $P0$ has to send the same message to three processes: $P1$, $P2$, and $P3$ (here each process is assumed to reside in a separate node).

If multicast communication primitives are not supported, the program structure of the communication pattern in Figure 5.7 is shown below.

```
P0: ......        P1: ......        P2: ......        P3: ......
    send(msg,P1)      ......            ......            ......
    send(msg,P2)      recv(msg,P0)      recv(msg,P0)      recv(msg,P0)
    send(msg,P3)      ......            ......            ......
```

As shown above, a multicast communication can be supported by many one-to-one communications. Assume that both **send** and **recv** are blocking operations. If $P0$ is executing **send(msg,P1)**, and $P1$ has not yet executed the **recv** statement, $P0$ is blocked. Meanwhile, $P2$ is executing the **recv** statement and is blocked because $P0$ has not yet executed the statement **send(msg,P2)**. Obviously, system resources are wasted due to the unnecessary blocking. Because of the nondeterministic and asynchronous properties of multicomputers, there is no way for $P0$ to predetermine a proper message-passing sequence. However, if $P0$ executed a single **multicast(msg,P1,P2,P3)** statement instead of three **send** statements, $P2$ would proceed as soon as it executed the **recv** statement.

Even if operations are not blocking, providing multicast operations may reduce communication latency considerably. In current multicomputers, software overhead accounts for a high percentage of communication latency [214]. Thus, replacing several **send** operations by a single **multicast** operation reduces software overhead. Therefore, supporting collective communication operations in software is useful even if those operations are not supported in hardware.

Furthermore, when a node sends the same message toward several destinations some of these replicated messages may traverse the same communication channels, creating more traffic than needed, as shown in the next example.

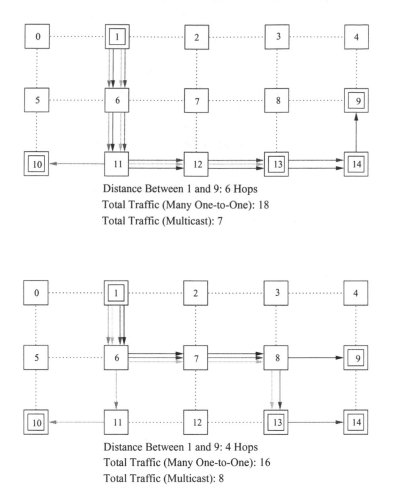

Figure 5.8. Different ways to perform multicast in a mesh network.

Example 5.2

Figure 5.8 shows different ways to perform multicast in a 3×5 mesh network. Node 1 wants to deliver the same message to nodes 9, 10, 13, and 14. Depending on the path followed, the total traffic in the network has different values. As shown in the figure, traffic can be considerably reduced by supporting multicast in hardware because the message is transmitted only once across each channel in the path.

The main problem here is that of determining which path(s) should be used to deliver a message from the source to all its destination(s). Since there are potentially many paths joining pairs of nodes in a parallel computer, different routes can be found depending on the criteria employed.

5.3.2   Evaluation Criteria

Two major routing design parameters are *traffic* and *time*. For a given multicast communication, the parameter "traffic" is quantified in the number of channels used to deliver the source message to all its destinations. This parameter takes into account the repeated use of some channels. The parameter "time" is the message communication latency. In an asynchronous multiprocessing environment, time should be considered from the destination node point of view because the receiving process can continue its execution as soon as the message is received. It is desirable to develop a routing mechanism that completes communication while minimizing both traffic and time. However, these two parameters are not, in general, totally independent; achieving a lower bound for one may prevent us from achieving the other. As illustrated in Figure 5.8, if multicast communication is supported, multiple messages traversing a channel can be reduced to one message transmission. Figure 5.8 shows two possible multicast communication patterns. In Figure 5.8a, the total traffic created is 7; while in Figure 5.8b, it is increased to 8. However, the distance between nodes 1 and 9 is reduced from 6 to 4.

The communication latency is dependent on the underlying switching technique. For SAF switching, the communication latency is linearly proportional to the number of channels between two nodes. Thus, the parameter time is usually represented by the number of channels traversed. In this case, minimizing time implies that for each destination node, the message should be delivered through a shortest path to that destination. In wormhole switching, the communication latency is almost independent of the number of hops between two nodes if there is no contention in the channels. However, deadlock-free routing becomes a critical issue.

An important metric used to evaluate a network is its communication latency, which is the sum of three component values: *start-up latency*, *network latency*, and *blocking time*. The *start-up latency*, T_s, is the time required for message framing/unframing, memory/buffer copying, validation, and so on, at both source and destination nodes. The start-up latency is mainly dependent on the design of system software within the nodes and the interface between nodes and routers. The *network latency* equals the elapsed time after the head of a message has entered the network at the source until the tail of the message emerges from the network at the destination. Given a source and destination node, the start-up and network latencies are static values, frequently used to characterize contention-free networks. The *blocking time* includes all possible delays encountered during the lifetime of a message. These delays are mainly due to conflicts over the use of shared resources, for example, a message encountering a busy channel or a full buffer. Blocking time reflects the dynamic behavior of the network due to the passing of multiple messages, and may be high if the network traffic is heavy or unevenly distributed.

Multicast latency refers to the elapsed time from when the source sends out its first copy of the message until the last destination has received its copy of the message. Multicast latency can be critical to program speed-up because, as in the case of barrier synchronization and data replication, the multicast operation may be performed in the serial component of the parallel algorithm.

5.4   Models for Multicast Communication

We shall use graphs to model the underlying topology of multicomputers. Let graph $G(V, E)$ denote a graph with node set V and edge set E. When G is known from context, the sets $V(G)$ and $E(G)$ will be referred to as V and E, respectively. A *path* with length n is a sequence of edges $e_1, e_2, \ldots, e_n$ such that

1. $e_i \neq e_j$ if $i \neq j$.

2. e_i and e_{i+1} have a common end-node.

3. If e_i is not the first or last edge, then it shares one of its end-nodes with e_{i-1} and the other with e_{i+1}.

Suppose $e_i = (v_i, v_{i+1})$ for $1 \leq i \leq n$. In the following discussion, a path with length n will be represented by its node visiting sequence $(v_1, v_2, \ldots, v_n, v_{n+1})$. A *cycle* is a path whose starting and ending nodes are the same, i.e., $v_1 = v_{n+1}$. Furthermore, we assume that for every pair of nodes in the path except v_1 and v_{n+1} are different. A graph is said to be *connected* if every pair of its nodes are joined by a path. A *tree* is a connected graph which contains no *cycles*. A graph $F(V, E)$ is a *subgraph* of another graph $G(V, E)$, if $V(F) \subseteq V(G)$ and $E(F) \subseteq E(G)$. A subgraph which is a tree is referred to as a *subtree*. For a pair of nodes u, v in $V(G)$, $d_G(u, v)$ denotes the length (the number of edges) of a shortest path from u to v in G.

The interconnection topology of a multicomputer is denoted by a host graph $G(V, E)$, where each vertex in V corresponds to a node and each edge in E corresponds to a communication channel (link). For a multicast communication, let u_0 denote the source node and $u_1, u_2, \ldots, u_k$ denote k destination nodes, where $k \geq 1$. The set $K = \{u_0, u_1, \ldots, u_k\}$, which is a subset of $V(G)$, is called a *multicast set*. Depending on the underlying communication paradigm and the routing method, the multicast communication problem in a multicomputer can be formulated as different graph theoretical problems.

Multicast Path Problem

In some communication mechanisms, replication of an incoming message in order to be forwarded to multiple neighboring nodes may involve too much overhead and is usually undesirable. Thus, the routing method does not allow each processor to replicate the message passing by. Also, a multicast path model provides better performance than the tree model (to be described below) when there is contention in the network. From switching technology point of view, the multicast path model is more suitable for wormhole switching.

The multicast communication problem becomes the problem of finding a shortest path starting from u_0 and visiting all k destination nodes. This optimization problem is the finding of an *optimal multicast path* (OMP) and is formally defined below.

Definition 5.1 *A multicast path* $(v_1, v_2, \ldots, v_n)$ *for a multicast set K in G is a subgraph $P(V, E)$ of G, where $V(P) = \{v_1, v_2, \ldots, v_n\}$ and $E(P) = \{(v_i, v_{i+1}) : 1 \leq i \leq n - 1\}$, such that $v_1 = u_0$ and $K \subseteq V(P)$. An OMP is a multicast path with the shortest total length.*

Multicast Cycle Problem

Reliable communication is essential to a message-passing system. Usually, a separate acknowledgment message is sent from every destination node to the source node on receipt of a message. One way to avoid the sending of $|K|$ separate acknowledgment messages is to have the source node itself receive a copy of the message it initiated after all destination nodes have been visited. Acknowledgments are provided in the form of error bits flagged by intermediate nodes when a transmission error is detected. Thus, the multicast communication problem is the problem of finding a shortest cycle, called *optimal multicast cycle* (OMC) for K.

Definition 5.2 *A multicast cycle* $(v_1, v_2, \ldots, v_n, v_1)$ *for K is a subgraph $C(V, E)$ of G, where $V(C) = \{v_1, v_2, \ldots, v_n\}$ and $E(C) = \{(v_n, v_1), (v_i, v_{i+1}) : 1 \leq i \leq n - 1\}$, such that $K \subseteq V(C)$. An OMC is a multicast cycle with the shortest total length.*

Steiner Tree Problem

Both OMC and OMP assume that the message will not be replicated by any node during transmission. However, message replication can be implemented by using some hardware approach [197]. If the major concern is to minimize traffic, the multicast problem becomes the well-known *Steiner tree* problem [122]. Formally, we restate the Steiner tree problem as follows.

Definition 5.3 *A Steiner tree, $S(V, E)$, for a multicast set K is a subtree of G, such that $K \subseteq V(S)$. A minimal Steiner tree (MST) is a Steiner tree with a minimal total length.*

Multicast Tree Problem

In the Steiner tree problem, it is not necessary using a shortest path from the source to a destination. If the distance between two nodes is not a major factor to the communication time, such as in VCT, wormhole, and circuit switching, the above optimization problem is appropriate. However, if the distance is a major factor to the communication time, such as in SAF switching, then we may like to minimize time first, then traffic. The multicast communication problem is then modeled as an *optimal multicast tree* (OMT). The OMT problem was originally defined in [195].

Definition 5.4 *An OMT, $T(V, E)$, for K is a subtree of G such that (a) $K \subseteq V(T)$, (b) $d_T(u_0, u_i) = d_G(u_0, u_i)$, for $1 \leq i \leq k$, and (c) $|E(T)|$ is as small as possible.*

The above graph optimization problems can be stated as follows:

> *Given a host graph G, a multicast set K, and an integer ℓ, does there exist an OMP (OMC, MST, OMT) for K with total length less than or equal to ℓ?*

Apparently, the complexity of each of the above optimization problems is directly dependent on the underlying host graph. The above graph optimization problems for the popular hypercube and 2-D mesh topologies were studied in [210, 212], showing that the OMC and OMP problems are NP-complete for those topologies. Also, it was shown that the MST and OMT problems are NP-complete for the hypercube topology [60, 136]. The MST problem for the 2-D mesh topology is equivalent to the *rectilinear Steiner tree* problem, which is NP-complete [121].

The NP completeness results indicate the necessity to develop heuristic multicast communication algorithms for popular interconnection topologies. Multicast communication may be supported in hardware, software, or both. Sections 5.5 and 5.7 will address hardware and software implementations, respectively, of multicast.

5.5 Hardware Implementations of Multicast

Hardware support of multicast communication in multicomputers requires increased functionality within the routers. This functionality may include interpretation of multicast addresses (or group ID) and forwarding of messages onto multiple outgoing channels (replication). The result is the capability for one local processor to efficiently send the same message to a specific set of destinations without requiring assistance from any other processor. The approaches used to implement such functionality are highly dependent on the network topology and may affect the design of the switching strategy used in the network. Before studying those approaches, some schemes to encode multiple destination addresses are described in the next section.

5.5.1   Multiaddress Encoding Schemes

The header of multidestination messages must carry the addresses of the destination nodes. The header information is an overhead to the system, increasing message latency and reducing the effective network bandwidth. A good multiaddress encoding scheme should minimize the message header length, also reducing the header processing time.

In wormhole and VCT switching, the routing algorithm is executed before the whole message arrives at the router. As the header may require several flits to encode the destination addresses, it is desirable that the routing decision in each router could be made as soon as possible to reduce message latency. Ideally, a message header should be processed on the fly as header flits arrive. When the number of destination addresses is variable, it is inefficient to use a counter to indicate the number of destinations. Such a counter should be placed at the beginning of a message header. Since the value of the counter may be changed at a router if the destination set is split into several subsets, it would prevent the processing of message headers on the fly. An alternative approach is to have an *end-of-header* (EOH) flit to indicate the end of a header. Another approach consists of using 1 bit in each flit to distinguish between header and data flits.

Figure 5.9 shows five different encoding schemes, namely, *all-destination* encoding, *bit string* encoding, *multiple-region broadcast* encoding, *multiple-region stride* encoding, and *multiple-region bit string* encoding. These schemes were proposed in [54].

The all-destination encoding is a simple scheme in which all destination addresses are carried by the header. This encoding scheme has two important advantages. First, the same routing hardware used for unicast messages can be used for multidestination messages. Second, the message header can be processed on the fly as address flits arrive. This scheme is good for a small number of addresses because the header length is proportional to the number of addresses. However, it produces a significant overhead when the number of destinations is large.

One way to limit the size of the header is to encode destination addresses as a bit string, where each bit corresponds to a destination ranged between node b and node e, as shown in Figure 5.9b.

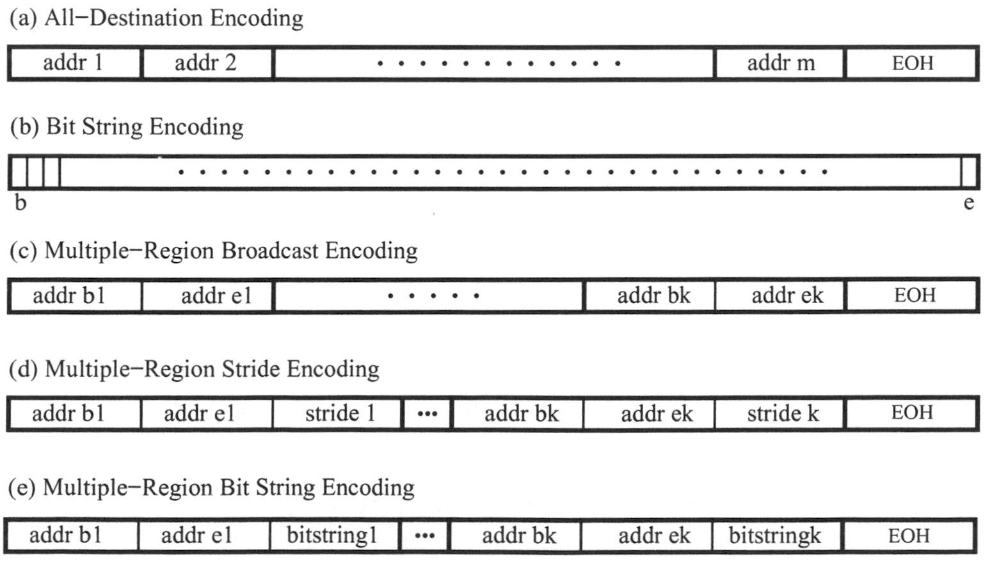

(a) All–Destination Encoding

| addr 1 | addr 2 | • • • • • • • • • • • | addr m | EOH |

(b) Bit String Encoding

| | | | | • | |
b   e

(c) Multiple–Region Broadcast Encoding

| addr b1 | addr e1 | • • • • • | addr bk | addr ek | EOH |

(d) Multiple–Region Stride Encoding

| addr b1 | addr e1 | stride 1 | ••• | addr bk | addr ek | stride k | EOH |

(e) Multiple–Region Bit String Encoding

| addr b1 | addr e1 | bitstring1 | ••• | addr bk | addr ek | bitstringk | EOH |

Figure 5.9. Multiaddress encoding schemes.

Since the length of the string in a system is predefined, the EOH field is not required. This encoding scheme is good when the average number of destinations is large. However, it is inefficient when the system is large and the number of destinations is small. The main drawback of the bit string encoding scheme is that a router usually has to buffer the entire bit string in order to make the routing decision and to generate the output bit string(s). Additionally, address decoding cannot be done with the same routing hardware as for unicast messages. Finally, the length of the string usually depends on network size, limiting the scalability of the system.

The remaining encoding schemes try to optimize the header length by considering ranges of addresses or *regions*. In Figure 5.9c, each region is specified by two fields: the beginning and ending addresses of the region. Within each region, the message is broadcast to all the addresses in the range. In some applications, a node may send a message to a set of destination addresses that have a constant distance between two adjacent addresses. A suitable encoding scheme for those applications consists of adding a stride to the definition of each region, as shown in Figure 5.9d. Finally, if the destination addresses are irregularly distributed but can be grouped into regions, each region can be specified by a bit string, in addition to the beginning and ending addresses (see Figure 5.9e). The main drawback of encoding schemes based on regions is that the routing hardware required to decode addresses is complex. Also, several header flits may be required to encode each region. Those flits should reach the router before starting a routing operation.

5.5.2 Tree-Based Multicast Routing

One approach to multicast routing is to deliver the message along a common path as far as possible, then replicate the message and forward each copy on a different channel bound for a unique set of destination nodes. The path followed by each copy may further branch in this manner until the message is delivered to every destination node. In such *tree-based* routing, the destination set is partitioned at the source, and separate copies are sent on one or more outgoing links. A message may be replicated at intermediate nodes and forwarded along multiple outgoing links toward disjoint subsets of destinations. The destination nodes can be either leaf nodes or intermediate nodes in the tree. In this approach, each node in the network should be able to replicate messages by sending copies out through different output channels. Message replication can be easily done by software in networks using SAF switching. This has been the traditional approach to support collective communication. Hardware replication of messages is much more complex, being suitable for networks using VCT or wormhole switching.

In order to replicate messages, the routing hardware requires several changes with respect to the router model described in Section 2.1. We assume that each destination address is encoded in a different flit, and that each message contains a set of destination address flits followed by data flits. Also, we assume that a single bit is used in each flit to distinguish between destination addresses and data flits. All the address flits are routed at each intermediate node, either reserving a new output channel or being transmitted through a previously reserved channel. Some status registers are required at the routing and arbitration unit to keep track of all the output channels reserved a message arriving on a given input channel. Once all the address flits have been routed, incoming data flits are simultaneously forwarded to all the output channels previously reserved by the address flits. Note that if the switch is a crossbar and it is implemented as a set of multiplexors (one for each switch output), it is possible to select the same input from several outputs. Therefore, the switch can be easily configured so that flits are simultaneously forwarded to several output channels from the same input channel. However, flow control is more complex than in unicast routing. Flit acknowledgment signals returned across all the output channels reserved by a message must be AND-ed because flits can only be forwarded when all the routers that should receive them have

---

Algorithm: Broadcast Tree for Hypercubes
  Input: s is the source node and v is the local node.
  Procedure:

  1. Let $d = v \oplus s$.

  2. Let $k = \text{FirstOne}(d)$.

  3. If $k = 0$, then exit.

  4. For $i = k - 1$ to 0, send a copy of the message to the neighboring node $v \oplus 2^i$ through the ith dimension output channel.

Figure 5.10. The broadcast algorithm for hypercubes.

confirmed buffer availability. Finally, the delivery buffer at each router should be designed in such a way that flits containing destination addresses are automatically discarded.

Although this section focuses on hardware support of multicast communication, we first describe a simple algorithm for broadcasting in hypercubes. This algorithm can be either implemented in hardware or software. It will serve to illustrate some drawbacks of tree-based multicast routing.

Broadcast Tree for Hypercube

Consider an n-cube topology. An original version of the following broadcast algorithm, which produces a *spanning binomial tree* based on the concept of recursive doubling, was proposed by Sullivan and Bashkow [333]. Each node in the system will receive the broadcast message exactly once and in no later than n time steps. Let s be the address of the source node and v be the node receiving a broadcast message. The broadcast algorithm is listed in Figure 5.10.

The function $\text{FirstOne}(v)$ indicates the location of the least significant 1 in an n-bit binary number v. If $v_k = 1$, and $v_j = 0$ for all $0 \le j \le k - 1$, then $\text{FirstOne}(v) = k$. If $v = 0$, then $k = n$.

Example 5.3

Figure 5.11 shows a broadcast tree rooted at node 0000 in a 4-cube. The numbers between square brackets indicate the time step for the corresponding message transmission.

Deadlock in Tree-Based Multicast Wormhole Switching

The spanning binomial tree is suitable for networks supporting SAF or VCT switching techniques. When combined with wormhole switching, tree-based multicast routing suffers from several drawbacks. Since there is no message buffering at routers, if one branch of the tree is blocked, then all are blocked (Figure 5.12). For the sake of clarity, input and output buffers in the figure have capacity for a single flit. Flit A at node $N5$ cannot advance because the next requested channel is busy. As a consequence, flit C cannot be replicated and forwarded to node $N5$. Blockage of any branch of the tree can prevent delivery of the message even to those destination nodes to which paths have been successfully established. For example, flits A and B at nodes $N3$ and $N2$ can advance and reach the destination node $N4$. However, flits at node $N1$ cannot advance. Tree-based multicast

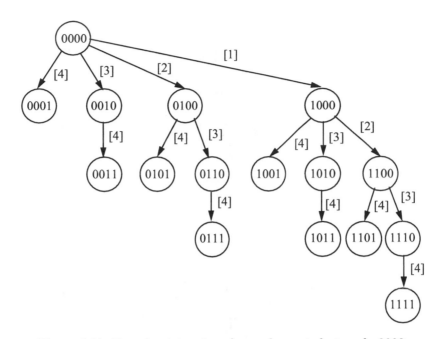

Figure 5.11. Broadcast tree in a four-cube rooted at node 0000.

routing may cause a message to hold many channels for extended periods, thereby increasing network contention. Moreover, deadlock can occur using such a routing scheme. The nCUBE-2 [247], a wormhole-switched hypercube, uses a spanning binomial tree approach to support broadcast and a restricted form of multicast in which the destinations form a subcube.

Figure 5.13 shows a deadlocked configuration on a 3-cube. Suppose that nodes 000 and 001 simultaneously attempt to transmit broadcast messages $M0$ and $M1$, respectively. The broadcast message $M0$ originating at host 000 has acquired channels $[000, 001]$, $[000, 010]$, and $[000, 100]$. The header flit has been duplicated at router 001 and is waiting on channels $[001, 011]$ and $[001, 101]$. The $M1$ broadcast has already acquired channels $[001, 011]$, $[001, 101]$, and $[001, 000]$ but is waiting on channels $[000, 010]$ and $[000, 100]$. The two broadcasts will block forever.

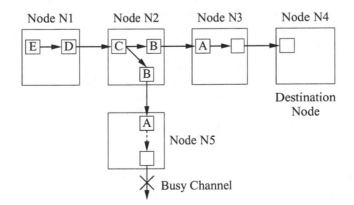

Figure 5.12. Message blocking in tree-based multicast routing.

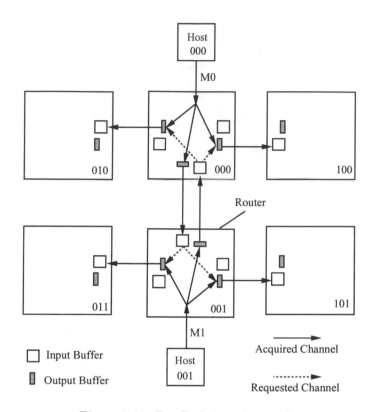

Figure 5.13. Deadlock in a three-cube.

In a similar manner, one may attempt to extend deadlock-free unicast routing on a 2-D mesh to encompass multicast. An extension of the XY routing method to include multicast is shown in Figure 5.14, in which the message is delivered to each destination in the manner described. As in the hypercube example, the progress of the tree requires that all branches be unblocked. For example, suppose that the header flit in Figure 5.14 is blocked due to the busy channel $[(4, 2), (4, 3)]$. Node $(4, 2)$ cannot buffer the entire message. As a result of this constraint, the progress of messages in the entire routing tree must be stopped. In turn, other messages requiring segments of this tree are also blocked. Network congestion may be increased, thereby degrading the performance of the network. Moreover, this routing algorithm can lead to deadlock. Figure 5.15 shows a deadlocked configuration with two multicasts, $M0$ and $M1$.

In Figure 5.15a, $M0$ has acquired channels $[(1, 1), (0, 1)]$ and $[(1, 1), (2, 1)]$, and requests channel $[(2, 1), (3, 1)]$, while $M1$ has acquired channels $[(2, 1), (3, 1)]$ and $[(2, 1), (1, 1)]$, and requests channel $[(1, 1), (0, 1)]$. Figure 5.15b shows the details of the situation for the nodes $(0, 1)$, $(1, 1)$, $(2, 1)$, and $(3, 1)$. Because neither node $(1, 1)$ nor node $(2, 1)$ buffers the blocked message, channels $[(1, 1), (0, 1)]$ and $[(2, 1), (3, 1)]$ cannot be released. Deadlock has occurred.

The next section presents a multicast wormhole routing algorithm based on the concept of network partitioning, which is equivalent to the concept of virtual networks presented in Section 4.4.3. A multicast operation is implemented as several submulticasts, each destined for a proper subset of the destinations and each routed in a different subnetwork. Because the subnetworks are disjoint and acyclic, no cyclic resource dependency can exist. Thus, the multicast routing algorithms are deadlock-free.

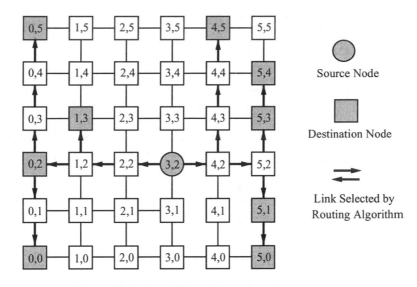

Figure 5.14. An *XY* multicast routing pattern.

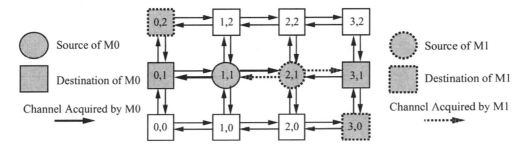

(a) Two Multicasts in Deadlock

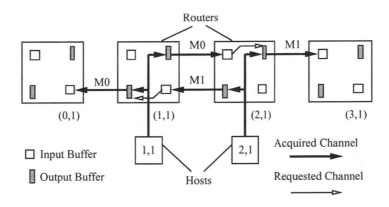

(b) Detailed Representation

Figure 5.15. A deadlock situation in a 3 × 4 mesh.

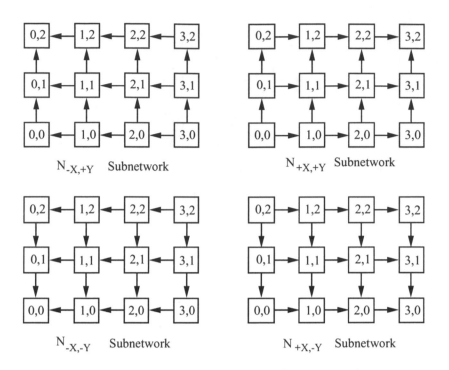

Figure 5.16. Network partitioning for 3×4 mesh.

Double-Channel XY Multicast Wormhole Routing

The following double-channel XY multicast routing algorithm for wormhole switching was proposed by Lin, McKinley, and Ni [206] for 2-D mesh.

The algorithm uses an extension of the XY routing algorithm, which was shown above to be susceptible to deadlock. In order to avoid cyclic channel dependencies, each channel in the 2-D mesh is doubled, and the network is partitioned into four subnetworks, $N_{+X,+Y}, N_{+X,-Y}, N_{-X,+Y}$, and $N_{-X,-Y}$, as in Section 4.4.3. Subnetwork $N_{+X,+Y}$ contains the unidirectional channels with addresses $[(i,j),(i+1,j)]$ and $[(i,j),(i,j+1)]$, subnetwork $N_{+X,-Y}$ contains channels with addresses $[(i,j),(i+1,j)]$ and $[(i,j),(i,j-1)]$, and so on. Figure 5.16 shows the partitioning of a 3×4 mesh into the four subnetworks.

For a given multicast, the destination node set D is divided into at most four subsets, $D_{+X,+Y}$, $D_{+X,-Y}$, $D_{-X,+Y}$, and $D_{-X,-Y}$ according to the relative positions of the destination nodes and the source node u_0. Set $D_{+X,+Y}$ contains the destination nodes to the upper right of u_0, $D_{+X,-Y}$ contains the destinations to the lower right of u_0, and so on.

The multicast is thus partitioned into at most four submulticasts from u_0 to each of $D_{+X,+Y}$, $D_{+X,-Y}$, $D_{-X,+Y}$, and $D_{-X,-Y}$. The submulticast to $D_{+X,+Y}$ will be implemented in subnetwork $N_{+X,+Y}$ using XY routing, $D_{+X,-Y}$ in subnetwork $N_{+X,-Y}$, and so on. The message routing algorithm is given in Figure 5.17. Example 5.4 illustrates the operation of the algorithm.

Example 5.4

Consider the 6×6 mesh given in Figure 5.14. At the source node $(3,2)$, the destination set
$$D = \{(0,0),(0,2),(0,5),(1,3),(4,5),(5,0),(5,1),(5,3),(5,4)\}$$

Algorithm: Double-Channel XY Routing for Subnetwork $N_{+X,+Y}$
Input: Destination set D', $D'=D_{+X,+Y}$, local address $v = (x,y)$;
Procedure:

1. If $x < \min \{x_i | (x_i, y_i) \in D'\}$, the message and the list D' are sent to node $(x+1, y)$. Stop.

2. If $(x,y) \in D'$, then $D' \leftarrow D' - \{(x,y)\}$ and a copy of the message is sent to the local node.

3. Let $D'_Y = \{(x_i, y_i) | x_i = x, (x_i, y_i) \in D'\}$. If $D'_Y \neq \emptyset$, the message and the list D'_Y are sent to node $(x, y+1)$; If $D' - D'_Y \neq \emptyset$, the message and the list $D' - D'_Y$ are sent to node $(x+1, y)$.

Figure 5.17. Double-channel XY routing algorithm.

is divided into four subsets

$D_{+X,+Y} = \{(4,5), (5,3), (5,4)\}$,
$D_{+X,-Y} = \{(5,0), (5,1)\}$,
$D_{-X,+Y} = \{(0,5), (1,3)\}$, and
$D_{-X,-Y} = \{(0,0), (0,2)\}$.

The message will be sent to the destinations in $D_{+X,+Y}$ through subnetwork $N_{+X,+Y}$, to the nodes in $D_{+X,-Y}$ using subnetwork $N_{+X,-Y}$, to the nodes in $D_{-X,+Y}$ using subnetwork $N_{-X,+Y}$, and to the nodes in $D_{-X,-Y}$ using subnetwork $N_{-X,-Y}$, respectively. The routing pattern is shown with solid arrows in Figure 5.18.

While this multicast tree approach avoids deadlock, a major disadvantage is the need for double channels. It may be possible to implement double channels with virtual channels, however, the signaling for multicast communication is more complex. Moreover, the number of subnetworks grows exponentially with the number of dimensions of the mesh, increasing the number of channels between every pair of nodes accordingly.

Tree-Based Multicast with Pruning

As mentioned in Section 5.5.2, tree-based multicast routing is more suitable for SAF or VCT switching than for wormhole switching. The reason is that when a branch of the tree is blocked, the remaining branches cannot advance if wormhole switching is used. There is a special case in which tree-based multicast routing is suitable for networks using wormhole switching: the implementation of invalidation or update commands in DSMs with coherent caches [224]. Taking into account the growing interest on these machines, it is worth studying this special case.

Message data only require a few flits. Typically, a single 32-bit flit containing a memory address is enough for invalidation commands. The command itself can be encoded in the first flit together with the destination node address. An update command usually requires one or two additional flits to carry the value of the word to be updated. Hence, it is possible to design compact hardware routers with buffers deep enough to store a whole message. However, when multicast routing is considered, the message header must encode the destination addresses. As a consequence, message size could be several times the data size. Moreover, messages have a very different size depending

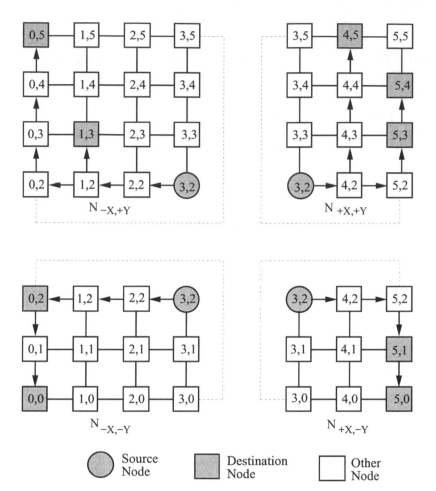

Figure 5.18. The routing pattern of the double-channel XY multicast tree.

on the number of destinations, therefore preventing the use of fixed-size hardware buffers to store a whole message. A possible solution consists of encoding destination addresses as a bit string (see Section 5.5.1) while limiting the number of destination nodes that can be reached by each message to a small value. This approach will be studied in Section 5.6 and applied to the implementation of barrier synchronization and reduction.

An alternative approach consists of using a fixed-size *input buffer* for flit pipelining (as in wormhole switching) and a small fixed-size *data buffer* to store the whole message data (as in VCT switching, except that destination addresses are not stored) [224]. This approach combines the advantages of wormhole switching and VCT switching. Its most important advantage is that a fixed and small buffer size is required for every channel, regardless of the number of destinations of the message. As a consequence, routers are compact and fast. As buffers are small, flits containing the destination addresses cannot be buffered at a single node, usually spanning several nodes. The main limitation of this mechanism is that it only works when message data can be completely buffered at each node.

In order to allow data flits to be buffered at a given node even when the next channel requested by the message is busy, a special message format is used. Figure 5.19 shows the format of a multicast

| d_n | ... | d_2 | Data | d_1 |

Figure 5.19. Message format for tree-based multicast routing.

message. The first flit of each message, d_1, encodes the first destination address. It is followed by the data flits of the message, and the remaining destination addresses, $d_2, d_3, \ldots, d_n$. As we will see, this message format will be kept while the message advances and produces new branches.

The architecture of a router supporting the message format described above is very similar to the one described in Section 5.5.2 for tree-based multicast routing. However, it requires a few changes. When the first flit of a message reaches a node, it is routed as usually, reserving the requested output channel if it is free. The next few flits contain the message data. As these flits arrive, they are copied to the *data buffer* of the input channel and transferred across the switch. The remaining flits, if any, contain additional destination addresses. These flits are routed in the same way as the first flit of the message. If the output channel requested by a destination address flit d_i was already reserved by a previously routed flit d_j, $1 \leq j < i$, then d_i is simply forwarded across the switch. Otherwise, d_i reserves a new output channel. In this case, d_i is forwarded across the switch, immediately followed by the message data flits previously stored in the data buffer. By doing so, the message forwarded across the new branch conforms to the format indicated in Figure 5.19. While data flits are being appended to the new branch of the message, incoming address flits are stored in the input buffer. Note that data only require a few flits. Also, routing each additional destination address flit d_i can be done in parallel with the transmission of d_{i-1} across the switch.

As indicated in Section 5.5.2, tree-based multicast routing is susceptible to deadlock. However, when message data only require a few flits, deadlock can be recovered from by pruning branches from the tree when a branch is blocked [224]. This mechanism relies on the use of data buffers to hold the message data, as described above. As shown in Figure 5.12, when a channel is busy, flit buffers are filled and flow control propagates backward, reaching the source node n_b of the branch. When this occurs, flits cannot be forwarded across any branch of the tree starting at n_b. The pruning mechanism consists of pruning all the branches of the tree at n_b except the one that was blocked. Pruning is only performed at the source node of the blocked branch. However, if flow control continues stopping flits at other nodes, pruning is also performed at those nodes.

Note that when using the described pruning mechanism, each pruned branch contains a message according to the format described in Figure 5.19. In particular, that message carries one or more destination address flits and all the data flits. Also, after pruning a branch it is possible to resume message transmission toward the remaining destination nodes because the data buffer contains a copy of all the data flits of the message.

The basic idea behind the pruning mechanism is that, once a tree has been completely pruned, the corresponding multicast message becomes a set of multiple unicast messages. Assuming that the base routing function for unicast routing is deadlock-free, multicast routing is also deadlock-free. However, not all the branches of a blocked tree need to be pruned. A deadlocked configuration requires a set of messages, each one waiting for a resource held by another message in the set. Therefore, only branches that cannot forward flits need to be pruned. Note that a branch may be unable to forward flits because another branch was blocked (see Figure 5.12). Moreover, it is useless to prune a blocked branch because flits will not be able to advance. As a result, pruning is only performed on branches that cannot forward flits but will be able to forward them as soon as they are pruned. By doing so, pruned branches will advance, freeing resources that may be needed by blocked branches of other multicast messages.

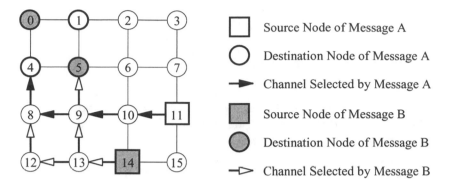

Figure 5.20. Deadlock recovery by pruning branches in tree-based multicast routing.

Example 5.5

Figure 5.20 shows an example of deadlock recovery by pruning branches in tree-based multicast routing. The routing algorithm is *XY* routing. As can be seen, message *A* cannot proceed because channel [9, 5] was previously reserved by message *B*. Similarly, message *B* cannot proceed because channel [8, 4] was previously reserved by message *A*. When node 9 routes the flit of message *A* containing the address of node 1, it finds that there is no free output channel for it. Then, a pruning of all the other branches of message *A* is performed at this node. In this case, the branch destined for node 4 is pruned, so that it can freely advance toward its destination. Such a pruning will release channels [9, 8] and [8, 4], which is blocking message *B*. Then, message *B* will advance, eventually releasing channel [9, 5], which is requested by message *A*. As a result, deadlock has been recovered from. In the event that flow control stopped the advancing of flits at node 13, message *B* would also prune its branch destined for node 5. This pruning is redundant but it shows that nodes performing a pruning do not need to synchronize.

Note that this example of deadlock recovery only serves to illustrate the pruning mechanism. It would not produce pruning in a real network unless the network were larger and each message would be destined for several additional nodes. The reason is that pruning would only take place at node 9 if there were more destination address flits in message *A* after the one destined for node 1. Similarly, pruning could only take place at node 13 if message *B* contained enough destination address flits to fill the buffers at nodes 8 and 12.

Tree-Based Multicast on Multistage Networks

The most natural way of implementing multicast/broadcast routing in multistage interconnection networks (MINs) is by using tree-based routing. Multicast can be implemented in a single pass through the network by simultaneously forwarding flits to several outputs at some switches. Broadcast can be implemented in a single pass by simultaneously forwarding flits to all the outputs at all the switches traversed by a message.

The replication of messages at some switches can be *synchronous* or *asynchronous*. In synchronous replication, the branches of a multidestination message can only forward if all the requested output channels are available. Hence, at a given time, all the message headers are at different switches of the same stage of the network. Synchronous replication requires a complex hardware signaling

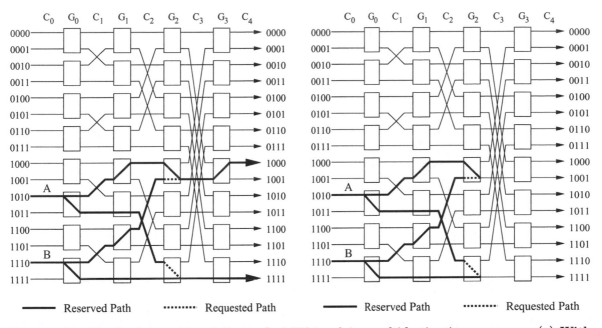

Figure 5.21. Deadlock in a 16-node butterfly MIN involving multidestination messages: (a) With asynchronous message replication. (b) With synchronous message replication.

mechanism, usually slowing down flit propagation. In asynchronous replication, each branch can forward independently without coordinating with other branches. As a consequence, hardware design is much simpler. However, bubbles may arise when some requested output channels are not available. The reason is that branches finding a free output channel are able to advance while branches finding a busy output channel are blocked. A similar situation for direct networks was shown in Figure 5.12.

The propagation of multidestination messages may easily lead to deadlock, regardless of whether synchronous or asynchronous message replication is performed, as shown in the following example.

Example 5.6

Figure 5.21a shows a deadlocked configuration in a 16-node butterfly MIN using asynchronous message replication. Figure 5.21b shows the same deadlocked configuration when messages are replicated synchronously. In each figure, two multidestination messages A and B, destined for nodes 1000 and 1111, are sent by nodes 1010 and 1110, respectively (see Example 4.7 to see how these messages are routed). In Figure 5.21a, the upper branch of message A successfully reserved the required output channel at stage G_2, proceeding toward node 1000. However, the upper branch of message B is blocked at stage G_2, requesting the same channel previously reserved by message A. On the other hand, the lower branch of message A is blocked at stage G_2, requesting a channel previously reserved by the lower branch of message B. The situation in Figure 5.21b is identical, except that the branches that successfully reserved the required output channels do not forward because all the branches of each tree must forward synchronously. Note that all the branches reached stage G_2 at the same time, and are routed simultaneously. However, the situation depicted in Figure 5.21b may occur depending on the priority of input channels at each switch.

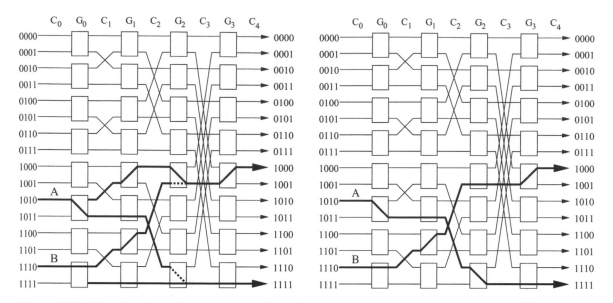

Figure 5.22. Pruning branches to recover from deadlock in a 16-node butterfly MIN: (a) Messages A and B detected at stage G_0 that one of their branches is blocked, pruning the branch that is not blocked. (b) The pruned branches have released the channels they were occupying and the blocked branches are able to proceed.

The tree-based multicast mechanism with pruning described in Section 5.5.2 and the associated message format also work on MINs. Indeed, that mechanism was first developed for MINs, and then adapted to direct networks. The behavior of the pruning mechanism is more intuitive when applied to a MIN, as can be seen in Example 5.7. Note that pruning a single branch from each deadlocked configuration is enough to recover from deadlock. However, switches would have to synchronize. Additionally, recovery from deadlock is faster if all the switches detecting blocked branches perform a pruning operation.

Example 5.7

Consider the deadlocked configuration shown in Figure 5.21a. Flow control propagates backward, stopping flit advance for the blocked branches at stages G_2, G_1, and G_0. As a consequence, the branch of message A that is not blocked is pruned at stage G_0. Similarly, the branch of message B that is not blocked is also pruned at stage G_0. The pruned branches advance, as shown in Figure 5.22a. Once the pruned branches have released the output channels they were occupying at stage G_2, the blocked branches are able to proceed reserving channels, as shown in Figure 5.22b. Note that in this example, the blocked branches have the same destinations as the pruned branches.

Alternative approaches have been proposed in [55, 321]. In [55], a scheme with synchronous replication of multidestination messages that uses a deadlock avoidance scheme at each intermediate switch has been proposed. This scheme is the only one up to now that has been developed for MINs using pure wormhole switching. However, this scheme is complex and requires considerable hardware support. In [321], deadlock is simply avoided by using VCT switching. However, this approach requires the use of buffers deep enough to store whole messages, including destination

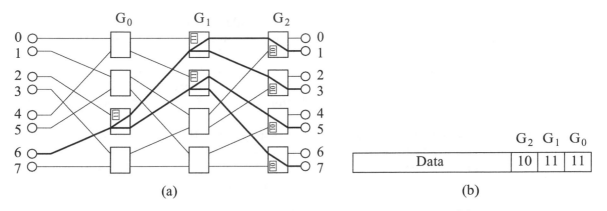

Figure 5.23. Multicast on multistage networks using multiport encoding: (a) Path followed by a multidestination message. (b) Message format using multiport encoding.

addresses. Therefore, this approach requires more buffering capacity than the pruning mechanism described in Section 5.5.2.

In order to alleviate the overhead of encoding many destination addresses, a multiport encoding mechanism has been proposed in [321]. In a MIN with n stages and $k \times k$ switches, this encoding requires n k-bit strings, one for each stage. Each k-bit string indicates the output ports to which the message must be forwarded at the corresponding switch. A 1 in the ith position of the k-bit string denotes that the message should be forwarded to output port i. Figure 5.23b shows an example of message format using multiport encoding. Figure 5.23a shows the path followed by this message when it is injected at node 6. The main drawback of this encoding scheme is that the same jth k-bit string must be used at all the switches in stage j that route the message. For example, in Figure 5.23a, all the switches in stage G_2 forward the message to the lower output of the switch. As a consequence, several passes through the network are usually required to deliver a message to a given destination set. However, the number of passes decreases beyond a certain number of destinations [321]. In particular, broadcast requires a single pass. So, this encoding scheme and the multicast mechanism proposed in [321] are more appropriate when the number of destinations is very high. For a small number of destinations, the message format and the pruning mechanism described in Section 5.5.2 usually perform better, also requiring smaller buffers. Anyway, the main limitation of both techniques is that message length is limited by the buffer capacity.

5.5.3 Path-Based Multicast Communication

To support deadlock-free multicast or broadcast wormhole routing, the tree-like communication pattern does not perform well unless messages are very short because the entire tree is blocked if any of its branches is blocked. A solution is to prohibit branching at intermediate nodes, leading to a multicast path pattern. To reduce the length of the multicast path, the destination node set can be divided into several disjoint subsets and send a copy of the source message down several separate multicast paths, each path for each subset of the destination nodes. This multidestination routing scheme will be referred to as *path-based* routing.

In path-based routing, the header of each copy of a message consists of multiple destinations. The source node arranges these destinations as an ordered list, depending on their intended order of traversal. As soon as the message is injected into the network, it is routed based on the address in the leading header flit corresponding to the first destination. Once the message header reaches the router of the first destination node, the flit containing this address is removed by the router. Now the message is routed to the node whose address is contained in the next header flit. This address corresponds to the second destination in the ordered list. While the flits are being forwarded by the router of the first destination node to its adjacent router, they are also copied flit by flit to the delivery buffer of this node. This process is carried out in each intermediate destination node of the ordered list. When the message reaches the last destination node, it is not routed any further and is completely consumed by that node.

The routing hardware requires a few changes with respect to the router model described in Section 2.1 to support path-based routing. We assume that each destination address is encoded in a different flit. Also, we assume that a single bit is used in each flit to distinguish between destination addresses and data flits. Some control logic is required to discard the current destination address and transmit the next destination flit to the routing and arbitration unit. Sending a single clock pulse to the corresponding input channel buffer so that flits advance one position is enough to discard the previous destination address. Then, the routing and arbitration unit is reset so that it looks for a destination address flit at the header of a buffer and starts a routing operation again. Also, note that if the switch is a crossbar and it is implemented as a set of multiplexors (one for each switch output), it is possible to select the same input from several outputs. Therefore, the switch can be easily configured so that flits are simultaneously forwarded to the next router and copied to the delivery buffer of the current node. Finally, the delivery buffer should be designed in such a way that flits containing destination addresses are automatically discarded and no flow control is required. This is to avoid conflicts with flow control signals from the next node when messages are simultaneously forwarded to the next router and copied to the delivery buffer.

A simple analysis shows that the probability that a message is blocked in path-based routing is lower than that for tree-based routing. Suppose that the probability that a message is blocked in each channel is p. Assume that at certain level of the tree-based routing the total number of branches is k. The tree requires all k channels be available at the same time. The probability that a message is blocked at this level would be $1 - (1-p)^k$. On the other hand, the probability of blocking for path-based routing is p since each multicast path only requests one channel at one moment. An important property of path-based routing is that, when one path is blocked, it will not block the message delivery on the other paths. For example, consider a 6-cube and suppose that p is 0.1. The second level of the broadcast routing tree has 6 branches. The probability that a message is blocked at this level is $1 - (1 - 0.1)^6$, which is 0.47, while the probability is only 0.1 for path-based routing.

On the other hand, path-based routing requires establishing an ordered list of destination addresses for each copy of a message. However, tree-based routing does not require any ordering among destinations. In many cases, the ordered destination list(s) can be computed at compile time. In some other cases, the compiler does not help because messages are dynamically generated by hardware. For example, messages are generated by the cache controller in distributed shared-memory multiprocessors (DSM) with coherent caches. In this case, a clever organization of the cache directory may considerably reduce the time required to prepare the ordered destination list [70]. Finally, when the list of destinations has to be explicitly ordered for each multidestination message, path-based routing should be the preferred over tree-based routing only if the additional cost of computing the ordered destination list(s) is compensated by a reduction in message latency.

In order to reduce the number of channels used for a given multicast, the subpath between the source and one of the destinations in a multicast path is not necessarily in a shortest path. Therefore, in path-based routing the average distance between the source and each destination is generally longer than that of tree-based routing. Note that in wormhole switching the network latency is almost independent of the length of a path. Moreover, path-based routing does not require replicating messages at each intermediate node, implying a less complex router.

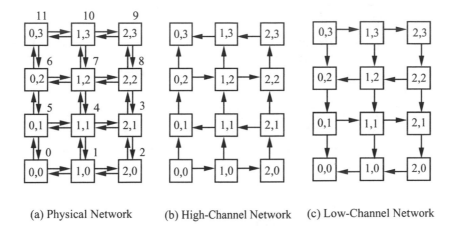

(a) Physical Network   (b) High-Channel Network   (c) Low-Channel Network

Figure 5.24. The labeling of a 4×3 mesh.

Routing Function Based on Hamiltonian Paths

A suitable network partitioning strategy for path-based routing is based on Hamiltonian paths. A *Hamiltonian path* visits every node in a graph exactly once [147]; a 2-D mesh has many Hamiltonian paths. Thus, each node u in a network is assigned a label, $\ell(u)$. In a network with N nodes, the assignment of the label to a node is based on the position of that node in a Hamiltonian path, where the first node in the path is labeled 0 and the last node in the path is labeled $N-1$. Figure 5.24a shows a possible labeling in a 4×3 mesh, in which each node is represented by its integer coordinate (x, y). The labeling effectively divides the network into two subnetworks. The *high-channel subnetwork* contains all of the channels whose direction is from lower-labeled nodes to higher-labeled nodes, and the *low-channel subnetwork* contains all of the channels whose direction is from higher-labeled nodes to lower-labeled nodes.

Unicast as well as multicast communication will use the labeling for routing. That is, a unicast message will follow a path based on the labeling instead of using XY routing. If the label of the destination node is greater than the label of the source node, the routing always takes place in the high-channel network; otherwise, it will take the low-channel network.

The label assignment function ℓ for a $m \times n$ mesh can be expressed in terms of the x and y coordinates of nodes as

$$\ell(x, y) = \begin{cases} yn + x & \text{if } y \text{ is even} \\ yn + n - x - 1 & \text{if } y \text{ is odd} \end{cases}$$

Let V be the node set of the 2-D mesh. The first step in finding a deadlock-free multicast algorithm for the 2-D mesh is to define a routing function $R : V \times V \to V$ that uses the two subnetworks in such a way as to avoid channel cycles. One such routing function, defined for a source node u and destination node v, is defined as $R(u, v) = w$, such that w is a neighboring node of u and,

$$\ell(w) = \begin{cases} \max\{\ell(z) : \ell(z) \le \ell(v) \text{ and } z \text{ is a neighboring node of } u\} & \text{if } \ell(u) < \ell(v) \\ \min\{\ell(z) : \ell(z) \ge \ell(v) \text{ and } z \text{ is a neighboring node of } u\} & \text{if } \ell(u) > \ell(v) \end{cases}$$

Given a source and a destination node, it can be observed from Figure 5.24 that a message is always routed along a shortest path. This is important because the same routing function is used for

Algorithm: Message Preparation for the Dual-Path Routing Algorithm
Input: Destination set D, local address u_0, and node label assignment function ℓ;
Output: Two sorted lists of destination nodes: D_H and D_L placed in message header.
Procedure:

1. Divide D into two sets D_H and D_L such that D_H contains the destination nodes with higher ℓ value than $\ell(u_0)$ and D_L the nodes with lower ℓ value than $\ell(u_0)$.

2. Sort the destination nodes in D_H, using the ℓ value as the key, in ascending order. Sort the destination nodes in D_L, using the ℓ value as the key, in descending order.

3. Construct two messages, one containing D_H as part of the header and the other containing D_L as part of the header.

Figure 5.25. Message preparation for the dual-path routing algorithm.

unicast and multicast communication. It was proved in [211] that for two arbitrary nodes u and v in a 2-D mesh, the path selected by the routing function R is a shortest path from u to v. Furthermore, if $\ell(u) < \ell(v)$, then the nodes along the path are visited in increasing order. If $\ell(u) > \ell(v)$, then the nodes along the path are visited in decreasing order. However, if the Hamiltonian path is defined in a different way, unicast communication may not follow shortest paths.

Next, two path-based multicast routing algorithms that use the routing function R are defined [211]. In these two algorithms, the source node partitions the set of destinations according to the subnetworks and sends one copy of the message into each subnetwork that contains one or more destinations. The message visits destination nodes sequentially according to the routing function R.

Dual-Path Multicast Routing

The first heuristic routing algorithm partitions the destination node set D into two subsets, D_H and D_L, where every node in D_H has a higher label than that of the source node u_0, and every node in D_L has lower label than that of u_0. Multicast messages from u_0 will be sent to the destination nodes in D_H using the high-channel network and to the destination nodes in D_L using the low-channel network.

The message preparation algorithm executed at the source node of the dual-path routing algorithm is given in Figure 5.25. The destination node set is divided into the two subsets, D_H and D_L, which are then sorted in ascending order and descending order, respectively, with the label of each node used as its key for sorting. Although the sorting algorithm may require $O(|D| \log |D|)$ time, it often need be executed only once for a given set of destinations, the cost being amortized over multiple messages. In fact, for algorithms with regular communication patterns, it may be possible to do the sorting at compile time. The path routing algorithm, shown in Figure 5.26, uses a distributed routing method. Upon receiving the message, each node first determines whether its address matches that of the first destination node in the message header. If so, the address is removed from the message header and the message is delivered to the host node. At this point, if the address field of the message header is not empty, the message is also forwarded toward the first destination node in the message header using the routing function R. It was proved in [211] that the dual-path multicast routing algorithm is deadlock-free.

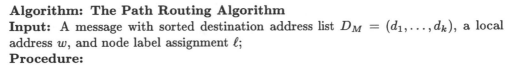

Algorithm: The Path Routing Algorithm

Input: A message with sorted destination address list $D_M = (d_1, \ldots, d_k)$, a local address w, and node label assignment ℓ;

Procedure:

1. If $w = d_1$, then $D'_M = D_M - \{d_1\}$ and a copy of the message is forwarded to the local node; otherwise, $D'_M = D_M$.

2. If $D'_M = \emptyset$, then terminate the message transmission.

3. Let d be the first address in D'_M, and let $w' = R(w, d)$.

4. The message is sent to node w' with address destination list D'_M in its header.

Figure 5.26. The path routing algorithm.

Example 5.8

Figure 5.27 shows an example of dual-path multicast routing in a 6×6 mesh. Each node x is labeled with $\ell(x)$ and its integer coordinates. First, the destination set is divided into two sets D_H and D_L at source node $(3, 2)$, with $D_H = \{(5, 3), (1, 3), (5, 4), (4, 5), (0, 5)\}$ and $D_L = \{(0, 2), (5, 1), (5, 0), (0, 0)\}$. Then, two copies of the message are sent along the paths shown in the figure. Note that the path between consecutive destinations is always minimal. However, the path may not be minimal when destinations are not consecutive.

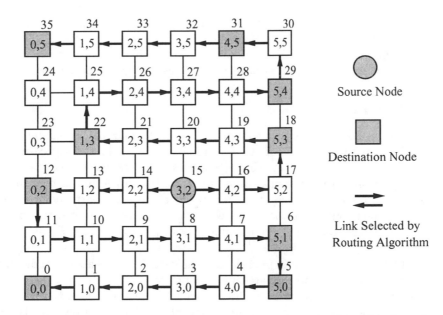

Figure 5.27. An example of dual-path multicast routing in a 6×6 mesh.

Algorithm: Message Preparation for the Multipath Routing Algorithm
Input: Destination set D, local address $u_0 = (x_0, y_0)$, and node assignment ℓ;
Output: Sorted destination node lists $D_{H1}, D_{H2}, D_{L1}, D_{L2}$ for four multicast paths.
Procedure:

1. Divide D into two sets D_H and D_L such that D_H contains the destination nodes with higher ℓ value than $\ell(u_0)$ and D_L the nodes with lower ℓ value than $\ell(u_0)$.

2. Sort the destination nodes in D_H, using the ℓ value as the key, in ascending order. Sort the destination nodes in D_L, using the ℓ value as the key, in descending order.

3. (Assume that $v_1 = (x_1, y_1)$ and $v_2 = (x_2, y_2)$ are the two neighboring nodes to u_0 with higher labels than that of u_0.)
   Divide D_H into two sets, D_{H1} and D_{H2} as follows:
   $D_{H1} = \{(x, y) | x \leq x_1 \text{ if } x_1 < x_2, \ x \geq x_1 \text{ if } x_1 > x_2\}$ and
   $D_{H2} = \{(x, y) | x \leq x_2 \text{ if } x_2 < x_1, \ x \geq x_1 \text{ if } x_2 > x_1\}$.
   Construct two messages, one containing D_{H1} as part of the header and send the message to v_1, and the other containing D_{H1} as part of the header and send the message to v_2.

4. Similarly, partition D_L into D_{L1} and D_{L2} and construct two messages.

Figure 5.28. Message preparation for the multipath routing algorithm.

The performance of the dual-path routing algorithm is dependent on the distribution of destination nodes in the network. The total number of channels used to deliver the message in Example 5.8 is 33 (18 in the high-channel network and 15 in the low-channel network). The maximum distance from the source to a destination is 18 hops. In order to reduce the average length of multicast paths and the number of channels used for a multicast, an alternative is to use a multipath multicast routing algorithm, in which the restriction of having at most two paths is relaxed.

Multipath Multicast Routing

In a 2-D mesh, most nodes have outgoing degree 4, so up to four paths can be used to deliver a message, depending on the locations of the destinations relative to the source node. The only difference between multipath and dual-path routing concerns message preparation at the source node. Figure 5.28 gives the message preparation of the multipath routing algorithm, in which the destination sets D_H and D_L of the dual-path algorithm are further partitioned. The set D_H is divided into two sets, one containing the nodes whose x coordinates are greater than or equal to that of u_0 and the other containing the remaining nodes in D_H. The set D_L is partitioned in a similar manner.

The rules by which ties are broken in partitioning the destination nodes depends on the location of the source node in the network and the particular labeling method used. For example, Figure 5.29a shows the partitioning of the destinations in the high-channel network when the source is the node labeled with 15. When the node labeled 8 is the source, the high-channel network is partitioned as shown in Figure 5.29b.

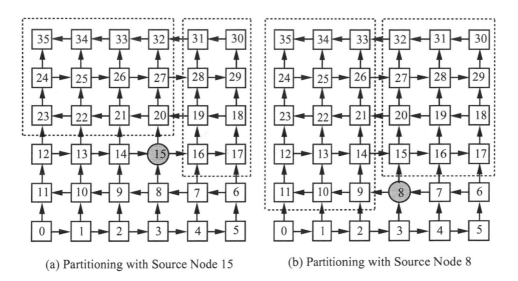

(a) Partitioning with Source Node 15 (b) Partitioning with Source Node 8

Figure 5.29. Multipath destination address partitioning.

Example 5.9

Figure 5.30 shows an example of multipath multicast routing in a 6×6 mesh. The source node and the destination set are the same as in Figure 5.27. The destination set is first divided into two sets D_H and D_L at source node $(3, 2)$, with $D_H = \{(5, 3), (1, 3), (5, 4), (4, 5), (0, 5)\}$ and $D_L = \{(0, 2), (5, 1), (5, 0), (0, 0)\}$. D_H is further divided into two subsets D_{H1} and D_{H2} at Step 3, with $D_{H1} = \{(5, 3), (5, 4), (4, 5)\}$ and $D_{H2} = \{(1, 3), (0, 5)\}$. D_L is also divided into $D_{L1} = \{(5, 1), (5, 0)\}$ and $D_{L2} = \{(0, 2), (0, 0)\}$. Then, the multicast is performed using four multicast paths, as shown in Figure 5.30. In this example, multipath routing requires only 21 channels, and the maximum distance from the source to destination is 6 hops.

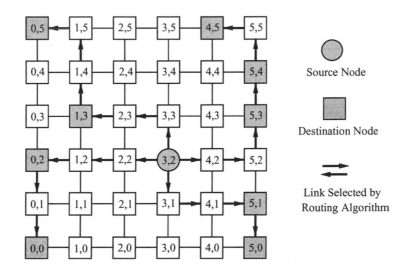

Figure 5.30. An example of multipath multicast routing in a 6×6 mesh.

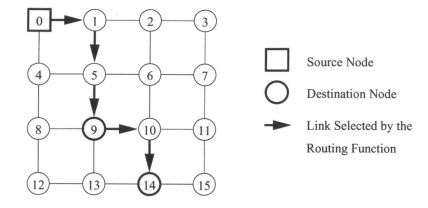

Figure 5.31. Multicast routing on a 2-D mesh with XY routing.

Example 5.9 shows that multipath routing can offer advantage over dual-path routing in terms of generated traffic and the maximum distance between the source and destination nodes. Also, multipath routing usually requires fewer channels than dual-path routing. Because the destinations are divided into four sets rather than two, they are reached more efficiently from the source, which is approximately centrally located among the sets. Thus, when the network load is not high, multipath routing offers slight improvement over dual-path routing due to the fact that multipath routing introduces less traffic to the network.

However, a potential disadvantage of multipath routing is not revealed until both the load and number of destinations are relatively high. When multipath routing is used to reach a relatively large set of destinations, the source node will likely send on all of its outgoing channels. Until this multicast transmission is complete, any flit from another multicast or unicast message that routes through that source node will be blocked at that point. In essence, the source node becomes a hot spot. In fact, every node currently sending a multicast message is likely to be a hot spot. If the load is very high, these hot spots may throttle system throughput and increase message latency. Hot spots are less likely to occur in dual-path routing, accounting for its stable behavior under high loads with large destination sets. Although all the outgoing channels at a node can be simultaneously busy, this can only result from two or more messages routing through that node. A detailed performance study can be found in [206, 208].

Multicast Channel Dependencies

As indicated in Section 3.1.3, there is a dependency between two channels when a packet or message is holding one of them, and then it requests the other channel. In path-based multicast routing, the delivery of the same message to several destinations may produce additional channel dependencies, as we show in the next example.

Let us consider a 2-D mesh using XY routing. This routing algorithm prevents the use of horizontal channels after using a vertical channel. Figure 5.31 shows an example of multicast routing on a 2-D mesh. A message is sent by node 0, destined for nodes 9 and 14. The XY routing algorithm first routes the message through horizontal channels until it reaches node 1. Then, it routes the message through vertical channels until the first destination is reached (node 9). Now, the message must be forwarded toward its next destination (node 14). The path requested by the XY routing algorithm contains a horizontal channel. So, there is a dependency from a vertical channel to a horizontal one. This dependency does not exist in unicast routing. It is due to the inclusion of multiple destinations in the message header. More precisely, after reaching an intermediate destination the message header is routed toward the next destination. As a consequence, it is forced to take a path that would not follow otherwise. For this reason, this dependency is referred to as *multicast dependency* [91, 97].

We studied four particular cases of channel dependency (direct, direct cross, indirect, and indirect cross dependencies) in Sections 3.1.4 and 3.1.5. For each of them we can define the corresponding multicast dependency, giving rise to *direct multicast*, *direct cross multicast*, *indirect multicast*, and *indirect cross multicast* dependencies. The only difference between these dependencies and the dependencies defined in Chapter 3 is that multicast dependencies are due to multicast messages reaching an intermediate destination. In other words, there is an intermediate destination in the path between the reserved channel and the requested channel.

The extended channel dependency graph defined in Section 3.1.3 can be extended by including multicast dependencies. The resulting graph is the *extended multicast channel dependency graph* [91, 97]. Similarly to Theorem 3.1, it is possible to define a condition for deadlock-free multicast routing based on that graph.

Before proposing the condition, it is necessary to define a few additional concepts. The message preparation algorithm executed at the source node splits the destination set for a message into one or more destination subsets, possibly reordering the nodes. This algorithm has been referred to as *split-and-sort function SS* [91, 97]. The destination subsets supplied by this function are referred to as *valid*.

A split-and-sort function SS and a connected routing function R form a *compatible pair* (SS, R) if and only if when a given message destined for the destination set D is being routed, the destination subset containing the destinations that have not been reached yet is a valid destination set for the node containing the message header. This definition imposes restrictions on both SS and R, because compatibility can be achieved either by defining SS according to this definition and/or by restricting the paths supplied by the routing function. Also, if (SS, R) is a compatible pair and R_1 is a connected routing subfunction of R, then (SS, R_1) is also a compatible pair.

The following theorem proposes a sufficient condition for deadlock-free path-based multicast routing [91, 97]. Whether it is also a necessary condition for deadlock-free multicast routing remains as an open problem.

Theorem 5.1 *A compatible pair (SS, R) for an interconnection network I, where R is connected, is deadlock-free if there exists a connected routing subfunction R_1 and the pair (SS, R_1) has no cycles in its extended multicast channel dependency graph.*

Adaptive Multicast Routing

This section describes two adaptive multicast routing functions based on the extension of the routing function presented in Section 5.5.3. The label-based dual-path (LD) adaptive multicast routing algorithm for 2-D meshes [205] is similar to the dual-path routing algorithm presented in Section 5.5.3. In addition to minimal paths between successive destination nodes, the LD algorithm also allows nonminimal paths as long as nodes are crossed in strictly increasing or decreasing label order.

The message preparation algorithm executed at the source node is identical to the one given in Figure 5.25 for the dual-path routing algorithm. The destination node set is divided into two subsets, D_H and D_L, which are then sorted in ascending order and descending order, respectively, with the label of each node used as its key for sorting. The LD algorithm for message routing is shown in Figure 5.32.

Algorithm: LD Algorithm for Message Routing

Input: A message with sorted destination address list $D_M = (d_1, \ldots, d_k)$, a local address w, and node label assignment ℓ;

Procedure:

1. If $w = d_1$, then $D'_M = D_M - \{d_1\}$ and a copy of the message is forwarded to the local node; otherwise, $D'_M = D_M$.

2. If $D'_M = \emptyset$, then terminate the message forwarding.

3. Let d be the first address in D'_M. Select any channel (w, w') such that $\ell(w) < \ell(w') \leq \ell(d_1)$.

4. The message is sent to node w' with address destination list D'_M in its header.

Figure 5.32. The LD algorithm for message routing.

Example 5.10

Figure 5.33 shows an example for the LD multicast routing algorithm in a 6×6 mesh. The destination set is divided into two sets D_H and D_L at source node $(3, 2)$, with $D_H = \{(4, 3), (1, 3), (4, 5), (0, 5)\}$ and $D_L = \{(1, 1), (5, 1), (0, 0)\}$. Then, two copies of the message are sent along the paths shown in the figure. In this example, nonminimal paths are used from node $(3, 2)$ to node $(4, 3)$, from $(1, 3)$ to $(4, 5)$, and from $(3, 2)$ to $(1, 1)$.

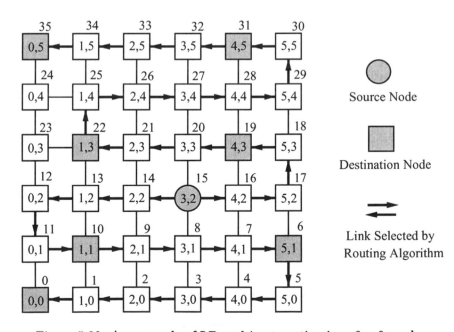

Figure 5.33. An example of LD multicast routing in a 6×6 mesh.

Another adaptive routing function was proposed in [91, 97]. It allows messages to use the alternative minimal paths between successive destinations offered by the interconnection network. This routing function can be used for meshes and hypercubes, once a suitable node labeling scheme is defined. It will serve as an example of the application of Theorem 5.1.

It is possible to define dual-path and multipath routing algorithms based on the routing function described below. This can be easily done by using the same message preparation algorithms as in Sections 5.5.3 and 5.5.3. For the sake of brevity, we will focus on the dual-path algorithm.

The routing function presented in Section 5.5.3 can be made adaptive by following a methodology similar to the one proposed in Section 4.4.4. This design methodology supplies a way to add channels following a regular pattern, also deriving the new routing function from the old one.

The routing function presented in Section 5.5.3 defines a minimal-path connected deterministic routing function R_1. It does not require virtual channels. From a logical point of view, we can consider that there is a single virtual channel per physical channel. Let C_1 be the set of (virtual) channels supplied by R_1. Now, each physical channel is split into two virtual channels. This is equivalent to adding one virtual channel to each physical channel. The additional virtual channels will be used for adaptive routing. Let C be the set of all the virtual channels in the network. Let C_{1H} be the set of virtual channels belonging to C_1 that connect lower-labeled nodes to higher-labeled nodes and let C_{1L} be the set of virtual channels belonging to C_1 that connect higher-labeled nodes to lower-labeled nodes. Let C_{xyH} be the set of output virtual channels from node x such that each channel belongs to a minimal path from x to y and the label of its destination node is not higher than the label of y. Let C_{xyL} be the set of output virtual channels from node x such that each channel belongs to a minimal path from x to y and the label of its destination node is not lower than the label of y. The adaptive routing function R is defined as follows:

$$\forall x, y \in N, \ R(x, y) = \begin{cases} R_1(x, y) \cup (C_{xyH} \cap (C - C_1)) & \text{if } \ell(x) < \ell(y) \\ R_1(x, y) \cup (C_{xyL} \cap (C - C_1)) & \text{if } \ell(x) > \ell(y) \end{cases}$$

In other words, the adaptive routing function can use any of the additional virtual channels belonging to a minimal path between successive destinations, except when a node with a label higher (for $\ell(x) < \ell(y)$) or lower (for $\ell(x) > \ell(y)$) than the label of the destination node is reached. Alternatively, the channels supplied by R_1 can also be used. This routing function can be easily extended for n-dimensional meshes as well as to support nonminimal paths. The extension for 3-D meshes was presented in [216]. The higher the number of dimensions, the higher the benefits from using adaptivity.

Example 5.11

Figure 5.34 shows the label assignment and a routing example for the adaptive routing function R in an 8×8 mesh. In what follows, we will refer to nodes using their labels instead of their integer coordinates. The destination set for the example has been split into two subsets, $D_H = \{41, 52, 53, 62\}$ and $D_L = \{1\}$. Solid arrows show the path supplied by the deterministic routing function R_1. Dashed arrows show the additional paths offered by the adaptive routing function R. Inside each path, all the additional virtual channels can be used by R.

As can be seen, R does not use all the minimal paths between successive destinations. For instance, when the next destination is node 41, the message is not allowed to reach nodes 44, 43, or 42, because they have a higher label value than the next destination node. However, R may route a message destined for a node with a higher label value through nodes with decreasing label values. This is the case when the next destination is node 41, allowing the

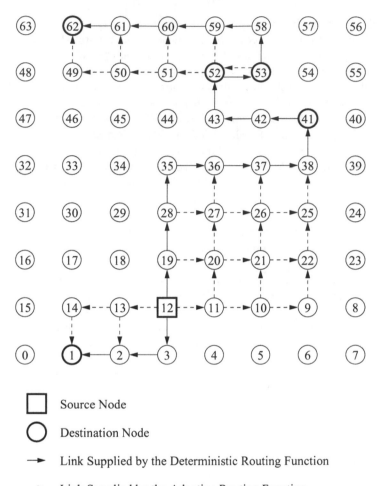

Source Node

Destination Node

→   Link Supplied by the Deterministic Routing Function

- →   Link Supplied by the Adaptive Routing Function

Figure 5.34. Label assignment and routing example for a 8 × 8 mesh.

message to be routed across channels $[12, 11]$, $[11, 10]$, $[10, 9]$, $[28, 27]$, $[27, 26]$, or $[26, 25]$. In these cases, R always uses virtual channels belonging to $C - C_1$. A similar situation arises when the next destination node has a lower label value than the source node. This is the case when the next destination is node 1.

Channels belonging to C_1 are used exactly in the same way by R and R_1. Therefore, there is not any cross-dependency between channels belonging to C_1. Let us analyze the indirect dependencies that appear in the example shown in Figure 5.34 by considering some paths supplied by R. For instance, if the header of the message destined for node 41 is at node 19, then it is routed to node 28 using a channel of C_1, then to node 27 using a channel of $C - C_1$ and then to node 36 using a channel of C_1, there is an indirect dependency between the channels of C_1. This dependency arises because R may route a message destined for a node with a higher label value through nodes with decreasing label values. If node 28 were a destination node, this example would correspond to an indirect multicast dependency.

Also, some indirect multicast dependencies exist between horizontal and vertical channels, due to messages that come back over their way after reaching an intermediate destination node. An example can be seen in Figure 5.34, when the message header is at node 52, and for instance, it is routed to node 53 using a channel of C_1, then to nodes 52 and 51 using channels of $C - C_1$, and finally, to node 60 using a channel of C_1.

The indirect and indirect multicast dependencies shown in the previous examples cannot be obtained by composing other dependencies. However, some indirect and indirect multicast dependencies can also be obtained by composing other direct and/or direct multicast dependencies. These dependencies do not add information to the channel dependency graphs.

Taking into account the definition of the split-and-sort function SS (message preparation algorithm) for the dual-path algorithm, a valid destination set for a source node n_s only contains nodes with label value higher (alternatively, lower) than $\ell(n_s)$. When the next destination node has a label value higher (lower) than the current node, the routing function cannot forward the message to a node with label value higher (lower) than the next destination node. Thus, the pair (SS, R) is compatible. However, if all the minimal paths between successive destination nodes were allowed, the pair would not be compatible. For instance, if after reaching node 41 the message of the example given in Figure 5.34 were allowed to reach node 54, the current destination set $D_{H1} = \{52, 53, 62\}$ is not a valid destination set for node 54.

There is not any dependency between channels belonging to C_{1H} and channels belonging to C_{1L}. However, if all the minimal paths between successive destinations were allowed, such dependencies would exist. The extended multicast channel dependency graph for (SS, R_1) consists of two subgraphs, each one containing the dependencies between channels belonging to C_{1H} and C_{1L}, respectively. Figure 5.35 shows part of the extended multicast channel dependency graph for (SS, R_1) and a 4×4 mesh. For the sake of clarity, the dependencies that do not add information to the graph have been removed. Also, only the subgraph for C_{1H} is displayed. The subgraph for C_{1L} is identical, except channel labeling. Channels have been labeled as Hs or Vs, where H and V indicate that the channel is horizontal and vertical, respectively, and s is the label assigned to the source node of the channel. It must be noted that there are two horizontal output channels belonging to C_1 for most nodes, but only one of them belongs to C_{1H}. The same consideration applies to vertical channels.

Solid arrows represent direct or direct multicast dependencies. Dashed arrows represent indirect or indirect multicast dependencies. Dotted arrows represent indirect multicast dependencies. The graph has been represented in such a way that it is easy to see that there are no cycles. Obviously, the routing subfunction R_1 is connected. As the pair (SS, R_1) has no cycles in its extended multicast channel dependency graph, by Theorem 5.1 the pair (SS, R) is deadlock-free.

Base Routing Conformed Path

Deadlock avoidance is considerably simplified if unicast and multicast routing use the same routing algorithm. Moreover, using the same routing hardware for unicast and multicast routing allows the design of compact and fast routers. The Hamiltonian path-based routing algorithms proposed in previous sections improve performance over multiple unicast routing. However, their development has been in a different track compared to e-cube and adaptive routing. Moreover, it makes no sense sacrificing the performance of unicast messages to improve the performance of multicast messages, which usually represent a much smaller percentage of network traffic. Therefore, as indicated in [268], it is unlikely that a system in the near future will be able to take advantage of Hamiltonian path-based routing.

The *Base Routing Conformed Path* (BRCP) model [268] defines multicast routing algorithms that are compatible with existing unicast routing algorithms. This model also uses path-based routing.

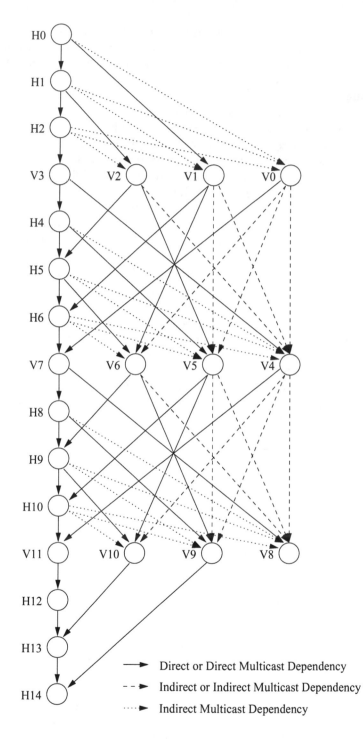

Figure 5.35. Extended multicast channel dependency graph for the pair (SS, R_1) and a 4×4 mesh. Only the channels in C_{1H} have been represented. (Hs = Horizontal channel from node s; Vs = Vertical channel from node s.)

The basic idea consists of allowing a multidestination message to be transmitted through any path in the network as long as it is a valid path conforming to the base routing scheme. For example, on a 2-D mesh with XY routing, a valid path can be any row, column, or row-column.

It is important to note that the BRCP model, as defined, cannot be directly applied on top of adaptive routing algorithms that allow cyclic dependencies between channels, like the ones described in Section 4.4.4. These algorithms divide the virtual channels of each physical channel into two classes: adaptive and escape. Adaptive channels allow fully adaptive routing while escape channels allow messages to escape from potential deadlocks. Escape channels can be selected by a message at any node. However, if the BRCP model allows all the valid paths conforming to the base routing scheme, destination nodes may be arranged along a path that can only be followed by using adaptive channels. As a consequence, messages may be forced to select adaptive channels to reach the next destination node, therefore preventing some messages from selecting escape channels to escape from a potential deadlock.

However, this does not mean that the BRCP model cannot be combined with fully adaptive routing algorithms that allow cyclic dependencies between channels. Simply, destination nodes should be arranged in such a way that multidestination messages could be transmitted through any valid path consisting of escape channels. It is not necessary to restrict multidestination messages to use only escape channels. Those messages are allowed to use adaptive channels. However, by arranging destinations as indicated above, we guarantee that any message can select an escape channel at any node. For example, consider a 2-D mesh using wormhole switching and the routing algorithm described in Example 3.8. In this algorithm, one set of virtual channels is used for fully adaptive minimal routing. The second set of virtual channels implements XY routing, and is used to escape from potential deadlocks. The BRCP model can be applied to the second set of virtual channels, exactly in the same way that it is applied to a 2-D mesh with XY routing. By doing so, multicast messages can take advantage of the BRCP model while unicast messages can benefit from fully adaptive routing.

The main goal of the BRCP model is providing support for multidestination messages without introducing additional channel dependencies with respect to the base routing algorithm used for unicast routing [268]. As indicated in Theorem 5.1, a compatible pair (SS, R) is deadlock-free if there exists a connected routing subfunction R_1 and the pair (SS, R_1) has no cycles in its extended multicast channel dependency graph. Instead of restricting the routing function R to satisfy this condition, the BRCP model restricts the split-and-sort function SS (message preparation algorithm) so that multicast dependencies do not produce any new channel dependency. Therefore, the extended multicast channel dependency graph and the extended channel dependency graph (defined in Section 3.1.3) are identical, and the condition proposed by Theorem 5.1 for deadlock-free routing is identical to the one for unicast routing (Theorem 3.1). As a consequence, if the base routing algorithm is deadlock-free, the multicast routing algorithm is also deadlock-free. The BRCP model can be formally defined as follows:

Definition 5.5 *A multidestination message from a source s with an ordered destination list $\{d_1, d_2, \ldots, d_{n-1}, d_n\}$ in a network supporting the routing function R conforms to this base routing if and only if the destination set $\{d_1, d_2, \ldots, d_{n-1}\}$ can be covered as intermediate nodes on one of the possible paths from s to d_n under the routing constraint R_1, where R_1 is a connected routing subfunction of R that has no cycles in its extended channel dependency graph.*

The routing subfunction R_1 supplies the escape channels mentioned above. If the routing function R has no cyclic dependencies between channels then R_1 can be made equal to R. In this case, a multidestination message can be transmitted through any path in the network as long as it is a valid path conforming to the base routing scheme defined by R.

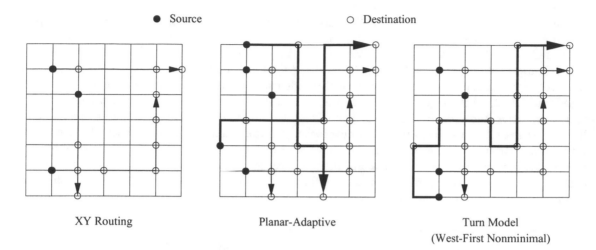

Figure 5.36. Examples of multidestination messages on a 2-D mesh under the BRCP model.

Example 5.12

Figure 5.36 shows examples of multidestination messages on a 2-D mesh under the BRCP model. If the network uses XY routing, a multidestination message can cover a set of destinations in row/column/row-column order. It should be noted that a set of destinations ordered in a column-row order manner is an invalid path under the BRCP model for XY routing. Similarly, in a network using planar-adaptive routing (see Section 4.3.1), a multidestination message can cover a set of destinations along any diagonal in addition to the flexibility supported by XY routing. Such additional paths are shown as bold lines in the figure. If the underlying routing scheme supports the west-first routing algorithm (see Section 4.3.2), it can provide further flexibility in covering many destinations using a single message. In this example, a nonminimal west-first routing algorithm is assumed. If the base routing scheme supports nonminimal routing then multidestination messages can also use nonminimal paths. This multicast routing algorithm conforming to nonminimal west-first routing was first proposed in [205]. Finally, if the base routing scheme supports fully adaptive routing, the set of destinations that can be covered by multidestination messages depends on the routing subfunction implemented by escape channels, as indicated above. Possible choices include XY routing as well as the west-first routing algorithm.

Once the set of valid paths for multidestination messages has been determined, it is necessary to define routing algorithms for collective communication. The *Hierarchical Leader-Based Scheme* (HL) has been proposed in [268] to implement multicast and broadcast. Given a multicast destination set, this scheme tries to group the destinations in a hierarchical manner so that the minimum number of messages are needed to cover all the destinations. Since the multidestination messages conform to paths supported by the base routing, the grouping scheme takes into account this routing scheme and the spatial positions of destination nodes to achieve the best grouping. Once the grouping is achieved multicast and broadcast take place by traversing nodes from the source in a reverse hierarchy.

Consider a multicast pattern from a source s with a destination set D. Let L_0 denote the set $D \cup \{s\}$. The hierarchical scheme, in its first step, partitions the set L_0 into disjoint subsets with a

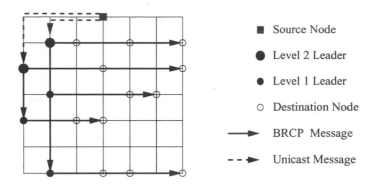

Figure 5.37. Example of multicast routing in a 2-D mesh using XY routing under hierarchical leader-based scheme.

leader node representing each subset. The leader node is chosen in such a way that it can forward a message to the members of its set using a single multidestination message under the BRCP model. For example, if a 2-D mesh implements XY routing then the partitioning is done such that the nodes in each set lie on a row, column, or row-column.

Let the leaders obtained by the above first-step partitioning be termed as *level-1* leaders and identified by a set L_1. This set L_1 can be further partitioned into disjoint subsets with a set of *level-2* leaders. This process of hierarchical grouping is continued as long as it is profitable, as indicated below. Assuming that the grouping is carried out for m steps, there will be m sets of leaders, satisfying that $L_m \subset L_{m-1} \subset \ldots L_1 \subset L_0$.

After the grouping is achieved, the multicast takes place in two phases. In the first phase, the source node performs unicast-based multicast (see Section 5.7) to the set L_m. The second phase involves m steps of multidestination message passing. It starts with the leaders in the set L_m and propagates down the hierarchical grouping in a reverse fashion to cover the lower-level leaders and finally, all the nodes in destination set D.

As mentioned above, the hierarchical grouping is continued as long as it is profitable in order to reduce the multicast latency. As start-up latency dominates communication latency in networks using pipelined data transmission, the minimum multicast latency is usually achieved by minimizing the number of communication steps. As will be seen in Section 5.7, unicast-based multicast requires $\lceil \log_2(|L_m| + 1) \rceil$ steps to reach all the leaders in the set L_m, assuming that the source node does not belong to that set. Therefore, the size of the set L_m should be reduced. However, while going from L_{m-1} to L_m, one additional step of multidestination communication is introduced into the multicast latency. Hence, it can be seen that when $\lceil \log_2(|L_{m-1}| + 1) \rceil > \lceil \log_2(|L_m| + 1) \rceil + 1$, it is profitable to go through an additional level of grouping. The previous expression assumes that the source node does not belong to L_{m-1}. If the source node belongs to L_{m-1} or L_m then the cardinal of the corresponding set must be reduced by one unit.

Example 5.13

Figure 5.37 shows an example of multicast routing in a 2-D mesh using XY routing under hierarchical leader-based scheme. Given a destination set, the first level grouping can be done along rows (dimension 0) to obtain the level-1 leaders as shown in the figure. The level-1 leaders can be grouped along columns (dimension 1) to form L_2 with two level-2 leaders. Note that each level-2 leader is also a level-1 leader. The multicast takes place in two phases. In the first phase, the source node uses unicast-based multicast to send unicast messages to the

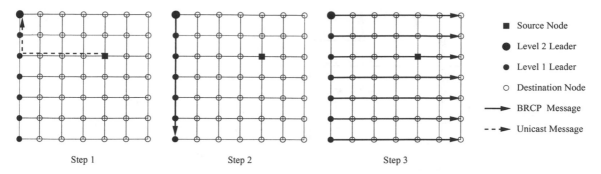

Figure 5.38. Broadcast routing in a 2-D mesh using XY routing under hierarchical leader-based scheme.

two level-2 leaders. In the next phase, these two level-2 leaders send multidestination messages along dimension 1 to cover the level-1 leaders. Finally, all the level-1 leaders (including the level-2 leaders) send multidestination messages along dimension 0 to cover the remaining destinations. In this example, the multicast takes four communication steps.

As the degree of multicasting increases, better grouping can be achieved while reducing L_1 to L_2. The best case is achieved for broadcast, as shown in Figure 5.38. In this case, all the level-1 leaders are reduced to a single level-2 leader. This indicates that broadcast from any arbitrary source can be done in three steps. A more efficient scheme to perform broadcast in two steps in a 2-D mesh using XY routing is shown in Figure 5.39a [267]. The number of steps to perform broadcasting can be further reduced by using the nonminimal west-first routing algorithm as the base routing, as shown in Figure 5.39b [267]. In this case, the message is first routed to the lower left corner of the network without delivering it to any destination. From that point the message crosses all the nodes in the network, delivering copies of the message as it advances. Although this scheme reduces the number of steps to one, the path traversed by the message is very long, usually resulting in a higher broadcast latency than two-step broadcast.

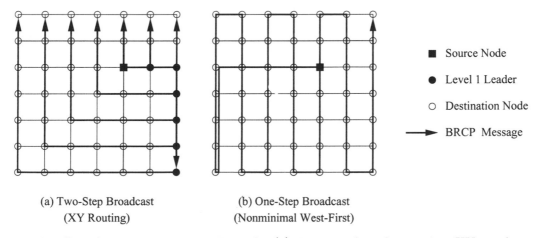

(a) Two-Step Broadcast
(XY Routing)

(b) One-Step Broadcast
(Nonminimal West-First)

Figure 5.39. Broadcast routing in a 2-D mesh: (a) Two-step broadcast using XY routing under hierarchical leader-based scheme. (b) One-step broadcast using nonminimal west-first routing.

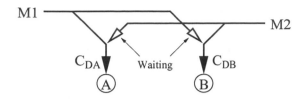

Figure 5.40. Deadlock produced by using a single delivery channel.

As defined, the HL scheme may produce considerable contention when several nodes send multicast messages concurrently. A method to reduce node contention is to make each multicast choose unique intermediate nodes, as different as possible from the rest. However, with dynamic multicast patterns, all concurrent multicasts are unaware of one another. This means that a multicast has no information whatsoever about the source and destinations of the other multicasts.

A good multicast algorithm should only use some local information to make its tree as unique as possible. A possible solution consists of using the position of the source node in the system [173]. This is unique for each multicast message. If each multicast constructs its tree based on the position of its corresponding source, then all the multicasts will end up with trees as unique as possible.

In the HL algorithm the multicast tree is generated using primarily the destination (distribution) information. It depends, to a very small degree, on the position of the source. So, it can be improved by choosing the leader sets for a multicast depending on the position of its source. In the *Source Quadrant-Based Hierarchical Leader* (SQHL) scheme [173], groupings are done exactly like in the HL scheme. However, the leader nodes are chosen in a different way. Consider a k-ary n-mesh. Let s_i be the ith coordinate of the source node s of a multicast. Consider the set of destinations or leaders of the previous level that only differ in the ith coordinate. They will be reached by a single multidestination message. If $s_i \leq k/2$ then the leader node will be the one in the set with the lowest coordinate in dimension i. Otherwise, the leader node will be the one with the highest coordinate in dimension i. For example, when grouping is performed along a given row in a 2-D mesh, the leader will be the leftmost destination in that row if the source node is located in the left half of the network. Otherwise, the leader will be the rightmost destination in that row. The remaining steps are the same as in the original HL scheme. The SQHL scheme allows multicast messages from source nodes in different quadrants of a mesh to proceed concurrently with minimal interference.

In the *Source-Centered Hierarchical Leader* (SCHL) scheme [173], each group g from the HL scheme is partitioned into at most two groups g_1 and g_2 based on the coordinates of the source node. Let s_i be the ith coordinate of the source node s of a multicast. Let us assume that destination nodes in g only differ in the coordinate corresponding to dimension i. All the nodes in that group with an ith coordinate lower than or equal to s_i will be in g_1. The remaining nodes will be in g_2. Leader nodes are chosen so that they have an ith coordinate as close as possible to s_i. Both the SQHL and SCHL schemes improve performance over the HL scheme, as will be seen in Chapter 9.

Deadlocks in Delivery Channels

The routing function R defined in Section 5.5.3 avoids deadlock by transmitting messages in such a way that nodes are crossed either in increasing or decreasing label order. However, deadlock is still possible because messages transmitted on the high-channel and low-channel subnetworks (see Figure 5.24) use the same delivery channels at every destination node [216, 268].

Figure 5.40 shows a deadlocked configuration in which two multidestination messages $M1$ and $M2$ are destined for nodes A and B. $M1$ and $M2$ are traveling in the high-channel and low-channel subnetworks, respectively. Assuming that $\ell(A) < \ell(B)$, $M1$ first reached node A, then node B.

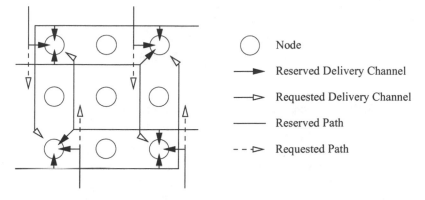

Figure 5.41. Deadlock produced in a 2-D mesh with three delivery channels per node. Multidestination routing uses the BRCP model and XY routing as the base routing.

Also, $M2$ first reached node B, then node A. As there is a single delivery channel at each node, each message has reserved one delivery channel and is waiting for the other delivery channel to become free. Note that $M1$ cannot be completely delivered to node A because wormhole switching is used.

Deadlocks may arise because messages traveling in the high-channel and low-channel subnetworks share the same delivery channels, thus producing cyclic dependencies between them. Effectively, message $M1$ in Figure 5.40 has reserved the delivery channel c_{DA} at node A, then requesting the delivery channel c_{DB} at node B. As a consequence, there is a dependency from c_{DA} to c_{DB}. Similarly, there is a dependency from c_{DB} to c_{DA}. This cyclic dependency can be easily broken by using different delivery channels for each subnetwork. In this case, two delivery channels at each node are enough to avoid deadlocks.

This situation may also arise when multidestination routing is based on the BRCP model. Consider an n-dimensional mesh with dimension-order routing for unicast messages. In this case, multidestination messages conforming to the base routing may be destined for sets of nodes along any dimension. As a consequence, the situation depicted in Figure 5.40 may occur in all the dimensions simultaneously. Figure 5.41 shows a deadlocked configuration for a 2-D mesh using XY routing where each node has three delivery channels. Note that each node has four input channels, which allow up to four messages requesting delivery channels at the same time.

As indicated in [267], the basic idea to avoid deadlock is to consider a given topology and routing function R, and determine the maximum number of multidestination messages that can enter a node simultaneously under the BRCP model. For example, if a base routing function R in an n-dimensional mesh requires v virtual channels per physical channel to support deadlock-free unicast routing, then $2nv$ delivery channels per node are sufficient for deadlock-free multidestination communication [267]. Note that each node has $2n$ input physical channels. Thus, each input virtual channel is associated with a dedicated delivery channel, therefore breaking all the dependencies between delivery channels.

It should be noted that virtual channels can also be used to reduce congestion. In this case, they are usually referred to as virtual lanes. Virtual lanes do not require additional delivery channels. Instead, each set of virtual lanes share a single delivery channel [267]. When a multidestination message arrived on a virtual lane and reserved a delivery channel, and another multidestination message arrives on another virtual lane in the same set, it must wait. This waiting cannot produce deadlock because both messages follow the same direction. Also, it should be noted that adaptive routing algorithms that allow cyclic dependencies between channels only require the escape channels to avoid deadlock. As indicated in Section 5.5.3, the BRCP model restricts routing for multidestination messages according to the paths defined by escape channels. As a consequence, only the escape channels need to be considered when computing the number of delivery channels required for those algorithms.

The high number of delivery channels required to implement deadlock-free multidestination communication under the BRCP model may restrict the applicability of this model. Fortunately, current trends in network topologies recommend the use of low-dimensional meshes or tori (two or three dimensions at most). Also, as shown in Sections 4.2 and 4.4.4, it is possible to design deterministic and fully adaptive routing algorithms with a very small number of virtual channels. One and two virtual channels per physical channel are enough for deterministic routing in n-dimensional meshes and k-ary n-cubes, respectively. For fully adaptive routing, the requirements for escape channels are identical to those for deterministic routing. As indicated in [267], four delivery channels are enough to support deadlock-free multidestination communication under the BRCP model in 2-D meshes when the base routing is either XY routing, nonminimal west-first or fully adaptive routing based on escape channels (described in Section 4.4.4). Moreover, there is very little blocking probability with all delivery channels being accessed simultaneously. Hence, delivery channels can be implemented as virtual channels by multiplexing the available bandwidth at the network interface.

5.6 Hardware Support for Barrier Synchronization and Reduction

In this section we describe algorithms and architectural support to perform barrier synchronization, reduction, and global combining. These algorithms have been proposed by Panda in [264, 265], and are based on the BRCP model described in Section 5.5.3.

5.6.1 Barrier Synchronization on a Linear Array

Barrier synchronization can be performed in two phases by using multidestination messages. The first phase implements *reporting* by using *gather* messages. The second phase implements *wake-up* by using *broadcasting* messages.

Consider a linear array of six processors as shown in Figure 5.42. Assume that four processors ($P0$, $P1$, $P2$, and $P4$) participate in a barrier. The rightmost processor $P4$, after reaching its barrier point, can send a multidestination gather message. The header of this message consists of an ordered destination list ($P2$, $P1$, and $P0$) with $P0$ as the final destination. As this message propagates toward $P0$, it can gather information from processors $P2$ and $P1$ regarding whether they have reached at the barrier or not. If this information is available at the router interface, the gather message need not be consumed and retransmitted at intermediate destinations.

As the message propagates, it checks for the arrival of information at every router interface of intermediate destinations. If the intermediate destination has already arrived at the barrier, the message proceeds ahead. Otherwise, it gets blocked at the respective router interface until the associated processor arrives at the barrier and provides information to the router interface. If a processor is not participating in a barrier, the message moves ahead at its router interface. Finally, the message is consumed at its final destination. In the example in Figure 5.42, the gather message from $P4$ will check the arrival of processors $P2$ and $P1$ at the barrier on its way and will finally get consumed at $P0$.

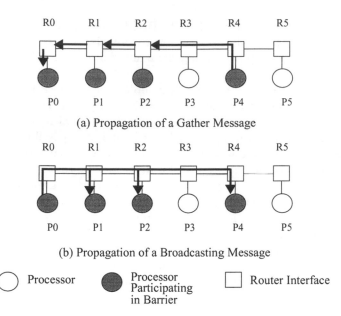

(a) Propagation of a Gather Message

(b) Propagation of a Broadcasting Message

Figure 5.42. Two-phase implementation of a barrier on a linear array of processors. (From [264].)

With the consumption of the gather message, processor $P0$ has information that all other participating processors ($P1$, $P2$, and $P4$) have arrived at the barrier. To implement the wake-up phase, $P0$ initiates a broadcasting message with $P1$, $P2$, and $P4$ as destinations. The propagation of this message, as shown in Figure 5.42b, is unconditional. It is very similar to the movement of a multidestination multicast/broadcast message as described in Section 5.5.3. The only difference is that, as this message passes through the routers of the intermediate participating processors ($P1$ and $P2$), it activates the wake-up signal to these processors. Processors $P0$ and $P4$ get waken-up after sending and receiving the broadcast message, respectively.

Architectural Support

In order to implement multidestination gather/broadcasting messages, some architectural support is required at the router interface. Similar to the concept of barrier registers [259], a set of buffers can be provided at each router interface of the system. Figure 5.43a shows a possible router interface organization with m buffers. Each buffer has a few bits for *synchronization id*, a flag *participate/not participate* (P), a flag *arrived/not arrived* (A), and some space for holding an incoming gather message. These buffers can be accessed by the associated processor. Note that by supporting m buffers at every router interface, a system can implement m concurrent barriers for an application at a given time.

Figure 5.43b shows a suitable format for gather/broadcasting messages. Each message carries a *msg type* field (2–3 bits) indicating whether it is a gather, broadcast, or unicast message. The width of *synchronization id* field depends on how many buffers can be incorporated into the router interface. The destination addresses are encoded as a bit string (see Section 5.5.1). For the linear array example being considered, 6 bits are sufficient to encode the addresses. Assuming processor 0 is identified as bit 0 of this address, the destination bit string of the gather message initiated by $P4$ will be 000111. Similarly, the broadcast message initiated by $P0$ will have a bit string of 010110.

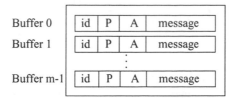

(a) Router Interface Organization Supporting Buffers

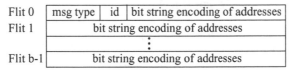

(b) Message Format

Figure 5.43. Architectural supports for implementing multidestination gather/broadcasting messages: (a) Synchronization buffers at a router interface. (b) Message format. (From [264].) (A = Arrived/not arrived; id = Synchronization id; P = Participate/not participate.)

Communication Sequence

Let us consider the communication sequence for the processors participating in a barrier using gather and broadcast messages. We assume static barriers [259] so that the processors participating in a barrier are known at compile time and the associated communication sequence can be generated before the program execution. A split-phase synchronization scheme [142, 260] with separate report and wake-up phases is assumed. Figure 5.44 shows the communication sequence to implement a barrier on a linear array. Before the execution of barrier x, $0 \leq x < m$, each intermediate processor specifies its desire for participating in the barrier by grabbing buffer x at its router interface, setting the associated *participate* flag to 1 and resetting the *arrived* flag to 0. These flags are reset by default, indicating that the associated processor does not participate. The *arrived* flag of buffer x at an intermediate router is set to 1 when the associated processor reaches its barrier point after computation.

The rightmost participating processor initiates a gather message with *synchronization id* = x. This gather message, while passing through the router of an intermediate destination, checks for the *participate* and *arrived* flags of the associated buffer x. If the processor is not participating then the message keeps on moving ahead. If the processor is participating and it has already arrived at the barrier then also the message proceeds ahead. If the processor is participating and it has not arrived at the barrier then the message gets blocked at the router interface. In this case, the message is stored in the *message* field of buffer x until the *arrived* flag is set to 1 by the processor. Then, the gather message is forwarded again into the network. Finally this gather message is consumed by the leftmost participating processor. Note that gather messages require the use of VCT switching. When a gather message is stored in the corresponding buffer at the router interface, it is removed from the network. This is required to avoid deadlock and to reduce network contention because a gather message may be waiting for long until a given processor reaches at the barrier.

After the gather phase is over, the leftmost processor initiates a broadcast message to the rightmost processor with intermediate processors as intermediate destinations. This message, as it passes through the routers of intermediate destinations, wakes up the associated processors, also resetting

Leftmost Participating Processor	*Intermediate Participating Processor*	*Rightmost Participating Processor*
compute;	compute; P[buff(x)]=1; A[buff(x)]=0; compute;	compute;
arrive at barrier point x;		arrive at barrier point x;
receive gather message from rightmost processor with id=x;	arrive at barrier point x; A[buff(x)]=1;	*send* gather message to leftmost processor and intermediate destinations with id=x;
send broadcast message to rightmost processor and intermediate destinations with id=x;	wait for wake-up; P[buff(x)]=0; A[buff(x)]=0;	*receive* broadcast message from leftmost processor with id=x;
compute;	compute;	compute;

Figure 5.44. Communication sequence of processors on a linear array while participating in a barrier with *synchronization id = x*, using gather and broadcast messages. (From [264].)

the *participate* and *arrived* flags of buffer x. The leftmost processor is done with the synchronization after sending the broadcast message. Similarly, the rightmost processor is done when it receives the broadcast message.

5.6.2   Barrier Synchronization on Meshes

Complete Barrier Synchronization

Consider a $k \times k$ mesh as shown in Figure 5.45. Complete barrier synchronization can be achieved by considering the mesh as a set of linear arrays [264]. A basic scheme using four steps is shown in Figure 5.45a. The first step uses gather message in all rows to collect information toward the first column. The second step uses a gather message on the first column. At the end of these two steps, the upper-left corner processor has information that all other processors have arrived at the barrier. Now it can initiate a broadcast message along the first column. During the final step, the nodes in the first column initiate broadcast messages along their respective rows. This requires four communication steps to implement barrier synchronization on a $k \times k$ mesh. For any k-ary n-cube system, similar dimensionwise gather and broadcast can be done to implement barrier synchronization with $2n$ communication steps. Note that under this basic scheme, the multidestination gather and broadcast messages need to move along a single dimension of the system only. As each multidestination message is destined for the nodes in a row or column, destination addresses can be encoded as a bit string of k bits. Hence, using 16-bit or 32-bit flits, destination addresses can be encoded into a few (1–3) flits for current network sizes.

An enhancement to this basic scheme can be done as shown in Figure 5.45b. The gather message initiated by the bottom row does not stop at the leftmost node of this row but continues along the first column to gather information from the leftmost leaders of all other rows. This will combine the first two gather steps into a single one. Hence, using such multidimensional gather message, complete barrier synchronization can be implemented on a 2-D mesh in three steps. This enhancement can

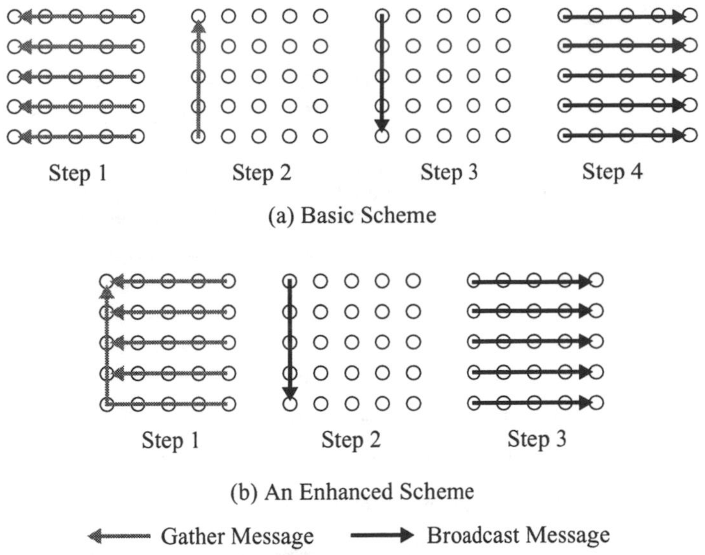

Figure 5.45. Complete barrier synchronization on a $k \times k$ mesh using: (a) A four-step basic scheme. (b) An enhanced scheme with three steps. (From [264].)

be easily extended to a higher number of dimensions. Note that such multidimensional message conforms to the BRCP model discussed in Section 5.5.3. The header of such multidimensional messages is longer in size because they need to carry more destinations in their headers. Though such a scheme is feasible, it requires additional logic at a router interface to wait for the arrival of multiple gather messages.

Arbitrary Set Barrier Synchronization

Consider a subset of nodes in a 2-D mesh trying to barrier synchronize as shown in Figure 5.46. If all processors belong to a single task then this subset barrier can be implemented as a complete barrier by forcing all processors to participate in each barrier. However, such an assumption is very restrictive. In this section, we describe a general scheme which allows for multiple subset barriers to be executed concurrently in a system and the operation for a given barrier involves only the processors participating in that barrier [264].

For a 2-D mesh, the scheme uses six phases as shown in Figure 5.46. The first phase consists of using gather messages within rows. For every row having at least two participating processors, a gather message is initiated by the rightmost participating processor and is consumed by the leftmost participating one. Let us designate the leftmost participating processors as row leaders. Now for every column having at least two row leaders, a gather message can be initiated by the bottom row leader to gather information along that column and finally be consumed by the top row leader. Let these top row leaders be designated as column leaders. After these two phases, information needs only to be gathered from the column leaders. It can be easily seen that these column leaders fall into disjoint rows and columns based on the grouping done. Hence no further reduction can be achieved with multidestination messages on systems supporting XY routing. If the base routing algorithm supports adaptivity then further reduction can still be achieved by using adaptive paths.

The third phase consists of unicast-based message passing. This phase implements gather among column leaders in a tree-like manner using unicast-based message passing in every step. Once this

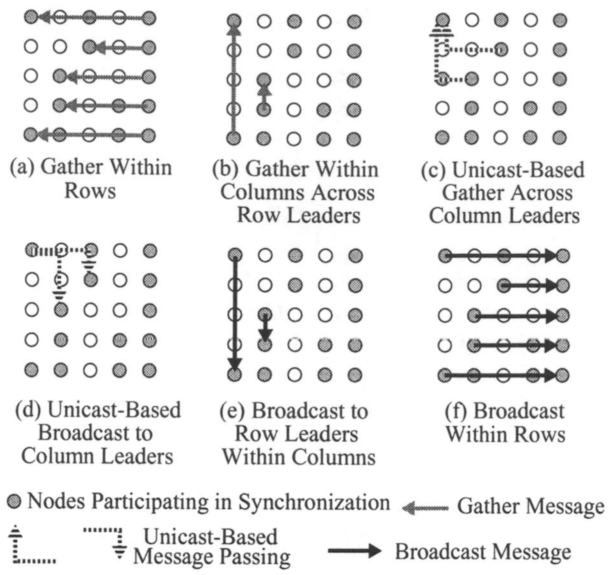

Figure 5.46. Barrier synchronization for an arbitrary subset of processors in a 2-D mesh using multi-destination gather and broadcasting messages together with unicast message passing. (From [264].)

reduction phase is over, the participating upper-left corner processor has information that all other processors have reached at their respective barriers. This completes the report phase of barrier synchronization. Now the wake-up phase of barrier synchronization can be achieved by a series of broadcast phases. The fourth phase involves broadcast from upper-left corner processor to column leaders in a tree-like manner using unicast-based multicast (see Section 5.7). The fifth phase involves broadcast by column leaders to row leaders using multidestination messages. During the final step, the row leaders use broadcast messages in their respective rows to wake-up the associated processors.

In this six-phase scheme, every phase except the third and the fourth needs only one communication step. The number of communication steps needed in the third and the fourth phases depend on the number of column leaders involved. This issue was discussed in Section 5.5.3.

5.6.3   Reduction and Global Combining

The reduction operation can be implemented by using multidestination gather messages. The basic name of this message indicates that it gathers information from multiple processors as it propagates. The reduction operation can be any associative and commutative function (sum, max, min, or user-defined) as defined under *collective communication* by the Message Passing Interface (MPI) standard [242]. Global combining can be achieved by broadcasting the result of the reduction operation to all the participating processors. This can be implemented by using multidestination broadcast/multicast messages. Barrier synchronization is a special case of global combining where there are no data (just an event). Hardware support for the broadcast/multicast operation has been described in Section 5.5.3. Hence, in this section we will mainly focus on the reduction operation.

Unlike gather messages for barrier synchronization, the reduction operation requires messages to carry some data. Also, the reduction operation to be performed on data must be encoded in the message. Figure 5.47a shows a suitable format for a gather message [265]. The *msg type* and *id* fields have already been described in Section 5.6.1. Also, destination addresses are encoded as bit

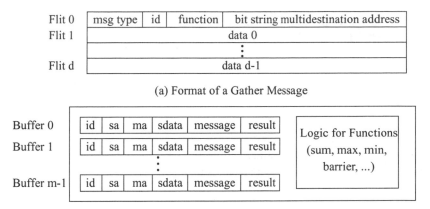

(a) Format of a Gather Message

(b) Router Interface Organization with Buffers

Figure 5.47. Architectural support for implementing the reduction operation: (a) Message format. (b) Message buffers and logic at the router interface. (From [265].) (id = Synchronization id; ma = Message arrived/not arrived; sa = Self arrived/not arrived; sdata = Self data.)

strings. The *function* field indicates the type of reduction operation (sum, max, min, etc.). Finally, the message contains some data flits on which the reduction operation will be performed.

The movement of gather messages through the network was described in Section 5.6.1. However, the tasks performed when a multidestination gather message arrives at an intermediate destination depend on the operation to be performed. In this section we give a more general description.

When several processors participate in a reduction operation, it may happen that a multidestination gather message reaches an intermediate processor and this processor has not reached the point when the reduction operation is executed. Similarly to barrier synchronization, the message must be stored in a buffer of the router interface, removing it from the network. Therefore, VCT switching is assumed.

The router interface organization required to implement the reduction operation also differs from the one presented in Section 5.6.1. Figure 5.47b shows a possible router interface organization with m buffers [265]. Each buffer has a few bits for *id*, a flag *sa* to indicate whether its associated processor has arrived at the reduction point during its execution or not, a flag *ma* indicating whether the message for the corresponding *id* has arrived or not, a buffer *sdata* to hold the data supplied by its associated processor, a buffer *message* to hold the incoming message, and a buffer *result* to hold the result. These buffers can be accessed by the associated processor.

A multidestination gather message, after arriving at the router interface of an intermediate destination, checks for the flag *sa* to be set on the buffer carrying the same *id* as that of itself. If this flag is set, it indicates that the processor has also arrived at its reduction execution point and has supplied data in the buffer *sdata*. Now the appropriate logic (indicated by the *function* field of the message) gets activated and operates on *sdata* and the data portion of the message to produce *result*. If the flag *sa* is not set, the processor has not supplied its data to the router interface yet. In this case, the message is stored in the *message* field of the buffer carrying the same *id* and the flag *ma* is set. The logic operation will start as soon as the processor arrives at its reduction execution point. Once the logic operation is over at the current router, the message is forwarded to the next destination while replacing *data* of the message with the *result*. Like this, the message moves ahead step by step while gathering results on its way. Finally, the message gets consumed by the router of the last destination and the gathered result is made available to the corresponding processor. The

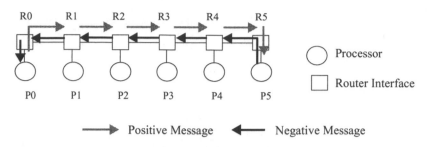

Figure 5.48. Implementation of the global combining operation on a linear array with a pair of positive and negative exchange messages. (From [265].)

operation of a gather message traversing k processors on a path can be expressed more formally as follows:

$$gather[0, k-1] = sdata_0 \odot sdata_1 \odot \ldots \odot sdata_{k-1}$$

where $sdata_i$ is the data item associated with processor p_i, the operation $\odot$ specifies the required reduction function and $gather[0, k-1]$ is the result gathered by the message. The *result* computed at the router interface can also be made available to each intermediate processor. Note that this result is the parallel prefix computation of operation $\odot$ over data items *sdata* associated with the processors already traversed by the message.

As mentioned above, global combining can be achieved by broadcasting the result of the reduction operation to all the participating processors. When performance is critical, global combining can be performed in half the number of steps by using *exchange* messages and a slightly different buffer structure at the router interface [265]. In particular, the single flag *ma* gets substituted by two flags (*pma* for positive message and *nma* for negative message). Similarly, the *message* field of each buffer gets replaced by two fields (*pmessage* and *nmessage*).

Figure 5.48 shows the implementation of the global combining operation on a linear array with a pair of positive and negative exchange messages. Each exchange message acts very much like a gather message. However, the router interface executes the reduction operation (sum, max, min, etc.) when the processor has arrived at its reduction execution point and both the positive and negative exchange messages have already arrived. It can be easily seen that the result of this operation at each router interface is the result of the global combining operation.

This scheme can be easily extended to meshes. Global combining can be achieved on a 2-D mesh by considering it as a set of linear arrays. As shown in Figure 5.49, exchange is first performed along all rows in parallel. At the end of this step, each processor has the result of all the processors in the same row. The second step involves a similar exchange operation along the columns in parallel and operates on the result of the first step. It can be easily seen that this two-step algorithm implements global combining over all processors with the final result being available to all processors.

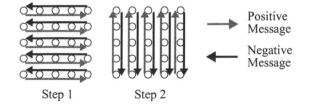

Figure 5.49. Global combining on a 2-D mesh in two steps using exchange messages. (From [265].)

5.7 Software Implementations of Multicast

Intuitively, hardware implementations of multicast communication are desirable as they would offer better performance. However, most existing wormhole-switched multicomputers support only unicast communication in hardware. In these environments, all communication operations must be implemented in software by sending one or more unicast messages. For instance, the multicast operation may be implemented by sending a separate copy of the message from the source to every destination. Depending on the number of destinations, such *separate addressing* may require excessive time, particularly in a one-port architecture in which a local processor may send only one message at a time. Assuming that the start-up latency dominates the communication latency, separate addressing achieves a communication latency that increases linearly with the number of destinations.

Performance may be improved by organizing the unicast messages as a *multicast tree*, whereby the source node sends the message directly to a subset of the destinations, each of which forwards the message to one or more other destinations. Eventually, all destinations will receive the message. The potential advantage of tree-based communication is apparent from the performance of various broadcast methods. For example, in the spanning binomial tree algorithm described in Section 5.5.2, the number of nodes that already received the broadcast message is doubled after each step. Hence, assuming a one-port architecture, communication latency increases logarithmically with the number of destinations.

It is possible to reduce latency even more if the router interface has several ports, allowing nodes to inject several messages simultaneously. However, in this section we will only consider algorithms for a one-port architecture because most commercial multicomputers have a single port. See [232] and [154, 231, 294, 341] for a survey and detailed descriptions of multicast/broadcast algorithms for multi-port architectures, respectively.

5.7.1 Desirable Features in Multicast Trees

Which types of multicast trees should be used depends on the switching technique and unicast routing algorithm. The following features are desirable in the software implementation of a multicast tree.

1. No local processors other than the source and destination processors should be involved in the implementation of the multicast tree.

2. The implementation should exploit the distance-insensitivity of wormhole switching.

3. The height of the multicast tree should be minimal. Specifically, for $m - 1$ destination nodes, the minimum height is $k = \lceil \log_2(m) \rceil$.

4. There should be no channel contention among the constituent messages of the multicast. In other words, the unicast messages involved should not simultaneously require the same channel. Note that this feature does not eliminate contention with other unicast or multicast messages.

How to achieve these goals depends on the switching technique and unicast routing algorithm of the network. Although the user has no control over the routing of individual messages, the designer may be able to reduce or eliminate channel contention by accounting for the routing algorithm in defining the set of unicast messages and the order in which they are transmitted. The following (small-scale) example illustrates the issues and difficulties involved in implementing efficient multicast communication in wormhole-switched networks that use dimension-ordered routing.

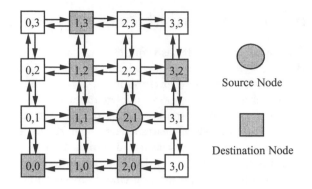

Figure 5.50. An example of multicast in a 4×4 mesh.

Example 5.14

Consider the 4×4 2-D mesh in Figure 5.50, and suppose that a multicast message is to be sent from node $(2,1)$ to seven destinations $\{(0,0), (1,0), (2,0), (1,1), (1,2), (3,2), (1,3)\}$.

In early direct network systems that used SAF switching, the procedure shown in Figure 5.51a could be used. At step 1, the source sends the message to node $(1,1)$. At step 2, nodes $(2,1)$ and $(1,1)$ inform nodes $(2,0)$ and $(1,2)$, respectively. Continuing in this fashion, this implementation requires four steps to reach all destinations. Node $(3,1)$ is required to relay the message, even though it is not a destination. Using the same routing strategy in a wormhole-switched network also requires four steps, as shown in Figure 5.51b. In this case, however, only the *router* at node $(3,1)$ is involved in forwarding the message. Hence, the message may be passed from $(2,1)$ to $(3,2)$ in one step, and no local processors other than the source and destinations are involved in sending the message.

In Figure 5.51c, the branches of the tree are rearranged to take advantage of the distance insensitivity of wormhole switching. The local processor at each destination receives the message exactly once. Using this method, the number of steps is apparently reduced to three. However, closer inspection reveals that the message sent from node $(1,0)$ to node $(1,2)$ and the message sent from node $(2,1)$ to node $(1,3)$ in step 3 use a common channel, namely, the $[(1,1),(1,2)]$ channel. Consequently, these two unicasts cannot take place during the same step, and again four steps are actually required.

This situation is rectified in Figure 5.51d, where only three steps are required. No local processors other than the source and destinations are involved, and the messages sent within a particular step do not contend for common channels. In practice, however, the message-passing steps of the multicast operation may not be ideally synchronized, and contention may arise among messages sent in *different* steps. As indicated in Section 5.2, start-up latency includes system call time at both the source and destination nodes; these latencies are termed the *sending latency* and *receiving latency*, respectively. If these latencies are large relative to the network latency, messages can be sent concurrently, but in different steps. For example, assuming that both sending latency and receiving latency have the same value, denoted by t, and that network latency is negligible, the labels in Figure 5.51d indicate when a copy of the message will enter and leave each node. Assuming a one-port architecture, the latency between two consecutive sends at a particular node is t. Leaf nodes in the tree do not send messages, and therefore encounter only receiving latency. For other destinations (intermediate nodes in the tree), both receiving latency and sending latency are incurred. Under these conditions,

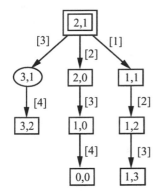

(a) A Multicast Tree Based on
Store–and–Forward Switching

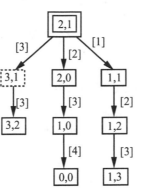

(b) A Multicast Tree Based
on Wormhole Switching

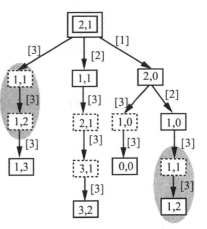

(c) Collision Occurs in Step 3 at the
Channel Between (1,1) and (1,2)

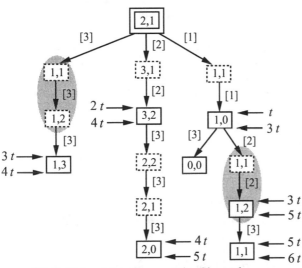

(d) Collision May Occur at the Channel
Between (1,1) and (1,2) if the Sending
and Receiving Latencies Are Large and
Approximately Equal in Value

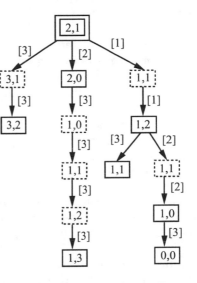

(e) Collision–Free Multicast Tree

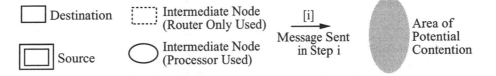

Figure 5.51. Unicast-based software multicast trees.

node $(1,0)$ may not have finished receiving the message from node $(2,1)$ until after node $(2,1)$ has finished sending to node $(3,2)$ and started sending to node $(1,3)$. If node $(1,0)$ sends to node $(1,2)$ at this time, $3t$, then contention will occur for the $[(1,1),(1,2)]$ channel. The multicast tree in Figure 5.51e, which is based on the methods presented in the following sections, is contention-free regardless of message length or receiving latency.

5.7.2   Dimension-Ordered Chains

Developing an algorithm that produces minimum-time, contention-free multicast implementations for a specific system requires a detailed understanding of potential conflicts among messages, which in turn are dependent on the routing algorithm used. This section formulates a method to avoid contention among unicast messages under the most common routing algorithm for wormhole-switched n-dimensional meshes, namely, dimension-order routing. This method was presented in [234].

A few preliminaries are in order. A node address x in a finite n-dimensional mesh is represented by $\sigma_{n-1}(x)\sigma_{n-2}(x)\ldots\sigma_0(x)$. Under a minimal deterministic routing algorithm, all messages transmitted from a node x to a node y will follow a unique shortest path between the two nodes. Let such a path be represented as $P(x,y) = (x; z_1, z_2, \ldots, z_k; y)$, where the z_is are the sequence of intermediate routers visited by the message. In order to simplify the presentation, we let $z_0 = x$ and $z_{k+1} = y$.

In order to characterize contention among messages transmitted under dimension-order routing, an ordering on nodes in an n-dimensional mesh is needed. The multicast algorithms described herein are based on lexicographic ordering of the source and destination nodes according to their address components. Actually, two such orderings are possible: one in which the subscripts of address components increase from right to left, and another in which the subscripts are reversed. Which ordering is appropriate for multicasting in a given system depends on whether addresses are resolved, under dimension-order routing, in decreasing or increasing dimension order. Here it is assumed that addresses are resolved in increasing dimension order, and we will refer to the ordering relation as *dimension order*.

Definition 5.6 *The binary relation* dimension order, *denoted* $<_d$, *is defined between two nodes* x *and* y *as follows:* $x <_d y$ *if and only if either* $x = y$ *or there exists an integer* j *such that* $\sigma_j(x) < \sigma_j(y)$ *and* $\sigma_i(x) = \sigma_i(y) \ \forall \ i, \ 0 \leq i \leq j-1$.

Since $<_d$ is just lexicographic ordering, it is a total ordering on the nodes in an n-dimensional mesh. Therefore, it is reflexive, antisymmetric, and transitive. Given a set of node addresses, they can be arranged in a unique, ordered sequence according to the $<_d$ relation.

Definition 5.7 *A sequence of nodes* $x_1, x_2, \ldots, x_m$ *is a* dimension-ordered chain *if and only if all the elements are distinct and either (1)* $x_i <_d x_{i+1}$ *for* $1 \leq i < m$ *or (2)* $x_i <_d x_{i-1}$ *for* $1 < i \leq m$.

The following lemmas address contention among messages sent between nodes whose addresses are arranged as a dimension-ordered chain [235].

Lemma 5.1 *If* $u <_d v <_d x <_d y$, *then dimension-ordered routes* $P(u,v)$ *and* $P(x,y)$ *are arc-disjoint.*

Lemma 5.2 *If* $u <_d v <_d x <_d y$, *then dimension-ordered routes* $P(y,x)$ *and* $P(v,u)$ *are arc-disjoint.*

Algorithm: The Chain Algorithm
Input: Dimension-ordered address sequence
$\{D_{left}, D_{left+1}, \ldots, D_{right}\}$, where D_{left} is the local address.
Output: Send $\lceil \log_2(right - left + 1) \rceil$ messages
Procedure:
while $left < right$ do
$center = left + \lceil \frac{right - left}{2} \rceil$;
$D = \{D_{center}, D_{center+1}, \ldots, D_{right}\}$;
Send a message to node D_{center} with the address field D;
$right = center - 1$
endwhile

Figure 5.52. The chain algorithm for multicast.

Lemmas 5.1 and 5.2 are critical to the development of efficient multicast algorithms because they indicate how channel contention may be avoided. The *chain algorithm* is a distributed algorithm that can be used to multicast a message from a source node to one or more destinations. The algorithm applies to situations in which the address of the source node is either less than or greater than those of all the destinations, according to the $<_d$ relation. Figure 5.52 gives the chain algorithm executed at each node. The source address and the destination addresses are arranged as a dimension-ordered chain in either increasing or decreasing order, with the source node occupying the position at the left end of the chain. The source node sends first to the destination node halfway across the chain, then to the destination node one quarter of the way across the chain, and so on. Each destination receives a copy of the message from its parent in the tree and may be responsible for forwarding the message to other destinations. The message carries the addresses of those nodes to be in the subtree rooted at the receiving node. The chain algorithm is designed to produce minimum-time multicast implementations on top of dimension-ordered unicast routing. Although some messages are passed through multiple routers before reaching their destinations, it turns out that channel contention will not occur among the messages, regardless of message length or start-up latency — referred to as *depth contention free*. The following theorem forms the basis for developing software-based multicast algorithms.

Theorem 5.2 *A multicast implementation resulting from the chain algorithm is a depth contention-free, minimum-time implementation.*

Example 5.15

Figure 5.53 shows the steps of a multicast implementation resulting from the chain algorithm in a 4×4 2-D mesh that uses XY routing. The set of nodes involved is the same as in Figure 5.50, however, node $(0,0)$ is the source rather than node $(2,1)$. The source node and the seven destinations have been arranged as a dimension-ordered chain. In this case, the X dimension is considered the low-order dimension, and the Y dimension is considered the high-order dimension.

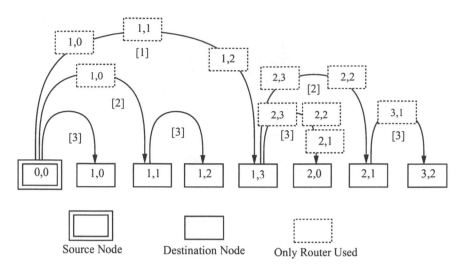

Figure 5.53. Multicast chain example in a 4×4 mesh.

5.7.3   Multicast in Hypercubes

As presented above, the chain algorithm is only applicable to those cases in which the source address is less than or greater than (according to $<_d$) all the destination addresses. Clearly, this situation is not true in general. For a hypercube network in which e-cube routing is used, it is straightforward to construct a depth contention-free multicast algorithm using the chain algorithm. Specifically, the symmetry of the hypercube effectively allows the source node to play the role of the first node in a dimension-ordered chain. The exclusive-OR operation, denoted $\oplus$, is used to carry out this task.

Definition 5.8 *A sequence $d_1, d_2, \ldots, d_{m-1}$ of hypercube addresses is called a d_0-relative dimension-ordered chain if and only if $d_0 \oplus d_1, d_0 \oplus d_2, \ldots, d_0 \oplus d_{m-1}$ is a dimension-ordered chain.*

Let d_0 be the address of the source of a multicast with $m - 1$ destinations. The source can easily sort the $m - 1$ destinations into a d_0-relative dimension-ordered chain, $\Phi = d_1, d_2, \ldots, d_{m-1}$. The source may then execute the chain algorithm using Φ instead of the original addresses. The multicast tree resulting from this method is called a *Unicast-cube*, or *U-cube*, tree. An interesting and useful property of the U-cube tree involves broadcast: the well-known binomial tree [333] is a special case of the U-cube tree when the source node and all destinations form a subcube. Also, the implementation constituting a U-cube tree is a depth contention-free, minimum-time implementation.

5.7.4   Multicast in Meshes

Unlike hypercubes, n-dimensional meshes are not symmetric. The source address may lie in the middle of a dimension-ordered chain of destination addresses, but the exclusive-OR operation is not applicable in the implementation of depth contention-free communication. However, another relatively simple method may be used, again based on the chain algorithm, to address this problem.

The *U-mesh* algorithm is given in Figure 5.54. The source and destination addresses are sorted into a dimension-ordered chain, denoted Φ, at the time when multicast is initiated by calling the U-mesh algorithm. The source node successively divides Φ in half. If the source is in the lower half, then it sends a copy of the message to the smallest node (with respect to $<_d$) in the upper

---

Algorithm: The U-Mesh Tree Algorithm
Inputs: Φ: dimension-ordered chain for source and destinations
$$\{D_{left}, D_{left+1}, \ldots, D_{right}\}$$
D_{source}: the address of source node
Output: Send $\lceil \log_2 (right - left + 1) \rceil$ messages
Procedure:
while $left < right$ **do**
 if $source < \frac{left+right}{2}$ **then** /* send right */
  $center = left + \lceil \frac{right-left}{2} \rceil$;
  $D = \{D_{center}, D_{center+1}, \ldots, D_{right}\}$;
  $right = center - 1$;
 else if $source > \frac{left+right}{2}$ **then** /* send left */
  $center = left + \lfloor \frac{right-left}{2} \rfloor$;
  $D = \{D_{left}, \ldots, D_{center-1}, D_{center}\}$;
  $left = center + 1$;
 else /* send left */
  $center = source - 1$;
  $D = \{D_{left}, \ldots, D_{center-1}, D_{center}\}$;
  $left = source$;
 endif
 Send a message to node D_{center} with the address field D;
endwhile

Figure 5.54. The U-mesh algorithm.

half. That node will be responsible for delivering the message to the other nodes in the upper half, using the same U-mesh algorithm. If the source is in the upper half, then it sends a copy of the message to the largest node in the lower half. In addition to the data, each message carries the addresses of the destinations for which the receiving node is responsible. At each step, the source deletes from Φ the receiving node and those nodes in the half not containing the source. The source continues this procedure until Φ contains only its own address. Note that if the source happens to lie at the beginning or end of Φ, then the U-mesh algorithm degenerates to the chain algorithm. In addition, when executed at an intermediate node in the tree, the U-mesh algorithm is simply the chain algorithm.

Example 5.16

Figure 5.55 depicts a multicast in a 6×6 mesh. Node $(3,3)$ is the source of a multicast message destined for the 16 shaded nodes. Figure 5.56 shows the result of the U-mesh algorithm for this example; intermediate routers are not shown. The source begins with a dimension-ordered chain $\Phi = (0,1), (0,2), (0,4), (1,0), (1,3), (1,5), (2,0), (2,2), (2,3), (2,5), (3,0), (3,2), (3,3), (3,4), (3,5), (4,1), (5,2)$. As shown in Figure 5.56, the source $(3,3)$ first sends to node $(2,3)$, the node with the highest address in the lower half of Φ. The lower half is deleted from Φ, and therefore the nodes remaining in Φ are $(2,5), (3,0), (3,2), (3,3), (3,4), (3,5), (4,1), (5,2)$. Node $(3,3)$ next sends to node $(3,4)$, the node with the lowest address in the upper

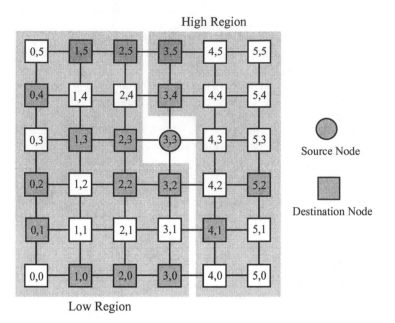

Figure 5.55. U-mesh regions for 16 destinations in a 2-D mesh.

half. The new sequence Φ becomes $(2,5)$, $(3,0)$, $(3,2)$, $(3,3)$. The next recipient is the node with the highest address in the lower half of Φ, namely $(3,0)$. Finally, node $(3,3)$ sends to node $(3,2)$. Each of the receiving nodes is likewise responsible for delivering the message to the nodes in its subtree using the chain algorithm. As shown in Figure 5.56, the multicast operation requires five steps.

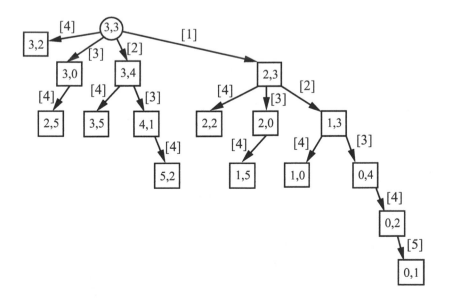

Figure 5.56. U-mesh tree for 16 destinations in a 2-D mesh.

Inspection of Figures 5.55 and 5.56 shows that if the constituent unicast messages follow XY routing, then no contention is possible among them. Two regions, *low* and *high*, are defined on either side (with respect to $<_d$) of the source node. By the construction of the U-mesh algorithm, any message sent by a node i in the high region will be destined for another node j, $i <_d j$, in the high region. Similarly, any message sent by a node i in the low region will be destined for another node j, $j <_d i$, in the low region. Stated in other terms, any reachable set includes nodes in either the low region or high region, but not both. This property can be used to prove depth contention-free message transmission within each region and, furthermore, that no channel contention can exist on the boundary between the two regions. This is stated by the following theorem:

Theorem 5.3 *The multicast implementation constituting a U-mesh tree is a minimum-time, depth contention-free implementation.*

However, contention may arise between concurrent multicast operations initiated by different nodes, specially when destination sets are identical. Contention can be reduced by modifying the dimension-ordered chain according to the position of the source node in the chain. The *Source-Partitioned U-mesh* (SPUmesh) algorithm [173] performs a *rotate-left* operation on the dimension-ordered chain Φ for a source and set of destinations. The rotation produces a new chain Φ_1 whose first element is the source of the multicast. Then, the U-mesh algorithm is performed on Φ_1.

5.8   Engineering Issues

When designing a parallel computer, the designer faces many trade-offs. One of them concerns providing support for collective communication. Depending on the architecture of the machine, different issues should be considered.

Multicomputers usually rely on message passing to implement communication and synchronization between processes executing on different processors. As indicated in Section 5.3.1, supporting collective communication operations may reduce communication latency even if those operations are not supported in hardware. The reason is that system calls and software overhead account for a large percentage of communication latency. Therefore, replacing several unicast message-passing operations by a single collective communication operation usually reduces latency significantly. For example, when a processor needs to send the same message to many different processors, a single multicast operation can replace many unicast message transmissions. Even if multicast is not supported in hardware, some steps like system call, buffer reservation in kernel space and message copy to the system buffer are performed only once. Also, when multicast is not supported in hardware, performance can be considerably improved by using the techniques described in Section 5.7 to organize the unicast messages as a multicast tree. Using those techniques, communication latency increases logarithmically with the number of destinations. Otherwise it would increase linearly. Obviously, implementing some hardware support for collective communication operations will speed up the execution of those operations even more.

On the other hand, communication between processes is usually performed in shared-memory multiprocessors by accessing shared variables. However, synchronization typically requires some hardware support. Barrier synchronization involves a reduce operation followed by a broadcast operation. Moreover, distributed shared-memory multiprocessors with coherent caches rely on a cache coherence protocol. Different copies of the same cache line are kept coherent by using write-invalidate or write-update protocols. Both invalidate and update commands may benefit from implementing hardware support for collective communication operations. Invalidations can be performed by sending a multicast message to all the caches having a copy of the block that is to be written to.

Acknowledgments can be gathered from those caches by performing a reduce operation. Updates can also be performed by sending a multicast message to all the caches having a copy of the block.

Adding hardware support for collective communication increases cost and hardware complexity, possibly slowing down the routing hardware. Now, the question is whether it is useful providing hardware support for collective communication or not. Some parallel computers provide support for a few operations. The nCUBE-2 (wormhole-switched hypercube) [247] supports broadcast within each subcube. The NEC Cenju-3 (wormhole-switched unidirectional MIN) [183] supports broadcast within each contiguous region. The TMC CM-5 [202] supports one multicast at a time via the control network. Unfortunately, in some cases that support was not properly designed. In the nCUBE-2 and the NEC Cenju-3 deadlock is possible if there are multiple multicasts.

One of the reasons for the lack of efficient hardware support for collective communication is that most collective communication algorithms proposed in the literature focused on networks with SAF switching. However, current multiprocessors and multicomputers implement wormhole switching. Path-based routing (see Section 5.5.3) was the first mechanism specifically developed to support multicast communication in direct networks implementing wormhole switching. However, the first path-based routing algorithms were based on Hamiltonian paths [211]. These algorithms are not compatible with the most common routing algorithms for unicast messages, namely, dimension-order routing. Therefore, it is unlikely that a system will take advantage of Hamiltonian path-based routing. Note that it makes no sense sacrificing the performance of unicast messages to improve the performance of multicast messages, which usually represent a smaller percentage of network traffic. Additionally, path-based routing requires a message preparation phase, splitting the destination set into several subsets and ordering those subsets. This overhead may outweigh the benefits from using hardware-supported multicast. Fortunately, in some cases it is possible to perform the message preparation phase at compile time.

More recently, the BRCP model (see Section 5.5.3) has been proposed [268]. In this model, the paths followed by multidestination messages conform to the base routing scheme, being compatible with unicast routing. Moreover, this model allows the implementation of multicast routing on top of both deterministic and adaptive unicast routing, therefore being suitable for current and future systems. So, it is likely to see some hardware implementations of multicast routing based on the BRCP model in future systems. However, more detailed performance evaluation studies are required to assess the benefits of hardware-supported multicast. Also, as indicated in Section 5.5.3, several delivery ports are required to avoid deadlock. This constraint may limit the applicability of the BRCP model.

Efficient barrier synchronization is critical to the performance of many parallel applications. Some parallel computers implement barrier synchronization in hardware. For example, the Cray T3D [258] uses a dedicated tree-based network with barrier registers to provide fast barrier synchronization. Instead of using a dedicated network, it is possible to use the same network as for unicast messages by implementing the hardware mechanisms described in Section 5.6.1. Again, these mechanisms have been proposed very recently, and a detailed evaluation is still required to assess their impact on performance.

As indicated above, protocols for cache coherence may improve performance if multicast and reduce operations are implemented in hardware. In this case, latency is critical. Multicast can be implemented by using the BRCP model described in Section 5.5.3. The multidestination gather messages introduced in Section 5.6.3 can be used to collect acknowledgments with minimum hardware overhead. This approach has been proposed and evaluated in [70]; up to a 15% reduction in overall execution time was obtained.

The cost of the message preparation phase can be reduced by using tree-based multicast routing because it is not necessary to order the destination set. Tree-based routing usually produces more channel contention than path-based routing, also being prone to deadlock. However, the average number of copies of each cache line is small, reducing contention considerably. Also, the pruning mechanism proposed in Section 5.5.2 can be used to recover from deadlock. Tree-based multicast routing with pruning has been specifically developed to support invalidations and updates efficiently [224]. This mechanism has some interesting advantages: it requires a single start-up regardless of the number of destinations, therefore achieving a very small latency; it requires a single delivery channel per node; also, it is able to deliver a message to all its destinations using only minimal paths. However, this mechanism only supports multicast. Support for the reduce operation is yet to be developed.

Most hardware mechanisms to support collective communication operations have been developed for direct networks. Recently some researchers focused on MINs. As shown in Section 5.5.2, MINs are very prone to deadlock when multicast is supported in hardware. Current proposals to avoid deadlock either require complex signaling mechanisms or large buffers to implement VCT switching. Up to now, no general solution has been proposed to this problem. Therefore, direct networks should be preferred if collective communication operations are going to be supported in hardware.

Finally, note that efficient mechanisms to support collective communication operations in hardware have been proposed very recently. Including hardware support for collective communication in the router may increase performance considerably if collective communications are requested frequently. However, in practice, most collective communication operations involve only a few nodes. In these cases, the performance gain achieved by supporting those operations in hardware is small. The only exception is barrier synchronization. In this case, hardware support reduces synchronization time considerably. Some manufacturers include dedicated hardware support for barrier synchronization. Whether hardware support should be specific for barrier synchronization or should support other collective communication operations remains an open question.

5.9   Commented References

Since the proposal of the spanning binomial tree broadcast algorithm [333] for hypercubes, broadcast communication and its extensions (gossiping and personalized broadcast) have been extensively studied [148, 153, 168]. Multicast communication was first studied in [195, 196] for hypercubes based on VCT switching. The theoretical foundation of optimal multicast problems was laid out in [60, 210, 212]. The multicast deadlock problem was studied in [47] for networks using VCT switching. Three multicast protocols, multi-unicast, resumable, and restricted-branch multicast were proposed to deal with the deadlock problem.

Hardware supported multicast routing in wormhole-switched networks was first studied in [211] for hypercubes and 2-D meshes, proposing the path-based multicast routing scheme and the dual-path and multipath algorithms. Detailed performance study of path-based multicast routing was reported in [206, 208]. These multicast algorithms were based on Hamiltonian paths. Path-based adaptive multicast routing was first studied in [205], where three adaptive multicast routing algorithms for 2-D meshes, called PM, FM, and LD, were proposed. In [204], a path-based multicast algorithm was proposed for the hypercube, also evaluating different strategies to order the destination sets. The first sufficient condition for deadlock-free adaptive multicast routing in wormhole-switched networks that allows cyclic dependencies between channels was proposed in [91, 97], where an adaptive multicast routing algorithm was also proposed. This algorithm was evaluated in [216] for 3-D meshes. The above-mentioned sufficient condition was used to propose efficient adaptive multicast routing algorithms for 2-D meshes in [110]. The path-based multicast mechanism was generalized in [342], where a trip-based model was proposed. This model can be applied to any connected network of arbitrary topology. Using this model, it is possible to construct trips such that at most two virtual channels per physical channel are needed to support multiple multicast on arbitrary network topologies.

The BRCP model for path-based multicast routing was first proposed in [268], where two schemes to implement multicast and broadcast, the hierarchical leader-based scheme and the multi-phase greedy scheme, were also proposed. The BRCP model was applied to the development of mechanisms for barrier synchronization [264], reduction, and global combining [265]. For this purpose, gather and exchange messages were proposed in addition to multicast messages. Gather and multicast messages were also proposed to support write-invalidate protocols for DSMs in [70], which presented a detailed performance evaluation study.

The problem of deadlocks produced by delivery channels was independently reported in [38, 216, 268]. A formal solution to this problem was proposed in [267].

Tree-based multicast routing algorithms for wormhole-switched 2-D meshes were first proposed in [206]. Since then, tree-based multicast routing has been discarded for direct networks implementing wormhole switching. However, tree-based multicast routing has been recently proposed for direct networks to support write-invalidate and write-update protocols for DSMs [224]. This routing scheme relies on a pruning mechanism to recover from deadlock.

Tree-based multicast routing has been recently studied on MINs with wormhole switching in [55], where a deadlock avoidance scheme for synchronous message replication was proposed. Asynchronous tree-based multicast routing was proposed in [345], avoiding deadlock by serializing the initiations of multicast operations in groups of switches. In [321], a multiport encoding mechanism was proposed for MINs using VCT switching.

Several approaches have been proposed to implement fast barrier synchronization in hardware [20, 108, 142, 259, 260, 264, 354].

Unicast-based multicast communication for direct networks implementing wormhole switching was studied in [233, 234], where the chain algorithm as well as the U-cube and the U-mesh algorithms were proposed. This work focused on one-port architectures. For multiport and all-port architectures, several multicast/broadcast algorithms have been proposed [154, 231, 294, 341]. Optimal multicast trees based on a parameterized communication model have been studied in [270]. Unicast-based multicast algorithms have also been proposed for bidirectional [352] and unidirectional multistage interconnection networks [56].

Several schemes to encode multiple destination addresses in the message header were proposed in [54]. Finally, see [251] and [266] for a discussion on the issues in designing efficient and practical algorithms for collective communication, and [232] for a recent survey on collective communication in wormhole-switched networks.

EXERCISES

5.1 Consider a hypercube implementing VCT switching, and the multicast set $K = \{u_0, u_1, \ldots, u_k\}$, where u_0 is the source node and $u_1, u_2, \ldots, u_k$ ($k \geq 1$) are k destination nodes. Propose a tree-based greedy multicast algorithm that works by sending a message through the dimension which can reach the most number of remaining destinations, and repeating the procedure until all destinations have been processed. If there is a tie in the number of destinations that can be reached, any selection policy may be used.

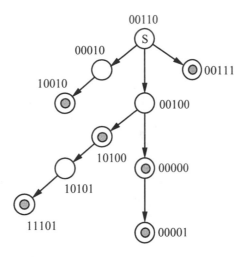

00110

00010

10010

S

00111

00100

10100

00000

10101

11101

00001

Figure 5.57. The multicast tree for the greedy multicast algorithm.

Solution   Assume that for a node u_i in an n-cube, its binary address is represented as $u_{i,n-1}, \ldots, u_{i0}$. The following greedy multicast algorithm, or LEN tree, was proposed by Lan, Esfahanian, and Ni (LEN) [195].

> **Algorithm: Greedy Multicast Algorithm (LEN Tree) for Hypercubes**
> **Input:** Local node address v and k destination addresses, $D = \{d_1, \ldots, d_k\}$.
> **Output:** g destination list(s): $D_1, \ldots, D_g$.
> **Procedure:**
> 1. Let $u_i = v \oplus d_i$ for $1 \le i \le k$.
> 2. If $u_i = 0$ for some i, send a copy of the message to the local processor, and set $D = D - \{d_i\}$.
> 3. Set $p = 1$.
> 4. Let $c_j = \sum_{i \in D} u_{ij}$ for $0 \le j \le n - 1$.
> 5. Find the smallest ℓ, such that $c_\ell \ge c_j$ for all $0 \le j \le n - 1$.
> 6. Set $D_p = \emptyset$.
> 7. For each $d_i \in D$, if $u_{i\ell} = 1$, then set $D_p = \{d_i\} \cup D_p$ and set $D = D - \{d_i\}$.
> 8. Put the destination sublist D_p into message header and send out the message through the ℓ-dimension output channel.
> 9. If $D = \emptyset$, then stop; otherwise, set $p = p + 1$ and go to Step 4.

5.2 Consider a 5-cube and a multicast communication, where source node is 00110 and the six destination nodes are 00111, 10100, 11101, 10010, 00001, and 00000. Show the multicast tree for the greedy multicast algorithm.

Solution   Figure 5.57 shows the multicast tree using the greedy multicast algorithm.

5.3 Consider a 5-cube and a multicast communication, where source node 01010 is sending to a set of six destinations {00111, 01011, 01101, 10001, 11010, 11110}. Compute the source-relative dimension-ordered chain and show the corresponding U-cube tree.

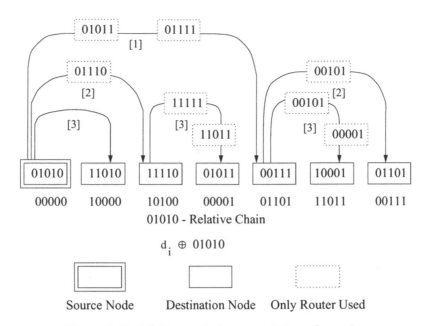

Figure 5.58. Multicast chain example in a five-cube.

Solution   Taking the exclusive-OR of each destination address with 01010 and sorting the results produces the (01010)-relative dimension-ordered chain $\Phi = 01010, 11010, 11110, 01011, 00111, 10001, 01101$. The corresponding U-cube tree is shown in Figure 5.58. It takes three steps for all destination processors to receive the message.

5.4 Consider a unidirectional MIN using wormhole switching. Suppose that path-based multicast routing is implemented in that network. Show that path-based multicast routing produces deadlock in MINs.

Solution   Figure 5.59 shows an example of deadlock for a path-based multicast: a path from node 0 to nodes 4 and 5.

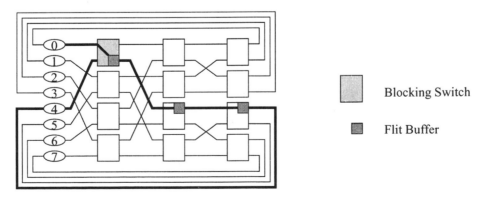

Figure 5.59. An example of deadlock for a path-based multicast.

5.5 Consider an implementation of tree-based multicast routing in a MIN using multiport encoding. The network has n stages and $k \times k$ switches. How many different destination sets can be reached in a single pass through the network?

Solution   Multiport encoding requires n k-bit strings, one for each stage. Each k-bit string indicates the output ports to which the message must be forwarded at the corresponding switch. The same jth k-bit string must be used at all the switches in stage j that route the message. So, a string with all 0s means that the message will not be forwarded through any port in any switch of the corresponding stage. Every other combination is a valid string and will deliver the message to one or more destinations. Therefore, if the network had a single stage, it would be possible to reach $2^k - 1$ different destination sets. For n stages, the number of different destination sets is $(2^k - 1)^n$.

PROBLEMS

5.1 Consider a 5-cube and a multicast communication, where node 01010 is the source and nodes 00000, 10111, 00111, 10101, 11111, 10000, and 00001 are destinations.

- Show the corresponding LEN tree.
- Show the corresponding U-cube tree.

5.2 Consider a 7×7 mesh and a multicast communication, where node $(1, 3)$ is the source and nodes $(0, 0)$, $(0, 6)$, $(6, 0)$, $(6, 6)$, $(3, 3)$, and $(3, 0)$ are six destinations.

- Show the corresponding U-mesh tree and the path followed by each message.
- Show the paths used by dual-path routing.
- Show the paths used by multipath routing.

5.3 Consider an implementation of multicast communication on a 2-D mesh based on the BRCP model. The base routing algorithm is north-last (see Section 4.3.2). Define a grouping strategy for destination nodes that minimizes the number of communication steps.

5.4 Consider a 2-D mesh using XY routing. Multicast communication is based on the BRCP model using XY routing as the base routing. Each node has four delivery channels to avoid deadlock, each one associated with the corresponding input channel. Now consider only the dependencies between delivery channels in adjacent nodes and draw the dependency graph for those channels on a 3×3 mesh. Compare this graph with the channel dependency graph for XY unicast routing (shown in Figure 3.20).

5.5 In a k-port communication model, each processor can simultaneously send messages (same or different) to k processors and simultaneously receive messages from k processors. Modify the chain algorithm for a two-port architecture.

5.6 Consider the architectural support for the implementation of barrier synchronization described in Section 5.6.1. Now consider the implementation of complete barrier synchronization in 2-D meshes as described in Section 5.6.2. Assume that the base routing is the west-first routing algorithm. Define a communication scheme to perform complete barrier synchronization in two steps. How does this scheme affect the architectural support?

5.7 In the study of various communication supports, most research has assumed a certain interconnect topology, such as mesh and hypercube. It is beneficial to study communication supports for a general communication model in order to obtain bounds for the communication latency. One such model is LogP which assumes a fully connected topology. Thus, it is equally efficient to send a message between any pair of processors. Furthermore, the communication is organized in steps. During each step, each processor is able to send k messages to k other processors and to receive k messages from k other processors, assuming a k-port architecture. Now consider a parallel machine with n processors. One processor has to broadcast m messages to other $n - 1$ processors. What is the minimum number of steps required to do such a broadcast for each of the following cases?

1. $n = 2^i$ for some i, $m = 1$, $k = 1$
2. Arbitrary n, $m = 1$, $k = 1$
3. Arbitrary n and m, $k = 1$
4. $n = 2^i$ for some i, $m = 1$, $k = 2$
5. Arbitrary n, $m = 1$, $k = 2$

5.8 Consider a fully connected topology with n processors and k ports per processor. How many steps are needed to perform a reduce operation? Show the corresponding algorithm as well.

5.9 Consider the implementation of path-based multicast routing in unidirectional MINs using wormhole switching. Even if deadlocks did not occur, would it be efficient?

5.10 Path-based routing was designed to support multicast communication. What modifications should be made in order to support scatter communication? What are the advantages and disadvantages of the proposed mechanism over multiple unicast routing?

5.11 Many of the proposed multicast routing algorithms were for mesh topologies. Consider the dual-path algorithm. Is it possible to modify this algorithm so that it works for torus topologies? If the answer is negative, explain the reasons. Otherwise, define a Hamiltonian path that takes advantage of wraparound channels and a multicast routing algorithm based on it.

5.12 Consider a 2-D torus network with two virtual unidirectional channels per physical unidirectional channel.

- Propose a dimension-ordered, deadlock-free unicast routing algorithm.
- Modify the above algorithm to support unicast-based multicast communication.

5.13 Discuss the advantages and disadvantages in using group ID (GID) instead of list of destination addresses in delivering a multicast message.

Chapter 6

Fault-Tolerant Routing

Performance and fault tolerance are two dominant issues facing the design of interconnection networks for large-scale multiprocessor architectures. Fault tolerance is the ability of the network to function in the presence of component failures. However, techniques used to realize fault tolerance are often at the expense of considerable performance degradation. Conversely, making high-performance communication techniques resilient to network faults poses challenging problems. The presence of faults renders existing solutions to deadlock and livelock-free routing ineffective. The result has been an evolution of techniques that must again address these basic issues in the presence of component failures.

The current generation of routers are very robust and do not appear to fail very often in practice. However, in some environments it is imperative that failures be anticipated and addressed, no matter how remote the possibility of component failures e.g., mission critical defense applications, space-borne systems, environmental controls, etc. These operating environments are characterized by differing component failure rates, ability for repair, and the feasibility of gracefully degraded operation. This has led to the development of a range of approaches to fault-tolerant routing in direct networks. This chapter presents a sampling of the various approaches with descriptions of specific routing algorithms. The ability to diagnose faults, particularly on-line, is a challenging problem and merits attention as a distinct research topic. The majority of techniques discussed in this chapter presume the existence of such diagnosis techniques, and focus on how the availability of such diagnosis information can be used to develop robust and reliable communication mechanisms. A few routing algorithms combine diagnosis and routing. The difficulty of on-line diagnosis is a function of the switching technique.

This chapter first examines the effect of faults on current solutions to deadlock-free routing, and establishes limits on the inherent redundancy of direct networks. This serves as the point of departure for the descriptions of the fault models and attendant routing algorithms.

6.1 Fault-Induced Deadlock and Livelock

It might initially appear that fully adaptive routing algorithms would enable messages to be routed around faulty regions. In reality, even the failure of a single link can destroy the deadlock freedom properties of adaptive routing algorithms. In this section, examples are presented to demonstrate how the occurrence of distinct classes of failures can lead to deadlock even for fully adaptive routing algorithms. Deadlocked configurations of messages are characterized and key issues that must be

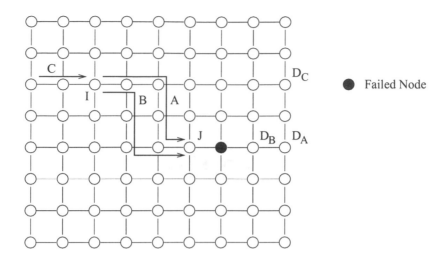

Figure 6.1. An example of the occurrence of deadlock due to faults in the presence of fully adaptive routing.

resolved are identified. In the remainder of this chapter, fault-tolerant routing techniques are then presented and discussed according to how they have chosen to address these issues.

Consider Duato's Protocol (DP), a fully adaptive, minimal-distance routing algorithm using wormhole switching in a 2-D mesh. This algorithm was shown in Figure 4.22. Recall that DP guarantees deadlock freedom by splitting each physical channel into two virtual channels: an adaptive channel and an escape channel. Fully adaptive routing is permitted using the adaptive channels, while deadlock is avoided by only permitting dimension-order routing on the escape channels.

Consider what happens when the router shown in Figure 6.1 fails. The figure shows three messages, A, B, and C. The destination nodes of these messages are also shown although the source nodes are not. Note that the state shown in the figure is not dependent on the location of the source nodes. The figure illustrates the network state at the point in time where all messages have only the last dimension to traverse. Since DP is a minimal-distance routing algorithm, in this last dimension a message has only two candidate virtual channels, and both of them traverse the same physical channel. Suppose that message A reserved adaptive channels from node I to node J, and that message B reserved the escape channel at node I, and then two vertical adaptive channels and two horizontal escape channels, reaching node J. It is apparent from the figure that message A can never make progress since the physical channel connected to the failed router is labeled faulty. Similarly, message B cannot make progress. In addition to blocking the messages requesting a faulty link, a faulty component can also block other messages. As can be seen in Figure 6.1, message C cannot make progress because the two virtual channels requested by it are occupied by messages A and B, respectively. Thus, the messages cannot advance and remain in an effectively deadlocked configuration even though cyclic dependencies between resources do not exist.

An equivalent situation can be constructed even if routers have multiple virtual channels and multiple virtual lanes in each channel. All lanes may be occupied by other messages. In general, if the fault is permanent, then any message waiting for the faulty component waits indefinitely, holding buffer and channel resources. The effect of the fault is propagated through permissible dependencies to affect messages that may not have to traverse the faulty component. These messages are said to form a *wait chain* [124]. Misrouting can avoid such deadlock, but must be controlled so that livelock is avoided and newly introduced dependencies do not produce deadlock. Fault-recovery mechanisms must (1) recover messages indefinitely blocked on faulty components, and (2) be propagated along wait chains to recover messages indirectly blocked on faulty components.

Pipelined switching mechanisms are particularly susceptible to faults due to the existence of dependencies across multiple routers. However, similar examples can be constructed with messages transmitted using packet switching or VCT switching. In this case, messages cannot make progress due to lack of buffer space in the next node along the path. Deadlock may be forestalled, but can eventually occur. While the above example portrays the effect of a static fault, dynamic faults can interrupt a message in progress and are more difficult to handle. Consider the failure of a link during the transmission of a data flit. Following data flits remain blocked in flit buffers with no routing information. These flits remain indefinitely in the network unless they are explicitly removed. Any other message that becomes blocked waiting for these buffers to become free starts the formation of a wait chain which can lead to deadlock.

From the above example, it is possible to identify several issues that must be addressed in the design of fault-tolerant routing algorithms.

1. If a header encounters a faulty component, messages must employ nonminimal routing. Misrouting must be controlled so that livelock is avoided and newly introduced dependencies do not produce deadlock among messages in the network. Typically this can be achieved with additional routing resources (e.g., virtual channels, packet buffers) and suitable routing restrictions among them. This is the minimum functionality required for tolerating static faults.

2. In case of dynamic faults where message transmission is interrupted and message contents possibly corrupted by a component failure, recovery mechanisms must traverse and eliminate or prevent all wait chains. Otherwise it is possible that these messages will remain in the network indefinitely, occupying resources and possibly lead to deadlock. Furthermore, some protocol is required either to recover the possibly corrupted message or to notify the source node so that a new copy of the message is transmitted.

As we might expect, solutions to these problems are dependent upon the type and pattern of the faulty components and the network topology. The next section shows how direct networks possess natural redundancy that can be exploited, by defining the redundancy level of the routing function. The remaining sections will demonstrate how the issues mentioned above are addressed in the context of distinct switching techniques.

6.2 Channel and Network Redundancy

This section presents a theoretical basis to answer a fundamental question regarding fault-tolerant routing in direct networks: What is the maximum number of simultaneous faulty channels tolerated by the routing algorithm? This question has been analyzed in [96], defining the redundancy level of the routing function, and proposing a necessary and sufficient condition to compute its value.

If a routing function tolerates f faulty channels, it must remain connected and deadlock-free for any number of faulty channels less than or equal to f. Note that, in addition to connectivity, deadlock freedom is also required. Otherwise, the network could reach a deadlocked configuration when some set of f channels fail.

The following definitions are required to support the discussion of the behavior of fault-tolerant routing algorithms. In conjunction with the fault model, the following terminology can be used to discuss and compare fault-tolerant routing algorithms.

Definition 6.1 *A network is said to be* connected *with respect to a routing algorithm if the routing function can route a message between any pair of nonfaulty routing nodes.*

This definition is useful since a network may be connected in the graph theoretic sense, where a physical path exists between a pair of nodes. However, routing restrictions may result in a routing function that precludes selection of links along that path.

Definition 6.2 *A channel is said to be* redundant *iff, after removing it, the resulting routing function is still connected and deadlock-free.*

This definition indicates the conditions to support the failure of a given channel. Fault-tolerant routing algorithms should be designed in such a way that all the channels are redundant, thus avoiding a single point of failure. However, even in this case, we cannot guarantee that the network will support two simultaneous faults. This issue is addressed by the following definitions.

Definition 6.3 *A routing algorithm is said to be* f fault-tolerant *if for any f failed components in the network, the routing function is still connected and deadlock-free.*

Definition 6.4 *A routing algorithm is said to be* f fault-recoverable *if for any f failed components in the network, a message that is undeliverable will not hold network resources indefinitely. If a network is fault-recoverable, the faults will not induce deadlock.*

Ideally, we would like the network to be f fault-tolerant for large values of f. Practically, however, we may be satisfied with a system that is f fault-recoverable for large values of f, and f_1 fault-tolerant for $f_1 << f$, so that only the functionality of a small part of the network suffers as a result of a failed component. Certainly, we want to avoid the situation where a few faults may cause a catastrophic failure of the entire network, or equivalently deadlocked configurations of messages. Finally, the next definition gives the redundancy level of the network.

Definition 6.5 *A routing algorithm has a* redundancy level *equal to r iff after removing any set of r channels, the routing function remains connected and deadlock-free, and there exists a set of $r + 1$ channels such that, after removing them, the routing function is no longer connected or it is not deadlock-free.*

Note that an algorithm has a redundancy level equal to r iff it is r fault-tolerant and it is not $r + 1$ fault-tolerant. The analysis of the redundancy level of the network is complex. Fortunately, there are some theoretical results which guarantee the absence of deadlock in the whole network by analyzing the behavior of the routing function R in a subset of channels C_1 (see Section 3.1.3). Additionally, that behavior does not change when some channels not belonging to C_1 are removed. That theory can be used to guarantee the absence of deadlock when some channels fail.

Suppose that there exists a routing subfunction R_1 that satisfies the conditions of Theorem 3.1. Let C_1 be the subset of channels supplied by R_1. Now, let us consider the effects of removing some channels from the network. It is easy to see that removing channels not belonging to C_1 does not add indirect dependencies between the channels belonging to C_1. It may actually remove indirect dependencies. In fact, when all the channels not belonging to C_1 are removed, there are no indirect dependencies between the channels belonging to C_1. Therefore removing channels not belonging to C_1 does not introduce cycles in the extended channel dependency graph of R_1. However, removing channels may disconnect the routing function. Fortunately, if a routing function is connected when

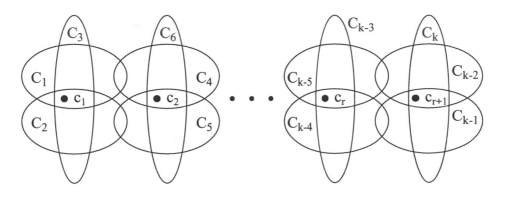

Figure 6.2. Channel sets supplied by all the minimally connected routing subfunctions of R and the corresponding elements in C_m.

it is restricted to use the channels in C_1, it will remain connected when some channels not belonging to C_1 are removed. Thus, if a routing function R satisfies the conditions proposed by Theorem 3.1, it will still satisfy them after removing some or all of the channels not belonging to C_1. In other words, it will remain connected and deadlock-free. So, we can conclude that all the channels not belonging to C_1 are redundant.

We can also reason in the opposite way. In general, there will exist several routing subfunctions satisfying the conditions proposed by Theorem 3.1. We will restrict our attention to the minimally connected routing subfunctions satisfying those conditions because they require a minimum number of channels to guarantee deadlock freedom. Let $R_1, R_2, \ldots, R_k$ be all the minimally connected routing subfunctions satisfying the conditions proposed by Theorem 3.1. Let $C_1, C_2, \ldots, C_k$ be the channel subsets supplied by those routing subfunctions. The set of redundant channels is given by

$$C_s = (C - C_1) \cup (C - C_2) \cup \ldots \cup (C - C_k) = C - (C_1 \cap C_2 \cap \ldots \cap C_k)$$

When $C_1 \cap C_2 \cap \ldots \cap C_k = \emptyset$ all the channels are redundant. Consider again the channel subsets $C_1, C_2, \ldots, C_k$. As the associated routing subfunctions are minimally connected, the failure of a single channel $c_j \in C_i$ will prevent us from using C_i to prove that R is deadlock-free. If the subsets $C_1, C_2, \ldots, C_k$ were disjoint, the routing function R would have a redundancy level equal to $k - 1$. Effectively, the worst case occurs when each faulty channel belongs to a different subset. The failure of $k - 1$ channels will still allow us to use one channel subset to prove deadlock freedom. However, when a channel from each subset fails we can no longer guarantee the absence of deadlock.

In general, the subsets $C_1, C_2, \ldots, C_k$ are not disjoint. In this case, the redundancy level will be less than $k - 1$. An example of channel subsets is shown in Figure 6.2. In order to compute the redundancy level of the network, it is only necessary to find the smallest set of channels $C_m = \{c_1, c_2, \ldots, c_{r+1}\}$ such that at least one channel in C_m belongs to C_i, $\forall i \in \{1, 2, \ldots, k\}$. If all the channels belonging to C_m fail, we cannot guarantee the absence of deadlock. Thus, the redundancy level is equal to the cardinality of C_m minus 1. This intuitive view is formalized by the following theorem:

Theorem 6.1 *A coherent routing function R for an interconnection network I has a redundancy level equal to r iff there exist $k > r$ minimally connected routing subfunctions $R_1, R_2, \ldots, R_k$, and these are the only such routing subfunctions that have no cycles in their corresponding extended* *channel dependency graphs, and there exists a subset of $r + 1$ channels $C_m \subset C$ such that it is the smallest subset of C satisfying that $\forall i \in \{1, 2, \ldots, k\}$, $C_m \cap C_i \neq \emptyset$, where $C_i = \bigcup_{\forall x, y \in N} R_i(x, y)$ is the set of channels supplied by the routing subfunction R_i.*

Theorem 6.1 is only applicable to physical channels if they are not split into virtual channels. If virtual channels are used, the theorem is only valid for virtual channels. However, it can be easily extended to support the failure of physical channels by considering that all the virtual channels belonging to a faulty physical channel will become faulty at the same time. Theorem 6.1 is based on Theorem 3.1. Therefore, it is valid for the same switching techniques as Theorem 3.1, as long as edge buffers are used.

6.3   Fault Models

The structure of fault-tolerant routing algorithms is a natural consequence of the types of faults that can occur and our ability to diagnose them. The patterns of component failures and expectations about the behavior of processors and routers in the presence of these failures determines the approaches to achieve deadlock and livelock freedom. This information is captured in the *fault model*. The fault-tolerant computing literature is extensive and thorough in the definition of fault models for the treatment of faulty digital systems. In this section we will focus on common fault models that have been employed in the design of fault-tolerant routing algorithms for reliable interprocessor networks.

One of the first considerations is the level at which components are diagnosed as having failed. Typically, detection mechanisms are assumed to have identified one of two classes of faults. Either the entire processing element (PE) and its associated router can fail, or any communication channel may fail. The former is referred to as a *node failure* and the latter as a *link failure*. On a node failure, all physical links incident on the failed node are also marked faulty at adjacent routers. When a physical link fails, all virtual channels on that particular physical link are marked faulty. Note that many types of failures will simply manifest themselves as link or node failures. For example, the failure of the link controller, or the virtual channel buffers, appear as a link failure. On the other hand, the failure of the router control unit or the associated PE effectively appears as a node failure. Even software errors in the messaging layer can lead to message handlers "locking up" the local interface and rendering the attached router inoperative, effectively resulting in a node fault. Hence, this failure model is not as restrictive as it may first appear.

This model of individual link and node failures leads to patterns of failed components. Adjacent faulty links and faulty nodes are coalesced into *fault regions*. Generally, it is assumed that fault regions do not disconnect the network, since each connected network component can be treated as a distinct network. Constraints may now be placed on the structure of these fault regions. The most common constraint employed is that these regions be convex. As will become apparent in this chapter, concave regions present unique difficulties for fault-tolerant routing algorithms. Some examples of fault regions are illustrated in Figure 6.3. Convex regions may be further constrained to be *block fault regions*: regions whose shape is rectangular. This distinction is meaningful only in some topologies, whereas in other topologies, convex faults imply a block structure. Given a pattern of random faults in a multidimensional k-ary n-cube, rectangular fault regions can be constructed by marking some functioning nodes as faulty to fill out the fault regions. This can be achieved in a fully distributed manner. The nodes are generally assumed to possess some ability for self-test as well as the ability to test neighboring nodes. We can envision an approach where in one step, each node performs a self-test and interrogates the status of its neighbors. If neighbors or links in two or more

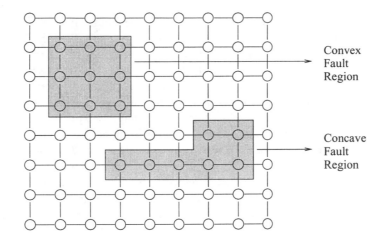

Figure 6.3. Examples of convex and concave fault regions in a 2-D mesh network.

dimensions are faulty, the node transitions to a faulty state, even though it may be nonfaulty. This diagnosis step is repeated. After a finite number of steps bounded by the diameter of the network, fault regions will have been created, and will be rectangular in shape. In multidimensional meshes and tori under the block fault model, fault-free nodes are adjacent to at most one faulty node, i.e., along only one dimension. Note that single component faults correspond to the block fault model with block sizes of 1.

The block fault model is particularly well suited to evolving trends in packaging technology and the use of low dimensional networks. We will continue to see subnetworks implemented in chips, multichip modules (MCM), and boards. Failures within these components will produce block faults at the chip, board and MCM level. Construction of block fault regions often naturally falls along chip, MCM, and board boundaries. For example, if submeshes are implemented on a chip, failure of two or more processors on a chip may result in marking the chip as faulty leading to a block fault region comprised of all of the processors on the chip. The advantages in doing so include simpler solutions to deadlock and livelock-free routing.

Failures may be either *static* or *dynamic*. Static failures are present in the network when the system is powered on. Dynamic failures appear at random during the operation of the system. Both types of faults are generally considered to be *permanent*, i.e., they remain in the system until it is repaired. Alternatively faults may be *transient*. As integrated circuit feature sizes continue to decrease and speeds continue to increase, problems arise with soft errors that are transient or dynamic in nature. The difficulty of designing for such faults is that they often cannot be reproduced. For example, soft errors that occur in flight tests of avionics hardware often cannot be reproduced on the ground. In addition, soft errors may become persistent, defying fault-tolerant schemes that rely on diagnosis of hard faults prior to system start-up. When dynamic or transient faults interrupt a message in progress, portions of messages may be left occupying message or flit buffers. Fault-recovery schemes are necessary to remove such message components from the network to avoid deadlock, particularly if such messages have become corrupted and can no longer be routed. e.g., the message header has been altered or has already been forwarded.

In addition to how components fail, techniques can depend on when they fail. There are a broad range of operational environments characterized by distinct rates at which components may fail. These rates can be measured by the mean time between failures (MTBF). Moreover the mean time to repair (MTTR) can vary significantly from on the order of hours or days for laboratory based machines, to years of unattended operation for space-based systems. It is unlikely that one set of fault-tolerant routing techniques will be cost effective or performance effective across a large range of such systems. For example, we may have MTTR $<<$ MTBF. In this case, the probability of the second or the third fault occurring before the first fault is repaired is very low. Therefore the maximum number of faulty components at any given time is expected to be small, e.g., a maximum of two to three faulty nodes or associated links. The system may be expected to continue operating, although with degraded interprocessor communication performance, until repair can be effected. Many commercial systems have been found to fit this characterization. For such relatively low fault rate environments, it may be feasible to employ lower-cost software-based approaches to handle the rerouting of messages that encounter faulty network components. Alternatively, for systems experiencing long periods of unattended operation such as spaceborne systems (effectively MTTR $\rightarrow \infty$), the number of concurrent failures can continue to grow. Thus, the attendant fault tolerance techniques must be more resilient and more expensive custom solutions may be appropriate.

The behavior of failed components is also important and the system implementation must preserve certain behaviors to ensure deadlock freedom. The failed node can no longer send or receive any messages and is effectively removed from the network. Otherwise messages destined for these nodes may block indefinitely holding buffers and leading to deadlock. In the absence of global information about the location of faults, this behavior can be preserved in practice by having routers adjacent to a failed node remove from the network messages destined for the failed router. It is also generally assumed that the faults are nonmalicious. Malicious injection of faults is not inherently an issue to be addressed by routing algorithms, although malicious faults can lead to flooding of the network with messages. Solutions in the presence of malicious or Byzantine faults can become complicated and involve interpretation of the messages and belong to higher-level protocol layers. This chapter is more concerned with routing messages around faulty components.

Finally, the fault model specifies the extent of the fault information that is available at a node. At one extreme, only the fault status of adjacent nodes is known. At the other extreme, the fault status of every node in the network is known. In the latter case, optimal routing decisions can be made at an intermediate node, i.e., messages can be forwarded along the shortest feasible path in the presence of faults. However, in practice it is difficult to provide global updates of fault information in a timely manner without some form of hardware support. The occurrence of faults during this update period necessitates complex synchronization protocols. Furthermore, the increased storage and computation time for globally optimal routing decisions have a significant impact on performance. At the other extreme, fault information is limited to the status of adjacent nodes. With only local fault information, routing decisions are relatively simple, and can be computed quickly. Also, updating the fault information of neighboring nodes can be performed simply. However, messages may be forwarded to a portion of the network with faulty components, ultimately leading to longer paths. In practice, routing algorithm design is typically a compromise between purely local and purely global fault status information. Figure 6.4 shows an example of the utility of having nonlocal fault information. The dashed line shows the path that would have been taken by a message from S to D. The solid line represents a path that the message could have been routed along had knowledge of the location of the faulty nodes been made available at the source. Finally, information aggregated at node may be more than a simple list of faulty links and nodes in the network or local neighborhood. For example, status information at a node may indicate the existence of a path(s) to all nodes at a distance of k links. Such a representation of node status implicitly encodes the location and distribution of faults. This is in contrast to a explicit list of faulty nodes or links within a k-neighborhood. Computation of such properties is a global operation, and we must be concerned about handling faults during that computation interval.

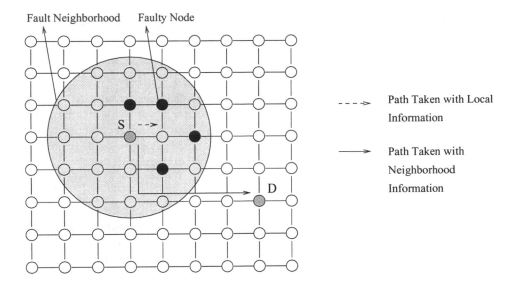

Figure 6.4. An example of using nonlocal fault information.

Developing algorithms for acquiring and maintaining fault information within a neighborhood is the problem of *fault diagnosis*. This is an important problem since diagnosis algorithms executing on-line consume network bandwidth and must provide timely updates to be useful. The notions of diagnosis within network fault models have been formalized in [27, 28]. In k-neighborhood diagnosis, each node records the status of all faulty nodes within distance k. In practice it may not be possible to determine the status of all nodes within distance k since some nodes may be unreachable due to faults. This leads to the less restrictive notion of k-*reachability* diagnosis [28]. In this case, each nonfaulty node can determine the status of each faulty node within distance k that is reachable via nonfaulty nodes. Algorithms for diagnosis are a function of the type of faults; dynamic fault environments will result in diagnosis algorithms different from those that occur in static fault environments.

In summary, the power and flexibility of fault-tolerant routing algorithms are heavily influenced by the characteristics of the fault model. The model in turn specifies alternatives for one or more attributes as discussed in this section. Examples are provided in Table 6.1.

Table 6.1. Examples of fault-tolerant model attributes.

Attribute	Options
Failure type	Node, physical or virtual link
Fault region	Block, convex, concave, random
Failure mode	Static, dynamic, transient
Failure time	MTTR, MTBF
Behavior of faulty components	Inoperable, receive, transmit
Fault neighborhood	Local, global, k-neighborhood, encoded

6.4   Fault-Tolerant Routing in SAF and VCT Networks

This section describes several useful paradigms for rerouting message packets in the presence of faulty network components. In SAF and VCT networks the issue of deadlock avoidance becomes one of buffer management. Packets cannot make forward progress if there are no buffers available at an adjacent router. Unless otherwise stated, the techniques described in this section generally address the issue of rerouting around faulty components under the assumption that the issue of deadlock freedom is guaranteed by appropriate buffer management techniques such as those described in Chapter 4. Rerouting around faulty components necessitates nonminimal routing and therefore the routing algorithms must ensure that livelock is avoided.

The early research on fault-tolerant routing in SAF and VCT networks largely focused on high-dimensional networks such as the the binary hypercube topology. This was in part due to the dependence of message latency on distance and the low average internode distance in such topologies. Additional benefits included low diameter, logarithmic number of ports per router, and an interconnection structure that matched the communication topology of many parallel algorithms. In principle, the techniques developed for binary hypercubes can be suitably extended to the more general k-ary n-cube and often the multidimensional mesh topologies.

In multidimensional direct networks, if the number of faulty components is less than the degree of a node, then the features of the topology can be exploited to find a path between any two nodes. For example, consider an n-dimensional binary hypercube with $f < n$ faulty components. In this topology there are n disjoint paths of length no greater than $n + 2$ between any pair of nodes [299]. As a result, $n - 1$ faulty components cannot physically disconnect the network and we expect to be able to describe an $(n - 1)$ fault-tolerant routing algorithm. The behavior of these algorithms is sensitive to the extent of the fault information available at an intermediate node. If the fault status of larger regions around the intermediate node are known, more informed routing decisions can be made with consequent improved performance. If only local information is available, routing decisions are fast and adjacent faulty regions can be avoided. However, the lack of any lookahead prevents choosing globally efficient routes and path lengths may be longer than necessary. The following routing algorithms differ in the manner in which global information about the location and distribution of faulty components is acquired and used.

6.4.1   Routing Algorithms Based on Local Information

Faulty components can be sidestepped by traversing a dimension orthogonal to the dimensions leading to the faulty components. Chen and Shin [53] describe such an algorithm for routing in binary hypercubes. Unlike k-ary n-cubes, messages in binary hypercubes ($k = 2$) need only traverse one link in each dimension (refer to the description in Chapter 1). If the source and destination node addresses differ in m bits, then the message will traverse m dimensions on a shortest path from the source to the destination. This sequence of dimensions is specified as a *coordinate sequence* and is represented as a list of dimensions. At an intermediate node, a dimension that is not on the shortest path to the destination is referred to as a *spare dimension*. When all of the shortest paths toward the destination from an intermediate node are blocked by faults, the message is transmitted across a spare dimension. The dimensions which were blocked by a fault, as well as those used as a spare dimension are recorded in an n-bit tag maintained in the message header. Note that the size of the tag accommodates at most $n - 1$ faulty components. The resulting message is comprised of several components: $(m, [c_1, c_2, \ldots, c_k], message, d)$. The value of m represents the distance to the

---

Algorithm: Fault-Tolerant Routing Using Spare Dimensions
Input: message $(m, [c_1, c_2, \ldots, c_k], message, d)$
Procedure:

1. If $m = 0$, then the destination has been reached.

2. For $j := 1$ to m, if link c_j is not faulty, then send $(m - 1, [c_1, c_2, \ldots, c_{j-1}, c_{j+1}, \ldots, c_m], message, d)$ along link c_j and stop.

3. If all of the dimensions along the shortest path are blocked by faults:

   a. For $j := 1$ to m, $d_{c_j} = 1$. /* record all blocked dimensions */

   b. Let h be the smallest spare dimension such that $d_h = 0$.

   c. $d_h = 1$ and send $(m + 1, [c_1, c_2, \ldots, c_m, h], message, d)$ along dimension h.

Figure 6.5. Fault-tolerant routing using spare dimensions.

destination. When $m = 0$, the router can assert that the local PE is the destination. The tag d is initialized to zero at the source. When an intermediate node receives a message, it is forwarded along one of the dimensions in the coordinate sequence. The header is updated to decrement m and eliminate the dimension being traversed from the coordinate sequence. When blocked by faults along all of the shortest paths, the value of m is incremented, the spare dimension added to the coordinate sequence, the tag d is updated, and the new message is misrouted along the spare dimension. This approach is $(n - 1)$ fault-tolerant. The routing algorithm is described in Figure 6.5.

In [53], the algorithm is shown to be able to route messages between any two nodes if the number of faulty components is less than n. In this case there is at least one spare dimension into the node that is nonfaulty, and the algorithm will find that spare dimension. This approach works well in high-dimensional networks. While the algorithm relies on purely local fault information, it can be extended to propagate fault information to nonneighboring nodes and to use this information effectively. Details can be found in [53].

Example 6.1

Consider an example of a message being routed from node 0010 to node 1101 in Figure 6.6. The original message is $(4, [3,2,1,0], message, 0000)$. The execution of the routing algorithm at the source sends the message with header $(3, [2,1,0], message, 0000)$ to node 1010. This node sends $(2,[1,0], message, 0000)$ to node 1110. At this point a fault on the next smaller dimension causes the message $(1, [1], message, 0000)$ to be forwarded to node 1111. The message must now be misrouted since the only path to the destination is blocked by a fault. The bit in the tag corresponding to this dimension is set, as well as the lowest available spare dimension. The message $(2, [1,0], message\ 0011)$ is sent to node 1110 where it is again routed back to node 1111 as $(1, [1], message\ 0011)$. This is due to the fact that no record of the previous traversal is maintained in the header. However, now at node 1111 dimension 2 is picked as the spare dimension since the tag value is 0011, in effect retaining some history information. The message $(2, [1,2], message, 0111)$ is routed to node 1011 where it can now be routed to node 1101 via dimension 1 and then dimension 2.

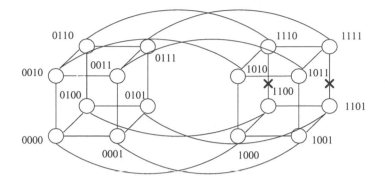

Figure 6.6. An example of SAF routing around faults.

The preceding approach relies on a fixed number of failures to guarantee message delivery, although the probability of delivery with values of $f > n$ is shown to be very high [53]. An alternative to deterministic approaches is the use of randomization to produce probabilistically livelock-free, nonminimal, fault-tolerant routing algorithms. The intuition behind the use of randomization is that repetitive sequences of link traversals typical of livelocked messages are avoided with a high probability. The thesis is that this can be achieved without the higher overhead costs in header size and routing decision logic of deterministic approaches to livelock freedom.

The Chaos router incorporates randomization to produce a nonminimal fault-tolerant routing algorithm using VCT switching. The use of VCT switching in conjunction with nonminimal routing and randomization is proposed as a means to produce very-high-speed, reliable communication substrates [187, 188, 189]. In *chaotic routing*, messages are normally routed along any profitable output channel. When a message resides in an input buffer for too long, blocked by busy output buffers, it is removed from the input buffer and stored in a local buffer pool. Messages in the local buffer pool are given a higher priority when output buffers become free, and messages from this pool are periodically reinjected into the network. In principal, if we have infinite storage at a node, removal of messages after a timeout breaks any cyclic dependencies and therefore prevents deadlock. In reality, the size of the buffer pool at a node is finite and is implemented as a queue. When this queue is full and a message must be stored in the queue, a random message is selected and misrouted. This is sufficient to prevent deadlock. However, livelock is still a source of concern. The key idea here is that a message has a nonzero probability of avoiding misrouting. This is in contrast to deterministic approaches wherein given specific router state, one fixed message is always selected for misrouting. The analysis of chaotic routing shows that the probability of infinite length paths approaches 0. Thus if a link is faulty, all messages using that link will be forwarded along other profitable links or misrouted around the faulty region.

Figure 6.7 provides a simplified illustration of the operation of a channel along a dimension using chaos routing. Each channel supports one input frame and one output frame to an adjacent router. Messages appearing in the input frames can be routed along any free profitable output dimension, if the corresponding output frame is free. If the message in the input frame cannot be forwarded, then it is stored in the local queue. If the queue is full, then a random message must be removed from the queue and misrouted. In this case, some output frame must be guaranteed to become free. The deroute buffers associated with the input frames ensure that this is indeed the case. This works as follows. When the message in input frame i in node P cannot be forwarded and the queue is full, that message is moved to the associated deroute buffer. We know that by freeing an input frame

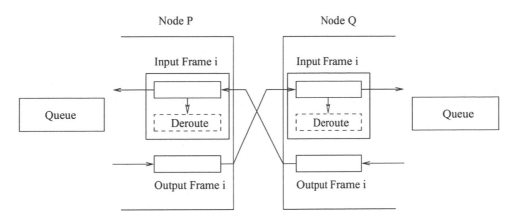

Figure 6.7. A functional view of the channel operation for chaotic routing.

along channel i, node P can receive a message from node Q. This permits progress in node Q's queue, and therefore the input frame i in node Q can be emptied. Consequently, the output frame i in node P can be emptied, can accommodate a message from the queue, and the rerouted message in the deroute buffer i can find its way into the queue. An alternative view toward understanding chaotic routing is to note that all six buffers across a dimension (e.g., as shown in Figure 6.7) cannot be occupied by messages concurrently. If dimensions are served in a round robin manner, then one output frame will eventually become free, permitting movement of messages from the queue to output frames, and therefore from input frames to output frames or the queue. Finally, we note that whenever an output frame becomes free, messages in the queue have priority over messages in the input frame. This exchange protocol across the channel guarantees deadlock freedom. A detailed description of the Chaos router can be found in Chapter 7.

If an adjacent channel is diagnosed or inferred as being faulty, the corresponding output frame will not empty. This frame is effectively unavailable and packets attempting to use this channel are naturally rerouted. There is the problem of recovering the packet that is in the output frame at the time the adjacent router has been diagnosed as faulty. Subsequent efforts have focused in augmenting the natural fault tolerance of chaotic routing with more efficient schemes that avoid losing a packet [355].

6.4.2 Routing Algorithms Based on Nonlocal Information

The preceding approaches assumed the availability of only local information with respect to faulty components – neighboring links and nodes. The greater the extent of the fault information that is available at a node, the more efficient routing decisions can be. Assume that each node has a list of faulty links and nodes within a *k-neighborhood* [198], i.e., all components within a distance of k links. The preceding routing algorithm might be modified as follows. Consider an intermediate node $X = (x_{n-1}, x_{n-2}, \ldots, x_1, x_0)$ that receives a message with a coordinate sequence $(c_1, c_2, \ldots, c_r)$ that describes the remaining sequence of dimensions to be traversed to the destination. From the coordinate sequence we can construct the addresses of all nodes on a minimum length path to the destination. For example, from intermediate node 0110, the coordinate sequence (0, 2, 3) describes a path through nodes 0111, 0011, and 1011. By examining all possible $r!$ orderings of the coordinate sequence we can generate all paths to the destination. If the first k elements of any such path are

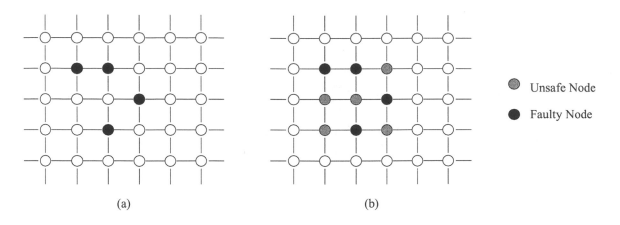

Figure 6.8. An example of the unsafe node designation.

nonfaulty, the message can be forwarded along this path. The complexity of this operation can be reduced by only examining the r disjoint paths to the destination. These disjoint paths correspond to the following coordinate sequences: $(c_1, c_2, \ldots, c_r)$, $(c_2, c_3, \ldots, c_r, c_1)$, $(c_3, c_4, \ldots, c_r, c_1, c_2)$, etc.

Rather than explicitly maintaining a list of faulty components in a k-neighborhood, an alternative method for expanding the extent of fault information is by encoding the state of a node. Lee and Hayes [198] introduced the notion of *unsafe* node. A nonfaulty node is unsafe if it is adjacent to two or more faulty or unsafe nodes. Each node now maintains two lists: one of faulty adjacent nodes, and one for unsafe adjacent nodes. With a fixed set of faulty components, the status of a node may be faulty, nonfaulty, or unsafe. The status can be computed for all nodes in parallel in $O(\log^3 N)$ steps for N nodes. Each node examines the state of its neighbors and changes its state if two or more are unsafe/faulty. A node need only transmit state information to the neighboring nodes if the local state has changed. This labeling algorithm will produce rectangular regions of nodes marked as faulty or unsafe. Figure 6.8 shows an example of the result of the labeling process in a 2-D mesh.

With fault distributions encoded in the state of the nodes, the approach toward routing now can be further modified. The unsafe status of nodes serve as a warning that messages may become

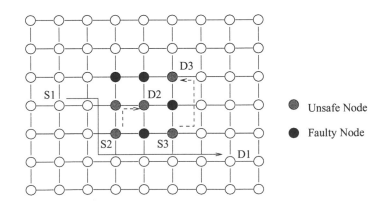

Figure 6.9. Examples of paths when routing in networks with unsafe/faulty nodes.

Algorithm: Fault-Tolerant Routing Using Unsafe Nodes
Procedure:

1. If a nonfaulty neighbor exists on a shortest path to the destination, forward the message to this neighbor. Stop.

2. If an unsafe neighbor exists on a shortest path to the destination, forward the message along this shortest path. Stop.

3. Forward the message to any nonfaulty neighbor. (With less than $\lceil \frac{n}{2} \rceil$ faults, such a neighbor is guaranteed to exist.) Stop.

Figure 6.10. Fault-tolerant routing using the unsafe designation.

trapped or delayed if routed via these nodes. Therefore the routing algorithm is structured to first route a message to an adjacent nonfaulty node on a shortest path to the destination. If such a node does not exist, the message is routed to an unsafe node on a shortest path to the destination. If no such neighboring node can be found, then the message is misrouted to any adjacent nonfaulty node. By construction, in binary hypercubes every nonfaulty and unsafe node must be connected to at least one nonfaulty node if the number of faulty components is less than $\lceil \frac{n}{2} \rceil$. This is not necessarily true for lower dimensional networks such as meshes, as shown in Figure 6.9. This algorithm is summarized in Figure 6.10. In this paradigm, since functioning nodes can be labeled as unsafe, messages may originate from or be destined to unsafe nodes. Step 2 of the algorithm ensures that such messages can be delivered. The overall structure of the algorithm is such that paths are generally constructed through fault-free nodes and around regions of unsafe and faulty nodes. An example of such routing around the rectangular fault regions that occur in 2-D meshes is shown in Figure 6.9. Note how paths between unsafe nodes are constructed.

Example 6.2

This example illustrates how the use of unsafe labels affects routing with the fault pattern shown in Figure 6.8a. Figure 6.9 shows nodes that become labeled unsafe. The solid line illustrates the path that is now taken by a message that is routed from $S1$ to $D1$. Note that the routing of messages through unsafe nodes is avoided. The figure also shows paths taken by messages from nodes $S2$ to $D2$ and from nodes $S3$ to $D3$. Note that the former message is forwarded through an unsafe node. Such routing decisions are preferred to misrouting. The message originating from node $S3$ must be misrouted since all shortest paths to the destination are blocked by faults.

The concept of a safe node captures the fault distribution within a neighborhood. A node is safe if all of the neighboring nodes and links are nonfaulty. This concept of safety can be extended to capture multiple distinct levels of safety in binary hypercubes [350]. A node has a *safety level* of k if any node at a distance of k can be reached by a path of length k. Safety levels can be viewed as a form of nonlocal state information. The location and distribution of faults is encoded in the safety level of a node. The exact locations of the faulty nodes are not specified. However, in practice, knowledge of fault locations is for the purpose of finding (preferably) minimal length paths. Safety levels can be used to realize this goal by exploiting the following properties. If the safety level of a

---

Algorithm: Fault-Tolerant Routing Using Safety Levels
Input: message $(message, Destination)$, tag $= Current\_Node \oplus Destination$, and D the distance to the Destination
Procedure:

1. If $tag = 0$, then the destination has been reached.

2. If there is at least one preferred neighbor with a safety level $\geq D - 1$, send the message to the preferred neighbor with the highest safety level.

3. If there is at least one spare neighbhor with a safety level $\geq D + 1$, update the tag and send the message to this neighbor.

Figure 6.11. Fault-tolerant routing in binary hypercubes using safety levels.

node is S, then for any message received by this node and destined for a node no more than distance S away, at least one neighbor on a shortest path to the destination will have safety level of $(S - 1)$. The neighbors on a shortest path to the destination will be referred to as *preferred* neighbors [350] and the remaining neighbors as *spare* neighbors. Clearly, if the message cannot be delivered to the destination, the safety levels of all of the preferred neighbors will be $< D - 1$, where D is the distance to the destination and that of the spare neighbors will be $< D$. Once the safety levels have been computed for each node, a message may be routed using the sequence of steps shown in Figure 6.11.

A faulty node has a safety level of 0. A safe node has a safety level of n (the diameter of the network). All nonfaulty nodes are initialized to a safety level of n. The levels of the other nodes are determined by the locations of faulty nodes. Intuitively, for a node to have a safety level of k, no more than $(n - k - 1)$ neighbors can have a safety level of less than $(k - 1)$. This will guarantee that for any incoming message destined to traverse k additional links, at least one neighbor along a preferred dimension will have a safety level of at least $k - 1$. It has been shown that this property enables the computation of safety levels of all nodes in $(n - 1)$ steps by a local algorithm that in each step updates the safety level of a node as a function of the safety level of its neighbors from the previous step.

Example 6.3

Consider a binary hypercube with four faulty nodes as shown in Figure 6.12 [350]. The nodes are labeled with their corresponding safety levels. Node 1100 has a safety level of 2. Thus every node at a distance of two hops from node 1100 can be reached by a path of length no more than 2. For example, consider a path to node 0110. If dimensions are traversed in increasing order, the dimension-order path is blocked by the faulty node 1010. However, an alternative path is available: via node 0100. Note that the node 0100 adjacent to node 1100 is on the shortest path to node 0110, and has a safety level of 4. This example illustrates the global nature of the safety level attribute. The exact distribution of the faults is unknown. However, the availability of shortest paths to nodes is encoded in the safety level and this can be used to make local decisions about routing.

Deadlock freedom can be preserved by using any of the techniques described in Chapter 4, e.g., the use of structured buffer pools.

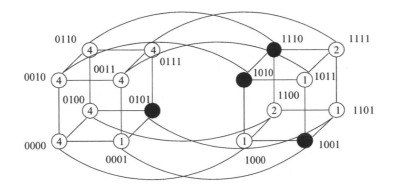

Figure 6.12. An example of computation of safety levels in a 16-node binary hypercube.

6.4.3 Routing Algorithms Based on Graph Search

Often it is not possible to guarantee that the number of faults will be less than $\left\lceil \frac{n}{2} \right\rceil$ or node degree. In this case, more flexible mechanisms are necessary to ensure that messages can be delivered if a physical path exists between two nodes. Routing algorithms based on graph search techniques provide the maximum flexibility. Message packets can be routed to traverse a set of links corresponding to a systematic search of all possible paths between a pair of nodes. Although the routing overhead is significant, the probability of message delivery in faulty networks is maximized. There have been several schemes for such search-based routing algorithms (e.g., [52, 62]). In the following we describe a fault-tolerant packet routing algorithm based on a depth-first traversal of binary hypercubes [52]. While specific computations may differ, the paradigm is certainly applicable to other point-to-point networks employing SAF or VCT switching mechanisms.

A major issue with exhaustive traversals of graphs or networks is that of visiting a node more than once. In the context of routing message packets in multipath networks, visiting a node more than once results in unnecessary overhead. Most approaches utilize state information maintained in the message header to avoid redundant visits. Consider a message structured as $(R, TD, message)$ [52]. R is an n-bit vector that serves as the routing tag. If bit i in R is set, the message must traverse dimension i. When $R = 0$, the message has arrived at its destination. TD is the set of dimensions that the message has traversed. It is initialized to 0 at the source. As the message progresses through intermediate nodes, R and TD are updated. Routing at an intermediate node proceeds in three steps. First the message is transmitted along a link on the shortest path to the destination. If all such paths are blocked by faulty components, the message must be misrouted to a neighboring node. However, we wish to avoid visiting any node more than once. This is realized as follows. In general, given an initial node, and a sequence of dimensions, $c_1, c_2, \ldots, c_k$, we can determine all of the nodes on the path from the source that are visited by traversing these dimensions. For example, starting from node 0110, a message traversing the dimensions 0, 2, and 3 will visit nodes 0111, 0011, and 1011, respectively. When a message is blocked by faults at an intermediate node, the list of dimensions traversed by the message up to this point can be used to compute the addresses of all of the nodes that have been visited by this message. Any adjacent nodes that belong in this set of nodes are no longer candidates for receiving the misrouted message. If all adjacent nodes have been visited or remain blocked by faults, the message backtracks to the previous node. Figure 6.14 shows an example of a search tree (i.e., sequence of nodes) generated by a message transmitted from node 0010 to node 1101. An algorithmic description of a routing algorithm based on depth-first search

---

Algorithm: Fault-Tolerant Routing with Depth-First Search

Input: message $(R, TD, message)$, where R is $(r_{n-1}, r_{n-2}, \ldots, r_1, r_0)$

Notation: $\oplus$ represents the exclusive-OR operation between binary vectors, e^i represents an n-bit vector with bit i set and all remaining bits $= 0$, and & represents the list concatenation operator.

Procedure:

1. If $R = 0$, destination has been reached

2. For $j := 0$ to $n - 1$, if $r_j = 1$ and link j is not faulty and the node adjacent in dimension j has not been visited before, send $(R \oplus e^i, TD\&j, message)$ across dimension j. Stop.

   /* message must be misrouted or backtracked */

3. If possible, pick the smallest dimension h such that the link crossing this dimension is nonfaulty and the node has not been visited before. Send the message $(R \oplus e^h, TD\&h, message)$ across dimension h. Stop.

   /* message backtracks to previous node on the path */

4. If this intermediate node received this message from the node across dimension g, the message $(R \oplus e^g, TD\&g, message)$ is sent back to the previous node on the path, i.e., the message backtracks to the previous node.

Figure 6.13. Fault-tolerant routing with depth-first search.

is provided in Figure 6.13. Optimizations to improve the efficiency of this implementation can be found in [52]. As in related approaches, each misrouting step lengthens the path between source and destination by two hops.

Example 6.4

Consider the path taken by a message from node 0010 to node 1101 in Figure 6.14. The sequence of nodes traversed by this message is (0010, 0011, 0001, 0000, 0001, 0011, 0111, 0101, 1101). The message initially traverses dimension 0, and then dimension 1 to arrive at node 0001. At this point failures in the profitable dimensions forces the message to misroute to node 0000. At node 0000, failures are detected on two outgoing links. The list of dimensions traversed by the message is recorded in the header. This list can be used to reconstruct all of the nodes visited by the message, and is used at node 0000 to determine that node 0010 has been visited (it is actually the source). This forces a backtrack to node 0001. At node 0001 all output channels have been searched. Therefore the message backtracks to node 0011 with message contents $(1110, [0, 1, 0, 0, 1], message)$. The routing algorithm at node 0011 will pick the lowest-numbered dimension that makes progress toward the destination. This is dimension 2, and therefore the message $(1010, [0, 1, 0, 0, 1, 2], message)$ is transmitted to node 0111. The message $(1000, [0, 1, 0, 0, 1, 2, 1], message)$ is sent to node 0101, where it can be forwarded to node 1101.

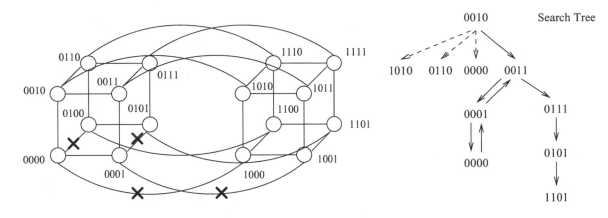

Figure 6.14. An example of depth-first search for fault-tolerant SAF routing.

Related algorithms that are also based on depth-first search, but differing in some of the optimizations can be found in [26, 28]. In particular, [28] describes an algorithm based on concurrent consideration of diagnosis and routing. The routing algorithm can proceed concurrently with on-line diagnosis of faulty nodes and links. The diagnosis algorithm is based on k-reachability and propagates fault information within a k-neighborhood. The approach is to devise a routing algorithm that can make use of concurrently available, and evolving, diagnostic information. As a result the initial message is injected into the network with a specification of the complete path from source to destination stored in the header. If no faults are encountered, the message is successfully routed to the destination along this path. At some intermediate node it may become evident that a node or link along this path has become faulty. This information may have just become available after the message has left the source. The intermediate node attempts to produce a new feasible path to the destination based on this updated diagnostic information. If such a path is not available and the message cannot be forwarded, the message is returned to the previous node on the path, i.e., a backtracking operation takes place. The routing algorithm is again invoked at this node. If the message is backtracked to the source, then it cannot be delivered. The result is an approach that produces a cooperative relationship between on-line k-reachability diagnosis and fault-tolerant routing.

The hyperswitch [62] is an adaptively routed network that supports circuit and packet switching and a set of backtracking routing algorithms for searching the network for uncongested and fault-free paths. The routing algorithm implemented by the hyperswitch is a best-first search heuristic. The routing probes for circuit-switched messages and the headers for packet-switched messages can be subjected to the same routing algorithm. Rather than an exhaustive depth-first search of the binary hypercube, the header maintains a channel history tag. The tag has n bits and records dimensions across which a header has backtracked. It can also be regarded as a record at a node, of the dimensions across which a header has unsuccessfully tried to find a path. When a backtracking header is received and forwarded across another dimension at an intermediate node, the channel history tag is forwarded along with the message. The setting of the dimensions in this tag prevents the message from making traversals along certain dimensions and therefore revisiting portions of the network that may already have been searched. Effectively, portions of the search tree shown in Figure 6.14 are pruned. In example 6.4 when the header backtracks to node 0011, the channel history tag might be set to 0010, and forwarded along with the message to node 0111. This will prevent the message from traversing dimension 1 at node 0111 and the header will be routed to node 1111 and then onto node 1101. The hyperswitch routing algorithm is programmable and can alternatively implement an exhaustive search or a hybrid search where the routing algorithm performs an exhaustive search when the message is within a specified distance from the destination. The hybrid approach is to prevent excessive (and unnecessary) backtracking in large networks when the message is far from the destination. The trade-off is between the probability of finding a path versus finding a longer path via backtracking.

6.4.4   Deadlock and Livelock Freedom Issues

In the description of the preceding SAF techniques, deadlock freedom was not discussed. With the exception of [198], the original descriptions did not directly address deadlock freedom. For SAF networks in general, there are standard techniques for resolving the issue of deadlock freedom, some of which were described in Chapter 3. The preceding routing algorithms could adopt the following approach. The message buffers within each router are partitioned into B classes. These classes are placed in a strict order (a partial order actually will suffice). For example, if the number of buffer classes is the same as the maximum path length of any message, then as messages are routed between nodes, they are constrained to occupy a buffer in a class equal to the distance traversed to that point. With a known maximum distance and a corresponding number of buffers at each node, buffers are occupied in strictly increasing order and deadlock is prevented. The approach described in [198] produces maximum path lengths of $(n+1)$, and thus $(n+2)$ buffer classes would suffice. Typically maximum path lengths, and therefore buffers at a node, depend upon the maximum number of faults. For routing algorithms based on graph search algorithms, the extent of the search would have to be controlled to bound the maximum path length, as a compromise between the probability of finding a path between any two nodes and the amount of buffer space required for deadlock freedom.

It is evident that fault-tolerant routing requires some form of misrouting to avoid faulty components. However, when messages are permitted to be routed farther away from the destination, the possibility of livelock must be addressed. The preceding techniques utilize deterministic approaches to prevent livelock by incorporating history information into the message header. A record of the history of the message is used in conjunction with knowledge of the structure of the network to bound the lifetime of a message packet in the network. The basic paradigm is one wherein the number of options for a message are guaranteed to be finite, and the routing algorithm ensures progress in exploring all of the options. A finite number of options can be created by using history information to ensure that nodes and links cannot be repeatedly visited by a message.

6.5   Fault-Tolerant Routing in Wormhole-Switched Networks

The use of small buffers in wormhole switching presents unique challenges in the design of fault-tolerant routing algorithms. Since blocked messages span multiple router nodes, the effects of faults are rapidly propagated through the routers and to other messages that compete for shared virtual channels. Since recovery from a fault is expensive in terms of time and resources, routing algorithms favor the incorporation of deadlock freedom by construction rather than recovery. The resulting algorithms are closely related to the permissible patterns of faulty components and the switching technique employed.

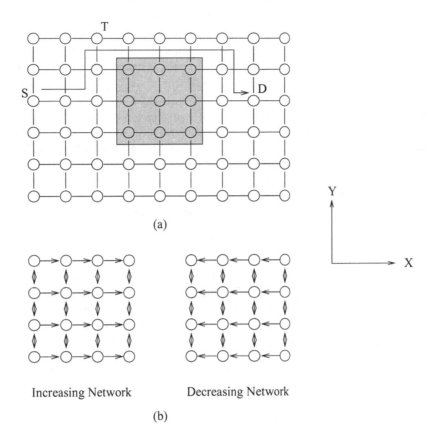

(a)

Increasing Network   Decreasing Network

(b)

Figure 6.15. Routing around block faults.

The most common approach is to route messages around fault regions, and to do so in a manner that avoids introducing new channel dependencies. The ability to successfully route messages around faulty regions depends on the shape of the fault region, and the base routing algorithm that is used, i.e., adaptive or oblivious. Approaches typically involve adding resources such as virtual channels and enforcing routing restrictions among them. The following sections discuss fault-tolerant routing algorithms that have evolved for wormhole-switched networks to accommodate different fault regions.

6.5.1 Rectangular Fault Regions

Consider the simplest fault model: block faults in a 2-D mesh network using the e-cube routing algorithm. Fault-free messages are routed in dimension order. When a block fault is encountered, the desired behavior of the routing algorithms is as shown in Figure 6.15a. The e-cube path of the message from node S to node D passes through the block fault region, and one alternative (nonminimal) path for the message is as shown in the figure. However, traversal of this path would require messages to be routed from a column to a row (e.g., at point T in the Figure 6.15). E-cube remains deadlock-free by preventing messages from traversing a row after traversing a column. Such traversals introduce new dependencies between channels in the vertical and horizontal direction, introduce cycles in the channel dependency graph, and therefore could lead to deadlocked message configurations. A solution to this problem for 2-D mesh networks proposed by Chien and Kim [58] is planar-adaptive routing which was described in Section 4.3.1. This approach adds one additional virtual channel in the vertical direction. Now the set of virtual channels can be partitioned into two virtual networks as shown in Figure 6.15b: the increasing network and the decreasing network. In the increasing (decreasing) network messages only travel in increasing (decreasing) X coordinates. The message shown in Figure 6.15a will be routed in the increasing virtual network. When the fault region is encountered, the message can be routed in the vertical direction to the top (or bottom) of the fault region. At this point the message may continue its progress in the horizontal direction.

Consider the example shown in the figure where the message uses the increasing network. Assume the virtual channel 0 is used in the Y direction in the increasing network. Since the fault regions are rectangular, messages only travel though intermediate nodes with nondecreasing values of the X coordinate. Further, if fault regions do not include boundary nodes, the ability to "turn the corner" around the fault region is guaranteed and messages traverse any given column in only one direction, i.e., there are no dependencies between the channels $d_{1,0}+$ and $d_{1,0}-$ (see Section 4.3.1 for notation). Thus, there are no cyclic dependencies among the channels in the Y direction. Since channels in the X direction are strictly in increasing coordinates, there can be no cyclic channel dependencies involving both X and Y channels. A similar argument can be made for the decreasing network. Since messages only travel in one network or the other, routing is deadlock-free.

The preceding technique is very powerful and can be extended in several ways. Since the networks are acyclic, messages can be adaptively routed [58] along shortest paths: at an intermediate node, a message may be routed along either dimension. The only case where a message will be misrouted is when the destination node is in the same column or row, and the message is blocked by a fault region. As the preceding discussion demonstrated, routing remains deadlock-free. The technique can also be extended to multidimensional meshes using planar-adaptive routing. Recall from Section 4.3.1 that in planar-adaptive routing messages are adaptively routed in successive planes A_i formed by two dimensions, d_i and d_{i+1}. When fault regions are constrained to be block faults, any two-dimensional cross section of the fault region will form a rectangular fault region, and will appear as shown in Figure 6.15a.

Note that when messages reduce the offset in dimension d_i to 0, they are routed in the next adaptive plane. Messages cannot be blocked by a fault region in dimension d_{i+1} having reduced the offset in dimension d_i to zero. Therefore messages are misrouted in only one dimension at a time. Since traffic in distinct adaptive planes that traverse the same physical link travel along separate virtual channels, and misrouting occurs only within one adaptive plane before messages are routed in the next adaptive plane, deadlock freedom is preserved. An algorithmic description of fault-tolerant planar-adaptive routing is provided in Figure 6.16.

The preceding techniques can be extended to tori as follows. Two virtual channels are required for each physical link to break the physical cycles created by the wraparound connections in the network. A solution for tori can be obtained simply by replacing each virtual channel in the mesh solution by two virtual channels. All of the arguments that characterize and demonstrate deadlock freedom for the mesh solution now apply to toroidal networks with appropriate routing restrictions over the wraparound channels to break the physical cycles. This solution requires six virtual channels for each physical channel.

The preceding techniques do encounter problems when fault regions occur adjacent to each other or include nodes on the boundary as shown in Figure 6.17. When messages being misrouted around a fault region reach a boundary node such as R, the direction of the message has to be reversed. This introduces dependencies from channels $d_{i,j}+$ to $d_{i,j}-$ and vice versa, creating cyclic dependencies among the virtual channels in dimension j, and cycles in the channel dependency graphs of the increasing and decreasing networks. The reason can be understood by observing that logically,

Algorithm: Fault-Tolerant Planar-Adaptive Routing for Meshes
Procedure:

1. For each adaptive plane A_i, for $0 \le i \le n - 1$, route the message using the following steps.

2. Route adaptively in dimensions d_i and $d_{(i+1) \bmod n}$ until progress is blocked by a fault.

3. If the offset in dimension d_i is reduced to 0, move to the next adaptive plane.

4. If blocked by a fault in dimension d_i and the offset in dimension d_{i+1} has been reduced to 0, then the message must be forwarded along a nonminimal path around the fault region. If the previous hop was in dimension d_{i+1}, continue in the same direction. Otherwise pick a direction in d_{i+1}.

5. Continue in dimension d_{i+1} until it is possible to turn into dimension d_i.

6. The message is routed in d_i until it is possible to correct in d_{i+1}.

7. Route in d_{i+1} until the offset in this dimension is reduced to zero.

8. Continue to route in dimension d_i.

9. When the offset in dimension d_i has been reduced to 0, move to the next adaptive plane.

Figure 6.16. Fault-tolerant planar-adaptive routing for meshes.

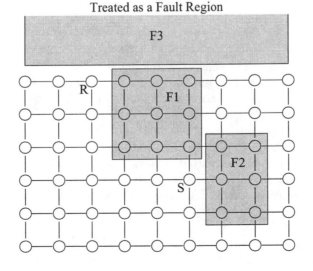

Figure 6.17. Adjacent and boundary fault regions.

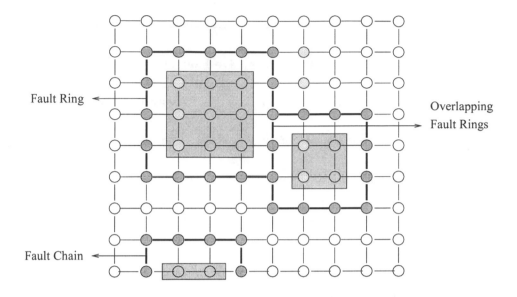

Figure 6.18. An example of fault rings and fault chains.

nodes on the boundary of a mesh are adjacent to a fault region of infinite extent. Messages cannot be routed around this fault region. The situation is equivalent to the occurrence of a concave fault region. Adjacent fault regions produce similar concavities as shown at node S. In the presence of concavities, paths in a 2-D mesh that are traversed by messages misrouted due to faults lose two important properties: (1) the X coordinate is no longer monotonically increasing or decreasing, and (2) new dependencies are introduced between channels in the vertical direction producing cycles in the channel dependency graph. Ensuring that fault regions remain convex will require marking fault-free nodes as faulty. In this example, construction of a rectangular fault region will necessitate marking the first five rows of nodes in Figure 6.17 faulty. Similar examples can be constructed for the multidimensional case. This is clearly an undesirable solution and motivates solutions that make more efficient use of nonfaulty nodes.

One such approach to reduce the number of functional nodes that must be marked as faulty was introduced by Chalasani and Boppana [49], and builds on the concept of *fault rings* to support more flexible routing around fault regions. Intuitively a fault ring is the sequence of links and nodes that are adjacent to, and surround a fault region. Rectangular fault regions will produce rectangular fault rings. Figure 6.18 shows an example of two fault rings and a fault chain. If a fault region includes boundary nodes, the fault ring reduces to a *fault chain*. The key idea is have messages that are blocked by a fault region, be misrouted along the fault rings and fault chains. For oblivious routing in 2-D meshes with nonoverlapping fault rings, and with no fault chains, two virtual channels suffice for deadlock-free routing around fault rings. These two channels form two virtual networks C_0 and C_1, each with acyclic channel dependencies, and messages travel in only one network (see Exercise 6.1).

However, this solution is inadequate in the presence of overlapping fault rings and fault chains. The reason is that the two virtual networks are no longer sufficient to remove cyclic dependencies between channels. Messages traveling in distinct fault rings share virtual channels as shown in Figure 6.18. As a result additional dependencies are introduced between the two virtual networks, leading to cycles. Furthermore, the occurrence of fault chains may cause messages that are initially

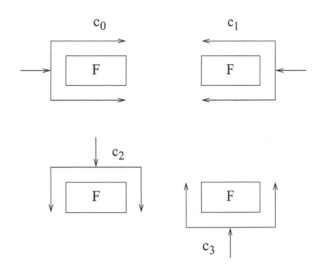

Figure 6.19. Routing restrictions around a fault region. (F = Fault region.)

routed toward the boundary nodes to be reversed. If we employed fault-tolerant planar-adaptive routing, such occurrences would introduce dependencies between the $d_{1,0}+$ and $d_{1,0}-$ virtual channels in dimension 1, creating cyclic dependencies between them.

The solution proposed by Chalasani and Boppana [49] is to provide additional virtual channels to create disjoint acyclic virtual networks. The effect is to separate the traffic of the two fault rings that traverse the shared links. This can be achieved by providing two additional virtual channels per link for a total of four virtual channels over each physical channel. Label these virtual channels c_0, c_1, c_2, and c_3. We may construct four virtual networks, each comprised of virtual channels of each type. Messages are assigned types based on the relative positions of the source and destinations and dimension-ordered routing. In a 2-D mesh, messages are typed as east-west (EW), west-east (WE), north-south (NS), or south-north (SN) based on the relative values of offsets in the first dimension. Routing is in dimension order until a message encounters a fault region. Depending on the type, the message is routed around the fault region as shown in Figure 6.19. The direction around the fault region is selected based on the relative position of the destination node. The WE messages use the c_0 channels, with the remaining messages using the other channels as shown. The EW and WE messages may become NS and SN messages. However, the converse is not true. Thus, dependencies between channel classes are acyclic. Since fault regions are rectangular, dependencies within a fault region are also acyclic — the arguments are similar to those provided for fault-tolerant planar-adaptive routing. A brief description of the routing algorithm is presented in Figure 6.20.

The extension to fully adaptive routing can be performed in a straightforward manner. Assume the existence of any base, fully adaptive routing algorithm and the associated set of virtual channels. The only instance in which the progress of an adaptively routed message is impeded is when the message need only be routed in the last dimension, and progress in this dimension is blocked by a fault region. In this case, with four additional virtual channels, the preceding solution for oblivious routing can be applied. There is no real loss in adaptivity since the message has only one dimension that remains to be traversed. This approach effectively adds four virtual channels to support oblivious routing around fault regions, and transitions to this solution as a last resort. Once a message enters these virtual channels, it remains in these channels until it is delivered to the destination.

Algorithm: Fault-Tolerant Routing Around Block Faults in 2-D Meshes Procedure:

1. Set and determine the message type (EW, WE, NS, or SN) based on the relative address of the destination.

2. At an intermediate node, a message is routed as follows:

   a. If the message has reached the destination deliver the message.

   b. If the message has reached the destination column set the message type to NS or SN.

   c. The message is forwarded along the dimension-order path if fault-free.

   d. The message has encountered a fault region. If this is the first hop in the fault ring or chain, the message picks a direction to follow along the fault ring or fault chain according to Figure 6.19 and the relative location of the destination.

   e. If a dimension-order path is not free, the message continues in the same direction along a fault ring or fault chain.

   f. If the message traversing the fault chain encounters the boundary, the direction of the message is reversed along the fault chain.

Figure 6.20. Fault-tolerant routing in overlapping rings in a 2-D mesh.

Example 6.5

Figure 6.21 shows an example of routing around regions with overlapping fault rings. Two messages A and B have destinations and sources as shown. The former is an EW message and the latter is a WE message. Message B is routed as a WE message around the fault region until it reaches the destination column where the type is changed to that of a NS message. The figure also illustrates the path taken by message A. Note that these two messages share a physical link where the fault rings overlap. Consider the shared link where both messages traverse the link in same direction. If virtual channels were not used to separate the messages in each fault ring, one of the messages could block the other. An EW message can block a WE message and vice versa, resulting in cyclic dependencies. The separation of the messages into four classes, the use of four distinct virtual networks, and acyclic dependencies between these networks prevents the occurrence of deadlock.

If fault rings do not overlap, the above approach is easily extended to fully adaptive routing in tori with the following simple modification. Let us assume there exists a base set of virtual channels that provides fully adaptive deadlock-free routing in 2-D meshes. From the preceding discussion, four additional virtual channels are provided for routing around the fault rings [50], creating the four virtual networks. From Figure 6.19 it is apparent that the channel dependency graph of virtual channels within each of the virtual networks is acyclic. The presence of wraparound channels in the torus destroys this property. The cyclic dependencies introduced in the torus can be eliminated through the use of routing restrictions. Messages traveling in a virtual network are

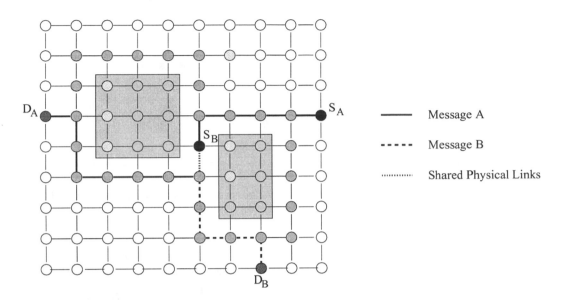

Figure 6.21. An example of routing around overlapping fault rings.

further distinguished by whether or not they will traverse the wraparound channel. These messages are routed in opposite directions around the fault region: messages that will (not) travel along the wraparound channel are routed in the counterclockwise (clockwise) direction around the fault region. Thus, the channel resources used by the message types are disjoint and cyclic dependencies are prevented from occurring between them. The routing algorithm is essentially the same as the extension to fully adaptive routing in 2-D meshes, modified to pick the correct orientation around the fault ring when a message is blocked by a fault.

However, if fault rings in tori overlap, then messages that use the wraparound links share virtual channels with messages that do not use the wraparound links. This sharing occurs over the physical channels corresponding the overlapping region of the fault rings. The virtual networks are no longer independent and cyclic dependencies can be created between the virtual networks and as a result, among messages. It follows from the preceding discussion that four more virtual channels [37] can be introduced across each physical link creating four additional networks to further separate the message traffic over shared links. This is a rather expensive solution. The alternative is to have the network functioning as a mesh. In this case the benefits of a toroidal connection are lost.

A different labeling procedure is used in [43] to permit misrouting around rectangular fault regions in mesh networks. Initially fault regions are grown in a manner similar to preceding schemes and all nonfaulty nodes that are marked as faulty are labeled as *deactivated*. Nonfaulty nodes on the boundary of the fault region are now labeled as *unsafe*. Thus, all unsafe nodes are adjacent to at least one nonfaulty node. An example of faulty, unsafe, and deactivated nodes is shown in Figure 6.22. There are three virtual channels traversing each physical channel. These virtual channels are partitioned into classes. Nodes adjacent to only nonfaulty nodes have the virtual channels labeled as two class 1 channels and one class 2 channel. Nodes adjacent to any other node type have the channels partitioned into class 2, class 3, and class 4 channels. In nonfaulty regions of the network, a message may traverse a class 1 channel along any shortest path to the destination. If no class 1 channel is available, class 2 channels are traversed in two phases. The first phase permits dimension-order traversal of positive direction channels and in the second phase negative direction

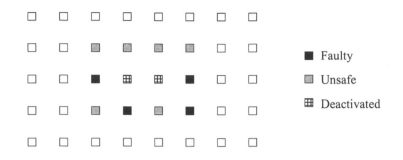

Figure 6.22. An example of adaptive fault-tolerant routing in meshes using three virtual channels.

class 2 channels can be traversed in any order (i.e., not in dimension order). The only time the fully adaptive variant of this algorithm must consider a fault region is when the last dimension to be traversed is blocked by a fault region necessitating nonminimal routing. Dimension $(i + 1)$ and dimension i channels are used to route the message around the fault region. Messages first attempt routing along a path using class 3 channels and class 2 channels in the positive direction. Subsequently messages utilize class 4 channels and class 2 channels in the negative direction. Note that class 3 and class 4 channels only exist across physical channels in the vicinity of faults. The routing restrictions prevent the occurrence of cyclic dependencies between the channels avoiding deadlock.

The paradigm adopted throughout the preceding examples has been to characterize messages by the direction of traversal in the network, and therefore the direction and virtual channels occupied by these message when misrouted around a fault ring. The addition of virtual channels for each message type ensures that these messages occupy disjoint virtual networks and therefore channel resources. Since the usage of resources within a network is orchestrated to be acyclic and transitions made by messages between networks remain acyclic, routing can be guaranteed to be deadlock-free. However, the addition of virtual channels affects the speed and complexity of the routers. Arbitration between virtual channels and the multiplexing of virtual channels across the physical channel can have a substantial impact on the flow control latency through the router [57]. This motivated investigations of solutions that did not rely on many (or any) virtual channels.

Origin-based fault-tolerant routing is a paradigm that enables fault-tolerant routing in mesh networks under a similar fault model, but without the addition of virtual channels [146]. The basic fault-free form of origin-based routing follows the paradigm of several adaptive routing algorithms proposed for binary hypercubes, and the turn model proposed for more general direct network topologies. Each message progresses through two phases. In the first phase, the message is adaptively routed toward a special node. On reaching this node, the message is adaptively routed to the destination in the second phase. In previous applications of this paradigm to binary hypercubes this special node could be the *zenith* node whose address is given by the logical OR of the source and destination addresses. Messages are first routed adaptively to their zenith and then adaptively toward the destination [184]. This phase ordering prevents the formation of cycles in the channel dependency graphs. Variants of this approach have also been proposed including the relaxation of ordering restrictions on the phases [59]. In origin-based routing in mesh networks this special node is the node that is designated as the origin according to the mesh coordinates. While the approach is directly extensible to multidimensional networks, the following description deals with 2-D meshes.

All of the physical channels are partitioned into two disjoint networks. The *IN* network consists of all of the unidirectional channels that are directed toward the origin, while the *OUT* network consists

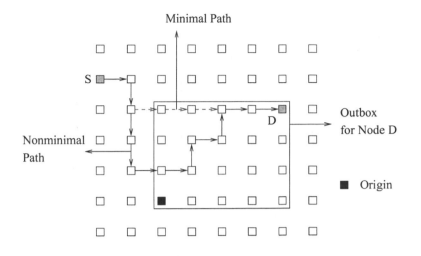

Figure 6.23. An example of origin-based routing in the mesh.

of all of the unidirectional channels directed away from the origin. The orientation of a channel can be determined by the node at the receiving end of the channel. If this node is closer to the origin that the sending end of the channel, the channel is in the *IN* network. Otherwise it is in the *OUT* network. The *outbox* for a node in the mesh is the submesh comprised of all nodes on a shortest path to the origin. An example of an outbox for a destination node *D* is shown in Figure 6.23. Messages are routed in two phases. In the first phase messages are routed adaptively toward the destination/origin, over any shortest path using channels in the *IN* network. When the header flit arrives at any node in the outbox for the destination, the message is now routed adaptively toward the destination using only channels in the *OUT* network. As shown in the example in Figure 6.23, the resulting complete path may not be a minimal path. The choice of minimal paths is easily enforced by restricting messages traversing the *IN* network to use channels that take the message closer to the destination. The result of enforcing such a restriction on the same (source, destination) pair is also shown in Figure 6.23. The choice of the origin node is important. Since all messages are first routed toward the origin, hot spots can develop around the origin. Congestion around the origin is minimized when it is placed at one of the corners of the mesh. In this case, origin-based routing is equivalent to the negative first algorithm derived from the turn model. We know from Chapter 4 that such routing algorithms are only partially adaptive. Placing the origin at the center will improve adaptivity, but increases hot spot contention in the vicinity.

The fault-tolerant implementation of origin-based routing requires the fault regions to be square. Square regions are formed by starting from the rectangular fault regions created by preceding techniques, and disabling additional nodes to ensure that the fault regions are square. A final step in setting up the mesh is for each nonfaulty node to compute and store the distance to the nearest fault region in the north, south, east, and west directions. The time required to compute this information and form the square fault regions depends on the network size, thus being bounded by the diameter of the mesh. Finally an origin node is selected such that the row and column containing the origin has no faulty nodes. If this is not possible, these techniques can be applied to the largest fault-free submesh, disabling all remaining nodes. Central to this routing algorithm is the identification of a set of nodes in the *diagonal band* of the destination. The diagonal band of a node *s* is the set of all nodes in the outbox of *s* that lie on a tridiagonal band toward the origin. The *X* and *Y* offsets from node *s* to any node in the diagonal band, differ by at most 1. An example of a diagonal band

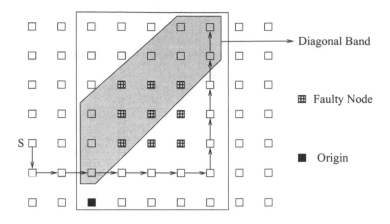

Figure 6.24. Fault-tolerant routing using origin-based routing.

is shown in Figure 6.24. The useful property of nodes in the diagonal band is that there exists a fault-free path from any one of these nodes to the destination node using channels in the *OUT* network [146]. Such nodes are referred to as *safe nodes*. The property of safety of nodes in the diagonal band is ensured by square fault regions. If fault regions are square then any message at a safe node that is blocked by a fault region is guaranteed of the existence of a path around the fault region, through nodes within the outbox, and reaching a destination node on the other side of the fault region. Square fault regions guarantee the safety of nodes in the diagonal band.

Fault-tolerant routing proceeds as follows. Messages are routed adaptively as before in the *IN* network toward the origin until it arrives at a node in the outbox of the destination or the origin (by definition the origin is in the outbox of the destination). Since the origin is in a fault-free column/row and fault regions are square, a free output channel in the *IN* network is guaranteed to exist during this phase. Once the message arrives at a node in the outbox of the destination, if the message is at a safe node then a path is guaranteed to be available to the destination using only channels in *OUT*. If the node is not at a safe node, routing continues in the *IN* network. At an intermediate node the distance to the nearest safe node in each direction can be computed. This is compared to the distance of the nearest fault in that direction. If the safe node is closer than fault regions, the message is routed to that node using only channels in *IN* or *OUT*. By virtue of their construction, safe nodes guarantee the availability of paths by routing around fault regions. If the message encounters a fault region, it can be routed around the fault region until it can be routed back up to the diagonal band. This case is illustrated in Figure 6.24.

Routing occurs in three phases with three successive goals: (1) route to the outbox, (2) route to a safe node in the outbox, and (3) route to the destination. This technique can be applied to meshes in the absence of virtual channels. Other optimizations such as increasing the size of the safe region in the outbox and trading adaptivity for simplicity and speed are described in [146]. A functional description of the algorithm is shown in Figure 6.25.

Rectangular and square fault regions provide some form of nondecreasing property in coordinates of misrouted messages. This property is exploited to prevent the occurrence of deadlocked message configurations. However, the construction of rectangular fault regions by the marking of fault-free routers and links as faulty can lead to significant under utilization of resources. While permitting arbitrary fault patterns is still an elusive goal, it would be desirable to relax the restrictions on the shape of the fault regions.

Algorithm: Fault-Tolerant Origin-Based Routing in 2-D Meshes
Procedure:

1. **Setup:** Source node s and destination node d. All fault-free nodes compute the distance to the nearest fault region and nearest safe node in each dimension.

2. **Phase 1:** The message is adaptively routed in the *IN* network from the source node until the message header arrives at a node in the outbox of d. If necessary, routing choices may be limited to shortest paths.

3. **Phase 2:** The header flit is in the outbox of d.

   a. If the header flit is not at a safe node, compute the distance to the nearest safe node in each direction.

   b. If a safe node is closer than the nearest faulty node in any direction, route the message to this node using only channels in *OUT* or only channels in *IN*.

   c. Otherwise, continue routing in the *IN* network.

4. **Phase 3:** The header flit is at a safe node.

   a. If the message is not blocked by a fault, route to an adjacent safe node that is on the path to the destination

   b. If the message is blocked by a fault, route the message along the faulty region until it can be turned back toward the nodes in the diagonal band. All nodes in the diagonal band are safe.

Figure 6.25. Fault-tolerant origin-based routing in 2-D meshes.

To help achieve this goal, the concept of fault rings can be extended in a minimal manner to account for certain classes of nonconvex fault regions [50]. Consider the class of fault regions in n-dimensional mesh networks where any 2-D cross-section of the fault region produces a single rectangular fault region. Such a fault model is referred to as a *solid fault model* [50]. Figure 6.26 provides an example of a nonconvex fault region that follows the solid fault model, and a message being routed along a fault ring around the fault region. As in previous techniques, for nonoverlapping fault rings and nonfaulty boundary nodes, messages types are distinguished by the relative position of the destination when the message is generated. For deterministic routing, we initially have EW and WE messages. When the message eventually arrives at the destination column, the message type is changed to NS or SN depending on the relative location of the destination. When a message encounters a fault, the rules for routing the message along the fault ring are shown in Table 6.2. There are four virtual channels over each physical channel: $c_0, c_1, c_2,$ and c_3. As in preceding techniques, each set of channels implements a distinct virtual network.

If a message must travel along a fault ring before encountering a fault region, i.e., as shown in the figure at node A, then the message must continue to be routed in the same direction along the fault ring. Otherwise the message follows the direction stated in Table 6.2. Each message type is routed in a distinct virtual network. From the routing rules we can observe that the channel dependency graph within a virtual network is acyclic. Further, messages can only transition from WE or EW

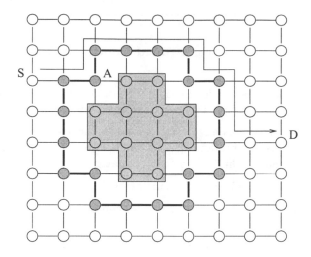

Figure 6.26. An example of routing around a solid fault.

channels to NS or SN channels but not vice versa. Thus, the relation between these virtual networks remains acyclic and therefore routing remains deadlock-free. Note that these rules apply to rings that do not overlap and that do not include nodes on the boundary of the mesh.

6.5.2   Software-Based Fault-Tolerant Routing

The addition of virtual channels and enforcement of routing restrictions between them impacts the design and implementation of the routers. However, in environments where the fault rates are relatively low, the use of expensive, custom, fault-tolerant routers often cannot be justified. Moreover, contemporary routers are compact, oblivious, and fast. Ideally, we wish to retain these features and minimize both the additional hardware support required in the routers and the impact on the router performance. It would also be advantageous to employ techniques that would not require expensive modifications to the routing control to implement rerouting restrictions. The development of these techniques is governed by the relationships between the MTBF and the MTTR. When MTTR $<<$ MTBF, the number of faulty components in a repair interval is small. In fact, the probability of the second or the third fault occurring before the first fault is repaired is very low. In such environments, *software-based rerouting* can be a cost-effective and viable alternative [332].

Table 6.2. Routing rules for solid fault regions.

Message Type	Position of Destination	F-Ring Orientation
WE	Row above current row	Clockwise
WE	Row below current row	Counterclockwise
EW	Row above current row	Counterclockwise
EW	Row below current row	Clockwise
NS or SN	Either	Either orientation

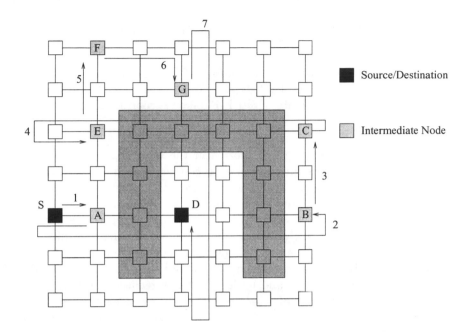

Figure 6.27. An example of software-based fault-tolerant routing (e-sft) in the presence of concave fault regions.

The software-based approach is based on the observation that the majority of messages do not encounter faults and should be minimally impacted while the relatively few messages that do encounter faults may experience substantially increased latency, although the network throughput may not be significantly affected. The basic idea is simple. When a message encounters a faulty link, it is removed from the network or *absorbed* by the local router and delivered to the messaging layer of the local node's operating system. The message-passing software either (1)modifies the header so that the message may follow an alternative path, or (2) computes an intermediate node address. In either case, the message is reinjected into the network. In the case that the message is transmitted to an intermediate node, it will be forwarded upon receipt to the final destination. A message may encounter multiple faults and pass through multiple intermediate nodes. The issues are distinct from adaptive packet routing in networks using packet switching or VCT switching. Since messages are routed using wormhole switching, rerouting algorithms and the selection of intermediate nodes must consider dependencies across multiple routers caused by small buffers (< message size) and pipelined dataflow. Since messages are reinjected into the network, dependencies are introduced between delivery channels at a router and the injection channels. These dependencies are introduced via local storage for absorbed packets. Memory allocation must ensure that sufficient buffer space can be allocated within the nodes or interfaces to avoid creating deadlock due to the introduction of these dependencies.

Since messages are removed from the network and reinjected, the problems of routing in the presence of concave fault regions are simplified. Consider the case of messages being routed obliviously using e-cube routing in a 2-D torus. Figure 6.27 illustrates an example of software-based rerouting in the presence of concave fault regions. The resulting routing algorithm has been referred to as *e-sft* [332]. In step 1 a message from the source is routed through an e-cube path to the destination, and encounters the fault region at node A. The message is absorbed at the node and

X-Dest	Y-Dest	F	X-Final	Y-Final	RT	DF	PF

Figure 6.28. Header format for software-based routing. (DF = Direction flag; F = Faulted status bit; PF = Prevent flag; RT = Reroute table; X-Dest = X coordinate offset; X-Final = X coordinate of the destination; Y-Dest = Y coordinate offset; Y-Final = Y coordinate of the destination.)

the header is modified by the messaging layer to reflect the reverse path in the same dimension, using the wraparound channels. The message again encounters the fault region at node B and is routed to an intermediate node in the vertical direction in an attempt to find a path around the fault region. This procedure is repeated at intermediate nodes E and F before the message is successfully routed around along the wraparound channels in the vertical dimension to the destination node D. While the path and sequence of routing decisions to find the path in the preceding example is easy to convey intuitively, the messaging layer must implement routing algorithms that can implement this decision process in a fully distributed manner with only local information about faults. These rerouting decisions must avoid deadlock and livelock. This is realized through the use of routing tables and by incorporating additional information in the routing header to capture history of encounters with fault regions by this message. The important characteristic of this approach is that messages are still routed in dimension order between any pair of intermediate nodes.

In order to keep track of the manner in which a message is rerouted, the header contains a 2-bit flag called the *Direction Flag* (DF). The DF is used to record the history of encounters with fault regions. For example, the message from S to D in Figure 6.27 will initially have a DF value of (00). When a fault region is encountered, DF is changed to (01), prior to routing in the reverse direction along the wraparound channel. Since fault-free routing is dimension order, a DF value of (10) would imply the message had attempted to traverse the X dimension in both directions and is now trying to traverse the Y dimension. The exception to this interpretation occurs when the source and destination nodes are in the same column. In this case the message will attempt the Y dimension first and the interpretation of DF is reversed, i.e., (00) and (01) ((10) and (11)) refer to the Y dimension (X dimension). A rerouted message may also encounter faults. The DF value in the header is only modified when the message is absorbed at a node. It enables e-sft routing to keep track of the directions along each dimension that have been attempted and therefore aid in rerouting decisions. There are three additional fields that are required in the header. A *Faulted Status* bit (F) indicates that the message has encountered at least one fault and is being rerouted. This bit enables a node to distinguish between messages destined for the local node and messages that must be forwarded. A *Prevent Flag* (PF) status bit is used to prevent the occurrence of certain livelock situations by recording a traversal through all DF values. A 2-bit *Reroute Table* field (RT) specifies one of three routing tables to be used for rerouting decisions. Finally, since messages may be routed through intermediate nodes, there must be two sets of address fields. The first records the final destination address (X-Final, Y-Final). This is an absolute address. The second is used for routing the messages and is an offset within each dimension (X-Dest, Y-Dest). The message header now appears as shown in Figure 6.28. Note that the routers only process the offset fields and set the F bit. All of the remaining header processing is done in software, and only when messages encounter faults. Thus, router operations are minimally impacted.

Let the coordinates of the destination node be (x_d, y_d) and the current node be (x_c, y_c). The offsets to the destination at any intermediate node can be computed as Δx and Δy in each dimension. The network hardware routes messages using traditional dimension-order routing based on the X-Dest and Y-Dest fields in the message header. If the outgoing channel at a router is faulty, the

Table 6.3. Rerouting rules when $\Delta y = 0$ (RT = 1).

Direction Flag	To/Via	Observations
00	$(x_d, y_d)_x^s$	DF = 01 if a fault is encountered
01	$(x_d, y_d)_x^l$	DF = 10 if a fault is encountered and if PF = 0 DF = 11 if a fault is encountered and if PF = 1
10	$(x_c, y_c + r)_y^s$	DF = 00 if no fault is encountered PF = 1 and DF = 11 if a fault is encountered
11	$(x_c, y_c - r)_y^s$	DF = 00 after it is received by a node

Table 6.4. Rerouting rules when $\Delta x = 0$ (RT = 2).

Direction Flag	To/Via	Observations
00	$(x_c, y_d)_y^s$	DF = 01 if a fault is encountered
01	$(x_c, y_d)_y^l$	DF = 10 if a fault is encountered and if PF = 0 DF = 11 if a fault is encountered and if PF = 1
10	$(x_c + r, y_c)_x^s$	DF = 00 if no fault is encountered PF = 1 and DF = 11 if a fault is encountered
11	$(x_c - r, y_c)_x^s$	DF = 00 after it is received by a node

Table 6.5. Rerouting rules when $\Delta y \neq 0$ and $\Delta x \neq 0$ (RT = 3).

Direction Flag	To/Via	Observations
00	$(x_d, y_d)_x^s$	DF = 01 if a fault is encountered
01	$(x_d, y_d)_x^l$	DF = 10 if a fault is encountered
10	$(x_c, y_d)_y^s$	DF = 00 if no fault is encountered DF = 11 if a fault is encountered
11	$(x_c, y_d)_y^l$	DF = 00 after it is received by a node

router sets the F bit, and routes the message to the local processor interface. This causes the message to be marked as a faulted message and ejected to the local messaging layer. If the F bit is set, the messaging software checks the X-Final and Y-Final fields to determine if the message is to be delivered locally. If the message is not to be delivered locally, a rerouting function is invoked. The X-Dest and Y-Dest fields are updated, and if necessary the DF, PF, and RT flags are modified. The initial rerouting function depends on the relative address of the first node where a fault is encountered and the final destination. Tables 6.3 – 6.5 describe the rerouting rules. The notation $(x_c, y_d)_y^s$, refers to the coordinates of the next node in the path using the short (i.e., s) path along the y dimension. The notation l refers to the choice of the longer path. The rerouting algorithm implemented in the messaging layer is described in Figure 6.29.

**Algorithm: Software-Based Fault-Tolerant Rerouting in 2-D Meshes
Procedure:**

1. If $((X\text{-Final}, Y\text{-Final}) == (X\text{-Mynode}, Y\text{-Mynode}))$ deliver locally;

2. Otherwise calculate Δx and Δy;

3. If $(\text{RT} == 0)$ set RT value based on Δx and Δy;

   Else switch (RT)

     Case 1: If $(\Delta x == 0)$, RT = 2; DF = 00; PF = 00;

     Case 2: If $(\Delta y == 0)$, RT = 1; DF = 00; PF = 00;

     Case 3: If $(\Delta x == 0)$, RT = 2; DF = 00; PF = 00;

       Else if $(\Delta y == 0)$, RT = 1; DF = 00; PF = 00;

4. Update DF and PF fields according to the appropriate routing table.

5. Compute new destination address and update the X-Dest and Y-Dest fields.

6. Reinject into the network

Figure 6.29. Software-based fault-tolerant rerouting in 2-D tori.

6.5.3   Unconstrained Fault Regions

Many of the early approaches to fault-tolerant routing did not adopt the approach of placing constraints on the shape of the fault regions. Rather these techniques focused on rerouting around single faulty nodes and links. Since complete knowledge of the patterns of occurrences of faults is not assumed, these techniques are not generally applicable to cases where larger fault regions must be supported. In these instances, the routing algorithms discussed here must rely on fault recovery techniques to prevent deadlock. Consequently guarantees of message delivery are made under conditions very different from those of the preceding techniques. However, these techniques have minimal impact on the design of the routers enabling them to remain compact and fast. Thus, they are attractive in environments with low fault rates.

The turn model described in Chapter 4 can be modified to handle the occurrence of faulty components. The example described here is the nonminimal version of the *negative first* routing algorithm for 2-D meshes. Recall that this algorithm operates in two phases: the message is routed in the negative direction in each of the dimensions in the first phase, and then messages are routed in the positive directions in the second phase. The fault-tolerant nonminimal version routes adaptively in the negative direction, even farther west or south than the destination. For example, this is the path taken by message A in Figure 6.30. During this phase the message is routed adaptively, and around faulty nodes or links. The exception occurs when a message being routed along the edge of the mesh in the negative direction encounters a faulty node. In the second phase, the message is routed adaptively in the positive directions to the destination, unless it reaches the destination column, in which case there is only one path to the destination. However, by permitting the message to be routed further west and south than the destination, more paths to the destination are created for the second phase increasing the possibility that messages can be routed around a single faulty component. Modifications to the routing logic of the base negative first algorithm are

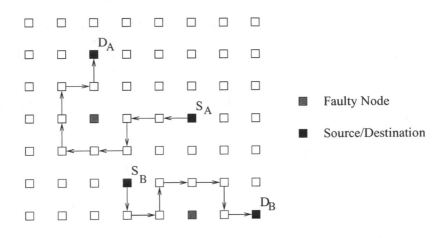

Figure 6.30. An example of fault-tolerant routing based on the turn model.

simply intended to increase the possibility of finding an alternative path when blocked by a faulty component, particularly along an edge of the mesh. The behavior that is permitted in this case is shown by message B in Figure 6.30. Such a single misroute to avoid a faulty component does avoid deadlock. The number of faults that can be tolerated is one less than the number of dimensions. This has been generalized to avoid up to $(n-1)$ faults in n-dimensional meshes [132]. The version of this algorithm for 2-D meshes is provided in Figure 6.31.

The advantage of this approach is that no virtual channels are required. From a practical point of view, in environments where the MTTR << MTBF, it is likely that no more than a single fault will occur within any repair interval. In this case the turn model approach can provide gracefully degraded communication performance in 2-D meshes until the faulty component can be replaced. Meanwhile the hardware architectures of the routers have been minimally impacted remaining compact and fast. For higher-fault-rate environments, more robust techniques that can provide delivery guarantees are desirable.

The *dimension reversal* (DR) approach defined by Dally and Aoki [74] produces gracefully degradable network performance in the presence of faults by dividing messages in classes. Each message

---

Algorithm: Fault-Tolerant Turn Model Routing in 2-D Meshes
Procedure:

1. **Phase 1:** The message is adaptively routed in the negative directions, avoiding the negative edges of the mesh as far as possible. If the message encounters a faulty node on the negative edge, route one hop perpendicular to the edge.

2. **Phase 2:** The message is adaptively routed in the positive directions towards the destination. If a faulty node on a negative edge of the mesh is encountered, the message is routed along a minimal distance path around that node.

Figure 6.31. Fault-tolerant turn model routing in 2-D meshes.

is permitted to be routed in any direction. However, if a message is routed from a channel in dimension d_i to a channel in dimension $d_j < d_i$, a DR counter maintained in the message header is incremented. This DR counter is used to prevent the occurrence of cycles in the channel dependency graph. A static approach to doing so in multidimensional meshes creates r virtual networks by using r virtual channels across each physical channel. All messages are initialized with their DR values equal to zero. Messages are injected into virtual network 0 and permitted to be routed in any direction toward the destination. Misrouting is also permitted, although it should be controlled to ensure livelock freedom. When a dimension reversal takes place, the message moves into the next virtual network. Messages that experience greater than $(r-1)$ dimension reversals are routed in dimension order, i.e., deterministic, nonadaptive routing, in the last virtual network. This approach can require a large number of virtual channels.

An alternative dynamic version of this approach has only two virtual networks: the adaptive network and the deterministic network. Messages are now injected into the adaptive network. These messages can be routed in any direction using only adaptive channels and with no constraints on the number of misroutes other than those required to ensure livelock freedom. However, if a message must block waiting for a free channel at any node, the message may only block on channels being used by messages with a higher value of the DR counter. If virtual channels are labeled with the DR value of the message currently using the channel, this is easy to check. If all outgoing channels are being used by messages with lower DR values, the message enters the deterministic network where it remains while following a fixed dimension-order path to the destination. The ordering of messages in the adaptive network prevents cycles of messages waiting on themselves. Messages only transition into the deterministic network and never the other way around. Therefore deadlock freedom is guaranteed in the fault-free case. Previous approaches have placed strict ordering requirements in resource usage, i.e., channels, to prevent cyclic dependencies. This approach is a bit different in that the message population in partitioned into groups by virtue of the values of their DR counters. Waiting is based on the DR values of the messages rather than channels or dimensions, and messages are prevented from waiting on themselves.

The simulation results provided in [74] show graceful degradation in average message latency and network throughput with relatively high fault rates. However, in the presence of faults, deadlock may still occur. If a physical channel fails, all messages that are constrained to use the deterministic network and cross that physical channel will be blocked indefinitely. These messages cannot be delivered and can eventually lead to deadlocked configurations of messages, although the routing freedom otherwise provided by the DR scheme makes this highly unlikely. To guarantee deadlock freedom in the presence of faults, some form of fault recovery mechanism will be necessary.

A closer look at existing wormhole switching algorithms can lead to several approaches to making these routing algorithms resilient to faults, although guaranteeing deadlock freedom is more difficult to achieve. Consider a minimal fully adaptive routing algorithm such as DP [92]. A simple extension permits an unprofitable adaptive channel to be used if no deterministic channel has been used by the message up to that point. This will permit the message to route around faulty regions with maximum flexibility before having made use of a deterministic channel. However, even if the message has traversed a deterministic channel, misrouting can still be permitted in dimensions lower than that of the last deterministic channel traversed. This will prevent cyclic dependencies from forming among deterministic channels and thus the extended channel dependency graph remains acyclic. However, from the point of view of guaranteeing deadlock freedom, situations may still arise where a message may have to block on a (deterministic) channel. If this channel is faulty, deadlock may result. In this case we would recommend coupling deadlock recovery schemes outlined in Section 6.7 with these schemes. This approach becomes more viable as the MTTR becomes increasingly smaller relative to the MTBF of the network components.

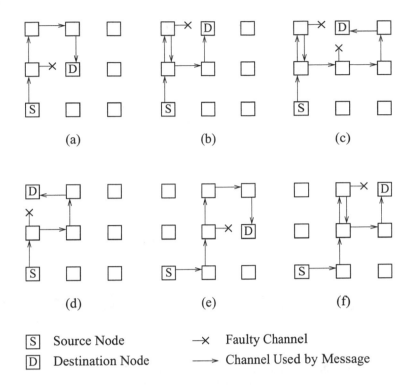

S Source Node   —× Faulty Channel

D Destination Node   ——→ Channel Used by Message

Figure 6.32. Routing examples with faulty channels on a 2-D mesh.

However, routing algorithms can be made more resilient to faults by combining routing techniques that support fully adaptive nonminimal routing. For example, it is possible to combine the theory of deadlock avoidance proposed in Section 3.1.3 with the turn model described in Section 4.3.2. This approach was followed in the fault-tolerant routing algorithm proposed in [94, 96] for n-dimensional meshes using wormhole switching. Each physical channel is split into four virtual channels. Virtual channels are grouped into four sets or virtual networks. The first virtual network consists of one virtual channel in each direction. It is used to send packets toward the east (X-positive). It will be referred to as *eastward* virtual network. The second virtual network also consists of one virtual channel in each direction. It is used to send packets toward the west (X-negative) and it will be referred to as *westward* virtual network. When the X coordinates of the source and destination nodes are equal, packets can be introduced in either virtual network. The routing algorithms for eastward and westward virtual networks are based on nonminimal west-last and east-last, respectively. Once a packet has used a west (east) channel in the eastward (westward) virtual network, it cannot turn again. However, 180-degree turns are allowed in Y channels except in the east (west) border. This routing algorithm is fully adaptive nonminimal. It is deadlock-free, as shown in Exercise 3.3 for 2-D meshes. While routing in the eastward (westward) virtual network, it tolerates faults except when routing on the east (west) border. In order to tolerate faults in the borders, two extra virtual networks are used. The extra eastward (westward) virtual network is used when a fault is met while routing on the west (east) border. The resulting routing algorithm is very resilient to faults under both the node failure and the link failure models [94, 96]. Figure 6.32 shows the paths followed when some channels fail. Figure 6.33 shows the paths followed when some nodes fail. Additionally this approach also supports rectangular fault regions.

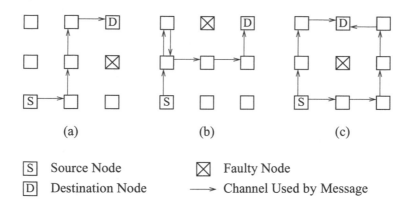

(a)   (b)   (c)

$\boxed{S}$ Source Node		$\boxtimes$ Faulty Node
$\boxed{D}$ Destination Node		$\longrightarrow$ Channel Used by Message

Figure 6.33. Routing examples with faulty nodes on a 2-D mesh. Case (c) shows two alternative paths.

6.6   Fault-Tolerant Routing in PCS and Scouting Networks

The PCS switching mechanism described in Chapter 2 supports the flexible routing of the header to avoid faulty regions of the network. Potential paths from the source to destination are searched by routing a header flit through the network along a path following a depth-first search of the network. The header acquires virtual links as it is routed adaptively toward the destination. When the header is blocked by a fault, and none of the output channels along a path to the destination are available, it may be routed along nonminimal paths. If all candidate output channels at an intermediate router are busy, the header backtracks over the last acquired virtual link, releases the link, and the search is continued from the previous node. History information can be maintained at each individual router rather than within the header to ensure that a particular physical path out of a router will not be searched by the same message more than once. Within each router a $2n$-bit mask, where n is the number of dimensions, is associated with each input virtual channel. This mask is initialized when the header first arrives at the router. When a header backtracks across a virtual channel and back to the router, the corresponding mask bit is set. Therefore, the routing function will prevent the header from being forwarded out across this channel if it backtracks to this node in the future. All channel masks are stored locally. While this approach will prevent a header from traversing the same link twice, without additional support it will not prevent the header from visiting the same node twice. In general, limiting misroutes can be more effective in preventing multiple visits to the same node, while keeping the header size small.

After the header arrives at the destination and a virtual circuit has been successfully established, data are pipelined from the source to the destination. The attractive feature of this approach is the ability to combine the high performance that can be achieved with pipelined data flow with the conservative approach to finding fault-free paths through the network. The advantage of this approach over algorithms using wormhole switching is that performance is less sensitive to the shape of the fault regions and deadlock freedom is independent of the shape of the fault region.

One approach to the use of PCS for fault-tolerant routing is found in a family of misrouting backtracking algorithms. This family is referred to as MB-m [127] and is a set of backtracking algorithms with the routing restriction that less than or equal to m unprofitable links may be

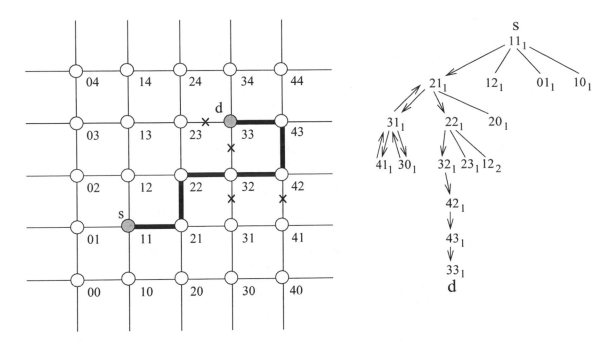

Figure 6.34. An example of a backtracking algorithm using PCS.

allowed in a path. With the history information distributed throughout the nodes, the header flit or probe consists of a vector of dimension offsets, a backtrack flag, and a misroute counter. Consider the following example of routing in a 2-D mesh as shown in Figure 6.34.

Example 6.6

In this example, the header is permitted one misroute in any path to the destination. The source is node 11 and the destination is node 33. The figure shows the final circuit established by the routing header. We see that the header is initially routed profitably from 11 to 31. At this point the header cannot progress along the minimal path to 32, and is misrouted to 41. Since only one misroute is permitted in the path, only profitable links at node 41 are candidate output channels. Since the only profitable links are either faulty, busy, or lead to a parent node, it is necessary to backtrack. A similar situation arises at node 30. Once the header has backtracked from 41 and 30, the history mask associated with the input channel (from node 21) indicates that all options available at 31 have been exhausted. Therefore, the header backtracks to node 21. From this node the header can be routed profitably to node 22, then to node 32. From 32 the probe is misrouted to 42 from which a profitable path can be constructed. Note that while the final path is limited to one misroute: a header may backtrack several times in setting up this path.

By permitting a larger number of misroutes, the algorithm can be made resilient to a larger number of faults. This family of algorithms is referred to as the misrouting backtracking with m misroutes (MB-m) class of algorithms. Deadlock freedom follows from the fact that the header does not block holding resources. Livelock freedom is guaranteed by limiting the number of misroutes.

Algorithm: Misrouting Backtracking Protocols with m Misroutes

Input: message header flit $([d_1, \ldots, d_n], b, m)$, where d_i is the offset the message must traverse in dimension i, b is the backtrack flag, and m is the misroute counter.

Procedure:

1. If the header is backtracking,

   a. Mask this channel by setting the corresponding bit in the history mask.

   b. Decrement the misroute counter m if the link was an unprofitable link.

   c. Otherwise initialize the history mask for this input channel.

2. Send the header over a valid nonmasked, output link. Such a link is one of the following:

   a. If a nonfaulty, profitable output link is available in dimension i, send $([d_1, \ldots, d_i \pm 1, d_n], b, m)$ along the correct direction in dimension i.

   b. Otherwise if m is less than the maximum number of allowed misroutes, select a nonfaulty link among the free, nonprofitable output links, and misroute $([d_1, \ldots, d_i \pm 1, \ldots, d_n], b, m + 1)$ along this link.

3. If a valid output channel is not available, the header must backtrack, and $([d_1, \ldots, d_p \pm 1, \ldots, d_n], b = 1, m)$ is transmitted to the parent node (assuming node is across dimension p).

Figure 6.35. The family of MB-m routing algorithms.

By keeping track of the outgoing links that have been searched at a node by a backtracking header, livelock is avoided although the header may eventually backtrack to the source when the network is congested. At this point some higher-level algorithm must be available to prevent unlimited retries. A description of the MB-m algorithm is shown in Figure 6.35.

The MB-m algorithms are very conservative in the sense that data flits are not injected into the network unless the path has been setup. The result is very robust algorithms for large numbers of faults. This is particularly desirable in systems that experience large periods of unattended operation or high fault rates, e.g., spaceborne embedded systems. However, when message sizes are small and fault rates relatively low, the overhead of an a priori path setup can be substantial. In such environments, an attractive option is to be able to dynamically configure the flow control protocols employed by the routers. Routing algorithms can be designed such that in the vicinity of faulty components messages use PCS style flow control, where controlled misrouting and backtracking can be used to avoid faults and deadlocked configurations. At the same time messages use wormhole switching flow control in fault-free portions of the network with the attendant performance advantages. Messages are routed in two phases — a fault-free phase and a faulty phase. Messages may transition between these two phases several times in the course of being routed between a source and destination node. Routing algorithms designed based on such flow control mechanisms are referred to as *multiphase routing algorithms* [80]. Such dynamically configurable flow control protocols can be configured using variants of scouting switching described in Chapter 2.

The following description presents a two-phase routing algorithm. Message routing proceeds in one of two phases: an optimistic phase for routing in fault-free network segments and a conservative

---

Algorithm: Two-Phase Routing
Procedure:

1. If the header is in DP mode then, pursue the following options in order.

   a. Select a safe profitable adaptive output channel. Stop.

   b. Select a safe deterministic output channel. Stop.

   c. If the safe deterministic channel is not faulty, block.

   d. If the deterministic channel is faulty, select an unsafe profitable adaptive channel and switch to scouting mode. Stop.

   e. Select an unsafe deterministic output channel, switch to scouting mode. Stop.

   f. Set header to detour mode.

2. If header is in detour mode then

   a. Select a profitable channel. Stop.

   b. If the number of misroutes $< m$, then misroute. Stop.

Figure 6.36. A two-phase fault-tolerant routing algorithm.

phase for routing in faulty segments. An example of a Two-Phase (TP) algorithm is shown in Figure 6.36. The optimistic phase uses a fully adaptive, minimal, deadlock-free routing function based on DP (see Section 4.4.4). The conservative phase uses a form of MB-m. The switching technique is scouting switching with a scouting distance of K.

The virtual channels on each physical link are partitioned into restricted and unrestricted partitions. Fully adaptive minimal routing is permitted on the unrestricted partition (adaptive channels) while only deterministic routing is allowed on the restricted partition (deterministic channels). Channels are marked as safe or unsafe [198, 350] depending on the number of faulty links/nodes within the immediate neighborhood. The definition of the extent of this neighborhood for determining the safe/unsafe designation can be quite flexible. The purpose is simply to serve as a warning that traversal of this channel will move the message into the vicinity of faulty nodes and links. Each output virtual channel is provided with a counter to keep track of positive and negative acknowledgments from the headers. The channel also maintains the current value of the scouting distance, K, for comparison with the counter value. Initializing this output value to 0 is equivalent to using wormhole switching.

The selection function uses a priority scheme in selecting candidate output channels at a router node. First, the selection function examines the safe adaptive channels. If one of these channels is not available, either due to the channel being faulty or busy, the selection function examines the available safe deterministic channel. If the safe deterministic channel is busy, the routing header must block and wait for that channel to become free. If a safe adaptive channel becomes free before a deterministic channel is freed, then the header is free to take the adaptive channel. If the deterministic channel is faulty, the selection function will return a profitable adaptive channel, regardless whether it is safe or unsafe. The selection function will not select an unsafe channel over an available safe channel. An unsafe channel is selected only if it is the only alternative other than misrouting or backtracking. When an unsafe profitable channel is selected as an output channel, the message enters the vicinity of a faulty network region. This is indicated by setting a status bit in the routing header. Subsequently, the counter values of every output channel traversed by the header are initialized to K to implement scouting switching and permit header backtracking to avoid faults if the need arises. Flow control is now more conservative, supporting more flexible algorithms in routing around faulty regions. If no unsafe profitable channel is available, the header changes to detour mode and records this status in the header.

In detour mode, the normal positive acknowledgments generated by scouting switching are not transmitted. Therefore data flits do not advance and the header is free to be routed around the faulty region. During the construction of the detour, the routing header performs a depth-first, backtracking search of the network using a maximum of m misroutes. Only adaptive channels are used to construct a detour. The detour is complete when all the misroutes made during the construction of the detour have been corrected or when the destination node is reached. When the detour is completed, acknowledgments flow again and data flits resume progress. Note that all channels (or none) in a detour are accepted before the data flits resume progress. This is required to ensure deadlock freedom.

It is clearly desirable to have messages that do not encounter faults to be routed optimistically with wormhole switching. With respect to the conservative phase, several alternatives are possible. For example, an alternative implementation for the conservative phase is to avoid the usage of the safe/unsafe designation for the channels and to continue optimistic routing using wormhole switching until forward progress is stopped due to faults. At this point, a detour can be constructed using only the header, and increased misrouting as necessary. When a detour is completed, one acknowledgment is sent to resume the flow of the data flits. Note that in this case we always have $K = 0$, and therefore no positive or negative acknowledgments are transmitted. Messages flow until either they are delivered or detours are the only option. In general, we expect that without the use of acknowledgments detours will have to be constructed more often. With the use of acknowledgments and a scouting distance, the header is permitted to backtrack a few links if necessary and potentially avoid costly detour construction. In general, this alternative for the conservative phase (i.e., detour construction only) is a trade-off between acknowledgment traffic bandwidth and the time spent in constructing detours.

Example 6.7

Figure 6.37 shows an example of two-phase routing with seven node failures and $m = 3$. With unsafe channels and K initially set to 0, the routing header routes to node B where it is forced to cross an unsafe channel. The value of K is increased to 3 and the header routes profitably to node A, with the data flits advancing until node B. At node A, the routing header cannot make progress toward the destination and therefore enters detour mode. The header is misrouted upward. After two additional misroutes the header can no longer be misrouted due to the limit on m. The routing header then is forced to backtrack to node A. Since there are no other output channels to select, the routing header is forced to backtrack to node C. From there, it is misrouted twice downward to where a profitable path to the destination can be found. In this example, the detour is completed when the destination is reached. Further, notice that data flits do not advance while the header is in detour mode. Thus, the first data flit is still at node B when the header is delivered to the destination.

The distinguishing features of this approach are: (1) it does not rely on additional virtual channels over that already needed for fully adaptive routing; (2) the performance is considerably better than

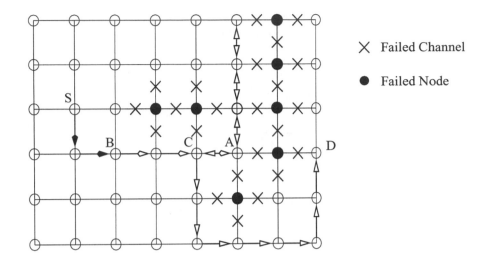

Figure 6.37. An example of two-phase routing.

conservative fault-tolerant routing algorithms with equivalent reliability; (3) it is based on a more flexible fault model, i.e., one that supports link and/or node faults and does not require convex fault regions; (4) it is compatible with existing techniques for recovery from dynamic or transient failures of links or switches (Section 6.7); and (5) it provides routing algorithms greater control over hardware message flow control, opening up new avenues for optimizing message-passing performance in the presence of faults. However, router complexity is increased although required architectural support does not appear to be on the critical path for router operation [80]. This approach does have a more complex channel model that can affect link speeds. From low to moderate number of faults, configurable flow control mechanisms can lead to deadlock-free fault-tolerant routing algorithms whose performance is superior to more conservative routing algorithms with comparable reliability. In a network with a large number of faults, the TP's partially optimistic behavior results in severe performance degradation [80].

6.7 Dynamic Fault Recovery

Often component failures can occur during network operation interrupting the transmission of messages across a link or router. We refer to such failures as dynamic failures. Dynamic failures may be permanent in nature. This is in contrast to transient failures where component operation may be intermittent. For example, a channel may periodically drop a flit or corrupt the contents of the message. In either case, failures may interrupt a message in progress across a link or router. Pipelined communication mechanisms such as wormhole switching or PCS are particularly susceptible to such faults since messages are buffered across multiple routers and data flits do not contain routing information. Packet switching mechanisms are amenable to link level error detection and retransmission with a copy of the packet on either side of the link to prevent loss of data, and eliminate the need for buffering data at the source. With any of the pipelined switching mechanisms, messages are spread over multiple links and present some unique difficulties in recovering from dynamic faults. This section focuses on techniques for recovery from such occurrences.

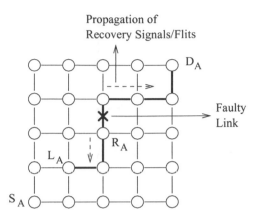

Figure 6.38. Recovery from dynamic failures.

6.7.1   Base Mechanisms

The ability to tolerate dynamic failures in message pipelines places additional requirements on the basic functionality of the network routers and interfaces. Consider the occurrence of a link failure as shown in Figure 6.38. The figure shows a message in transit between nodes S_A and D_A. The last flit of the message has left S_A and is currently in node L_A. The link marked in the network now fails. The portions of the message above the failed link continue to make progress toward the destination. The portions of the message below the failed link, starting with the flits in the output buffers of router R_A, block in place. These data flits have no routing information associated with them. Therefore they cannot be rerouted and block indefinitely holding resources, possibly leading to deadlock as shown in Figure 6.1.

This situation places new requirements on the functionality of switching techniques and associated routing algorithms. There are at least two basic approaches to deal with such orphaned data flits. In one approach, header information is maintained through the routers that contain flits of the message. When messages are interrupted, a new message can be constructed with the stored header information and the (relatively) smaller message can be forwarded along an alternative path to the destination. This will be referred to as *flit-level recovery*. Messages are injected only once into the network and recover from link-level dynamic and transient failures. Alternatively, the blocked data flits can be recovered and discarded from the network, the router buffers freed, and the message retransmitted from the source. In this case, the source and destination must synchronize message delivery or drop messages. This requires that the message be buffered at the source until it can be asserted that it has been delivered either explicitly through acknowledgments or implicitly through other mechanisms. This will referred to as *message-level recovery* to denote the level at which recovery takes place. Implementations of each basic approach are described in the following.

6.7.2   Flit-Level Recovery

Reliable message delivery can be handled by end-to-end protocols that utilize acknowledgments and message retransmission to synchronize delivery of messages. Messages remain buffered at the source until it can be asserted that the message has been delivered. If we consider packet switching, more efficient alternatives exist for ensuring reliable end-to-end message delivery. Error detection and retransmission/rerouting can be implemented at the link level. A message must be successfully transmitted across a link before it is forwarded. With some a priori knowledge of the component failure rates, fault-tolerant routing algorithms can be developed where packets are injected into the network exactly once, and guaranteed to be delivered to the destination by rerouting around faulty components. The difficulty in applying the same approach to wormhole-switched messages has been that the message packets cannot be completely buffered at each router, and are spread across multiple routers when the header flit blocks. Thus, link level monitoring and retransmission are difficult to realize on a message packet basis. The Reliable Router developed at the Massachussets Institute of Technology (MIT) [75, 76] has implemented a novel approach utilizing a flit level copying and forwarding algorithm to solve this problem and realize *exactly-once* injection and subsequent delivery of all packets in wormhole-switched networks.

Networks of reliable routers utilize three virtual networks. Five virtual channels are provided across each physical channel. Two of these virtual channels are used to implement an adaptive network where messages may utilize any outgoing channel from a router. Two more virtual channels are utilized to implement a dimension-ordered network where messages traverse links in dimension order. The two sets of dimension-order channels are used by packets at two priority levels. The two priorities are used with distinct resources to prevent software deadlocks. The remaining virtual channel is used as part of a network that implements the turn model for fault-tolerant routing. The adaptive and dimension-ordered networks together implement DP (see Section 4.4.4) for fully adaptive routing. When a message cannot acquire an adaptive channel, it attempts the dimension-order channel. If this channel is also busy, the message blocks for one cycle, and then first attempts to route along the adaptive channel. When a message can no longer progress due to a fault on the outgoing dimension-ordered link, the message employs nonminimal turn model style routing in the fault handling network to route around the fault (except for 180-degree turns). At the adjacent router, the message may transition back to the adaptive and dimension-ordered networks, or may remain in the fault handling network until it is delivered to the destination. This choice depends on the dimension across which the failed channel was encountered. If the packet traversed a nonminimal link in the y direction, this dimension traversal can be subsequently corrected without violating the x-y ordering in the dimension-order virtual network. However, nonminimal traversals in the x dimension result in the packet remaining in the fault handling network until it has reached its destination. This restriction is necessary to ensure deadlock freedom. Based on this overall routing strategy, dynamic faults are handled as described below.

Link-level monitoring and retransmission is used to guarantee the successful progress of data flits across links and between routers. This implies that a copy of each data flit is maintained by the sending router until it can be asserted that the flit was received error-free. The flit level flow control ensures that there always exist exactly two copies of every flit in the network at all times. Thus, when a data flit successfully advances, flow control information must travel in the reverse direction to free the oldest copy of the flit. If a link fails, the message can now be partitioned into two messages. Data flits on the header side of the fault continue toward the destination. Data flits on the other side of the failure must construct a new header and reroute this new message along an alternative path. This requires that copies of the header flit exist in each router containing a data flit of the message. Finally a special token defines the end of the message. The flit-level flow control and copying is illustrated in Figure 6.39.

Each message is comprised of four components: a header, tail, data, and the token signifying the end of the message. Figure 6.39a shows the state of a message just prior to failure of the link. Now assume that a link failure has been detected. Figure 6.39b shows the state of the routers two cycles later. One side of the failed link has the header and a single data flit. A token is generated (not shown), appended to the data flit, and this new message can now continue toward the destination.

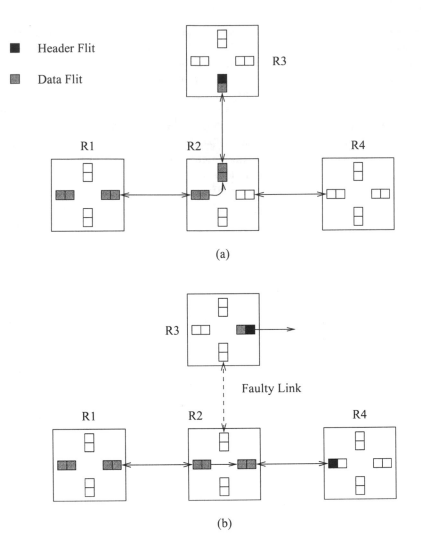

Figure 6.39. An example of flit-level copying and forwarding for exactly-once message delivery.

The data flits on the other side of the fault are orphaned. A new header is constructed, prepended to the first data flit, and routed as a new message. The token of the original message serves as the token for this message. Header reconstruction is supported by maintaining a copy of the header in all of the routers with a data flit from the message (not shown in the figure). When the message token passes through the router the copies of the header flit can be cleared. To facilitate reconstruction of the message at the destination, the headers are distinguished (*original* and *restart*) as are the token types (*unique* and *replica*). Finally, although not shown, a copy of every flit is maintained on both sides of a link. Flit-level flow control must enable the correct release of flit copies. Whenever router $R2$ successfully transmits a flit to router $R3$, a copied signal is transmitted to $R1$ so that $R1$ may invalidate its copy of the flit. In this way exactly two copies of each data flit are maintained in the network at all times. A more detailed description of the architecture of the router implementation can be found in Chapter 7.

6.7.3   Message-Level Recovery

An alternative to flit-level recovery is to find and discard the interrupted message components and retransmit the message from the source. Recovery is at the level of complete messages rather than at the flit level. The PCS-based solutions exploit the fact that a separate control network comprised of the control channels exists. Consider a message pipeline where a fault is detected on a reserved virtual link or physical channel as shown in Figure 6.38. The link is marked faulty. The link controller at the source end of the faulty virtual link introduces a *release flit* (referred to as *kill flit* in [124]) into the complementary virtual control channel of the virtual link upstream from the fault. This release flit is routed back to the source router. The link controller at the destination end of the faulty virtual link introduces a release flit into the corresponding virtual control channel of the virtual link downstream from the failed virtual link. This release flit is propagated along toward the destination. When a release flit arrives at a node, the input and output virtual links associated with the message are released and the flit is propagated toward the source (or destination). If multiple faults occur in one message pipeline, this mechanism is applied recursively to fault-free segments.

When a release flit arrives at an intermediate router node, the set of actions taken by that node will depend on the state of the interrupted message pipeline in that node. We have the following rules that are to be implemented by each router node. In all of the following steps it is implicit that virtual links and associated buffers are released. If two control flits for the same message arrive at a router node (from opposite directions along the path), the two control flits collide at that router node. A flit in progress toward the destination (source) is referred to as a *forward* (*reverse*) flit. The following rules govern the collision of control flits and are based on the assumption [124] that paths are removed by message acknowledgments from the destination rather than by the last flit of the message. Thus, a path is not removed until the last flit has been delivered to the destination. This behavior guarantees message delivery in the presence of dynamic or transient faults.

1. If a forward release flit collides with a reverse release flit, remove both release flits from the network. This may occur with multiple faults within the same message pipeline.

2. If a forward release flit collides with a message header (during the setup phase), remove both the routing header and the release flit.

3. If a release flit reaches the source, inform the message handler that the message transmission has failed. The handler may choose to retransmit or to invoke some higher-level fault handling algorithm.

4. If a release flit reaches the destination the partially received message is discarded.

5. If a forward release flit collides with a setup acknowledgment, the acknowledgment is removed from the network and the release flit is allowed to continue along the path toward the destination.

6. If a forward release flit collides with a message acknowledgment both are removed from the network.

Release flits are injected into the network only on the occurrence of faults. Since faults are a dynamic phenomenon, they may occur at any time during path setup, message transmission, or message acknowledgment. The interaction of control flits produces the actions defined above to ensure proper recovery. In the fault-free case each virtual circuit contains at most one control flit at a time. Therefore, it is necessary to add additional buffer space for one reverse and one forward release flit per virtual control channel. Since nonheader control flits are allowed to pass blocked

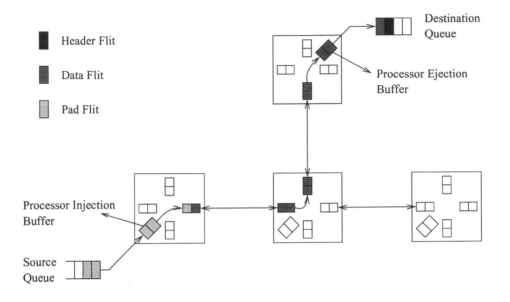

Figure 6.40. An example of compressionless routing.

headers, release flits will not wait and therefore cannot create chains of blocked flits as shown in Figure 6.1. Header flits using backtracking PCS algorithms do not block on faults. Thus, no flit in the network blocks indefinitely on a fault. As a result, release flits cannot induce deadlock in the presence of faults and the existing routing algorithm is deadlock-free.

As long as a path exists between the source and destination, if a fault interrupts the message, both the source and destination will be notified. However, it is possible that an inconsistent state can develop between a source and destination where the destination has received the message intact, but the source believes the message was lost and must retransmit. This situation develops when a dynamic fault occurs in the virtual circuit after the last flit is delivered, but before the final message acknowledgment reaches the source. This situation can be remedied at the operating system level by assigning identification tags to messages. If the source is prevented from sending the next message until the previous message has been successfully received, the destination can detect and discard duplicate messages relatively easily.

The above approach requires the use of virtual channels to support recovery traffic. The use of virtual channels can complicate routing decisions and channel control leading to an increase in the flow control latency through the router and across the channel. Fault tolerant implementations of *compressionless routing* have been proposed [179] motivated by a desire to simplify router design to enable adaptive routing and fault recovery with speeds comparable to oblivious routers. Compressionless routing exploits the small amount of buffering within the network routers to be able to indirectly determine when the header of a message has reached the destination. For example, assume that each router can only buffer two flits at the input and output of a router. If a message is to traverse three routers to the destination, once the 12th flit has been injected into the network the source node can assert that the header has been received into the destination node queue. Figure 6.40 illustrates this case, with the exception that the message is actually comprised of 10 flits. When the last data flit is injected into the network the header will not have reached the destination node. Therefore the message is padded with *pad flits*. The number of pad flits that must be added is a function of the distance to the destination and the message size. A separate pad signal enables

Figure 6.41. Control of padded messages.

the routers to distinguish between data flits and pad flits and is also used to remove the path when message transmission is complete. Thus, every message is padded with one pad flit as the tail flit. The pad signal appears as shown in Figure 6.41.

Fault-tolerant routing can now be realized as follows. The sender maintains a counter for the number of injected flits and a timer for recording the time a message remains blocked. The flit counter enables the sender to determine whether the header has reached the destination. For the static fault model, once the header flit has been delivered it can be asserted that the message will be delivered. If the header encounters a fault it can be rerouted. Misrouting can be accommodated by limiting the number of nonminimal steps that are permitted and correspondingly increasing the number of required pad flits. No routing restrictions are enforced to prevent deadlock and therefore routing is maximally adaptive. Rather, deadlock detection is employed. A timer is used to determine if a message has been blocked too long and is therefore possibly deadlocked. When the timer expires at the source an *FKILL* control signal is transmitted from the source to release the path and buffers. The message is then retransmitted. Compressionless routing is based on the experimental observation that algorithms with a high degree of adaptivity rarely result in deadlocked message configurations. The occurrence of static faults is indistinguishable from deadlock due to cyclic dependencies.

In the case of dynamic faults, messages may be interrupted by faults, and therefore the algorithm requires some modification. Now messages are padded such that the path is held until the last data flit has reached the destination. If a fault interrupts a message in progress, the detecting router transmits *FKILL* and *BKILL* signals toward the destination and source routers respectively, to release the path. When the destination receives an *FKILL* signal, it can be asserted that the received message is incomplete and can be discarded. The reception of a *BKILL* signal by the source causes retransmission by the source. Faults occurring on links that are transmitting pad flits do not require transmission of recovery signals.

Compressionless routing does not require virtual channels, and is applicable to a wide variety of topologies. The *KILL* signals can be used for buffer allocation and for determining the immediate status of adaptively routed messages, i.e., whether they have been delivered or not. This latter property can be used to guarantee in-order delivery of multiple messages. The overall result is a simpler and therefore faster router design. However, pad flits use real bandwidth. If messages tend to be short and networks low-dimensional and large, the increase in router speed is traded off against a drop in network utilization. An alternative view is that compressionless routing encourages the use of higher-dimensional networks with low average interprocessor distance.

6.7.4 Miscellaneous Issues

All of the approaches described in this section utilize bandwidth in different ways to enable recovery from dynamic faults and for synchronization between the source and destination to detect or avoid duplicate messages. These techniques do so while providing for fully distributed recovery of orphan flits. In PCS-based dynamic fault tolerance, network bandwidth is consumed by release flits and message acknowledgments for synchronization as well as recovery. In compressionless-routing-based recovery, network bandwidth is consumed by pad flits and a few extra control signals (which represent bandwidth that could otherwise have been used for data transmission). Exactly-once delivery appears to require the least amount of additional bandwidth for fault recovery at the expense of increased storage within the router. The increase in the number of messages produces an increase in the number of message headers. The headers utilize more bandwidth and storage within the routers for copies. However, with increasingly larger routers becoming feasible this does not appear to be a limiting factor. The increased message population changes the blocking probabilities experienced by all messages and can have some impact on average message latency and throughput. At low loads this impact would not appear to be significant.

Timeout mechanisms have been proposed for use at the link level as well as the message level. Link-level timeouts are often used to determine if flit transmission across a channel has been successful and the timeout interval is generally easier to establish. Node-level timeouts have been used to determine if messages have been received. There are several issues with using timeouts at the node level. It is is difficult to determine the appropriate value of the timeout interval since it is sensitive to traffic conditions and fault patterns. In the presence of dynamic communication traffic that varies across applications, conservative estimates of timeout intervals lead to long recovery times while small timeout intervals lead to false recovery, i.e., network congestion is erroneously interpreted as a deadlock situation. Further, buffering requirements at the source node increase with timeout interval since messages must be maintained for a longer period of time. Most importantly, the use of timeouts does not address the problem of recovering orphaned data flits in the network.

The availability of such distributed recovery mechanisms enables several existing adaptive routing algorithms based on wormhole switching to become fault recoverable. Consider fully adaptive routing algorithms under the wormhole switching model. Under the static fault model, if a wormhole-switched header blocks on a faulty virtual link, deadlock may occur. Thus, adaptive wormhole-switched routing algorithms that rely on deterministic subnetworks become deadlock-prone. If recovery mechanisms were supported, then if the header is forced to block waiting on a faulty link in a deterministic subnetwork, the recovery mechanism can be invoked to remove this message. Since the fault occurs at the location of the header flit, only the source node is informed that the route failed. The message may now be retransmitted or a higher-level fault handler may be invoked. Since the base routing algorithm is adaptive, a retransmitted message may possibly find a different path to the destination. However, since generally no memory of the past route is maintained, routing algorithms based on wormhole switching are likely to repeat their last route. Randomizing the choice of adaptive output channels will make these routing algorithms more robust. A final message acknowledgment is necessary to remove the message path and ensure delivery of the last flit.

6.8 Engineering Issues

The design of a reliable communication fabric arises naturally in the design of dependable systems. These emerging classes of systems can be relied upon to deliver services in the presence of failures. Attributes of dependable systems include availability, reliability, and security. Reliable interconnection networks form a natural component of such a system. For a given probability of failure for an isolated component, the probability of the failure of at least one component in a network grows as the size of the system increases. As described above, such failures can lead to deadlock, particularly in obliviously routed networks. Thus, the expectation is that dependable systems will incorporate some degree of fault-tolerant routing. The hard questions relate to the choice of technique and the cost/performance/reliability trade-offs.

The effective design of fault-tolerant networks must proceed from the initial specification of application requirements that specify system MTBF, acceptable message latency and network bandwidth, and system failure conditions. The application environment will determine the fault model. One effective methodology [155] proceeds from this point through a selection of fault-tolerant routing techniques, establishment of fault tolerance/performance trade-offs, and culminates in the validation and verification of the design. Effective fault-tolerant network design requires that fault tolerance be considered from the outset and not added after a performance based design.

The application requirements determine the fault model: the nature and the types of faults that can occur, their frequency of occurrence, and how they manifest themselves as errors. The routing algorithms described in this section assume that faults manifest themselves as failed links and routers. The pattern and rate of these failures depend on lower-level fault models that can be derived from the applications requirements. For example, faults may characterized as follows.

- Hard faults, e.g., radiation-induced, natural failures, etc.

- Transient faults e.g., radiation-induced, switching transients, etc.

- Design faults, e.g., hardware and software

The specific faults and their manifestations (e.g., single-event upset and bit errors) must be derived from the target application environment. The description will include the rates at which these faults will occur and the requirements on MTTR, MTBF, acceptable degradation in message latency, etc. These rates may vary by fault type. For example, soft faults may occur at different rates than hard faults. Soft faults can occur on the order of minutes to hours (e.g., in a space environment) while hard faults can occur on the order of months. One of the difficulties with establishing requirements is that they may also depend on the mode of operation. A system may move from operational to degraded mode after the occurrence of the first failure. The requirements on recovery latency may be more stringent in degraded mode. Requirements may be stronger during bursty traffic situations than under low-load conditions. Information from the application environment is used to establish the fault model and place constraints on fault recovery times.

Once the fault model has been established, decisions must be made on how the fault information is to be managed. Examples of alternatives include: (1) the location and type of faults are globally known, (2) at each node, only the fault status of neighboring nodes are available, or (3) at each node the fault status of nodes within a k-distance neighborhood are known. The availability of global fault information will enable the computation and selection of optimal routes. The difficulty arises in the time and space overhead of maintaining this information and recomputing these global routes on-line. The use of global information also requires support for the reliable broadcast of fault information. This lengthens the recovery time, thus increasing the probability of the occurrence of a second fault before the system is finished recovering from the first. The use of purely local information enables fast rerouting decisions but the lack of any form of lookahead can lead to network hot spots and resulting performance degradation. Natural trade-offs involve propagating fault information to a neighborhood and using this information in rerouting decisions.

Once the fault model and extent of fault location information has been determined, the major difficulty now is in choosing between the diverse set of fault-tolerant routing techniques. One set of guidelines can be obtained by considering the relationship between MTTR and MTBF as illustrated in Figure 6.42. Consider the case where the MTTR << MTBF. In this case we would expect the probability of the failure of two network components in the repair interval to be fairly low. During this time it may be permissible for the network to operate with degraded latency/throughput

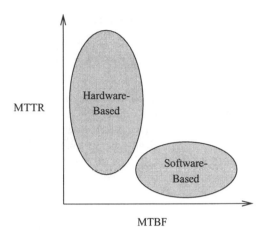

Figure 6.42. Choosing a fault-tolerant routing approach.

characteristics. In fact, depending on the network load, performance may not even be significantly degraded. Many machines operating in a commercial environment share these characteristics where the MTTR is on the order of hours to days while MTBF is on the order of months. In this case, software-based techniques for rerouting messages may be preferred. The emerging switch-based networks such as Myrinet [30] and TNet [156] appear to have these characteristics. The Myrinet network is in fact automatically configured based on routing packets that determine interconnection topology. This is feasible since failures are not occurring at a rapid rate. The software-based approaches have minimal impact on the router design: messages encountering faults are simply ejected to the messaging layer of the local node. Messages that do not encounter faults remain unaffected (there may be second-order effects due to increased traffic as a result of rerouted messages). However, in the presence of even a single fault the messages that do encounter this failed component experience significant increase in latency, more so than in corresponding hardware implemented rerouting schemes.

On the other hand, consider embedded systems with real-time requirements where MTTR $>>$ MTBF. One such example is space-borne embedded computing systems where repair is infeasible and therefore MTTR is effectively infinite. In this case an investment in hardware solutions may be justified. If we do consider hardware solutions then the specific choice depends on the fault model. Packet switching and PCS in conjunction with backtracking and misrouting algorithms are the most robust and can tolerate large numbers of failures but extract both performance and cost overheads. The wormhole-switched routing algorithms based on block fault models are less expensive and simpler but are not as robust and require the construction of block fault regions. Both classes of solutions require custom routers. In addition to the probability of message delivery we must consider the impact on performance. Hardware solutions tend to provide better latency/throughput performance. Even a single fault leads to much higher message latencies for software-based rerouting. Thus, even if MTTR $<<$ MTBF, performance constraints such as the need for real-time communication may favor hardware-based solutions.

Between these two extremes (software versus custom hardware) there are compromise approaches that utilize some form of spatial and temporal redundancy with different trade-offs between cost and performance. For example, each message may be replicated and transmitted along a disjoint path through the network. The ability to route messages along disjoint paths requires source routing: the header contains the output port addresses of each intermediate router rather than the destination address or offset. A routing table at each source stores headers for each set of disjoint paths for every destination node. The design of these routing tables must be such that routing is guaranteed to be deadlock-free for multipacket transmission. This approach requires that routers be modified to be source-routed (many commercial chips already are) and that network bandwidth be sacrificed for reliability. Sacrificing bandwidth may be feasible since most networks are usually limited by interface and software overheads rather than raw link bandwidths. The challenge here is creating routing tables that are deadlock-free in the presence of this style of traffic. Depending on the degree of replication, e.g., only two messages transmitted between nodes, recomputation of routing tables may be necessary if both paths are interrupted by a fault. Note that a message that cannot be delivered must be removed from the network to avoid deadlock. Other alternatives include dual redundant networks or routers. This is an expensive solution that may be infeasible in some environments due to cost or size, weight, or power constraints (e.g., embedded systems).

Many of the approaches described in this chapter rely on the absence of faults during some small interval of time during which system state is being updated, e.g., constructing block fault regions or updating routing tables. What happens if faults occur during this interval? What is the probability of such an occurrence? How does one make a choice between various approaches? Simulation-based modeling appears to be the approach of choice to evaluate the performance of these networks in pursuit of answers to these questions. It is useful to have tools that would permit empirical fault injection studies for a relatively more accurate analysis of the effect of faults and the ability of the system network to detect and respond to them in a timely fashion. Coverage analysis can be invaluable in designing the network. For example, fault injection studies can reveal the type of network error states that occur due to bit errors that corrupt the routing header. Tools such as DEPEND [338] can be used to utilize fault dictionaries that capture the manner in which errors are manifested due to various types of faults. These fault dictionaries can be used in fault injection studies to evaluate alternatives for fault-tolerant routing. For example, using realistic fault injection models the analysis may discover that software-based rerouting provides the same level of fault coverage as more expensive hardware-based schemes and with acceptable rerouting message latency.

Evaluation tools should extend the analysis to the impact of faults on the execution of application programs. Reliable communications is a means to enable the execution of application programs. The primary consideration in the design of the network is the effect of faults and the fault-tolerant routing techniques on the execution of programs. In the presence of faults, message delivery may no longer be guaranteed. In this case the program execution may fail. Delivery probabilities can be estimated via simulation driven by communication traces of application programs or representative kernels. Formal models can also establish the ability of routing algorithms to find paths based on a known and fixed number or pattern of faults, e.g., up to the node degree. Most routing algorithms attempt to at least guarantee delivery when the number of faulty components is less than the node degree of the interconnection network.

A second effect of faults is on message latency, which is more of a concern in real-time systems. Virtual channels can have a significant impact on message latency. The failures of routers and links produces congestion in their vicinity as messages are rerouted. These messages will experience increased blocking delays as they compete for access to a smaller number of links. The presence of virtual channels will reduce the blocking delay and increase the overall network throughput. With backtracking routing algorithms, the presence of additional virtual channels affects the probability that a message is delivered since these algorithms do not block on busy channels. Thus, while studies have shown that the presence of virtual channels can affect the flow control latency through the routers, in the presence of faults they can have a substantial positive effect on latency.

The execution time performance of faulty networks depends on whether the network is operating at saturation, in the low-load region, or just at the brink of saturation. The performance/reliability trade-offs tend to be different for each operating region. The intuitive explanation follows from the fact that the message population consists of two types of messages: those that have encountered faults and those that have not. Consider operation with message destinations uniformly distributed in a mesh network. When operating in the low-load region, increasing the injection rate for a fixed number of faults may not significantly change the percentage of messages that encounter a faulty component. Thus, average latencies may not appear to be affected as the load increases. However, as we get closer to saturation the effects start to become more pronounced as congestion in the vicinity of faults makes the performance sensitive to the number of available channels and the use of oblivious or adaptive routing. Alternatively, for a fixed injection rate, as we increase the number of faults, the performance characteristics depend upon the routing techniques. With the use of software-based rerouting and a base oblivious routing algorithm, performance is significantly affected with each additional failure since a greater percentage of the message population encounters faulty components. However, adaptively routed networks will observe little change in message characteristics since the network initially has enough redundant bandwidth. As injection rates approach those corresponding to saturation, the occurrence of additional faults has a substantial impact on performance. For a fixed number of faults, when the network is in saturation the performance is dominated by the steady-state behavior of the messages that do not encounter faults. Each additional fault increases the percentage of the message population that has to be rerouted contributing to congestion and further degradation in performance. The performance also depends on the buffering available at the individual nodes. These buffers provide a natural throttling mechanism and in effect control the saturation behavior of the network.

The difficulty is in determining the operating region for a set of applications. One way of deriving these requirements from an application is by developing an injection model that specifies the size of messages and the rate at which nodes can be expected to inject these messages into the network. This model is essentially a profile of the communication demands to be placed on the network. From this profile one can construct models to determine the demand on the bisection bandwidth and the demand on network bandwidth in general (see Chapter 9 for examples of how to specify performance in a topology-independent manner). From the injection model and physical network characteristics we can make some assessment of what region the network is operating in for the target applications. The injection model will depend on the processor speeds, the average number of instructions between communication commands, and the internal node bandwidth to the network interface.

A critical issue that has not been addressed in this chapter is fault detection. Although it is beyond the scope of this book, a few general points can be made. General fault tolerance and digital systems techniques are applicable within the routers, interfaces, and software layers. These detection mechanisms identify failed links or routers in keeping with the fault models for networks used here. In addition, link failures can be detected either by adding some redundant information in every transmission, by exercising some tests while the link is idle, or both. Adding redundant information requires a few additional wires per link. In the simplest case, a parity bit requires a single wire. However, this method allows the immediate detection of permanent as well as transient faults. As transient faults are more frequent in many designs, a simple algorithm may allow the retransmission of the information. On the other hand, testing idle links does not require additional wires (the receiving node retransmits the information back to the sender). Using otherwise idle bandwidth in this fashion permits a wider range of tests and consequently a more detailed analysis of link behavior. However, it does not detect the transmission of incorrect (i.e., corrupted) data. Both techniques complement each other very well. Other common techniques include protecting the packet header, data, or both with cyclic redundancy checks. By recomputing the checks for packets on the fly as they pass through a node it is possible to detect failed links. Phits traversing a channel can also be encoded to transmit error detection patterns. More extensive use of coding can correct certain classes of errors. Hard errors such as link failures or router failures are usually detected with timeouts. Similar techniques are also used for end-to-end flow control by using positive acknowledgments with timeouts although in this case it may not be possible to determine the location of the failure.

Although the majority of proposals for fault-tolerant routing algorithms consider static faults, faults may occur at any time in real systems. Designers must consider handling dynamic faults. When a fault interrupts a message in transit, the message cannot be delivered, and a fragment of the message may remain in the network indefinitely, leading to deadlock. Support for dynamic faults must perform two different actions: removal of fragments of interrupted messages, and notification of the source and destination nodes that message delivery has failed, thereby permitting retransmission and reception of the complete message. The latter action can be supported at higher-level protocol layers by message sizes in the header, message level acknowledgments, and retransmission on failures. Router nodes then simply have to discard fragments of interrupted messages. The alternative is hardware support for recovery, usually by transmitting control information toward the destination and source nodes from the location of the fault. Such an approach does create some nontrivial synchronization problems, e.g., preventing the notification from overtaking the message header. Solutions have been proposed for these problems but do exact some costs in hardware implementation. Adding support to remove fragments of interrupted messages is very convenient because it does not slow down normal operation significantly (as opposed to retransmission based on higher-level protocols) and deadlocks produced by interrupted messages are avoided. However, notifying the source node produces an extra use of resources for every transmitted message, therefore degrading performance significantly even in the absence of faults. Considering the probability of interrupted messages a trade-off must be made between the probability of dropping packets vs. loss in performance.

Finally, if the network is designed to operate in an unattended environment, repair is not possible. In addition to selecting an appropriate switching technique and routing algorithm to meet the requirements on MTBF, it is useful for the network to be designed with higher numbers of dimensions. This will increase the number of disjoint paths between processors. The degradation in latency/throughput performance is expected to occur at a slower rate with a higher number of dimensions, increasing the likelihood of meeting requirements for a longer period of time.

6.9 Commented References

The notion of fault-tolerant routing has existed as long as there have been communication networks. In the context of multiprocessors some of the early work was naturally based on the early switching techniques, packet switching and circuit switching. While there has been a substantial amount of work in fault tolerance in indirect networks, this text has largely concentrated on the emerging systems using direct networks.

As direct network based multiprocessors evolved based on binary hypercubes, substantial analysis focused on the properties of this network. This topology was highly popular until low-dimensional networks became the topology of choice. A great deal of the analysis for fault tolerance focused on the connectivity properties of the binary hypercube in the presence of faults as opposed to the development of deadlock- and livelock-free routing algorithms. Thus, much of that literature has been omitted from this text in favor of what we hope are a few representative examples of routing techniques in faulty networks. In packet-switched binary hypercube networks, fault-tolerant routing algorithms tended to either exploit the unique topological properties of hypercubes or to employ some form of graph search. For example, Chen and Shin used the concept of spare dimensions [53] to route around faulty regions. The spare dimension transported the message in a direction "orthogonal" to the faulty node. Routing was based on purely local information about the fault status of the neighboring nodes. Lee and Hayes [198] extended the state designation of a node to include the unsafe state. The unsafe state was used to serve as a warning that messages may become trapped or delayed if routed via nodes marked as unsafe. Lee and Hayes demonstrated that this approach can be used in the formulation of deadlock-free wormhole-switched routing algorithms. Other routing algorithms followed that found ways to utilize the unsafe designation effectively, as well as extending the binary safe/unsafe designation to the notion of a range of safety levels [350].

The use of graph search techniques also led to the design of many adaptive fault-tolerant SAF routing algorithms. The critical issue here was how the state of the search was maintained and utilized to avoid repeated searches as well as the discovery of a path if one existed. Different techniques for maintaining the state of the network led to different routing algorithms, each exploiting the multidimensional structure of the hypercube in a different way. The Jet Propulsion Laboratory (JPL) Mark III hypercube [62] supported multiple modes of communication including both circuit switching and packet switching. Both modes operated with path setup following a best-first heuristic search for finding a path through the network around congested or faulty nodes. Chen and Shin [52] proposed a strategy that relied on a depth-first search of the network. In contrast to organized search, randomization was proposed as deadlock avoidance technique for adaptive fault-tolerant routing [34, 188]. Messages can be adaptively routed, and when blocking occurs a randomly chosen message is misrouted. The formal analysis ensures that infinite paths are avoided and the messages are not indefinitely blocked. Simulation studies establish that adaptive routing is a viable approach toward avoiding faulty components. However, messages can still be completely buffered within a node. The use of small buffers in wormhole switching creates a new set of problems.

The first algorithms based on wormhole switching focused on fault regions that were convex and block-structured, marking fault-free nodes as faulty if necessary. Messages could be routed around faulty regions without introducing cyclic dependencies with the aid of virtual channels — often organized explicitly as fault rings [37] — or by restricting adaptivity [58]. Both oblivious as well as adaptive routing algorithms could be adapted to this fault model. Subsequent work relaxed constraints on the location and relationship between fault regions. The basic principle underlying these approaches was to establish the minimal number of virtual networks necessary to separate traffic along the links. Traffic was usually characterized by the relationship between the source and destination by direction of traversal along each dimension. If message flows around a fault region could be separated and prevented from interacting, then routing could remain deadlock free. A similar thought process has extended this approach to routing around certain classes of nonconvex fault regions[50].

While the preceding techniques used virtual channels, there was increasing interest in techniques for fault-tolerant routing using wormhole switching without the overhead of virtual channels. The turn model was extended to enable messages to be routed around faults by relying on a local relabeling scheme in the vicinity of faults [132]. Origin-based routing in meshes was also introduced for this purpose and is a generalization of turn model routing[146]. Messages are first routed toward the origin and then toward the destination. By placing the origin at different places within the mesh, messages could be routed around fault-free regions in a deadlock-free manner without the aid of virtual channels, although there are some constraints on the relative locations of fault regions.

More recent algorithms attempt to combine the flexibility of circuit-switched routing algorithms and wormhole-switched routing algorithms by using PCS switching and its variants [80, 127]. The resulting misrouting backtracking algorithms have fault-tolerance properties similar to their packet-switched counterparts, but the performance is substantially better due to the pipelined data flow, particularly for large messages. While these approaches do not rely on virtual channels, they do rely on the availability of a distinct control channel across each physical channel.

All of the approaches described here assume the implementation of routing and selection functions within the network routers to implement the fault-tolerant routing algorithms, resulting in expensive custom solutions. Suh et al. [332] point out that in some low-fault-rate environments, software-based rerouting is a viable option when repair times are short relative to network component MTBF. The network can operate in degraded mode until repair. The challenge here is devising rerouting strategies that are deadlock- and livelock-free in the presence of a wide range of fault patterns. Certain pathological fault patterns may pose a problem while exhaustive search techniques may still find paths. It is interesting to note that such a strategy also accommodates a wider range of fault patterns for both adaptive and oblivious routing, however, the performance penalty for rerouted messages is high.

Finally while rerouting is acceptable for statically known component failures, the occurrence of failures that disrupt messages necessitate recovery mechanisms. Two very similar techniques include compressionless routing [179] and acknowledged PCS [124]. Both recover messages in a distributed fashion although they use network bandwidth in different ways. The reliable router from MIT has an exactly-once delivery philosophy [75]. Interrupted messages form smaller messages which are independently routed through the network to their destinations. No retransmission is involved. In general, these recovery mechanisms can complement any one of the existing routing algorithms based on pipelined switching mechanisms. We can now expect to see techniques evolve that will accommodate collective communication operations, and we can expect to see irregular topologies that will be designed for the clustered workstation environment.

EXERCISES

6.1 Show that for dimension-ordered routing in a 2-D mesh, only two virtual channels are required for routing around rectangular fault regions with nonoverlapping fault rings. How would this change if fault rings are allowed to overlap?

Solution   Figure 6.43 illustrates the routing restrictions necessary for deadlock-free routing [37]. Since messages traveling in the horizontal dimension and messages traveling in the vertical dimension use a distinct set of channels, deadlock can only occur due to cyclic dependencies between messages within each group (i.e., horizontal or vertical). From the figure

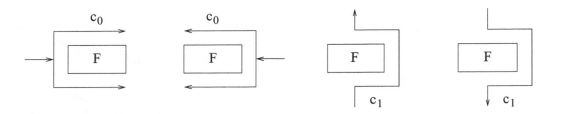

Figure 6.43. Routing restrictions for e-cube routing on a 2-D mesh. (F = Fault region.)

we see that eastbound and westbound messages always traverse a disjoint set of c_0 channels. Thus, they do not interfere with each other. Since the topology is a mesh and there are no wraparound channels there are no cyclic dependencies between c_0 channels. Now consider the northbound and southbound channels messages which use the c_1 channels. Note that these messages are restricted to following a clockwise or counterclockwise orientation around the fault regions. Thus, a message in one group cannot block on a channel held by a message in the other group. In the absence of wraparound channels, north bound and south bound messages do not form cyclic channel dependencies. Thus, the solution shown in the figure is deadlock-free.

Now if fault rings were allowed to overlap, the eastbound messages traversing a fault region in the clockwise direction may share a channel with (and therefore block) a message traversing an adjacent fault region in the counterclockwise direction. Thus, east bound and westbound messages can form cyclic dependencies. The solution is to introduce additional virtual channels to further separate the traffic on a link. Two additional virtual channels per link will suffice.

6.2 Consider a k-ary n-cube network with f faults. What is the maximum number of consecutive links that a PCS header will have to backtrack in any single source-destination path?

Solution If there have been no previous misroutes, the header flit is allowed to misroute in the presence of faults even when the number of misroutes is limited. Thus, the header will only backtrack when the only healthy channel is the one previously used to reach the node. In the case of a k-ary n-cube, every node has $2n$ channels incident on a distinct node. Since the header arrived from a nonfaulty node, it will be forced to backtrack if $(2n - 1)$ channels are faulty. At the next node, since the header has backtracked from a nonfaulty node and originally arrived from a nonfaulty node it will be forced to backtrack if the remaining $(2n - 2)$ channels are faulty. Each additional backtracking step will be forced by $(2n - 2)$ additional failed channels. Thus we have:

$$f = 2n - 1 + (b - 1)(2n - 2)$$
$$b = (f - 1)div(2n - 2) \tag{6.1}$$

6.3 Now consider a multidimensional mesh-connected network with a backtracking misrouting packet-switched routing algorithm. What is the maximum number of consecutive links that the message will backtrack, in the presence of f faulty links or nodes?

Solution If there have been no previous misrouting operations, the message is allowed to misroute in the presence of faults, even if the maximum number of misrouting operations is limited. There are several possible cases:

1. The routing probe is at a node with 2n channels. This is the same case as with a torus-connected k-ary n-cube. Hence, the number of faults required to force the first backtrack is $(2n - 1)$. To force additional backtracks, $(2n - 2)$ additional faults are required per additional backtrack.

2. The probe is at a node with less than 2n channels. As with the earlier cases, all channels except the one used to reach the node can be used in case of faults (either for routing or misrouting). The worst case occurs when the node has the minimum number of channels. In an n-dimensional mesh, nodes located at the corners only have n channels. One of the

channels was used by the probe to reach the node. Hence, the failure of $(n-1)$ channels or nodes causes the routing probe to backtrack. The probe is now on the edge of the mesh, where each node has $(n+1)$ channels. One channel was already used to reach the node the first time and another one for the previous backtracking operation, therefore only $(n-1)$ channels are available for routing. These channels must all be faulty to force a backtrack operation. Thus, the maximum number of mandatory backtrack operations is $f \, div(n-1)$.

3. A turn from a corner into a dead end. In order to cause the initial backtrack, there need to be n faults. $(n-2)$ faults are required to cause a backtrack at the corner node. Each additional backtrack requires $(n-1)$ faults. Hence, the maximum number of backtracking operations is $(f+1)div(n-1)$.

6.4 In a binary hypercube with $N = 2^n$ nodes, given a list of dimensions that have been traversed by a message as $[1, 3, 6, 2, 3, 1, 5]$, and a current intermediate node as 24. An outgoing link across dimension 4 is a candidate output link for this message. Has this node been visited by this message?

Solution   By reversing the coordinate sequence we can reconstruct the sequence of nodes that has been visited by this message. The previous node is given by $0011000 \oplus 010000 = 0111000 =$ node 56. The other nodes on the path include 58, 50, 54, 118, 126, and 124.

PROBLEMS

6.1 In a binary hypercube with $N = 2^n$ nodes, how many shortest paths are affected by the failure of a single link?

6.2 Modify DP to permit misrouting in any dimension lower than the last dimension traversed in the escape network. Show that such an algorithm can tolerate all single-node or single-link faults except in the last dimension.

6.3 Consider the use of fault rings for fault-tolerant oblivious routing in 2-D meshes using four virtual channels per link. Fault rings may overlap. Draw the channel dependencies between the input virtual channels and output virtual channels at a router node.

6.4 Consider a k-ary n-cube network with f faults. What is the maximum number of consecutive links that a PCS header will have to backtrack in any single source destination path?

6.5 Show that with at most three faulty components e-sft is livelock-free. With such a small number of components, you can ignore the PF flag.

6.6 The negative-first or north-last turn model routing algorithms have limited adaptivity for some source destination pairs, and therefore are deadlock-prone without fault recovery. Combine two turn model routing algorithms to produce a fully adaptive fault-tolerant routing algorithm.

Hint   Use distinct virtual networks. Specify constraints on the traversal of a message between networks to realize deadlock freedom.

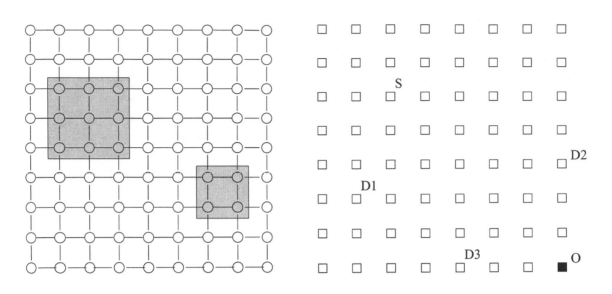

Figure 6.44. An example faulty 2-D mesh.   Figure 6.45. Origin-based routing.

6.7 Consider the fault regions shown in Figure 6.44 in a 2-D mesh. Show the channels used by EW, WE, NS, and SN meshes assuming dimension-order routing. The purpose of this exercise to be able to observe that each group of messages utilize a disjoint set of channels, and that the channel dependencies within each group are acyclic.

6.8 Given the location of the origin as shown in Figure 6.45, identify the possible paths taken by a message from the source (S) to each of the destinations, $D1$, $D2$, and $D3$, in origin-based routing.

6.9 Show how you can include fault recovery to make the routing algorithm of Dally and Aoki [74] deadlock-free in the presence of faults.

6.10 In a k-ary n-cube with $f < 2n$ faults, what is the maximum path length of a packet-switched message routed using an algorithm that permits a maximum of m misroutes?

6.11 Consider a routing algorithm in binary hypercubes where the dimensions to be traversed by a message are partitioned into two groups — the set of UP dimensions (the $0 \to 1$ direction across a dimension) and the set of $DOWN$ dimensions. Routing proceeds by routing across UP dimensions in any order and across $DOWN$ dimensions in strictly dimension order. What is the maximum number of faults that can be tolerated by adaptively routing in this fashion?

Chapter 7

Network Architectures

In many instances, particularly in fine-grained parallel machines, the performance of the applications are communication-limited rather than computation-limited. In this case, the design of the network architecture is crucial. By network architecture we refer to the topology of interconnection between the processing nodes, and the data and control path of the routers within the individual nodes. The design of the network architecture is fundamentally a process of making trade-offs between performance parameters such cost, latency, and throughput, and physical constraints such as area, wireability, and I/O limitations. Since physical constraints are continually evolving with advances in fabrication and packaging technology, so too are the appropriate choices of network topology and design alternatives for the router architecture. This chapter discusses basic issues facing the choice of network topologies and presents the design of router architectures that have been successfully employed within these topologies.

Chapter 1 describes many distinct topologies that have been proposed for use in multiprocessor architectures. The majority of these topologies are either configurations of, or isomorphic to, k-ary n-cube networks. These include the binary hypercube, tori, rings, and meshes. Indirect networks such as the indirect binary n-cube and Omega networks are also topologically closely related to these networks. Low dimensional k-ary n-cube networks possess desirable features with respect to their physical implementations, such as constant degree and ease of embedding in physical space. They also possess desirable properties with respect to message performance such as simple distributed routing algorithms. As a result, these networks have been used in the majority of commercial systems developed in the past decade. These include the iPSC series of machines from Intel, the Cray T3D and T3E, the Ametek 2010, MasPar MP-1 and MP-2, and Thinking Machines CM-1 and CM-2. These networks have formed the communications substrate of many commercial machines and are therefore the focus of this chapter. We observed that the network topology is primarily influenced by the packaging technology which places constraints on the wiring density, chip pin-out, and wire lengths. In the presence of these constraints, topological design issues must reconcile conflicting demands in choices of channel width, network dimensionality, and wire length. Thus, this chapter initially focuses on the optimization of the network topology.

While the architecture of the routers is certainly related to the topology of the interconnect, their design is primarily influenced by the switching technique that they are designed to support. Generic issues can be broadly classified into those dealing with internal data and control paths and those dealing with the design of the interrouter physical links. Specific design choices include internal switch design, buffer management, use of virtual channels, and physical channel flow control strategies. The remainder of the chapter presents descriptions of several modern router architectures as examples of specific design choices. Rather than present a comprehensive coverage of available architectures, we have tried to select illustrative examples from the range of currently available architectures.

7.1 Network Topology and Physical Constraints

For a fixed number of nodes, the choice of the number of dimensions of a k-ary n-cube represents a fundamental trade-off between network diameter and node degree. This choice of network dimension also places different demands on physical resources such as wiring area and number of chip I/Os. For a given implementation technology, practical constraints on these physical resources will determine architectural features such as channel widths, and as a result determine the *no-load message latency*: message latency in the absence of traffic. Similarly, these constraints will also determine the degree of congestion in the network for a given communication pattern, although accurate modeling of such dynamic behavior is more difficult. It thus becomes important to model the relationships between physical constraints and topology, and the resulting impact on performance. Network optimization is the process of utilizing these models in selecting topologies that best match the physical constraints of the implementation. The following subsections discuss the dominant constraints and the construction of analytic models that incorporate their effects on the no-load message latency.

7.1.1 Bisection Bandwidth Constraints

One of the physical constraints facing the implementation of interconnection networks is the available wiring area. The available wiring area is determined by the packaging technology, i.e., does the network reside on a chip, multichip module or printed circuit board. In particular, VLSI systems are generally wire-limited: the silicon area required by these systems is determined by interconnect area and the performance is limited by the delay of these interconnections. Since these networks must be implemented in three dimensions, for an N node network the available wiring space grows as $N^{\frac{2}{3}}$ while the network traffic can grow as N. Clearly machines cannot be scaled to arbitrarily large sizes without eventually encountering wiring limits. The choice of network dimension is influenced by how well the resulting topology makes use of available wiring area. Such an analysis requires performance measures that can relate network topology to the wiring constraints.

On such performance measure is the *bisection width* of a network: the minimum number of wires that must be cut when the network is divided into two equal sets of nodes. Since the primary goal is one of assessing bandwidth and resulting wiring demands, only wires carrying data are generally counted, excluding control, power, and ground signals. However, these effects are relatively easy to incorporate in the following analysis. The collective bandwidth over these wires is referred to as the *bisection bandwidth*. For example, consider a 2-D torus with $N = k^2$ nodes. Assume that each pair of adjacent nodes are connected with one bidirectional data channel of width W bits. If this network is divided into two halves, there will be $2W\sqrt{N}$ wires crossing this bisection. The factor of 2 is due to the wraparound channels. Imagine what happens when we bisect a 3-D torus with $N = k^3$ nodes. Each half comprises of $\frac{k^3}{2}$ nodes. A 2-D plane of k^2 nodes has links crossing the bisection, leading to a bisection width of $2Wk^2 = 2Wk^{n-1}$. These cases are illustrated in Figure 7.1. For the sake of clarity the wraparound links in the 3-D topology are not shown. In general, a bisection of a k-ary n-cube will cut channels from a k-ary $(n-1)$-cube leading to a bisection width of $2Wk^{n-1}$.

Using the above approach we can compute the bisection width of a number of popular topologies. These are summarized in Table 7.1. The implicit assumption here is that all of these topologies are regular, i.e., each dimension has the same radix. Consider the case of networks with $N =$

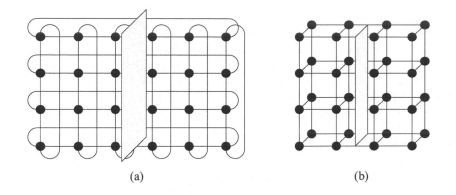

Figure 7.1. Examples of the computation of bisection width: (a) 2-D torus. (b) 3-D torus (wraparound links not shown).

$k_1 \times k_2 \times \ldots \times k_n$ nodes. In this case the minimum bisection width is orthogonal to the dimension with the largest radix. For example, this is the case shown in Figure 7.1. If the largest radix is k_m, then we have $\frac{N}{k_m}$ nodes with channels across this bisection. Thus, the bisection width can be expressed as $\frac{2WN}{k_m}$ bits.

The above computation assumes that each node devotes W pins to communication with a neighbor along a dimension. No assumptions are made about how these pins are used. In general, given a set of W pins between adjacent nodes, these may be utilized as two (opposite) $\frac{W}{2}$ bit unidirectional channels, one W-bit bidirectional channel, or one W-bit unidirectional channel. In the computing bisection width, the manner is which these channels are used is not particularly important. However, it is central to the evaluation of performance since channel widths directly impact message latency. We will see in later sections that assumptions about how these pins are used must be unambiguous and clearly stated.

7.1.2 Node Size Constraints

In addition to wiring space, a second physical constraint is the number of I/Os available per router. This is referred to as the *node size*. The construction of networks under a constant channel width for an arbitrary number of dimensions is impractical since the node size is linear in the number of dimensions. For example, consider a 2-D network and assume a baseline channel width of 16 data

Table 7.1. Examples of bisection width and node size of some common networks ($t \times t$ switches are assumed in the Omega network).

Network	Bisection Width	Node Size
k-ary n-cube	$2Wk^{n-1}$	$2Wn$
Binary n-cube	$\frac{NW}{2}$	nW
n-dimensional mesh	Wk^{n-1}	$2Wn$
Omega network	NW	$2tW$

bits, 8 control bits, and full-duplex channels, i.e., two unidirectional channels between adjacent nodes. This would correspond to 192 signal pins not including power, ground, and some miscellaneous I/Os. This is certainly feasible in current technology. For an n-dimensional network, the router will have 48 pins in each direction in each dimension for a total pin-out of $96n$. If we consider a 10-D network with the same channel width, we will require 960 pins, or close to 500 pins just for the channels in a more modest 5-D network. As we progress to 32-bit channels, the feasible network dimension becomes smaller. Thus, practical considerations place limits on channel width as a function of dimensionality [1, 3].

Even if we consider the bisection width constraints and networks being wiring area limited, it is likely that before networks encounter a bisection width limit, they may encounter the pin-out limit. This is evident from the following observation. Consider the implementation of a k-ary n-cube with the bisection width constrained to be N bits. The maximum channel width determined by this bisection width is given by

$$\text{Bisection width} = 2Wk^{n-1} = N \Rightarrow W = \frac{k}{2} \tag{7.1}$$

Note that this is the maximum channel width permitted under this bisection width constraint. A router does not have to provide this number of pins across each channel. However, if it does, the router will have a channel width of W bits between adjacent routers in each direction in each dimension for a total pin-out of $2nW = nk$. A network of 2^{20} nodes will have a pin-out of 2,048 in a 2-D configuration and a pin-out of 128 in a 4-D configuration. The former is certainly infeasible in 1997 technology for commercial single-chip packaging. In general, both the maximum number of available pins and the wiring area constraint as represented by the bisection width place upper bounds on the channel width. If the maximum number of pins available for data channels is given by P, and the bisection width is given by B, then the channel width is constrained by the following two relations. The feasible channel width is the smaller of the two.

$$W \leq \frac{P}{2n}$$

$$W \leq \frac{B}{2k^{n-1}} \tag{7.2}$$

To understand the effect of channel width on message latency consider the following. For a fixed pin-out, higher-dimensional networks will have smaller channel widths: a fixed number of pins partitioned across a higher number of dimensions. As we reduce the number of dimensions, the channel width increases. For example, if the channel width of an n-dimensional binary hypercube is W_h, then the total number of pins is nW_h (note the absence of the factor of 2 since $k = 2$ is special case with no wraparound channels). If we keep this pin-out constant, then for an m-dimensional torus with k_1^m nodes, the pin-out is $2mW_m$. The channel width of the torus is given by

$$W_m = W_h \times \frac{n}{2} \times \frac{1}{m} \tag{7.3}$$

However, if we keep the number of nodes constant, we have

$$N = 2^n = k_1^m \Rightarrow k_1 = N^{\frac{1}{m}} \tag{7.4}$$

Therefore we see that as the dimension decreases, the linear increase in channel width is offset by an exponential increase in the distance traveled by a message in each dimension. Expressions for message latency must capture these effects in enabling the analysis of trade-offs between bisection width, pin-out, and wiring length.

7.1.3 Wire Delay Constraints

As pointed out in [71], in VLSI systems the cycle time of the network is determined by the maximum wire delay, while the majority of the power is expended in driving these wires. Thus, topologies that can be embedded in two and three dimensions with short wires will be preferred. While even low-dimensional networks may logically appear to have long wires due to the wraparound connections, these can be avoided by interleaving nodes as shown in Figure 7.2 [258, 312]. However, when higher-dimensional networks are embedded in two and three dimensions, longer long wires do result. For the purposes of analyzing the effect of wire length we can determine this increase in wire length as follows [3]. The following analysis is based on an embedding in two dimensions, although it can be extended to three dimensions in a straightforward manner.

A k-ary n-cube is embedded in two dimensions by embedding $\frac{n}{2}$ dimensions of the network into each of the two physical dimensions (assuming an even number of dimensions). After embedding the first two dimensions each additional dimension increases the number of nodes in the network by a factor of k. Embedding in two dimensions provides an increase in the number nodes in each physical dimension by a factor of $\sqrt{k}$. If we ignore wire width and wiring density effects, the length of the longest wire in each physical dimension is also increased by a factor of $\sqrt{k}$. Note that if we had to account for the thickness of the wires, the length of the longest wire would actually grow faster than $\sqrt{k}$ as we increase the number of dimensions (see [3] for a good discussion). Ignoring wire width effects, the length of the longest wire in a 2-D embedding of an n-dimensional network increases by a factor of $k^{\frac{n-2}{2}}$ over the maximum wire length of a 2-D network. For a generalization to embedding in three dimensions and higher, refer to Exercise 7.3.

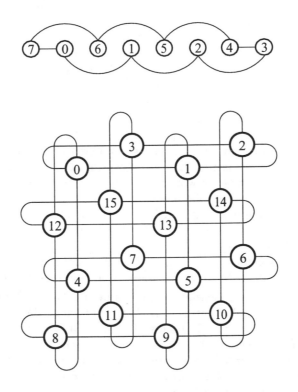

Figure 7.2. Interleaving nodes to avoid the long wire lengths due to the wraparound connections.

The delay along the wire may follow one of several models depending upon the length, the implementation medium, e.g., aluminum on silicon, copper on polyimide, etc. The three common wire delay models include the linear, logarithmic, and constant delay models.

$$\text{Delay} \propto \log_e l \quad \text{Logarithmic delay model}$$
$$\text{Delay} \propto l \quad\quad \text{Linear delay model}$$
$$\text{Delay} \propto C \quad\quad \text{Constant delay model}$$

where l is the wire length. These delay models are incorporated into a model of average message latency developed in the following section.

7.1.4 A Latency Model

Given the impact of the preceding physical constraints, we can now develop a model of the no-load latency of a message in a k-ary n-cube in the presence of these constraints. Such relationships between performance and implementation constraints help us make informed trade-offs in the choice of network topology. In the following we assume a wormhole-switched network, and the development follows that provided in [3].

Consider the base latency of a wormhole-switched message from Equation 2.4.

$$t_{wormhole} = D(t_r + t_s + t_w) + \max(t_s, t_w) \left\lceil \frac{L}{W} \right\rceil \tag{7.5}$$

where t_r is the time to make a routing decision, t_s is the delay through the switch, and t_w is the wire delay across the physical channel. The first term in the right hand side of the expression represents the delay due to the distance between the source and destination. The major components are the routing, switch, and link delays. The routing protocols discussed in Chapter 4 implement decisions that can be quite complex relative to the no-load delay of a data flit through the switch. While the impact of this routing delay is reduced for long messages, it may be nonnegligible for small messages, and is represented by t_r. It is sometimes the case that the switch delays (t_s) are greater than the link delays, and as a result have a nonnegligible impact on the performance of the network. The development of the latency model in this section assumes switch delays dominate wire delays and follows the approach in [3]. Later in this chapter we consider the case where wire delays dominate switch delays. Finally, t_w represents the wire delay across the physical link. The above expression is based on a router architecture where the inputs and outputs are buffered. Thus, once a message pipeline has been set up, the period of this pipeline is determined by the greater of the switch delay and wire delay. If we had used an input only buffered switch, then $\max(t_s, t_w)$ would have simply been replaced by $(t_s + t_w)$.

Under random traffic, the value of the distance D above can be replaced by the average distance between any pair of nodes. With bidirectional links, in an n-dimensional network a message will travel an average of $\frac{k}{4}$ links in a dimension when k is even and $\frac{(k^2-1)}{4k}$ links when k is odd. To capture the effect of wire delays the routing, switching, and wire delays can be normalized to the wire delay between adjacent nodes in a 2-D network. This will permit analysis that would remain relevant with improvements in technology. As new packaging techniques, materials, and interconnect media evolve, wire delays between adjacent nodes in a 2-D embedding will improve. The latency expression using normalized delays will represent performance relative to this improved base 2-D case. Let the switch delay and routing delay be represented as integer multiples of the wire delay in a 2-D network: s and r, respectively. From the earlier discussion, we know the value of t_w relative to a 2-D network. Thus, the latency expression can be written as follows (for networks where k is even):

$$t_{wormhole} = n\frac{k}{4}(r + s + k^{\frac{n}{2}-1}) + \max(s, k^{\frac{n}{2}-1})\left\lceil \frac{L}{W} \right\rceil \qquad (7.6)$$

The above expression is based on a linear delay model for wires. For short wires, delay is logarithmic [71] and for comparison purposes, it is useful (though perhaps unrealistic) to have model based on constant wire delay. The above expression is normalized to the wire delay in a 2-D mesh. Therefore, in the constant delay model, wire delay simply remains at 1. In the logarithmic delay model, delay is a logarithmic function of wire length, i.e., $1 + \log_e l$ [71]. The latency expression under the logarithmic wire delay model can be written as

$$t_{wormhole} = n\frac{k}{4}\left[r + s + 1 + \left(\frac{n}{2} - 1\right)\log_e k\right] + \max\left[s, 1 + \left(\frac{n}{2} - 1\right)\log_e k\right]\left\lceil \frac{L}{W} \right\rceil \qquad (7.7)$$

For the constant wire delay model the latency expression is

$$t_{wormhole} = n\frac{k}{4}(r + s + 1) + s\left\lceil \frac{L}{W} \right\rceil \qquad (7.8)$$

The latency expressions can be viewed as the sum of two components: a *distance component* which is the delay experienced by the header flit, and a *message component*, which is the delay due to the length of the message. The expressions also include terms representing physical constraints (wire length, channel widths), network topology (dimensions, average distance), applications (message lengths) and router architecture (routing and switching delays). Although in the above expression routing and switching delays are constants, we could model them as an increasing function of network dimension. This appeals to intuition since a larger number of dimensions may make routing decisions more complex, and increase the delay through internal networks that must switch between a larger number of router inputs and outputs. We revisit this issue in the exercises at the end of this chapter.

The above expression provides us with insight into selecting the appropriate number of dimensions for a fixed number of nodes. The minimum latency is realized when the component due to distance is equal to the component due message length. The choice of parameters such as the switching and routing delays, channel widths, and message lengths determine the dimension at which this minimum is realized. The parameters themselves are not independent and are related by implementation constraints. Examples of such analysis are presented in the following sections.

7.1.5   Analysis

In this section we focus on the selection of the optimal dimension given a fixed number of nodes. The optimal dimension realizes the minimal value of the no-load latency. The choice of the optimal dimension is dependent on the technological parameters. Wiring density, pin-out, and wire delays each individually define a dimension that minimizes the no-load latency performance of the network. The following analysis is intended to demonstrate how the topological features of the network are dependent on constraints on each these three physical features, and thus enable us to select the topology that optimizes the performance of an implementation.

Constant Bisection Width

We first consider the case where the wiring area is limited, and this limited wiring resource is represented by a fixed bisection width. For the purposes of this analysis, let us assume this fixed resource is assumed to be equivalent to that of a k-ary n-cube with $k = 2$, and single-bit channels between adjacent nodes. Substituting $k = 2$ and $W = 1$ in the expression in Table 7.1, we obtain this constant bisection width as N. Note that this value differs from the expression for the special case of the n-dimensional binary hypercube in that wrap-around channels are assumed. The following analysis could just as easily be performed with with any known bisection width. From Section 7.1.2, we know that the corresponding channel width that fully utilizes this bisection width is $\frac{k}{2}$. Thus, the latency expression under the constant bisection width constraint can be obtained by substituting for W and can be written as

$$t_{wormhole} = n\frac{k}{4}(r + s + k^{\frac{n}{2}-1}) + \max(s, k^{\frac{n}{2}-1})\left\lceil\frac{2L}{k}\right\rceil \tag{7.9}$$

In the above latency expression we implicitly assume that all of the W signals devoted to the channel between a pair of routers is used for message transmission, i.e., half-duplex channels. We could have assumed that the W signals were organized as two unidirectional physical channels — one in each direction across the channel. In this case the channel width in the above expression would have been replaced by $\frac{k}{4}$ rather than $\frac{k}{2}$. This illustrates the necessity of being careful about what exactly a W-bit channel refers to in order to maintain fair comparisons between networks. Comparing W-bit bidirectional channels and W-bit, dual, unidirectional channels is clearly not a fair comparison. Although both instances are sometimes described as W-bit channels between adjacent nodes, the latter has twice as many signals as the former. From the perspective of packaging and wiring area demands, we are simply interested in the number of pins devoted to communication with a neighbor in a dimension. A fair comparison between two networks would ensure the same number of signals devoted to communication between neighboring nodes in a dimension.

As we increase the number of dimensions, when the network is laid out in the plane (or even in three dimensions for that matter), the number of interprocessor channels that cross the bisection increases. If this bisection width is held constant, then the individual channel width must decrease, effectively making messages longer and increasing the component of message latency due to message length. The length of the longest wire also increases with increasing dimension increasing the distance component of the latency expression for higher dimensions. For a constant number of nodes, increasing the dimension increases the wire length by a factor of $N^{\frac{1}{(n+1)n}}$. The cumulative effect of all of these trade-offs is illustrated in Figure 7.3. It is apparent that for larger-size systems, the distance component of message latency dominates at low dimensions, thus favoring networks of dimension 3 or less. Smaller message sizes also effectively increase the impact of switching and routing delays. Thus, increasing r, s, and reducing L for the larger size systems (e.g., 2^{20} and 2^{16} nodes) will further increase the optimal dimension to 4 but not much further. For smaller systems (i.e., 2^8) the optimal number of dimensions remains at three since the latency in these systems is less dependent on the distance component. This behavior appeals to intuition since messages must travel through a greater number of routers in larger systems and thus would be more sensitive to switching and routing delays. Note that the large values of latency are due to the model component that provides an exponential penalty for wire length at high dimensions.

In general, we find that the trade-offs are a bit different for a larger number of nodes versus a smaller number of nodes. Larger systems are more sensitive to switch and wire delays and when these are large, can encourage the use of a larger number of dimensions, e.g., three to six. Smaller message sizes also have the effect of increasing the impact of switch and routing delays. Smaller

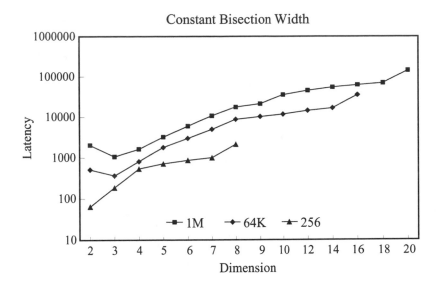

Figure 7.3. Effect of constant bisection width on the no-load message latency.

size systems are less sensitive to these delays. Rather, the relative impact of narrower channels has a greater effect on message latency than the switching and routing delays. The optimal number of dimensions for smaller systems tends to be about two to three. Finally, the use of linear wire delay models penalizes higher-dimension networks. However, use of the logarithmic wire delay models does not change the results appreciably. The optimal number of dimensions for large systems ($> 1K$) ranges from three to six, and for small systems (< 512) remains at two for realistic wire delay models. For small systems, the (unrealistic) constant delay model and small message sizes increases the optimal number of dimensions. However for the case of 16K and 1M nodes, the optimal number of dimensions rises to 9. These results are summarized in Tables 7.2a and 7.2b.

Finally we note that the behavior is dependent on two additional factors. The latency expressions are based on the no-load latency. The presence of link congestion and blocking within the network can produce markedly different behavior, particularly if the message destinations and lengths are nonuniform. Reference [3] presents one approach to incorporating models of network congestion into the latency expressions. A second issue is the design of the routers. If routers employ input

Table 7.2. Optimal number of dimensions for constant bisection bandwidth and: (a) Message size of 32 bits. (b) Message size of 256 bits.

(a)

Wire Delay Model	1M	16K	256
Linear	3	3	2
Logarithmic	7	6	2
Constant	9	7	3

(b)

Wire Delay Model	1M	16K	256
Linear	3	3	2
Logarithmic	4	3	2
Constant	6	4	2

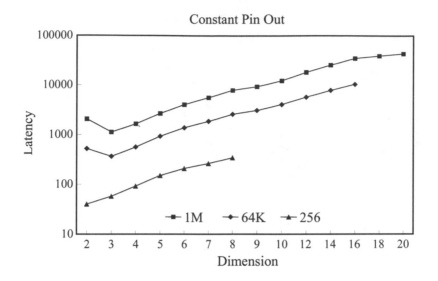

Figure 7.4. Effect of constant pin-out on the no-load message latency.

buffering, the cycle time of the message pipeline is the sum of the switch (t_s) and wire (t_w) delays. When both input and output buffering is employed, the cycle time is reduced to max (t_s, t_w). Thus, the latter model would favor higher dimensions since it is less dependent on wire delays particularly when switching delays are relatively large.

Constant Node Size

The preceding analysis can lead to designs where the individual nodes must have extremely large pin-out (often impractical in 1996–1997 technology) to make full use of the bisection bandwidth. In these instances network performance is limited not by the wiring resource but chip I/O or pin resources [1]. As we did for bisection width, we can re-write the latency expression to capture the dependency of latency on the network dimension assuming the number of chip I/Os are fixed. The following expression is written assuming linear wire delay and P pins per chip devoted to communication channels. Each router is assumed to communicate over W signals with an adjacent router in each direction in each dimension. Thus $P = 2nW$ and substituting $W = \frac{P}{2n}$ the no-load latency expression using a linear wire delay model becomes

$$t_{wormhole} = n\frac{k}{4}(r + s + k^{\frac{n}{2}-1}) + \max(s, k^{\frac{n}{2}-1})\left\lceil \frac{2nL}{P} \right\rceil \tag{7.10}$$

The factor of 2 comes from the availability of channels in each direction within a dimension, and the use of W signals between adjacent nodes. For binary hypercubes we would have $W = \frac{P}{n}$ since there is only one direction in each dimension. A plot illustrating the optimal number of dimensions is shown in Figure 7.4 for the linear wire delay model provided in the above equation, parameterized as shown in the figure. The message size is fixed to that of a nominal-sized cache line in a shared-memory system, or medium size message (32 bytes) and we assume a nominal number of pins devoted to communication (256 pins). The optimal number of dimensions for large numbers of nodes with message size of 256 bits is 3, whereas for the smaller-sized system it is 2. If the wire delay model is

Table 7.3. Optimal number of dimensions for constant pin-out and: (a) Message size of 32 bits. (b) Message size of 256 bits.

(a)

Wire Delay Model	1M	16K	256
Linear	3	3	3
Logarithmic	9	7	4
Constant	9	8	4

(b)

Wire Delay Model	1M	16K	256
Linear	3	3	2
Logarithmic	6	4	2
Constant	9	7	3

changed to the logarithmic delay model the optimal number of dimensions increases to 6, 4, and 2 for the 1M, 16K, and 256-node systems respectively. Reducing the message size has a substantial effect further increasing the optimal number of dimensions. These results are summarized in Tables 7.3a and 7.3b.

The exponential increase in the distance in each dimension overshadows the linear increase in channel width as the network dimension is reduced. Under the constant node size constraint model, higher dimensionality is more important than wider channels [1]. The use of input and output buffering further encourages the use of higher dimensions. This model is also particularly sensitive to wire delays as shown in Figure 7.4.

This analysis is very dependent upon the structure of the physical channel. The model assumes that the number of pins devoted to communication with a neighboring node in a dimension is organized as a single bidirectional channel of width W bits. The channel width is a major determinant of message latency. The pins could have been organized as two unidirectional channels of width $\frac{W}{2}$ bits each, significantly altering the impact of message size. Our expectation is that with the use of bidirectional channels, the network would be relatively more sensitive to traffic patterns and load since messages can only cross the physical channel in one direction at a time. Such conflicts may be reduced by using full-duplex channels, or making the channels unidirectional. In the latter case the average distance a message travels within a dimensions is doubled (to $\frac{k-1}{2}$), and overall average message distance would be increased. The preceding analysis could be easily repeated for any of these relevant cases with appropriate adjustments to the expression that relates channel widths to the number of available data pins. The important point to note is that when pin resources are limited, they can be used in different ways with consequently differing impact on performance.

It is also important to note that while the analysis has been under a single constraint, the bisection width and node size are not independent. A fixed node size and dimensionality will produce a fixed bisection width. Using the model of the physical channel between adjacent routers as described in the preceding paragraphs, we observe that the channel width $W = \frac{P}{2n}$. Based on this channel width, the relationship between node size and bisection width can be written from Table 7.1 as

$$Bisection\ width = \frac{P}{n}\ k^{n-1} \qquad (7.11)$$

Bisection width is linearly related to node size and inversely related to the network dimensionality. As networks are scaled to larger sizes, the technology-dependent question is one of whether bisection width or node size limits are encountered first. The answer is based on a moving target, and may be different at any given point in the technology curve.

Constant Wire Throughput

The analysis described in the preceding sections were based on the assumption that switching delays were dominant. Therefore the latency model represented these delays (and routing delays) as values normalized to the wire delay of between adjacent routers in a 2-D implementation. As the speed of operation continues to rise and systems employ larger networks, wire delays begin to dominate. This section develops the latency model in the case where it is wire delays that are dominant rather than switching delays.

When the delay along the wire is small relative to the speed of transmission through the wire media and propagation delay through the drivers, the lines can be modeled as simple capacitive loads. This is the case for lower-dimensional networks. When higher-dimensional networks are laid out in 2 or 3 dimensions, the propagation delay along the longest wire can be substantial. In reality, a signal connection actually operates as a transmission line. As the speeds of network operation increase, and high-dimensional networks are mapped to two and three dimensions producing longer wires, a more accurate analysis utilizes models of physical channel behavior based on transmission lines. Consider the following analysis [31]. A signal propagates along a wire at a speed given by the following expression.

$$v = \frac{c_0}{\sqrt{\epsilon_r}} \tag{7.12}$$

The value of c_0 is the speed of light in vacuum and ϵ_r is the relative permittivity of the dielectric material of the transmission line. If the wire is long enough relative to the signal transition times, a second signal can be driven onto the line before the first signal has been received at the source. The maximum number of bits on the wire is a function of the frequency of operation, wire length, and signal velocity. These factors are related by the following expression:

$$n = \frac{fl}{v} \tag{7.13}$$

where f is the clock frequency, l is the length of the line, and v is the signal velocity.

Given the number of dimensions and layout of the network, the maximum number of bits that can be placed on the wire can be computed from this expression. Typical values for v have been reported as $0.1 - 0.2$ m/s [16, 31]. These values provide maximum wire lengths for nonpipelined channels for a 1 GHz switching speed. For $v = 0.2$ m/s and a switching speed of 1 GHz, a wire of length one meter can support the concurrent transmission of 5 bits. While link pipelining has been use in local area networks, until recently its use in multiprocessor interconnects has been quite limited. This is rapidly changing with the continuing increase in clock speeds and confluence of traditional local area interconnect and multiprocessor backplane interconnect technologies [30, 156].

While latency remains unaffected, link throughput would now be decoupled from wire delay and limited by the switching speeds of the drivers and wire media rather than physical length of the wires. Multiple bits can concurrently be in transmission along a wire. From the latency equations developed in earlier sections, it is clear that wire delays play an important role, and as a result, link pipelining fundamentally changes the trade-offs that dictates the optimal number of dimensions. Channel bandwidth is now limited by switching speed rather than wire lengths. Scott and Goodman [310] performed a detailed modeling and analysis of the benefits of link pipelining in tightly coupled multiprocessor interconnects. Their analysis utilized a base case of a 3-D unidirectional torus. To remain consistent with the preceding discussion, we apply their analysis techniques to the 2-D case and latency expressions developed above. Thus, we will be able to compare the effects of link pipelining, switch delays, wiring constraints, and pin-out on the optimal choice of network dimension. The preceding latency expression for wormhole-switched networks can be rewritten as

$$t_{wormhole} = n\frac{k}{4}(r + s + w_{avg}) + s\left\lceil\frac{L}{W}\right\rceil \tag{7.14}$$

The above expression is normalized to the delay between adjacent nodes in a 2-D network. The value of w_{avg} is the average wire delay expressed relative to this base time period. Note the latency term due to message length is now dependent only on the switching delay which determines the rate at which bits can be placed on the wire.

While nonpipelined networks have their clock cycle time dictated by the maximum wire length, pipelined networks have the clock cycle time determined by the switching speed of the routers. The distance component of message latency depends on the length of the wires traversed by the message. However, the wire length between adjacent nodes will depend on the dimension being traversed. The average wire length can be computed as follows [310].

To avoid the long wires due to the wraparound channels, node positions are interleaved as shown in Figure 7.2. Recall that the wire length is computed relative to the wire length between two adjacent nodes in a 2-D mesh. Let the wire length between two nonadjacent nodes in Figure 7.2 be denoted by l_2. In this case there are $(k - 2)$ links of length l_2 and two links of length equal to the base wire length in a 2-D layout (see the 1-D interleaved placement in Figure 7.2). If we assume that this base wire length is one unit and that l_2 is twice the base wire length between adjacent nodes, we can write the average wire length in this dimension as

$$\text{Average wire length} = l_2\frac{k - 1}{k} = 2\frac{k - 1}{k} \tag{7.15}$$

In practice, l_2 may be a bit longer than twice the base wire length. In the following we retain the variable l_2 in the expressions. Consider topologies with an even number of dimensions. When an n-dimensional topology is mapped into the plane, $\frac{n}{2}$ dimensions are mapped into each physical dimension. As each pair of dimensions are added, the number of nodes in each physical dimension is increased by a factor of k and the average wire length in each dimension grows by a factor of k. Mapping each additional pair of dimensions increases this average wire length in each physical dimension by a factor of k. Consider all the logical dimensions mapped to one of the two physical dimensions. The sum of the mean wire lengths in each of these dimensions is given by

$$l_2\frac{k - 1}{k} + l_2\frac{k - 1}{k}k + l_2\frac{k - 1}{k}k^2 + \ldots + l_2\frac{k - 1}{k}k^{\frac{n-2}{2}} \tag{7.16}$$

We can similarly compute the sum of the mean wire length in each dimension mapped to the other physical dimension. The sum of these two expressions divided by the total number of dimensions gives the average wire length of the topology. This simplified expression appears as

$$l_2\frac{k - 1}{k}(1 + k + \ldots + k^{\frac{n-2}{2}})\frac{2}{n} \tag{7.17}$$

Using the sum of the geometric series and simplifying, we have

$$w_{avg} = \frac{2l_2(N^{\frac{1}{2}} - 1)}{nk} = \frac{4(N^{\frac{1}{2}} - 1)}{nk} \tag{7.18}$$

Substituting in the equation for latency, we have an expression for the latency in a link-pipelined network that is embedded in two dimensions.

Optimal Number of Dimensions — Summary

To generate an intuition about the effect of physical constraints on network performance we can make the following observations. Message latency can viewed as the sum of two components: a distance component and a message size component represented as

$$\text{Message latency } = \alpha \times Dist(n) + \beta \times Msg\_Length(n) \tag{7.19}$$

For a fixed number of nodes, the function $Dist(n)$ decreases as the network dimension increases. Under bisection width and constant pin-out constraints the function $Msg\_Length(n)$ increases with increasing network dimension since channel widths decrease. Minimum latency is achieved when the components are equal. The coefficient of the distance component is a function of switching, routing, and wire delays: α determines how fast the distance component of latency reduces with increasing dimension. This appeals to intuition as large switching delays encourage the use of a smaller number of intermediate routers by a message, i.e., a larger number of dimensions. Similarly, β, which is a function of switching and wire delay, determines how fast the message component increases with increasing network dimension. The optimal number of dimensions is determined as a result of specific values of router architecture and implementation technology that fix the values of α and β.

It is important to note that these models provide the optimal number of dimensions in the absence of contention. This analysis must be coupled with the detailed performance analysis usually via simulation as described in Chapter 9, or analytic models of contention(e.g., as in [1, 3, 128]).

7.1.6   Packaging Constraints

It is clear that physical constraints have a substantial impact on the performance of the interconnection network. In practice, electronic packaging is a major determinant of these physical constraints. By *packaging* we refer to the hierarchy of interconnections between computational elements. Systems start with communicating elements sharing a silicon surface. Bare die may then be packaged in single-chip carrier or a multichip module [302], which in turn may be mounted on one or both sides of a printed circuit board. Multiple boards are mounted in a card cage, and multiple card cages may be connected and so on. This is graphically illustrated in Figure 7.5. The materials and fabrication technology at each level of this hierarchy are distinct, leading to interconnects with very different physical characteristics and constraints. For example, wire pitch may vary from a few micrometers on a die to a few hundred micrometers on a printed circuit board. Such parameters clearly determine available wiring area and therefore achievable bisection bandwidth. With multichip modules and area array I/Os the number of I/Os available out of a die becomes proportional to chip area rather than chip perimeter [301]. As the preceding analysis has demonstrated, the choice of topology is strongly influenced by such physical constraints and therefore by the packaging technology.

Packaging technology continues to evolve, keeping pace with rapid advances in semiconductor technology. The advent of new packaging technologies, e.g., low-cost multichip modules (MCM), 3-D chip stacks, etc. will lead to major changes in the relationship between these physical constraints, and as a result significantly impact the cost, performance, and reliability of the next generation of systems in general, and multiprocessor interconnects in particular [84, 123]. An accurate analysis of the effect of packaging technology and options will enable the identification of topologies that effectively utilize available packaging technology, where "form fits function [71]."

From the point of view of the network topology, the fundamental packaging question concerns the placement of die, package, board, and subsystem boundaries and the subsequent performance impact of these choices. Die boundaries may be determined in part by technology as we see advances

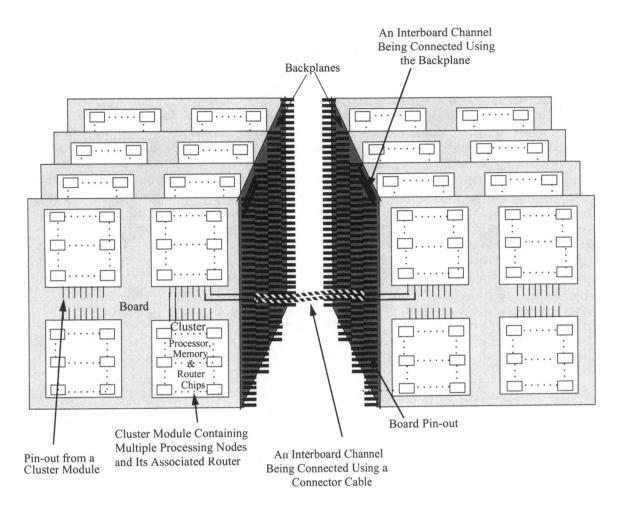

Figure 7.5. Illustration of a packaging hierarchy. (From [19].)

that place multiple processors and the associated routers and interconnect on a single chip. The placement of other boundaries such as multichip carriers and boards are determined by trade-offs in cost, performance, thermal density, reliability, pin-out, etc. For example, the network used to connect 16 processors on a single chip may be quite different from that used on a printed circuit board to connect 64 such chips. Therefore these partitioning decisions are critical. To make the most effective use of packaging technology, we need accurate models of performance to predict the impact of a specific choice of partitions for a given network topology. In a more general setting, such models have been used as elements of a "design for packageability" style of system-level design [84]

Technology projections from groups such as the Semiconductor Industries Association provide assessments of the evolution of implementation technology parameters such as feature size, wafer sizes, clock rates, etc. There have been several recent efforts aimed at assessing the impact of packaging technology on the design and optimization of future network topologies. As a representative example of a relatively new arena of work, the following discussion presents one such approach to assessing the impact of packaging technology on network design.

Basak and Panda [18, 19] provide a model and framework for designing clustered multiprocessor systems in a two-level packaging hierarchy. A k-ary n-cube cluster-c topology is proposed, where each cluster consists of c nodes. While the intracluster network is left undefined and open, the intercluster network is a k-ary n-cube with k^n clusters for a total of $N = k^n \times c$ nodes. With a fixed number of nodes, by varying the number of clusters one can change the physical characteristics of the intercluster and intracluster networks. For example, with single-chip nodes the intracluster network may occupy the surface a board while the intercluster network may appear between boards. In the authors' terminology, the state of the art in packaging at each level offers or supplies physical resources such as bisection bandwidth and pin-out capability. A specific clustering of nodes produces a demand for bisection width, area, and pin-out at each level, e.g., board or chip. The proposed design paradigm is one of reconciling the demand and supply in the most efficient manner possible. Towards this end, analytic models are developed for supplied and demanded resources such as bisection bandwidth, node pin out, and area. Optimization algorithms can utilize these models to produce the most efficient designs.

For example, the demanded bisection bandwidth of an N node system is estimated as follows. Assume that each node injects λ bits/cycle into the network, where a cycle is the wire delay between adjacent routers. As in preceding sections this cycle time is assumed to be normalized to that of the delay between adjacent nodes in a 2-D mesh. On the average, we have $c\lambda$ bits generated within a cluster. With random destinations, a $(1 - \frac{c}{N})$ fraction of these injected bits traverse the intercluster network, and half of this traffic crosses the bisection. Aggregating over all nodes, the demanded bisection bandwidth of a k-ary n-cube cluster-c topology in bits/cycle is

$$\text{Demanded bisection bandwidth} = \frac{N\lambda(1 - \frac{c}{N})}{2} \tag{7.20}$$

As described in [19], the value of λ can be derived from various projections of computation to communication ratios, processor speeds, and emerging network link speeds. Typical estimates can be found in [298]. Now consider the available bisection bandwidth of a packaged clustered network. From the expressions in Table 7.1, we have the bisection bandwidth of the intercluster network as

$$\text{Bisection bandwidth} = \frac{2\frac{N}{c}W}{k_{max}} \tag{7.21}$$

In a regular network where $k_1 = k_2 = \ldots = k_n, k_{max} = (\frac{N}{c})^{\frac{1}{n}}$. The issue here is that the channel width is limited by the pin-out at the chip or board level. In the following, the constraints on the channel width are derived based on a regular network where $k_1 = k_2 = \ldots = k_n$. The extension to distinct radices is straightforward [19]. Consider boards with a capacity of $B = b^n$ clusters, where $b < k$, i.e., no dimension can completely fit on a board and traversal of any dimension forces a interboard communication. Along each dimension we have b^{n-1} nodes with channels traversing interboard boundaries (since the cross section in this dimension has b^{n-1} nodes). Including channels in both directions, the total number of signals coming off the board is given by

$$\text{Board pinout requirements} = 2\sum_{i=1}^{n} b^{n-1}W = 2nb^{n-1}W \tag{7.22}$$

By equating the above to the number of available board-level pins, we can derive the constraint on channel width. The number of available pins may be a function of the perimeter of the board as found in conventional technology, or it may be proportional to the area of the board representing the use of free-space optical communication or the use of elastomeric connectors [255]. The above derivation is based on the assumption that the intraboard bisection width is not the limiting factor

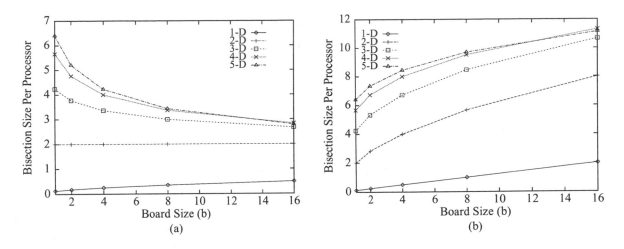

Figure 7.6. Examples of the effect of packaging technology: (a) Periphery pin-out technology. (b) Surface pin-out technology. (From [19].)

on channel width, but rather the interboard pin-out is the limiting factor. This appears to be reasonable in 1997 technology. The alternative is easily modeled by using the intraboard bisection bandwidth as the limiting factor for channel width. Assuming a maximum available board-level pin-out of P_B, we have

$$W = \frac{P_B}{2nb^{n-1}} = \frac{P_B}{2nBb^{-1}} \tag{7.23}$$

Note that B, the number of clusters on a board is a function of the of the board size and cluster size, and therefore a function of packaging technology. By substituting the above expression for channel width in the expression for bisection width, the dependency between bisection width, board size, cluster size, and pin-out can be studied. These expressions relate parameters that define a generation of packaging technology with architectural features that define the network in manner that permits the analysis of the impact of packaging constraints.

An example of the trade-offs that can be studied is illustrated in Figure 7.6. Based on the preceding expressions, these curves from [19] illustrate the relationship between the board size and offered intercluster bisection bandwidth on a per processor basis. This relationship is shown for the cases where the number of I/Os is proportional to board periphery and board area. For the former case, the analysis indicates that for higher-dimensional networks, smaller board sizes offer a higher per-processor bisection bandwidth. The converse is true for the case where the number of I/Os is proportional to board area. A detailed study of the relationships between network and packaging parameters, as well as a precise definitions of the packaging parameters captured in these models can be found in [19].

7.2 Router Architectures

The router architecture is largely determined by the switching technique that is supported. The majority of modern commercial routers found in high performance multiprocessor architectures and emerging switched networks for workstation clusters utilize some form of cut-through switching

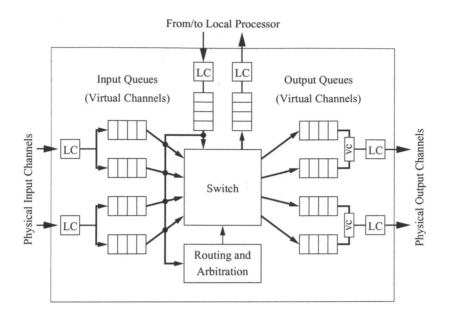

Figure 7.7. Canonical router architecture.

or some variant of it, e.g., VCT switching, wormhole switching, buffered wormhole switching, etc. Therefore this chapter largely focuses on a discussion of issues and designs of such routers. While the router implementations for wormhole and VCT switching differ in many of the architectural trade-offs, they share many common features derived from the use of some form of cut-through switching. The common issues and features facing the design of routers can be categorized as intrarouter or interrouter, and are discussed below. This discussion is followed by descriptions of recent router designs, emphasizing their unique features and reinforcing the commonly held trade-offs.

7.2.1   Intrarouter Performance

In an effort to capture the commonalities and enable quantifiable comparisons, Chien [57] developed an abstract model for the architecture of routers in wormhole-switched k-ary n-cubes. This model is largely concentrated on the intrarouter architecture while the performance of interrouter link operation is very sensitive to packaging implementations. The basic wormhole router functions can be captured in an abstract router architecture as shown in Figure 7.7. We are interested in the implementation complexity of each of the components in the figure.

- *Crossbar switch.* This component is responsible for connecting router input buffers to router output buffers. High-speed routers will utilize crossbar networks with full connectivity, while lower-speed implementations may utilize networks that do not provide full connectivity between input buffers and output buffers.

- *Link controller (LC).* Flow control across the physical channel between adjacent routers is implemented by this unit. The link controllers on either side of a channel coordinate to transfer flow control units. Sufficient buffering must be provided on the receiving side to account for delays in propagation of data and flow control signals. When a flow control event signaling a full buffer is transmitted to the sending controller, there must still be sufficient buffering at the receiver to store all of the phits in transit, as well as all of the phits that will be injected during the time it takes for the flow control signal to propagate back to the sender. If virtual channels are present, the controller is also responsible for decoding the destination channel of the received phit.

- *Virtual channel controller (VC).* This component is responsible for multiplexing the contents of the virtual channels onto the physical channel. With tree-based arbitration, the delay can be expected to be logarithmic in the number of channels.

- *Routing and arbitration unit.* This logic implements the *routing function*. For adaptive routing protocols, the message headers are processed to compute the set of candidate output channels, and generate requests for these channels. If relative addressing is being used in the network, the new headers, one for each candidate output channel, must be generated. For oblivious routing protocols header update is a very simple operation. Alternatively, if absolute addressing is used, header processing is reduced since new headers do not need to be generated.

  This unit also implements the *selection function* component of the routing algorithm: selecting the output link for an incoming message. Output channel status is combined with input channel requests. Conflicts for the same output must be arbitrated (in logarithmic time), and if relative addressing is used, a header must be selected. If the requested buffer(s) is (are) busy, the incoming message remains in the input buffer until a requested output becomes free. The figure shows a full crossbar that connects all input virtual channels to all output virtual channels. Alternatively, the router may use a design where full connectivity is only provided between physical channels and virtual channels arbitrate for crossbar input ports. Fast arbitration policies are crucial to maintaining a low flow control latency through the switch.

- *Buffers.* These are FIFO buffers for storing messages in transit. In the above model, a buffer is associated with both the input physical channels and output physical channels. The buffer size is an integral number of flow control units. In alternative designs, buffers may be associated only with inputs (input buffering) or outputs (output buffering). In VCT switching sufficient buffer space is available for a complete message packet. For a fixed buffer size, insertion and removal from the buffer is usually not on the router critical path.

- *Processor interface.* This component simply implements a physical channel interface to the processor rather than to an adjacent router. It consists of one or more injection channels from the processor and one or more ejection channels to the processor. Ejection channels are also referred to as delivery channels or consumption channels.

While the above router model is representative of routers constructed to date, router architectures are evolving with different implementations. The routing and arbitration unit may be replicated to reduce arbitration time and channels may share ports on the crossbar. The basic functions appear largely unaltered but with distinct implementations to match the current generation of technology.

If the routers support adaptive routing, the presence of multiple choices makes the routing decision more complex. There is a need to generate information corresponding to these choices and to select among these choices. This naturally incurs some overhead in time as well as resources, e.g., chip area. Similarly, the use of virtual channels, while reducing header blocking delays in the network, makes the link controllers more complex by requiring arbitration and more complex flow control mechanisms.

Table 7.4. A parameterization of the component delays in a wormhole-switched router. (From [57].)

Module	Parameter	Gate Count	Delay
Crossbar	P (ports)	$O(P^2)$	$c_0 + c_1 \times \log P$
Flow control unit	None	$O(1)$	c_2
Address decoder	None	$O(1)$	c_3
Routing decision	F (freedom)	$O(F^2)$	$c_4 + c_5 \times \log F$
Header selection	F (freedom)	$O(\log F)$	$c_6 + c_7 \times \log F$
VC controllers	V (#VCs)	$O(V)$	$c_8 + c_9 \times \log V$

The two main measures of intrarouter performance [57] are the routing latency or header latency, and the flow control latency. From Figure 7.7 it is apparent that the latency experienced by the header flit(s) through a router is comprised of several components. After the header has been received, it must be decoded and the connection request generated. Since multiple headers may arrive simultaneously, the routing and arbitration unit arbitrates among multiple requests and one of the headers is selected, and routed. This involves computing an output and if it is available, setting the crossbar. The updated header and subsequent data may now be driven through the switch, and will experience some multiplexing delay through the link controllers as they multiplex multiple virtual channels across the physical channel. Once a path has been set up, data flits may now flow through the router with no further involvement with the routing and arbitration unit, but may compete for physical channel bandwidth with other virtual channels.

The flow control latency determines the rate at which flits can be transmitted along the path. In the terminology of pipelines, the flow control latency is the message pipeline stage time. From the figure, we can see that the flow control latency experienced by a data flit is the sum of the delay through the channel flow control, the time to drive the flit through the crossbar, and the multiplexing delay experienced through the link controller, as well as the time to read and write the FIFO buffers. The delay through the link controller is often referred to as the *flit multiplexing delay* or *channel multiplexing delay*. A general model for these delays is quite difficult to derive since the latencies are sensitive to the implementation. One approach to developing such model for wormhole-switched networks is described in [57]. A canonical model of a wormhole-switched router is developed, containing units for address decoding, flow control, and switching. Implementations of the various components (e.g., tree of gates, or selectors for each output) are modeled and expressions for the implementation complexity of each component are derived, but parameterized by technology dependent constants. The parameterized model is illustrated in Table 7.4. By instantiating the constants with values based on a particular implementation technology, realistic delays can be computed for comparing alternative designs. In [57], the values are instantiated for a class of implementations based on gate arrays to derive estimates of flow control latency through the router. The utility of the model stems from the application to many classes of routers. Other router architectures using similar components for partially adaptive or fully adaptive routing can be constructed, and the parameterized model used to estimate and compare intrarouter latencies. In fact, comparisons are possible across technology implementations.

A major determinant of the intrarouter delays is the size and structure of the switch. The use of a crossbar switch to connect all input virtual channels to all output virtual channels is feasible for low-dimensional networks with a small number of virtual channels. A 2-D network with four

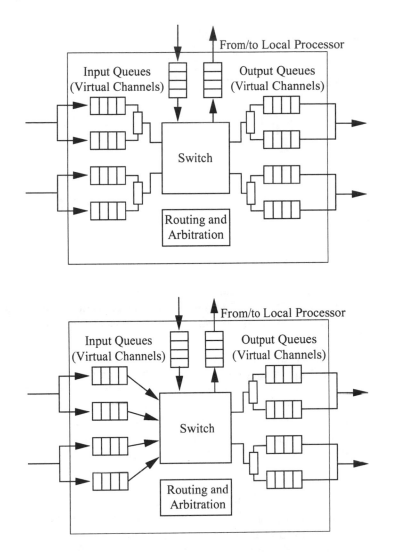

Figure 7.8. Alternative router switch organizations.

virtual channels per link would require a 16×16 crossbar and a 3-D network would require a 24×24 switch. Considering that these channels may be byte or word wide, it is apparent that alternatives begin to become attractive. One alternative is to have the switch size determined by the number of physical channels. The data rate into and out of the switch is limited by the bandwidth of the physical channels, while virtual channels decouple buffer resources (and therefore messages) from the physical channel. Thus, channel utilization can remain high, while the construction of crossbar switches remains feasible for higher-dimensional networks. However, input messages must now arbitrate for both switch inputs and outputs. In adaptively routed networks, this arbitration cost grows quadratically with the degree of adaptivity. An intermediate organization provides switch inputs for each input virtual channel, but outputs only for each physical channel. Thus, arbitration is simplified by only having inputs arbitrate for ports on one side of the switch. These alternatives are illustrated in Figure 7.8.

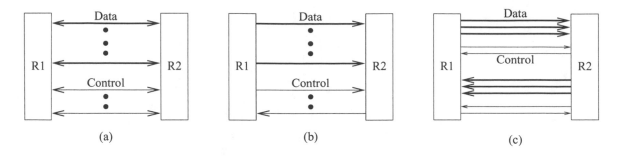

Figure 7.9. An example of: (a) Half-duplex organization. (b) Unidirectional organization. (c) Full-duplex organization.

7.2.2   Physical Channel Issues

The behavioral aspects of interrouter flow control, particularly in the presence of virtual channels is discussed at some length by Dally [73] and Bolding [31] as well as in detail in the descriptions of the individual routers. The following discussion of the issues in physical channel design is largely drawn from these efforts.

In Chapter 2 we have seen that flow control is performed at two levels. Message flow control manipulates logical units of information such as flits. These logical units are the granularity of information for sharing network resources such as interrouter links, intrarouter data paths, and allocating buffers. For example, when a virtual channel competes for, and acquires a physical link, a flit is transferred in its entirety before the control of the channel is relinquished. The transfer of a single flit is not interleaved with other flits. The granularity of a flit determines the effectiveness with which messages share buffers, links, and datapaths. The considerations and performance implications are similar to those facing the choice of thread granularity for multithreaded programs sharing a CPU.

Physical channel flow control may require several cycles to transfer a flit across the channel, e.g., a 64-bit flit across a 16-bit-wide physical channel. In this case, the physical flow control operates on 16-bit phits. By making the flit and phit sizes equivalent, simpler protocols can be used for operating the physical channel. The synchronization of physical transfers can also be used to signify the transfer of flits and the availability of buffer space. Otherwise the message flow control across the channel for blocking messages and allocating and freeing buffers must operate at a different rate than the physical channel signaling rate, increasing the complexity of the router interfaces and intrarouter data paths. In packet-switched and VCT-switched networks, buffer allocation is clearly at the level of logical units such as packets, while channel flow control is typically at finer granularities. In circuit-switched networks, the issue of flow control between routers is encountered during path setup. Once the hardware path has been established message flow control operations are performed between the source and destination routers.

The fixed number of pins devoted to communication between adjacent routers may be organized in several ways. The channel may be organized as (1) a bidirectional half-duplex channel, (2) a unidirectional channel, or (3) a bidirectional full-duplex channel. An example of the three alternatives is illustrated in Figure 7.9. The use of bidirectional half-duplex or unidirectional channels maximizes channel widths. With the exception of pins devoted to control, message transmission between adjacent routers can make full use of the available pins between two routers. However, with unidirectional channels, the topology must be a tori or similar "wrapped" topology to ensure that all

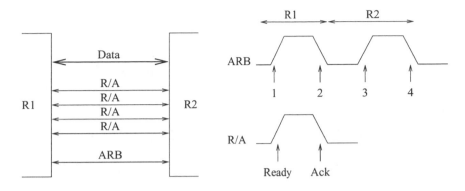

Figure 7.10. An example of the operation of a half-duplex channel.

pairs of nodes may communicate. As a result, the use of unidirectional channels doubles the average distance traveled by a message in tori, increasing the distance component of message latency. Half-duplex links have the disadvantage that both sides of the link must arbitrate for the use of the link. The arbitration must be fair and provide access to both sides of the channel when data are available to be transmitted. Fair arbitration requires status information to be transmitted across the channel to indicate the availability of data to be transmitted. Such traffic may consume bandwidth through messages (in-band transmission) or may be signaled using dedicated pins (out-of-band transmission). We would like this arbitration to be efficient in that the link bandwidth devoted to arbitration signals is minimized. In addition to consuming bandwidth, this arbitration time can increase the flow control latency across the link reducing link utilization as traffic increases. In contrast, this arbitration overhead is avoided in unidirectional full-duplex links, and therefore links can generally be run faster. However, channel widths are reduced i.e., approximately halved as bandwidth is statically allocated in each direction. When the data are being transmitted in only one direction across the channel, 50% of the pin bandwidth is unused. A full-duplex link is only fully utilized when messages are being transmitted in both directions. Depending on the exact pin counts and channel protocol, this organization also serves to roughly double message length and the corresponding component of message latency.

If virtual channels are used, additional bits/signals must be used to distinguish between virtual channels that share the physical channel. These additional bits may use bandwidth or be transmitted across dedicated control pins. An example of the operation of a physical channel that supports multiple virtual channels is provided in Example 7.1.

Example 7.1

The Network Design Frame [79] utilizes half-duplex physical channels to support two virtual channels. The sequence of operations involved in a transfer across this channel are illustrated in Figure 7.10. The channel consists of an 11-bit bidirectional data channel. At power up, one side of the channel is the default owner and has the privilege to transmit information. When the idle side of the channel wishes to transmit a flit, a request is generated by driving the ARB signal high. Channel ownership is transferred when the current owner drives the signal low, and roles are reversed. For example, in the figure $R1$ owns the channel at time 1 and ownership is transferred to $R2$ at time 2. Now $R1$ drives the ARB signal high at time 3 to request ownership and becomes the owner again at time 4. A flit transfer is synchronized

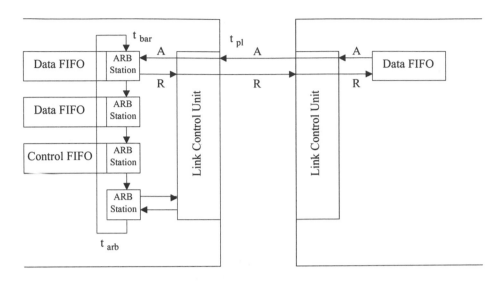

Figure 7.11. An example of overlapping channel arbitration and channel transmission.

using a single request/acknowledge (R/A) signal for each virtual channel in each direction across the physical channel, leading to a total of four R/A signals. A transfer is initiated by driving the corresponding R/A signal high. When the receiving side of the channel is ready to accept another flit, the receiver pulls the R/A signal low.

In the Network Design Frame, one virtual channel has a higher priority than the other. Demand-driven, fair allocation of bandwidth across the physical channel to multiple virtual channels on both sides of the link will require fast, fair arbitration schemes. Ideally we would like arbitration delays to be completely overlapped with transmission and therefore completely hidden. The following example provides one solution for hiding arbitration delays in self-timed router architectures.

Example 7.2

The channel structure and operation of the Ariadne router is illustrated in Figure 7.11 [7]. The operation of this channel is also self-timed, and each virtual channel is granted access to the physical channel using a demand-driven mutual exclusion ring [303]. Within a router output port, each virtual channel owns an arbitration station on the mutual exclusion ring. In addition there is a station on the ring corresponding to the port on the other end of the channel. A signal representing the privilege to drive the physical channel circulates around this ring. The cycle time across a physical link is determined by the interaction between two activities. The first is the arbitration among virtual channels competing for the physical channel. The second is the handshake cycle time for transmission of a flit across the physical channel. A barrier synchronization between these activities can be implemented as part of the channel flow control mechanism as illustrated in Figure 7.11.

The efficiency of this approach can be captured in the following expression. Let t_{arb} represent the period of the arbitration oscillator, i.e., the time for the privilege to circulate through all stations on one side of the channel. Let t_{pl} represents the handshake time to transfer a phit over the physical link and place a request to send the next phit. When a virtual channel is granted the privilege from its ARB Station, phit transmission is stalled until the previous transmission has been completed. When transmission begins, the privilege can be released, serving to overlap transmission latency with the next round of arbitration. When more than one channel is contending for the link, arbitration can be completely hidden. When only one virtual channel is transmitting, the privilege may circulate all the way around the ring before the next phit can be transmitted, potentially slowing down transmission. The privilege is available at intervals of t_{arb}, except the first time when it is available after $\frac{3}{4}t_{arb}$. Thus in general, with one virtual channel transmitting, the privilege is available at points in time of $\frac{3}{4}t_{arb} + mt_{arb}$ for some $m > 0$. Once the physical cycle is complete and the privilege has returned, a small barrier synchronization latency t_{bar} is incurred before the privilege is again released. Thus, the link cycle time with one active virtual channel is

$$t_c = \frac{3}{4}t_{arb} + mt_{arb} + t_{bar}$$

for the minimum m such that $\frac{3}{4}t_{arb} + mt_{arb} + t_{bar} > t_{pl}$. The value of $t_c - t_{pl}$ represents the degree to which arbitration cannot be overlapped with flit transmission across the link.

At low loads, half-duplex links are advantageous since they deliver the full bandwidth of the available pins to the messages whereas full-duplex links remain under utilized. However, at high loads the full bandwidth of the link is utilized in both cases, although arbitration traffic in the case the half-duplex links will produce relatively lower utilization. The disparity in performance is greater when link pipelining is employed [31]. When channel ownership must be switched in the case of a half-duplex link, transmission can begin only after the channel has been drained of the bits currently in transit. In addition, the first phit transmitted in the new direction incurs the full latency of the physical link. Thus, arbitration overheads relative to full-duplex operation correspondingly increase since a greater percentage of time is spent in switching directions across the channel. A second problem is in the propagation of status information. With pipelined links, the received status of flow control information may not reflect the actual status at the time it is received. This is an issue for both half-duplex and full-duplex pipelined links.

For example, the transmission of flow control information to indicate the lack of buffer space arrives too late at the sender: multiple phits are already in transit and will be dropped due to lack of space. However, full link utilization can be maintained without loss with a buffer on the receiver of sufficient depth to store all the phits in transit across the channel. The relationship between the buffer depth, wire delay, bandwidth, etc. can be derived as follows [107]. Assume that propagation delay is specified as P ns per unit length and the length of the wire in the channel is L units. When the receiver requests the sender to stop transmitting, there may be LPB phits in transit on a channel running at B Gphits/s. In addition, by the time the flow control signal propagates to the sender, an additional LPB phits may be placed in the channel. Finally, if the processing time at the receiver is F ns (e.g., flow control operation latency), this delay permits the sender to place another FB phits on the channel. The available buffer space in the receiver must be large enough to receive all of these phits when a *stop* signal is transmitted to the sender. These *slack buffers* [314] serve to hide the wire latency and the flow control latency. The size of the buffers can be estimated as follows.

$$\text{Available buffer space} = 2LPB + FB \text{ phits} \tag{7.24}$$

In cases where long wire latencies dominate, the use of link pipelining favors the use of full-duplex channels, particularly under high loads. This is typically the case in the emerging class of low latency interconnects for workstation/PC clusters. To reduce the wiring costs of long interconnects as well

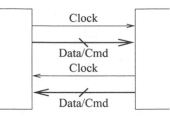

Figure 7.12. An example of the operation of a full-duplex channel with data/command encoding.

as maintain high link utilization, full-duplex channel techniques have been developed using slack buffers and pin-efficient flow control. An example is described in Example 7.3.

Example 7.3

The structure of an example full-duplex channel is shown in Figure 7.12. This channel is used in the routing fabric of Tandem's ServerNet [156], and differs from the preceding example is several ways. Physical channel flow control is synchronous and the clock is transmitted across the link. At the transmitting end of the channel, the clock is sent through similar delay paths as the data so that it may be used to sample the data at the receiver. Buffer management and message-level flow control is via commands that are transmitted in the reverse direction across the 9-bit data/command channel. The 9-bit encoding provides for 256 data symbols and 20 command symbols. The specific encoding used in ServerNet is shown below.

Bit 8	Bit 7	Bit 6	Function
0	0	0	Command
0	0	1	Error
0	1	0	Error
1	0	0	Error
0	1	1	Data $<7{:}6> = 00$
1	0	1	Data $<7{:}6> = 01$
1	1	0	Data $<7{:}6> = 10$
1	1	1	Data $<7{:}6> = 11$

The most significant 3 bits determine how the remaining 6 bits will be interpreted. For command words, these 6 bits are encoded as a 3-of-6 code where all command words have exactly three 1s and three 0s, resulting in 20 such command words. Examples of command symbols that may be used include *STOP, SEND, END-OF-MSG*, and *IDLE*. The data symbols are encoded as four groups of 64 symbols. For example, from the above table reception of 011101011 would be interpreted as the data word 00101011, while reception of 110101011 would be interpreted as 10101011. The error codes are used to ensure a minimum Hamming distance of two between command symbols and data symbols. Commands interspersed within the data stream are used for buffer management and message flow control in addition to error signaling. Slack buffers are used to hide the latency of the transmission of flow control commands.

A similar physical channel structure and approach is used within the routers for Myrinet. Both Tandem's ServerNet and Myricom's Myrinet bring traditional multiprocessor network technology to the workstation and PC cluster environment. Interconnects can be substantially longer and therefore the delays for asynchronous handshaking signals become larger. The use of synchronous channels and slack buffers to overlap flow control delays as described above is motivated in part by operation in this high latency environment. Another advantage of encoding commands is the reduction in pin-out requirements. The percentage of pins devoted to data is higher although some of the bandwidth is now devoted to control.

There are also many other technological features that impact the choice of full- or half-duplex links. We point to one technique for maximizing the use of available pins on the router chips: simultaneous bidirectional signaling [48, 76, 193]. This technique allows simultaneous signaling between two routers across a single signal line. Thus, full-duplex bidirectional communication of a single bit between two routers can be realized with one pin (signal) rather than two signals. This is achieved by transmitting [76] a logic 1 (0) as a positive (negative) current. The received signal is the superposition of the two signals transmitted from both sides of the channel. Each transmitter generates a reference signal which is subtracted from the superimposed signal to generate the received signal. The result is a considerable savings over the number of I/O pins required, and consequent reduction in the packaging cost. The low voltage swing employed in the Reliable Router [76] results in additional reduction in power consumption, but necessitates different noise reduction techniques. This approach would enable wider, half-duplex links and larger number of dimensions. Currently the main difficulty with this scheme is the complexity of the signaling mechanism and the susceptibility to noise. Both of these disadvantages can be expected to be mitigated as the technology matures.

Collectively, from the preceding observations we can make the following general observations. For large systems with a higher number of dimensions, wire delays would dominate. The use of higher clock speeds, communication intensive applications and the use of pipelined links in this environment would favor full-duplex links. Lower dimensionality, and communication traffic below network saturation would tend to favor the use of half-duplex links. Cost considerations would encourage the use of low(er) cost packaging which would also favor half-duplex links and the use of command/data encodings to reduce the overall pin count and therefore package cost.

7.2.3 Wormhole Routers

A Generic Dimension-Ordered Router and its Derivatives

A generic dimension-ordered router can be represented as shown in Figure 7.13 [57]. The abstract router design in Figure 7.7 can be refined to take advantage of the structure of dimension-ordered routing. In dimension-ordered routing, messages complete traversal in a dimension prior to changing dimension. Thus, it is not necessary to provide paths from any input link to any output link. An incoming message on dimension X will either continue along dimension X (continuing in either the positive or negative direction), or proceed to the next dimension to be traversed. Thus, each dimension can be serviced by a 3×3 crossbar as shown in Figure 7.13 for a 2-D router. The first dimension accepts messages from the local node and the last dimension ejects messages to the local node. A message must cut through each dimension crossbar. For example, consider a message that is injected into the network that must only traverse the Y dimension. It is injected into the X dimension crossbar where routing logic forwards it to the Y dimension crossbar, and subsequently out along the Y dimension link.

If dimension offsets are used in the header, routing decisions are considerably simplified. A check for zero determines if the traversal within the dimension has been completed. The header

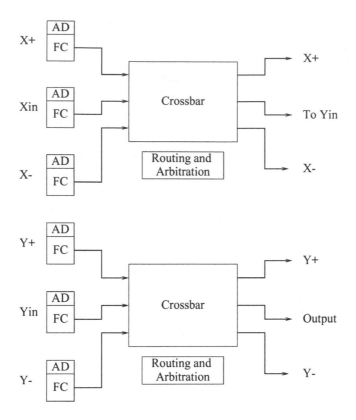

Figure 7.13. Organization of a canonical wormhole router. (AD = Address decoder; FC = Flow control.)

is updated and forwarded through the output port. An example of a router that uses such a partitioned data path is the network design frame [79]. This is a router designed for use in 2-D mesh-connected networks. Each physical channel is an 11-bit bidirectional channel supported by five control lines to implement channel flow control. Each link supports two virtual channels in each direction. Four of the control signals are bidirectional lines used for request/acknowledge flow control for each virtual channel. The fifth bidirectional control line is used to implement a token-passing protocol to control access to the bidirectional data lines. The physical channel flow control protocol is described in Example 7.1. The two virtual channels implement two virtual networks, at two priority levels. Latency-sensitive traffic uses the higher priority network. Since physical bandwidth is rarely completely utilized, the use of virtual channels to separate traffic is an attractive alternative to two distinct physical networks. Within the router, each virtual network implementation is well represented by the canonical organization shown in Figure 7.13. A 3×3 nonblocking switch (reference the multistage topologies in Chapter 1) can be implemented with four 2×2 switches. Using the partitioned design in Figure 7.13, the four crossbar switches can be implemented using twelve 2×2 switching elements, rather than having a 9×9 full crossbar switch with 11-bit channels at each port. This represents an area savings of approximately 95%.

The first two flits of the message header contain the offsets in the X and Y direction respectively. The routing units perform sign and zero checks to determine if the message is to continue in the same dimension, transition to the next dimension, or be ejected. Output link controllers perform

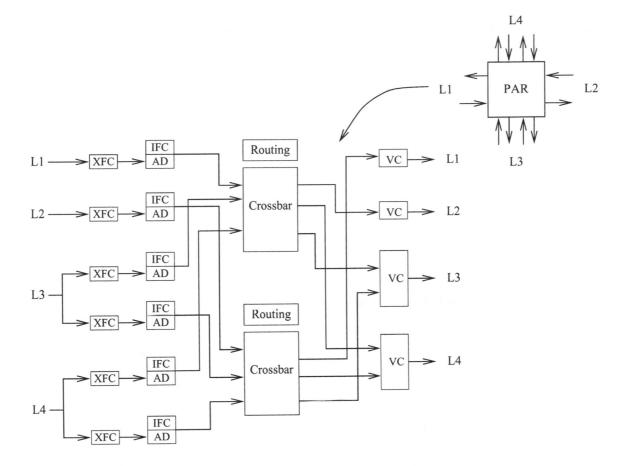

Figure 7.14. Organization of a planar-adaptive router. (AD = Address decoder; IFC = Internal flow control; PAR = Planar-adaptive router; VC = Virtual channel controller; XFC = External flow control.)

arbitration between the two virtual channels to grant access to the physical link. If the router does not have access to the bidirectional channel, there is a delay before the token is requested and transferred from the other side of the channel.

These wormhole routers exploit the routing restrictions of dimension-ordered routing to realize efficient router architectures. If adaptive routing is permitted, the internal router architectures begin to become more complex, especially as the number of dimensions and the number of virtual channels increase. This is simply a direct result of the increased routing flexibility. However, the idea of using partitioned datapaths to reduce the implementation complexity can still be applied if adaptivity can be controlled. The advantages of the partitioned datapath found in dimension-ordered routers can be combined with limited adaptive routing to achieve a more balanced, less complex design. The planar-adaptive routing techniques described in Chapter 4 is an attempt to balance hardware complexity with potential advantages of increased routing freedom. The basic strategy is to adaptively route in a sequence of adaptive planes. The block diagram of a 2-D router is shown in Figure 7.14 [11]. Note how the datapath is partitioned. Each crossbar provides the switching for the increasing or decreasing network. Messages only travel in one or the other. Higher-dimensional networks can be supported by providing the same basic organization in each successive pair of dimensions. This technique can also be generalized to support higher degrees of adaptivity by increasing the number of dimensions within which adaptive routing is permitted. Figure 7.14 illustrates the organization for adaptive routing in two dimensions at a time. Alternatives may permit adaptive routing in three dimensions at a time. A 5-D network may permit adaptive routing in successive 3-D cubes. These routers are referred to as *f-flat* routers, where the parameter f signifies the number of dimensions within which adaptive routing is permitted at any one time. Aoyama and Chien [11] use this baseline design to study the performance impact of adaptive routing via the design of f-flat routers. While performance may be expected to improve with increasing adaptivity, the hardware complexity certainly grows with increasing f.

This idea of using partitioned datapaths to reduce internal router complexity can be used in fully adaptive routers as well in order to offset the competing factors of increased adaptivity and low router delay. The internal router architecture can be designed to fully exploit the expected routing behavior as well as the capabilities of the underlying routing algorithm to achieve highest possible performance. For instance, if most packets tend not to change dimensions or virtual channel classes frequently during routing (i.e., routing locality in dimension or in virtual channel class), then it is not necessary for the internal datapath to provide packets with direct access to all output virtual channels, even in fully adaptive routing. Each crossbar switch may provide access to all the virtual channels in the same dimension. Alternatively, a given crossbar switch may provide access to a single virtual channel in each dimension. In both cases, each switch must provide a connection to the next switch.

For instance, in the Hierarchical Adaptive Router [215], the internal datapath is partitioned into ordered virtual channel networks which includes all dimensions and directions. Deadlock is avoided by enforcing routing restrictions in the lowest virtual network. Although this router architecture exploits routing locality in virtual channel class, the lowest virtual channel network (the escape resource) presents a potential bottleneck. While this ordering between virtual channel networks is required for deadlock avoidance-based routing, it is a restriction that can be relaxed in recovery-based routing. Choi and Pinkston [61] proposed such an enhancement for a Disha deadlock recovery-based router design.

The Intel Teraflops Router

The Teraflops system is an architecture being designed by Intel Corporation in an effort to produce a machine capable of a sustained performance of 10^{12} floating-point operations per second and a peak performance of 1.8×10^{12} floating-point operations per second. *Cavallino* is the name for the network interface chip and router that forms the communication fabric for this machine [48]. The network is a k-ary 3-cube, with a distinct radix in each dimension. Up to eight hops are permitted in the Z dimension, 256 hops in the X dimension and 64 hops in the Y dimension. The router has six ports and the interface design supports 2-D configurations where the two ports in the Z dimension are connected to two processing nodes rather than other routers. This architecture provides a flexible basis for constructing a variety of topologies.

Unlike most other routers, Cavallino uses simultaneous bidirectional signaling. Physical channels are half-duplex. A receiver interprets incoming data with respect to the reference levels received and the data being driven to determine the value being received. The physical channel is 16 bits wide (phits). Message flits are 64 bits and require four clock cycles to traverse the channel. Three additional signals across the channel provide virtual channel and flow control information. The buffer status transmitted back to the sending virtual channel is interpreted as almost full rather than an exact number of available locations. This scheme allows for some slack in the protocols to

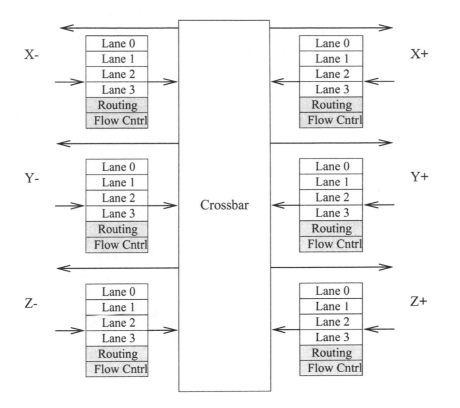

Figure 7.15. Architecture of the Intel teraflops router.

tolerate signaling errors. The physical channel operates at 200 MHz, providing an aggregate data rate of 400 Mbytes/s in each direction across the link. Four virtual channels are multiplexed in each direction across a physical link.

The internal structure of the router is shown in Figure 7.15. A message enters along one virtual channel and is destined for one output virtual channel. The routing header contains offsets in each dimension. In fact, routing order is $Z - X - Y - Z$. Using offsets permits fast routing decisions within each node as a message either turns to a new dimension or continues along the same dimension. The router is input buffered. With six input links and four virtual channels/link, a 24-to-1 arbitration is required on each crossbar output. The speed of operation and the length of the signal paths led to the adoption of a two-stage arbitration scheme. The first stage arbitrates between corresponding virtual channels from the six inputs, e.g., a 6-to-1 arbiter for virtual channel 0 on each link. The second stage is a 4-to-1 arbitration for all channels with valid data competing for the same physical output link. The internal data paths are 16 bits, matched to the output links. The ports were designed such that they could be reset while the network was operational. This would enable removal and replacement of routers and CPU boards while the network was active.

A block diagram of the network interface is shown in Figure 7.16. The router side of the interface utilizes portions of the router architecture configured as a three-port design. One port is used for message injection and ejection while two other ports are used for connection to two routers. This flexibility permits the construction of more complex topologies. This is often desired for the purposes of fault tolerance or simply increased bandwidth. Each output virtual channel is 384 bytes deep while

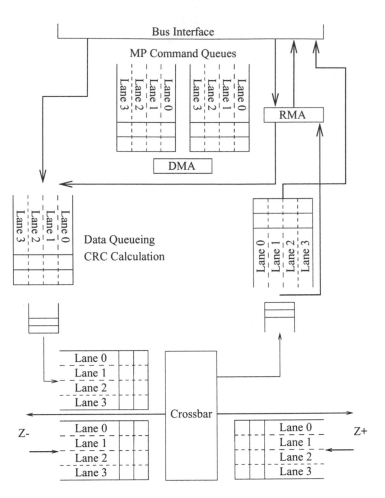

Figure 7.16. Interface architecture for the Cavallino router. (CRC = Cyclic redundancy check.)

each input virtual channel is 256 bytes deep. There are two additional interesting components of the interface. The first is the remote memory access (RMA) engine. The RMA engine has access to a memory-resident mapping table that maps processor addresses into the physical addresses of remote nodes. Request messages are created for remote accesses and response messages are created to service remote requests. The RMA engine also provides support for remotely accessible atomic operations, e.g., read and clear. This functionality supports synchronization operations. The second interesting feature is the direct memory access (DMA) interface. The DMA engine supports eight channels and corresponding command queues (one for each input and output virtual channel). Each channel can store up to eight commands. This volume of posted work is supported by command switching by the DMA engine, e.g., when injection is blocked due to congestion. The access to the control of the DMA engine is memory-mapped, and user access is permitted to support the implementation of low-overhead, lightweight messaging layers. Throughput through the DMA engine approaches 400 Mbytes/s.

While forming the backbone of the Teraflops machine, the Cavallino chip set is also regarded as a high-performance chip set that can be used for configuring high-performance NOWs.

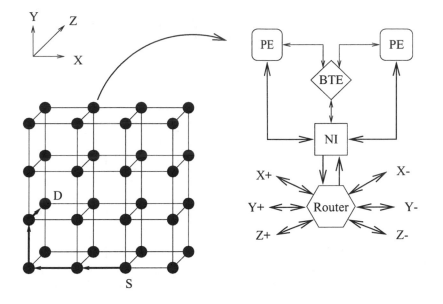

Figure 7.17. Organization of the T3D system. (BTE = Block transfer engine; NI = Network interface.)

The Cray T3D

The Cray T3D utilizes a k-ary 3-cube interconnect. An example of a $4 \times 4 \times 2$ configuration of processing element (PE) nodes is is illustrated in Figure 7.17. Each PE node consists of two DEC Alpha 150 MHz processors sharing a single network interface to the local router. The network has a maximum radix of 8 in the X and Z dimensions and 16 in the Y dimension. Therefore, the maximum configuration is 1,024 PE nodes or 2,048 processors. The system is packaged with two PE nodes per board. This choice of radix is not arbitrary. Rather it is based on the observation that under random traffic, messages will travel $\frac{1}{4}$ the way around each dimension in the presence of bidirectional links. If we consider only the packets that travel in say, the $X+$ direction, then the average distance traveled by these packets will be $\frac{1}{8}$ the distance in that direction. If the injection and ejection ports of the network interface have the same capacity as the individual links then a radix of 8 in each dimension can be expected to produce a balanced demand on the links and ports.

The router architecture is based on fixed-path, dimension-order wormhole switching. The organization of the relevant components is shown in Figure 7.18. There are four unidirectional virtual channels in each direction over a physical link. These four virtual channels are partitioned into two virtual networks with two virtual channels/link. One network is referred to as the request network and transmits *request packets*. The second network is the reply network carrying only *reply packets*. The two virtual channels within each network prevent deadlock due to the wraparound channels as described below. Adjacent routers communicate over a bidirectional, full-duplex physical channel, with each direction comprised of 16 data bits and 8 control bits as shown in Figure 7.18. The 4 forward control channel bits are used to identify the type of message packet (request or response) and the destination virtual channel buffer. The four acknowledge control signals are used for flow control and signify empty buffers on the receiving router. Due to the time required for channel flow control (e.g., generation of acknowledgments), as long as messages are integral multiples of 16 bits (see message formats below), full link utilization can be achieved. Otherwise some idle physical

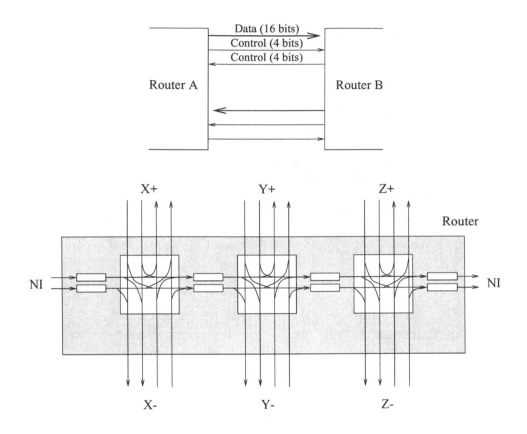

Figure 7.18. Architecture and operation of the T3D router.

channel cycles are possible. The router is physically partitioned into three switches as shown in the figure. Messages are routed to first correct the offset in X, then Y, and finally Z dimensions. The first switch is connected to the injection channel from the network interface and is used to forward the message in the $X+$ or $X-$ directions. When the message has completed traversal in the X dimension, the message moves to the next switch in the intermediate router for forwarding along the Y dimension, and then to the Z dimension. Message transition between switches is via *interdimensional virtual channels*. For the sake of clarity the figure omits some of the virtual channels.

Message packets comprise of a header and body. Sample formats are shown in Figure 7.19. The header is an integral number of 16-bit phits that contain routing information, control information for the remote PE, and possibly source information as well. The body makes use of check bits to detect errors. For example, a 64-bit word will be augmented with 14 check bits (hence the 5-phit body in Figure 7.19) and four-word message bodies will have 56 check bits (necessitating 20-phit bodies). The messages are organized as sequences of flits, with each flit comprised of 8 phits. Virtual channel buffers are 1 flit deep.

The T3D utilizes *source routing*. Header information identifies the sequence of virtual channels that the message will traverse in each dimension. In order to understand the routing strategy, we must first be familiar with the PE addressing scheme. While all PEs have physical addresses, they also possess logical addresses and virtual addresses. Logical addresses are based on the logical

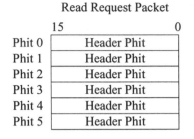

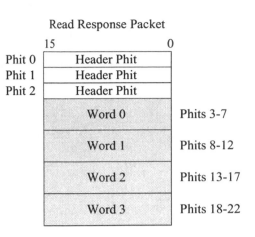

Figure 7.19. T3D packet formats.

topology of the installation. Thus, nodes can be addressed by the coordinate of their logical position in this topology, and are in principle independent of their physical location. This approach permits spare nodes to be mapped into the network to replace failed nodes by assigning the spare node the same logical address. The virtual address is assigned to nodes within a partition allocated to a job. The virtual address is interpreted according to the shape of the allocated partition. For example, 16 nodes can be allocated as an $8 \times 2 \times 1$ topology, or as a $4 \times 2 \times 2$ topology. In the latter case the first 2 bits of the virtual address are allocated to the X offset and the remaining 2 bits to the Y and Z offsets. When a message is transmitted, the operating system or hardware translates the virtual PE address to a logical PE address. This logical PE address is used as an index into a table that provides the offsets in each dimension to forward the message to the correct node. In this manner if a spare PE is mapped in to replace a faulty PE, the routing tables at each node simply need to be updated.

Dimension-order routing prevents cyclic dependencies between dimensions. Deadlock within a dimension is avoided by preventing cyclic channel dependencies as shown in Figure 7.20. One channel is identified by the software as the *dateline* communication link. Consider a request message that

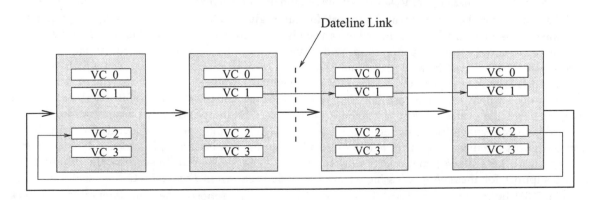

Figure 7.20. Deadlock avoidance within a dimension. (VC = Virtual channel.)

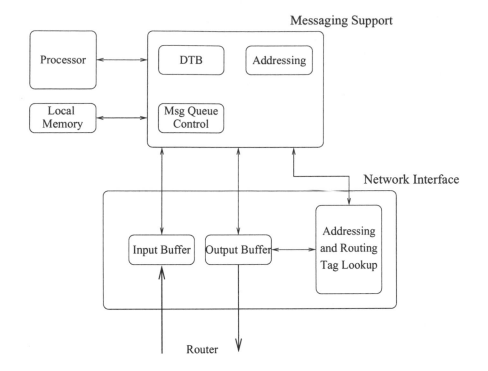

Figure 7.21. Message processing datapath. (DTB = Data translation buffer.)

must traverse this dimension. If the message will traverse the dateline communication link, it will be forwarded along virtual channel 1, otherwise it will be forwarded along virtual channel 0. The message does not switch between virtual channels within a dimension. The dateline effectively identifies the wraparound channel, and the routing restrictions implement the Dally and Seitz [78] restrictions to guarantee deadlock-free routing. When the routing tables are constructed, they implement these restrictions. Such restrictions, while realizing deadlock-free routing, result in unbalanced utilization of the virtual channels. The flexibility of source-based routing enables static optimization of the message paths to balance traffic across virtual channels and further improve link utilization [311].

The T3D provides architectural support for messaging. The routing tables are supported in hardware, as is virtual to logical PE address translation prior to routing tag lookup. Message headers are constructed after the processor provides the data and address information. When a message is received, it is placed in a message queue in a reserved portion of memory and an interrupt is generated. If the store operation to the message queue fails, a negative acknowledgment is returned to the source where messages are buffered to enable retransmission. Successful insertion into the queue generates a positive acknowledgment to the source. Request and reply packets can implement a shared address space (not coherent shared memory). When the processor generates a memory address, support circuitry maps that address into a local or nonlocal address. Nonlocal references result in request packets being generated to remote nodes. A block diagram illustrating the organization of the support for message processing within the node is shown in Figure 7.21.

The T3D links operate at 150 MHz or 300 Mbytes/s. The reported per hop latency is two clock cycles [311] while the maximum sustained data bandwidth into the node (i.e., excluding packet headers, acknowledgments, etc) is 150 Mbytes/s per node or 75 Mbytes/s per processor.

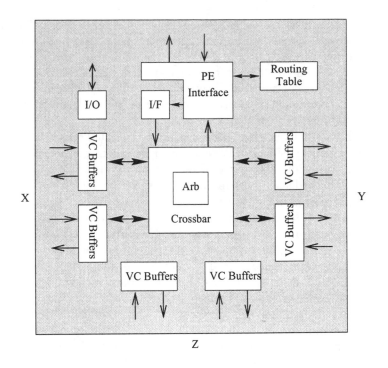

Figure 7.22. Architecture of the T3E router. (Arb = Arbitrator; I/F = Interface.)

The Cray T3E

The T3E represents a second-generation multiprocessor system [309, 312]. The network and router architecture of the T3E retains many of the operational characteristics of the T3D but is very different in other ways. The system design evolved to substantially improve latency tolerance, resulting in a shift in emphasis in the design of the network from reducing latency to providing sustained bandwidth. This resulted a change in the balance between processors and network bandwidth — only one processor/network node in the T3E — and the use of standard-cell CMOS (single-chip) rather than ECL (three-chip) technology. Along with doubling of the link bandwidth, this produces a factor of four increase in the per processor bandwidth. The topology is still that of a 3-D torus with a maximum radix of 8, 32, and 8 in the X, Y, and Z dimensions, respectively. A block diagram of the T3E router is shown in Figure 7.22.

A T3E packet is 1 – 10 flits, and each flit is 5 phits. The network physical channel is full-duplex with 14-bit data producing a flit size of 70 bits. A flit can carry one 64-bit word with some additional control information. The router operates on a 75 MHz clock. During each clock cycle 5 phits are transmitted across the channel, leading to a link transmission rate of 375MHz and link bandwidth of 600 Mbytes/s.

Five virtual channels are multiplexed in each direction over each physical channel. Four of the channels essentially function as they do in the T3D (with differences identified below) while the fifth channel is used for fully adaptive routing. Each adaptive channel can buffer up to 22 flits while each of the regular channels can buffer up to 12 flits. The channels utilize credit based flow control for buffer management with acknowledgments in the reverse direction being piggybacked on other messages or transmitted as idle flits. Round-robin scheduling across active virtual channels within a group determines which channel will compete for crossbar outputs. The winning channel can request a virtual channel in the deterministic direction, or an adaptive channel in the highest-ordered direction yet to be satisfied. If both are available, the adaptive channel is used. Once an output virtual channel is allocated, it must remain allocated, while other virtual channel inputs may still request and use the same physical output channel. Finally, output virtual channels must arbitrate for the physical channel. This process is also round robin although the adaptive channel has the lowest priority to start transmitting.

Routing is fully adaptive. The deterministic paths use four virtual channels for the request/reply network as in the T3D. However, the path is determined by ordering dimensions *and* the direction of traversal within each dimension. This style of routing can be regarded as *direction order* rather than dimension order. The ordering used in the T3E is $X+$, $Y+$, $Z+$, $X-$, $Y-$, and $Z-$. In general, any other ordering would work just as well. By applying the concept of channel classes from Chapter 3, it is apparent that each direction corresponds to a class of channels, and the order in which channel classes are used by a message is acyclic. Thus, routing is deadlock-free. In addition, the network supports an initial hop in any positive direction, and permits one final hop in the $Z-$ direction at the end of the route. These initial and final hops add routing flexibility and are only necessary if a normal direction-order route does not exist. Each message has a fixed path that is determined at the source router. A message can be routed along the statically configured path, or along the adaptive virtual channel over any physical link along a minimal path to the destination. However, the implementation does not require the extended channel dependency graph to be acyclic. The adaptive virtual channels are large enough to buffer two maximal messages. Therefore indirect dependencies between deterministic channels do not exist. This permits optimizations in the manner in which virtual channels are assigned to improve virtual channel utilization and minimize imbalance due to routing restrictions. Finally, adaptive routing can be turned off via control fields within the routing tables, and on an individual packet basis through a single bit recorded in the message. Since adaptively routed messages may arrive out of order at the destination, the latter capability enables the processor to issue sequences of messages that are delivered in order.

Memory management and the network interface operation have been made more flexible than the first-generation support found in the T3D. An arbitrary number of message queues are supported in both user memory and system memory. Message queues can be set up to be interrupt-driven, polled, or interrupt-driven based on some threshold on the number of messages. In general, message passing is more tightly coupled with operations for the support of shared-memory abstractions.

The Reliable Router

The Reliable Router chip is targeted for fault-tolerant operation in 2-D mesh topologies [76]. The block diagram of the Reliable Router is shown in Figure 7.23. There are are six input channels corresponding to the four physical directions in the 2-D mesh, and two additional physical ports: the local processor interface, and a separate port for diagnostics. The input and output channels are connected through a full crossbar switch, although some input/output connections may be prohibited by the routing function.

While message packets can be of arbitrary length, the flit length is 64 bits. There are four flit types: head, data, tail, and token. The format of the head flit is as shown in Figure 7.24. The size of the physical channel or phit size is 23 bits. The channel structure is illustrated in Figure 7.23. To permit the use of chip carriers with fewer than 300 pins, these physical channels utilize half-duplex channels with simultaneous bidirectional signaling. Flits are transferred in one direction across the physical channel as four 23-bit phits called *frames*, producing 92-bit transfers. The format of a data flit and its constituent frames are as shown in Figure 7.25. The 28 bits in excess of the flit size are

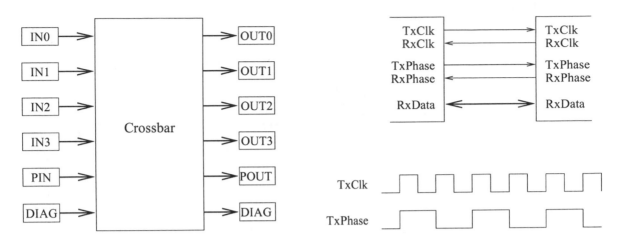

Figure 7.23. Block diagram of the Reliable Router.

used for byte parity bits (BP), kind of flit (Kind), virtual channel identification (VCI), flow control to implement the unique token protocol (Copied Kind, Copied VCI, Freed), to communicate link status information (U/D, PE), and two user bits (USR1, USR0). For a given direction of transfer, the clock is transmitted along with the four data frames as illustrated in the figure. Data are driven on both edges of the clock. To enable the receiver to distinguish between the four frames and re-assemble them into a flit, the transmitting side of the channel also sends a pulse on the *TxPhase* signal which has the relative timing as shown. The flit is then assembled and presented to the routing logic. This reassembly process takes two cycles. Each router runs off a locally generated 100 MHz clock removing the problems with distributing a single global clock. Reassembled flits pass through a synchronization module for transferring flits from the transmit clock domain to the receive clock domain with a worst-case penalty of one cycle (see [76] for a detailed description of the data synchronization protocol). The aggregate physical bandwidth in one direction across the channel is 3.2 Gbits/s.

Bit Field	63:12	11	10	9:5	4:0
Contents	User info	Priority	Diagnostic	Address in Y	Address in X

Figure 7.24. Reliable Router head flit format.

Bit Field	22	21	20:18	17	16	15:0
Frame 0	PE	USR0	VCI	BP1	BP0	Data[15:0]
Frame 1	Copied kind		Copied VCI	BP3	BP2	Data[31:16]
Frame 2	U/D	USR1	Kind	BP5	BP4	Data[47:32]
Frame 3	Freed			BP7	BP6	Data[63:48]

Figure 7.25. Reliable Router frame format for data flits.

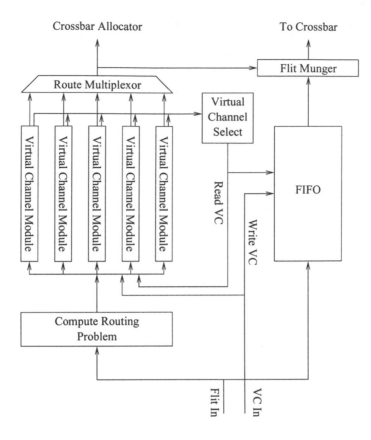

Figure 7.26. Block diagram of the input controller.

While the output controllers simply transmit the flit across the channel, generating the appropriate control and error checking signals, the input controllers contain the core functionality of the chip, and are organized as illustrated in Figure 7.26. The crossbar provides switching between the physical input channels and the physical output channels. Each physical channel supports five virtual channels, which share a single crossbar port: two channels for fully adaptive routing, two channels for dimension-ordered routing, and one for fault handling. The fault handling channels utilize turn model routing. The two dimension-ordered channels support two priority levels for user packets. The router is input buffered. The FIFO block is actually partitioned into five distinct FIFO buffers — one corresponding to each virtual channel. Each FIFO buffer is 16 flits deep. Bandwidth allocation is demand driven: only allocated channels with data to be transmitted or channels with new requests (i.e., head flits) compete for bandwidth. Virtual channels with message packets are accorded access to the crossbar bandwidth in a round robin fashion by the scheduler in the Virtual Channel Controller. Data flits simply flow through the virtual channel FIFO buffers, and the virtual channel number is appended to the flit prior to the transmission of the flit through the crossbar and across the physical channel to the next router. Flow control guarantees the presence of buffer space. When buffers at the adjacent node are full, the corresponding virtual channel does not compete for crossbar bandwidth.

A more involved sequence of operations takes place in routing a head flit. On arrival the head flit is transferred to both the FIFO buffer and a block that compares the destination address with the local node address. The result is the *routing problem* which contains all of the information used to route the message. This information is stored in the virtual channel module, along with routing information: the address of the output controller and the virtual channel ID. Recall from the protocol description provided in Section 6.7.2, the header information must be retained in the router to construct additional messages in the presence of a fault. To minimize the time spent in arbitration for various shared resources, the routing logic is replicated within each virtual channel module. This eliminates the serialized access to the routing logic and only leaves arbitration for the output controllers which is handled by the crossbar allocator. The routing logic first attempts to route a message along an adaptive channel, failing which a dimension-order channel is requested. If the packet fails in arbitration, on the next flit cycle, the router again first attempts an adaptive channel. The virtual channel module uses counters and status signals from adjacent nodes (see *Freed* bits in Figure 7.25) to keep track of buffer availability in adjacent routers. A virtual channel module is eligible to bid for access to the crossbar output only if the channel is routed, buffer space is available on the adjacent node, and there is data to be transmitted. When a fault occurs during transmission, the channel switches to a state where computation for retransmission occurs. After a period of two cycles, the channel switches back to a regular state and competes for access to the crossbar outputs. A header can be routed and the crossbar allocated in two cycles, i.e., 20 ns. The worst case latency through the router is projected to be eight cycles or 80 ns.

Arbitration is limited to the output of the crossbar, and is resolved via three packet priority levels: two user priority levels, and the highest level reserved for system packets. Starvation is prevented by changing the packet priority to level 3 after an input controller has failed to gain access to an output controller after seven tries. Packet selection within a priority level is randomized.

The implementation of the unique token protocol for reliable transmission necessitates some special handling and architectural support. The token at the end of a message must be forwarded only after the corresponding flit queue has successfully emptied. Retransmission on failure involves generation of duplicate tokens. Finally, flow control must span two routers to ensure that a duplicate copy of each data flit is maintained at all times in adjacent routers. When a data flit is successfully transmitted across a channel, the copy of the data flit two routers upstream must be deallocated. The relevant flow control signals are passed through frames as captured in Figure 7.25.

SGI SPIDER

The SGI SPIDER (Scalable Pipelined Interconnect for Distributed Endpoint Routing) [118] was designed with multiple missions in mind: as part of a conventional multiprocessor switch fabric, as a building block for large-scale nonblocking central switches, and as a high-bandwidth communication fabric for distributed graphics applications. The physical links are full-duplex channels with 20 data bits, a frame signal, and a differential clock signal in each direction. Data are transferred on both edges of a 200 MHz clock realizing a raw data rate of 1 Gbyte/s in each direction. The chip core operates at 100 MHz, providing 80-bit units that are serialized into 20-bit phits for transmission over the channel. The organization of the SPIDER chip is shown in Figure 7.27.

The router implements four 256-byte virtual channels over each physical link. The units of buffer management and transmission are referred to as *micropackets*, equivalent to the notion of a flit. Each micropacket is comprised of 128 bits of data, 8 bits of sequencing information, 8 bits of virtual channel flow control information, and 16 CRC bits to protect against errors. The links implement automatic retransmission on errors until the sequence number of the transmitted flit is acknowledged. The micropacket format is shown in Figure 7.28. The number on top of each field indicates the field size in bits. Virtual channel buffer management utilizes credit-based flow control. On initialization, all channels credit their counterparts with buffer space corresponding to their size.

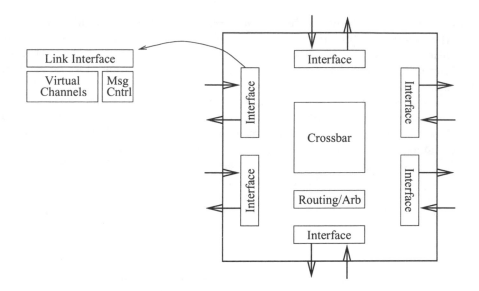

Figure 7.27. Organization of the SGI SPIDER chip.

The 8 bits of virtual channel flow control information are used to identify the virtual channel number of the transmitted micropacket, the address of the virtual channel being credited with additional buffer space, and the amount of credit. An interesting feature of SPIDER links is the transparent negotiation across the link to determine the width of the channel. For example, the router can negotiate to use only the lower 10 bits of the channel. The interface to the chip core remains the same, while the data rate will be a function of the negotiated port width.

The SPIDER chip supports two styles of routing. The first is source routing which is referred to as *vector routing*. This mechanism is utilized for network configuration information and administration. The second style is table-driven routing. The organization of the tables is based on a structured view of the network as a set of metadomains, and local networks within each domain. The topology of the interdomain network and the local network can be different. Messages are first routed to the correct destination domain and then to the correct node within a domain. Routing is organized as shown in Figure 7.29. The destination address is a 9-bit field, comprised of two subfields: a 5-bit metadomain field and a 4-bit local field. The tables map these indices into 4-bit router port addresses, thereby supporting routers with up to 16 ports. Access to the metatable provides a port address to route the message toward the correct domain. If the message is already in the correct domain as determined by comparison with the local meta ID, the local address table is used to determine the output port that will take the message towards the destination node. Not shown in the figure is a mode to force

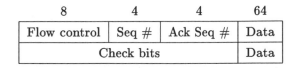

Figure 7.28. SPIDER data micropacket format.

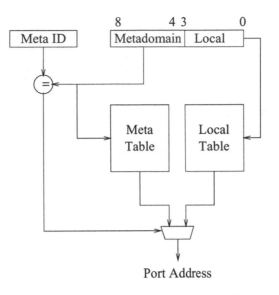

Figure 7.29. SPIDER routing tables.

the message to use the local address. Table-driven routing is oblivious and forces messages to use fixed paths. The table entries are computed to avoid deadlock and can be reinitialized in response to faults. Messages using vector routing can be used to reload the tables.

Normally arbitration for the output of the crossbar is not possible until the routing operation has been completed and has returned a crossbar output port address. In order to overlap arbitration and table lookup, the routing operation described above produces the output port address at the next router. This 4-bit port address (Dir) is passed along with the message. At the adjacent router, the port address is extracted from the header and can be immediately submitted for crossbar output arbitration while table lookup progresses in parallel. This overlap saves one cycle. The header is encoded into the 128 data bits of a micropacket. The overall header organization is shown in Figure 7.30. The number on top of each field indicates the field size in bits. The age field establishes message priorities for arbitration (see below) and the CC (congestion control) field permits the use of multiple virtual channels.

To maximize crossbar bandwidth each input virtual channel buffer is organized as a set of linked lists of messages, one for each output port (five in this chip). This organization prevents messages blocked on an output port from blocking other messages in the same buffer destined for a different output port. With 24 input virtual channels, there are potentially 120 candidates for arbitration. To avoid starvation, messages in the router are aged at a programmable rate and arbitration is priority-driven. The top 16 priority levels of a total of 255 levels are reserved.

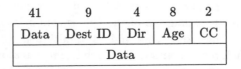

Figure 7.30. SPIDER header micropacket format.

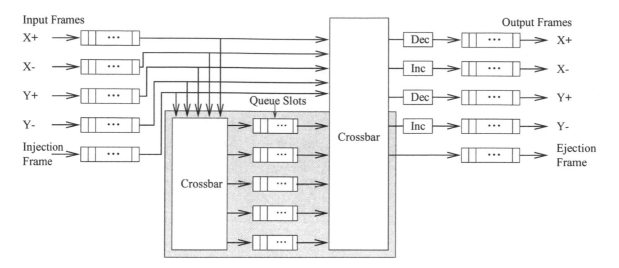

Figure 7.31. Block diagram of the Chaos router. (Dec = Decrementer; Inc = Incrementer.)

Support is provided within the chip to track message statistics such as retransmission rates on links so that problematic links can be identified and may be shut down. Timers support the detection of error conditions and potential deadlock situations, e.g., those due to errors. Timer expiration may result in either micropackets injected into the message stream for message recovery, or in resetting of a router port. A real-time clock is also distributed through the network to support tight synchronization. The pad-to-pad no-load latency through the chip is is estimated to be 40 ns, while the latency from input on a router to the input on the adjacent router is estimated to be 50 ns.

7.2.4 VCT Routers

Routers supporting VCT switching share many of the attributes of wormhole routers. The principal distinguishing feature is the availability of sufficient space for buffering complete message packets. As a result, deadlock freedom is generally achieved through buffer management rather than routing restrictions. The following examples discuss three router architectures currently under development.

The Chaos Router

The Chaos router chip is an example of a router designed for VCT switching for operation in a 2-D mesh. To reduce pin count, each channel is a 16-bit, half-duplex bidirectional channel. The chip was designed for a cycle time of 15 ns. The latency for the common case of cut-through routing (no misrouting) is four cycles from input to output. This performance compares favorably to that found in more compact oblivious routers, and has been achieved by keeping the misrouting and buffering logic off of the critical path. A block diagram of the Chaos router is shown in Figure 7.31.

The router is comprised of the router core and the multiqueue [32]. The core connects *input frames* to *output frames* through a crossbar switch. Each frame can store one 20-flit message packet. Each flit is 16 bits wide and corresponds to the width of the physical channel. The architecture of the core is very similar to that of contemporary oblivious routers, with the additional ability to buffer complete 20-flit packets in each input and output frame. Under low load conditions, the majority of the traffic flows through this core, and therefore considerable attention was paid to the optimization of the performance of the core datapath and control flow. However, when the network starts to become congested, messages may be moved from input frames to the multiqueue, and subsequently from the multiqueue to an output frame. When a packet is stalled in an input frame waiting for an output frame to become free, this packet is moved to the multiqueue to free channel resources to be used by other messages. To prevent deadlock, packets may also be moved from input frames to the multiqueue if the output frame on the same channel has a packet to be transmitted. This ensures that both receiving and transmitting buffers on both sides of a channel are not occupied, ensuring progress (reference the discussion of chaotic routing in Chapter 6) and avoiding deadlocked configurations of messages. Thus, messages may be transmitted to output frames either from an input frame or from the multiqueue, with the latter having priority. If the multiqueue is full and a message must be inserted, a randomly chosen message is misrouted.

Although several messages may be arriving simultaneously, the routing decisions are serialized by traversing the output channels in order. The *action dimension* is the current dimension under consideration (both positive and negative directions are distinguished). Packets in the multiqueue have priority in being routed to the output frame. If a packet in the multiqueue requires the active dimension output and the output frame is empty, the packet is moved to the output frame. If the queue is full and the output frame is empty, a randomly selected packet is misrouted to this output frame. Misrouting is the longest operation and takes five cycles. If the multiqueue operations do not generate movement, then any packet in an input frame requesting this output dimension can be switched through the crossbar. This operation takes a single cycle. The routing delay experienced by a header is two cycles. Finally, if the input frame of the active dimension is full, it is read into the multiqueue. This implements the policy of handling stalled packets and the deadlock avoidance protocol. The preceding steps encompass the process of routing the message. The no-load latency through the router is four cycles: one cycle for the header to arrive on the input, two cycles for the routing decision, and one cycle to be switched through the crossbar to the output frame [32]. If a message is misrouted, the routing decision takes five cycles.

Logically, the multiqueue contains messages partially ordered according to the output channel that the messages are waiting to traverse. The above routing procedure requires complete knowledge of the contents of the multiqueue and relative age of the messages. The current implementation realizes a five-packet multiqueue. This logically corresponds to five queues: one for each output including the output to the processor. Since messages are adaptively routed, a message may wait on one of several output channels, and therefore must logically be entered in more than one queue. When a free output frame is available for transfers from the multiqueue, determination of the oldest message waiting on this output must be readily available. The state of the multiqueue is maintained in a destination scoreboard.

The logical structure of the destination scoreboard is illustrated in Figure 7.32 for a multiqueue with six slots. This scoreboard keeps track of the relationship between the messages in the multiqueue, their FIFO order, and the destination outputs. Each row corresponds to an output frame in a particular dimension or to the local processor. Each column corresponds to one of the five slots in the multiqueue. When a packet enters the tail of the queue, its status enters from the left, i.e., in the first column. In this column, each row entry is set to signify that the corresponding output channel is a candidate output channel for this packet. For example, the packet that is located at the tail of the queue can be transmitted out along the $Y+$ or $X-$ directions, whichever becomes available. As packets exit the multiqueue, the columns in the scoreboard are shifted right. When an output frame is freed, the first message destined for that frame is dequeued from the central queue. Thus, messages may not necessarily be removed from the head of the queue. In this case some column in the middle of the matrix is reset, and all columns are compressed right corresponding to

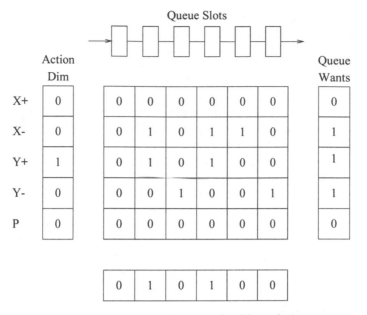

Figure 7.32. Tracking messages in the Chaos multiqueue.

the compression in the queue when a message is removed from the middle. It is apparent that taking the logical OR of row elements indicates if there is a message in the queue for the corresponding output frame. Given a specific dimension (e.g., the action dimension) it is apparent that row and column logical operations will produce a vector indicating messages that are queued for the action dimension. The relative positions of the bits set in this vector determines the relative age of the multiple messages and is used to select the oldest. Thus, all messages are queued in FIFO order, while messages destined for a particular output are considered in the order that they appear in this FIFO buffer.

The maximum routing delay for a message packet is five cycles, and occurs when messages are misrouted. This delay can be experienced for each of the four outputs in a 2-D mesh (the processor channel is excluded). Since routing is serialized by output, each output will be visited at least once every 20 cycles. Thus, messages are 20 flits to maintain maximum throughput. In reality, the bidirectional channels add another factor of 2, therefore in the worst case we have 40 cycles between routing operations on a channel.

Finally, the router includes a number of features in support of fault-tolerant routing. Timers on the channels are used to identify adjacent faulty channels/nodes. Packets bodies are protected by checksums while the header portion is protected by parity checks. A header that fails a parity check at an intermediate node, is ejected and handled in software. A separate single bit signal on each channel is used to propagate a fault detection signal throughout the network. When a router receives this signal, message injections are halted and the network is allowed to "drain" [35]. Messages which do not successfully drain from the network are detected using a timer and ejected to the local processor. When all messages have been removed from the faulty network, the system enters a diagnostic and recovery phase. Recovery is realized by masking out faulty links. This is achieved within the routing decision logic by performing the logical AND of a functional channel

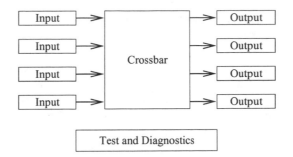

Figure 7.33. The Arctic routing chip.

mask with a vector of candidate output channels computed from the routing header. This will only permit consideration of nonfaulty output channels. If the result indicates that no candidate channels exist (this may occur due to faults), the packet is immediately misrouted.

Currently an active project is underway to implement a version of the Chaos router as a LAN switch. This switch will be constructed using a new version of the Chaos router chip and will utilize 72-byte packets and full-duplex, bidirectional channels with 8-bit wide links. As described in Section 7.2.2, the arbitration between two sides of a half-duplex pipelined channel carries substantial performance penalties. With LAN links being potentially quite long, half-duplex links represented a poor design choice. The projected speed of operation is 180 Mhz using the byte-wide channels for a bidirectional channel bandwidth of 360 Mbytes/s. The LAN switch will be constructed using a network of Chaos router chips. For example, a 16-port switch can be constructed using a 4×4 torus network of Chaos routers. Routing internal to the switch is expected to be normal Chaos routing while switch to switch routing is expected to use source routing and standard FIFO channels with link pipelining, if the links are long enough. Packet-level acknowledgments will be used for flow control across the LAN links. With the design of a special-purpose interface, the goal is to obtain host-to-host latencies down in the 10–20 μs range. This new-generation chip design is being streamlined with clock cycle times approaching 5.6 ns (simulated). This would produce a minimal delay through the router of four cycles or 22.4 ns. Packet formats and channel control have also been smoothed in this next generation chip to streamline the message pipeline implementation.

Arctic Router

The Arctic routing chip is a flexible router architecture that is targeted for use in several types of networks, including the fat tree network used in the *T multiprocessor [269]. The basic organization of the router is illustrated in Figure 7.33, and the current prototype is being used as part of a network with PowerPC compute nodes. Four input *sections* can be switched to any one of four output sections. The router is input-buffered and each input section is comprised of three buffers. Each buffer is capable of storing one maximum sized packet of 96 bytes in support of VCT switching. The crossbar switch connects the 12 inputs to four outputs. Message packets have one of two priority levels. The buffers within an input unit are managed such that the last empty buffer is reserved for a priority packet.

The physical channels are 16-bit full-duplex links operating at 50 MHz, providing a bandwidth of 200 Mbytes/s for each link. The internal router datapaths are 32 bits wide. The Arctic physical channel interface includes a clock and frame signal as well as a flow control signal in the reverse direction. The flow control is used to enable counter increment/decrement in the transmitter to keep track of buffer availability on the other side of the channel. The initial value of this counter is configurable enabling the chip to interface with other routers that support different buffer sizes.

Routing is source-based, and networks can be configured for fat trees, Omega, and grid topologies. In general, two subfields of the header (perhaps single bits) are compared with two reference values. Based on the results of this comparison, 2 bits are selected from the packet header, or some combination of header and constant 0/1 bits are used to produce a 2-bit number to select the output channel. For the fat tree routing implementation, 8 bytes of the message are devoted routing, control, and CRC. The routing header is comprised of two fields with a maximum width of 30 bits: 14 bits for the path up the tree, and 16 bits for the path down the tree to the destination. Since routing is source-based, and multiple alternative paths exist up the tree, the first field is a random string. Portions of this field are used to randomize the choice of the up path. Otherwise a portion of the second field is used to select an appropriate output headed down the tree to the destination. Rather than randomizing all of the bits in the first field, by fixing the values of some of the bits such as the first few bits, messages can be steered through regions of the lower levels of the network. Source based routing can be utilized in a very flexible way to enforce some load balancing within the network. For example, I/O traffic could be steered through distinct parts of a network to minimize interference with data traffic. Messages traversing the Arctic fabric experience a minimum latency of six cycles/hop.

The Arctic chip devotes substantial circuitry to test and diagnostics. CRC checks are performed on each packet, and channel control signals are encoded. Idle patterns are continuously transmitted when channels are not in use to support error detection. On-chip circuitry and external interfaces support static configuration in response to errors: ports can be selectively disabled and flushed and the route tables used for source routing can be recomputed to avoid faulty regions. An interesting feature of the chip is the presence of counters to record message counts for analysis of the overall network behavior.

R2 Router

The R2 router evolved as a router for a second-generation system in support of low-latency high-performance interprocessor communication. The current network prototype provides for interprocessor communication between Hewlett-Packard commercial workstations. The R2 interconnect topology is a 2-D hexagonal interconnect and the current router is designed to support a system of 91 nodes. Each router has seven ports: six to neighboring routers and one to a local network interface (referred to as the fabric interface component or FIC). The topology is wrapped, i.e., routers at the edge of the network have wraparound links to routers at the opposite end of the dimension. The network topology is shown in Figure 7.34. For clarity, only one wrapped link is illustrated. As in multidimensional tori, the network topology provides multiple shortest paths between each pair of routers. However, unlike tori, there are also two *no-farther* paths. When a message traverses a link along a no-farther path, the distance to the destination is neither increased nor decreased. The result is an increase in the number of routing options available at an intermediate router.

The physical channel is organized as a half-duplex channel with 16 bits for data and 9 bits for control. One side of each link is a router port with an arbiter which governs channel mastership. The routers and channels are fully self-timed, eliminating the need for a global clock. There are no local clocks and resynchronization with the local node processor clocks is performed in the network interface. The rate at which the R2 ports can toggle is estimated to be approximately 5 – 10 ns corresponding to an equivalent synchronous transmission rate of 100 – 200 MHz.

Message packets may be of variable length and upto a maximum of 160 bytes. Each packet has a 3-byte header that contains addressing information, and a 16-byte protocol header that contains

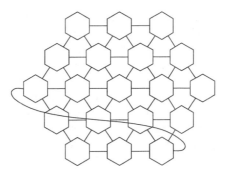

Figure 7.34. Wrapped hexagonal interconnect used in the R2-based network.

information necessary to implement a novel *sender-based protocol* for low-latency messaging. A 4-byte CRC trailer rounds out the message packet format. Two types of messages are supported: normal messages and priority messages. While normal messages may be as large as 64K packets in length, priority messages are limited to a single packet. Typically priority messages are used by the operating system while normal messages are generated by the applications.

A block diagram of the R2 router is illustrated in Figure 7.35. In the figure the ports are drawn as distinct inputs and outputs to emphasize the data path, although they are bidirectional. Each FIFO buffer is capable of storing one maximum-length packet. There are 12 FIFO buffers for normal packets and three FIFO buffers for storing priority packets. Two 7×15 crossbars provide switching between the buffers and the bidirectional ports. Each of the FIFO buffers has a routing controller. Routing decisions use the destination address in the packet header and the local node ID. Buffer management and ordered use of buffers provides deadlock freedom. The implementation is self-timed, and the time to receive a packet header and to compute the address of an output port is estimated to take between 60 and 120 ns.

Routing is controlled at the sender by specifying a number of *adaptive credits*. Each adaptive credit permits the message packet to traverse one link that takes the packet no further from the

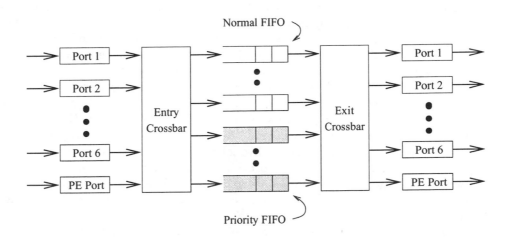

Figure 7.35. Organization of the R2 router.

destination. At any node, there are always two no-farther directions. The adaptive credit field in the header is decremented each time a message takes an adaptive step and further adaptive routing is not permitted once this value is reduced to zero. Shortest paths are given priority in packet routing. Priority packets are only routed along shortest paths. When all outputs for a priority packet are blocked by a normal packet, the priority packet is embedded in the normal packet byte stream being transmitted along one of the shortest paths, analogous to the implementation of virtual channels. An interesting feature of the R2 router is the support for message throttling. Packet headers are monitored and in the presence of congestion, rapid injection of packets from a source can cause negative acknowledgments to be propagated back to the source to throttle injection.

Error handling was considered at the outset during the initial design, and basic mechanisms were provided to detect packets which could not be delivered. Once detected, these packets were ejected at the local node to be handled in software by higher-level protocols. A variety of conditions may cause message exceptions. For example, the message packet headers contain a field that keeps track of the maximum number of hops. This field is decremented at each intermediate router, and when this value becomes negative, the message is ejected. An ejection field in the header is used to mark packets that must be forwarded by the router to the local processor interface. The router also contains watchdog timers that monitor the ports/links. If detection protocols time out, a fault register marks the port/link as faulty. If, the faulty port leads to a packet destination, this status is recorded in the header and the packet is forwarded to another router adjacent to the destination. If the second port/link to the destination is also found to be faulty, the packet is ejected.

7.2.5   Circuit Switching

Circuit switching along with packet switching represent the first switching techniques used in multiprocessor architectures. This section presents one such example and some more recent ideas toward improving the performance of the next generation of circuit-switched networks.

Intel iPSC Direct Connect Module (DCM)

The second generation network from Intel included in the iPSC/2 series machines utilized a router that implements circuit switching. Although most machines currently use some form of cut-through routing, circuit-switched networks do present some advantages. For example, once a path is setup, data can be transmitted at the full physical bandwidth without delays due sharing of links. The system can also operate completely synchronously without the need for flow control buffering of data between adjacent routers. While the previous generation of circuit-switched networks may have been limited by the path lengths, the use of link pipelining offers new opportunities.

The network topology used in the iPSC series machines is that of a binary hypercube. The router is implemented in a module referred to as the *direct connect module* (DCM). The DCM implements dimension-ordered routing and supports up to a maximum of eight dimensions. One router port is reserved for direct connections to external devices. The remaining router ports support topologies of up to 128 nodes. The node architecture and physical channel structure is shown in Figure 7.36. Individual links are bit-serial, full-duplex, and provide a link bandwidth of 2.8 Mbytes/s. Data, control, and status information are multiplexed across the serial data link. The strobe lines supply the clock from the source. The synchronous nature of the channel precludes the need for any handshaking signals between routers.

When a message is ready to be transmitted, a 32-bit word is transferred to the DCM. The least significant byte contains the routing tag — the exclusive-OR of the source and destination addresses. These bits are examined in ascending order by each routing element. A bit value of 1 signifies that

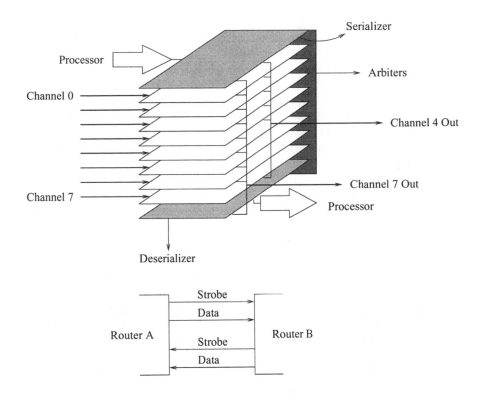

Figure 7.36. The iPSC/2 circuit switched router organization.

the message must traverse the corresponding dimension. The input Serializer generates a request for the channel in the dimension corresponding to the least significant asserted bit in the routing tag. Subsequent routing elements at intermediate nodes receive the header, and make similar requests to output channels. Multiple requests for the same output channel are arbitrated and resolved in a round-robin fashion. Note the connectivity at the outputs in Figure 7.36. An outgoing channel can expect to receive a message only from lower-numbered channels. This significantly reduces the design complexity of the routing elements. Channel status information is continually multiplexed across the data lines in the reverse direction. The status information corresponds to *RDY* or *EOM* (end of message) signals. These signals achieve end-to-end flow control. For example, when the destination DCM receives a routing header, the *RDY* status signal transmitted back to the source DCM initiates the actual transfer of data. The *EOM* status signal appended to the message causes the reserved links to be freed as it traverses the path. The propagation of status signals through the DCM from input to output is achieved by keeping track of the channel grants generated during the setup of the original message path. This end-to-end flow control also permits the propagation of "not ready" status information to the source to enable throttling of message injections.

Optimizing Circuit Switching

Communication requirements heavily depend on the application running on the parallel machine and the mapping scheme used. Many applications exhibit both spatial and temporal communication locality. If the router architecture supports circuit switching, conceivably compile time analysis could permit the generation of instructions to set up and retain a path or circuit that will be heavily used over a certain period of time. It is possible to design a router architecture such that a circuit is set up and left open for future transmission of data items. This technique was proposed in [39] for systolic communication. It has also been proposed in [159] for message passing and extended in [82]. The underlying idea behind preestablished circuits is similar to the use of cache memory in a processor: a set of channels is reserved once and used several times to transmit messages.

In structured message-passing programs, it may be feasible to identify and set up circuits prior to actual use. This set up may be overlapped with useful computation. When data are available, the circuit would have already been established, and permit lower latency message delivery. However, setting up a circuit in advance only eliminates some source software overheads such as buffer allocation, as well as routing time and contention. This may be a relatively small advantage compared to the bandwidth wasted by channels that have been reserved but are not currently used. Circuits could be really useful if they performed like caches, i.e., preestablished circuits actually operate faster. Link-level pipelining can be employed in a rather unique way to ensure this cache-like behavior. We use the term *wave pipelining* [102] to represent data transmission along such high-speed circuits.

It is possible to use wave pipelining across switches and physical channels, enabling very high clock rates. With a preestablished circuit, careful design is required to minimize the skew between wires in a wave-pipelined parallel data path. Synchronizers are required at each delivery channel. Synchronizers may also be required at each switch input to reduce the skew. Clock frequency is limited by delivery bandwidth, by signal skew, and by latch setup time. With a proper router and memory design, this frequency can potentially be higher than that employed in current routers, increasing channel bandwidth and network throughput accordingly. Spice simulations [102] show that up to a factor of four increase in clock speed is feasible. Implementations would be necessary to validate the models. The use of pipelined channels allows the designer to compute clock frequency independently of wire delay, limited by routing delay and switch delay. An example of a router organization that permits the use of higher clock frequencies based on the use of wave pipelining across both switches and channels is shown in Figure 7.37.

Each physical channel in switch S_0 is split into $k + w$ virtual channels. Among them, k channels are the control channels associated with the corresponding physical channels in switches $S_1, \ldots, S_k$. Control channels are only used to set up and tear down physical circuits. These channels have capacity for a single flit and only transmit control flits. Control channels are set up using pipelined circuit switching and handled by the PCS routing control unit. The remaining w virtual channels are used to transmit messages using wormhole switching and require deeper buffers. They are handled by the wormhole routing control unit. The hybrid switching technique implemented by this router architecture was referred to as *wave switching* [102]. With such a router architecture, it is possible to conceive of approaches to optimizing the allocation of link bandwidth in support of real-time communication, priority traffic, or high throughput.

7.2.6   Pipelined Circuit Switching

The implementation of routing protocols based on pipelined circuit switching present different challenges from those presented by wormhole-switched routers, notably in the need to provide support for backtracking and the distinction between control flit traffic and data flit traffic. Ariadne [7] is a router for PCS supporting the MB-m family of fault-tolerant routing protocols. The current implementation is for a k-ary 2-cube with 8-bit-wide, half-duplex physical data channels. There are two virtual data channels and one virtual control channel in each direction across each physical link. The router is fully asynchronous and is comprised of three major components — the control path, the physical link interface, and the data path.

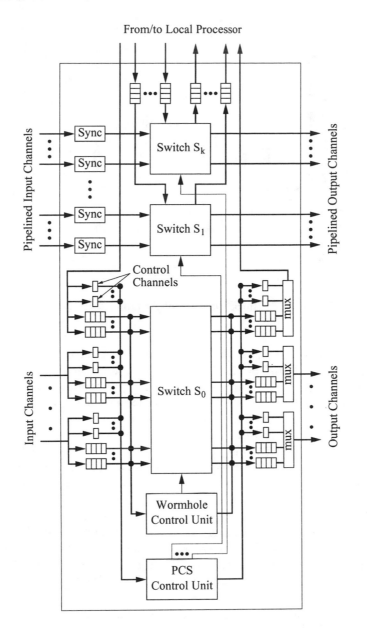

Figure 7.37. Organization of a router employing wave pipelining. (Mux = Multiplexer; PCS = Pipelined circuit switching; Sync = Synchronizer.)

Figure 7.38 illustrates the block diagram of the architecture of the Ariadne chip. Each physical link has an associated link control unit (LCU). These LCUs are split in the diagram with the input half on the left and the output half on the right. Each input LCU feeds a data input buffer unit (DIBU) and a control input buffer unit (CIBU). The buffer units contain FIFO buffers for each virtual channel over the link. The data FIFO buffers feed directly into distinct inputs of the 9×9 crossbar.

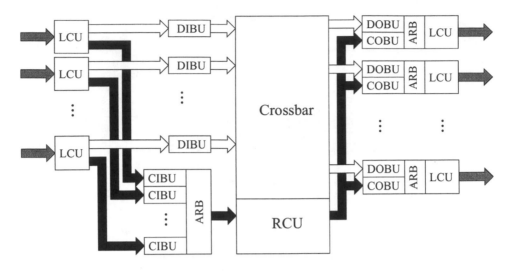

Figure 7.38. Block diagram of Ariadne: a PCS router.

The internal control path is indicated by the solid arrows. Control and data flits arrive over the physical link and are differentiated by the LCU. Control flits are first directed to the CIBUs. The CIBUs send their flits to the router control unit (RCU) via a common bus. The CIBUs arbitrate for use of the bus via a distributed, mutual exclusion mechanism. Once a CIBU has acquired the privilege to use the bus, it presents its routing header and virtual channel address. When the RCU receives a routing header, a routing decision is made, a crossbar mapping is modified, and the header is directed to a control output buffer unit (COBU) via a common output bus.

Figure 7.39 illustrates the signals that comprise each physical link. There are four pairs of request (R) and acknowledge (A) lines. Since the links are half-duplex, nodes must arbitrate for the privilege to send data over the link. One request/acknowledge pair for each side is used in the arbitration protocol (R_{ARBn}, A_{ARBn}). Once a node has the privilege to send, the other request/acknowledge pair is used in the data transfer (R_{DATAn}, A_{DATAn}). An *Accept* line is used to indicate whether or not the flit was accepted by the receiving node or rejected due to input buffer overflow. While there are more pin-efficient methods of implementing these internode handshaking protocols [193], the use of a self-timed design and new switching technique led to the adoption of a more conservative approach.

Virtual channels are granted access to the physical channel using a demand-driven mutual exclusion ring. A signal representing the privilege to drive the physical channel circulates around this ring. Each virtual channel has a station on the ring and will take the privilege if the channel has data to send. In addition, there is also a station on the ring that represents the routing node on the other side of the link (these are half-duplex channels). If the other node has data to send, the privilege will be taken, and the other node will be given control of the link. This scheme multiplexes data in a true demand-driven, rotating fashion among all virtual channels in both directions over the physical link.

While PCS requires one control channel for each virtual data channel, Ariadne combines all control channels into one common virtual control channel. Originally done to reduce circuit area, it also reduces the number of stations on the arbitration rings devoted to control flit FIFO buffers. While it may increase the control flit latency to the RCU, the control flit traffic through the network

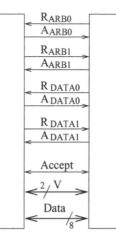

Figure 7.39. Physical link.

is substantially less than the data flit traffic. Each message creates two control flits (the header and acknowledgment flits) and any number of data flits. For most realistic message sizes, it is the data flit population that will be the determinant of message throughput and latency. The larger the message, the smaller the effect of collapsing control channels into a single channel. For example, with 32-flit messages, control flits will represent about 6% of the offered load.

Backtracking protocols must use history information. Rather than carry this information within the routing header, leading to large headers [52, 62], history information is stored locally at a router when necessary. With each virtual data channel we associate a history mask containing a bit for each physical channel. Backtracking protocols use the history mask to record the state of the search at an intermediate node. For example, when a header flit arrives on a virtual channel, say f, the history mask for virtual channel f is initialized to 0, except for the bit corresponding to the physical link of f. The header is routed along some outgoing physical link, say g and the bit for link g is set in the history mask of f. If eventually the header returns to the node backtracking across g, the routing header is prevented from attempting link g again because the bit for g in the history mask of f is set.

The current control flit format is shown in Figure 7.40. All header flits have the Header bit set. Headers will have the Backtrack bit set or cleared depending on whether they are moving forward or backtracking. Acknowledgment flits will have the Header bit cleared and the Backtrack bit set. The next implementation of Ariadne is expected to use 16-bit flits which will allow for larger X and Y offsets as well as an increase in the number of misroutes that are permitted.

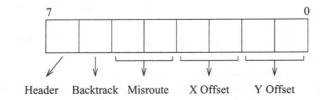

Figure 7.40. Control flit format.

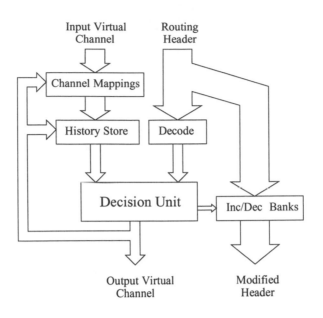

Figure 7.41. Routing control unit.

The routing control unit is more complex than in wormhole-switched routers since history information must be extracted, and the routing protocols are fully adaptive necessitating the selection of one output channel from several candidates. Figure 7.41 shows a block diagram of the RCU. The first step in routing is decoding the routing header and fetching history information. When a forward going routing header enters a node, the history mask is initialized. When a routing header is backtracking, its history mask must be retrieved from the history store. Since the history mask is associated with the virtual channel the header first arrived on, the RCU must first determine the header's point of origination from the crossbar. Once the history information is either initialized or retrieved, a routing decision is made and the values in the outgoing header flit are modified accordingly. The necessary offsets are selected after the routing function has been computed [57]. The selection function favors profitable directions over misrouting.

Data flits are directed to the DIBUs by the LCU. The data input FIFO buffers feed the input ports of a 9×9 crossbar. It is a full virtual-to-virtual channel crossbar — four physical channels with two virtual channels/physical channel and one channel to the processor. The data output FIFO buffers receive their inputs from the output ports of the crossbar. The crossbar is constructed in such a way that the mapped status of every input and output can be read by the RCU. In addition, the RCU may query the crossbar to determine the input that is mapped to an output. Thus, the RCU can obtain the information necessary to direct backtracking headers and acknowledgment flits to their parent node in the path.

Critical sections of the design were simulated using Spice with the level three CMOS transistor models provided by MOSIS for the HP CMOS26B 0.8 μm process. Due to the self-timed nature of the router, the intranode delays incurred by control and data flits is nondeterministic due the arbitration for the RCU and physical links. Since routing headers follow a different path through the router than data flits, the delays are presented in separate tables. The routing header delay is provided in Table 7.5. Adding all of the components, the intranode latency of routing headers ranges from 21 to 48 ns (line 1, Table 7.5). Note that this includes both intranode delay and pad

Table 7.5. Simulated (Spice) timing: Path setup.

Parameter	Time
Control path	13.75 ns + RCU + $2t_{arb}$
RCU (Forward-going header)	13.0 − 16.0 ns
RCU (Acknowledgment)	7.5 ns
RCU (Backtracking header)	16.0 − 19.0 ns

Table 7.6. Simulated (Spice) timing: Data path.

Parameter	Time
Data path	8.5 ns + t_{arb}
Link cycle time (1 active channel)	16.4 ns + t_{synch} + $2t_l$
Link cycle time (>1 active channels)	13.65 ns + $2t_l$
Link idle time for direction change	4.3 ns + t_l

delays as well as channel arbitration delays. Table 7.6 summarizes the major delay components for data flits in Ariadne. In the table, t_{synch} represents the portion of the channel delay that cannot be overlapped with arbitration while t_{arb} represents the worst-case delay in arbitration. Modeled datapath bandwidths are in the vicinity of 50–75 Mbytes/s depending on traffic and message distribution.

7.2.7   Buffered Wormhole Switching

This variant of wormhole switching is employed in the SP-2 interconnection network: a bidirectional multistage interconnection network constructed from 4 × 4 bidirectional buffered crossbar switches. Two stages of four switches each, are organized into a *frame* that supports up to 16 processors. The architecture of a frame is shown in Figure 7.42. Each crossbar switch has four bidirectional inputs and four bidirectional outputs, and therefore operates as an 8 × 8 crossbar. In this two-stage organization, except for processors on the same switch, there are four paths between every pair of processors connected to the same frame. The use of bidirectional links avoids the need for costly (i.e., long) wraparound links from the outputs back to the inputs. Multiple frames can be connected as shown in Figure 7.42 to connect larger numbers of processors, either by directly connecting frames (up to 5 frames or 80 processors) or by cascading frames together. In the cascaded organization, switch frames are used in the last stage to provide wraparound links as shown in Figure 7.42. As the systems grow larger, the number of paths between any pair of processors grows. For example, the 128-node configuration provides 16 paths between any pair of frames.

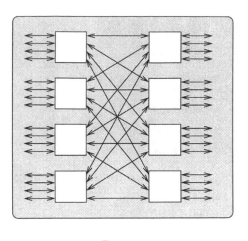

Frame

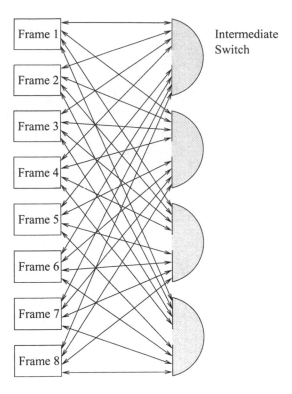

Figure 7.42. System interconnect using an SP-2 frame.

The SP-2 physical channel appears as shown in Figure 7.43. The data channel is 8 bits wide, with a single-bit tag signal and a single-bit token signal in the reverse direction. With the addition of a clock signal, the channel is 11 bits wide. SP-2 flits are matched to the channel width at 8 bits. An active tag signifies valid token on the channel. Tokens are encoded in two cycle frames: a sequence of 0–1 represents no tokens and 1–0 represents two tokens. The token sequence is used to increment a counter in the receiving port. The counter keeps track of the number of flits that can be sent and is decremented each time a flit is transmitted. The other patterns are used for error detection.

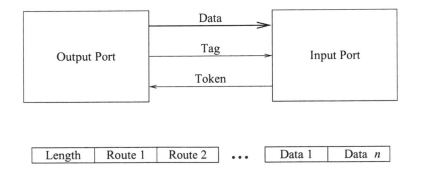

Figure 7.43. SP-2 physical channel and message packet formats.

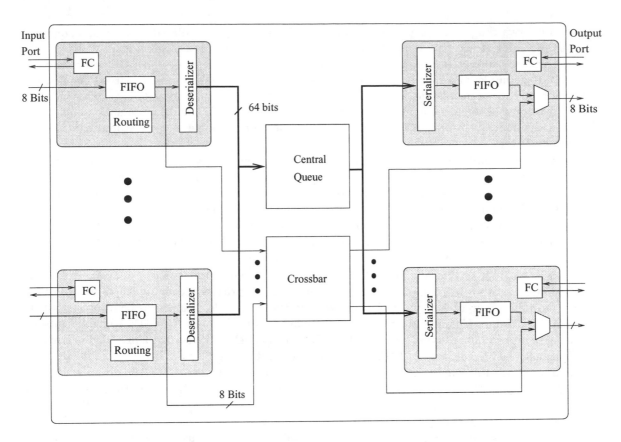

Figure 7.44. Architecture of the SP-2 router. (FC = Flow control.)

Due to propagation delays on the physical link, the input port must be able to buffer a number of flits greater than twice the channel delay: buffers are 31 flits or bytes. The transmitting side of the link consumes a token for each flit transmitted on the channel. The first flit of the message is a byte that contains the message length in flits, thus limiting message sizes to a maximum of 255 flits. Successive flits contain routing information, one routing flit for each frame (two switches) traversed by the message.

Figure 7.44 illustrates the block diagram of the architecture of the SP-2 switch. The behavior of buffered wormhole routing was described in Chapter 2. Messages are routed using source routing. Message flits are received into an input FIFO queue where the first router flit is decoded to request an output port, and CRC checks are performed. Bits 6–4 determine the output port on the first switch in a frame, while bits 2–0 determine the output port of the second switch in a frame. Bit 7 determines which of these two fields is used by the switch — when it is cleared, bits 6–4 are used. When bit 7 is set bits 2–0 are used, and the input port logic discards the routing flit and decrements the length flit in the message. Thus the message becomes smaller as it progresses toward the destination. It takes one cycle to request an output port and receive permission to transmit. If the requested port is available, it is a single cycle through the crossbar to move a flit. If the output port is not free or the request not granted by the time a chunk is received, the chunk must be buffered in the central queue. Such a chunk is referred to as a critical chunk since it is ready for immediate forwarding to an output port. Note that if any message is buffered in the central queue, a output port will not accept a request from the corresponding input port. Subsequent chunks of the message will be buffered in the central queue as space is available. Such chunks are noncritical. As the preceding chunks of a message are transmitted, noncritical chunks become critical chunks, i.e., they are ready for transmission. Storage in the central queue is allocated as follows. One chunk is statically allocated to each output port (to hold the current critical chunk). Remaining chunks are allocated dynamically to incoming messages as they become available and are stored as described in Chapter 2.

Output ports arbitrate among crossbar requests from input ports according to a least-recently-served discipline. Output port requests for the next message chunk from the central queue are also served according to a least-recently-served discipline. Note that the internal data path to the central buffer is 64 bits wide, i.e., 8 flits. Thus, one receiver can be served every cycle, with one chunk being transmitted to the central queue or the output port in one cycle. One transmitter can also be served every cycle. Each chunk is 8 flits, which takes eight cycles to receive. Thus, the bandwidth into the central queue is matched to the bandwidth out of the queue.

The SP-2 switch interface is controlled by a powerful communications coprocessor — a 64-bit Intel i860 CPU with 8 Mbytes of memory. On one side, this processor communicates with an SP-2 switch through a pair of 2-Kbyte FIFO queues. On the other side, the processor interfaces to the RS/6000 CPU Micro Channel bus via a pair of 2 Kbyte FIFO channels. One DMA engine transfers messages to and from the co-processor card and Micro Channel, and a second DMA engine transfers data between the Micro Channel FIFO buffers and the switch interface FIFO buffers. This interface can achieve bandwidths approaching that of the switch links [328].

Like the Cray T3D, the SP-2 employs source routing. The route tables are statically constructed and stored in memory to be used by the messaging software. The construction and use of the routes is performed in a manner that prevents deadlock and promotes balanced use of multiple paths between pairs of processors. In this manner an attempt is made to fully use the available wire bandwidth.

At the time of this writing the next generation of IBM switches were becoming available. The new switches utilize 16-bit flits and the crossbar path is 16 bits wide. Internally the switches operate at 75 MHz as opposed to 40 MHz in the current router. The physical channel structure remains the same, except that differential signaling results in doubling the number of signals per port to 22. The physical channel also operates at 150 MHz. Chunks are now 128 bits wide and the central queue can store 256 chunks for a total of 4 Kbytes. Since the flit size and clock speed has doubled, so have the buffers on the input ports. Flow control and buffer management necessitates 63-flit buffers, or 126 bytes. With the wider internal switch data paths and higher clock rates, the memory-to-memory bandwidth, including Micro Channel transfers, is approaching 100 Mbytes/s for large messages.

7.2.8   Network of Workstations

The first half of the 90s has seen a relentless, and large (close to doubling every 1.5 years) improvement in the price/performance ratio of workstations and personal computers. There is no evidence of this trend fading any time soon. With the concurrent trends in portable parallel programming standards, there has been an explosive growth in research and development efforts seeking to harness these commodity parts to create commercial off-the-shelf multiprocessors. A major architectural challenge in configuring such systems has been in providing the low latency and high throughput interprocessor communication traditionally afforded by multiprocessor backplanes and interconnects in a cluster of workstations/PCs. We are now seeing a migration of this interconnect technology into the cluster computing arena. This section discusses two examples of such networks.

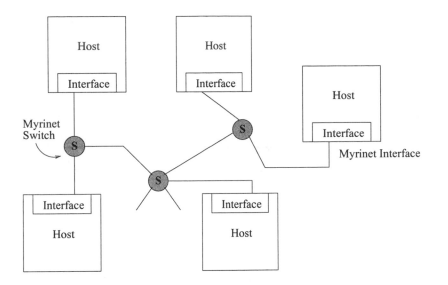

Figure 7.45. An example of a network configured with Myrinet.

Myrinet

Myrinet is a switching fabric that grew out of two previous research efforts, the CalTech Mosaic Project [314] and the USC/ISI ATOMIC LAN [107] project. The distinguishing features of Myrinet includes the support of high performance wormhole switching in arbitrary LAN topologies. A Myrinet network comprises of host interfaces and switches. The switches may be connected to other host interfaces and other switches as illustrated in Figure 7.45, leading to arbitrary topologies.

Each Myrinet physical link is a full-duplex link with 9-bit-wide channels operating at 80 MHz. The 9-bit character may be a data byte or one of several control characters used to implement the physical channel flow control protocol. Each byte transmission is individually acknowledged. However, due to the length of the cable up to 23 characters may be in transit in both directions at any given time. As in the SP-2, these delays are accommodated with sufficient buffering at the receiver. The *STOP* and *GO* control characters are generated at the receiver and multiplexed along the reverse channel (data may be flowing along this channel) to implement flow control. This slack buffer [314] is organized as shown in Figure 7.46c. As the buffer fills up from the bottom, the *STOP* control character is transmitted to the source when the buffer crosses the *STOP* line. There is enough remaining buffer space for all of the flits in transit as well as the flits that will be injected before the *STOP* character arrives at the source. Once the buffer has drained sufficiently (i.e., crosses the *GO* line) a *GO* character is transmitted and the sender resumes data flow. The placement of the *STOP* and *GO* points within the buffer are designed to prevent constant oscillation between *STOP* and *GO* states, and reduce flow control traffic. A separate control character (*GAP*) is used to signify the end-of-message. To enable detection of faulty links or deadlocked messages, non-*IDLE* characters must be periodically transmitted across each channel. Longer timeout intervals are use to detect potentially deadlocked packets. For example, this may occur over a nonfaulty link due to bit errors in the header. In this case, after 50 ms the blocked part of the packet is dropped, and a forward reset signal is generated to the receiver and the link buffers reset.

Myrinet employs wormhole switching with source routing. The message packets may be of variable length and are structured as shown in Figure 7.46c. The first few flits of the message header

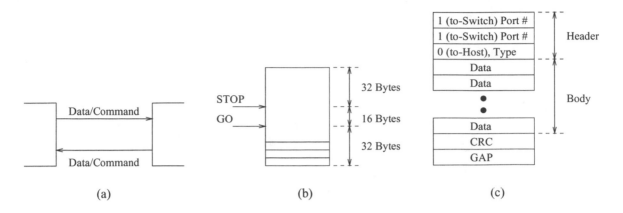

Figure 7.46. (a) The Myrinet physical link. (b) Organization of the receiver buffer. (c) Myrinet message packet format.

contain the address of the switch ports on intermediate switches. In a manner similar to the SP-2 switches, each flit addresses one of the output ports in a switch. Each switch strips off the leading flit as the message arrives and uses the contents to address an output port. Conflicts for the same output port are resolved using a recirculating token arbitration mechanism to ensure fairness. The remaining flits of the message are transmitted though the selected output port. Once the message reaches the destination, the Myrinet interface examines the leading flit of the message. This flit contains information about the contents of the packet, e.g. control information, data encoding, etc. For example, this encoding permits the message to be interpreted as an Internet Protocol (IP) packet. The most significant bit determines if the flit is to be interpreted by the host interface or a switch. The header flits are followed by a variable number of data flits, an 8-bit CRC, and the *GAP* character signifying the end of the message.

The switches themselves are based on two chips: a pipelined crossbar chip and the interface chip that implements the link-level protocols. The maximum routing latency through an eight-port switch is 550 ns [30]. At the time of this writing, four-port and eight-port switches are available with 16- and 32-port switches under development. The Myrinet host interface resembles a full-fledged processor with memory and is shown in Figure 7.47. Executing in this interface is the Myrinet control program (MCP). The interface also supports DMA access to the host memory. Given this basic infrastructure, and the programmability of the interface it is possible to conceive of a variety of implementations for the messaging layer and indeed, several have been attempted in addition to the Myrinet implementation. A generic implementation involves a host process communicating with the interface through a pair of command and acknowledgment queues. Commands to the interface cause data to be accessed from regions in memory, transferred to the interface memory, packetized, and transmitted out the physical channel. Acknowledgment of completion is by a message in the acknowledgment queue, or optionally the generation of an interrupt. Message reception follows a similar sequence of events where the header is interpreted, data transferred to locations in host memory, and an acknowledgment (or interrupt) generated. Typically a set of unswappable pages are allocated in host memory to serve as the destination and source of the interface DMA engine. In general, the Myrinet interface is capable of conducting transfers between the interface and both host and kernel memory. The MCP contains information mapping network addresses to routes, and performs the header generation. In any Myrinet network, one of the interfaces serves as the *mapper*: it is responsible for sending mapping packets to other interfaces. This map of the network is

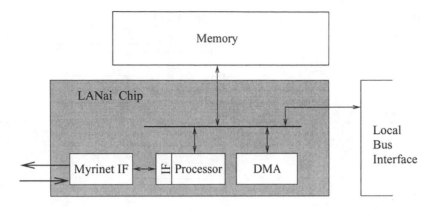

Figure 7.47. Architecture of the Myrinet interface. (DMA = Direct memory access; IF = Interface.)

distributed to all of the other interfaces. Now all routes can be created locally by each interface. The network maps are computed in a manner that is guaranteed to provide only deadlock-free routes. The attractive feature of the Myrinet network is that should the mapper interface be removed or faulty links separate the network, a new mapper is selected automatically. Periodic remapping of the network is performed to detect faulty links and switches, and distribute this information throughout the network.

More recently, Myrinet designs have evolved to a three-chip set. The single-chip crossbar is used for system area networks (SAN) where the distances are less than 3 meters. For longer distances, custom VLSI chips convert to formats suitable for longer distances of up to 8 meters typically used in LANs. A third chip provides a 32-bit FIFO interface for configurations as classical multicomputer nodes. Switches can be configured with combinations of SAN and LAN ports producing configurations with varying bisection bandwidth and power requirements. The building blocks are very flexible and permit a variety of multiprocessor configurations as well as opportunities for subsequently growing an existing network. For example, a Myrinet switch configured as a LAN switch has a cut-through latency of 300 ns while a SAN switch has a cut-through latency of 100 ns. Thus, small tightly coupled multiprocessor systems can be configured with commercial processors to be used a parallel engines. Alternatively, low latency communication can be achieved within existing workstation and PC clusters that may distributed over a larger area.

ServerNet

ServerNet [15, 156, 157, 158] is a SAN that provides the interconnection fabric for supporting interprocessor, processor-I/O and I/O-I/O communication. The goal is to provide a flexible interconnect fabric that can reliably provide scalable bandwidth. ServerNet is built on a network of switches that employ wormhole switching. Figure 7.48 illustrates the structure of the physical channel and the organization of the router. Like Myrinet, ServerNet is based on point-to-point switched networks to produce low latency communication. The structure and design of ServerNet was heavily influenced by the need to integrate I/O transfers and interprocessor communication transfers within the same network fabric.

The structure and operation of the physical channel was described in Example 7.3. The choice of 8-bit channels and command encoding was motivated by the corresponding reduction in pin-out and complexity of control logic for fault detection. The link speed of 50 MHz presents a compromise

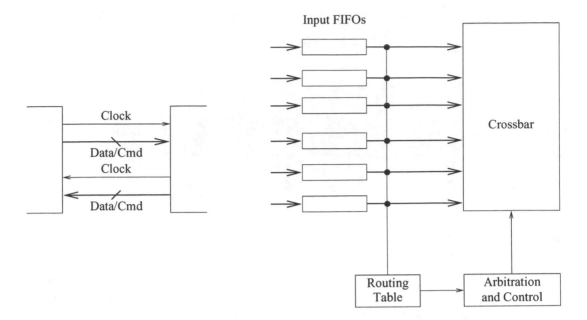

Figure 7.48. The ServerNet channel and router organization. (CMD = Command.)

between cost and the performance of modern peripheral devices. If increased bandwidth is required between end points, additional links can be added to the network. The router is a six-port, wormhole-switched router as shown in Figure 7.48. Virtual channels are not used. Since source clocking is employed to transmit flits, a synchronizing FIFO is used to receive flits at the sender's clock and output flits on the receivers clock to the input buffers. The flit buffers are 64 bytes deep. As described in Example 7.3, flow control for buffer management is implemented via commands in the reverse direction. A 1,024-entry routing table uses the destination address in the header to determine the output port. The packet now enters arbitration for the output port. Each input possesses an accumulator that determines the priority of the input channel during arbitration. The channel that gains the output channel has the associated accumulator value reduced by an amount equal to the sum of the accumulators of the remaining channels that are seeking access. The channels losing arbitration increment the value of their accumulator. This scheme avoids starvation. Deadlock freedom is achieved by design in computing the values of routing table entries. The latency through the router is on the order of 300 ns and the measured latency for a zero length packet through one switch is on the order of 3 μs.

Message headers consist of an 8-byte header which contains 20-bit source and destination IDs, message length, and additional control and transaction type information. The message header is followed by an optional 4-byte ServerNet address, variable-sized data field, and a trailing CRC. The ServerNet address is used to address a location in the destination node's address space. For interprocessor communication, the host interface will map this address to a local physical address. In this manner processor nodes can provide controlled and protected access to other nodes. All messages generate acknowledgments. Timers are used to enforce timeouts on acknowledgments. There are four message types: read request (17 bytes), read response ($13 + N$ bytes), write request ($17 + N$ bytes) and write response (13 bytes). The value of N represents the data size. The maximum data size is 64 bytes.

The six-port architecture can be used to create many different topologies including the traditional mesh, tree, and hypercube topologies. ServerNet is structured to use two disjoint networks: the X network and the Y network. Duplication in conjunction with acknowledgments for each packet, and error checking by means of CRC are used to realize reliable operation.

7.3 Engineering Issues

The discussions of the network optimizations and router architectures have necessarily included engineering issues and trade-offs. In this section we speculate on important trends and their impact on future networks. The design of a scalable, reliable computing system is fundamentally about the optimization of metrics such as cost, performance, and reliability in the presence of physical constraints. The emerging advances in packaging technologies, e.g., low cost MCMs, 3-D chip stacks, etc. will lead to major changes in the relationship between these physical constraints, and as a result significantly impact the cost, performance, and reliability of the next generation of interconnection networks. An accurate analysis of the effect of packaging technology and options early in the system design process will enable the implementation of systems that effectively utilize available packaging technology.

Provided with a high-level design, the fundamental question relates to where should we place die, multichip module, board, and subsystem boundaries. Die boundaries may be determined by the use of commercial parts. MCM boundaries may be determined by cost, performance, or thermal density. These partitioning decisions are critical. To make the most effective use of packaging technology we must be able to predict the impact of packaging technology on a particular design. The type of trade-offs that can be made at the packaging level include the following.

- High packaging densities (80–90%) can be realized with flip chip bonding and MCMs. This process is also more expensive and must be weighed against the reliability of a larger number of I/Os. If the implementation strategy is one of an active backplane, high-density multipath networks become viable, particularly in embedded multiprocessor applications.

- High wiring densities (50 μm pitch vs. 500 μm pitch) can be achieved in multichip packaged substrates. This has a direct, positive effect on the achievable bisection bandwidth of the network but is achieved at a higher cost and possibly entails greater power densities.

- Area array bonding can provide higher chip pin-out changing the fundamental trade-offs of what goes on- and off-chip. Off-chip speed penalties may no longer be as severe depending on the package substrate materials, e.g., organic polymer dielectric layers and copper interconnects.

- Due to the nonlinear cost/yield relationships, monolithic designs may be more cost-effectively implemented on multiple smaller die. Thus larger switches and increased buffering may become viable architectural options.

- Global interconnects on MCM substrates are not as lossy as intrachip interconnects. As a result, comparable or better performance can be obtained via the use of MCM interconnects. Furthermore, large reductions in interchip delays are possible due to lower parasitics involved in the MCM die attach technologies, hence redefining the partitioning of designs across multiple die. Several smaller die may be a cost-effective option to a larger monolithic die. This off-chip penalty has historically motivated several generations of computer architecture designs.

The above trade-offs must be made once node design and interconnect options have been proposed. These packaging technologies are making the use of multiprocessor architectures in embedded sensor processing applications quite feasible in the foreseeable future. However, doing so will require the optimization of the topologies for these new constraints.

A second issue is embedded in the advent of cluster-based computing with workstations and PCs. We are seeing the migration of the expertise gained from the design of several generations of high speed multiprocessor interconnects, to the design of low-latency, robust cluster interconnects. Among the many architectural issues being resolved in this context is the point at which the network is integrated into the local node (e.g., memory, as an I/O device, etc.), software/hardware interface to network bandwidth, and the design of message layers that realize low-latency communication when constrained to use commodity parts. Some of the software issues arc discussed in Chapter 8.

7.4   Commented References

Dally [71] originally studied the design of k-ary n-cube networks under the assumption of VLSI implementations wherein network implementations were wire-limited. Wiring constraints were captured in the form of bisection width constraints. Networks were compared by fixing the available bisection width to that of a binary hypercube with bit-wide, full-duplex, data channels. Under different wire delay models the analysis concluded that low-dimensional networks provided a better fit between form and function, resulting in better overall latency and throughput characteristics. Subsequently, Abraham and Padmanabhan [1] studied the problem under the assumption of fixed pin-out constraints. In this environment, the wider channel widths of low-dimensional networks were offset by the greater distances. Thus, their analysis tended to favor higher-dimensional networks. Bolding and Konstantinidou [33] observed that the maximum available pin-out is not independent of the bisection width. Thus, they proposed using the product of the bisection width and pin-out as a measure of the cost of the network. Thus comparisons could be made between two (quantifiable) equal-cost networks. Agarwal's [3] analysis included the effect of switch delays, which was missing from prior analysis. In this model, the analysis favored slightly higher-dimensional networks than Dally's analysis [71]. One of the principal inhibitors of the use of higher-dimensional networks has been the wire delay due to the long wires that result when these networks are laid out in the plane. Scott and Goodman [310] studied the ability to pipeline bits on the wire, effectively using these long propagation delays as storage to create pipelined wires. As result, their analysis too favored higher-dimensional networks. These techniques are reflected in the switching fabric that is produced in current generation networks. Finally, the continuous evolution of high-density packaging with area-bonded die is resulting in the capability for producing chips with very high number of I/O connections. This relaxation of the pin constraint will no doubt favor lower-dimensional networks due to the constraints on bisection width.

The first routers were packet-switched and circuit-switched, following from previous experiences with multicomputer communications in the LAN environment. While packet-switched networks enabled deadlock-free routing via structured memory allocation, message latencies in tightly coupled multiprocessors were very high due to the linear relationship between interprocessor distance and latency. The advent of cut-through routing significantly reduced this latency, but the need to buffer packets at the nodes required the involvement of the node processors: we can expect this trend to be quite inefficient in the tightly coupled multiprocessor world. The advent of small-buffer cut-through or wormhole switching made it feasible to construct single-chip, compact, fast routers that did not require the services of intermediate nodes. A generation of router chips were based on this approach [77, 79, 255]. As densities continued to increase, it was possible to include enough buffer space on the single chip to support VCT switching [41, 83, 188]. With better understanding of the advantages as well as limitations of cut-through switching, efforts started focusing on optimizations to further improve the performance or reliability leading to new router architectures [7, 316, 327].

Finally, we are seeing a convergence of techniques for routing in LANs and multiprocessor backplanes. As clusters of workstations become economically viable, focus has shifted to the support of efficient messaging mechanisms and hardware support. The new generation of router architectures reflects this trend [30, 156]. We can expect this trend to continue, further blurring the distinctions between clusters of workstations and tightly coupled multiprocessor backplanes.

E X E R C I S E S

7.1 Rewrite the expression for the no-load message latency in a k-ary n-ary cube under the following assumptions. Rather than a router architecture that is buffered at the input and output, assume that the router has input buffering only. Thus, in a single cycle, a flit can progress from an input buffer on one router to an input buffer of another router, if the corresponding output link at the first router is free. Furthermore, assume that the routing delay and the switch delay scale logarithmically with the network dimension.

Solution   We have the equation for the no-load latency given by

$$t_{wormhole} = n\frac{k}{4}\left[r + s + 1 + \left(\frac{n}{2} - 1\right)\log_e k\right] + \max\left[s, 1 + \left(\frac{n}{2} - 1\right)\log_e k\right]\left\lceil\frac{L}{W}\right\rceil \quad (7.25)$$

Each stage of the message pipeline from the source to the destination now consists of transmission across the router and the link. Therefore, the coefficient of the second term becomes the sum of the wire delay and switch delay. The new expression is

$$t_{wormhole} = n\frac{k}{4}\left[r + s + 1 + \left(\frac{n}{2} - 1\right)\log_e k\right] + \left[s + 1 + \left(\frac{n}{2} - 1\right)\log_e k\right]\left\lceil\frac{L}{W}\right\rceil \quad (7.26)$$

This equation can be rewritten as

$$t_{wormhole} = rn\frac{k}{4} + \left[s + 1 + \left(\frac{n}{2} - 1\right)\log_e k\right]\left(n\frac{k}{4} + \left\lceil\frac{L}{W}\right\rceil\right) \quad (7.27)$$

The first term is the component due to routing delays (in the absence of contention). The coefficient of the second term corresponds to the clock cycle time of the network.

7.2 Individual analysis of the networks has been based on their use of a single resource, e.g., wiring density or pin-out. Actually both node degree and bisection are related. A better measure of network cost/performance appears to be the product of node degree and bisection width proposed in [33]. Determine the relationship between channel widths of two networks of equal cost using this performance metric. Compare a binary hypercube and an equivalent-sized 2-D mesh using this metric.

Solution   In general, consider two topologies of dimension r and s with the same number of nodes. We know that the product of their bisection bandwidth and pin count are equal. The width of each dimension in the r-dimensional topology is given by $N^{\frac{1}{r}}$. This formula is derived from the relation $N = k_m^r$. The pin-out is given by (including only data pins) $2rw_r$ where w_r is the channel width. We can now write the products of the bisection bandwidth and pin-out as

$$(2w_r N^{1-\frac{1}{r}})(2rw_r) = (2w_s N^{1-\frac{1}{s}})(2sw_s)$$

From the above expression we have

$$\frac{w_r}{w_s} = \sqrt{\frac{sN^{1-\frac{1}{s}}}{rN^{1-\frac{1}{r}}}}$$

Substituting the correct number of dimensions for a binary hypercube and a 2-D mesh, we have

$$\frac{w_{hyp}}{w_{mesh}} = \sqrt{\frac{2N^{1-\frac{1}{2}}}{rN^{1-\frac{1}{r}}}}$$

which simplifies to

$$\frac{w_{hyp}}{w_{mesh}} = \sqrt{\frac{4\sqrt{N}}{N \log_2 N}}$$

7.3 Early in this chapter, an expression was provided for the relative length of the longest wire in a k-ary n-cube when embedded in two dimensions. Repeat this analysis when a k-ary n-cube is embedded in three dimensions.

Solution   Consider the base case of of a 3-D cube with each dimension interleaved as shown in Figure 7.2. A k-ary n-cube is embedded in three dimensions by embedding $\frac{n}{3}$ dimensions of the network into each of the three physical dimensions. Let us assume that the number of dimensions is a multiple of 3. Each additional dimension beyond the first three increases the number of nodes in the network by a factor of k. Embedding in three dimensions provides an increase in the number nodes in each physical dimension by a factor of $k^{\frac{1}{3}}$. If we ignore wire width and wiring density effects, the length of the longest wire in each physical dimension is also increased by a factor of $k^{\frac{1}{3}}$. Therefore for n dimensions the longest wire will grow by a factor of $k^{\frac{n-3}{3}} = k^{\frac{n}{3}-1}$. Note that similar arguments lead to the general case of the wire length of embeddings in d dimensions being $k^{\frac{n}{d}-1}$.

PROBLEMS

7.1 Cascading is employed to configure a 512-node IBM SP-2 system. How many disjoint paths exist between any pair of processors?

7.2 Flow control operations across a link take a finite amount of time. A message may be in transit during this period. In pipelined links, several messages may be in transit. The receive buffer size must be large enough to store the phits in progress over a link. Given the maximum number of phits in transit on a physical channel, write an expression for the minimum receive buffer size in phits to prevent any loss of data.

7.3 Consider an m-dimensional and n-dimensional tori of equal cost, where cost is given by the product of the bisection width and pin-out that utilizes this bisection width. Write analytical expressions for the relationships between the channel widths of the two networks and the bisection bandwidths of the two networks.

7.4 Consider embedding a k-ary n-cube in three dimensions rather than two dimensions. Rewrite the expression for average message latency by modifying the expressions that capture the effect of wire length. Compare this to the expression derived in this chapter.

7.5 We are interested in determining the maximum message injection rate for a given bisection bandwidth. Assume we have a 16×16 torus with 1-flit-wide, half-duplex channels. Message destinations are uniformly distributed. Find the maximum message injection rate in flits/node/cycle.

Hint   Every message generated by a node is equally likely to cross the bisection, or be addressed to a node in the same half of the network.

7.6 A $4 \times 4 \times 8$ Cray T3D system experiences a single node failure. There are no spare nodes. All of the routing tables are updated to use the longer path in the dimension. Now we are concerned about deadlock. Is deadlock possible? Justify your answer with a proof or an example.

7.7 Source routing as described in the Cray T3D can cause imbalance in the use of virtual channels. For an eight-node ring, compute the degree of imbalance across each physical link. The degree of imbalance across a physical link is defined as the ratio of (1) the difference in the number of source-destination pairs that use virtual channel 0 and virtual channel 1 across the link, and (2) the total number of source-destination pairs that use the link. The choice of the dateline link does not matter.

7.8 What is the bisection bandwidth in bytes of the following machine configurations?

1. A $4 \times 8 \times 4$ Cray T3D
2. An 8×14 Intel Paragon
3. A 64-node IBM SP-2

7.9 Using the following values for the constants in the parameterized cost model shown in Table 7.4, compute the routing latency and the maximum flit bandwidth available to a message.

Constant	c_0	c_1	c_2	c_3	c_4	c_5	c_6	c_7	c_8	c_9
Value (ns)	0.4	0.6	2.2	2.7	0.6	0.6	1.4	0.6	1.24	0.6

Chapter 8

Messaging Layer Software

The majority of this text has been concentrated on issues facing the design of the interconnection network: switching, routing, and supporting router architectures. However, from the user's perspective the experienced latency/throughput performance is not only a function of the network, but also of the operations performed at the source and destination processors to inject and receive messages from the network. End-to-end performance can be measured from data located in the memory of the sending process, to data in the memory of the receiving process. This includes the process of preparing data for transmission (e.g., computation of packet headers and check sums) and injecting/ejecting messages into/out of the network. In most systems, a large segment of this functionality is implemented in software: the *messaging layer*. With the dramatic improvements in raw link bandwidths, the time on the wire experienced by messages has become overshadowed by the software overheads at the sender/receiver.

These software overheads are determined by the functionality to be provided by the messaging layer, and the hardware features that are available in the network and node interfaces to support this desired functionality. For example, the overhead in transferring message data from the local memory to the network interface is determined by the internal node design and the availability of services such as DMA, interrupts, or memory-mapped interfaces. This chapter first discusses the major functions that are provided by current message layers and then discusses how the implementation of these functions are affected by the services provided by the network hardware and the internal node architecture. The services of this messaging layer is the basis on which user-level message-passing libraries can be constructed. The chapter focuses on the message-passing programming model and does not include issues concerning the support of shared memory abstractions on distributed memory architectures. The data transfer requirements for implementing shared address spaces have similarities with the requirements of message-passing implementations, and several current research efforts are studying the integration of shared-memory and message-passing communication within a common framework. However, there appears to be a greater consensus on the requirements for supporting message-passing models, and this chapter focuses on examples from this domain.

Generally an application programmers interface (API) provides access to the services of the messaging layer through a set of library procedures and functions. A desirable API is one that presents clear semantics, is independent of a specific platform, and presents high-level abstractions that are easy to use. The Messaging Passing Interface (MPI) represents a standard message-passing API that has evolved out of the collective efforts of many people in academia, industry, and government over the past several years. It captures many of the desirable features of a message-passing API gleaned from collective experience with the development with several message-passing libraries. It is

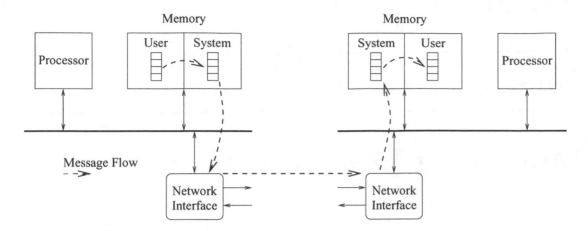

Figure 8.1. A model for message transmission/reception.

rapidly becoming the API of choice for portable parallel message-passing programming. Therefore a brief introduction to MPI is provided in the latter half of this chapter. A full introduction to the MPI standard can be found in many excellent texts and papers (e.g., [139, 324]). An understanding of the design and implementation of the messaging layer can help motivate and clarify the semantics of the MPI interface, and aid in developing efficient MPI-based programs.

8.1 Functionality of the Messaging Layer

The design of the messaging layer follows from an identification of the functions that must be performed in the delivery of a message. An example of the flow of data from the location in the source node's memory to the destination node's memory location is illustrated in Figure 8.1. While this represents only one implementation, it is fairly generic and captures functions found in many implementations. Let us suppose that a user process starts with a single word to be transmitted to a process being executed on another node. Transmission of this word is initiated via a call to a message passing procedure such as send(buf, nbytes, dest), where buf contains the nbytes of data to be transmitted to node dest. A message packet must be created (*packetization*) with a header containing information required to correctly route the packet to its destination. This packet may also include other information (e.g., CRC codes) in addition to the data. Access to the network interface may not be immediately available. Therefore the message may be buffered in system memory (*copying* and *buffering*) prior to injection into the network while the send() call returns to the main program. Until recently, network interfaces were largely treated as I/O devices. Traditionally, drivers that control such devices (*interface_control*) were privileged, and were available only through a system call (*User/Kernel Transitions*). More recently, the high overhead of such an approach has evolved into more efficient schemes for transferring control to message handlers that execute in the user address space. Once the network interface has the message packet, it is injected into the network where the routers cooperate in delivering the message to the destination node interface. When the message is received at the node, there must be some way to invoke the messaging layer software, e.g., interrupts, polled access, etc. Similar device driver services may then be invoked to transfer the message from the network interface into temporary system buffers (copied later into the user buffers), or transmitted directly to user buffers. Message transfer is now complete.

We can view each of the above functions as essential to the process of transmitting messages. Collectively they determine the minimum latency of a message, and the slowest component (invariably a software component) determines the maximum bandwidth. Consider the issues in each of these steps.

8.1.1 Packetization

Computation of the message headers, sequence numbers, parity, CRC, checks sums, etc. are overhead operations. When these operations are implemented in software they can exact significant performance penalties. Most interfaces now implement the majority, if not all, packetization functions in hardware. For example, in the Cray T3D, the interface hardware performs a table lookup to generate the routing tag [258], while it is possible to compute the CRC while copying data between buffers or during a DMA transfer [30]. Packetization overheads have been largely minimized in modern machines.

8.1.2 Network Interface Control

As an I/O device, control of the network interface can take one of many forms. Data may be transferred to/from the interface using direct memory access (DMA). In this case the software must initialize the appropriate DMA channel and initiate DMA access. This can be as simple as requiring two instructions: one to load the starting address and one to load the counter ([106] for the nCUBE-2). If DMA is only allowed into certain portions of memory, then interaction with operating system may be required. Pages used as targets of DMA or used to hold network interface data structures such as queues should be pinned down to prevent them from being swapped out.

Alternatively the interface may be memory-mapped and accessible from user space. The messaging software may initialize the interface with stores to memory locations corresponding to control registers. Message packets may be similarly transferred to interface memory. When a message is received, the messaging software may be invoked via interrupts, or polling. Programmed I/O is yet another way to access the network interface if it is treated as an I/O device. Note that these software overheads corresponding to network interface control are a function of mechanisms provided with the design of the node to transfer data to/from memory from/to I/O devices.

However, the network interface may not be on the I/O bus, but rather higher in the hierarchy such as on the memory bus [240] or integrated into the processor [40]. Such tightly coupled interfaces are capable of delivering a higher percentage of the physical network bandwidth, but remain specialized. Such organizations are also less likely to be compatible with evolving node architecture designs, but eliminate the performance bottleneck of slow (relatively) I/O buses. Examples of alternatives for integrating the network interface into a common node architecture are illustrated in Figure 8.2. However, this approach of interfacing via the I/O bus is becoming increasingly popular due to the ease with which it can be used with commercial off-the-shelf processor and memory systems, as well as widely used bus and interface standards.

8.1.3 User/Kernel Interface

A major performance issue is whether the message software must execute in the kernel context or whether it can be run from the user level. Early message layer implementations had the message handlers execute in the kernel necessitating expensive context swaps on each invocation. Messages

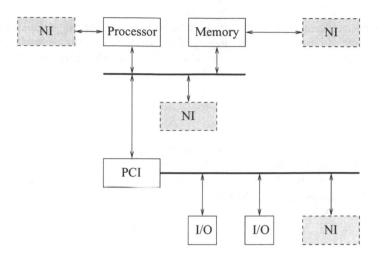

Figure 8.2. Examples of the placement on network interfaces. (NI = Network interface; PCI = Peripheral component interconnect.)

from the network were first read into system buffers and them copied into user memory data structures. There are active efforts in the design of several current-generation message layers seeking implementations where the message handlers execute in the user context and have direct access to the network interfaces from the user level. In addition to the substantial savings in buffering and copying, the high overhead of frequent context switches is avoided.

Some node architectures (e.g., Intel Paragon) make use of a coprocessor to execute all message-passing functions. The interaction of the coprocessor with the compute processor may be interrupt driven or polled. This permits significant overlap between the message processing and computation, however may do little for latency. Since the message processor controls the network interface similar considerations about protected communications arise when seeking to run message handlers in user context rather than the kernel on the coprocessor.

8.1.4   Copying and Buffering

Buffering policies are extremely important to the design of the message layer. They are crucial to both correctness as well as performance. Network routing protocols remain deadlock free under the *consumption assumption*: all messages destined for a node are eventually consumed. Deadlock freedom proofs that rely on this assumption (as do virtually all such proofs), are based on memory of infinite extent. In reality, memory is necessarily limited, and therefore some flow control between senders and receivers is necessary to ensure that a fixed amount of storage can be allocated, deallocated and reused over large numbers of messages while avoiding the loss of messages. Credit-based flow control, windowing schemes, etc. are examples of techniques for managing a limited amount of memory.

To ensure the availability of buffer space, the Intel iPSC/2 machines employed a three-trip protocol for sending long messages (> 100 bytes). An initial request message is transmitted to the receiver to allocate buffer space. On receiving a reply message, the message can be transmitted. Various token protocols can be employed where each node has a number of tokens corresponding to buffers. To send a message a processor must have a token from the destination. Tokens can be returned by piggybacking on other messages. The Fast Message library [263] uses a *return-to-sender* optimistic flow control protocol for buffer management. Packets are optimistically transmitted after allocating buffer space *at the source* for the packet. If the packet cannot be received due to the lack of buffer space, it is returned to the sender where it can be retransmitted, and buffer space is guaranteed to be available to receive the rejected packet. If the packet is successfully delivered, acknowledgments are used to free buffer space at the source. This scheme has the advantage of requiring buffer space proportional to the number of outstanding message packets rather than having to preallocate space proportional to the number of nodes.

The overhead of buffer management can be measured as the time spent in the message handlers to acquire and release buffers, performing status updates such marking buffers as allocated and free, and updating data structures that track available buffers. Generally memory is statically allocated to keep these management costs down.

In addition to the above functions, interprocessor communication is often expected to preserve other properties that may require additional functionality within the message layer. A detailed study of the source of software overheads in the message layer by Karamcheti and Chien [171] identified several functions implemented in the messaging layer to provide services that are not provided by the network, but are expected by the user-level programs. Detailed breakdowns of the cost of the message layer were also presented by Martin [225]. The analysis presented in these studies provides the following insights.

8.1.5 In-Order Message Delivery

Very large messages must be segmented into multiple packets for transmission and delivery. If the network does not guarantee delivery order, then some mechanism is necessary to reassemble the message at the destination. For example, adaptive routing may cause packets to arrive out of order since they may be routed along different paths. The use of virtual channels and virtual lanes may cause packets to overtake one another in transit. Reordering message packets may entail the use sequence numbers within the message packet headers to enable reconstruction at the destination. The messaging layer may have to buffer out-of-order packets so that packets may be delivered to the user-level programs in order incurring additional buffering delays. The costs occur as (1) time to place sequence numbers within packet headers, (2) latency/bandwidth effects due to larger headers, (3) buffering costs at the destination, and (4) checks for sequencing.

8.1.6 Reliable Message Delivery

Most message-passing programs are predicated upon the reliable delivery of messages to ensure correct execution. Reliable delivery may be ensured by acknowledgments from the destination and may require buffering messages until such acknowledgments are received. The cost of managing these buffers and the processing of acknowledgments can be charged as overhead due to to reliable delivery. The time to compute various checks e.g., CRC, if implemented in software is also charged to this category. Further, messages may be ejected from the network and rerouted in software in the presence of failures. These rerouting decisions are made by the messaging layer at the intermediate nodes. To detect messages that have been dropped in the network, the handlers may maintain timestamps of outstanding messages that were recorded when the message was injected into the network. Subsequent query of the timestamp and comparison with the current time involves a few handler instructions to detect lost packets.

8.1.7   Protection

The state of messages may be maintained in the network interface or in special pages in memory. In a multiprogrammed environment programs must be prevented from interfering with the message-passing state of other programs. When message handlers operate in the kernel context, this can be achieved via traditional mechanisms. When handlers operate in the user address space this can be more difficult to do. One approach [225] is to have a user scheduler that manages the network interface. Each process now must have a unique ID that is part of the message. When the message handlers receive a message, this ID is checked. If the message is not destined for the currently active process, it is stored in a separate queue. This queue is accessed by the scheduler, and stored as part of the saved network interface state for that process. From the point of view of assessing software overheads, the instructions for extracting and checking process IDs and storing messages can be attributed to process protection mechanisms.

The preceding discussion was the result of experiences with the design and implementation of messaging layers that focused solely on message transport. If we consider the support of message-passing APIs with additional semantics, other operations may have to be supported that will further contribute to the software overheads. The MPI standard presented in Section 8.4 will provide several examples of such useful semantics for message-passing applications.

8.2   Impact of Message Processing Delays

The aggregation of the various overheads produced by the software messaging layer as described above has a considerable impact on the performance of the interconnection network. An increase of the software overhead directly affects the communication latency. Moreover, it can even limit the throughput achieved by the interconnection network since the injection rate decreases as software overhead increases.

Consider an interconnection network with N nodes. Assuming that each node has a single injection/delivery port, a new message cannot be injected until the currently injected message has left the node. We are going to compute an upper bound for channel utilization as a function of communication start-up latency. In what follows, we will use the following notation:

N Number of nodes in the network

B_N Network bisection bandwidth

B_c Channel bandwidth

t_s Start-up latency

t_I Injection time

L Message length

p_B Probability of a message crossing the bisection

u Channel utilization in the network bisection

Assuming that there is no contention in the network and there is no pipelining in the network interface, the time required at the source node to inject a message is given by $t_I = t_s + L/B_c$. As each node has a single port, the maximum injection rate is $1/t_I$. For the sake of simplicity

Table 8.1. Upper bound for the average channel utilization as a function of message length.

Message Length (bytes)	4	16	64	256	1K	4K
Channel Utilization	0.0016	0.0064	0.0254	0.0998	0.3716	1.1623

let us assume a message destination distribution in which the probability of a message crossing the network bisection is p_B. Assuming that there is no contention in the network, the average utilization of channels in the network bisection is

$$u = \frac{N p_B L}{t_I B_N}$$

Now, let us compute channel utilization by using values taken from some real machine. We assume the following values:

$$
\begin{aligned}
N &= 256 \\
B_N &= 6,400 \text{ Mbytes/s} \\
B_c &= 200 \text{ Mbytes/s} \\
t_s &= 50 \ \mu s
\end{aligned}
$$

It should be noted that channel utilization decreases as communication locality increases. So, for this study we assume a uniform distribution of message destinations. For this distribution, we have $p_B \approx 0.5$. For these values, channel utilization is

$$u = \frac{256 \times 0.5 L}{\left(50 \times 10^{-6} + \frac{L}{200 \times 10^6}\right) \times 6,400 \times 10^6} = \frac{128L}{320,000 + 32L} = \frac{4L}{10,000 + L}$$

Table 8.1 shows the average channel utilization for different message lengths. Note that these values are upper bounds because they assume that there is no contention in the network. Obviously, channel utilization cannot be higher than one. Thus, the value displayed in the table for channel utilization when message length is 4 Kbytes means that the start-up latency is not the limiting factor in this case. Instead, channel utilization is limited by channel contention.

As can be seen in Table 8.1, channel utilization is very low for messages shorter than 256 bytes. Therefore, when messages are short network performance is limited by software overhead. In this case, there is no benefit in increasing channel bandwidth. The minimum message length required to achieve the maximum channel utilization in the absence of network contention is

$$L = \frac{10,000}{8 p_B - 1}$$

This length is equal to 3,333 bytes for a uniform distribution. This expression also indicates that when communication locality increases, the minimum message length required to achieve the maximum channel utilization also increases. Moreover, for traffic exhibiting a high degree of locality, full channel utilization cannot be achieved regardless of message length. This occurs when $p_B \leq 0.125$ for this example.

8.3   Implementation of the Messaging Layer

Traditionally, interprocessor communication has been treated in the same manner as input/output operations. The network interface was essentially a fast I/O device. Access to this device was protected and was granted through the operating system. This is still true for intercomputer communication in a LAN environment. However, the resulting high latency is difficult to absorb in parallel programs. This has spurred activity in the implementation of low-overhead messaging layers. Two notable examples include the Active Message layer [105, 106] and the Fast Message layer [263]. To motivate the implementation of these approaches consider the operational model of previous (and some current generation) message-passing machines illustrated in Figure 8.3.

While the user program nonblocking `send()` and `receive()` procedures execute asynchronously, the message layer is responsible for synchronizing the transport of messages. A nonblocking `send()` call immediately returns to the user program, but the message layer may need to buffer the message until the network interface is available. In this case the message is copied into system buffers to allow the program execution to proceed. Reception of a message will generate an interrupt to invoke the operating system handler that extracts the message from the network interface and buffers the message until a matching `receive()` is executed by the user program. At this point the message is copied into the user program data structures. The advantage of this approach is that messages can be consumed in an arbitrary order and at arbitrary points in time.

The designers of the first generation of streamlined messaging layers point out that this programming model is mismatched to the hardware capabilities leading to high overheads due to repeated transitions across the user/operating system interface and excessive copying and buffer management [106]. A closer look reveals that messages are transmitted by handlers and received by handlers. If these handlers were integrated into the programs themselves and user-level access provided to the network interface, computation could be smoothly integrated with computation. Buffering/copying can be minimized as well as the overheads due to system calls. This streamlined implementation can result in over an order of magnitude reduction in software overhead. Active Messages [105, 106] and Fast Messages [263] represent this approach to the implementation of the messaging layer.

Such messaging layer implementations are necessarily at a lower level of abstraction resembling interrupt handlers in invocation and use. Therefore, these procedures tend to serve better as targets for compilers and library developers than as a user-level API. Further, the use of industry standard

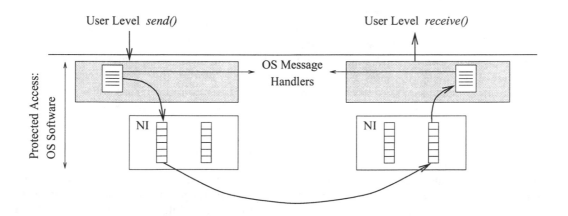

Figure 8.3. Messaging layer implementation. (NI = Network interface; OS = Operating system.)

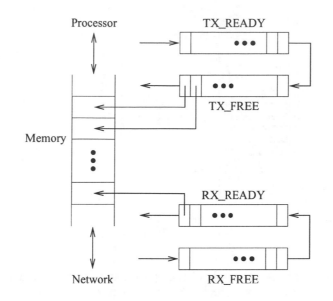

Figure 8.4. A model of the Medusa network interface.

APIs is very important for portability and development cost. Nonetheless, these lean message layers are available for the implementation of finely tuned, efficient parallel programs as well as serving as a target for portable message-passing APIs. The following two sections describe examples of implementations of Active messages and Fast Messages.

8.3.1 Example: Active Messages

The basic principle underlying active messages is that the message itself contains the address of a user-level handler which is to be executed on message reception [106]. Consider how this might work for the transmission of a one-word message. Let us suppose that the network interface is mapped into the user address space so that user programs have access to the control registers and buffer memory within the interface. The network interface receives a message into the local buffer within the interface. The message interrupts the processor and the handler specified within the message is invoked. This handler may read the message data in the buffer and assign it to a local program variable. Alternatively, if the message data provide a request for a value, the handler can immediately transmit a reply. In either case, the message need not be extracted from the interface and buffered locally in memory. Rather than using interrupts, the user program may be periodically polling the interface seeking messages. In this case, no interrupt is generated. There is no buffering and no invocation of the operating system. Execution of the handler is extremely fast. Compare this scenario with the one described in conjunction with Figure 8.3.

Given this basic model the following presents a synopsis of the design of an active message layer for the HP workstations (HPAM) using the Medusa network interface [225]. The network interface is mapped into the address space of the processor and is comprised of 1 Mbyte of VRAM partitioned into 8 Kbyte blocks (one per message). Four queues control the buffering and transmission of messages as shown in Figure 8.4. Queue entries are comprised of a memory block number and message length pair. Transmission proceeds with the construction of a message in a block and insertion of

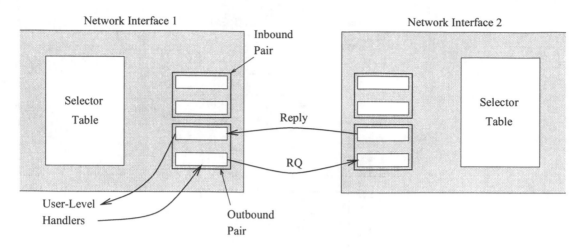

Figure 8.5. An example of the operation of active messages.

the corresponding queue entry in the TX_READY queue to initiate transmission. Completion of the transmission causes the queue entry to move to the TX_FREE queue. Messages are received by removing entries from the RX_READY queue and accessing VRAM. When the message block is empty the queue entry moves to the RX_FREE queue to be used by the interface to place incoming network packets in free blocks.

Active message implementations are based on a request-reply model of communication [106]. Every message generates a reply. Some messages naturally generate a reply such as remote read operations. However other messages do not, in which case a reply must be automatically generated. The HPAM implementation is unique in that it supports an all-to-all communication model. All buffers and book keeping storage are statically allocated. The following description describes a sequence of operations for implementing point-to-point communication.

The single request-reply protocol requires two pairs of buffers for communicating with each processor as shown in Figure 8.5. The outbound pair is used to transmit a message and store the reply. Similarly the inbound pair is used to store an incoming message and the locally generated reply. A descriptor table contains status information for each buffer, e.g., busy/free, time busy, etc. When a message is to be transmitted, the outbound buffer is marked as busy and the timestamp of the message stored in the descriptor table entry. The buffer remains allocated until a reply is received. Busy buffers cause handlers to block while still receiving other messages: to preserve deadlock freedom active message handlers cannot be preempted. Retransmission occurs after a timeout period. When a message is received (on an inbound channel), it contains a pointer into the descriptor table to enable checks prior to invoking the handler specified in the message, e.g., does it belong to the currently active process? This handler may now read the data in the inbound buffer, copying it to local data structures. The handler generates a reply if necessary (or one is generated automatically). All HPAM functions automatically poll the interface to avoid the high cost of the interrupts (approximately 10 μs in this case).

The preceding description is simplified, omitting many important checks and features unique to the specific implementation. However, the description does cover important aspects of the active message implementation: the implementation of a request-reply protocol, buffer management, and reliable message delivery mechanisms. Detailed issues deal with retransmission protocols, handling lost packets, and synchronized access to the interface in a multiprogramming environment. This

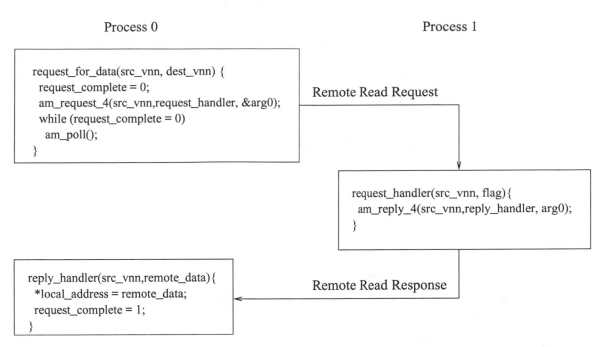

Figure 8.6. An example of the use of active messages.

latter issue is of particular concern in the design of the messaging layer. What happens when a message arrives for a process that has been swapped out? In this case the handler cannot be invoked. The HPAM implementation solves this problem by enforcing protection via an external scheduling daemon that is responsible for saving and restoring the network interface card state on each context switch. When a message arrives for a blocked process it is stored in a special queue for the blocked process. When the process is restored the HPAM layer first checks for messages in this queue.

The preceding example has provided an implementation of a message layer that permits user-level messaging with very low latencies: on the order of 29 μs per message. In other environments, e.g., networks using ATM communication, it may not be feasible to be granted user-level access to the network interfaces. In this case, careful streamlined implementation of the user/kernel interface is necessary for efficient implementations. Buffering/copying costs can still be significantly reduced.

Example 8.1

Figure 8.6 illustrates the logical flow of information through handlers in an implementation of the active message paradigm. Process 0 makes a request for remote data. The source handler initializes a completion flag (*request_complete*) and calls the active message procedure *am_request_4()*. The source now polls waiting for completion of the remote read. The message contains the name of the handler to be invoked by the destination process on message reception. This handler responds to the request message with a read operation to return the data value. This handler runs to completion. Note no buffering is necessary at this point. Similarly reception of the message at the host invokes the reply handler which assigns the message contents to a local memory location. Buffering and copying of message contents is avoided.

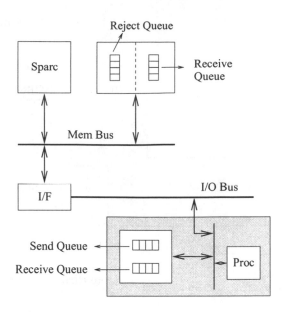

Figure 8.7. Implementation of FM on Myrinet.

The request handler within the destination process is only permitted access to the network to reply to messages, while the reply handler at the source process is prevented from accessing the network. This helps prevent cyclic dependencies and certain deadlock situations.

8.3.2   Example: Illinois Fast Messages

A second example of a streamlined messaging layer implementation is the Fast Messages (FM) library from the University of Illinois [263]. The FM procedures are similar to active messages in that a handler is specified within the message. However, there is no notion of request-reply message pairs. There are also no restrictions on the actions that a handler can take. Thus, program properties such as deadlock freedom are the responsibility of, and must be guaranteed by, the programmer. The reduced constraints can lead to very efficient implementations. In this regard it can be a viewed as low-level messaging library suitable as a target for compilers and library developers, rather than as a general-purpose user-level API.

The following description is of the FM implementation on Myrinet using Sun Sparcstations [263]. The Myrinet interface (the LANai) incorporates a processor datapath that executes a control program for injecting/ejecting messages from the network interface and setting up transfers to and from the host. The LANai memory is mapped into the host address space. Communication between the host and the LANai is across the memory and I/O buses of the Sparc. The implementation of the message function is via four queues as shown in Figure 8.7. The send and receive queues are in the network interface and the reject and receive queues are in host memory. The FM send functions write directly into the send queues in the network interfaces, initiating transmission. However on a receive, the interface will DMA the message into the receive queue in kernel memory (DMA is allowed only to/from kernel pages). DMA on reception permits overlap of computation and communication while direct stores to the interface on send calls removes the overhead of copying to the

DMA region. This is a good example of how precise trade-offs are clearly a function of the node architecture and operating system constraints.

The reject queue is used for implementation of the optimistic buffer allocation policy. Since there is no request-reply coupling, there is no running knowledge of the availability of buffer space on remote nodes. Therefore when a message is sent, buffer space is first allocated locally (the reject queue) prior to transmission. When a message is received and no buffer space is available, the message is rejected. The returned message is guaranteed to be received. In the current implementation, the distinction between request and rejected packets is not made in the interface but is done at the host. This choice was influenced by the relatively slow speed of the network interface processor and the ability to make use of block DMA transfers if messages were simply packed together without being interpreted at the interface. The user programs must ensure that the handlers that receive messages are invoked often enough to reduce the number of rejected packets. This approach requires acknowledgment of received packets to release buffers at the source. The current FM implementation optimizes acknowledgments by piggybacking these messages on top of normal traffic. The FM handler when invoked extracts all of the messages from the queue, and programs are expected to poll regularly to remove pending messages.

8.4 Application Programming Layer: The Message Passing Interface

The early success of the message-passing programming model in constructing applications led to several commercial as well as public domain efforts towards the implementation of message-passing libraries. Examples include Intel's NX/2 [275], PVM [334], and p4 [45, 46]. These concurrent efforts naturally shared many common attributes by virtue of support for a common programming model, while necessarily presenting distinctions in syntax, semantics, and constraints on their usage due to their developmental and evolutionary heritage. The ability to provide a portable implementation of message-passing libraries was demonstrated in principal with several of these packages. However, the diversity of available libraries remained a hindrance to the development of truly portable message-passing programs. Thus, a forum was created with members from academia, industry, and government. Through an open participatory process, the first Message Passing Interface (MPI) standard evolved and was completed in June 1994. A second revision subsequently appeared in June 1995 as the MPI version 1.1 standard.

The MPI standard is an application programming interface, not an implementation. "The MPI standard defines the user interface and functionality for a wide range of message-passing capabilities" [324]. In defining the syntax and semantics of the interface, the designers had to balance the impact of the specification on portability, efficiency, and ease of use. For example, data type information appears in the interface to permit support across heterogeneous environments where the value of an operand may have distinct representations on different machines, e.g., byte ordering. The standard refrains from specifying how operations must be performed, focusing on the logical behavior and what must be performed. The stated goals of MPI are illustrative and summarized from [324] below.

- The interface should reflect the needs of applications.

- The interface should not constrain the implementation, i.e., permit optimizations that may eliminate buffering, use extensive buffering, support concurrent communication and computation, etc.

- The specification should permit support for a heterogeneous environment.

- The semantics should be language-independent.

- The user should be relieved from the responsibility for reliable communication, i.e., checking or creating acknowledgments.

- Usage should not require much deviation from well-understood current practice.

- The interface design should be supportive of thread safety.

The standard remains focused on the logical aspects of message passing and avoids specifying or addressing system specific operations such as I/O operations, task management, and other operating system specific features. The standard also avoids explicitly addressing shared memory operations, although MPI can be (and has been) implemented on shared memory machines. Some of these (non-MPI) features could conceivably be offered as extensions with a specific vendor implementation. There are several excellent texts and publications that describe in some detail the rationale and specification of the MPI standard [139, 324], as well as tutorial descriptions on the use of MPI [139]. There is also a continually growing set of web pages that provides information on the standard, updates of evolving efforts, and links to a variety of tutorials, texts, and papers. An excellent place to start is at [243]. The purpose of this chapter is to merely highlight major features of the standard, and where possible, relate the interface features to the implementation of the messaging layer. As a result, we briefly describe some of the novel features of MPI. This includes general concepts, the structure of point-to-point communication, support for collective communication, and the availability of virtual process topologies.

8.4.1   General Concepts

An MPI program consists of autonomous processes, executing their own code in either the MIMD or SPMD programming paradigms. Each process usually executes in its own address space and communicates via MPI communication primitives. The basic communication mechanism within MPI is point-to-point communication between pairs of processes. The model assumes the use of a reliable user-level message transmission protocol. Furthermore, messages are *nonovertaking*. The implication of these semantics is that if single-threaded programs are written with point-to-point message-passing calls with source and destination process addresses explicitly specified, program execution is deterministic.

The community experience with the development of many successful message-passing library packages led to the precise definition and adoption of several logical concepts as an aid in thinking about and writing correct, efficient, parallel programs. At the highest level MPI specifies the notion of a communication domain. This domain is a set of n processes, which are implementation dependent objects. From the programmer's perspective, each process is assigned a rank in this group between $0 \ldots (n-1)$. Message-passing programs are written to send messages to processes identified by their rank. The group of processes is identified by an object called a *communicator*. Each process within a group can be thought of as possessing a communicator for the communication domain within which it is a member. The communicator is logically a set of links to other processes within the same group, i.e., communication domain, and is referred to as an intracommunicator. The relationship between intracommunicators in a communication domain is illustrated in Figure 8.8.

The notion of a communicator provides a very simple concept with which to structure groups of processes. Often it is desirable to allocate one subgroup of processes to a specific subtask while

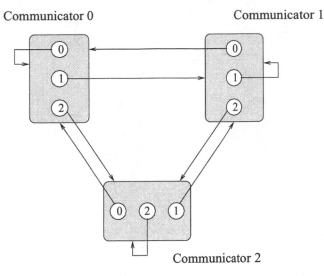

Figure 8.8. Representation of intracommunicators.

another subgroup of processes are tasked with a distinct computation. Processes within subgroups will communicate among themselves. There will also usually be communication between processes in distinct subgroups. In MPI terminology, each subgroup will have intracommunicators for communication within the subgroup. Each process must also possess *intercommunicators* for communication between subgroups. Logically the intercommunicator used by processes within one group can be thought of as links to processes within the other group and vice versa. This information captured within intercommunicators is illustrated in Figure 8.9.

The linear rank of a process within a group provides no information about the structure of the problem and a great deal of mental book keeping is often required to orchestrate interprocessor communication to follow the structure of the problem. We often keep a mental map or even a physical drawing of how processes must communicate. To facilitate such thinking, MPI provides for the specification and use of *virtual topologies* of processes within a group. This virtual topology can be used for realizing efficient assignments of processes to processors, or for writing scalable programs. A substantial body of work exists on algorithms for mapping parallel programs onto parallel architectures. Optimal mapping algorithms exist for many structured programs and networks. The specification of virtual topologies effectively provides hints to the run-time system about the communication structure of the program, enabling the optimization of program mappings. The fact that a logical communication topology is specified does not preclude communication between any pair of processes not connected within this topology. It simply means that this existence of communication between these two processes cannot be made known to the run-time system for use in computing process assignments. The use of topologies can also make it easier to write scalable parallel programs. Many parallel algorithms, particularly those that involve domain decomposition over large data sets, are structured with regular communication patterns. If programs are written parameterized by the topology, implementations are easily scaled to larger data sets. The availability of MPI functions to query and extract the rank of neighboring processes makes the development of such general-purpose programs relatively easy. While explicit support is available for the support of various multidimensional orthogonal topologies, MPI functions facilitate the specification and use of arbitrary logical process communication structures as well.

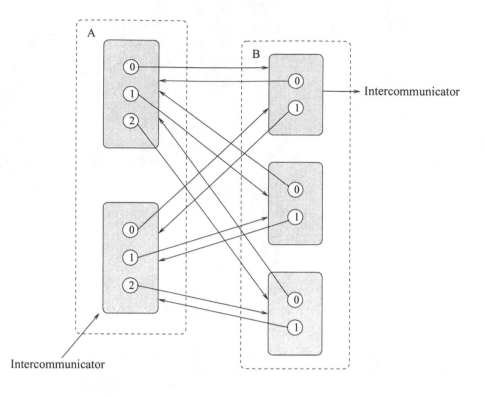

Figure 8.9. Representation of intercommunicators.

8.4.2   Point-to-Point Communication

With process groups, communicators, and logical topologies we have a set of logical concepts with which to describe the point-to-point and collective communication semantics of MPI. The basic constructs of MPI are best illustrated by examining an example MPI function. Consider the following blocking send procedure [324]:

MPLSEND(buf, count, datatype, dest, tag, comm)

IN	**buf**	Initial address of send buffer
IN	**count**	Number of entries to send
IN	**datatype**	Datatype of each entry
IN	**dest**	Rank of the destination
IN	**tag**	Message tag
IN	**comm**	Communicator

The above procedure transmits **count** number of entries starting at address **buf** to node **dest**. Note that the message size is specified as a number of entries and not as a number of bytes. Usage in conjunction with the **datatype** argument promotes a portable implementation. The language support provides definitions for a host of predefined data types, e.g., for the C language there exist MPI_CHAR, MPI_FLOAT, MPI_BYTE, etc. Facilities are also available for the user to define new datatypes.

In addition to specifying the source of message data, the call also specifies the dest, tag, and comm fields, which with the addition the source address form the *message envelope*. The comm argument is the communicator, and dest is the rank of the receiving process within this communication domain. If the communicator is an intercommunicator, then dest is the rank of the process in the destination domain (we must be careful since processes can belong to more than one domain and have different ranks in each domain). Thus, comm and dest serve to uniquely identify the destination process. The tag is simply an integer valued argument that can be used by the receiving processes to distinguish between messages.

The blocking semantics are with respect to buffer usage rather than temporal relationship between between send and matching receive operations. When a blocking send procedure returns, this does not necessarily imply that the matching receive procedure has started executing. A blocking send call returns as soon as the send buffer can be safely reused. Depending upon the implementation this may be the case after the message has been copied directly into the receive buffer, or after it has been copied into a system buffer for subsequent transmission. In the latter case the send may return before the matching receive has even begun executing, which may run counter to our expectations for blocking operations. A blocking receive returns when the buffer contains the message data. The blocking receive is shown below.

MPI_RECV(buf, count, datatype, source, tag, comm, status)

OUT	buf	Initial address of receive buffer
IN	count	Number of entries to receive
IN	datatype	Datatype of each entry
IN	source	Rank of the source
IN	tag	Message tag
IN	comm	Communicator
OUT	status	Return status

The receiver uses the message envelope to specify the sources from which messages will be received. Only messages whose envelopes match the receiver's request will be accepted. Receivers also control message reception via type matching. The source field may be a wild card, e.g., the predefined string MPI_ANY_SOURCE. In this instance, a message may be received from any source and it may not be possible to know a priori the exact size of the message. Therefore the buffer size is an upper bound on the required storage. Query functions are available to obtain information about received messages, e.g., MPI_GET_COUNT() returns the number of received entries in the receive buffer. The status field is a structure that contains additional information for the receiver.

There are a host of nonblocking calls that return immediately to permit overlap of communication and computation. These calls are supported by query functions that are used to determine if the operation has actually completed. Such calls are a necessary prelude to the reuse of buffers used in the nonblocking calls. These functions include MPI_WAIT() and MPI_TEST(). A common structure is to initiate a nonblocking send operation and continue with computation that is overlapped with the transmission. When the program reaches a point where the send buffer must be reused, queries are used to establish the completion of the previously issued send operation.

It is clear that the choice of buffering strategy has a significant impact on performance, particularly if there are known features of the application that can be exploited. To enable the programmer to influence the buffering strategy and thus performance, MPI offers several modes for send/receive operations. The preceding descriptions were that of *standard mode* send/receive calls. In this case, no assumption can be made with regard to whether the message is buffered or not. In *buffered mode* buffering can be provided within the user program. Therefore the user can guarantee that some buffering is available. *Synchronous mode* realizes the semantics of a rendezvous operation and ensures that a matching receive has executed. Finally, in *ready* mode, the user can assert that the matching receive has been posted. These distinct modes enable to user to exploit some knowledge of the application implementation in influencing the choice of the message transfer protocol used in a communication operation.

When communication repeatedly occurs between processes, e.g., in loops, some of the overhead involved in the message-passing implementation may be shared across multiple messages by using features for *persistent communication*. Calls to MPI functions are used to set up and retain the local parameters used for communication. The setup procedures (e.g., MPI_SEND_INIT () and MPI_RECV_INIT ()) return handles bound to arguments. These handles are used in subsequent MPI_START () calls. The semantics of each pair of persistent communication procedure calls is identical to that of a nonblocking send or receive.

It is important to understand that while the send and receive call semantics are well defined, this does not preclude the programmer from constructing erroneous programs. In particular, errant use of blocking receive calls can lead to deadlocked programs. There is also no notion of fairness in how receive calls match messages. These considerations should be taken into account when constructing programs.

8.4.3   Collective Communication

A specific class of communication patterns that have received increasing attention in the recent past has been the class of collective communication operations. As the name suggests, collective communication involves the aggregation or dissemination of data from/to multiple processes. The importance of collective communications is derived from the fact that many frequently used parallel algorithms such as sorting, searching, and matrix manipulation share data among groups of processes. Transmission of data to multiple destinations can be implemented with multiple calls for point-to-point transmission. However, these patterns of sharing data are very regular, and are important enough to merit special procedures.

In general, collective communication involves one or more senders and one or more receivers. Examples include broadcast of a single data item from one process to all other processes, broadcast of unique items from one process to all other processes, and the inverse operation: gathering data from a group of processes. There are also other operations that are collective in nature although no data are communicated, i.e., barrier synchronization. In general, we can identify the following common collective communication operations:

- Broadcast: a source process sends identical data to all other processes.

- Scatter: a source process sends a distinct message to all other processes.

- Gather: this operation is the reverse of scatter.

- All-to-all broadcast: every process communicates the same data to every other process.

- All-to-all personalized exchange: every process communicates unique data to each other process.

The MPI standard specifies support for all of these collective communication operations as well as other global operations such as reduce and scan operations. As an example, consider the following MPI call:

MPI_ALLTOALL(sendbuf, sendcount, sendtype, recvbuf, recvcount, recvtype, comm)

IN	sendbuf	Starting address of the send buffer
IN	sendcount	Number of elements sent to each process
IN	sendtype	Datatype of send buffer elements
OUT	recvbuf	Address of receive buffer
IN	recvcount	Number of elements received from any process
IN	recvtype	Datatype of receive buffer elements
IN	comm	Communicator

This operation is executed by all of the processes in the group. Each process sends a distinct block of data to each other process. The jth block in process i is sent to process j where it is stored in the ith block. The receiver buffer must be large enough to store sendcount elements from each process. This is the most general collective communication primitive. Suitable restrictions on messages, senders, and receivers realize the remaining collective communication operations. Corresponding MPI calls exist for each of these operations.

Another useful operation that does not involve the transfer of any data between processes is the barrier synchronization operation. The call appears as follows:

MPI_BARRIER(comm)

This procedure blocks until all processes within the group have made the call. The semantics of the collective communication operations are consistent with those of point-to-point operations, but are more restrictive in several ways. The message sizes must be known and match the receiver specified buffer sizes. These calls are all blocking calls and therefore must appear in the same order in all processes. Note that the tag does not appear in the above (or other) calls. These calls are also only available in the equivalent of standard mode. When a collective communication call returns, buffers can be reused (as in point-to-point calls). However, no assertion can be made about the status of other processes. Even though the operations are collective in nature, and logically may be thought of as occurring simultaneously, a user cannot assume that these operations synchronize processes in the same way that a barrier synchronization operation does.

The preceding description provides a brief overview of the major concepts underlying the MPI standard. Both Active Messages and Fast Messages present candidate implementation techniques for MPI. We can see that the abstractions supported by a user-level API are richer and more complex than the performance-driven, memory-to-memory data transfer view of lower level messaging layers. However, understanding their differences and relationships can be helpful in writing efficient programs. The complete list of MPI procedures can be found in [324] and many useful links to MPI-related material can be found on the Web at [243].

The following discussion presents an example of an MPI program template that contains the basic elements typically found in a message-passing parallel program. This template is for creating a parallel program based on a master-slave model of parallel program execution. This excellent template is presented at [245] and is shown below with a few additions. A more detailed exposition of such a template as well as the description of the local area multicomputer (LAM) implementation and development environment for MPI can be found at [245]. By filling in portions of this template with correct code we can create an executable MPI program.

```c
#include <stdio.h>
#include <string.h>
#include <sys/types.h>
#include <mpi.h>
#define WORKTAG         1
#define DIETAG          2

main(argc, argv)
int                     argc;
char                    *argv[];
{
    int                 pool_size, node_name_length, myrank;
    char                my_node_name[BUFSIZ];
    MPI_Init(&argc, &argv);     /* initialize MPI */
    MPI_Comm_size ( MPI_COMM_WORLD, &pool_size );
    MPI_Comm_rank(
            MPI_COMM_WORLD,     /* always use this */
            &myrank);           /* process rank, 0 thru N-1 */
    MPI_Get_processor_name ( my_node_name, &node_name_length );
    if (myrank == 0) {
        master();
    } else {
        slave();
    }
    MPI_Finalize();             /* cleanup MPI */
}


master()
{
    int                 ntasks, rank, work;
    double              result;
    MPI_Status          status;
    MPI_Comm_size(
            MPI_COMM_WORLD,     /* always use this */
            &ntasks);           /* #processes in application */
/*
 * Seed the slaves.
 */
    for (rank = 1; rank < ntasks; ++rank) {
        work = /* get_next_work_request */;
        MPI_Send(&work,         /* message buffer */
                1,              /* one data item */
                MPI_INT,        /* data item is an integer */
                rank,           /* destination process rank */
                WORKTAG,        /* user chosen message tag */
                MPI_COMM_WORLD);/* always use this */
    }
```

```
    /* Receive a result from any slave and dispatch a new work
     * request until work requests have been exhausted.
     */
        work = /* get_next_work_request */;
        while (/* valid new work request */) {
            MPI_Recv(&result,         /* message buffer */
                     1,               /* one data item */
                     MPI_DOUBLE,      /* of type double real */
                     MPI_ANY_SOURCE,  /* receive from any sender */
                     MPI_ANY_TAG,     /* any type of message */
                     MPI_COMM_WORLD,  /* always use this */
                     &status);        /* received message info */
            MPI_Send(&work, 1, MPI_INT, status.MPI_SOURCE,
                     WORKTAG, MPI_COMM_WORLD);
            work = /* get_next_work_request */;
        }
    /*
     * Receive results for outstanding work requests.
     */
        for (rank = 1; rank < ntasks; ++rank) {
            MPI_Recv(&result, 1, MPI_DOUBLE, MPI_ANY_SOURCE,
                     MPI_ANY_TAG, MPI_COMM_WORLD, &status);
        }
    /*
     * Tell all the slaves to exit.
     */
        for (rank = 1; rank < ntasks; ++rank) {
            MPI_Send(0, 0, MPI_INT, rank, DIETAG, MPI_COMM_WORLD);
        }
}


slave()
{
    double            result;
    int               work;
    MPI_Status        status;
    for (;;) {
        MPI_Recv(&work, 1, MPI_INT, 0, MPI_ANY_TAG, MPI_COMM_WORLD, &status);
    /*
     * Check the tag of the received message.
     */
        if (status.MPI_TAG == DIETAG) {
            return;
        }
        result = /* do the work */;
        MPI_Send(&result, 1, MPI_DOUBLE, 0, 0, MPI_COMM_WORLD);
    }
}
```

Example 8.2

This example utilizes the master-slave paradigm for implementing parallel computations. A master process farms out units of work to a set of slave processes. When all units of work have been completed, the master process sends messages that cause the slaves to terminate execution. This simple example contains elements that are representative of a variety of MPI programs. All MPI programs begin with an MPI_Init () and end with an MPI_Finalize (). Any MPI-related processing must be contained within the program between these two calls. Since each process executes the same code, the next two MPI calls determine the number of processes in this communication domain and the rank of the current process in this pool. The first three MPI calls above are generally found at the beginning of every MPI program and enable process specific execution. The fourth call can be used to obtain the processor node name of the executing process.

A process now first checks to determine if it is serving as the master or as a slave. We set the process of rank 0 to serve as the master. Accordingly one of the two procedures is called. Consider the procedure that implements the behavior of the master. The master process sends units of work to all of the slaves. Note that the first call in the master procedure determines the total number of processes in the domain. The next iterative set of calls uses point-to-point communication to send units of work to all slave processes. As long as there is work to be done, the master process receives results of work from the slaves and continues to provide each such slave an additional unit of work. When all units of work have been farmed out, the master process waits for the results from each slave, and sends a termination message to each slave as their final results come in. The slave processes simply receive messages and return results until they are informed that all work is completed and they may terminate. Note that on procedure return the last call made by both master and slave processes is MPI_Finalize ().

All communication is performed using point-to-point send and receive procedures. We can also think of an alternative approach where the master process utilizes an MPI_Bcast() call to terminate all slave processes after all results have been received.

The preceding example illustrates how processes can be written to have different behaviors as a function of their rank and of the environment in general. Care must be taken in reasoning about the concurrent execution of MPI programs. It is usually not possible to make assertions about what events in different processes are *taking place* concurrently. Rather it is usually only possible to make assertions about relative orders of events based on the partial sequencing produced by message-passing calls.

8.5   Engineering Issues

The goal is to get as close to the "bandwidth on the wire" as possible. The messaging layer software is a major determinant of how close we can actually get. The design of the messaging layer software is strongly influenced by the node architecture, and the set of services that the message layer is to provide to user programs. First consider the network interface. A portion of the message handler is devoted to interaction with the network interface in the transfer of messages to and from the interface. The cost of this interaction and consequent software overhead depends on how this interface is accessed. Interfaces may be memory mapped, register mapped, or tightly integrated within the memory hierarchy. Coordination of transfers between the interface and memory may involve polling, direct memory access, or interrupts.

In most commodity systems interrupts are expensive. Avoidance of interrupts will typically require the processor to poll the interface to receive messages. User programs must ensure that the polling frequency is tied to the available buffer space to prevent buffer overflow and/or substantial buffer management traffic between nodes. Flow control at this level must avoid loss of message packets due to lack of buffer space. Given the varying speeds of the processors, interfaces, and networks, sufficient buffer space will decouple the operation of all three components. Larger buffers will support lower polling frequencies. If packets are buffered for retransmission, increasing the memory can actually have the effect of reducing source buffering requirements for retransmission.

It is desirable that access to the network interface not be through the operating system. Invoking the operating system for services is expensive. While these costs can be amortized over large messages, short messages incur a significant penalty. The traditional justification for operating system access to the network interface is for maintaining protection between programs that share the interface. There have been recent techniques evolving toward minimizing the operating system interaction while still being able to provide protection between programs. One approach [29] is for programs to access the interface through system calls to set up protected information that is used on subsequent user-level transfers. For a sequence of transfers between a pair of nodes, these system calls need be made only once. A second approach is to implement protection mechanisms outside of the operating system and tag messages with what are effectively process IDs. The handlers that access the interface perform the appropriate checks before modifying any of the interface state [225].

However, in some systems there may be constraints derived from the operating system design that make it necessary to access interfaces through the operating system. For example, DMA mechanisms may be permitted only between the interface and kernel mapped portions of memory [263]. In the implementation of Fast Messages over Myrinet, this presented the choice between copying messages to kernel memory to use the DMA mechanism versus memory-mapped writes across the I/O bus to the interface. Pakin, Lauria and Chien argue that asymmetry in the manner in which send and receive operations are supported may be desirable. Any involvement by the node processor is time taken away from useful computation. However, rather than copying messages into system buffers for concurrent transmission, it may be just as efficient for the node processor to be involved in send operations, particularly for short messages, However, receive operations should use the interface mechanisms such as DMA since it can be overlapped with useful computation on a node. The node processor and handler software does not have to be invoked until the message is completely in memory. The utility of such asymmetry in the manner in which send and receive operations are handled is a function of the node architecture and operating system constraints. These may not be as much of an issue if the system is being designed from bottom up rather than having to use existing commercial systems.

In designing the message layer, there is a question of where the responsibility is placed for correctness, e.g., deadlock freedom. It is possible to design buffer management protocols that are fast but prone to deadlock if their use is not carefully orchestrated. Alternatively, buffer management protocols can be designed to prevent the loss of messages due lack of buffer space at the expense of additional checks and/or messages. For example, the request-reply protocol followed by active messages serves to prevent forms of deadlock. The choice is often resolved based on the user of the messaging layer. If the implementation is to serve as a target for library developers and compilers, implementors may choose faster options at the expense of relying on correctness by construction. If the implementation is to serve as an application level programming interface, preventive techniques may be used to ensure correctness with some relative loss in performance.

In addition to interface and buffer management, Karamcheti and Chien [171] identified several classes of services that may be enforced within the messaging layer, and therefore incur overhead. These include checks for in-order message packet delivery (reordering out of sequence packets), and reliable message delivery (handling and generating acknowledgments). If we were to closely examine the code for a typical message handler we could find instructions devoted to one or more of the following functions:

- Network interface control for transmission and reception

- Kernel interaction

- Buffer allocation/deallocation

- Copying

- Reliable message delivery

- Protected access to the network interface

- In-order delivery of message packets

- Deadlock freedom

When user-level handlers are used, in multiprogrammed systems messages may arrive for a process that is swapped out. The maximum performance from implementations such as active messages and fast messages is obtained when process scheduling across multiple nodes is coordinated with messaging operations [263]. This continues to be an active area of current research. The continuing gap between memory and processor speeds and the interest in shared memory parallel architectures has led to extensive analysis and characterization of the memory hierarchy. There are well understood techniques for managing this hierarchy and integrating the management within the compiler and run time systems. A similar set of techniques does not yet exist for the hierarchy of delays encountered by messages within the network. Interprocessor communication is still treated more like I/O operations rather than memory accesses, although attention has been drawn to this fact and we can expect to see increased activity in this area particularly as workstations clusters become viable parallel computing platforms.

8.6   Commented References

It is clear that software costs will be determined by the architecture of the network interface and the manner in which it will be integrated into the processing nodes. Several research projects have been studying efficient communication support by focusing on the design of the network interface. Central themes have included support for both the shared memory and message-passing paradigms, low overhead message initiation, overlapping communication and computation, and integrating I/O and interprocessor communication. Developments in these areas certainly will impact the design of future messaging layers.

An emerging class of flexible network interface architectures are those based on the use of an integer datapath in the network interface to run message handling software. Commercial examples include Myrinet [30] and ServerNet [156] while research examples include the Stanford FLASH [149] and Wisconsin Typhoon [289]. The Stanford FLASH project uses a special-purpose chip — the MAGIC chip — for handling communication, I/O, and memory transfers. The MAGIC chip comprises a cache-based processor operating in parallel with a fast pipelined datapath to handle data transfers. Protocol handlers for synchronization, message passing, and other operations execute within MAGIC out of local memory. The control path is faster than the datapath so the handlers themselves are not a performance bottleneck. The important property here is that the network is optimized to handle cache line size transfers. Message passing is really implemented on top of an optimized shared memory communication mechanism. Typhoon is a similar network interface and supports the Tempest user interface for both shared memory and message passing operations. Both projects explore the support of multiple communication paradigms and the customization of communication policies. We can think of active message handlers executing within such an interface although the FLASH interface does not support user-level handlers within MAGIC. Given the increasing high wire bandwidth of commercial networks, such datapaths must be quite fast so as not to be the bottleneck in injecting/ejecting messages to/from the network.

More tightly coupled register-mapped interfaces have been proposed in [151] and provides an abstract machine optimized for the support of short messages, such as those found in shared memory operations. Longer messages can also be handled although in this case the tight coupling with the processor datapath may encourage more efficient alternatives. The SHRIMP project [29] supports communication by mapping virtual memory pages of the sending process into the address space of the destination processes. Accesses to these pages can now be transparently captured and transmitted to the remote process, or can be buffered and explicitly transmitted with send() operations. System calls set up this mapping information and enforce protection policies in a multiprogramming environment. A tightly coupled network interface unit enables fast message initiation and support is readily provided for user-level messaging.

The availability of such interfaces serve to provide more efficient support for message passing. User programs still expect a certain set of services in support of the semantics of the message-passing libraries. The Active Messages [106] and Fast Messages [263] paradigms are really independent of the specific node architecture, although the efficiency of the implementations certainly depends on the node architectures.

PROBLEMS

8.1 Similar to the metric employed in the evaluation of vector machines, we can define the $n_{\frac{1}{2}}$ metric as the message length required to achieve 50% of the maximum channel utilization. Write an expression for this metric in terms of the model parameters provided in Section 8.2.

8.2 Assume the network is an $N = k^2$ node torus and that each physical link is implemented as two unidirectional, single-flit-wide channels. With uniformly distributed message destinations and B flit messages, write an expression for the injection rate in flits/node/cycle that will saturate the bisection bandwidth. Compute this value for a 1,024-node network with 32-flit messages.

8.3 Processor speeds have historically outpaced network speeds although that is changing. Suppose the processor speed doubles between system generations while the network bisection bandwidth increases by 50%, and the memory-network interface bandwidth remains constant. Discuss the effects on channel utilization and network throughput from one generation of the system to the next.

8.4 Often message-passing programs exhibit a great deal of temporal locality: many messages are transferred between a pair of processes with short intermessage intervals. What overheads in managing this message transmission can be shared across multiple messages, i.e., what benefits can be gained from MPI's concept of persistent communication.

8.5 Develop a simple model to quantify the benefits of persistent communication in terms of its effect on channel utilization.

Hint   Persistent communication effectively reduces the value of t_s in proportion to the number of messages that can share this overhead (Section 8.2).

8.6 Construct an example of the occurrence of deadlock using active message handlers that can be preempted.

8.7 The HPAM active message layer for the HP workstations statically allocates a request-reply buffer pair for every potential destination processor since the communication model is based on all-to-all communication. An outbound channel reserves a buffer for the expected reply. However, why is a reply buffer used for an inbound channel? You would expect that when a request message arrived, a reply would be automatically generated and transmitted by the handler. Why does this reply have to be saved in a buffer? When can this buffer be freed?

Hint   Consider the issue of reliable communication.

Chapter 9

Performance Evaluation

This chapter studies the performance of interconnection networks, analyzing the effect of network traffic and the impact of many design parameters discussed in previous chapters. Whenever possible, suggestions will be given for some design parameters. However, we do not intend to study the whole design space. Therefore, this chapter also presents general aspects of network evaluation, so that the reader can evaluate the effect of parameters that are not considered in this chapter.

As indicated in Chapter 8, a high percentage of the communication latency in multicomputers is produced by the overhead in the software messaging layer. At first glance, it may seem that spending time in improving the performance of the interconnection network hardware is useless. However, for very long messages, communication latency is still dominated by the network hardware latency. In this case, networks with a higher channel bandwidth may achieve a higher performance. On the other hand, messages are usually sent by the cache controller in distributed shared-memory multiprocessors with coherent caches. In this architecture there is no software messaging layer. Therefore, the performance of the interconnection network hardware is much more critical. As a consequence, in this chapter we will mainly evaluate the performance of the interconnection network hardware. We will consider the overhead of the software messaging layer in Section 9.12.

Network load has a very strong influence on performance. In general, for a given distribution of destinations, the average message latency of a wormhole-switched network is more heavily affected by network load than by any design parameter, provided that a reasonable choice is made for those parameters. Also, throughput is heavily affected by the traffic pattern (distribution of destinations). Therefore, modeling the network workload is very important. Most performance evaluation results only considered a uniform distribution of message destinations. However, several researchers have considered other synthetic workloads, trying to model the behavior of real applications. Up to now, very few researchers have evaluated networks using the traffic patterns produced by real applications. Therefore, in this chapter we will mainly present results obtained by using synthetic workloads.

Most evaluation results presented in this chapter do not consider the impact of design parameters on clock frequency. However, some design choices may considerably increase router complexity, therefore reducing clock frequency accordingly. Router delay is mostly affected by the number of dimensions of the network, the routing algorithm and the number of virtual channel per physical channel. The evaluation presented in Section 9.10 considers a very detailed model, trying to be as close as possible to the real behavior of the networks. As will be seen, conclusions are a bit different when the impact of design parameters on clock frequency is considered.

In addition to unicast messages, many parallel applications perform some collective communication operations. Providing support for those operations may reduce latency significantly. Collective communication schemes range from software approaches based on unicast messages to specific hardware support for multidestination messages. These schemes are evaluated in Section 9.11.

Finally, most network evaluations only focus on performance. However, reliability is also important. A wide spectrum of routing protocols has been proposed to tolerate faulty components in the network, ranging from software approaches for wormhole switching to very resilient mechanisms based on different switching techniques. Thus, we will also present some results concerning network fault tolerance in Section 9.13.

9.1   Performance Metrics and Normalized Results

This section introduces performance metrics and defines some standard ways to illustrate performance results. In the absence of faults, the most important performance metrics of an interconnection network are latency and throughput. *Latency* is the time elapsed since the message transmission is initiated until the message is received at the destination node. This general definition is vague, and can be interpreted in different ways. If the study only considers the network hardware, latency is usually defined as the time elapsed since the message header is injected into the network at the source node until the last unit of information is received at the destination node. If the study also considers the injection queues, the queuing time at the source node is added to the latency. This queuing time is usually negligible unless the network is close to its saturation point. When the messaging layer is also being considered, latency is defined as the time elapsed since the system call to send a message is initiated at the source node until the system call to receive that message returns control to the user program at the destination node.

Latency can also be defined for collective communication operations. In this case, latency is usually measured since the operation starts at some node until all the nodes involved in that operation have completed their task. For example, when only the network hardware is being considered, the latency of a multicast operation is the time elapsed since the first fragment of the message header is injected into the network at the source node until the last unit of information is received at the last destination node.

The latency of individual messages is not important, especially when the study is performed using synthetic workloads. In most cases, the designer is interested in the average value of the latency. The standard deviation is also important because the execution time of parallel programs may increase considerably if some messages experience a much higher latency than the average value. A high value of the standard deviation usually indicates that some messages are blocked for long in the network. The peak value of the latency can also help in identifying these situations.

Latency is measured in time units. However, when comparing several design choices, the absolute value is not important. As many comparisons are performed by using network simulators, latency can be measured in simulator clock cycles. Unless otherwise stated, the latency plots presented in this chapter for unicast messages will measure the average value of the time elapsed since the message header is injected into the network at the source node until the last unit of information is received at the destination node. In most cases, the simulator clock cycle will be the unit of measurement. However in Section 9.10, latency will be measured in nanoseconds.

Throughput is the maximum amount of information delivered per time unit. It can also be defined as the maximum traffic accepted by the network, where *traffic*, or *accepted traffic* is the amount of information delivered per time unit. Throughput could be measured in messages per second or messages per clock cycle, depending on whether absolute or relative timing is used. However, throughput would depend on message and network size. So, throughput is usually normalized, dividing it by message size and network size. As a result, throughput can be measured in bits per node and microsecond, or in bits per node and clock cycle. Again, when comparing different design choices by simulation, and assuming that channel width is equal to flit size, throughput can be measured in flits per node and clock cycle. Alternatively, accepted traffic and throughput can be measured as a fraction of *network capacity*. A uniformly loaded network is operating at capacity if the most heavily loaded channel is used 100% of the time [73]. Again, network capacity depends on the communication pattern.

A standard way to measure accepted traffic and throughput was proposed at the Workshop on Parallel Computer Routing and Communication (PCRCW'94). It consists of representing them as a fraction of the network capacity for a uniform distribution of destinations, assuming that the most heavily loaded channels are located in the network bisection. This network capacity is referred to as *normalized bandwidth*. So, regardless of the communication pattern used, it is recommended to measure applied load, accepted traffic and throughput as a fraction of normalized bandwidth. Normalized bandwidth can be easily derived by considering that 50% of uniform random traffic crosses the bisection of the network. Thus, if a network has bisection bandwidth B bits/s, each node in an N-node network can inject $2B/N$ bits/s at the maximum load. Unless otherwise stated, accepted traffic and throughput will be measured as a fraction of normalized bandwidth. While this is acceptable when comparing different design choices in the same network, it should be taken into account that those choices may lead to different clock cycles. In this case, each set of design parameters may produce a different bisection bandwidth, therefore invalidating the normalized bandwidth as a traffic unit. In that case, accepted traffic and throughput can be measured in bits (flits) per node and microsecond. We will use this unit in Section 9.10.

A common misconception consists of using throughput instead of traffic. As mentioned above, throughput is the maximum accepted traffic. Another misconception consists of considering throughput or traffic as input parameters instead of measurements, even representing latency as a function of traffic. When running simulations with synthetic workload, the *applied load* (also known as *offered traffic*, *generation rate*, or *injection rate*) is an input parameter while latency and accepted traffic are measurements. So, latency-traffic graphs do not represent functions. It should be noted that the network may be unstable when accepted traffic reaches its maximum value. In this case, increasing the applied load may reduce the accepted traffic until a stable point is reached. As a consequence, for some values of the accepted traffic there exist two values for the latency, clearly indicating that the graph does not represent a function.

In the presence of faults, both performance and reliability are important. When presenting performance plots, the Chaos Normal Form (CNF) format (to be described below) should be preferred in order to analyze accepted traffic as a function of applied load. Plots can be represented for different values of the number of faults. In this case, accepted traffic can be smaller than applied load because the network is saturated or because some messages cannot be delivered in the presence of faults. Another interesting measure is the probability of message delivery as a function of the number of failures.

The next sections describe two standard formats to represent performance results. These formats were proposed at PCRCW'94. The Burton Normal Form (BNF) uses a single latency versus accepted traffic graph. The CNF requires paired accepted traffic versus applied load and latency versus applied load graphs. Use of only latency (including source queuing) versus applied load is discouraged because it is impossible to gain any data about performance above saturation using such graphs.

Burton Normal Form (BNF)

BNF graphs, advocated by Burton Smith, provide a single-graph plot of both latency and accepted traffic. The X-axis corresponds to accepted traffic, and the Y-axis corresponds to latency. Because the X-axis is a dependent variable, the resulting plot may not be a function. This causes the graph to be a bit hard to comprehend at first glance.

Format

- X-axis: Normalized accepted traffic.

- Y-axis: Latency (not including source queuing).

- Labels: Points labeled with normalized applied load. For the sake of clarity, labels may be omitted when accepted traffic is equal to applied load.

Advantages

- BNF shows both accepted traffic and latency, before and after saturation.

- BNF requires only one graph.

- Easily shows curves of equal network population.

Disadvantages

- BNF graphs are more difficult for novices to interpret.

- Labels for normalized applied load can be distracting, especially when multiple curves are plotted on the same graph.

Chaos Normal Form (CNF)

CNF graphs display accepted traffic on one graph and network latency on a second graph. In both graphs, the X-axis corresponds to normalized applied load. By using two graphs, the latency is shown both below and above saturation, and the accepted traffic above saturation is visible. While BNF graphs show the same data, CNF graphs are more clear in their presentation of the data.

Format of first graph

- X-axis: Normalized applied load.

- Y-axis: Normalized accepted traffic.

Format of second graph

- X-axis: Normalized applied load.

- Y-axis: Latency (not including source queuing).

Advantages

- CNF shows both accepted traffic and latency, before and after saturation.

- CNF graphs are easily understood.

Disadvantages

- CNF requires two graphs to show performance data.

9.2 Workload Models

The evaluation of interconnection networks requires the definition of representative workload models. This is a difficult task because the behavior of the network may differ considerably from one architecture to another, and from one application to another. For example, some applications running in multicomputers generate very long messages while distributed shared-memory multiprocessors with coherent caches generate very short messages. Moreover, in general, performance is more heavily affected by traffic conditions than by design parameters.

Up to now, there has been no agreement on a set of standard traces that could be used for network evaluation. Most performance analysis used synthetic workloads with different characteristics. In what follows, we describe the most frequently used workload models. These models can be used in the absence of more detailed information about the applications.

The workload model is basically defined by three parameters: *distribution of destinations*, *injection rate* and *message length*. The distribution of destinations indicates the destination for the next message at each node. The most frequently used distribution is the *uniform* one. In this distribution, the probability of node i sending a message to node j is the same for all i and j, $i \neq j$ [287]. The case of nodes sending messages to themselves is excluded because we are interested in message transfers that use the network. The uniform distribution makes no assumptions about the type of computation generating the messages. In the study of interconnection networks, it is the most frequently used distribution. The uniform distribution provides what is likely to be an upper bound on the mean internode distance because most computations exhibit some degree of communication locality.

Communication locality can be classified as *spatial* or *temporal* [287]. An application exhibits spatial locality when the mean internode distance is smaller than in the uniform distribution. As a result, each message consumes less resources, also reducing contention. An application has temporal locality when it exhibits communication affinity among a subset of nodes. As a consequence, the probability of sending messages to nodes that were recently used as destinations for other messages is higher than for other nodes. It should be noted that nodes exhibiting communication affinity need not be near one another in the network.

When network traffic is not uniform, we would expect any reasonable mapping of a parallel computation to place those tasks that exchange messages with high frequency in close physical locations. Two simple distributions to model spatial locality are the *sphere of locality* and the *decreasing probability distribution* [287]. In the former, a node sends messages to nodes inside a sphere centered on the source node with some usually high probability ϕ, and to nodes outside the sphere with probability $1-\phi$. All the nodes inside the sphere have the same probability to be reached. The same occurs for the nodes outside the sphere. It should be noted that when the network size varies, the ratio between the number of nodes inside and outside the sphere is not constant. This distribution models the communication locality typical of programs solving structured problems (e.g., the nearest-neighbor communication typical of iterative partial differential equation solvers coupled with global communication for convergence checking). In practice, the sphere can be replaced by other geometric figures depending on the topology. For example, it could become a square or a cube in 2-D and 3-D meshes, respectively.

In the decreasing probability distribution, the probability of sending a message to a node decreases as the distance between the source and destination nodes increases. Reed and Grunwald [287] proposed the distribution function $\Phi(d) = Decay(l, dmax) \times l^d$, $0 < l < 1$, where d is the distance between the source and destination nodes, $dmax$ is the network diameter and l is a locality parameter. $Decay(l, dmax)$ is a normalizing constant for the probability Φ, chosen such that the sum of the probabilities is equal to one. Small values of the locality parameter l mean a high degree of locality whereas larger values of l mean that messages can travel larger distances. In particular, when l is equal to $1/e$, we obtain an exponential distribution. As l approaches one, the distribution function Φ approaches the uniform distribution. Conversely, as l approaches zero, Φ approaches a nearest-neighbor communication pattern. It should be noted that the decreasing probability distribution is adequate for the analysis of networks of different sizes. Simply, $Decay(l, dmax)$ should be computed for each network.

The distributions described above exhibit different degrees of spatial locality but have no temporal locality. Recently, several specific communication patterns between pairs of nodes have been used to evaluate the performance of interconnection networks: bit-reversal, perfect-shuffle, butterfly, matrix transpose, complement. These communication patterns take into account the permutations that are usually performed in parallel numerical algorithms [175, 200, 239]. In these patterns, the destination node for the messages generated by a given node is always the same. Therefore, the utilization factor of all the network links is not uniform. However, these distributions achieve the maximum degree of temporal locality. These communication patterns can be defined as follows:

- *Bit-reversal.* The node with binary coordinates $a_{n-1}, a_{n-2}, ..., a_1, a_0$ communicates with the node $a_0, a_1, ..., a_{n-2}, a_{n-1}$

- *Perfect-shuffle.* The node with binary coordinates $a_{n-1}, a_{n-2}, ..., a_1, a_0$ communicates with the node $a_{n-2}, a_{n-3}, ..., a_0, a_{n-1}$ (rotate left 1 bit).

- *Butterfly.* The node with binary coordinates $a_{n-1}, a_{n-2}, ..., a_1, a_0$ communicates with the node $a_0, a_{n-2}, ..., a_1, a_{n-1}$ (swap the most and least significant bits).

- *Matrix transpose.* The node with binary coordinates $a_{n-1}, a_{n-2}, ..., a_1, a_0$ communicates with the node $a_{\frac{n}{2}-1}, ..., a_0, a_{n-1}, ..., a_{\frac{n}{2}}$

- *Complement.* The node with binary coordinates $a_{n-1}, a_{n-2}, ..., a_1, a_0$ communicates with the node $\overline{a_{n-1}, a_{n-2}, ..., a_1, a_0}$.

Finally, a distribution based on a *least recently used stack model* has been proposed in [287] to model temporal locality. In this model, each node has its own stack containing the m nodes that were most recently sent messages. For each position in the stack there is a probability of sending a message to the node in that position. The sum of probabilities for nodes in the stack is less than 1. Therefore, a node not currently in the stack may be chosen as the destination for the next transmission. In this case, after sending the message, its destination node will be included in the stack, replacing the least recently used destination.

For synthetic workloads, the injection rate is usually the same for all the nodes. In most cases, each node is chosen to generate messages according to an exponential distribution. The parameter λ of this distribution is referred to as injection rate. Other possible distributions include a uniform distribution within an interval, bursty traffic and traces from parallel applications. For the uniform distribution, the injection rate is the mean value of the interval. Bursty traffic can be generated either by injecting a burst a messages every time a node has to inject information into the network, or by changing the injection rate periodically.

The network may use some congestion control mechanism. This mechanism can be implemented by placing a limit on the size of the buffer on the injection channels [36], by restricting injected messages to use some predetermined virtual channel(s) [74] or by waiting until the number of free output virtual channels at a node is higher than a threshold [220]. If a congestion control mechanism is used, the effective injection rate is limited when the network approaches the saturation point. This situation should be taken into account when analyzing performance graphs.

Message length can also be modeled in different ways. In most simulation runs, message length is chosen to be fixed. In this case, message length may be varied from one run to another in order to study the effect of message length. Also, message length can be computed according to a normal distribution or a uniform distribution within an interval. In some cases, it is interesting to analyze the mutual effect of messages with very different lengths. For example, injecting even a small fraction of very long messages in the network may increase the latency of some short messages considerably, therefore increasing the standard deviation of latency. In these cases, a weighed mix of short and long messages should be used. Both short and long messages may be of fixed size, or be normally or uniformly distributed as indicated above. Finally, it should be noted that message length has a considerable influence on network performance. So, the selected message length distribution should be representative of the intended applications. Obviously, application traces should be used if available.

In addition to the workload parameters described above, collective communication requires the generation of the set of nodes involved in each collective communication operation. The number of nodes involved in the operation may be fixed or randomly generated. Once the number of nodes has been determined, node addresses can be computed according to any of the models described above. For example, a multicast operation may start by computing the number of destinations using some statistical distribution. Then, the address of each destination can be computed according to a uniform distribution. Although most performance analysis have been performed by executing only collective communication operations both unicast messages and multidestination messages coexist in real traffic. Therefore, workload models for collective communication operations should consider a mixture of unicast and multidestination messages. Both the percentage of multidestination messages and the number of nodes involved in the collective communication operation should match as much as possible the characteristics of the intended applications.

9.3   Comparison of Switching Techniques

In this section, we compare the performance of several switching techniques. In particular, we analyze the performance of networks using packet switching, VCT switching, and wormhole switching. Previous comparisons [293] showed that VCT and wormhole switching achieve similar latency for low loads. For packet switching, latency is much higher. On the other hand, VCT and packet switching achieve similar throughput. This throughput is more than twice the value achieved by wormhole switching, which saturates at a lower applied load.

In this section, we take into account the effect of adding virtual channels. We will mainly focus on the comparison between VCT and wormhole switching. As mentioned in Chapter 2, routers implementing wormhole switching are simpler and can be clocked at a higher frequency. In this comparison, we are not taking into account the impact of the delay of router components on clock frequency. However, in order to make the comparison more fair, we assume that VCT and packet switching use edge buffers instead of central buffers. By doing so, the complexity of the flow-control hardware is similar for all the switching techniques. Also, as packet switching does not pipeline packet transmission, it is assumed that there are no output buffers, transmitting data directly from an input edge buffer through the switch to the corresponding output channel.

For packet switching, we consider edge buffers with capacities for four packets. For VCT, we consider edge buffers with capacities for one, two and four packets. For wormhole switching, we show the effect of adding virtual channels. The number of virtual channels is varied from one to four. In this comparison, the buffer capacity of each virtual channel is kept constant (4 flits) regardless of the number of virtual channels. Therefore, adding virtual channels also increases the total buffer

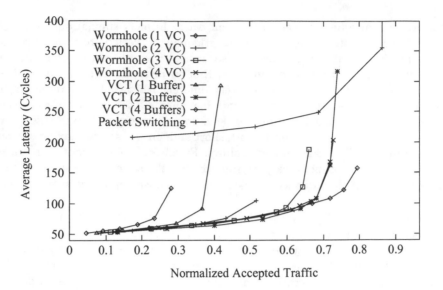

Figure 9.1. Average packet latency vs. normalized accepted traffic on a 16×16 mesh for different switching techniques and buffer capacities. (VC = Virtual channel; VCT = Virtual cut-through.)

capacity associated with each physical channel. The effect of adding virtual channels while keeping the total buffer capacity constant will be studied in Sections 9.7.1 and 9.10.5. The total buffer capacity per physical channel is equal to one packet when using four virtual channels. Note that a blocked packet will span four channels in wormhole switching regardless of the number of virtual channels used. Total buffer capacity will differ from one plot to another. The remaining router parameters (routing time, channel bandwidth, etc.) are the same for all the switching techniques.

Figure 9.1 shows the average packet latency versus normalized accepted traffic for different switching techniques on a 16×16 mesh using dimension-order routing, 16-flit packets and a uniform distribution of message destinations. As expected from the expressions for the base latency in Chapter 2, VCT and wormhole switching achieve the same latency for low traffic. This latency is much lower than the one for packet switching. However, when traffic increases wormhole switching without virtual channels quickly saturates the network, resulting in low channel utilization.

The low channel utilization of wormhole switching can be improved by adding virtual channels. As virtual channels are added, network throughput increases accordingly. As shown in [73], adding more virtual channels yields diminishing returns. Similarly, increasing queue size for VCT switching also increases throughput considerably. An interesting observation is that the average latency for VCT and for wormhole switching with virtual channels is almost identical for all the range of applied load until one of the curves reaches the saturation point. Moreover, when the total buffer capacity per physical channel is the same as in VCT, wormhole switching with virtual channels achieves a much higher throughput. It should be noted that in this case wormhole switching uses four virtual channels. However, VCT switching has capacity for a single packet per physical channel. Thus, the channel remains busy until the packet is completely forwarded. Although blocked packets in wormhole switching span multiple channels, the use of virtual channels allow other packets to pass blocked packets.

When VCT switching is implemented by using edge queues with capacity for several packets, channels are freed after transmitting each packet. Therefore, a blocked packet does not prevent the use of the channel by other packets. As a consequence, network throughput is higher than the one for wormhole switching with four virtual channels. Note however that the improvement is relatively small, despite the fact that the total buffer capacity for VCT switching is two or four times the buffer capacity for wormhole switching. In particular, we obtained the same results for wormhole switching with four virtual channels and VCT switching with two buffers per channel. We also run simulations for longer packets, keeping the size of the flit buffers used in wormhole switching. In this case, results are more favorable to VCT switching but buffer requirements also increase accordingly.

Finally, when the network reaches the saturation point, VCT switching has to buffer packets very frequently, therefore preventing pipelining. As a consequence, VCT and packet switching with the same number of buffers achieve similar throughput when the network reaches the saturation point.

The most important conclusion is that wormhole switching is able to achieve latency and throughput comparable to those of VCT switching, provided that enough virtual channels are used and total buffer capacity is similar. If buffer capacity is higher for VCT switching then this switching technique achieves better performance but the difference is small if enough virtual channels are used in wormhole switching. These conclusions differ from the ones obtained in previous comparisons because virtual channels were not considered [293]. An additional advantage of wormhole switching is that it is able to handle messages of any size without splitting them into packets. However, VCT switching limits packet size, especially when buffers are implemented in hardware.

As we will see in Section 9.10.5, adding virtual channels increases router delay, decreasing clock frequency accordingly. However, similar considerations can be made when adding buffer space for VCT switching. In what follows we will focus on networks using wormhole switching unless otherwise stated.

9.4 Comparison of Routing Algorithms

In this section we analyze the performance of deterministic and adaptive routing algorithms on several topologies under different traffic conditions. The number of topologies and routing algorithms proposed in the literature is so high that it could take years evaluating all of them. Therefore, we do not intend to present an exhaustive evaluation. Instead, we will focus on a few topologies and routing algorithms, showing the methodology that can be applied to obtain some preliminary evaluation results. These results are obtained by simulating the behavior of the network under synthetic loads. A detailed evaluation requires the use of representative traces from intended applications.

Most current multicomputers and multiprocessors use low-dimensional (2-D or 3-D) meshes (Intel Paragon [165], Stanford DASH [203], Stanford FLASH [192], MIT Alewife [4], MIT J-Machine [255], MIT Reliable Router [75]), or tori (Cray T3D [258], Cray T3E [312]). Therefore, we will use 2-D and 3-D meshes and tori for the evaluation presented in this section. Also, most multicomputers and multiprocessors use dimension-order routing. However, fully adaptive routing has been recently introduced in both experimental and commercial machines. This is the case for the MIT Reliable Router and the Cray T3E. These routing algorithms are based on the design methodology presented in Section 4.4.4. Therefore, the evaluation presented in this section analyzes the behavior of dimension-order routing algorithms and fully adaptive routing algorithms requiring two sets of virtual channels: one set for dimension-order routing and another set for fully adaptive minimal routing. We also include some performance results for true fully adaptive routing algorithms based on deadlock recovery techniques.

A brief description of the routing algorithms follows. The deterministic routing algorithm for meshes crosses dimensions in increasing order. It does not require virtual channels. When virtual channels are used, the first free virtual channel is selected. The fully adaptive routing algorithm for meshes was presented in Example 3.8. When there are several free output channels, preference is given to the fully adaptive channel in the lowest useful dimension, followed by adaptive channels in increasing useful dimensions. When more than two virtual channels are used, all the additional virtual channels allow fully adaptive routing. In this case, virtual channels are selected in such a way that channel multiplexing is minimized. The deterministic routing algorithm for tori requires two virtual channels per physical channel. It was presented in Example 4.1 for unidirectional channels. The algorithm evaluated in this section uses bidirectional channels. When more than two virtual channels are used, every pair of additional channels have the same routing functionality as the first pair. As this algorithm produces a low channel utilization, we also evaluate a dimension-order routing algorithm that allows a higher flexibility in the use of virtual channels. This algorithm is based on the extension of the routing algorithm presented in Example 3.3 for unidirectional rings. The extended algorithm uses bidirectional channels following minimal paths. Also, dimensions are crossed in ascending order. This algorithm will be referred to as partially adaptive because it offers two routing choices for many destinations. The fully adaptive routing algorithm for tori requires one additional virtual channel for fully adaptive minimal routing. The remaining channels are used as in the partially adaptive algorithm. This algorithm was described in Exercise 4.4. Again, when there are several free output channels, preference is given to the fully adaptive channel in the lowest useful dimension, followed by adaptive channels in increasing useful dimensions. When more than two virtual channels are used, all the additional virtual channels allow fully adaptive routing. In this case, virtual channels are selected in such a way that channel multiplexing is minimized. Finally, the true fully adaptive routing algorithm allows fully adaptive minimal routing on all the virtual channels. Again, virtual channels are selected in such a way that channel multiplexing is minimized. This algorithm was described in Section 4.5.3. Deadlocks may occur, and are handled by using Disha (see Section 3.6).

Unless otherwise stated, simulations were run using the following parameters. It takes one clock cycle to compute the routing algorithm, to transfer one flit from an input buffer to an output buffer, or to transfer one flit across a physical channel. Input and output flit buffers have a variable capacity, so that the total buffer capacity per physical channel is kept constant. Each node has four injection and four delivery channels. Also, unless otherwise stated, message length is kept constant and equal to 16 flits (plus 1 header flit).

9.4.1 Performance Under Uniform Traffic

Deterministic Versus Adaptive Routing

Figure 9.2 shows the average message latency versus normalized accepted traffic on a 2-D mesh when using a uniform distribution for message destination. The graph shows the performance of deterministic routing with one and two virtual channels, and fully adaptive routing (with two virtual channels). As can be seen, the use of two virtual channels almost doubles the throughput of the deterministic routing algorithm. The main reason is that when messages block, channel bandwidth is not wasted because other messages are allowed to use that bandwidth. Therefore adding a few virtual channels reduces contention and increases channel utilization. The adaptive algorithm achieves 88% of the throughput achieved by the deterministic algorithm with the same number of virtual channels. However, latency is almost identical, being slightly lower for the adaptive algorithm. So, the additional flexibility of fully adaptive routing is not able to improve performance when traffic is uniformly distributed. The reason is that the network is almost uniformly loaded. Additionally, meshes are not regular, and adaptive algorithms tend to concentrate traffic in the central part of the network bisection, thus reducing channel utilization in the borders of the mesh.

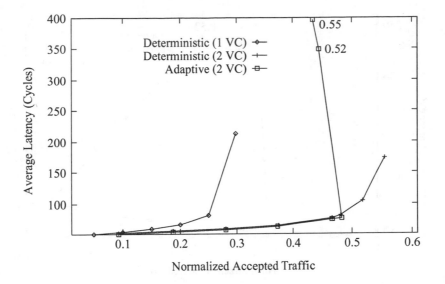

Figure 9.2. Average message latency vs. normalized accepted traffic on a 16×16 mesh for a uniform distribution of message destinations.

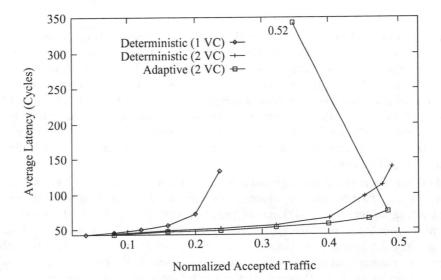

Figure 9.3. Average message latency vs. normalized accepted traffic on an $8 \times 8 \times 8$ mesh for a uniform distribution of message destinations.

It should be noted that there is a small performance degradation when the adaptive algorithm reaches the saturation point. If injection rate is sustained at this point, latency increases considerably while accepted traffic decreases. This behavior is typical of routing algorithms that allow cyclic dependencies between channels, and will be studied in Section 9.9.

Figure 9.3 shows the average message latency versus normalized accepted traffic on a 3-D mesh

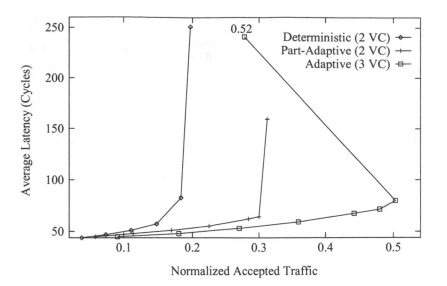

Figure 9.4. Average message latency vs. normalized accepted traffic on a 16×16 torus for a uniform distribution of message destinations.

when using a uniform distribution for message destination. This graph is quite similar to the one for 2-D meshes. However, there are some significant differences. The advantages of using two virtual channels in the deterministic algorithm are more noticeable on 3-D meshes. In this case, throughput is doubled. Also, the fully adaptive algorithm achieves the same throughput as the deterministic algorithm with the same number of virtual channels. The latency reduction achieved by the fully adaptive routing algorithm is also more noticeable on 3-D meshes. The reason is that messages have an additional channel to choose from at most intermediate nodes. Again, there is some performance degradation when the adaptive algorithm reaches the saturation point. This degradation is more noticeable than on 2-D meshes.

Figure 9.4 shows the average message latency versus normalized accepted traffic on a 2-D torus when using a uniform distribution for message destination. The graph shows the performance of deterministic routing with two virtual channels, partially adaptive routing with two virtual channels, and fully adaptive routing with three virtual channels. Both partially adaptive and fully adaptive algorithms considerably increase performance over the deterministic one. The partially adaptive algorithm increases throughput by 56%. The reason is that channel utilization is unbalanced in the deterministic routing algorithm. However, the partially adaptive algorithm allows most messages to choose between two virtual channels instead of one, therefore reducing contention and increasing channel utilization. Note that the additional flexibility is achieved without increasing the number of virtual channels. The fully adaptive algorithm increases throughput over the deterministic one by a factor of 2.5. This considerable improvement is mainly due to the ability to cross dimensions in any order. Unlike meshes, tori are regular topologies. So, adaptive algorithms are able to improve channel utilization by distributing traffic more uniformly across the network. Partially adaptive and fully adaptive algorithms also achieve a reduction in message latency with respect to the deterministic one for the full range of network load. Similarly, the fully adaptive algorithm reduces latency with respect to the partially adaptive one. However, performance degradation beyond the saturation point reduces accepted traffic to 55% of its maximum value.

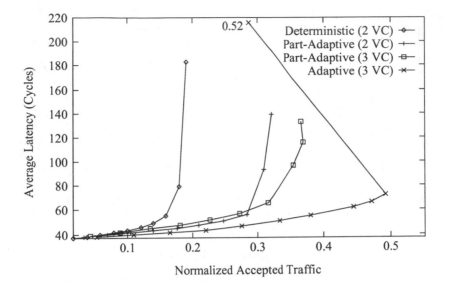

Figure 9.5. Average message latency vs. normalized accepted traffic on an $8 \times 8 \times 8$ torus for a uniform distribution of message destinations.

Figure 9.5 shows the average message latency versus normalized accepted traffic on a 3-D torus when using a uniform distribution for message destination. In addition to the routing algorithms analyzed in Figure 9.4, this graph also shows the performance of the partially adaptive routing algorithm with three virtual channels. Similarly to meshes, adaptive routing algorithms perform comparatively better on a 3-D torus than on a 2-D torus. In this case, the partially adaptive and fully adaptive algorithms increase throughput by factors of 1.7 and 2.6, respectively, over the deterministic one. Latency reduction is also more noticeable than on 2-D torus. This graph also shows that adding one virtual channel to the partially adaptive algorithm does not improve performance significantly. Although throughput increases by 18%, latency is also increased. The reason is that the partially adaptive algorithm with two virtual channels already allows the use of two virtual channels to most messages, therefore allowing them to share channel bandwidth. So, adding another virtual channel has a small impact on performance. The effect of adding virtual channels will be analyzed in more detail in Section 9.7.1. This result is similar for other traffic distributions. Therefore, in what follows we will only consider the partially adaptive algorithm with two virtual channels. This result also confirms that the improvement achieved by the fully adaptive algorithm is mainly due to the ability to cross dimensions in any order.

The relative behavior of deterministic and adaptive routing algorithms on 2-D and 3-D meshes and tori when message destinations are uniformly distributed is similar for other traffic distributions. In what follows, we will only present simulation results for a single topology. We have chosen the 3-D torus because most performance results published up to now focused on meshes. So, unless otherwise stated, performance results correspond to a 512-node 3-D torus.

Figure 9.6 shows the standard deviation of latency versus normalized accepted traffic on a 3-D torus when using a uniform distribution for message destination. The scale for the Y-axis has been selected to make differences more visible. As can be seen, a higher degree of adaptivity also reduces the deviation with respect to the mean value. The reason is that adaptive routing considerably reduces contention at intermediate nodes, making latency more predictable. This occurs in all the

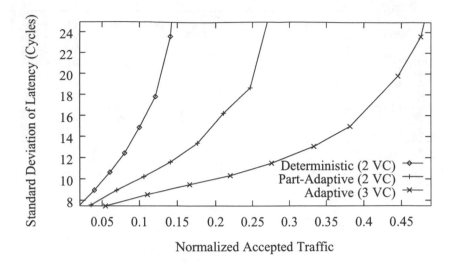

Figure 9.6. Standard deviation of latency vs. normalized accepted traffic on an $8 \times 8 \times 8$ torus for a uniform distribution of destinations.

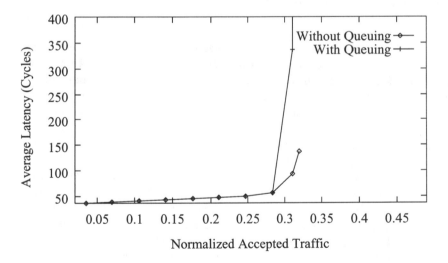

Figure 9.7. Average message latency vs. normalized accepted traffic considering and without considering queuing time at the source node.

simulations we run. So, in what follows, we will only present graphs for the average message latency.

In Figure 9.5, latency is measured since a message is injected into the network. It does not consider queuing time at the source node. When queuing time is considered, latency should not differ significantly unless the network is close to saturation. When the network is close to saturation, queuing time increases considerably. Figure 9.7 shows the average message latency versus normalized accepted traffic for the partially adaptive algorithm on a 3-D torus. This figure shows that latency is not affected by queuing time unless the network is close to saturation.

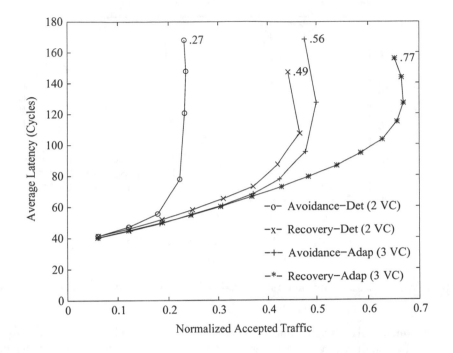

Figure 9.8. Average message latency vs. normalized accepted traffic on an $8 \times 8 \times 8$ torus for a uniform distribution of message destinations.

Deadlock Avoidance Versus Deadlock Recovery

Figure 9.8 plots the average message latency versus normalized accepted traffic for deadlock recovery-based and avoidance-based deterministic and adaptive routing algorithms. The simulations are based on a 3-D torus (512 nodes) with uniform traffic distribution and 16-flit messages. Each node has a single injection and delivery channel. The timeout used for deadlock detection is 25 cycles. The recovery-based deterministic routing algorithm with two virtual channels is able to use both of the virtual channels without restriction and is therefore able to achieve a 100% improvement in throughput over avoidance-based deterministic routing. Avoidance-based fully adaptive routing is able to achieve a slightly higher throughput and lower latency than recovery-based deterministic routing when using an additional virtual channel. Note that this algorithm allows unrestricted adaptive routing on only one of its three virtual channels. By freely using all three virtual channels, recovery-based true fully adaptive routing is able to achieve a 34% higher throughput than its avoidance-based counterpart.

These results show the potential improvement that can be achieved by using deadlock recovery techniques like Disha to handle deadlocks. It should be noted however that a single injection/delivery channel per node has been used in the simulations. If the number of injection/delivery channels per node is increased, the additional traffic injected into the network increases the probability of deadlock detection at saturation, and deadlock buffers are unable to recover from deadlock fast enough. Similarly, when messages are long, deadlock buffers are occupied for long time every time a deadlock is recovered from, thus degrading performance considerably when the network reaches saturation. In this case, avoidance-based adaptive routing algorithms usually achieve better performance than recovery-based algorithms. This does not mean that recovery-based algorithms are not useful as

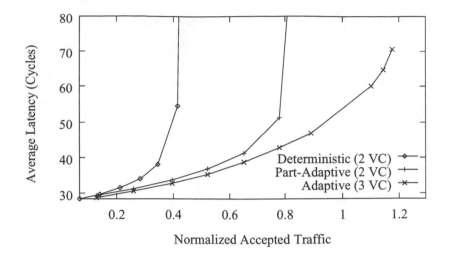

Figure 9.9. Average message latency vs. normalized accepted traffic for local traffic (side = 4).

general purpose routing algorithms. Simply, currently available techniques are not able to recover from deadlock fast enough when messages are long or when several injection/delivery channels per node are used. The main reason is that currently available deadlock detection techniques detect many false deadlocks, therefore saturating the bandwidth provided by the deadlock buffers. However, this situation may change when more powerful techniques for deadlock detection are developed. In what follows, we will only analyze avoidance-based routing algorithms.

9.4.2   Performance Under Local Traffic

Figure 9.9 shows the average message latency versus normalized accepted traffic when messages are sent locally. In this case, message destinations are uniformly distributed inside a cube centered at the source node with side equal to four channels.

The partially adaptive algorithm doubles throughput with respect to the deterministic one when messages are sent locally. The fully adaptive algorithm performs even better, reaching a throughput three times higher than the deterministic algorithm, and 50% higher than the partially adaptive algorithm. Latency is also smaller for the full range of accepted traffic.

When locality increases even more, the benefits of using adaptive algorithms are smaller because the distance between source and destination nodes are short, and the number of alternative paths is much smaller. Figure 9.10 shows the average message latency versus normalized accepted traffic when messages are uniformly distributed inside a cube centered at the source node with side equal to two channels. In this case, partially and fully adaptive algorithms perform almost the same. All the improvement with respect to the deterministic algorithm comes from a better utilization of virtual channels.

9.4.3   Performance Under Nonuniform Traffic

As stated in [74], adaptive routing is especially interesting when traffic is not uniform. Figures 9.11 and 9.12 compare the performance of routing algorithms for the bit-reversal and perfect-shuffle

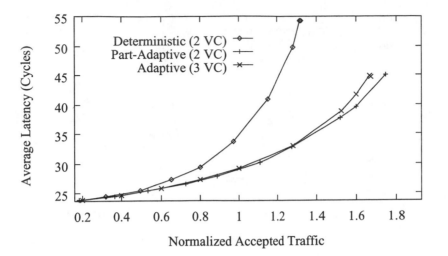

Figure 9.10. Average message latency vs. normalized accepted traffic for local traffic (side = 2).

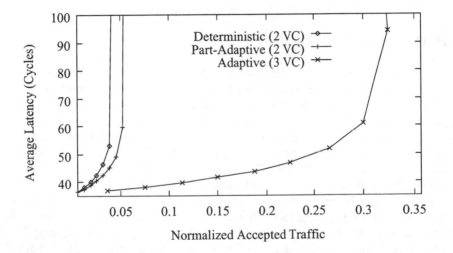

Figure 9.11. Average message latency vs. normalized accepted traffic for the bit-reversal traffic pattern.

communication patterns, respectively. In both cases, the deterministic and partially adaptive algorithms achieve poor performance because both of them offer a single physical path for every source/destination pair.

The fully adaptive algorithm increases throughput by a factor of 2.25 with respect to the deterministic algorithm when using the perfect-shuffle communication pattern, and it increases throughput by a factor of 8 in the bit-reversal communication pattern. Standard deviation of message latency is also much smaller for the fully adaptive algorithm. Finally, note that there is no significant performance degradation when the fully adaptive algorithm reaches the saturation point, especially for the perfect-shuffle communication pattern.

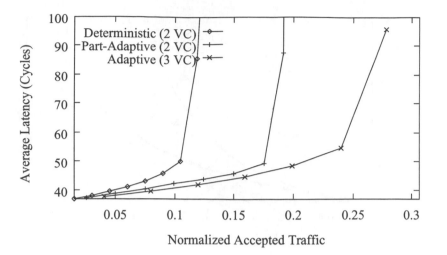

Figure 9.12. Average message latency vs. normalized accepted traffic for the perfect-shuffle traffic pattern.

9.5   Effect of Message Length

In this section we analyze the effect of message length on performance. We will only consider the traffic patterns for which the adaptive algorithm behaves more differently: uniform distribution and very local traffic (side = 2). Figures 9.13 and 9.14 show the average message latency divided by message length for uniform and local traffic, respectively. For the sake of clarity, plots only show the behavior of deterministic and fully adaptive algorithms with short (16 flits) and long (256 flits) messages. We also run simulations for other message lengths. For 64-flit messages, plots were close to the plots for 256-flit messages. For 128-flit messages, plots almost overlapped to ones for 256-flit messages. Similar results were obtained for messages longer than 256 flits.

The average flit latency is smaller for long messages. The reason is that messages are pipelined. Path setup time is amortized among more flits when messages are long. Moreover, data flits can advance faster than message headers because headers have to be routed, waiting for the routing control unit to compute the output channel, and possibly waiting for the output channel to become free. Therefore, when the header reaches the destination node, data flits advance faster, thus favoring long messages. Throughput is also smaller for short messages when the deterministic algorithm is used. However, the fully adaptive algorithm performs comparatively better for short messages, achieving almost the same throughput for short and long messages. Hence, this routing algorithm is more robust against variations in message size. This is due to the ability of the adaptive algorithm to use alternative paths. As a consequence, header blocking time is much smaller than for the deterministic algorithm, achieving a better channel utilization.

9.6   Effect of Network Size

In this section we study the performance of routing algorithms when network size increases. Figure 9.15 shows the average message latency versus normalized accepted traffic on a 16-ary 3-cube (4096 nodes) when using a uniform distribution for message destination.

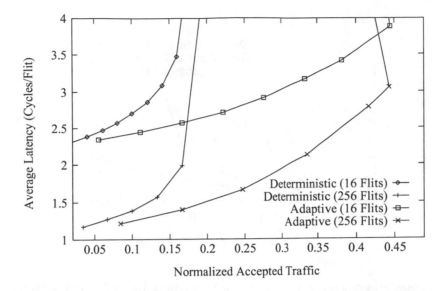

Figure 9.13. Average message latency divided by message length vs. normalized accepted traffic for a uniform distribution of message destinations.

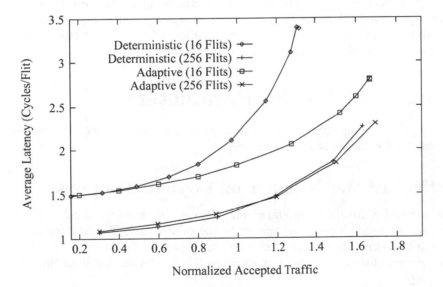

Figure 9.14. Average message latency divided by message length vs. normalized accepted traffic for local traffic (side = 2).

The shape of the plots and the relative behavior of routing algorithms are similar to the ones for networks with 512 nodes (Figure 9.5). Although normalized throughput is approximately the same, absolute throughput is approximately half the value obtained for 512 nodes. The reason is that there are twice as many nodes in each dimension and the average distance traveled by each message is doubled. Also, bisection bandwidth increases by a factor of four while the number of nodes

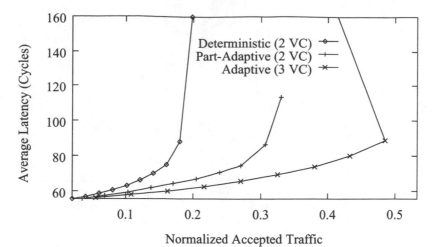

Figure 9.15. Average message latency vs. normalized accepted traffic for a uniform distribution of message destinations. Network size = 4K nodes.

sending messages across the bisection increases by a factor of eight. However, latency only increases by 45% on average, clearly showing the advantages of message pipelining across the network. In summary, scalability is acceptable when traffic is uniformly distributed. However, the only way to make networks really scalable is by exploiting communication locality.

9.7 Impact of Design Parameters

This section analyzes the impact of several design parameters on network performance: number of virtual channels, number of ports and buffer size.

9.7.1 Effect of the Number of Virtual Channels

Splitting each physical channel into several virtual channels increases the number of routing choices, allowing messages to pass blocked messages. On the other hand, flits from several messages are multiplexed onto the same physical channel, slowing down both messages. The effect of increasing the number of virtual channels has been analyzed in [73] for deterministic routing algorithms on a 2-D mesh topology.

In this section, we analyze the effect of increasing the number of virtual channels on all the algorithms under study, using a uniform distribution of message destinations. As in [73], we assume that the total buffer capacity associated with each physical channel is kept constant, and equal to 16 flits (15 flits and 18 flits for three and six virtual channels, respectively).

Figure 9.16 shows the behavior of the deterministic algorithm with two, four, six, and eight virtual channels per physical channel. Note that the number of virtual channels for this algorithm must be even. The higher the number of virtual channels, the higher the throughput. However, the highest increment is produced when changing from two to four virtual channels. Also, latency slightly increases when adding virtual channels. These results are very similar to the ones obtained in [73]. The explanation is simple: Adding the first few virtual channels allows messages to pass

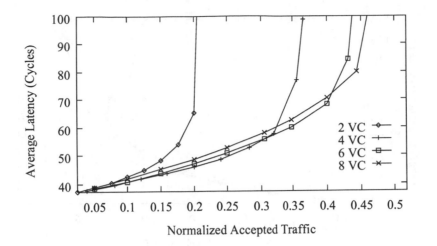

Figure 9.16. Effect of the number of virtual channels on the deterministic algorithm. Plots show the average message latency vs. normalized accepted traffic for a uniform distribution of message destinations.

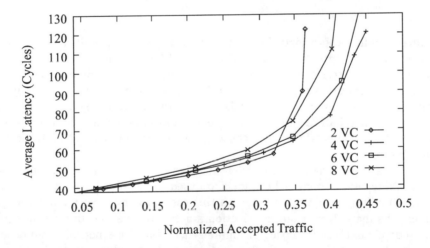

Figure 9.17. Effect of the number of virtual channels on the partially adaptive algorithm. Plots show the average message latency vs. normalized accepted traffic for a uniform distribution of message destinations.

blocked messages, increasing channel utilization and throughput. Adding more virtual channels does not increase routing flexibility considerably. Moreover, buffer size is smaller and blocked messages occupy more channels. As a result, throughput increases by a small amount. Adding virtual channels also has a negative effect [89]. Bandwidth is shared among several messages. However, bandwidth sharing is not uniform. A message may be crossing several physical channels with different degrees of multiplexing. The more multiplexed channel becomes a bottleneck, slightly increasing latency.

Figure 9.17 shows the behavior of the partially adaptive algorithm with two, four, six, and eight virtual channels. In this case, adding two virtual channels increases throughput by a small

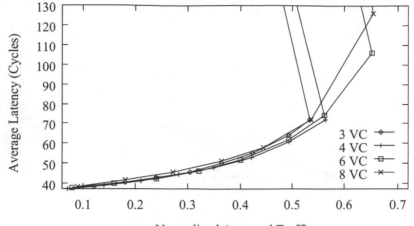

Figure 9.18. Effect of the number of virtual channels on the fully adaptive algorithm. Plots show the average message latency vs. normalized accepted traffic for a uniform distribution of message destinations.

amount. However, adding more virtual channels increases latency, and even reduces throughput. Moreover, the partially adaptive algorithm with two and four virtual channels achieves almost the same throughput as the deterministic algorithm with four and eight virtual channels, respectively. Note that the partially adaptive algorithm is identical to the deterministic one, except that it allows most messages to share all the virtual channels. Therefore, it effectively allows the same degree of channel multiplexing using half the number of virtual channels as the deterministic algorithm. When more than four virtual channels are used, the negative effects of channel multiplexing mentioned above outweigh the benefits.

Figure 9.18 shows the behavior of the fully adaptive algorithm with three, four, six, and eight virtual channels. Note that two virtual channels are used for deadlock avoidance and the remaining channels are used for fully adaptive routing. In this case, latency is very similar regardless of the number of virtual channels. Note that the selection function selects the output channel for a message in such a way that channel multiplexing is minimized. As a consequence, channel multiplexing is more uniform and channel utilization is higher, obtaining a higher throughput than the other routing algorithms. As indicated in Section 9.4.1, throughput decreases when the fully adaptive algorithm reaches the saturation point. This degradation can be clearly observed in Figure 9.18. Also, as indicated in [92], it can be seen that increasing the number of virtual channels increases throughput, and even removes performance degradation.

9.7.2   Effect of the Number of Ports

Network hardware has become very fast. In some cases, network performance may be limited by the bandwidth available at source and destination nodes to inject and deliver messages, respectively. In this section, we analyze the effect of that bandwidth. As fully adaptive algorithms achieve a higher throughput, this issue is more critical when adaptive routing is used. Therefore, we will restrict our study to fully adaptive algorithms. Injection and delivery channels are usually referred to as *ports*. In this study, we assume that each port has a bandwidth equal to the channel bandwidth.

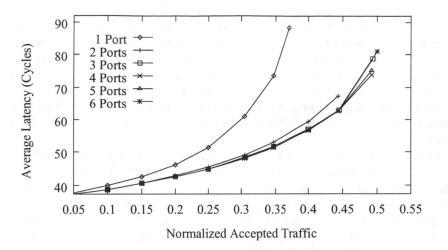

Figure 9.19. Effect of the number of ports for a uniform distribution of message destinations. Plots show the average message latency vs. normalized accepted traffic.

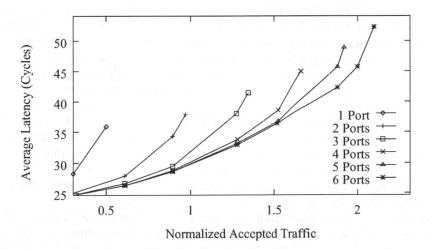

Figure 9.20. Effect of the number of ports for local traffic (side = 2). Plots show the average message latency vs. normalized accepted traffic.

Figure 9.19 shows the effect of the number of ports for a uniform distribution of message destinations. For the sake of clarity, we removed the part of the plots corresponding to the performance degradation of the adaptive algorithm close to saturation. As can be seen, the network interface is a clear bottleneck when using a single port. Adding a second port decreases latency and increases throughput considerably. Adding a third port increases throughput by a small amount, and adding more ports does not modify the performance. It should be noted that latency does not consider source queuing time. When a single port is used, latency is higher because messages block when the header reaches the destination node, waiting for a free port. Those blocked messages remain in the network, therefore reducing channel utilization and throughput.

As can be expected, more bandwidth is required at the network interface when messages are sent locally. Figure 9.20 shows the effect of the number of ports for local traffic with side $= 2$ (see Section 9.4.2). In this case, the number of ports has a considerable influence on performance. It has a stronger impact on throughput than the routing algorithm, or even the topology used. The higher the number of ports, the higher the throughput. However, as the number of ports increases, adding more ports has a smaller impact on performance. Therefore, in order to avoid mixing the effect of different design parameters, we run all the simulations in the remaining sections of this chapter by using four ports.

Taking into account that the only way to make parallel machines really scalable is by exploiting locality, the effect of the number of ports is extremely important. However, most current multi-computers have a single port. In most cases, the limited bandwidth at the network interface does not limit the performance. The reason is that there is an even more important bottleneck in the network interface: the software messaging layer (see Section 9.12). The latency of the messaging layer reduces network utilization, hiding the effect of the number of ports. However, the number of ports may become the bottleneck in distributed shared-memory multiprocessors.

9.7.3   Effect of Buffer Size

In this section, we analyze the effect of buffer size on performance. Buffers are required to allow continuous flit injection at the source node in the absence of contention, therefore hiding routing time and allowing windowing protocols between adjacent routers. Also, if messages are short enough, using deeper buffers allows messages to occupy a smaller number of channels when contention arises and buffers are filled. As a consequence, contention is reduced and throughput should increase. Finally, buffers are required to hold flits while a physical channel is transmitting flits from other buffers (virtual channels).

If buffers are kept small, buffer size does not affect clock frequency. However, using very deep buffers may slow-down clock frequency. So there is a trade-off. Figure 9.21 shows the effect of input and output buffer size on performance using the fully adaptive routing algorithm with three virtual channels. In this case, no windowing protocol has been implemented. Minimum buffer size is two flits because flit transmission across physical channels is asynchronous. Using smaller buffers would produce bubbles in the message pipeline.

As expected, the average message latency decreases when buffer size increases. However, the effect of buffer size on performance is small. The only significant improvement occurs when the total flit capacity changes from 4 to 5 flits. Adding more flits to buffer capacity yields diminishing returns as buffer size increases. Increasing input buffer size produces almost the same effect as increasing output buffer size, as far as total buffer size remains the same. The reason is that there is a balance between the benefits of increasing the size of each buffer. On one hand, increasing the input buffer size allows more data flits to make progress if the routing header is blocked for some cycles until an output channel is available. On the other hand, increasing the output buffer size allows more data flits to cross the switch while the physical channel is assigned to other virtual channels. Moreover, when a message blocks, buffers are filled. In this case, it does not matter how total buffer capacity is split among input and output buffers. The only important issue is whether buffers are deep enough to allow the blocked message to leave the source node so that some channels are freed.

Note that the plots in Figure 9.21 correspond to short messages (16 flits). We also run simulations for longer messages. In this case, buffer size has a more noticeable impact on performance. However, increasing buffer capacity does not increase performance significantly if messages are longer than the diameter of the network times the total buffer capacity of a virtual channel. The reason is that a blocked message keeps all the channels it previously reserved regardless of buffer size.

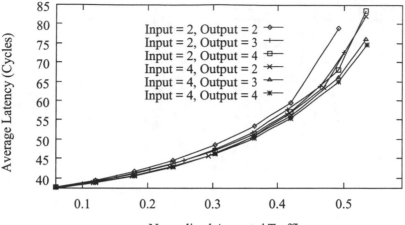

Figure 9.21. Effect of input and output buffer size. Plots show the average message latency vs. normalized accepted traffic for the fully adaptive routing algorithm with three virtual channels using a uniform distribution of message destinations.

9.8 Comparison of Routing Algorithms for Irregular Topologies

In this section we analyze the performance of the routing algorithms described in Section 4.9 on switch-based networks with randomly generated irregular topologies under uniform traffic. We also study the influence of network size and message length.

A brief description of the routing algorithms follows. A breadth-first spanning tree on the network graph is computed first using a distributed algorithm. Routing is based on an assignment of direction to the operational links. The up end of each link is defined as: (1) the end whose switch is closer to the root in the spanning tree; (2) the end whose switch has the lower ID, if both ends are at switches at the same tree level. The up/down routing algorithm uses the following up/down rule: a legal route must traverse zero or more links in the up direction followed by zero or more links in the down direction. We will refer to this routing scheme as UD. It does not require virtual channels. When virtual channels are used, the first free virtual channel is selected. We will refer to as UD-2VC the up/down routing scheme in which physical channels are split into two virtual channels.

The adaptive routing algorithm proposed in [319] also splits each physical channel into two virtual channels (original and new channels). Newly injected messages can use the new channels following any minimal path but the original channels can only be used according to the up/down rule. However, once a message reserves one of the original channels, it can no longer reserve any of the new channels again. When a message can choose among new and original channels, a higher priority is given to the new channels at any intermediate switch. We will refer to this routing algorithm as A-2VC.

Finally, an enhanced version of the A-2VC algorithm can be obtained as follows [318]: Newly injected messages can only leave the source switch using new channels belonging to minimal paths, and never using original channels. When a message arrives at a switch from another switch through a new channel, the routing function gives a higher priority to the new channels belonging to minimal

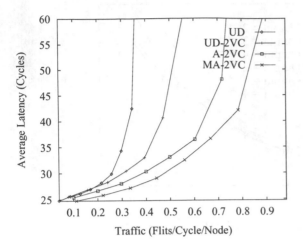

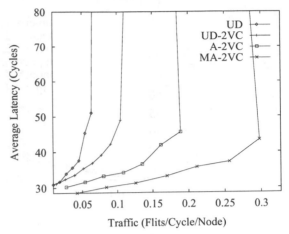

Figure 9.22. Average message latency vs. accepted traffic for an irregular network with 16 switches. Message length is 16 flits.

Figure 9.23. Average message latency vs. accepted traffic for an irregular network with 64 switches. Message length is 16 flits.

paths. If all of them are busy, then the routing algorithm selects an original channel belonging to a minimal path (if any). If none of the original channels provides minimal routing, then the original channel that provides the shortest path will be used. We will refer to this routing scheme as MA-2VC, since it provides minimal adaptive routing with two virtual channels.

Unless otherwise stated, simulations were run using the following parameters. Network topology is completely irregular and was generated randomly. However, for the sake of simplicity, we imposed three restrictions to the topologies that can be generated. First, we assumed that there are exactly four nodes (processors) connected to each switch. Also, two neighboring switches are connected by a single link. Finally, all the switches in the network have the same size. We assumed eight-port switches, thus leaving four ports available to connect to other switches. We evaluated networks with a size ranging from 16 switches (64 nodes) to 64 switches (256 nodes). For each network size, several distinct irregular topologies were analyzed. However, the average latency values achieved by each topology for each traffic rate were almost the same. The only differences arose when the networks were heavily loaded, close to saturation. Additionally, the throughput achieved by all the topologies was almost the same. Hence, we only show the results obtained by one of those topologies, chosen randomly. Input and output flit buffers have capacity for 4 flits. Each node has one injection and one delivery channel. For message length, 16-, 64-, and 256-flit messages were considered. Finally, it takes one clock cycle to compute the routing algorithm, to transfer one flit from an input buffer to an output buffer, or to transfer one flit across a physical channel.

It is important to note that we assumed that virtual channel multiplexing can be efficiently implemented. In practice, implementing virtual channels is not trivial because switch-based networks with irregular topology are usually used in the context of networks of workstations. In this environment, link wires may be long, increasing signal propagation delay and making flow control more complex.

Figure 9.22 shows the average message latency versus accepted traffic for each routing scheme on a randomly generated irregular network with 16 switches. Message size is 16 flits. It should be noted that accepted traffic has not been normalized because normalized bandwidth differs from one

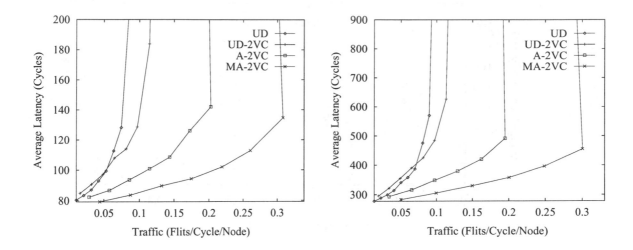

Figure 9.24. Average message latency vs. accepted traffic for an irregular network with 64 switches. Message length is 64 flits.

Figure 9.25. Average message latency vs. accepted traffic for an irregular network with 64 switches. Message length is 256 flits.

network to another even for the same size. As can be seen, when virtual channels are used in the up/down routing scheme (UD-2VC), throughput increases by a factor of 1.5. The A-2VC routing algorithm doubles throughput and reduces latency with respect to the up/down routing scheme. The improvement with respect to UD-2VC is due to the additional adaptivity provided by A-2VC. When the MA-2VC routing scheme is used, throughput is almost tripled. Moreover, the latency achieved by MA-2VC is lower than the one for the rest of routing strategies for the whole range of traffic. The improvement achieved by MA-2VC with respect to A-2VC is due to the use of shorter paths. This explains the reduction in latency as well as the increment in throughput because less bandwidth is wasted in nonminimal paths.

The MA-2VC routing scheme scales very well with network size. Figure 9.23 shows the results obtained on a network with 64 switches. In this network, throughput increases by factors of 4.2 and 2.7 with respect to the UD and UD-2VC schemes, respectively, when using the MA-2VC scheme. Latency is also reduced for the whole range of traffic. However, the factor of improvement in throughput achieved by the A-2VC scheme with respect to UD is only 2.6. Hence, when network size increases, the performance improvement achieved by the MA-2VC scheme also increases because there are larger differences among the minimal distance between any two switches and the routing distance imposed by the up/down routing algorithm.

Figures 9.23, 9.24, and 9.25 show the influence of message size on the behavior of the routing schemes. Message size ranges from 16 to 256 flits. As message size increases, the benefits of using virtual channels become smaller. In particular, the UD-2VC routing scheme exhibits a higher latency than the UD scheme for low to medium network traffic. This is due to the fact that when a long message waits for a channel occupied by a long message, it is delayed. However, when two long messages share the channel bandwidth, both of them are delayed. Also, the UD routing scheme increases throughput by a small amount as message size increases. The routing schemes using virtual channels, and in particular the adaptive ones, achieve a similar performance regardless of message size. This behavior matches the one for regular topologies, as indicated in Section 9.5. These results show the robustness of the UD-2VC, A-2VC, and MA-2VC routing schemes against

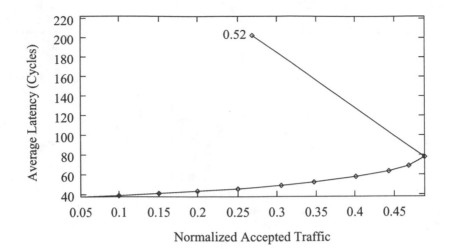

Figure 9.26. Average message latency vs. normalized accepted traffic for the fully adaptive algorithm using four ports and a uniform distribution of message destinations.

message size variation. Additionally, the MA-2VC routing scheme achieves the highest throughput and lowest latency for all message sizes.

Finally, it should be noted that the improvement achieved by using the theory proposed in Section 3.1.3 for the design of adaptive routing algorithms is much higher in irregular topologies than in regular ones. This is mainly due to the fact that most paths in irregular networks are nonminimal if those techniques are not used.

9.9   Injection Limitation

As indicated in previous sections, the performance of the fully adaptive algorithm degrades considerably when the saturation point is reached. Figure 9.26 shows the average message latency versus normalized accepted traffic for a uniform distribution of message destinations. This plot was already shown in Figure 9.5. Note that each point in the plot corresponds to a stable working point of the network (i.e., the network has reached a steady state). Also, note that Figure 9.26 does not represent a function. The average message latency is not a function of accepted traffic (traffic received at destination nodes). Both average message latency and accepted traffic are functions of the applied load.

Figure 9.27 shows the normalized accepted traffic as a function of normalized applied load. As can be seen, accepted traffic increases linearly with the applied load until the saturation point is reached. Indeed, they have the same value because each point corresponds to a steady state. However, when the saturation point is reached, accepted traffic decreases considerably. Further increments of the applied load do not modify accepted traffic. Simply, injection buffers at source nodes grow continuously. Also, average message latency increases by an order of magnitude when the saturation point is reached, remaining constant as applied load increases further. Note that latency does not include source queuing time.

This behavior typically arises when the routing algorithm allows cyclic dependencies between resources. As indicated in Chapter 3, deadlocks are avoided by using a subset of channels without

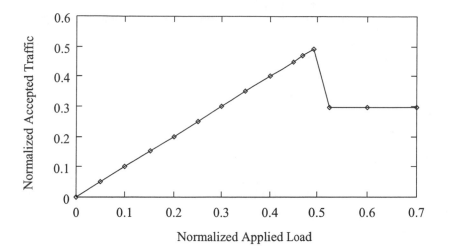

Figure 9.27. Normalized accepted traffic as a function of normalized applied load for the fully adaptive algorithm using four ports and a uniform distribution of message destinations.

cyclic dependencies between them to escape from cyclic waiting chains (*escape channels*). The bandwidth provided by the escape channels should be high enough to drain messages from cyclic waiting chains as fast as they are formed. The speed at which waiting chains are formed depends on network traffic. The worst case occurs when the network is beyond saturation. At this point congestion is very high. As a consequence, the probability of messages blocking cyclically is not negligible. Escape channels should be able to drain at least one message from each cyclic waiting chain fast enough so that those escape channels are free when they are requested by another possibly deadlocked message. Otherwise, performance degrades and throughput is considerably reduced. The resulting accepted traffic at this point depends on the bandwidth offered by the escape channels.

An interesting issue is that the probability of messages blocking cyclically not only depends on applied load. Increasing the number of virtual channels per physical channel decreases that probability. Reducing the number of injection/delivery ports also decreases that probability. However, those solutions may degrade performance considerably. Also, as indicated in Section 9.4.3, some communication patterns do not produce performance degradation. For those traffic patterns, messages do not block cyclically or do it very infrequently.

The best solution consists of designing the network correctly. A good network design should provide enough bandwidth for the intended applications. The network should not work close to the saturation point because contention at this point is high, increasing message latency and decreasing the overall performance. Even if the network reaches the saturation point for a short period of time, performance will not degrade as much as indicated in Figures 9.26 and 9.27. Note that the points beyond saturation correspond to steady states, requiring a sustained message generation rate higher than the one corresponding to saturation. Moreover, the simulation time required to reach a steady state for those points is an order of magnitude higher than for other points in the plot, indicating that performance degradation does not occur immediately after reaching the saturation point. Also, after reaching the saturation point for some period of time, performance improves again when message generation rate falls below the value at the saturation point.

If the traffic requirements of the intended applications are not known in advance, it is still possible to avoid performance degradation by using simple hardware mechanisms. A very effective solution

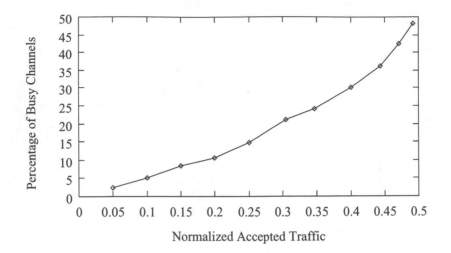

Figure 9.28. Percentage of busy output virtual channels vs. normalized accepted traffic for a uniform distribution of message destinations.

consists of limiting message injection when network traffic is high. For efficiency reasons, traffic should be estimated locally. Injection can be limited by placing a limit on the size of the buffer on the injection channels [36], by restricting injected messages to use some predetermined virtual channel(s) [74], or by waiting until the number of free output virtual channels at a node is higher than a threshold [220]. This mechanism can be implemented by keeping a count of the number of free virtual channels at each router. When this count is higher than a given threshold, message injection is allowed. Otherwise, messages have to wait at the source queue. Note that these mechanisms have no relationship with the injection limitation mechanism described in Section 3.3.3. Injection limitation mechanisms may produce starvation if the network works beyond the saturation point for long periods of time.

The injection limitation mechanism described above requires defining a suitable threshold for the number of free output virtual channels. Additionally, this threshold should be independent of the traffic pattern. Figures 9.28, 9.29, and 9.30 show the percentage of busy output virtual channels versus normalized accepted traffic for a uniform distribution, local traffic (side = 2), and the bit-reversal traffic pattern, respectively. Interestingly enough, the percentage of busy output virtual channels at the saturation point is similar for all the distributions of destinations. It ranges from 40 to 48%. Other traffic patterns exhibit a similar behavior. As a 3-D torus with three virtual channels per physical channel has 18 output virtual channels per router, seven or eight virtual channels are occupied. Therefore, 10 or 11 virtual channels are free on average at the saturation point. Thus, messages should only be injected if 11 or more virtual channels are free at the current router. The latency/traffic plots obtained for different traffic patterns when injection is limited are almost identical to the ones without injection limitation, except that throughput does not decrease and latency does not increase beyond the saturation point.

Despite the simplicity and effectiveness of the injection limitation mechanism described above, it has not been tried with traffic produced by real applications. Extensive simulations should be run before deciding to include it in a router design. Moreover, if network bandwidth is high enough, this mechanism is not necessary, as indicated above. Nevertheless, new and more powerful injection limitation mechanisms are currently being developed.

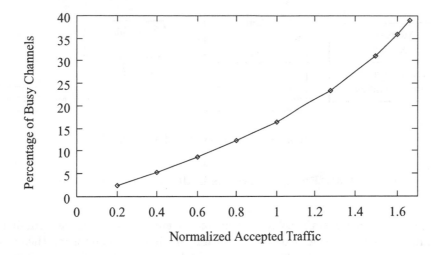

Figure 9.29. Percentage of busy output virtual channels vs. normalized accepted traffic for local traffic (side = 2).

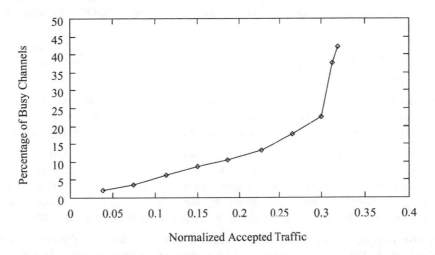

Figure 9.30. Percentage of busy output virtual channels vs. normalized accepted traffic for the bit-reversal traffic pattern.

9.10 Impact of Router Delays on Performance

9.10.1 A Speed Model

Most network simulators written up to now for wormhole switching work at the flit level. Writing a simulator that works at the gate level or at the transistor level is a complex task. Moreover, execution time would be extremely high, considerably reducing the design space that can be studied. A reasonable approximation to study the effect of design parameters on the performance of the interconnection network consists of modeling the delay of each component of the router. Then, for

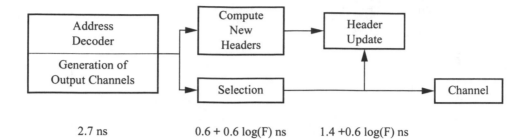

Figure 9.31. Propagation delays in the routing control unit.

a given set of design parameters, the delay of each component is computed, determining the critical path and the number of clock cycles required for each operation, and computing the clock frequency for the router. Then, the simulation is run using a flit-level simulator. Finally, simulation results are corrected by using the previously computed clock frequency.

Consider the router model described in Section 2.1. We assume that all the operations inside each router are synchronized by its local clock signal. To compute the clock frequency of each router, we will use the delay model proposed in [57]. It assumes 0.8 μm CMOS gate array technology for the implementation.

- *Routing control unit.* Routing a message involves the following operations: address decoding, routing decision, and header selection.

  The first operation extracts the message header and generates requests of acceptable outputs based on the routing algorithm. In other words, the address decoder implements the routing function. According to [57], the address decoder delay is constant and equal to 2.7 ns.

  The routing decision logic takes as inputs the possible output channels generated by the address decoder, and the status of the output channels. In other words, this logic implements the selection function. This circuit has a delay that grows logarithmically with the number of alternatives, or degree of freedom, offered by the routing algorithm. Representing by F the degree of freedom, this circuit has a delay value given by $0.6 + 0.6 \log F$ ns.

  Finally, the routing control unit must compute the new header, depending on the output channel selected. While new headers can be computed in parallel with the routing decision, it is necessary to select the appropriate one when this decision is made. This operation has a delay that grows logarithmically with the degree of freedom. Thus, this delay will be $1.4 + 0.6 \log F$ ns.

  The operations and the associated delays are shown in Figure 9.31.

  The total routing time will be the sum of all delays, yielding

  $t_r = 2.7 + 0.6 + 0.6 \log F + 1.4 + 0.6 \log F = 4.7 + 1.2 \log F$ ns

- *Switch.* The time required to transfer a flit from one input channel to the corresponding output channel is the sum of the delay involved in the internal flow control unit, the delay of the crossbar, and the setup time of the output channel latch.

  The flow control unit manages the buffers, preventing overflow and underflow. It has a constant delay equal to 2.2 ns.

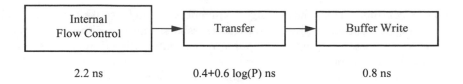

Figure 9.32. Propagation delays in the switch.

The crossbar is usually implemented using a tree of selectors for each output. Thus, its delay grows logarithmically with the number of ports. Assuming that P is the number of ports of the crossbar, its delay is given by $0.4 + 0.6 \log P$ ns.

Finally, the setup time of a latch is 0.8 ns.

The operations and the associated delays are shown in Figure 9.32.

The switch delay is

$$t_s = 2.2 + 0.4 + 0.6 \log P + 0.8 = 3.4 + 0.6 \log P \text{ ns}$$

- *Channels.* The time required to transfer a flit across a physical channel includes the off-chip delay across the wires, and the time required to latch it onto the destination. Assuming that channel width and flit size are identical, this time is the sum of the output buffer, input buffer, input latch, and synchronizer delays. Typical values for the technology used are 2.5 (with 25 pF load), 0.6, 0.8, and 1.0 ns, respectively, yielding 4.9 ns per flit. The output buffer delay includes the propagation time across the wires, assuming that they are short. This is the case for a 3-D torus when it is assembled in three dimensions.

If virtual channels are used, the time required to arbitrate and select one of the ready flits must be added. The virtual channel controller has a delay logarithmic in the number of virtual channels per physical channel. Notice that we do not include any additional delay to decode the virtual channel number at the input of the next node, because virtual channels are usually identified using one signal for each one [77]. If V is the number of virtual channels per physical channel, virtual channel controller delay is $1.24 + 0.6 \log V$ ns.

The operations and the associated delays are shown in Figure 9.33.

The total channel delay yields

$$t_w = 4.9 + 1.24 + 0.6 \log V = 6.14 + 0.6 \log V \text{ ns}$$

Now, these times are instantiated for every routing algorithm evaluated:

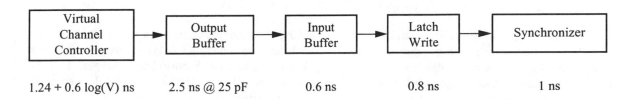

Figure 9.33. Propagation delays across physical channels.

1. *Deterministic routing.* This routing algorithm offers a single routing choice. The switch is usually made by cascading several low-size crossbars, one per dimension. Each of these crossbars switches messages going in the positive or negative direction of the same dimension, or crossing to the next dimension. As there are two virtual channels per physical channel and two directions per dimension, the first crossbar in the cascade has eight ports, including four injection ports. Taking into account that dimensions are crossed in order, most messages will continue in the same dimension. Thus, the number of crossbars traversed will be one most of the times. So, for the deterministic routing algorithm, we have $F = 1$, $P = 8$, and $V = 2$, and we obtain the following delays for router, switch, and channel, respectively

   $t_r = 4.7 + 1.2 \log 1 = 4.7$ ns

   $t_s = 3.4 + 0.6 \log 8 = 5.2$ ns

   $t_w = 6.14 + 0.6 \log 2 = 6.74$ ns

2. *Partially adaptive routing.* The number of routing choices is equal to two, because there are two virtual channels per physical channel that can be used in most cases, but dimensions are crossed in order. Because dimensions are crossed in order, the switch can be the same as for the deterministic algorithm. Substituting $F = 2$, $P = 8$, and $V = 2$

   $t_r = 4.7 + 1.2 \log 2 = 5.9$ ns

   $t_s = 3.4 + 0.6 \log 8 = 5.2$ ns

   $t_w = 6.14 + 0.6 \log 2 = 6.74$ ns

3. *Fully adaptive routing.* In this case, the number of routing choices is five, because we have one virtual channel in each dimension that can be used to cross the dimensions in any order, and also the two channels provided by the partially adaptive algorithm. As there are two channels per dimension, with three virtual channels per physical channel, plus four injection/delivery ports, the switch is a 22-port crossbar. Thus, we have $F = 5$, $P = 22$, and $V = 3$. Substituting

   $t_r = 4.7 + 1.2 \log 5 \approx 7.49$ ns

   $t_s = 3.4 + 0.6 \log 22 \approx 6.1$ ns

   $t_w = 6.14 + 0.6 \log 3 \approx 7.1$ ns

Taking into account that all the delays for each routing algorithm are similar, the corresponding router can be implemented by performing each operation in one clock cycle. In this case, the clock period is determined by the slowest operation. Hence

1. $t_{deterministic} = \max(t_r, t_s, t_w) = \max(4.7, 5.2, 6.74) = 6.74$ ns

2. $t_{partially\_adaptive} = \max(t_r, t_s, t_w) = \max(5.9, 5.2, 6.74) = 6.74$ ns

3. $t_{fully\_adaptive} = \max(t_r, t_s, t_w) = \max(7.49, 6.1, 7.1) = 7.49$ ns

The deterministic and the partially adaptive routing algorithms require the same clock period of 6.74 ns. Although routing delay is greater in the latter case, channel delay dominates in both cases, therefore being the bottleneck. For the adaptive algorithm, clock period increases up to 7.49 ns, slowing down clock frequency by 10% with respect to the other algorithms. It should be noted that clock frequency would be the same if a single injection/delivery port were used.

   The following sections show the effect of router delays on performance. Note that plots in those sections are identical to the ones shown in Sections 9.4.1, 9.4.2, and 9.4.3, except that plots for each

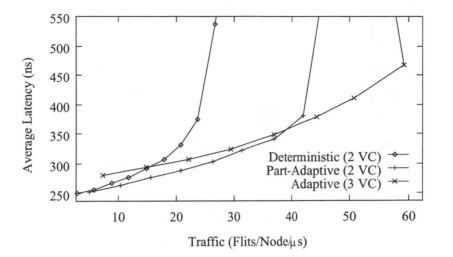

Figure 9.34. Average message latency vs. accepted traffic for a uniform distribution of message destinations.

routing algorithm have been scaled by using the corresponding clock period. As the deterministic and the partially adaptive algorithms have the same clock frequency, comments will focus on the relative performance of the fully adaptive routing algorithm. Finally, note that as VLSI technology improves, channel propagation delay is becoming the only bottleneck. As a consequence the impact of router complexity on performance will decrease over time, therefore favoring the use of fully adaptive routers.

9.10.2 Performance Under Uniform Traffic

Figure 9.34 shows the average message latency versus accepted traffic when using a uniform distribution for message destination. Latency and traffic are measured in ns and flits/node/μs, respectively. Note that in this case, accepted traffic has not been normalized because the normalizing factor is different for each routing algorithm.

As expected, the lower clock frequency of the fully adaptive router produces a comparatively higher latency and lower throughput for the fully adaptive algorithm. Nevertheless, this algorithm still increases throughput by 103% and 28% with respect to the deterministic and the partially adaptive algorithms. However, for low loads, these algorithms achieve a latency up to 10% lower than the fully adaptive one. When the network is heavily loaded, the fully adaptive algorithm offers more routing options, achieving the lowest latency. Moreover, this algorithm also obtains a lower standard deviation of the latency (not shown) for the whole range of traffic.

9.10.3 Performance Under Local Traffic

Figures 9.35 and 9.36 show the average message latency versus accepted traffic when message destinations are uniformly distributed inside a cube centered at the source node with side equal to four and two channels, respectively.

The relative behavior of the routing algorithms heavily depends on the average distance traveled by messages. When side = 4, the fully adaptive routing algorithm increases throughput by a factor of

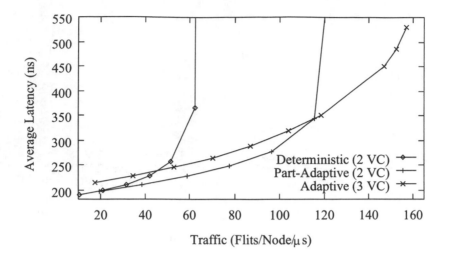

Figure 9.35. Average message latency vs. accepted traffic for local traffic (side = 4).

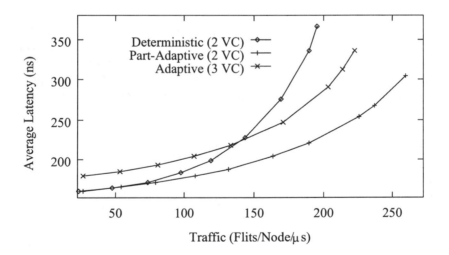

Figure 9.36. Average message latency vs. accepted traffic for local traffic (side = 2).

2.5 with respect to the deterministic algorithm. However, the fully adaptive algorithm only achieves the lowest latency when the partially adaptive algorithm is close to saturation. Here, the negative effect of the lower clock frequency on performance can be clearly observed.

When traffic is very local, the partially adaptive algorithm achieves the highest throughput, also offering the lowest latency for the whole range of traffic. Nevertheless, it only improves throughput by 32% with respect to the deterministic algorithm. The fully adaptive algorithm exhibits the highest latency until accepted traffic reaches a 60% of the maximum throughput. In this case, the negative effect of the lower clock frequency on performance is even more noticeable. As a consequence, adaptive routing is not useful when most messages are sent locally.

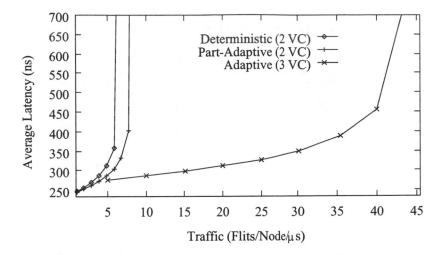

Figure 9.37. Average message latency vs. accepted traffic for the bit-reversal traffic pattern.

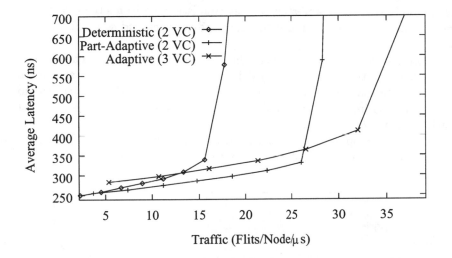

Figure 9.38. Average message latency vs. accepted traffic for the perfect-shuffle traffic pattern.

9.10.4 Performance Under Nonuniform Traffic

Figures 9.37 and 9.38 show the average message latency versus accepted traffic for the bit-reversal and the perfect-shuffle traffic patterns, respectively.

Despite the lower clock frequency, the fully adaptive algorithm increases throughput by a factor of 6.9 over the deterministic algorithm when the bit-reversal communication pattern is used. For the perfect-shuffle communication pattern, the fully adaptive algorithm doubles throughput with respect to the deterministic one. However, it only increases throughput by 35% over the partially adaptive algorithm. Also, this algorithm achieves a slightly lower latency than the fully adaptive one until it is close to the saturation point.

Table 9.1. Clock period of the router as a function of the number of virtual channels.

Virtual	Clock Period (ns)		
Channels	Deterministic	Partially Adaptive	Fully Adaptive
2	6.74 (t_w)	6.74 (t_w)	–
3	–	7.09 (t_w)	7.49 (t_r)
4	7.34 (t_w)	7.34 (t_w)	8.30 (t_r)
6	7.69 (t_w)	7.80 (t_r)	9.27 (t_r)
8	7.94 (t_w)	8.30 (t_r)	9.89 (t_r)

9.10.5   Effect of the Number of Virtual Channels

Section 9.7.1 showed that splitting physical channels into several virtual channels usually increases throughput but may increase latency when too many virtual channels are added. Also, it showed that virtual channels are more interesting for deterministic algorithms than for adaptive algorithms. In summary, the use of virtual channels has some advantages and some disadvantages. Therefore there is a trade-off.

In this section a more realistic analysis of the effect of adding virtual channels is presented. This study considers the additional propagation delay introduced by the circuits required to implement virtual channels. Note that increasing the number of virtual channels increases channel propagation delay. Moreover, it also increases the number of routing options and switch size, increasing routing delay and switch delay accordingly.

Assuming that all the operations are performed in a single clock cycle, Table 9.1 shows the clock period of the router as a function of the number of virtual channels per physical channel for the

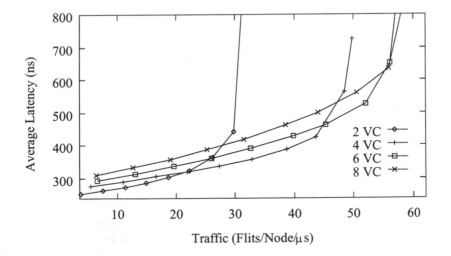

Figure 9.39. Average message latency vs. accepted traffic as a function of the number of virtual channels. Deterministic routing algorithm.

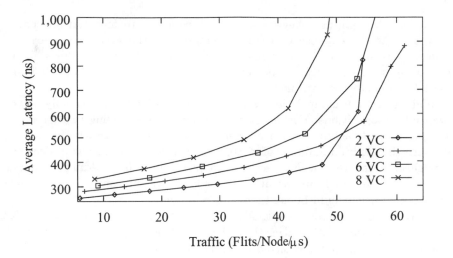

Figure 9.40. Average message latency vs. accepted traffic as a function of the number of virtual channels. Partially adaptive routing algorithm.

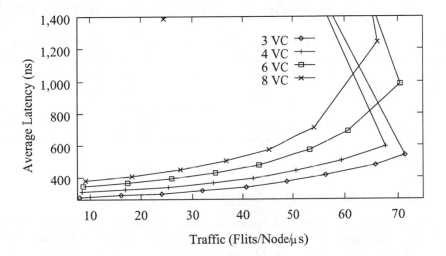

Figure 9.41. Average message latency vs. accepted traffic as a function of the number of virtual channels. Fully adaptive routing algorithm.

three routing algorithms under study. It has been computed according to the model presented in Section 9.10.1. For each value of the clock period, the slowest operation (t_r, t_s, or t_w) is indicated.

Figures 9.39, 9.40, and 9.41 show the effect of adding virtual channels to the deterministic, partially adaptive and fully adaptive routing algorithms, respectively. Plots show the average message latency versus accepted traffic for a uniform distribution of message destinations.

For the deterministic algorithm there is a trade-off between latency and throughput. Adding virtual channels increases throughput but it also increases latency. Therefore, depending on the requirements of the applications, the designer has to choose between achieving a lower latency or supporting a higher throughput. Anyway, changing from two to four virtual channels increases throughput by 52% at the expense of a small increment in the average latency. The standard deviation of latency is also reduced. The reason is that the additional channels allow messages to pass blocked messages. On the other hand, using eight or more virtual channels is not interesting at all because latency increases with no benefit.

However, adding virtual channels is not interesting at all for the partially adaptive and the fully adaptive routing algorithms. For the partially adaptive one, adding two virtual channels only increases throughput by 13%. Adding more virtual channels even decreases throughput. Moreover, the algorithm with the minimum number of virtual channels achieves the lowest latency except when the network is close to saturation. For the fully adaptive algorithm, adding virtual channels does not increase throughput at all. Moreover, it increases latency significantly. Therefore, the minimum number of virtual channels should be used for both adaptive algorithms.

A similar study can be done for meshes. Although results are not shown, the conclusions are the same. For the deterministic routing algorithm, it is worth adding one virtual channel (for a total of two). Using three virtual channels increases throughput by a small amount but it also increases latency. For the fully adaptive routing algorithm, using the minimum number of virtual channels (two channels) achieves the lowest latency. It is not worth adding more virtual channels.

9.11   Performance of Collective Communication

In this section, we present some evaluation results for networks implementing support for collective communication operations. Taking into account that communication start-up latency is very high in most multicomputers, we can expect a significant improvement in the performance of collective communication operations when some support for these operations is implemented in a parallel computer. However, the usefulness of implementing such a support depends on how frequently collective communication operations are performed and on the number of nodes involved in each of those operations. So, depending on the applications running on the parallel computer, it may be useful or not implementing such a support.

9.11.1   Comparison with Separate Addressing

Figure 9.42 compares the measured performance of separate addressing and a multicast tree algorithm (specifically, the spanning binomial tree presented in Section 5.5.2) for subcubes of different sizes on a 64-node nCUBE-2. The message length is fixed at 100 bytes. The tree approach offers substantial performance improvement over separate addressing.

The U-mesh algorithm described in Section 5.7.4 was evaluated in [234]. The evaluation was performed on a 168-node Symult 2010 multicomputer, based on a 12×14 2-D mesh topology. A set of tests was conducted to compare the U-mesh algorithm with separate addressing and the Symult 2010 system-provided multidestination service *Xmsend*. In separate addressing, the source nodes sends an individual copy of the message to every destination. The Xmsend function was implemented to exploit whatever efficient hardware mechanisms may exist in a given system to accomplish multiple-destination sends. In the case of lacking any such mechanism, it is implemented as a library function that performs the necessary copying and multiple unicast calls.

Figure 9.43 plots the multicast latency values for implementations of the three methods. A large sample of destination sets were randomly chosen in these experiments. The message length was 200 bytes. The multicast latency with separate addressing increases linearly with the number of destinations. With the U-mesh algorithm, the latency increases logarithmically with the number

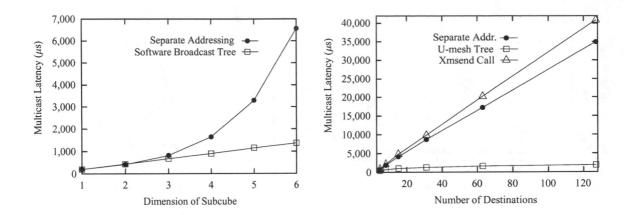

Figure 9.42. Comparison of 100-byte broadcasts on a 64-node nCUBE-2.

Figure 9.43. Multicast comparison on a 168-node Symult 2010.

of destinations. These experimental results demonstrate the superiority of the U-mesh multicast algorithm. Taking into account these results and that the U-mesh algorithm requires no hardware support, we can conclude that multicomputers should at least include a software implementation of multicast, regardless of how frequently this operation is performed.

9.11.2 Comparing Tree-Based and Path-Based Algorithms

This section compares the performance of the double-channel XY multicast routing algorithm presented in Section 5.5.2, and the dual-path and multipath multicast algorithms presented in Section 5.5.3. These results were presented in [208]. The performance of a multicast routing algorithm depends not only on the delay and traffic resulting from single multicast message, but also on the interaction of the multicast message with other network traffic. In order to study these effects on the performance of multicast routing algorithms, some simulations were run on an 8×8 mesh network. The simulation program modeled multicast communication in 2-D mesh networks. The destinations for each multicast message were uniformly distributed. All simulations were executed until the confidence interval was smaller than 5% of the mean, using 95% confidence intervals, which are not shown in the figures.

In order to compare the tree-based and path-based algorithms fairly, each algorithm was simulated on a network that contained double channels. Figure 9.44 gives the plot of average network latency for various network loads. The average number of destinations for a multicast is 10, and the message size is 128 bytes. The speed of each channel is 20 Mbytes/s. All three algorithms exhibit good performance at low loads. The path-based algorithms, however, are less sensitive to increased load than the tree-based algorithm. This result occurs because in tree-based routing, when one branch is blocked the entire tree is blocked, increasing contention considerably. This type of dependency does not exist in path-based routing. Multipath routing exhibits lower latency than dual-path routing because, as shown above, paths tend to be shorter, generating less traffic. Hence, the network will not saturate as quickly. Although not shown in the figure, the variance of message latency using multipath routing was smaller than that of dual-path routing, indicating that the former is also generally more fair.

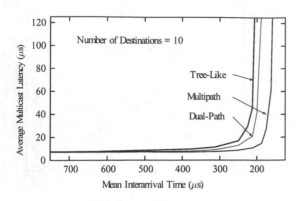

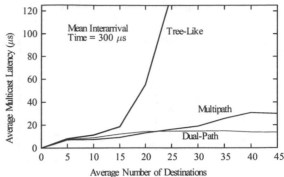

Figure 9.44. Performance under different loads on a double-channel mesh.

Figure 9.45. Performance of different number of destinations on a double-channel mesh.

The disadvantage of tree-based routing increases with the number of destinations. Figure 9.45 compares the three algorithms, again using double channels. The average number of destinations is varied from 1 to 45. In this set of tests, every node generates multicast messages with an average time between messages of 300 μs. The other parameters are the same as for the previous figure. With larger sets of destinations, the dependencies among branches of the tree become more critical to performance and cause the delay to increase rapidly. The conclusion from Figures 9.44 and 9.45 is that tree-based routing is not particularly well suited for 2-D mesh networks when messages are relatively long. The path algorithms still perform well, however. Note that the dual-path algorithm results in lower latency than the multipath algorithm for large destination sets. The reason is somewhat subtle. When multipath routing is used to reach a relatively large set of destinations, the source node will likely send on all of its outgoing channels. Until this multicast transmission is complete, any flit from another multicast or unicast message that routes through that source node will be blocked at that point. In essence, the source node becomes a hot spot. In fact, every node currently sending a multicast message is likely to be a hot spot. If the load is very high, these hot spots may throttle system throughput and increase message latency. Hot spots are less likely to occur in dual-path routing, accounting for its stable behavior under high loads with large destination sets. Although all the outgoing channels at a node can be simultaneously busy, this can only result from two or more messages routing through that node.

Simulations were also run for multipath and dual-path routing with single channels and an average of 10 destinations. As the load increased, multipath routing offered slight improvement over dual-path routing. However, both routing algorithms saturated at a much lower load than with double channels (approximately for an average arrival time between messages of 350 μs), resulting in much lower performance than the tree-based algorithm with double channels. This result agrees with the performance evaluation presented in Section 9.4.1, which showed the advantage of using two virtual channels on 2-D meshes.

Finally, tree-based multicast with pruning (see Section 5.5.2) performs better than path-based multicast routing algorithms when messages are very short and the number of destinations is less than half the number of nodes in the network [224]. This makes tree-based multicast with pruning especially suitable for the implementation of cache coherent protocols in distributed shared-memory multiprocessors.

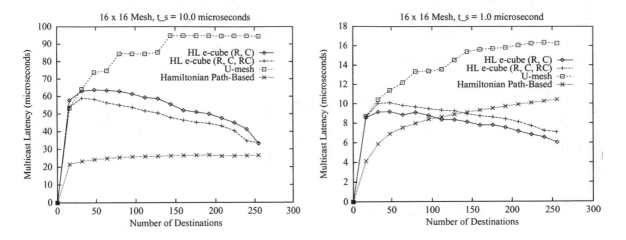

Figure 9.46. Comparison of single-source multicast latency on 16×16 meshes with two different communication start-up (t_s) values. (From [267].)

In summary, path-based multicast routing algorithms perform better than tree-based algorithms for long messages, especially for large destination sets. However, tree-based multicast performs better than path-based multicast when messages are very short. Finally, other design parameters like the number of virtual channels may have a stronger influence on performance than the choice of the multicast algorithm.

9.11.3 Performance of Base Routing Conformed Path Multicast

This section presents performance evaluation results for hardware supported multicast operations based on the Base Routing Conformed Path (BRCP) model described in Section 5.5.3. For comparison purposes, the U-mesh and the Hamiltonian path-based routing algorithms are also evaluated. These results were presented in [267].

To verify the effectiveness of the BRCP model, single-source broadcasting and multicasting was simulated at the flit-level. Two values for communication start-up time (t_s) were used: 1 and 10 μs. Link propagation time (t_p) was assumed to be 5 ns for 200 Mbytes/s link. For unicast message passing, router delay (t_{node}) was assumed as 20 ns. For multidestination message passing a higher value of router delay, 40 ns, was considered. For a fair comparison, $2n$ consumption channels were assumed for both multidestination and unicast message passing, where n is the number of dimensions of the network. Each experiment was carried out 40 times to obtain average results.

Figures 9.46 and 9.47 compare the latency of single-source multicast on 2-D meshes for two network sizes and two t_s values. Four different schemes were considered: hierarchical leader-based (HL) scheme using (R, C) and (R, C, RC) paths, U-mesh, and Hamiltonian path-based scheme. The simulation results show that the BRCP model is capable of reducing multicast latency as the number of destinations participating in the multicast increases beyond a certain number. This cutoff number was observed to be 16 and 32 nodes for the two network sizes considered. For large number of destinations the HL schemes are able to reduce multicast latency by a factor of 2 to 3.5 compared to the U-mesh scheme. The Hamiltonian path-based scheme performs best for smaller system size,

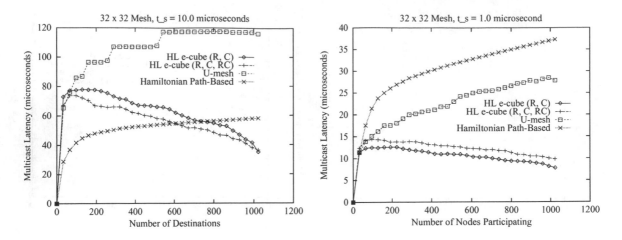

Figure 9.47. Comparison of single-source multicast latency on 32×32 meshes with two different communication start-up (t_s) values. (From [267].)

higher t_s, and less number of destinations per multicast. However, the HL schemes perform better than the Hamiltonian path-based scheme as the system size increases, t_s reduces, and the number of destinations per multicast increases.

For systems with higher t_s (10 μs), the HL scheme with RC paths was observed to implement multicast faster than using R and C paths. However, for systems with $t_s = 1$ μs, the scheme using R and C paths performed better. This is because a multidestination worm along a RC path encounters longer propagation delay (up to $2k$ hops in a $k \times k$ network) compared to that along a R/C path (up to k hops). The propagation delay dominates for systems with lower t_s. Thus, the HL scheme with R and C paths is better for systems with lower t_s value, whereas the RC path-based scheme is better for other systems.

9.11.4   Performance of Optimized Multicast Routing

This section evaluates the performance of several optimizations described in Chapter 5. In particular, the Source-Partitioned U-mesh (SPUmesh) algorithm introduced in Section 5.7.4, and the Source Quadrant-based Hierarchical Leader (SQHL) and Source-Centered Hierarchical Leader (SCHL) schemes described in Section 5.5.3 are compared to the U-mesh and Hierarchical Leader-based (HL) algorithms described in the same sections. The performance results presented in this section were reported in [173].

A flit-level simulator was used to model a 2-D mesh and evaluate the algorithms for multiple multicast. The parameters used were: t_s (communication start-up time) = 5 μs, t_p (link propagation time) = 5 ns, t_{node} (router delay at node) = 20 ns, t_{sw} (switching time across the router crossbar) = 5 ns, t_{inj} (time to inject message into network) = 5 ns and t_{cons} (time to consume message from network) = 5 ns. The message length was assumed to be a constant 50 flits and a 16×16 mesh was chosen. Each experiment was carried out 30 times to obtain average results. For each simulation, destination sets were randomly generated for each multicast message. Multicast latency is plotted against (a) number of sources (s), while keeping number of destinations (d) fixed, and (b) d, while keeping s fixed. The former shows the effect of the number of multicasts on latency, while the latter shows the effect of the size of the multicasts on latency.

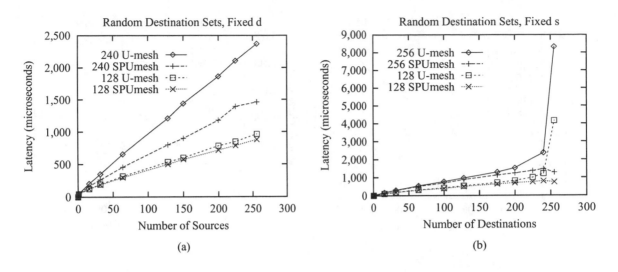

Figure 9.48. Multiple multicast latency on a 16×16 mesh using U-mesh and SPUmesh algorithms. Randomly generated destination sets with: (a) Fixed d (128, 240) with varying s. (b) Fixed s (128, 256) with varying d. (From [173].)

It can be observed in Figure 9.48a that the SPUmesh algorithm outperforms the U-mesh algorithm for large d by a factor of about 1.6. For small to moderate values of d, performance is similar. This is clear in Figure 9.48b where the U-mesh latency shoots up for larger d, whereas the SPUmesh latency remains more or less constant. The U-mesh algorithm behaves in this way because increasing d increases the number of start-ups the common center node will have to sequentialize. However, the SPUmesh algorithm performs equally well for both large and small d. This is because increasing d does not increase the node contention, as the multicast trees are perfectly staggered for identical destination sets.

It can be observed in Figure 9.49a that the SCHL scheme does about two to three times better than the SQHL scheme and about five to seven times better than the HL scheme. The HL scheme undergoes a large degree of node contention even for randomly chosen destinations. A property of the HL scheme observed in Section 9.11.3 is that latency reduces with increase in d. This basic property of the HL scheme is best exploited by the SCHL scheme. This can be noticed in Figure 9.49b where on increasing d the latency of SCHL drops. However, the SQHL scheme outperforms the SCHL scheme for small d, since the number of start-ups at the U-mesh stage of the multicast will be more for the SCHL scheme. There is a crossover point after which the SCHL scheme performs better. This can be seen Figure 9.49b. The above results lead to the conclusion that node contention is one of the principal reasons for poor performance of existing multicast algorithms. Reducing node contention should be the primary focus while designing multicast algorithms.

9.11.5 Performance of Unicast-Based and Multidestination-Based Schemes

This section compares multicast algorithms using unicast messages with those using multidestination messages. This measures the potential additional benefits that a system provides if it supports multidestination wormhole routing in hardware. The multicast algorithms selected for comparison

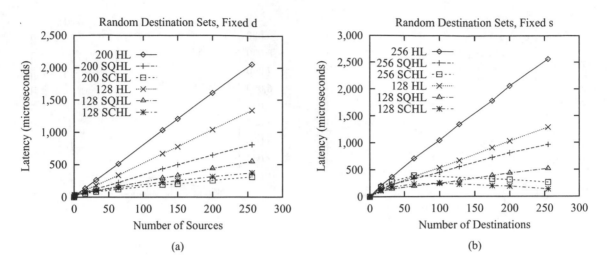

Figure 9.49. Multiple multicast latency on a 16×16 mesh using HL, SQHL, and SCHL schemes. Randomly generated destination sets with: (a) Fixed d (128, 200) with varying s. (b) Fixed s (128, 256) with varying d. (From [173].)

are the ones that achieved the best performance in Section 9.11.4 (the SPUmesh and the SCHL schemes), using the same parameters as in that section. The performance results presented in this section were reported in [173].

As expected, the SCHL scheme outperforms the SPUmesh algorithm for both large and small d. This can be seen in Figure 9.50. Since the destination sets are completely random, there is no node contention to degrade the performance of the SCHL scheme. There is a crossover point at around $d = 100$, after which the SCHL scheme keeps improving as d increases. The reason is that hierarchical grouping of destinations gives relatively large leader sets for small d. This is because the destinations are randomly scattered in the mesh. On the other hand, SPUmesh generates perfectly staggered trees for identical destination sets. But, as d increases, leader sets become smaller and the advantage of efficient grouping in the SCHL scheme overcomes the node contention. This results in a factor of about 4–6 improvement over the SPUmesh algorithm when the number of sources and destinations is very high.

These results lead to the conclusion that systems implementing multidestination message passing in hardware can support more efficient multicast than systems providing unicast message passing only. However, when the number of destinations for multicast messages is relatively small, the performance benefits of supporting multidestination message passing are small. So the additional cost and complexity of supporting multidestination message passing is only worth it if multicast messages represent an important fraction of network traffic and the average number of destinations for multicast messages is high.

9.11.6   Performance of Path-Based Barrier Synchronization

This section compares the performance of unicast-based barrier synchronization [354] and the barrier synchronization mechanism described in Section 5.6.2. These performance results were reported in [264].

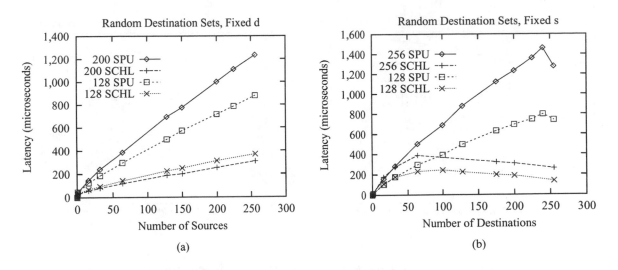

Figure 9.50. Multiple multicast latency on a 16×16 mesh using SPUmesh and SCHL. Randomly generated destination sets with: (a) Fixed d (128, 200) with varying s. (b) Fixed s (128, 256) with varying d. (From [173].)

A flit-level simulator was used to evaluate the algorithms for barrier synchronization. The following parameters were assumed: t_s (communication start-up time) as 1 and 10 μs, t_p (link propagation time) as 5 ns, and channel width as 32 bits. For multidestination gather and broadcast worms, bit-string encoding was used. The node delay (t_{node}) was assumed to be 20 ns for unicast-based message passing. Though the node delay for multidestination worm (using bit manipulation logic) may be similar to that of unicast messages, three different values of node delay were simulated. In the simulation graphs, these values are indicated by 20 ns ($1\times$ node delay), 30 ns ($1.5\times$ node delay), and 40 ns ($2\times$ node delay). The processors were assumed to be arriving at a barrier simultaneously. For arbitrary set barrier synchronization, the participating processors were chosen randomly. Each experiment was repeated 40 times and the average synchronization latency was determined.

Complete Barrier

Complete barrier synchronization schemes were evaluated for the following 2-D mesh configurations with e-cube routing: 4×4, 8×4, 8×8, 16×8, 16×16, 32×16, 32×32, 64×32, and 64×64. Evaluations were done for $t_s = 1$ μs and $t_s = 10$ μs. Figure 9.51 shows the comparison. It can be observed that the multidestination scheme outperforms unicast-based scheme for all system sizes. As the system size grows, the cost of synchronization increases very little for multidestination scheme compared to the unicast-based scheme. The costs for 64×32 and 64×64 configurations are higher because the worm length increases by 1 flit to accommodate bit-encoded addresses with 32-bit channel width. With 1 μs communication start-up time, the multidestination scheme with $1\times$ node delay is able to barrier synchronize 4K processors in just 11.68 μs. The unicast-based scheme also performs very well, being able to synchronize the same number of processors in 31 μs with no hardware support. For higher communication start-up, the cost with multidestination scheme remains practically constant with increase in system size. This shows the effectiveness of multidestination scheme to perform low cost barrier synchronization in a large system in spite of higher communication start-up time.

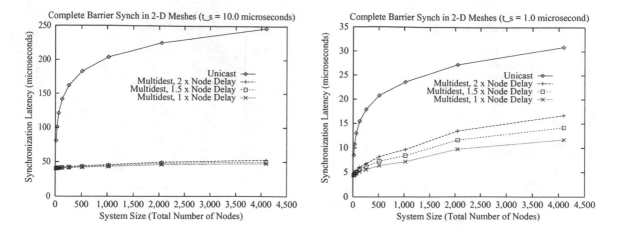

Figure 9.51. Comparison of unicast-based and multidestination-based schemes to implement complete barrier synchronization on 2-D meshes. (From [264].)

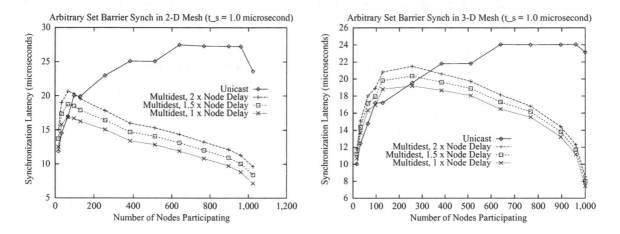

Figure 9.52. Comparison of unicast-based and multidestination-based schemes to implement arbitrary set barrier synchronization on 2-D and 3-D meshes. (From [264].)

Arbitrary Subset Barrier

The cost of arbitrary subset barrier synchronization was evaluated on 32×32 and $10 \times 10 \times 10$ systems with different number of participating processors. Communication start-up time of $1~\mu$s with varying node delays for the multidestination scheme were assumed. Figure 9.52 shows the comparison. It can be seen that as the number of participating processors increases beyond certain number, the multidestination scheme is able to implement a barrier with reduced cost. This is the most unique strength of this scheme. It shows the potential to implement dense barrier synchronization with reduced cost. Such crossover depends on system size, topology, communication start-up time, and node delay. For $1\times$ node delay, the crossover was observed at 96 nodes for 32×32 system, and 256 nodes for $10 \times 10 \times 10$ system. The crossover point is smaller for 2-D mesh compared to 3-D mesh.

With less number of processors participating in a barrier, the multidestination scheme performs little worse due to longer paths traveled by multidestination worms. Beyond the crossover point, the multidestination scheme demonstrates steady reduction in cost over unicast-based scheme. For 75% nodes participating in a barrier, with the technological parameters considered, the multidestination scheme reduces the synchronization cost by a factor of 1.4–2.7 compared to the unicast-based scheme. For higher communication start-up time and system size, the improvement will be higher.

9.12 Software Messaging Layer

9.12.1 Overhead of the Software Messaging Layer

The overhead of the software messaging layer and its contribution to the overall communication latency has been evaluated by several researchers on different parallel computers [86, 170, 171, 214, 353]. Here we present some recent performance evaluation results obtained by running benchmarks on an IBM SP2. These results have been reported in [238]. In the next section, we will show the drastic reduction in latency that can be achieved by establishing virtual circuits between nodes before data are available and by reusing those circuits for all the messages exchanged between those nodes.

The SP2 communication subsystem is composed of the high-performance switch plus the adapters that connect the nodes to the switch [5, 328, 329]. The adapter contains an on-board microprocessor to offload some of the work of passing messages from node to node, and some memory to provide buffer space. DMA engines are used to move information from the node to the memory of the adapter, and from there to the switch link.

Three different configurations of the communication subsystem of the IBM SP2 were evaluated. In the first configuration, the adapters were based on an Intel i860, providing a peak bandwidth of 80 Mbytes/s. The links connecting to the high-performance switch provided 40 Mbytes/s peak bandwidth in each direction, with a node-to-node latency of 0.5 μs for systems with up to 80 nodes. The operating system was AIX version 3, which included MPL, a proprietary message-passing library [323]. An implementation of the MPI interface [44] was available as a software layer over MPL. In the second configuration, communication hardware was identical to the one in the first configuration. However, the operating system was replaced by AIX version 4, which includes an optimized implementation of MPI. In the third configuration, the network hardware was updated, keeping AIX version 4. The new adapters are based on a PowerPC 601, achieving a peak transfer bandwidth of 160 Mbytes/s. The new switch offers 300 Mbytes/s peak bidirectional bandwidth, with latencies lower than 1.2 μs for systems with up to 80 nodes.

The performance of point-to-point communication was measured using the code provided in [86] for systems using MPI. The performance of the IBM SP2 is shown in Table 9.2 for the three configurations described above and different message lengths (L). The words "old" and "new" refer to the communications hardware, and "v3" and "v4" indicate the version of the operating system. As can be seen, software overhead dominates communication latency for very short messages. Minimum latency ranges from 40 to 60 μs while hardware latency is on the order of 1 μs. As a consequence, software optimization has a stronger effect on reducing latency for short messages than improving network hardware. This is the case for messages shorter than 4 Kbytes. However, for messages longer than 4 Kbytes the new version of the operating system performs worse. The reason is that for messages shorter than 4 Kbytes an eager protocol is used, sending messages immediately, while for longer messages a rendezvous protocol is used, sending a message only when the receiver node agrees to receive it. Switching to the rendezvous protocol incurs in higher start-up costs but reduces

Table 9.2. Average values of latency and throughput for point-to-point communication. (From [238].)

L	Latency (μs)			Throughput (Mbytes/s)		
(Bytes)	Old–v3	Old–v4	New–v4	Old–v3	Old–v4	New–v4
0	59.37	43.59	39.39	0	0	0
8	59.30	45.33	44.38	0.13	0.18	0.18
16	59.42	45.31	42.78	0.27	0.35	0.37
32	60.10	46.90	46.31	0.53	0.68	0.69
64	61.66	47.11	44.84	1.04	1.36	1.43
128	64.54	50.54	49.58	1.98	2.53	2.58
256	80.38	63.16	51.79	3.19	4.05	4.94
512	95.59	78.16	61.95	5.36	6.55	8.27
1,024	118.95	97.40	87.68	8.61	10.51	11.68
2,048	165.12	134.44	114.83	12.40	15.23	17.83
4,096	229.33	197.40	164.69	17.86	20.75	24.87
8,192	359.22	393.11	319.74	22.81	20.84	25.62
10^4	415.45	448.76	351.56	24.07	22.28	28.45
10^5	2,964.40	2,997.40	1,693.90	33.73	33.36	59.04
10^6	28,318.00	28,364.00	11,587.00	35.31	35.26	86.30

the number of times information is copied when using the new hardware, thus reducing the cost per byte for the third configuration. Finally, the higher peak bandwidth of the new hardware can be clearly appreciated for messages longer than 10 Kbytes.

An interesting observation is that the message length required to achieve half the maximum throughput is approximately 3 Kbytes for the old hardware configuration and around 32 Kbytes for the new network hardware. Thus, improving network bandwidth without reducing software overhead makes even more difficult to take advantage of the higher network performance. Therefore, the true benefits of improving network hardware will depend on the average message size.

Several parallel kernels have been executed on an IBM SP2 with 16 Thin2 nodes. These kernels include four benchmarks (MG, LU, SP, and BT) from the NAS Parallel Benchmarks (NPB) version 2 [14] and a shallow water modeling code (SWM) from the ParkBench suite of benchmarks [349]. Only the first and third configurations described above for the communication subsystem were evaluated (referred to as old and new, respectively).

Figure 9.53 shows the execution time in seconds and the average computation power achieved for the different benchmarks. It can be clearly seen that the performance of all the applications is almost the same for the old and new configurations because average message lengths are shorter than 10 Kbytes.

Therefore, software overhead has a major impact on the performance of parallel computers using message-passing libraries. Improving network hardware will have an almost negligible impact on performance unless the latency of the messaging layer is considerably reduced.

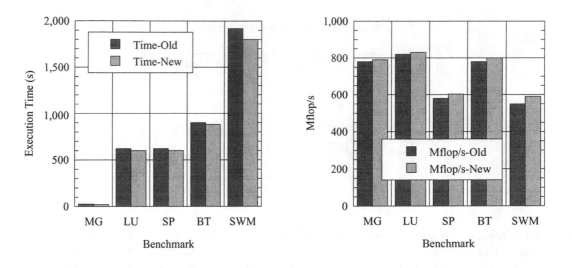

Figure 9.53. Execution time and average computation power achieved for the different benchmarks on an IBM SP2 with 16 Thin2 nodes. (From [238].)

9.12.2   Optimizations in the Software Messaging Layer

In this section we present some performance evaluation results showing the advantages of establishing virtual circuits between nodes, and caching and reusing those circuits. This technique is referred to as *virtual circuit caching* (VCC). VCC is implemented by allocating buffers for message transmission at source and destination nodes before data are available. Those buffers are reused for all the subsequent transmissions between the same nodes, therefore reducing software overhead considerably. A directory of cached virtual circuits is kept at each node. The evaluation results presented in this section are based on [82].

The simulation study has been performed using a time-step simulator written in C. The simulated topology is a k-ary n-cube. A simulator cycle is normalized to the time to transmit one flit across a physical link. In addition, the size of one flit is 2 bytes. Since the VCC mechanism exploits communication locality, performance evaluation was performed using traces of parallel programs. Traces were gathered for several parallel kernels executing on a 256-processor system.

The communication traces were collected using an execution-driven simulator from the SPASM toolset [322]. The parallel kernels are the (1) broadcast-and-roll parallel matrix multiply (MM), (2) a NAS kernel (EP), (3) a fast Fourier transform (FFT), (4) a Kalman filter (Kalman), and (5) a multigrid solver for computing a 3-D field (MG). The algorithm kernels display different communication traffic patterns.

Locality Metrics

The following metric attempts to capture communication locality by computing the average number of messages that are transmitted between a pair of processors:

$$Avg\_Message\_Density = 1 - \frac{Number\_of\_Source\_Destination\_Pairs}{Total\_Number\_of\_Messages}$$

This metric gives a measure of the number of messages that can use the same circuit, which as a result may be worth caching. However, this measure does not incorporate any sense of time, i.e.,

Table 9.3. Message density for various traces.

Communication Trace	Message Density
EP	0.0
FFT	0.0
Kalman	0.848
MG	0.0
MM	0.466

there is no information about when each of the individual messages are actually sent relative to each other. In analyzing a trace for communication locality, we can compute the expression above over smaller intervals of time and produce a value that would be the average message density per unit of time. If parallel algorithms are structured to incorporate some temporal locality, i.e., messages from one processor to another tend to be clustered in time, then this measure will reflect communication locality. A trace with a high value of message density is expected to benefit from the use of the cacheable channels. Table 9.3 shows the computed values of the average message density for the traces under study. The traces with a value of 0.0 (EP, FFT, MG) possess no locality. They have no (source, destination) pairs that send more than one message to each other. The other traces have nonzero values, implying that reuse of circuits is beneficial.

The Effects of Locality

An uncached message transmission was modeled as the sum of the messaging layer overhead (including the path setup time) and the time to transmit a message. The overhead includes both the actual system software overhead and the network interface overhead. For example, this overhead was measured on an Intel Paragon, giving an approximate value of 2,600 simulator cycles. However, the selected value for the overhead was 100 simulator cycles, corresponding to approximate reported measured times for active message implementations [106]. A cached message transmission is modeled as the sum of the time to transmit the message (the actual data transmission time) and a small overhead to model the time spent in moving the message from user space to the network interface and from the network interface back into the user space. In addition, there is overhead associated with each call to set up a virtual circuit. This overhead is equivalent to that of an uncached transmission. There is also overhead associated with the execution of the directive to release a virtual circuit.

The effect of VCC is shown in Table 9.4. The differences are rather substantial but there are several caveats with respect to these results. The VCC latencies do not include the amortized software overhead, but rather only network latencies. The reason is the following. The full software overhead (approximately 100 cycles) is only experienced by the first message to a processor. Subsequent messages experience latencies shown in Table 9.4. Moreover, if virtual circuits are established before they are needed, it is possible to overlap path setup with computation. In this case, the VCC latencies shown in Table 9.4 are the latencies actually experienced by messages. Since these traces were simulated and optimized by manual insertion of directives in the trace, almost complete overlap was possible due to the predictable nature of many references. It is not clear that automated compiler techniques could do near as well and the values should be viewed in that light. The VCC

Table 9.4. The effect of virtual circuit caching. Latencies are measured in cycles.

Program	EP	FFT	Kalman	MG	MM
VCC Latency	32.27	30.17	47.00	32.27	27.26
Non-VCC Latency	133.26	137.64	147.99	133.42	174.28

entries in the table are the average experienced latencies without including path setup time. The non-VCC latencies show the effect of experiencing overhead with every transmission. Although EP, FFT, and MG do not exhibit a great degree of locality, the results exhibit benefit from overlapping path setup with computation. Finally, the overhead of 100 cycles is only representative of what is being reported these days with the active message [106] and the fast message [263] implementations. Anyway, the latency reduction achieved by using VCC in multicomputers is higher than the reduction achieved by other techniques.

9.13   Performance of Fault-Tolerant Algorithms

In this section, we present evaluation results for several fault-tolerant routing protocols. This evaluation study analyzes the performance of the network in the presence of faults using synthetic workloads. Also, the probability of completion for some parallel kernels in the presence of faults is studied. A wide range of solutions to increase fault tolerance has been considered, covering from software-based fault-tolerant routing protocols to very resilient protocols based on PCS. Although some of these results have been published recently [80, 127, 332], some other results are new.

9.13.1   Software-Based Fault-Tolerant Routing

In this section we evaluate the performance of the software-based fault-tolerant routing protocols presented in Section 6.5.2. These techniques can be used on top of any deadlock-free routing algorithm, including oblivious e-cube routing and fully adaptive Duato's protocol (DP). The resulting fault-tolerant routing protocols are referred to as *e-sft* and *DP-sft*, respectively.

The performance of e-sft and DP-sft was evaluated with flit-level simulation studies of message passing in a 16-ary 2-cube with 16-flit messages, a single flit routing header, and eight virtual channels per physical channel. Message destination traffic was uniformly distributed. Simulation runs were made repeatedly until the 95% confidence intervals for the sample means were acceptable (less than 5% of the mean values). The simulation model was validated using deterministic communication patterns. We use a congestion control mechanism (similar to [36]) by placing a limit on the size of the buffer on the injection channels. If the input buffers are filled, messages cannot be injected into the network until a message in the buffer has been routed. Injection rates are normalized.

Cost of e-sft and DP-sft

The header format for e-sft and DP-sft was shown in Figure 6.28. A 32-bit header enables routing within a 64 × 64 torus. The flags require 6 bits and the offsets require 6 bits each. We assume the use of half-duplex channels. With half-duplex channels, 32-bit channels are comparable to the number of data pins devoted to interrouter communication in modern machines (e.g., there are two

16-bit full-duplex channels in the Intel Paragon router). A flit crosses a channel in a single cycle, and traverses a router from input to output in a single cycle. Use of 16-bit full-duplex channels would double the number of cycles to transmit the routing header. Routing decisions are assumed to take a single cycle with the network operating with a 50 MHz clock and 20 ns cycle time. The software cost for absorbing and reinjecting a message is derived from measured times on an Intel Paragon and reported work with active message implementations [106]. Based on these studies we assess this cost nominally at 25 μs per absorption/injection or 50 μs each time a message must be processed by the messaging software at an intermediate node. If the message encounters busy injection buffers when it is being reinjected, it is requeued for reinjection at a later time. Absorbed messages have priority over new messages to prevent starvation.

The router hardware can retain the same basic architecture as the canonical form for dimension-order routers or adaptive routers presented in Section 7.2.1 which captures the basic organization of several commercial and research designs. The only additional functionality required is of the Routing and Arbitration Unit. When a message is routed to a faulty output channel, the F bit must be set and the $X - Dest$ and $Y - Dest$ fields reset to 0 to cause the message to be absorbed. One side effect of the increased header size is a possible increase in virtual channel buffer size and the width of the internal datapaths, although 32-bit datapaths appear to be reasonable for the next generation of routers. Finally, as with any approach for fault-tolerant routing, support for testing of channels and nodes must be available. The remaining required functionality of e-sft and DP-sft is implemented in the messaging layer software.

Simulation Results

In a fault-free network the behavior of e-cube and e-sft is identical, with slightly lower performance for e-sft due to the larger header size. Simulation experiments placed a single fault region within the network. Performance of e-sft and DP-sft are shown in Figure 9.54 for a nine-node convex fault region and for an 11-node concave fault region. Due to the greater difficulty in entering and exiting a concave fault region, the average message latency is substantially greater in the presence of concave fault regions than for equivalent sized convex fault regions. The message latency for DP-sft is significantly lower than the message latency for e-sft. The reason is that when a fault is encountered, DP-sft is able to find an alternative fault-free path in most cases. However, the only choice for e-sft is absorbing the message. The curves also indicate that for each of the fault configurations the latency remains relatively constant as the accepted traffic increases. As network load increases, the number of messages each node injects and receives increases, but the percentage of messages that encounter the fault region remains relatively constant. Therefore, the latency remains relatively flat. Another factor is that the high latencies of rerouted messages mask some of the growth in the latency of messages that do not encounter faults, though a close inspection of the graphs reveals a small but steady growth in average latency. For the concave fault region and DP-sft, this growth rate is larger. This is due to the fact that with adaptive routing, the number of messages that encounter a fault increases with load. The high latencies of these messages contributes to the faster growth in average message latency.

Figure 9.55 shows the performance of e-sft and DP-sft in the presence of a single convex fault region ranging in size from 1 to 21 failed nodes. For each plot the message injection rate (normalized applied load) is indicated between parentheses. The latency plots indicate that when the network is below saturation traffic the increase in the size of the fault block causes significant increases in the average message latency for e-sft. This is due to the increase in the number of messages encountering fault regions (a 1-node fault region represents 0.4% of the total number of nodes in the network, while a 21-node fault region represents 8.2% of the total number of nodes). On the contrary, in DP-sft the

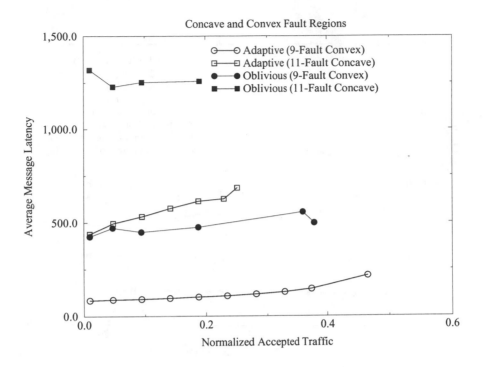

Figure 9.54. Average message latency vs. normalized accepted traffic for e-sft and DP-sft with a 9-node convex fault block and an 11-node concave fault block.

average message latencies remain relatively constant since at low loads a larger percentage (relative to e-sft) of messages can be routed around the fault regions and can avoid being absorbed. The latency and accepted traffic curves for high injection rate (0.576) represent an interesting case. Latency and accepted traffic for e-sft appear to remain relatively constant. At high injection rates and larger fault regions, more messages become absorbed and rerouted. However, the limited buffer size provides a natural throttling mechanism for both new messages as well as absorbed messages waiting to be reinjected. As a result, active faulted messages in the network form a smaller percentage of the traffic and both the latency and accepted traffic characteristics are dominated by the steady-state values of traffic unaffected by faults. The initial drop in accepted traffic for small number of faults is due to the fact that initially a higher percentage of faulted messages are delivered, reducing accepted traffic. These results suggest that sufficient buffering of faulted messages and priorities in reinjecting them have a significant impact on the performance of faulted messages. However, for high injection rate (0.576) and DP-sft the average message latency increases and the accepted traffic decreases as the number of faults is increased. At high injection rates congestion increases. Messages encountering a fault may also find that all the alternative paths offered by DP-sft are busy. As messages are not allowed to block if the channel used to escape from deadlock is faulty, those messages are absorbed. Thus, the percentage of messages that are absorbed after encountering a fault increases with applied load, therefore increasing latency and reducing accepted traffic. At low injection rates, the accepted traffic remains relatively constant independent of the size of the fault blocks since fault blocks only increase the latency of the messages. Note that for lower injection rates the accepted traffic curves for e-sft and DP-sft are identical. Since messages are guaranteed delivery when operating well below saturation, the network quickly reaches the steady state for accepted traffic.

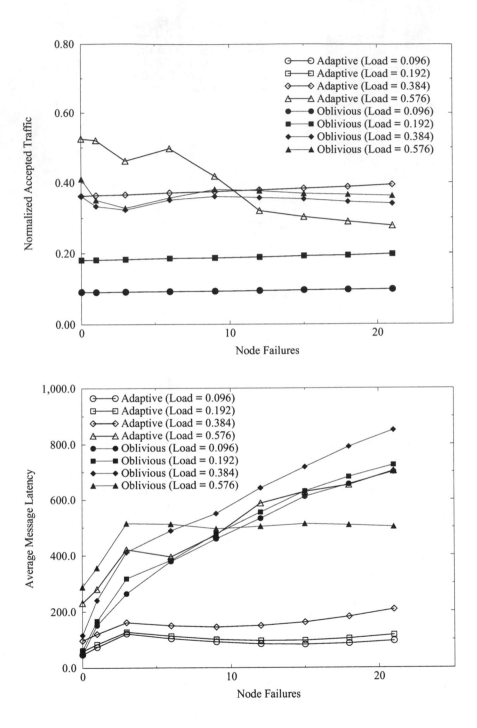

Figure 9.55. Normalized accepted traffic and average message latency as a function of node failures (convex regions).

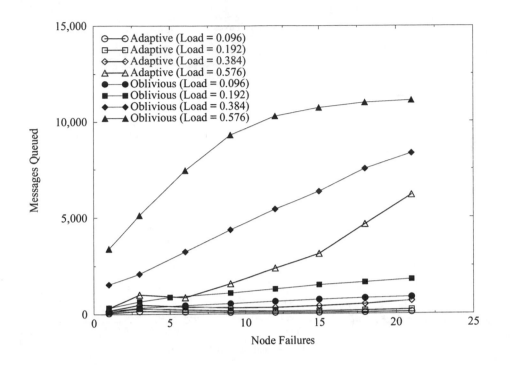

Figure 9.56. Number of messages queued as a function of node failures (convex regions).

The plots in Figure 9.56 show the number of messages queued by message absorbing nodes for message injection rates (normalized applied load) of 0.096, 0.192, 0.384, and 0.576, in the presence of a single convex fault region ranging in size from 1 to 21 failed nodes. This is simply a count of the number of messages absorbed due to faults. A given message contributes more than once to this count if it is absorbed multiple times. As expected, the number of messages queued increases as the number of node faults increases. Also, the number of messages queued is much higher for e-sft than for DP-sft. At lower injection rates the number of messages absorbed increases rather slowly, remaining relatively constant for DP-sft while approximately doubling for e-sft. This number increases rapidly for higher injection rates. At an injection rate of 0.576, the rate of increase decreases as the number of faults increases for e-sft. Note that DP-sft displays contrasting behavior. Eventually, the number of absorbed messages is limited by the buffering capacity for faulted messages. This limit is reached by e-sft much earlier compared to DP-sft. Figure 9.57 shows similar behavior in the presence of convex and concave regions, i.e., on the average, concave regions cause more messages to be absorbed.

In general, the number of times a message is rerouted is relatively small. In practice, the probability of multiple router failures before repair is very low in most systems. In these systems, the large majority of faulted messages will not have to pass through more than one node. This makes these techniques attractive for next-generation wormhole-routed networks. In summary, it can be observed that the performance of rerouted messages is significantly affected by techniques for buffering and reinjection. At low to moderate loads, the performance of adaptive routing protocols provides substantial performance improvements over oblivious protocols. At high fault rates and loads beyond saturation, increased adaptivity can cause severe performance degradation due to increased congestion. At high loads and high fault rates, oblivious protocols are limited by buffering capacity while adaptive protocols are limited by congestion.

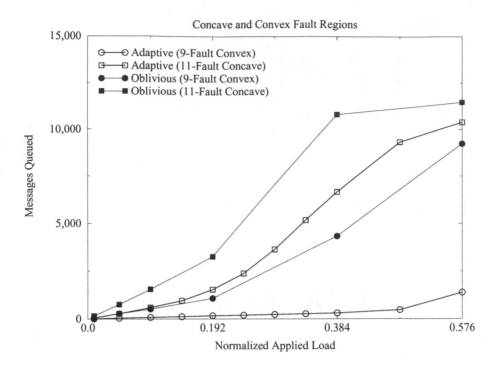

Figure 9.57. Number of messages queued as a function of applied load.

9.13.2   Routing Algorithms for PCS

This section evaluates the performance of two backtracking protocols using pipelined circuit switching (PCS), and compares them with three routing protocols using wormhole switching. Performance is analyzed both in fault-free networks and in the presence of static faults. The backtracking protocols analyzed in this section are exhaustive profitable backtracking (EPB), and misrouting backtracking with m misroutes (MB-m). These protocols were described in Section 4.7. The wormhole protocols analyzed here are Duato's protocol (DP), dimension reversal routing (DR), and negative-first (NF). These protocols were described in Sections 4.4.4 and 4.3.2.

Given a source-destination pair (s, d), let s_i, d_i be the ith dimension coordinates for s and d, respectively. Let $|s_i - d_i|_k$ denote the torus dimension distance from s_i to d_i defined by

$$|s_i - d_i|_k = \min\{|s_i - d_i|, k - |s_i - d_i|\}.$$

We performed simulation studies on 16-ary 2-cubes to evaluate the performance of each protocol. Experiments were conducted with and without static physical link faults under a variety of network loads and message sizes. For all routing protocols except NF, a processor s was allowed to communicate to other processors in the subcube defined by $\{d : |s_i - d_i|_k \leq 4, i = 1, ..., n\}$. This corresponds to a neighborhood of about one half the network diameter. Destinations were picked uniformly through this neighborhood. Since NF is not allowed to use end-around connections, the communication neighborhood was defined by $\{d : |s_i - d_i| \leq 4, i = 1, ..., n\}$. Thus, the diameter of the communication patterns were comparable for all routing protocols. A simulator cycle was normalized to the time to transmit one flit across a physical link. Each simulation was run for 30,000 global clock cycles, discarding information occurring during a 10,000-clock-cycle warmup

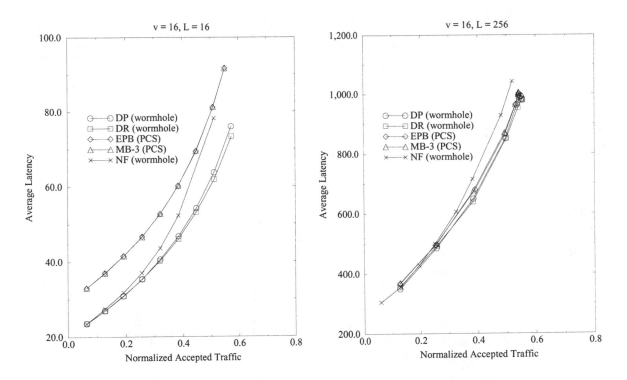

Figure 9.58. Fault-free performance graphs.

period. The transient start-up period was determined by monitoring variations in the values of performance parameters. We noted that after a duration of 10,000 network cycles, the computed parameter values did not deviate more than 2%. The recorded values in the start-up interval were discarded. In a moderately loaded network, in the 20,000 clock cycles over which statistics were gathered, over 800,000 flits were moved through the network. Each simulation was run repeatedly to obtain a sample mean and a sample variance for each measured value. Runs were repeated until the confidence intervals for the sample means were acceptable. The simulation model was validated using deterministic communication patterns. Simulations on single messages in traffic-free networks gave the theoretical latencies and setup times for wormhole and PCS messages. In addition, tests were performed on individual links to ensure that the simulated mechanisms for link arbitration in the presence of multiple virtual circuits over the link functioned correctly.

Fault-Free Performance

In this study we performed experiments on fault-free 16-ary 2-cubes. Each physical link multiplexed 16 virtual channels in each direction. We ran the simulations for message sizes of 16 and 256 flits. The primary purpose of this study was to show the relative performance of PCS and wormhole switching under fault-free conditions. Figure 9.58 shows average latency versus normalized accepted traffic for the protocols under study. Latency is measured in clock cycles. If we assume normal distributions, the 95% confidence intervals for the normalized accepted traffic and latency data points were all within 5% of their values.

We see from the graphs that the added overhead of PCS causes a significant performance penalty over wormhole switching at lower message sizes. This penalty grows with the average number of

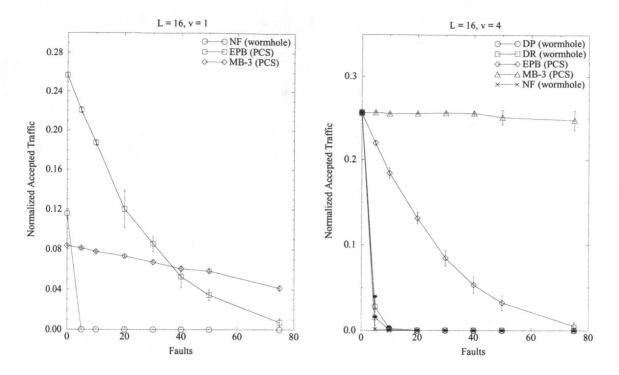

Figure 9.59. Normalized accepted traffic vs. network faults ($v = 1, 4$).

links in the communication path. It is also interesting to note that the penalty appears to be relatively flat across the range of network loads. The relative network throughput capacity is not significantly reduced by the use of PCS. And, as message sizes get large, PCS has performance approaching that of wormhole switching since the overhead is a much smaller fraction of the total communication latency. A similar set of experiments were performed using uniformly distributed destination addresses. The overall trends were identical to that found in Figure 9.58. Since the average path length is larger in the uniformly distributed message pattern, the performance penalty for PCS was proportionately larger.

Fault-Tolerant Performance

In this study we performed experiments on 16-ary 2-cubes with faulty physical links. We use physical link faults to address the performance of the protocols under changes in network topology. We are primarily concerned with overall network throughput (measured by accepted traffic) rather than delivery of individual messages and therefore focus on the effect of failures causing a change in network topology. Figures 9.59 and 9.60 show the normalized accepted traffic of each protocol as physical link faults in the system increase for a moderate network load. The network load is defined by establishing a desired normalized injection rate λ_i. We chose $\lambda_i \approx 0.26$ since that is close to half of the normalized network throughput capacity (from Figure 9.58 we see that normalized network throughput appears to lie between 0.5 and 0.6). The four graphs correspond to networks with 1, 4, 8, and 16 virtual channels per physical link direction, respectively. Assuming the measured accepted traffic is normally distributed, the 95% confidence intervals for each point on the graph is indicated by the error bars.

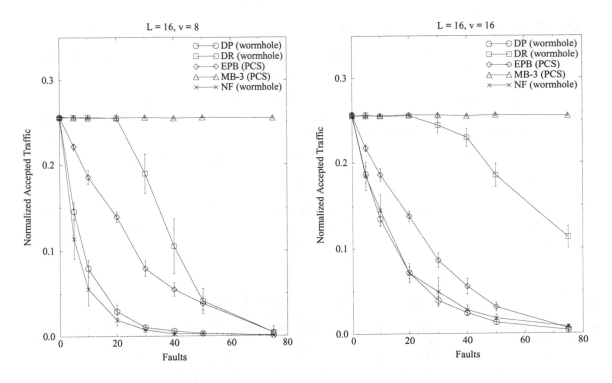

Figure 9.60. Normalized accepted traffic vs. network faults ($v = 8, 16$).

In networks with only one virtual channel per physical link direction, only NF, EPB, and MB-3 were studied since DP and DR require multiple virtual channels per physical link. In the graph with $v = 1$, we see that the cost of misrouting in networks without multiple virtual channels is very high. The realizable network throughput for NF was less than half of the desired injection rate. For MB-3 it was only a third of λ_i. Despite its poor throughput, MB-3 displays good relative performance as the number of faulty links in the network increases. The sustainable throughput for NF with $v = 1$ is 0 for 5 or more physical link faults in the network. The realizable network throughput for EPB declines steadily as faults are introduced into the network.

For $v = 4$, the picture changes considerably. Using multiple virtual channels significantly reduces the cost and likelihood of misrouting. The misrouting protocols NF, MB-3, and DR can all sustain the desired injection rate in networks with no faulty links. With five faulty physical links, however, all of the progressive (wormhole) protocols display extremely reduced throughput. With 10 or more faulty physical links, the wormhole protocols are frequently deadlocked. MB-3 demonstrates a very flat normalized accepted traffic up to 75 failed physical links (14.65% of the physical links).

As the number of virtual channels grows even higher, we see that the wormhole protocols develop more resilience to faults. With $v = 8$, DR is able to sustain the desired network throughput up to 20 link failures. NF and DP show marginal improvement. DP suffers due to the fact that it is unable to misroute. Thus, any failed link will disconnect some portion of the network. Eventually, a message will stall on a faulty link and cause deadlock. Similarly NF suffers from the fact that misrouting is disabled after the first positive going link is used. With $v = 16$, DR, NF, and DP show further marginal improvement. Recent studies have shown that the implementation and performance costs of using virtual channels can be significant [57]. Such results favor the use of protocols that work well with smaller numbers of virtual channels.

Overall, we can make the following observations:

1. As a rule, protocols that have great freedom in misrouting (DR, MB-3) tolerate faults better than those with limited or no misrouting (NF, DP, EPB).

2. The progressive protocols for wormhole switching benefit from increased numbers of virtual channels, while the fault-tolerant performance of backtracking PCS protocols are relatively insensitive to the number of virtual channels.

3. DR needs many virtual channels to provide higher levels of fault-tolerant behavior.

4. MB-3 provides the best overall fault-tolerant performance.

5. For fine-grained message passing, the performance of PCS protocols relative to wormhole switching drops off rapidly and the primary benefit is better fault tolerance properties. For larger ratios of message sizes to message distance, performance approaches that of wormhole switching.

9.13.3   Routing Algorithms for Scouting

In this section we evaluate the performance of the two-phase (TP) routing protocol described in Section 6.6. When no faults are present in the network, TP routing uses $K = 0$ and the same routing restrictions as DP. This results in performance that is identical to that of DP. To measure the fault tolerance of TP, it is compared with misrouting, backtracking with m misroutes (MB-m).

Fault-Tolerant Performance

The performance of the fault-tolerant protocols was evaluated with simulation studies of message passing in a 16-ary 2-cube with 32-flit messages. The routing header was 1 flit long. The message destination traffic was uniformly distributed. Simulation runs were made repeatedly until the 95% confidence intervals for the sample means were acceptable (less than 5% of the mean values). The simulation model was validated using deterministic communication patterns. We use a congestion control mechanism (similar to [36]) by placing a limit on the size of the buffer (eight buffers per injection channel) on the injection channels. If the input buffers are filled, messages cannot be injected into the network until a message in the buffer has been routed. A flit crosses a link in one cycle. The metrics used to measure the performance of TP are average message latency and accepted traffic.

The fault performance of TP is evaluated with a configuration of TP that uses $K = 0$ in fault-free segments. It also uses $K = 0$ in the faulty regions, i.e., it does not use unsafe channels, and then it uses misrouting backtracking search to construct detours when the header cannot advance.

Figure 9.61 is a plot of the latency-traffic curves of TP and MB-m with 1, 10, and 20 failed nodes randomly placed throughout the network. The performance of both routing protocols drops as the number of failed nodes increases, since the number of undeliverable messages increases as the number of faults increases. MB-m degrades gracefully with steady but small drops in the network throughput as the number of faults increases. However, the latency of TP-routed messages for a given network load remains 30 − 40% lower than that of MB-m routed messages.

Figure 9.62 shows the normalized accepted traffic and average latency of TP and MB-m as a function of node failures under varying applied loads. This figure shows that the latency of messages successfully routed via MB-m remains relatively flat regardless of the number of faults in the system. The number in parenthesis indicates the normalized applied load. However, with the normalized

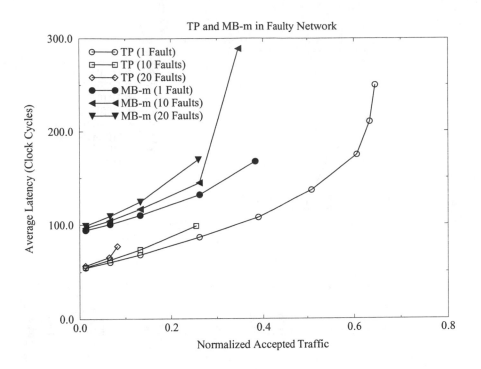

Figure 9.61. Average message latency vs. normalized accepted traffic of TP and MB-*m* with faults.

applied load at 0.384, the latency increased considerably as the number of faults increased. This is because with a low number of faults in the system, an applied load of 0.384 is at the saturation point of the network. With the congestion control mechanism provided in the simulator, any additional applied load is not accepted. However, at the saturation point, any increase in the number of faults will cause the aggregate bandwidth of the network to increase beyond saturation and therefore cause the message latency to increase and the network throughput to drop. When the applied load was at 0.64, the network was already beyond saturation so the increase in the number of faults had a lesser effect.

At low to moderate loads and even at high loads with a low number of faults, the latency and accepted traffic characteristics of TP are significantly superior to that of MB-*m*. The majority of the benefit is derived from messages in fault-free segments of the network transmitting with $K = 0$ (i.e., wormhole switching). TP however, performed poorly at high loads as the number of faults increased. While saturation traffic with one failed node was 0.64, it dropped to slightly over 0 with 20 failed nodes. It should be noted that in the simulated system (a 16-ary 2-cube), 20 failed nodes is much greater than the limit for which TP was designed. Anyway, the performance of TP with a high number of faults is very good as long as the applied load is low to moderate. At higher loads and increased number of faults, the effect of the positive acknowledgments due to the detour construction becomes magnified and performance begins to drop. This is due to the increased number of searches that the routing header has to perform before a path is successfully established and the corresponding increase in the distance from the source node to the destination. The trade-off in this version of TP is the increased number of detours constructed versus the performance of messages in fault-free sections of the network. With larger numbers of faults, the former eventually dominates. In this region, purely conservative protocols like MB-*m* appear to work better.

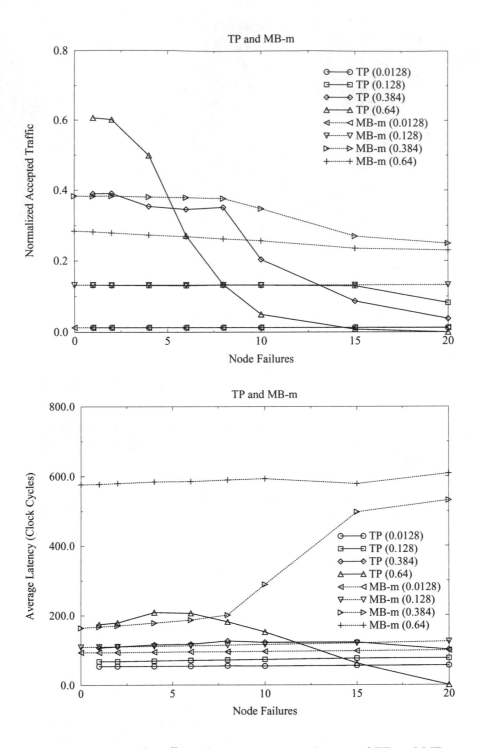

Figure 9.62. Normalized accepted traffic and average message latency of TP and MB-*m* as function of node faults.

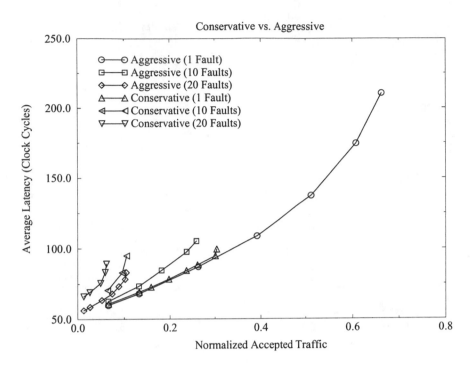

Figure 9.63. Comparison of aggressive ($K = 0$) and conservative ($K = 3$) routing behavior of TP.

In summary, at low fault rates and below network saturation loads, TP performs better than MB-m. We also note that TP protocol used in the experiments was designed for three faults ($2n - 1$ in a 2-D network). A relatively more conservative version could have been configured. Figure 9.63 compares the performance of TP with $K = 0$ and $K = 3$. With only one fault in the network and low network traffic, both versions realize similar performance. However, with high network traffic and larger number of faults, the aggressive TP performs considerably better. This is due to the fact that with $K > 0$, substantial acknowledgment flit traffic can be introduced into the network, dominating the effect of an increased number of detours.

Cost of Supporting Dynamic Faults

When dynamic faults occur, messages may become interrupted. In Section 6.7 a special type of control flit, called *release flit*, was introduced to permit distributed recovery in the presence of dynamic faults.

These control flits release any reserved buffers, notify the source that the message was not delivered, and notify the destination to ignore the message currently being received. If we are also interested in guaranteeing message delivery in the presence of dynamic faults, the complete path must be held until the last flit is delivered to the destination. A message acknowledgment sent from the destination removes the path and flushes the copy of the message at the source. Here we are only interested in the impact on the performance of TP. Figure 9.64 illustrates the overhead of this recovery and reliable message delivery mechanism.

The additional message acknowledgment introduces additional control flit traffic into the system. Message acknowledgments tend to have a throttling effect on injection of new messages. As a

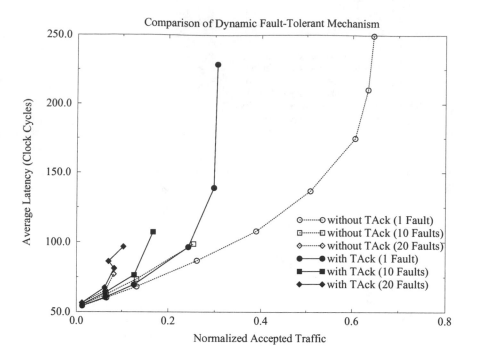

Figure 9.64. Comparison of TP with and without tail-acknowledgment flits.

result, TP routing using the mechanism saturates at lower network loads and delivered messages have higher latencies. From the simulation results shown in Figure 9.64, we see that at low loads the performance impact of support for dynamic fault recovery is not very significant. However, as applied load increases, the additional traffic generated by the recovery mechanism and the use of message acknowledgments begins to produce a substantial impact on performance. The point of interest here is that dynamic fault recovery has a useful range of feasible operating loads for TP protocols. In fact, this range extends almost to saturation traffic.

Trace-Driven Simulation

The true measure of the performance of an interconnection network is how well it performs under real communication patterns generated by actual applications. The network is considered to have failed if the program is prevented from completing due to undeliverable messages. Communication traces derived from two different application programs: EP (Gaussian Deviates), and MMP (Matrix Multiply). These program traces were generated using the SPASM execution-driven simulator [322].

Communication trace driven simulations were performed allowing only physical link failures. Node failures would require the remapping of the processes, with the resulting remapping affecting performance. No recovery mechanisms were used for recovery of undeliverable messages. The traces were generated from applications executing on a 16-ary 2-cube. The simulated network was a 16-ary 2-cube with 8 and 16 virtual channels per physical link. The aggressive version of TP was used, i.e., no unsafe channels were used. Figure 9.65 shows plots of the probability of completion for the two different program traces with differing values of misrouting (m). A trace is said to have completed when all trace messages have been delivered. If even one message cannot be delivered,

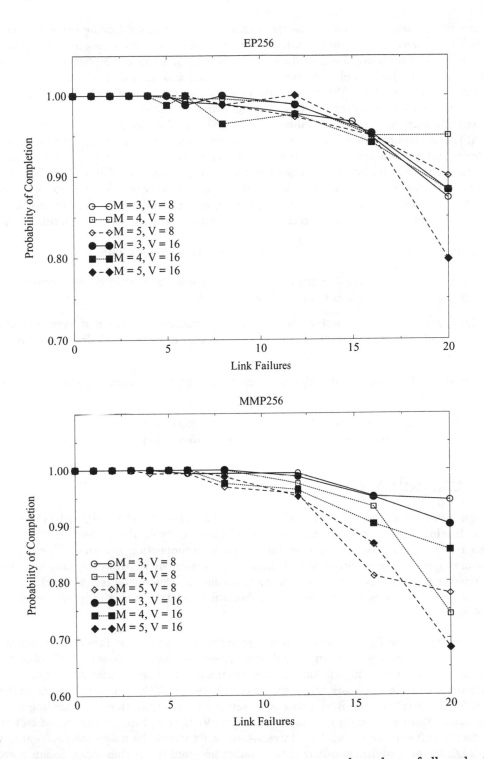

Figure 9.65. Probability of completion for various program traces and numbers of allowed misroutes.

program execution cannot complete. The results show the effect of not having recovery mechanisms. These simulations were implemented with no retries attempted when a message backtracks to the source or the node containing the first data flit. This is responsible for probabilities of completion below 1.0 for even a small number of faults. The performance effects of the recovery mechanism was illustrated in Figure 9.64. We expect that two or three retries will be sufficient in practice to maintain completion probabilities of 1.0 for a larger number of faults.

In some instances, an increased number of misroutes resulted in poorer completion rates. We believe that this is primarily due to the lack of recovery mechanisms and retries. Increased misrouting causes more network resources to be reserved by a message. This may in turn increase the probability that other messages will be forced to backtrack due to busy resources. Without retries, completion rates suffer. Again we see the importance of implementing relatively simple heuristics such as a small number of retries. Finally, the larger number of virtual channels offered better performance since it provided an increase of network resources and hence reduced the amount of searching required by routing headers.

Specifically, the performance evaluation provided the following insights:

1. The cost of positive acknowledgments in TP dominates the cost of detour construction, suggesting the use of low values of K, preferably $K = 0$.

2. Configurable flow control enables substantial performance improvement over PCS for low to modest number of faults since the majority of traffic is in the fault-free portions, realizing performance close to that of wormhole switching.

3. For low to modest number of faults, the performance cost of recovery mechanisms is relatively low.

4. At very high fault rates, we still must use more conservative protocols like MB-m to ensure reliable message delivery and application program completion.

9.14   Conclusions

When designing an interconnection network for a parallel computer, the designer has to face several trade-offs. In this section we present some considerations about the impact of different design parameters on the performance and reliability of an interconnection network. These parameters have been arranged by decreasing order of impact on performance. However, this ordering is not strict. Whenever possible, we will give recommendations for different design parameters.

From the performance point of view, the evaluation presented in this chapter provided the following insights:

- *Software messaging layer.* A high percentage of the communication latency in multicomputers is produced by the overhead in the software messaging layer. Reducing or hiding this overhead is likely to have a higher impact on performance than the remaining design parameters, especially when messages are relatively short. The use of VCC can eliminate or hide most of the software overhead by overlapping path setup with computation, and caching and retaining virtual circuits for use by multiple messages. VCC complements the use of techniques to reduce the software overhead, like active messages. It should be noted that software overhead is so high in some multicomputers that it makes no sense improving other design parameters. However, once this overhead has been removed or hidden, the remaining design parameters become much more important.

- *Software support for collective communication.* Collective communication operations considerably benefit from using specific algorithms. Using separate addressing, latency increases linearly with the number of participating nodes. However, when algorithms for collective communication are implemented in software, latency is considerably reduced, increasing logarithmically with the number of participating nodes. This improvement is achieved with no additional hardware cost and no overhead for unicast messages.

- *Number of ports.* If the software overhead has been removed or hidden, the number of ports has a considerable influence on performance, especially when messages are sent locally. If the number of ports is too small, the network interface is likely to be a bottleneck for the network. The optimal number of ports heavily depends on the spatial locality of traffic patterns.

- *Switching technique.* Nowadays, most commercial and experimental parallel computers implement wormhole switching. Although VCT switching achieves a higher throughput, the performance improvement is small when virtual channels are used in wormhole switching. Additionally, VCT switching requires splitting messages into packets not exceeding buffer capacity. If messages are longer than buffer size, wormhole switching should be preferred. However, when messages are shorter than or equal to buffer size, VCT switching performs slightly better than wormhole switching, also simplifying deadlock avoidance. This is the case for distributed shared-memory multiprocessors. VCT switching is also preferable when it is not easy to avoid deadlock in wormhole switching (multicast routing in multistage networks), or in some applications requiring real-time communication [293]. Finally, a combination of wormhole switching and circuit switching with wave-pipelined switches and channels has the potential to increase performance, especially when messages are very long [102].

- *Packet size.* For pipelined switching techniques, filling the pipeline produces some overhead. Also, routing a header usually takes longer than transmitting a data flit across a switch. Finally, splitting messages into packets and reassembling them at the destination node also produces some overhead. These overheads can be amortized if packets are long enough. However, once packets are long enough to amortize the overhead, it is not convenient to increase packet size even more because blocking time for some packets will be high. On the other hand, switching techniques like VCT may limit packet size, especially when packet buffers are implemented in hardware. Finally, it should be noted that this parameter only makes sense when messages are long. If they are shorter than the optimal packet size, messages should not be split into packets. This is the case for DSMs.

- *Deadlock handling technique.* Current deadlock avoidance techniques allow fully adaptive routing across physical channels. However, some buffer resources (usually some virtual channels) must be dedicated to avoid deadlock by providing escape paths to messages blocking cyclically. On the other hand, progressive deadlock recovery techniques require a minimum amount of dedicated hardware to deliver deadlocked packets. Deadlock recovery techniques do not restrict routing at all, therefore allowing the use of all the virtual channels to increase routing freedom, achieving the highest performance when packets are short. However, when packets are long or have very different lengths and the network approaches the saturation point, the small bandwidth offered by the recovery hardware may saturate. In this case, some deadlocked packets may have to wait for long, thus degrading performance and making latency less predictable. Also, recovery techniques require efficient deadlock detection mechanisms. Currently available detection techniques only work efficiently when all the packets are short and have a similar length. Otherwise, many false deadlocks are detected, quickly saturating the bandwidth of the recovery hardware. The poor behavior of current deadlock detection mechanisms considerably limits the practical applicability of deadlock recovery techniques unless all the packets are short. This may change when more accurate distributed deadlock detection mechanisms are developed.

- *Routing algorithm.* For regular topologies and uniform traffic, the difference between deterministic and fully adaptive routing algorithms is small. However, for switch-based networks with irregular topology and uniform traffic, adaptive routing algorithms considerably improve performance over deterministic or partially adaptive ones because the latter usually route many messages across nonminimal paths. Moreover, for nonuniform traffic patterns, adaptive routing considerably increases throughput over deterministic routing algorithms, regardless of network topology. On the other hand, adaptive routing does not reduce latency when traffic is low to moderate because contention is small and base latency is the same for deterministic and fully adaptive routing, provided that both algorithms only use minimal paths. So, for real applications, the best choice depends on the application requirements. If most applications exhibit a high degree of communication locality, fully adaptive routing does not help. If the traffic produced by the applications does not saturate the network (regardless of the routing algorithm) and latency is critical, then adaptive routing will not increase performance. However, when multiprocessors implement latency hiding mechanisms and application performance mainly depends on the throughput achievable by the interconnection network, then adaptive routing is expected to achieve higher performance than deterministic routing. In case of using adaptive routing, the additional cost of implementing fully adaptive routing should be kept small. Therefore, routing algorithms that require few resources to avoid deadlock or to recover from it, like the ones evaluated in this chapter, should be preferred. For these routing algorithms, the additional complexity of fully adaptive routing usually produces a small reduction in clock frequency.

- *Number of virtual channels.* In wormhole switching, when no virtual channels are used, blocked messages do not allow other messages to use the bandwidth of the physical channels they are occupying. Adding the first additional virtual channel usually increases throughput considerably at the expense of a small increase in latency. On the other hand, adding more virtual channels produces a much smaller increment in throughput while increasing hardware delays considerably. For deterministic routing in meshes, two virtual channels provide a good trade-off. For tori, the partially adaptive algorithm evaluated in this chapter with two virtual channels also provides a good trade-off, achieving the advantages of channel multiplexing without increasing the number of virtual channels with respect to the deterministic algorithm. If fully adaptive routing is preferred, the minimum number of virtual channels should be used. Fully adaptive routing requires a minimum of two (three) virtual channels to avoid deadlock in meshes (tori). Again, for applications that require low latency and produce a relatively small amount of traffic, adding virtual channels does not help. Virtual channels only increase performance when applications benefit from a higher network throughput.

- *Hardware support for collective communication.* Adding hardware support for multidestination message passing usually reduces the latency of collective communication operations with respect to software algorithms. However, this reduction is very small (if any) when the number of participating nodes is small. When many nodes participate and traffic is only composed of multidestination messages, latency reduction ranges from 2 to 7, depending on several parameters. In real applications, traffic for collective communication operations usually represents a much smaller fraction of network traffic. Also, the number of participating nodes may considerably vary from one application to another. In general, this number is small except for broadcast and barrier synchronization. In summary, whether adding hardware support for collective communication is worth its cost depends on the application requirements.

- *Injection limitation mechanism.* When fully adaptive routing is used, network interfaces should include some mechanism to limit the injection of new messages when the network is heavily loaded. Otherwise, increasing applied load above the saturation point may degrade performance severely. In some cases, the start-up latency is so high that it effectively limits the injection rate. When the start-up latency does not prevent network saturation, simple mechanisms like restricting injected messages to use some predetermined virtual channel(s) or waiting until the number of free output virtual channels at a node is higher than a threshold are enough. Injection limitation mechanisms are especially recommended when using routing algorithms that allow cyclic dependencies between channels, and to limit the frequency of deadlock when using deadlock recovery mechanisms.

- *Buffer size.* For wormhole switching and short messages, increasing buffer size above a certain threshold does not improve performance significantly. For long messages (or packets), increasing buffer size increases performance because blocked messages occupy fewer channels. However, when messages are very long increasing buffer size only helps if buffers are deep enough to allow blocked messages to leave the source node and release some channels. It should be noted that communication locality may prevent most messages from leaving the source node before reaching their destination even when using deep buffers. Therefore, in most cases small buffers are enough to achieve good performance. However, this analysis assumes that flits are individually acknowledged. Indeed, buffer size in wormhole switching is mainly determined by the requirements of the flow control mechanism. Optimizations like block acknowledgments require a certain buffer capacity to perform efficiently. Moreover, when channels are pipelined, buffers must be deep enough to store all the flits in transit across the physical link plus the flits injected into the link during the propagation of the flow control signals. Some additional capacity is required for the flow control mechanism to operate without introducing bubbles in the message pipeline. Thus, when channels are pipelined buffer size mainly depends on the degree of channel pipelining. For VCT switching, throughput increases considerably when moving from one to two packet buffers. Adding more buffers yields diminishing returns.

From the reliability point of view, the evaluation presented in this chapter provided the following insights:

- *Reliability/performance trade-offs.* An interconnection network should be reliable. Depending on the intended applications and the relative value of $MTBF$ and $MTTR$, different trade-offs are possible. When $MTTR << MTBF$, the probability of the second or the third fault occurring before the first fault is repaired is very low. In such environments, software based rerouting is a cost-effective and viable alternative. This technique supports many fault patterns and requires minimum hardware support. However, performance degrades significantly when faults occur, increasing latency for messages that meet faults by a factor of $2 - 4$. When faults are more frequent or performance degradation is not acceptable, a more complex hardware support is required. The fault tolerance properties of the routing algorithm are constrained by the underlying switching technique, as indicated in the next item.

- *Switching technique.* If performance is more important than reliability, fault tolerance should be achieved without modifying the switching technique. In this case, additional resources (usually virtual channels) are required to implement limited misrouting and route messages in the presence of faults. If reliability is more important than performance, PCS has the potential to increase fault tolerance considerably at the cost of some overhead in path setup. PCS can be combined with misrouting backtracking protocols, achieving an excellent level of tolerance to static faults. Finally, dynamically configurable flow control techniques, like scouting, offer an excellent performance/reliability trade-off at the expense of a more complex hardware support. This switching technique achieves performance similar to that of wormhole switching in the absence of faults, and reliability halfway between wormhole switching and PCS.

- *Support for dynamic faults.* Faults may occur at any time. When a fault interrupts a message in transit the message cannot be delivered, and a fragment of the message may remain in the network forever, therefore producing deadlock. So, hardware support for dynamic faults has to perform two different actions: removing fragments of interrupted messages and notifying the source node so that the message is transmitted again. Adding support to remove fragments of interrupted messages is very convenient because it does not slow down normal operation significantly, and deadlocks produced by interrupted messages are avoided. However, notifying the source node produces an extra use of resources for every transmitted message, therefore degrading performance significantly even in the absence of faults. So, this additional support for reliable transmission should only be included when reliability is more important than performance.

9.15   Commented References

Many researchers evaluated the performance of interconnection networks with different combinations of design parameters. In this section, we briefly comment on some of those results. These references may be useful as pointers for further reading.

Several evaluation studies compared the relative performance of different routing algorithms or analyzed the performance of some proposed routing algorithm. Most recent studies focused on wormhole switching [24, 36, 74, 92, 175, 343], also existing results for packet switching [277], VCT switching [33, 189, 248, 250], hybrid switching [316], PCS [126, 127], scouting [80, 100] and wave pipelining [102]. Although most results were obtained for direct networks, multistage networks [253], and switch-based interconnects with irregular topologies [30, 284, 318, 319] were also considered.

Some studies analyzed the impact of the network topology on performance, considering implementation constraints [1, 3, 71, 103, 249, 310]. Hierarchical topologies were also studied [18, 161]. Also, some researchers compared the performance of different switching techniques [126, 292, 293].

Some performance evaluations analyzed the impact of using virtual channels [73, 89, 311]. Several selection functions were compared in [74]. The effect of the number of delivery ports was studied in [17, 189]. Injection limitation techniques to prevent performance degradation with loads above the saturation point were evaluated in [74, 220, 221].

Deadlock avoidance techniques were evaluated in [92, 137]. Deadlock recovery techniques were analyzed in [9, 179, 226, 288]. Detailed cost and speed models for routers and links were proposed in [11, 57]. Some evaluation studies considered this model in order to perform a more realistic evaluation [101].

Some performance studies analyzed the impact of message length and hybrid traffic [176, 185], packetization [177], and channel allocation policies [185]. The behavior of networks supporting real-time communication was studied in [291].

The performance of different support for collective communication operations was reported in [110, 173, 208, 224, 234, 264, 267]. The overhead of the software messaging layer was studied in [170, 171, 214]. In [238], it is shown that doubling network bandwidth may not improve the performance of parallel computers if software overhead is too high.

Also, the fault tolerance performance of several combinations of switching techniques and routing algorithms was evaluated in [37, 74, 80, 100, 127]. Hardware support for dynamic faults was evaluated in [124].

Several analytical models of the behavior of interconnection networks were proposed [2, 3, 71, 128, 178, 310], analyzing the effect of several topological parameters. Several distributions for message destinations were proposed in [287]. Detailed performance measurements and trace-driven simulations were reported in [160, 214]. Finally, several network simulators have been developed. Some descriptions of network simulation tools can be found in [21, 85, 169, 230, 261, 290, 292]. Also, a technique to reduce the number of simulations required for a performance study was presented in [219].

Appendix A

Formal Definitions for Deadlock Avoidance

In this appendix we present a formal definition of most concepts defined in Section 3.1. These definitions are mainly based on [98]. This theory proposes a necessary and sufficient condition for an adaptive routing function to be deadlock-free. It is valid for networks using wormhole switching and routing functions that only consider the current and destination nodes in their domain. The domain of the routing function can be extended by considering the input buffer containing the message header. This extension considerably changes the definitions. These changes can be found in [99], where a necessary and sufficient condition for deadlock avoidance is proposed for VCT and SAF switching. The view presented in Section 3.1 unifies the theories proposed in [98] and [99]. These theories are based on a sufficient condition for deadlock avoidance presented in [92]. Other extensions of this theory include support for path-based multicast routing [97] and for a mixed set of resources (edge and central buffers) [10].

This theory is valid when messages are split into packets. However, we will consider that messages are not split. Otherwise, the assumptions and definitions proposed below should refer to packets.

A.1 Assumptions

1. A node can generate messages of arbitrary length destined for any other node at any rate.

2. A message arriving at its destination node is eventually consumed. As a consequence, a node cannot forward a message destined for itself through the network.

3. Wormhole switching is used. So, once a queue accepts the first flit of a message, it must accept the remainder of the message before accepting any flits from another message. Also, a message may occupy several channels simultaneously.

4. The routing control unit may arbitrate between messages that request it, but may not choose among waiting messages.

5. A queue cannot contain flits belonging to different messages. Thus, when a message is blocked, its header flit will always occupy the head of a queue.

6. The route taken by a message depends on its destination and the status of output channels (free or busy). At a given node, an adaptive routing function supplies a set of output channels based on the current and destination nodes. A selection from this set is made based on the status of output channels at the current node. This selection is performed in such a way that a free channel (if any) is supplied. If all the output channels are busy, the message header will be routed again until it is able to reserve a channel, thus getting the first channel that becomes free.

7. When several messages are waiting for a free output channel, they are routed following a round-robin strategy, thus preventing starvation.

8. The routing function may allow messages to follow nonminimal paths.

9. For each source-destination pair, the routing function will supply at least one minimal path. This assumption is only required to prove the necessary condition for deadlock-freedom.

A.2   Definitions

Definition A.1 *An* interconnection network I *is a strongly connected directed multigraph,* $I = G(N, C)$. *The vertices of the multigraph N represent the set of processing nodes. The arcs of the multigraph C represent the set of communication channels. More than a single channel is allowed to connect a given pair of nodes. Each channel c_i has an associated queue with capacity $cap(c_i)$. The source and destination nodes of channel c_i are denoted s_i and d_i, respectively. For the sake of simplicity, an enumeration of arbitrary channels is denoted $c_1, c_2, \ldots, c_k$ instead of $c_{n_1}, c_{n_2}, \ldots, c_{n_k}$. An enumeration does not imply any channel ordering.*

Definition A.2 *Let F be the set of valid* channel status, $F = \{free, busy\}$.

Definition A.3 *An* adaptive routing function $R : N \times N \to \mathcal{P}(C)$, *where $\mathcal{P}(C)$ is the power set of C, supplies a set of alternative output channels to send a message from the current node n_c to the destination node n_d, $R(n_c, n_d) = \{c_1, c_2, \ldots, c_p\}$. By definition, $R(n, n) = \emptyset$, $\forall n \in N$.*

Definition A.4 *A* selection function $S : \mathcal{P}(C \times F) \to C$ *selects a free output channel (if any) from the set supplied by the routing function. From the definition, S takes into account the status of all the channels belonging to the set supplied by the routing function. The selection can be random or based on static or dynamic priorities. It must be noticed that starvation is prevented using a round-robin strategy when several message headers are waiting for the router, according to assumption 7. The selection function will only affect performance.*

Definition A.5 *A routing function R for a given interconnection network I is* connected *iff*

$$\forall x, y \in N, x \neq y, \exists c_1, c_2, \ldots, c_k \in C \text{ such that } \begin{cases} c_1 \in R(x, y) \\ c_{m+1} \in R(d_m, y), \quad m = 1, \ldots, k-1 \\ d_k = y \end{cases}$$

In other words, it is possible to establish a *path* $P(x, y) \in \mathcal{P}(C)$ between x and y using channels belonging to the sets supplied by R.

Definition A.6 *Given an interconnection network I, a routing function R, and a pair of adjacent channels* $c_i, c_j \in C$, *there is a* direct dependency *from* c_i *to* c_j *iff*

$$\exists x \in N \text{ such that } c_i \in R(s_i, x) \text{ and } c_j \in R(d_i, x)$$

That is, c_j can be requested immediately after using c_i by messages destined for some node x. Adjacency means that $d_i = s_j$.

Definition A.7 *A* channel dependency graph D *for a given interconnection network I and routing function R, is a directed graph,* $D = G(C, E)$. *The vertices of D are the channels of I. The arcs of D are the pairs of channels* (c_i, c_j) *such that there is a direct dependency from* c_i *to* c_j.

Definition A.8 *A* sink *channel for a given interconnection network I and routing function R is a channel* c_i *such that*

$$x \in N, c_i \in R(s_i, x) \Rightarrow x = d_i$$

In other words, all the flits that enter a sink channel reach their destination in a single hop.

Definition A.9 *A* configuration *is an assignment of a set of flits to each queue. All of the flits in any one queue belong to the same message (assumption 5). The number of flits in the queue for channel* c_i *is denoted* $size(c_i)$. *If the first flit in the queue for channel* c_i *is destined for node* n_d, *then* $head(c_i) = n_d$. *If the first flit is not a header and the next channel reserved by its header is* c_j, *then* $next(c_i) = c_j$. *Let* $C_h \subseteq C$ *be the set of channels containing a header flit at their queue head. Let* $C_d \subseteq C$ *be the set of channels containing a data or tail flit at their queue head. A configuration is* legal *iff*

$$\forall c_i \in C \begin{cases} size(c_i) \leq cap(c_i) \\ size(c_i) > 0 \Rightarrow c_i \in R(s_i, head(c_i)) \end{cases}$$

For each channel, the queue capacity is not exceeded and all the flits stored in the queue (if any), can reach the channel from the previous node using the routing function.

Definition A.10 *A* deadlocked configuration *for a given interconnection network I and routing function R is a nonempty legal configuration verifying the following conditions:*

1) $C_h \neq \emptyset$

2) $\forall c_i \in C_h \begin{cases} head(c_i) \neq d_i \\ size(c_j) > 0 \quad \forall c_j \in R(d_i, head(c_i)) \end{cases}$

3) $\forall c_i \in C_d \begin{cases} head(c_i) \neq d_i \\ size(next(c_i)) = cap(next(c_i)) \end{cases}$

In a deadlocked configuration there is no message whose header flit has already arrived at its destination. Header flits cannot advance because the queues for all the alternative output channels supplied by the routing function are not empty (see assumption 5). Data and tail flits cannot advance because the next channel reserved by their message header has a full queue. No condition is imposed on empty channels. It must be noticed that a data flit can be blocked at a node even if there are free output channels to reach its destination because data flits must follow the path reserved by their header.

Definition A.11 *A routing function R for an interconnection network I is* deadlock-free *iff there is not any deadlocked configuration for that routing function on that network.*

Definition A.12 *A routing subfunction R_1 for a given routing function R is a routing function defined on the same domain as R that supplies a subset of the channels supplied by R*

$$R_1(x,y) \subseteq R(x,y) \quad \forall x, y \in N$$

The set of all the channels supplied by R_1 is $C_1 = \bigcup_{\forall x,y \in N} R_1(x,y)$. Also, the complementary routing subfunction of R_1 will be denoted as

$$R_1^R(x,y) = R(x,y) - R_1(x,y) \quad \forall x, y \in N$$

Thus, R_1 is a restriction of R. It should be noted that this definition allows the restriction of channel routing capability instead of simply removing channels. In other words, it is possible to restrict the use of a channel c_i when R_1 routes messages to some destinations while still allowing the use of c_i when routing messages to other destinations.

Definition A.13 *Given an interconnection network I, a routing function R, a routing subfunction R_1, and a pair of nonadjacent channels $c_i, c_j \in C_1$, there is an* indirect dependency *from c_i to c_j iff*

$$\exists x \in N, \ \exists c_1, c_2, \ldots, c_k \in C \text{ such that } \begin{cases} c_i \in R_1(s_i, x) \\ c_1 \in R_1^R(d_i, x) \\ c_{m+1} \in R_1^R(d_m, x), \quad m = 1, \ldots, k-1 \\ c_j \in R_1(d_k, x) \end{cases}$$

That is, it is possible to establish a path from s_i to d_j for messages destined for some node x, and c_i and c_j are the first and last channels in that path and the only ones in that path supplied by R_1 for the destination of the message. Therefore, c_j can be requested after using c_i by some messages. As c_i and c_j are not adjacent, some other channels not supplied by R_1 for the destination of the message are reserved while establishing the path between them. Those channels are supplied by R.

Definition A.14 *Given an interconnection network I, a routing function R, a routing subfunction R_1, and a pair of adjacent channels $c_i, c_j \in C_1$, there is a* direct cross-dependency *from c_i to c_j iff*

$$\exists x, y \in N \text{ such that } \begin{cases} c_i \in R_1(s_i, x) \\ c_i \in R_1^R(s_i, y) \\ c_j \in R_1(d_i, y) \end{cases}$$

That is, c_j can be requested immediately after using c_i by messages destined for some node y, c_j is supplied by R_1 for the destination of the message, and c_i cannot be supplied by R_1 for that destination. However, c_i is supplied by R_1 for some other destination(s).

Definition A.15 *Given an interconnection network I, a routing function R, a routing subfunction R_1, and a pair of nonadjacent channels $c_i, c_j \in C_1$, there is an* indirect cross-dependency *from c_i to c_j iff*

$$\exists x, y \in N, \ \exists c_1, c_2, \ldots, c_k \in C \text{ such that } \begin{cases} c_i \in R_1(s_i, x) \\ c_i \in R_1^R(s_i, y) \\ c_1 \in R_1^R(d_i, y) \\ c_{m+1} \in R_1^R(d_m, y), \quad m = 1, \ldots, k-1 \\ c_j \in R_1(d_k, y) \end{cases}$$

That is, it is possible to establish a path from s_i to d_j for messages destined for some node y, c_i and c_j are the first and last channels in that path, c_j is the only channel in that path supplied by R_1 for the destination of the message, and c_i cannot be supplied by R_1 for that destination. However, c_i is supplied by R_1 for some other destination(s). Therefore, c_j can be requested after using c_i by some messages. As c_i and c_j are not adjacent, some other channels not supplied by R_1 for the destination of the message are reserved while establishing the path between them.

Definition A.16 *An* extended channel dependency graph D_E *for a given interconnection network I and routing subfunction R_1 of a routing function R, is a directed graph, $D_E = G(C_1, E_E)$. The vertices of D_E are the channels supplied by the routing subfunction R_1 for some destinations. The arcs of D_E are the pairs of channels (c_i, c_j) such that there is either a direct, indirect, direct cross- or indirect cross-dependency from c_i to c_j.*

The following definition is only required to prove the necessary condition for deadlock freedom.

Definition A.17 *A routing function R for a given interconnection network I is* coherent *iff for every pair of nodes $x, y \in N, x \neq y$ and for every path $P(x, y) = \{c_1, c_2, \ldots, c_k\}$ that can be established by R between them*

$$\forall i \in \{1, \ldots, k\}, \quad c_{m+1} \in R(d_m, d_i), \quad m = 0, \ldots, i-1, \quad \text{where } d_0 = x$$

That is, for every path P that can be established by R, every prefix of P is also a path of R. In other words, if a routing function R can establish a path $P(x, y)$ between x and y, it can also establish a path between x and any intermediate node crossed by $P(x, y)$ using a subset of the channels used by $P(x, y)$. If the routing function R is coherent, there is not any loop (1-cycle) in the extended channel dependency graph of any routing subfunction. Otherwise, there would be a destination node for which a message is allowed to cross a channel c_i (and its source node s_i) twice. Taking into account assumption 2, the subpath starting and ending at s_i is not allowed. Thus, that routing function would not be coherent.

A.3 Theorems

The following theorem proposes a sufficient condition for an adaptive routing function to be deadlock-free.

Theorem A.1 *A connected and adaptive routing function R for an interconnection network I is deadlock-free if there exists a routing subfunction R_1 that is connected and has no cycles in its extended channel dependency graph D_E.*

For coherent routing functions, this condition becomes a necessary and sufficient one, as indicated by the following theorem.

Theorem A.2 *A coherent, connected and adaptive routing function R for an interconnection network I is deadlock-free iff there exists a routing subfunction R_1 that is connected and has no cycles in its extended channel dependency graph D_E.*

Appendix B

List of Acronyms

1-D	= One-dimensional
2-D	= Two-dimensional
3-D	= Three-dimensional
AM	= Active messages
API	= Application programmers interface
ATM	= Asynchronous transfer mode
BFS	= Breadth-first spanning tree
BMIN	= Bidirectional multistage interconnection network
BNF	= Burton normal form
BRCP	= Base routing conformed path
BWS	= Buffered wormhole switching
CAD	= Computer-aided design
CIBU	= Control input buffer
CMOS	= Complementary metal oxide semiconductor
CMU	= Carnegie Mellon University
CNF	= Chaos normal form
COBU	= Control output buffer
CPU	= Central processing unit
CRC	= Cyclic redundancy check
CSMA/CD	= Carrier-sense multiple access with collision detection
CWG	= Channel wait-for graph
DASH	= Directory architecture for shared-memory
DCM	= Direct connect module
DCSH	= Distributed crossbar switch hypermesh
DEC	= Digital Equipment Corp.
DIBU	= Data input buffer
DMA	= Direct memory access
DMIN	= Dilated multistage interconnection network
DOBU	= Data output buffer
DP	= Duato's protocol (Duato's routing algorithm)
DR	= Dimension reversal
DSM	= Distributed shared-memory multiprocessor

DTB   = Data translation buffer
ECL   = Emitter-coupled logic
EMB   = Exhaustive misrouting backtracking
EOH   = End-of-header
EPB   = Exhaustive profitable backtracking
FDDI   = Fiber Distributed Data Interface
FIFO   = First-in-first-out
FM   = Fast messages
GID   = Group ID
HL   = Hierarchical leader-based
HP   = Hewlett-Packard
HPF   = High Performance Fortran
IBM   = International Business Machines
I/O   = Input/output
IP   = Internet protocol
ISI   = Information Sciences Institute
KSR   = Kendall Square Research
LAN   = Local area network
LC   = Link controller
LCU   = Link control unit
LD   = Label-based dual-path
LEN   = Lan, Esfahanian, and Ni
MAGIC   = Memory and general interconnect controller
MB-m = Misrouting backtracking protocol with m misroutes
MCM   = Multichip module
MCP   = Myrinet control program
MIMD   = Multiple-instruction multiple-data
MIN   = Multistage interconnection network
MIT   = Massachusetts Institute of Technology
MPI   = Message passing interface
MST   = Minimal Steiner tree
MTBF   = Mean time between failures
MTTR   = Mean time to repair
NEC   = Nippon Electric Company
NI   = Network interface
NOW   = Network of workstations
NP   = Non polynomial
NPB   = NAS Parallel Benchmarks
NUMA   = Nonuniform memory access
OMC   = Optimal multicast cycle
OMP   = Optimal multicast path
OMT   = Optimal multicast tree
PAR   = Planar-adaptive routing
PC   = Personal computer
PCI   = Peripheral component interconnect
PCS   = Pipelined circuit switching
PE   = Processing element
PVM   = Parallel virtual machine

RAID	=	Redundant arrays of inexpensive disks
RCU	=	Router control unit
RHS	=	Right-hand side
RMA	=	Remote memory access
RST	=	Rectilinear Steiner tree
SAF	=	Store-and-forward
SAN	=	System area network
SCHL	=	Source-centered hierarchical leader
SCI	=	Scalable coherent interface
SGI	=	Silicon Graphics Inc.
SHRIMP	=	Scalable high-performance really inexpensive multiprocessor
SIMD	=	Single-instruction multiple-data
SPASM	=	Simulator for parallel architectural scalability measurements
SPIDER	=	Scalable pipelined interconnect for distributed endpoint routing
SPMD	=	Single-program multiple-data
SPUmesh	=	Source partitioned U-mesh
SQHL	=	Source quadrant-based hierarchical leader
SWM	=	Shallow water modeling
TMC	=	Thinking Machines Corp.
TMIN	=	Traditional multistage interconnection network
TP	=	Two-phase routing algorithm
TPB-u	=	Two-phase backtracking
UMA	=	Uniform memory access
USC	=	University of Southern California
VC	=	Virtual channel or virtual channel controller
VCC	=	Virtual circuit caching
VCT	=	Virtual cut-through
VLSI	=	Very large-scale integration
VRAM	=	Video random-access memory

References

[1] S. Abraham and K. Padmanabhan, "Performance of multicomputer networks under pin-out constraints," *Journal of Parallel and Distributed Computing*, vol. 12, no. 3, pp. 237–248, July 1991.

[2] V. S. Adve and M. K. Vernon, "Performance analysis of mesh interconnection networks with deterministic routing," *IEEE Transactions on Parallel and Distributed Systems*, vol. 5, no. 3, pp. 225–246, March 1994.

[3] A. Agarwal, "Limits on interconnection network performance," *IEEE Transactions on Parallel and Distributed Systems*, vol. 2, no. 4, pp. 398–412, October 1991.

[4] A. Agarwal, et al., "APRIL: A processor architecture for multiprocessing," *Proceedings of the 17th International Symposium on Computer Architecture*, pp. 104–14, June 1990.

[5] T. Agerwala, et al., "SP2 system architecture," *IBM Systems Journal*, vol. 34, no. 2, pp. 152–184, 1995.

[6] S. B. Akers and B. Krishnamurthy, "A group-theoretic model for symmetric interconnection networks," *IEEE Transactions on Computers*, vol. C-38, no. 4, pp. 555–566, April 1989.

[7] J. D. Allen, et al., "Ariadne - an adaptive router for fault-tolerant multicomputers," *Proceedings of the 21st International Symposium on Computer Architecture*, pp. 278–288, April 1994.

[8] Anjan K. V. and T. M. Pinkston, "DISHA: A deadlock recovery scheme for fully adaptive routing," *Proceedings of the 9th International Parallel Processing Symposium*, pp. 537–543, April 1995.

[9] Anjan K. V. and T. M. Pinkston, An efficient fully adaptive deadlock recovery scheme: DISHA," *Proceedings of the 22nd International Symposium on Computer Architecture*, pp. 201–210, June 1995.

[10] Anjan K. V., T. M. Pinkston, and J. Duato, "Generalized theory for deadlock-free adaptive routing and its application to Disha Concurrent," *Proceedings of the 10th International Parallel Processing Symposium*, pp. 815–821, April 1996.

[11] K. Aoyama and A. A. Chien, "The cost of adaptivity and virtual lanes in a wormhole router," Technical Report, Department of Computer Science, University of Illinois at Urbana-Champaign, 1994.

[12] Arvind and R. S. Nikhil, "Executing a program on the MIT tagged token dataflow architecture," *Proceedings of the PARLE Conference*, published as *Lecture Notes in Computer Science*, vol. 2, pp. 1–29, Springer-Verlag, Eindhoven, 1987.

[13] W. C. Athas and C. L. Seitz, "Multicomputers: Message-passing concurrent computers," *IEEE Computer*, vol. 21, no. 8, pp. 9–24, August 1988.

[14] D. Bailey, et al., "The NAS parallel benchmarks 2.0," Technical Report NAS-95-020, December 1995. Available from *http://www.nas.nasa.gov/NAS/NPB*.

[15] W. E. Baker, et al., "A flexible ServerNet-based fault tolerant architecture," *Proceedings of the Fault Tolerant Computing Symposium*, pp. 2–11, June 1995.

[16] H. B. Bakoglu, *Circuits, Interconnections, and Packaging for VLSI*, Addison-Wesley, Reading, MA, 1990.

[17] S. Balakrishnan and D. K. Panda, "Impact of multiple consumption channels on wormhole routed k-ary n-cube networks," *Proceedings of the 7th International Parallel Processing Symposium*, pp. 163–167, April 1993.

[18] D. Basak and D. K. Panda, "Scalable architectures with k-ary n-cube cluster-c organization," *Proceedings of the 5th IEEE Symposium on Parallel and Distributed Processing*, pp. 780–787, December 1993.

[19] D. Basak and D. K. Panda, "Designing clustered multiprocessor systems under packaging and technological advancements," *IEEE Transactions on Parallel and Distributed Systems*, vol. 7, no. 9, pp. 962–978, September 1996.

[20] C. J. Beckmann and C. D. Polychronopoulos, "Fast barrier synchronization hardware," *Proceedings of Supercomputing'90*, pp. 180–189, November 1990.

[21] R. C. Bedichek, "Talisman: Fast and accurate multicomputer simulation," *Proceedings of ACM Joint International Conference on Measurement and Modeling of Computer Systems/ SIGMETRICS'95*, and *Performance Evaluation Review*, vol. 23, no. 1, pp. 14–24, May 1995

[22] J. Beecroft, M. Homewood, and M. McLaren, "Meiko CS-2 interconnect elan-elite design," *Parallel Computing*, vol. 20, no. 10–11, pp. 1627–1638, November 1994.

[23] C. Berge, *Graphs and Hypergraphs*, North-Holland, 1973.

[24] P. E. Berman, et.al, "Adaptive deadlock- and livelock-free routing with all minimal paths in torus networks," in *Proceedings of the 4th Annual ACM Symposium on Parallel Algorithms and Architectures*, pp. 3–12, June 1992.

[25] L. M. Bhuyan and D. P. Agrawal, "Generalized hypercube and hyperbus structures for a computer network," *IEEE Transactions on Computers*, vol. C-33, no. 4, pp. 323–333, April 1984.

[26] D. Blough and N. Bagherzadeh, "Near-optimal message routing and broadcasting in faulty hypercubes," *International Journal of Parallel Programming*, vol. 19, no. 5, pp. 405–423, October 1990.

[27] D. Blough and S. Najand, "Fault tolerant multiprocessor system routing using incomplete diagnostic information," *Proceedings of the 6th International Parallel Processing Symposium*, pp. 398–402, April 1992.

[28] D. Blough and H. Wang, "Cooperative diagnosis and routing in fault-tolerant multiprocessor systems," *Journal of Parallel and Distributed Computing*, vol. 27, pp. 205–211, June 1995.

[29] M. A. Blumrich, et al., "Virtual memory mapped network interface for the SHRIMP multicomputer," *Proceedings of the 21st International Symposium on Computer Architecture*, pp. 142–153, April 1994.

[30] N. J. Boden, et al., "Myrinet - A gigabit per second local area network," *IEEE Micro*, pp. 29–36, February 1995.

[31] K. Bolding, "Multicomputer interconnection network channel design," Technical Report UW-CSE-93-12-03, Department of Computer Science and Engineering, University of Washington, 1993.

[32] K. Bolding, et al., "The Chaos router chip: Design and implementation of an adaptive router," *Proceedings of the International Conference on VLSI'93*, September 1993, and in *IFIP Transactions A*, vol. A-42, pp. 311–320, 1994.

[33] K. Bolding and S. Kostantinidou, "On the comparison of hypercube and torus networks," *Proceedings of the 1992 International Conference on Parallel Processing*, vol I, pp. 62–66, August 1992.

[34] K. Bolding and L. Snyder, "Mesh and torus chaotic routing," *Proceedings of the MIT/Brown Conference on Advanced Research in VLSI*, 1992.

[35] K. Bolding and W. Yost, "Design of a router for fault tolerant networks," *Proceedings of the Workshop on Parallel Computer Routing, and Communication*, pp. 226–240, May 1994.

[36] R. V. Boppana and S. Chalasani, "A comparison of adaptive wormhole routing algorithms," *Proceedings of the 20th International Symposium on Computer Architecture*, pp. 351–360, May 1993.

[37] R. V. Boppana and S. Chalasani, "Fault-tolerant wormhole routing algorithms for mesh networks," *IEEE Transactions on Computers*, vol. 44, no. 7, pp. 848–864, July 1995.

[38] R. V. Boppana, S. Chalasani and C. S. Raghavendra, "On multicast wormhole routing in multicomputer networks," *Proceedings of the 6th IEEE Symposium on Parallel and Distributed Processing*, pp. 722–729, Dallas, October 1994.

[39] S. Borkar, et al., "iWarp: An integrated solution to high-speed parallel computing," *Proceedings of Supercomputing'88*, pp. 330–339, November 1988.

[40] S. Borkar, et al., "Supporting systolic and memory communication in iWarp," *Proceedings of the 17th International Symposium on Computer Architecture*, pp. 70–81, May 1990.

[41] G. A. Boughton, "Arctic routing chip," *Proceedings of the Workshop on Parallel Computer Routing and Communication*, pp. 310–317, May 1994.

[42] Y. M. Boura and C. R. Das, "Efficient fully adaptive wormhole routing in n-dimensional meshes," *Proceedings of the 14th International Conference on Distributed Computing Systems*, pp. 589–596, June 1994.

[43] Y. M. Boura and C. R. Das, "Fault-tolerant routing in mesh networks," *Proceedings of the 1995 International Conference on Parallel Processing*, vol I, pp. 106–109, August 1995.

[44] P. Bridges et al., *User's Guide to MPICH, a Portable Implementation of MPI*, Argonne National Laboratory, Argonne, 1995.

[45] R. Butler and E. Lusk, "Users guide to the p4 programming system," Technical Report TM-ANL-92-17, Argonne National Laboratory, Argonne, 1992.

[46] R. Butler and E. Lusk, "Monitors, messages, and cluster: the p4 parallel programming system," *Journal of Parallel and Distributed Computing*, vol. 20, no. 4, pp. 547–564, April 1994.

[47] G. T. Byrd, N. P. Saraiya, and B. A. Delagi, "Multicast communication in multiprocessor systems," *Proceedings of the 1989 International Conference on Parallel Processing*, vol. I, pp. 196–200, August 1989.

[48] J. Carbonaro and F. Verhoorn, "Cavallino: The teraflops router and NIC," *Proceedings of Hot Interconnects Symposium IV*, August 1996.

[49] S. Chalasani and R. V. Boppana, "Fault-Tolerant wormhole routing in tori," *Proceedings of the 8th International Conference on Supercomputing*, pp. 146–155, July 1994.

[50] S. Chalasani and R. V. Boppana, "Communication in multicomputers with nonconvex faults," *Proceedings of Euro-Par'95*, pp. 673–684, August 1995.

[51] S. Chandra, J. R. Larus and A. Rogers, "Where is time spent in message-passing and shared-memory programs," *Proceedings of the 6th International Conference on the Architectural Support for Programming Languages and Operating Systems*, pp. 61–73, October 1994.

[52] M.-S. Chen and K. G. Shin, "Depth-first search approach for fault-tolerant routing in hypercube multicomputers," *IEEE Transactions on Parallel and Distributed Systems*, vol. 1, no. 2, pp. 152–159, April 1990.

[53] M.-S. Chen and K. G. Shin, "Adaptive fault-tolerant routing in hypercube multicomputers," *IEEE Transactions on Computers*, vol. C–39, no. 12, pp. 1406–1416, December 1990.

[54] C.-M. Chiang and L. M. Ni, "Multi-address encoding for multicast," *Proceedings of the Workshop on Parallel Computer Routing and Communication*, pp. 146–160, May 1994.

[55] C.-M. Chiang and L. M. Ni, "Deadlock-free multi-head wormhole routing," *Proceedings of the First High Performance Computing-Asia*, 1995.

[56] C.-M. Chiang and L. M. Ni, "Efficient software multicast in wormhole-routed unidirectional multistage networks," in *Proceedings of the 7th IEEE Symposium on Parallel and Distributed Processing*, pp. 106–113, 1995.

[57] A. A. Chien, "A cost and speed model for k-ary n-cube wormhole routers," *Proceedings of Hot Interconnects'93*, August 1993.

[58] A. A. Chien and J. H. Kim, "Planar-adaptive routing: Low-cost adaptive networks for multiprocessors," *Proceedings of the 19th International Symposium on Computer Architecture*, pp. 268–277, May 1992.

[59] G. Chiu, S. Chalasani and C. S. Raghavendra, "Flexible, fault-tolerant routing criteria for circuit switched hypercubes," *Proceedings of the 11th International Conference on Distributed Systems*, pp. 582–589, July 1991.

[60] H. A. Choi and A. H. Esfahanian, "On complexity of a message-routing strategy for multicomputer systems," *Proceedings of the 16th International Workshop on Graph-Theoretic Concepts in Computer Science*, pp. 170–181, June 1990.

[61] Y. Choi and T. M. Pinkston, "Crossbar analysis for optimal deadlock recovery router architecture," *Proceedings of the 11th International Parallel Processing Symposium*, pp. 583–588, April 1997.

[62] E. Chow, et al., "Hyperswitch network for the hypercube computer," *Proceedings of the 15th International Symposium on Computer Architecture*, pp. 90–99, May–June 1988.

[63] Special issue on Interconnection Networks, *IEEE Computer*, vol. 20, no. 6, June 1987.

[64] R. Cypher and L. Gravano, "Requirements for deadlock-free, adaptive packet routing," *Proceedings of the 11th ACM Symposium on Principles of Distributed Computing*, pp. 25–33, August 1992.

[65] R. Cypher and L. Gravano, "Adaptive, deadlock-free packet routing in torus networks with minimal storage," *Proceedings of the 1992 International Conference on Parallel Processing*, vol. III, pp. 204–211, August 1992.

[66] R. Cypher and L. Gravano, "Storage-efficient, deadlock-free packet routing algorithms for torus networks," *IEEE Transactions on Computers*, vol. 43, no. 12, pp. 1376–1385, December 1994.

[67] R. Cypher, A. Ho, S. Konstantinidou and P. Messina, "Architectural requirements of parallel scientific applications with explicit communication," *Proceedings of the 20th International Symposium on Computer Architecture*, pp. 2–13, May 1993.

[68] R. Cypher and S. Konstantinidou, "Bounds on the efficiency of message passing protocols for parallel computers," *Proceedings of the 5th Annual ACM Symposium on Parallel Algorithms and Architectures*, pp. 173–181, 1993.

[69] R. Cypher and S. Konstantinidou, "Bounds on the efficiency of message passing protocols for parallel computers," *SIAM Journal of Computing*, vol. 25, no. 5, pp. 1082–1104, October 1996.

[70] D. Dai and D. K. Panda, "Reducing cache invalidation overheads in wormhole routed DSMs using multidestination message passing," *Proceedings of the 1996 International Conference on Parallel Processing*, pp. 138–145, August 1996.

[71] W. J. Dally, "Performance analysis of k-ary n-cube interconnection networks," *IEEE Transactions on Computers*, vol. C–39, no. 6, pp. 775–785, June 1990.

[72] W. J. Dally, "Express cubes: Improving the performance of k-ary n-cube interconnection networks," *IEEE Transactions on Computers*, vol. C–40, no. 9, pp. 1016–1023, September 1991.

[73] W. J. Dally, "Virtual-channel flow control," *IEEE Transactions on Parallel and Distributed Systems*, vol. 3, no. 2, pp. 194–205, March 1992.

[74] W. J. Dally and H. Aoki, "Deadlock-free adaptive routing in multicomputer networks using virtual channels," *IEEE Transactions on Parallel and Distributed Systems*, vol. 4, no. 4, pp. 466–475, April 1993.

[75] W. J. Dally, et al., "The Reliable Router: A reliable and high-performance communication substrate for parallel computers," *Proceedings of the Workshop on Parallel Computer Routing and Communication*, pp. 241–255, May 1994.

[76] W. J. Dally, et al., "Architecture and implementation of the Reliable Router," *Proceedings of Hot Interconnects Symposium II*, August 1994.

[77] W. J. Dally and C. L. Seitz, "The torus routing chip," *Journal of Distributed Computing*, vol. 1, no. 3, pp. 187–196, October 1986.

[78] W. J. Dally and C. L. Seitz, "Deadlock-free message routing in multiprocessor interconnection networks," *IEEE Transactions on Computers*, vol. C–36, no. 5, pp. 547–553, May 1987.

[79] W. J. Dally and P. Song, "Design of self-timed VLSI multicomputer communication controller," *Proceedings of the International Conference on Computer Design*, pp. 230–234, October 1987.

[80] B. V. Dao, J. Duato and S. Yalamanchili, "Configurable flow control mechanisms for fault-tolerant routing," *Proceedings of the 22nd International Symposium on Computer Architecture*, pp. 220–229, June 1995.

[81] B. V. Dao, J. Duato and S. Yalamanchili, "Dynamically configurable flow control protocols for fault tolerant routing," *IEEE Transactions on Parallel and Distributed Systems* (submitted for publication).

[82] B. V. Dao, S. Yalamanchili and J. Duato, "Architectural support for reducing communication overhead in multiprocessor interconnection networks," *Proceedings of the Third International Symposium on High-Performance Computer Architecture*, pp. 343–352, February 1997.

[83] A. Davis, et al., "R2: A damped adaptive router design," *Proceedings of the Workshop on Parallel Computer Routing and Communication*, pp. 295–309, May 1994.

[84] P. Dehkordi, K. Ramamurthi and D. Bouldin, "Early cost/performance cache analysis of a split MCM based MicroSparc CPU," *Proceedings of the Multi-Chip Module Conference*, pp. 148–153, February 1996.

[85] P. M. Dickens, P. Heidelberger and D. M. Nicol, "Parallelized network simulators for message passing parallel programs," *Proceedings of the International Workshop on Modeling, Analysis, Simulation of Computer and Telecommunication Systems*, pp. 72–76, 1995.

[86] J. J. Dongarra and T. Dunigan, "Message-passing performance of various computers," Technical Report UT–CS–95–229, Computer Science Department, University of Tennessee, 1995. Available at *http://www.cs.utk.edu/ library/1995.html.* The benchmark for point-to-point communication is available at *http://www.netlib.org/benchmark/comm.shar.*

[87] J. Duato, "On the design of deadlock-free adaptive routing algorithms for multicomputers: Design methodologies," *Proceedings of Parallel Architectures and Languages Europe*, pp. 390–405, June 1991.

[88] J. Duato, "Deadlock-free adaptive routing algorithms for multicomputers: Evaluation of a new algorithm," in *Proceedings of the 3rd IEEE Symposium on Parallel and Distributed Processing*, pp. 840–847, December 1991.

[89] J. Duato, "Improving the efficiency of virtual channels with time-dependent selection functions," *Proceedings of Parallel Architectures and Languages Europe*, pp. 635–650, June 1992.

[90] J. Duato, "Channel classes: A new concept for deadlock avoidance in wormhole networks," *Parallel Processing Letters*, vol. 2, no. 4, pp. 347–354, December 1992.

[91] J. Duato, "A new theory of deadlock-free adaptive multicast routing in wormhole networks," *Proceedings of the 5th IEEE Symposium on Parallel and Distributed Processing*, pp. 64–71, December 1993.

[92] J. Duato, "A new theory of deadlock-free adaptive routing in wormhole networks," *IEEE Transactions on Parallel and Distributed Systems*, vol. 4, no. 12, pp. 1320–1331, December 1993.

[93] J. Duato, "A necessary and sufficient condition for deadlock-free adaptive routing in wormhole networks," *Proceedings of the 1994 International Conference on Parallel Processing*, vol. I, pp. 142-149, August 1994.

[94] J. Duato, "A theory to increase the effective redundancy in wormhole networks," *Parallel Processing Letters*, vol. 4, nos. 1 and 2, pp. 125–138, June 1994.

[95] J. Duato, "Improving the efficiency of virtual channels with time-dependent selection functions," *Future Generation Computer Systems*, vol. 10, no. 1, pp. 45–58, April 1994.

[96] J. Duato, "A theory of fault-tolerant routing in wormhole networks," *Proceedings of the International Conference on Parallel and Distributed Systems*, pp. 600–607, December 1994.

[97] J. Duato, "A theory of deadlock-free adaptive multicast routing in wormhole networks," *IEEE Transactions on Parallel and Distributed Systems*, vol. 6, no. 9, pp. 976–987, September 1995.

[98] J. Duato, "A necessary and sufficient condition for deadlock-free adaptive routing in wormhole networks," *IEEE Transactions on Parallel and Distributed Systems*, vol. 6, no. 10, pp. 1055–1067, October 1995.

[99] J. Duato, "A necessary and sufficient condition for deadlock-free routing in cut-through and store-and-forward networks," *IEEE Transactions on Parallel and Distributed Systems*, vol. 7, no. 8, pp. 841–854, August 1996.

[100] J. Duato, et al., "Scouting: Fully adaptive, deadlock-free routing in faulty pipelined networks," *Proceedings of the International Conference on Parallel and Distributed Systems*, pp. 608–613, December 1994.

[101] J. Duato and P. López, "Performance evaluation of adaptive routing algorithms for k-ary n-cubes," *Proceedings of the Workshop on Parallel Computer Routing and Communication*, pp. 45–59, May 1994.

[102] J. Duato, et al., "A high performance router architecture for interconnection networks," *Proceedings of the 1996 International Conference on Parallel Processing*, vol. I, pp. 61–68, August 1996.

[103] J. Duato and M. P. Malumbres, "Optimal topology for distributed shared-memory multiprocessors: Hypercubes again?", in *Proceedings of Euro-Par'96*, vol. 1, pp. 205–212, August 1996.

[104] C. Dubnicki, K. Li and M. Mesarina, "Network interface support for user-level buffer management," *Proceedings of the Workshop on Parallel Computer Routing and Communication*, pp. 256–265, May 1994.

[105] T. von Eicken, A. Basu, and V. Buch, "Low latency communication over ATM networks using active messages," *IEEE Micro*, vol. 15, no. 1, pp. 46–53, February 1995.

[106] T. von Eicken, et al., "Active messages: A mechanism for integrated communication and computation," *Proceedings of the 19th International Symposium on Computer Architecture*,pp. 256–266, May 1992.

[107] R. E. Felderman, et al., "ATOMIC: A high-speed local communication architecture," *Journal of High Speed Networks*, vol. 3, no. 1, pp. 1–28, January 1994.

[108] A. Feldmann, et al., "Subset barrier synchronization on a private memory parallel system," *Proceedings of the 4th Annual ACM Symposium on Parallel Algorithms and Architectures*, pp. 209–218, June 1992.

[109] C. M. Flaig, "VLSI mesh routing systems," Technical Report 5241:TR:87, Dept. of Computer Science, California Institute of Technology, 1987.

[110] E. Fleury and P. Fraigniaud, "Strategies for multicasting in meshes," *Proceedings of the 1994 International Conference on Parallel Processing*, vol. III, pp. 151–158, August 1994.

[111] E. Fleury and P. Fraigniaud, "Deadlocks in adaptive wormhole routing," *IEEE Transactions on Parallel and Distributed Systems* (submitted for publication).

[112] M. Flynn, *Computer Architecture: Pipelined and Parallel Processor Design*, pp. 63-140, Jones and Bartlett, Boston, MA., 1995.

[113] T. J. Fountain and M. J. Shute (eds.), *Multiprocessor Computer Architectures*, North-Holland, 1990.

[114] G. Fox, et al., "Fortran D language specification," Technical Report COMP TR90-141, Rice University, Department of Computer Science, Houston, TX., December 1990.

[115] G. C. Fox, et al., *Solving Problems on Concurrent Processors. Volume I: General Techniques and Regular Problems*, Englewood Cliffs, NJ, Prentice Hall, 1988.

[116] M. I. Frank and M. K. Vernon, "A hybrid shared memory/message passing parallel machine," *Proceedings of the 1993 International Conference on Parallel Processing*, vol. I, pp. 232–236, August 1993.

[117] M. L. Fulgham and L. Snyder, "A comparison of input and output driven routers," *Proceedings of Euro-Par'96*, vol. 1, pp. 195-204, August 1996.

[118] M. Galles, "Scalable pipelined interconnect for distributed endpoint routing: The SPIDER chip," *Proceedings of Hot Interconnects Symposium IV*, August 1996.

[119] M. Galles, "Spider: A high speed network interconnect", *IEEE Micro*, vol. 17, no. 1, pp. 34–39, January-February 1997.

[120] J. M. García and J. Duato, "An algorithm for dynamic reconfiguration of a multicomputer network," *Proceedings of the 3rd IEEE Symposium on Parallel and Distributed Processing*, pp. 848-855, December 1991.

[121] M. R. Garey and D. S. Johnson, "The rectilinear Steiner tree problem is NP-complete," *SIAM Journal of Applied Math*, vol. 32, pp. 826–834, 1977.

[122] M. R. Garey and D. S. Johnson, *Computer and Intractability, A Guide to the Theory of NP-Completeness*, San Francisco, CA, W. H. Freeman and Co., 1979.

[123] V. Garg, et al., "Incorporating multi-chip module packaging constraints into system design," *Proceedings of the European Design and Test Conference*, March 1996.

[124] P. T. Gaughan, et al., "Distributed, deadlock-free routing in faulty, pipelined, direct interconnection networks," *IEEE Transactions on Computers*, vol. 45, no. 6, pp. 651–665, June 1996.

[125] P. T. Gaughan and S. Yalamanchili, "Pipelined circuit-switching: A fault-tolerant variant of wormhole routing," in *Proceedings of the 4th IEEE Symposium on Parallel and Distributed Processing*, pp. 148–155, December 1992.

[126] P. T. Gaughan and S. Yalamanchili, "Adaptive routing protocols for hypercube interconnection networks," *IEEE Computer*, vol. 26, no. 5, pp. 12–23, May 1993.

[127] P. T. Gaughan and S. Yalamanchili, "A family of fault-tolerant routing protocols for direct multiprocessor networks," *IEEE Transactions on Parallel and Distributed Systems*, vol. 6, no. 5, pp. 482–497, May 1995.

[128] P. T. Gaughan and S. Yalamanchili, "A performance model of pipelined k-ary n-cubes," *IEEE Transactions on Computers*, vol. 44, no. 8, pp. 1059–1063, August 1995.

[129] D. Gelernter, "A DAG-based algorithm for prevention of store-and-forward deadlock in packet networks," *IEEE Transactions on Computers*, vol. C–30, pp. 709–715, October 1981.

[130] C. J. Glass and L. M. Ni, "The turn model for adaptive routing," *Proceedings of the 19th International Symposium on Computer Architecture*, pp. 278-287, May 1992.

[131] C. J. Glass and L. M. Ni, "Maximally fully adaptive routing in 2D meshes," *Proceedings of the 1992 International Conference on Parallel Processing*, August 1992.

[132] C. J. Glass and L. M. Ni, "Fault-tolerant wormhole routing in meshes," *Proceedings of the 23rd International Symposium on Fault-Tolerant Computing*, pp. 240-249, June 1993.

[133] L. R. Goke and G. J. Lipovski, "Banyan networks for partitioning multiprocessing systems," *Proceedings of the First International Symposium on Computer Architecture*, pp. 21–28, 1973.

[134] I. S. Gopal, "Prevention of store-and-forward deadlock in computer networks," *IEEE Transactions on Communications*, vol. COM–33, no. 12, pp. 1258–1264, December 1985.

[135] J. M. Gordon and Q. F. Stout, "Hypercube message routing in the presence of faults," *Proceedings of the Third Conference on Hypercube Concurrent Computers and Applications*, pp. 318–327, January 1988.

[136] R. L. Graham and L. R. Foulds, "Unlikelihood that minimal phylogenies for realistic biological study can be constructed in reasonable computational time," *Mathematical Biosciences*, vol. 60, pp. 133–142, 1982.

[137] L. Gravano, et al., "Adaptive deadlock- and livelock-free routing with all minimal paths in torus networks," *IEEE Transactions on Parallel and Distributed Systems*, vol. 5, no. 12, pp. 1233–1251, December 1994.

[138] A. G. Greenberg and B. Hajek, "Deflection routing in hypercube networks," *IEEE Transactions on Communications*, vol. COM–40, no. 6, pp. 1070–1081, June 1992.

[139] W. Gropp, E. Lusk and A. Skejellum, *Using MPI: Portable Parallel Programming with the Message Passing Interface*. Cambridge, MA., MIT Press, 1994.

[140] D. Grunwald and D. A. Reed, "Analysis of backtracking routing in binary hypercube computers," Technical Report-UIUC-DCS-R-89-1486, Department of Computer Science, University of Illinois at Urbana-Champaign, Urbana, IL, February 1989.

[141] K. D. Gunther, "Prevention of deadlocks in packet-switched data transport systems," *IEEE Transactions on Communications*, vol. COM–29, pp. 512–524, April 1981.

[142] R. Gupta, "The fuzzy barrier: A mechanism for the high speed synchronization of processors," *Proceedings of the 3rd International Conference on Architectural Support for Programming Languages and Operating Systems*, pp. 54–63, April 1989.

[143] A. Gupta, et al., "Comparative evaluation of latency reducing and tolerating techniques," *Proceedings of the 18th International Symposium on Computer Architecture*, pp. 254–263, June 1991.

[144] J. Gurd, C. C. Kirkham and A. P. Boehm, "The Manchester Dataflow Computing System," *Experimental Parallel Computing Systems*, J. Dongarra (ed.). North-Holland, 1987.

[145] J. Gurd, C. C. Kirkham and I. Watson, "The Manchester prototype dataflow computer," *Communications of the ACM*, vol. 28, no. 1, pp. 34–52, January 1985.

[146] R. L. Hadas and E. Brandt, "Origin-based fault-tolerant routing in the mesh," *Proceedings of the First International Symposium on High-Performance Computer Architecture*, pp. 102–111, January 1995.

[147] F. Harary, *Graph Theory*, Addison-Wesley, 1972.

[148] S. M. Hedetniemi, S. T. Hedetniemi, and A. L. Liestman, "A survey of gossiping and broadcasting in communication networks," *Networks*, vol. 18, no. 4, pp. 319–349, Winter 1988.

[149] J. Heinlein, et al., "Integration of message passing and shared memory in the Stanford FLASH multiprocessor," *Proceedings of the 6th International Conference on the Architectural Support for Programming Languages and Operating Systems*, pp. 38–50, November 1994.

[150] S. Heller, "Congestion-free routing on the CM-5 data router," *Proceedings of the Workshop on Parallel Computer Routing and Communication*, pp. 176–184, May 1994.

[151] D. S. Henry and C. F. Joerg, "A tightly coupled processor-network interface," *Proceedings of the 5th International Conference on Architectural Support for Programming Languages and Operating Systems*, pp. 111–122, October 1992.

[152] High Performance Fortran Forum, "High Performance Fortran language specification (version 1.0, draft)," January 1993.

[153] C.-T. Ho and S. L. Johnsson, "Distributed routing algorithms for broadcasting and personalized communication in hypercubes," *Proceedings of the 1986 International Conference on Parallel Processing*, pp. 640–648, August 1986.

[154] C.-T. Ho and M. Kao, "Optimal broadcast in all-port wormhole-routed hypercubes," *IEEE Transactions on Parallel and Distributed Systems*, vol. 6, no. 2, pp. 200–204, February 1995.

[155] Honeywell Inc., "Remote exploration and experimentation (REE) project study phase: Interim technical report," National Aeronautics and Space Administration/Jet Propulsion Laboratory, August 1996.

[156] R. Horst, "TNet: A reliable system area network," *IEEE Micro*, vol. 15, no. 1, pp. 36–44, February 1995.

[157] R. Horst, "ServerNet deadlock avoidance and fractahedral topologies," *Proceedings of the 10th International Parallel Processing Symposium*, pp. 274–280, April 1996.

[158] R. Horst, et al., "Performance modeling of ServerNet topologies," *Proceedings of the 10th International Parallel Processing Symposium*, pp. 518–523, April 1996.

[159] J.-M. Hsu and P. Banerjee, "Hardware support for message routing in a distributed memory multicomputer," *Proceedings of the 1990 International Conference on Parallel Processing*, vol. I, pp. 508–515, August 1990.

[160] J.-M. Hsu and P. Banerjee, "Performance measurement and trace driven simulation of parallel CAD and numeric applications on a hypercube multicomputer," *IEEE Transactions on Parallel and Distributed Systems*, vol. 3, no. 4, pp. 451–464, July 1992.

[161] W. T. Hsu and P. C. Yew, "The impact of wiring constraints on hierarchical network performance," *Proceedings of the 6th International Parallel Processing Symposium*, pp. 580–588, March 1992.

[162] K. Hwang, *Advanced Computer Architecture*, McGraw-Hill, New York, NY, 1993.

[163] K. Hwang and F. A. Briggs, *Computer Architecture and Parallel Processing*, New York, NY, McGraw-Hill, 1984.

[164] Intel iPSC/1 Reference Manual, Beaverton. OR, 1986.

[165] *Paragon XP/S Product Overview*, Beaverton, OR, Intel Corporation, Supercomputer Systems Division, 1991.

[166] C. Izu, et al., "A router node architecture for cut-through torus networks." Technical Report, Departamento de Arquitectura y Tecnologia de Computadores, Universidad del Pais Vasco, Spain, 1994.

[167] C. R. Jesshope, P. R. Miller, and J. T. Yantchev, "High performance communications in processor networks," *Proceedings of the 16th International Symposium on Computer Architecture*, pp. 150–157, May–June 1989.

[168] S. L. Johnsson and C.-T. Ho, "Optimum broadcasting and personalized communication in hypercubes," *IEEE Transactions on Computers*, vol. C-38, no. 9, pp. 1249–1268, September 1989.

[169] J. R. Jump and S. Lakshmanamurthy, "NETSIM: A general-purpose interconnection network simulator," *Proceedings of the International Workshop on Modeling, Analysis, Simulation of Computer and Telecommunication Systems*, pp. 121–125, January 1993.

[170] V. Karamcheti and A. A. Chien, "Do faster routers imply faster communication?," *Proceedings of the Workshop on Parallel Computer Routing and Communication*, pp. 1–15, May 1994.

[171] V. Karamcheti and A. A. Chien, "Software overhead in messaging layers: Where does the time go?," *Proceedings of the 6th International Conference on Architectural Support for Programming Languages and Operating Systems*, pp. 51–60, October 1994.

[172] P. Kermani and L. Kleinrock, "Virtual cut-through: A new computer communication switching technique," *Computer Networks*, vol. 3, pp. 267–286, 1979.

[173] R. Kesavan and D. K. Panda, "Minimizing node contention in multiple multicast on wormhole k-ary n-cube networks," *Proceedings of the 1996 International Conference on Parallel Processing*, vol. 1, pp. 188–195, August 1996.

[174] R. E. Kessler and J. L. Schwarzmeier, "CRAY T3D: A new dimension for Cray Research," *Proceedings of Compcon*, pp. 176–182, Spring 1993.

[175] J. H. Kim and A. A. Chien, "An evaluation of the planar/adaptive routing," *Proceedings of the 4th IEEE Symposium on Parallel and Distributed Processing*, pp. 470–478, December 1992.

[176] J. H. Kim and A. A. Chien, "Evaluation of wormhole-routed networks under hybrid traffic loads," *Proceedings of the 26th Hawaii International Conference on System Sciences*, pp. 276–285, January 1993.

[177] J. H. Kim and A. A. Chien, "The impact of packetization in wormhole-routed networks," *Proceedings of Parallel Architectures and Languages Europe 93*, pp. 242–253, June 1993.

[178] J. Kim and C. R. Das, "Hypercube communication delay with wormhole routing," *IEEE Transactions on Computers*, vol. C-43, no. 7, pp. 806–814, July 1994.

[179] J. H. Kim, Z. Liu and A. A. Chien, "Compressionless routing: A framework for adaptive and fault-tolerant routing," in *Proceedings of the 21st International Symposium on Computer Architecture*, pp. 289–300, April 1994.

[180] J. H. Kim, Z. Liu and A. A. Chien, "Compressionless routing: A framework for adaptive and fault-tolerant routing," in *IEEE Transactions on Parallel and Distributed Systems*, vol. 8, no.3, pp. 229–244, March 1997.

[181] J.-Y. Kim, et al., "Drop-and-reroute: A new flow control policy for adaptive wormhole routing," *Proceedings of the 1995 International Conference on Parallel Processing*, vol. I, pp. 60–67, August 1995.

[182] T. F. Knight and A. Krymm, "A self-terminating low-voltage swing CMOS output driver," *IEEE Journal of Solid-State Circuits*, vol. 23, no. 2, pp. 457–464, April 1988.

[183] N. Koike, "NEC Cenju-3: A microprocessor-based parallel computer," *Proceedings of the 8th International Parallel Processing Symposium*, pp. 396–401, April 1994.

[184] S. Konstantinidou, "Adaptive, minimal routing in hypercubes," *Proceedings of the Sixth MIT Conference on Advanced Research in VLSI*, pp. 139–153, April 1990.

[185] S. Konstantinidou, "On the effect of queues sizes and channel scheduling policies in the segment router," *Proceedings of the Workshop on Parallel Computer Routing and Communication*, pp. 72–85, May 1994.

[186] S. Konstantinidou, "Segment router: A novel router design for parallel computers," *Proceedings of the 6th Annual ACM Symposium on Parallel Algorithms and Architectures*, pp. 3643–373, June 1994.

[187] S. Konstantinidou and L. Snyder, "The Chaos router: A practical application of randomization in network routing," *Proceedings 2nd Annual ACM Symposium on Parallel Algorithms and Architectures*, pp. 21–31, July 1990.

[188] S. Konstantinidou and L. Snyder, "Chaos router: Architecture and performance," *Proceedings of the 18th International Symposium on Computer Architecture*, pp. 79–88, June 1991.

[189] S. Konstantinidou and L. Snyder, "The Chaos router," *IEEE Transactions on Computers*, vol. 43, no. 12, pp. 1386–1397, December 1994.

[190] J. S. Kowalik (ed.), *Parallel MIMD Computation: HEP Supercomputer and its Applications*, MIT Press, 1985.

[191] C. Kruskal and M. Snir, "The performance of multistage interconnection networks for multiprocessors," *IEEE Transactions on Computers*, vol. C-32, no. 12, pp. 1091–1098, December 1983.

[192] J. Kushkin, et al., "The Stanford FLASH multiprocessor," *Proceedings of the 21st International Symposium on Computer Architecture*, pp. 302–313, April 1994.

[193] K. Lam, L. R. Dennison, and W. J. Dally, "Simultaneous bidirectional signaling for IC systems," *Proceedings of the International Conference on Computer Design*, pp. 430–433, Cambridge, MA., September 1990.

[194] Y. Lan, "Multicast in faulty hypercubes," *Proceedings of the 1992 International Conference on Parallel Processing*, vol. I, pp. 58–61, August 1992.

[195] Y. Lan, A. H. Esfahanian, and L. M. Ni, "Distributed multi-destination routing in hypercube multiprocessors," *Proceedings of the Third Conference on Hypercube Concurrent Computers and Applications*, pp. 631–639, January 1988.

[196] Y. Lan, A. H. Esfahanian, and L. M. Ni, "Multicast in hypercube multiprocessors," *Journal of Parallel and Distributed Computing*, vol. 8, no. 1, pp. 30–41, January 1990.

[197] Y. Lan, L. M. Ni, and A. H. Esfahanian, "A VLSI router design for hypercube multiprocessors," *Integration: The VLSI Journal*, vol. 7, pp. 103–125, August 1989.

[198] T. Lee and J. P. Hayes, "A fault-tolerant communication scheme for hypercube computers," *IEEE Transactions on Computers*, vol. C–41, no. 10, pp. 1242–1256, October 1992.

[199] J. van Leeuwen and R. B. Tan, "Interval routing," *The Computer Journal*, vol. 30, no. 4, pp. 298–307, August 1987.

[200] F. T. Leighton, *Introduction to Parallel Algorithms and Architectures: Arrays, Trees, Hypercubes*, Morgan Kaufmann Publishers, 1992.

[201] C. E. Leiserson, "Fat-trees: Universal networks for hardware-efficient supercomputing," *IEEE Transactions on Computers*, vol. C-34, pp. 892–901, October 1985.

[202] C. E. Leiserson, et al., "The network architecture of the Connection Machine CM-5," *Proceedings of the 4th Annual ACM Symposium on Parallel Algorithms and Architectures*, pp. 272–285, June–July 1992.

[203] D. Lenoski, et al., "The Stanford DASH multiprocessor," *IEEE Computer*, vol. 25, no. 3, pp. 63–79, March 1992.

[204] X. Lin, et al., "Adaptive wormhole routing in hypercube multicomputers," *Proceedings of the 5th IEEE Symposium on Parallel and Distributed Processing*, pp. 72–79, December 1993.

[205] X. Lin, P. K. McKinley, and A. H. Esfahanian, "Adaptive multicast wormhole routing in 2D mesh multicomputers," in *Proceedings of Parallel Architectures and Languages Europe 93*, pp. 228–241, June 1993.

[206] X. Lin, P. K. McKinley, and L. M. Ni, "Performance evaluation of multicast wormhole routing in 2D-mesh multicomputers," *Proceedings of the 1991 International Conference on Parallel Processing*, vol. I, pp. 435–442, August 1991.

[207] X. Lin, P. K. McKinley, and L. M. Ni, "The message flow model for routing in wormhole-routed networks," *Proceedings of the 1993 International Conference on Parallel Processing*, vol. I, pp. 294–297, August 1993.

[208] X. Lin, P. K. McKinley, and L. M. Ni, "Deadlock-free multicast wormhole routing in 2D mesh multicomputers," *IEEE Transactions on Parallel and Distributed Systems*, vol. 5, no. 8, pp. 793–804, August 1994.

[209] X. Lin, P. K. McKinley, and L. M. Ni, "The message flow model for routing in wormhole-routed networks," *IEEE Transactions on Parallel and Distributed Systems*, vol. 6, no. 7, pp. 755–760, July 1995.

[210] X. Lin and L. M. Ni, "Multicast communication in multicomputers networks," *Proceedings of the 1990 International Conference on Parallel Processing*, vol. III, pp. 114–118, August 1990.

[211] X. Lin and L. M. Ni, "Deadlock-free multicast wormhole routing in multicomputer networks," *Proceedings of the 18th International Symposium on Computer Architecture*, pp. 116–125, May 1991.

[212] X. Lin and L. M. Ni, "Multicast communication in multicomputer networks," *IEEE Transactions on Parallel and Distributed Systems*, vol. 4, no. 10, pp. 1104–1117, October 1993.

[213] D. H. Linder and J. C. Harden, "An adaptive and fault tolerant wormhole routing strategy for k-ary n-cubes," *IEEE Transactions on Computers*, vol. C–40, no. 1, pp. 2–12, January 1991.

[214] R. J. Littlefield, "Characterizing and tuning communications performance for real applications," *Proceedings of the First Intel DELTA Applications Workshop*, February 1992.

[215] Z. Liu and A. A. Chien, "Hierarchical adaptive routing," *Proceedings of the 6th IEEE International Symposium on Parallel and Distributed Processing*, pp. 688–695, October 1994.

[216] Z. Liu and J. Duato, Adaptive unicast and multicast in 3D mesh networks, *Proceedings of the 27th Hawaii International Conference on System Sciences*, pp. 173–182, January 1994.

[217] Z. Liu, J. Duato and L.-E. Thorelli, "Grouping virtual channels for deadlock-free adaptive wormhole routing," in *Proceedings of Parallel Architectures and Languages Europe 93*, pp. 254–265, June 1993.

[218] P. López, Diseño de un Circuito de Comunicaciones de Altas Prestaciones para Redes de Interconexión con Control de Flujo "Wormhole". Ph.D. Dissertation, Polytechnical University of Valencia, Spain, 1995.

[219] P. López, et al., "A methodology to speed-up the evaluation of interconnection networks," *IEEE Technical Committee on Computer Architecture Newsletter*, pp. 32–37, August 1995.

[220] P. López and J. Duato, "Deadlock-free adaptive routing algorithms for the 3D-torus: Limitations and solutions," in *Proceedings of Parallel Architectures and Languages Europe 93*, pp. 684-687, June 1993.

[221] P. López and J. Duato, "Deadlock-free fully-adaptive minimal routing algorithms: Limitations and solutions," *Computers and Artificial Intelligence*, vol. 14, no. 1, pp. 105–125, 1995.

[222] S. Loucif, M. Ould-Khaoua and L. M. Mackenzie, "The express channel concept in hypermeshes and k-ary n-cubes," in *Proceedings of the 8th IEEE Symposium on Parallel and Distributed Processing*, pp. 566–569, October 1996.

[223] L. M. Mackenzie, et al., "COBRA: A high-performance interconnection network for large multicomputers," Technical Report 119/R19, Computer Science Department, University of Glasgow, 1991.

[224] M. P. Malumbres, J. Duato and J. Torrellas, "An efficient implementation of tree-based multicast routing in distributed shared-memory multiprocessors," *Proceedings of the 8th IEEE Symposium on Parallel and Distributed Processing*, pp. 186–189, October 1996.

[225] R. Martin, "HPAM: An active message layer for a network of HP workstations," *Proceedings of Hot Interconnects Symposium II*, 1994.
Available from *ftp://ftp.cs.berkeley.edu/CASTLE/Active_Messages/hotipaper.ps*.

[226] J. M. Martínez, et al., "Software-based deadlock recovery technique for true fully adaptive routing in wormhole networks," *Proceedings of the 1997 International Conference on Parallel Processing*, August 1997.

[227] M. D. May, "The next generation transputers and beyond," *Proceedings of the 2nd European Distributed Memory Computing Conference*, pp. 7–22, April 1991.

[228] M. D. May, P. W. Thompson and P. H. Welch (eds.), *Networks, Routers and Transputers: Function, Performance and Application*, IOS Press, 1993.

[229] N. R. McKenzie, et al., "Cranium: An interface for message passing on adaptive packet routing networks," *Proceedings of the Workshop on Parallel Computer Routing and Communication*, pp. 266–281, May 1994.

[230] P. K. McKinley and C. Trefftz, "MultiSim: A simulation tool for the study of large-scale multiprocessors," in *Proceedings of the International Workshop on Modeling, Analysis, Simulation of Computer and Telecommunication Systems*, pp. 57–62, January 1993.

[231] P. K. McKinley and C. Trefftz, "Efficient broadcast in all-port wormhole-routed hypercubes," *Proceedings of the 1993 International Conference on Parallel Processing*, vol. II, pp. 288–291, August 1993.

[232] P. K. McKinley, Y.-J. Tsai and D. F. Robinson, "Collective communication in wormhole-routed massively parallel computers," *IEEE Computer*, vol. 28, no. 12, pp. 39–50, December 1995.

[233] P. K. McKinley, et al., "Unicast-based multicast communication in wormhole-routed networks," *Proceedings of the 1992 International Conference on Parallel Processing*, August 1992.

[234] P. K. McKinley, et al., "Unicast-based multicast communication in wormhole-routed networks," *IEEE Transactions on Parallel and Distributed Systems*, vol. 5, no. 12, pp. 1252–1265, December 1994.

[235] P. K. McKinley, et al., "ComPaSS: Efficient communication services for scalable architectures," *Proceedings of Supercomputing'92*, pp. 478–487, November 1992.

[236] J. Merlin, "Techniques for the automatic parallelization of Distributed Fortran 90," Technical Report SNARC 92-02, University of Southampton, Southampton Novel Architecture Research Center, 1992.

[237] P. M. Merlin and P. J. Schweitzer, "Deadlock avoidance in store-and-forward networks – I: Store-and-forward deadlock," *IEEE Transactions on Communications*, vol. COM–28, pp. 345–354, March 1980.

[238] J. Miguel, et al., "Assessing the performance of the new IBM SP2 communication subsystem," Technical Report 96–06–01, Department of Electrical and Computer Engineering, University of California, Irvine, June 1996.

[239] P. R. Miller, *Efficient Communications for Fine-Grain Distributed Computers*. Ph.D. Dissertation, Southampton University, U.K., 1991.

[240] R. Minnich, D. Burns and F. Hady, "The memory-integrated network interface," *IEEE Micro*, vol. 15, no. 1, pp. 11–20, February 1995.

[241] P. Mohapatra, "Wormhole routing techniques in multicomputer systems," Technical Report TR-ACAR-95-03, Department of Electrical and Computer Engineering, Iowa State University, 1995.

[242] Message Passing Interface Forum, "MPI: A message-passing interface standard," *International Journal of Supercomputer Applications and High Performance Computing*, vol. 8, no. 3/4, 1994. Available at *ftp://www.netlib.org/mpi/mpi-report.ps*.

[243] Web page at *URL http://www.erc.mstate.edu/mpi*.

[244] Web page at *URL http://cisr.anu.edu.au/pub/papers/meglicki/mpi/tutorial/mpi*.

[245] Web page at *URL http://www.osc.edu/Lam/mpi/mpi_ezstart.html*.

[246] T. N. Mudge, J. P. Hayes and D. C. Winsor, "Multiple bus architectures," *IEEE Computer*, vol. 20, no. 6, pp. 42–48, June 1987.

[247] *NCUBE 6400 Processor Manual*, NCUBE Corporation, 1990.

[248] J. Y. Ngai and C. L. Seitz, "A framework for adaptive routing in multicomputer networks," *Proceedings of the 1st Annual ACM Symposium on Parallel Algorithms and Architectures*, pp. 1–9, June 1989.

[249] J. Nguyen, J. Pezaris, G. Pratt and S. Ward, "Three-dimensional network topologies," *Proceedings of the Workshop on Parallel Computer Routing and Communication*, pp. 101–115, May 1994.

[250] T. D. Nguyen and L. Snyder, "Performance analysis of a minimal adaptive router," *Proceedings of the Workshop on Parallel Computer Routing and Communication*, pp. 31–44, May 1994.

[251] L. M. Ni, "Should scalable parallel computers support efficient hardware multicast?," *Proceedings of the 1995 ICPP Workshop on Challenges for Parallel Processing*, pp. 2–7, August 1995.

[252] L. M. Ni, "Issues in designing truly scalable interconnection networks," *Proceedings of the 1996 ICPP Workshop on Challenges for Parallel Processing*, pp. 74–83, August 1996.

[253] L. M. Ni, Y. Gui and S. Moore, "Performance evaluation of switch-based wormhole networks," *Proceedings of the 1995 International Conference on Parallel Processing*, vol. 1, pp. 32–40, August 1995.

[254] L. M. Ni and P. K. McKinley, "A survey of wormhole routing techniques in direct networks," *IEEE Computer*, vol. 26, no. 2, pp. 62–76, February 1993.

[255] M. Noakes, D. A. Wallach and W. J. Dally, "The J-Machine multicomputer: An architectural evaluation," *Proceedings of the 20th International Symposium on Computer Architecture*, pp. 224–235, May 1993.

[256] A. G. Nowatzyk, et al., "S-Connect: From networks of workstations to supercomputer performance," *Proceedings of the 22nd International Symposium on Computer Architecture*, pp. 71–82, June 1995.

[257] S. Nugent, "The iPSC/2 direct connect communications technology," *Proceedings of the Third Conference on Hypercube Concurrent Computers and Applications*, pp. 51–59, January 1988.

[258] W. Oed, "The Cray Research Massively Parallel Processing System: Cray T3D," Cray Research, 1993.

[259] M. T. O'Keefe and H. G. Dietz, "Hardware barrier synchronization: Static barrier MIMD (SBM)," *Proceedings of the 1990 International Conference on Parallel Processing*, pp. 35–42, August 1990.

[260] M. T. O'Keefe and H. G. Dietz, "Hardware barrier synchronization: Dynamic barrier MIMD (DBM)," *Proceedings of the 1990 International Conference on Parallel Processing*, pp. 43–46, August 1990.

[261] E. Olk, "PARSE: Simulation of message passing communication networks," *Proceedings of the 27th Annual Simulation Symposium*, pp. 115–124, April 1994.

[262] A. Y. Oruç, "Multiple tracks of research on interconnection networks," *Proceedings of the 1995 ICPP Workshop on Challenges for Parallel Processing*, pp. 16–23, August 1995.

[263] S. Pakin, M. Lauria and A. A. Chien, "High performance messaging on workstations: Illinois fast messages on Myrinet," *Proceedings of Supercomputing 95*, November 1995.

[264] D. K. Panda, "Fast barrier synchronization in wormhole k-ary n-cube networks with multidestination worms," *Proceedings of the First International Symposium on High-Performance Computer Architecture*, pp. 200–209, January 1995.

[265] D. K. Panda, "Global reduction in wormhole k-ary n-cube networks with multidestination exchange worms," *Proceedings of the 10th International Parallel Processing Symposium*, pp. 652–659, April 1995.

[266] D. K. Panda, "Issues in designing efficient and practical algorithms for collective communication on wormhole-routed systems," *Proceedings of the 1995 ICPP Workshop on Challenges for Parallel Processing*, pp. 8–15, August 1995.

[267] D. K. Panda, S. Singal, and R. Kesavan, "Multidestination message passing in wormhole k-ary n-cube networks with base routing conformed paths." Technical Report OSU-CISRC-12/95-TR54, Ohio State University, December 1995. *IEEE Transactions on Parallel and Distributed Systems* (submitted for publication).

[268] D. K. Panda, S. Singal, and P. Prabhakaran, "Multidestination message passing mechanism conforming to base wormhole routing scheme," *Proceedings of the Workshop on Parallel Computer Routing and Communication*, pp. 131–145, May 1994.

[269] G. Papadopoulos, et al., "*T: Integrating building blocks for parallel computing," *Proceedings of Supercomputing'93*, pp. 624–635, November 1993.

[270] J. Park, et al., "Construction of optimal multicast trees based on the parameterized communication model," *Proceedings of the 1996 International Conference on Parallel Processing*, vol. I, pp. 180–187, August 1996.

[271] D. M. Pase, "MPP Fortran programming model," Technical Report, Cray Research, January 1992.

[272] J. H. Patel, "Performance of processor-memory interconnections for multiprocessors," *IEEE Transactions on Computers*, vol. C-30, pp. 771–780, October 1981.

[273] F. Petrini and M. Vanneschi, "Performance analysis of minimal adaptive wormhole routing with time-dependent deadlock recovery," *Proceedings of the 11th International Parallel Processing Symposium*, pp. 589–595, April 1997.

[274] G. Pfister and A. Norton, "Hot spot contention and combining in multistage interconnect networks," *IEEE Transactions on Computers*, vol. C-34, pp. 943–948, October 1985.

[275] P. Pierce, "The NX/2 operating system," *Proceedings of the 3rd Conference on Hypercube Concurrent Computers and Applications*, pp. 384–390, January 1988.

[276] G. D. Pifarré, et al., "Fully-adaptive minimal deadlock-free packet routing in hypercubes, meshes and other networks," *Proceedings of the 3rd Annual ACM Symposium on Parallel Algorithms and Architectures*, pp. 278–290, June 1991.

[277] G. D. Pifarré, et al., "Fully adaptive minimal deadlock-free packet routing in hypercubes, meshes, and other networks: Algorithms and simulations," *IEEE Transactions on Parallel and Distributed Systems*, vol. 5, no. 3, pp. 247–263, March 1994.

[278] T. M. Pinkston, J. Borsody, and W. Kostis, "Turn selection enhancements to deadlock recovery algorithms," Technical Report CENG–96–34, University of Southern California, December 1996.

[279] T. M. Pinkston and J.-H. Ha, "SPEED DMON: Cache coherence on an optical multi-channel interconnect architecture," *Journal of Parallel and Distributed Computing*, vol. 41, no. 1, February 1997.

[280] T. M. Pinkston, M. Raksapatcharawong and Y. Choi, "Smart-pixel implementation of network router deadlock handling mechanisms," *Spring Topical Meeting on Optics in Computing Technical Digest*, March 1997.

[281] T. M. Pinkston, M. Raksapatcharawong and C. Kuznia, "An asynchronous optical token smart-pixel design based on hybrid CMOS/SEED integration," *IEEE/LEOS 1996 Summer Topical Meeting on Smart Pixels Technical Digest*, pp. 40–41, August 1996.

[282] T. M. Pinkston and S. Warnakulasuriya, "On deadlocks in interconnection networks," *Proceedings of the 24th International Symposium on Computer Architecture*, June 1997.

[283] F. P. Preparata and J. Vuillemin, "The cube-connected cycles: A versatile network for parallel computation," *Communications of the ACM*, vol. 24, no. 5, pp. 300–309, May 1981.

[284] W. Qiao and L. M. Ni, "Adaptive routing in irregular networks using cut-through switches," *Proceedings of the 1996 International Conference on Parallel Processing*, vol. I, pp. 52–60, August 1996.

[285] C. S. Raghavendra, P.-J. Yang and S.-B. Tien, "Free dimensions, an effective approach to achieving fault tolerance in hypercubes," *Proceedings of the 22nd International Symposium on Fault-Tolerant Computing*, pp. 170–177, July 1992.

[286] C. S. Raghavendra, P.-J. Yang and S.-B. Tien, "Free dimensions, an effective approach to achieving fault tolerance in hypercubes," *IEEE Transactions on Computers*, vol. 44, no. 9, pp. 1152–1157, September 1995.

[287] D. A. Reed and D. C. Grunwald, "The performance of multicomputer interconnection networks," *IEEE Computer*, vol. 20, no. 6, pp. 63–73, June 1987.

[288] D. S. Reeves, E. F. Gehringer and A. Chandiramani, "Adaptive routing and deadlock recovery: A simulation study," in *Proceedings of the 4th Conference on Hypercube Concurrent Computers and Applications*, pp. 331–337, March 1989.

[289] S. K. Reinhardt, J. R. Larus, and D. A. Wood, "Tempest and Typhoon: User-level shared memory," *Proceedings of the 21st International Symposium on Computer Architecture*, pp. 325–336, April 1994.

[290] J. Rexford, et al., "PP-MESS-SIM: A simulator for evaluating multicomputer interconnection networks," *Proceedings of the Simulation Symposium*, pp. 84–93, April 1995.

[291] J. Rexford, J. Dolter and K. G. Shin, "Hardware support for controlled interaction of guaranteed and best-effort communication," *Proceedings of the Workshop on Parallel and Distributed Real-Time Systems*, pp. 188–193, April 1994.

[292] J. Rexford, et al., "PP-MESS-SIM: A flexible and extensible simulator for evaluating multicomputer networks," *IEEE Transactions on Parallel and Distributed Systems*, vol. 8, no. 1, pp. 25–40, January 1997.

[293] J. Rexford and K. G. Shin, "Support for multiple classes of traffic in multicomputer routers," *Proceedings of the Workshop on Parallel Computer Routing and Communication*, pp. 116–130, May 1994.

[294] D. F. Robinson, et al., "Efficient collective data distribution in all-port wormhole-routed hypercubes," *Proceedings of Supercomputing'93*, pp. 792–801, November 1993.

[295] D. F. Robinson, et al., "Efficient multicast in all-port wormhole-routed hypercubes," *Journal of Parallel and Distributed Computing*, vol. 31, no.2, pp. 126–140, December 1995.

[296] A. Robles and J. Duato, "Multilinks: A new approach to the design of adaptive routing algorithms for multicomputers," *Proceedings of the IMACS-IFAC Symposium on Parallel and Distributed Computing in Engineering Systems*, pp. 405–410. June 1991.

[297] A. W. Roscoe, "Routing messages through networks: An exercise in deadlock avoidance," Oxford University Computing Laboratory Report, 1987.

[298] E. Rothberg, J. P. Singh, and A. Gupta, "Working sets, cache sizes, and node granularity issues for large scale multiprocessors," *Proceedings of the 20th International Symposium on Computer Architecture*, pp. 14–25, June 1993.

[299] Y. Saad and M. H. Schultz, "Topological properties of hypercubes," *IEEE Transactions on Computers*, vol. C-37, no. 7, pp. 867–872, July 1988.

[300] M. R. Samatham and D. K. Pradhan, "The de Bruijn multiprocessor network: A versatile parallel processing and sorting network for VLSI," *IEEE Transactions on Computers*, vol. C-38, no. 4, pp. 567–581, April 1989.

[301] P. A. Sandborn, M. S. Abadir, and C. F. Murphy, "The trade-off between peripheral and area array bonding of components in multi-chip modules," *IEEE Transactions on Components, Packaging, and Manufacturing Technologies*, vol. 17, no. 2, pp. 249–256, June 1994.

[302] P. A. Sandborn and H. Moreno, *Conceptual Design of Multi-chip Modules and Systems*, Boston, MA., Kluwer Academic Publishers, 1994.

[303] D. E. Schimmel, J. D. Allen, and P. T. Gaughan, "Efficient self-timed distributed mutual exclusion," Technical Report GIT/CSRL-94/1, Georgia Institute of Technology, available via anonymous ftp at *ftp.ee.gatech.edu:pub/csrl*, February 1994.

[304] M. D. Schroeder et al., "Autonet: A high-speed, self-configuring local area network using point-to-point links," Technical Report SRC research report 59, DEC, April 1990.

[305] L. Schwiebert and D. N. Jayasimha, "Optimal fully adaptive wormhole routing for meshes," *Proceedings of Supercomputing'93*, pp. 782–791, November 1993.

[306] L. Schwiebert and D. N. Jayasimha, "A universal proof technique for deadlock-free routing in interconnection networks," *Proceedings of the Symposium on Parallel Algorithms and Architectures*, pp. 175–184, July 1995.

[307] L. Schwiebert and D. N. Jayasimha, "Optimally fully adaptive minimal wormhole routing for meshes," *Journal of Parallel and Distributed Computing*, vol. 27, pp. 56–70, May 1995.

[308] L. Schwiebert and D. N. Jayasimha, "A necessary and sufficient condition for deadlock-free wormhole routing," *Journal of Parallel and Distributed Computing*, vol. 32, no. 1, pp. 103–117, January 1996.

[309] S. L. Scott, "Synchronization and communication in the T3E multiprocessor," *Proceedings of the 7th International Conference on Architectural Support for Programming Languages and Operating Systems*, pp. 26–36, October 1996.

[310] S. L. Scott and J. R. Goodman, "The impact of pipelined channels on k-ary n-cube networks," *IEEE Transactions on Parallel and Distributed Systems*, vol. 5, no. 1, pp. 2–16, January 1994.

[311] S. L. Scott and G. Thorson, "Optimized routing in the Cray T3D," *Proceedings of the Workshop on Parallel Computer Routing and Communication*, pp. 281–294, May 1994.

[312] S. L. Scott and G. Thorson, "The Cray T3E network: adaptive routing in a high performance 3D torus," *Proceedings of Hot Interconnects Symposium IV*, August 1996.

[313] C. L. Seitz, "The Cosmic Cube," *Communications of the ACM*, vol. 28, no. 1, pp. 22–33, January 1985.

[314] C. L. Seitz and W. Su, "A family of routing and communication chips based on the Mosaic," *Proceedings of the Washington Symposium on Integrated Systems*, 1993.

[315] S. Shafer and K. Ghose, "Improving parallel program execution time with message consolidation," *Proceedings of the 8th International Parallel Processing Symposium*, pp. 736–742, April 1994.

[316] K. G. Shin and S. W. Daniel, "Analysis and implementation of hybrid switching," *IEEE Transactions on Computers*, vol. C-45, no. 6, pp. 684–692, June 1996.

[317] H. J. Siegel, et al., "Using the multistage cube network topology in parallel supercomputers," *Proceedings of the IEEE*, vol. 77, pp. 1932–1953, December 1989.

[318] F. Silla and J. Duato, "Improving the efficiency of adaptive routing in networks with irregular topology," *Proceedings of the 1997 Conference on High Performance Computing*, December 1997.

[319] F. Silla, et al., "Efficient adaptive routing in networks of workstations with irregular topology," *Proceedings of the Workshop on Communications and Architectural Support for Network-based Parallel Computing*, pp. 46–60, February 1997.

[320] M. Singhal, "Deadlock detection in distributed systems," *IEEE Computer*, vol. 22, no. 11, pp. 37–48, November 1989.

[321] R. Sivaram, D. K. Panda, and C. B. Stunkel, "Efficient broadcast and multicast on multistage interconnection networks using multiport encoding," *Proceedings of the 8th IEEE Symposium on Parallel and Distributed Processing*, pp. 36–45, October 1996.

[322] A. Sivasubramaniam, et al., "Machine abstractions and locality issues in studying parallel systems," Technical Report GIT–CC–93/63, Georgia Institute of Technology, October 1993.

[323] M. Snir et al., "The communication software and parallel environment of the IBM SP2," *IBM Systems Journal*, vol. 34, no. 2, pp. 205–221, 1995.

[324] M. Snir, et al., *MPI: The Complete Reference*, Cambridge, MA, MIT Press, 1996.

[325] H. S. Stone, "Parallel processing with the perfect shuffle," *IEEE Transactions on Computers*, vol. 20, pp. 153–161, February 1971.

[326] C. B. Stunkel, et al., "Architecture and implementation of Vulcan," *Proceedings of the 8th International Parallel Processing Symposium*, pp. 266–274, April 1994.

[327] C. B. Stunkel, et al., "The SP1 high-performance switch," *Proceedings of the Scalable High Performance Computing Conference*, pp. 150–157, May 1994.

[328] C. B. Stunkel, et al., "The SP-2 communication subsystem," Technical Report, IBM T. J. Watson Research Center, August 1994.

[329] C. B. Stunkel, et al., "The SP2 high-performance switch," *IBM Systems Journal*, vol. 34, no. 2, pp. 185–204, February 1995.

[330] C. Su and K. G. Shin, "Adaptive deadlock-free routing in multicomputers using only one extra channel," *Proceedings of the 1993 International Conference on Parallel Processing*, August 1993.

[331] C. Su and K. G. Shin, "Adaptive fault-tolerant deadlock-free routing in meshes and hypercubes," *IEEE Transactions on Computers*, vol. 45, no. 6, pp. 666–683, June 1996.

[332] Y.-J. Suh, et al., "Software based fault-tolerant oblivious routing in pipelined networks," *Proceedings of the 1995 International Conference on Parallel Processing*, vol. 1. pp. 101–105, August 1995.

[333] H. Sullivan and T. R. Bashkow, "A large scale, homogeneous, fully distributed parallel machine," *Proceedings of the 4th International Symposium on Computer Architecture*, March 1977.

[334] V. S. Sunderam, et al., "The PVM concurrent computing system: Evolution, experiences, and trends," *Parallel Computing*, vol. 20, no. 4, pp. 531–545, April 1994.

[335] T. Szymanski, "Hypermeshes: Optical interconnection networks for parallel processing," *Journal of Parallel and Distributed Computing*, vol. 26, pp. 1–23, January 1995.

[336] N. Tanabe, et al, "Base-m n-cube: High performance interconnection networks for highly parallel computer PRODIGY," *Proceedings of the 1991 International Conference on Parallel Processing*, August 1991.

[337] A. S. Tanenbaum, *Computer Networks*, (2nd ed.), Englewood Cliffs, NJ, Prentice-Hall, 1988.

[338] D. Tang and R. Iyer, "Dependability measurement and modeling of computer systems," *IEEE Transactions on Computers*, vol. 42, no. 1, pp. 62–75, January 1993.

[339] Thinking Machines Corporation, *CM Fortran Programming Guide*, January 1991.

[340] Thinking Machines Corporation, *The Connection Machine CM-5 Technical Summary*, October 1991.

[341] Y.-J. Tsai and P. K. McKinley, "An extended dominating node approach to collective communication in wormhole-routed 2D meshes," *Proceedings of the Scalable High-Performance Computing Conference*, pp. 199–206, May 1994.

[342] Y.-C. Tseng, D. K. Panda, and T.-H. Lai, "A trip-based multicasting model in wormhole-routed networks with virtual channels," *IEEE Transactions on Parallel and Distributed Systems*, vol. 7, no. 2, pp. 138–150, February 1996.

[343] J. H. Upadhyay, V. Varavithya, and P. Mohapatra, "An efficient and balanced routing in two-dimensional meshes," in *Proceedings of the First International Symposium on High-Performance Computer Architecture*, pp. 112–121, January 1995.

[344] L. G. Valiant, "A scheme for fast parallel communication," *SIAM Journal on Computing*, vol. 11, pp. 350–361, 1982.

[345] V. Varavithya and P. Mohapatra, "Tree-based multicasting on wormhole routed multistage interconnection networks," *Proceedings of the 1997 International Conference on Parallel Processing*, August 1997.

[346] S. Warnakulasuriya and T. M. Pinkston, "Characterization of deadlocks in interconnection networks," *Proceedings of the 11th International Parallel Processing Symposium*, pp. 80–86, April 1997.

[347] S. Wills, et al., "The offset cube: An optoelectronic interconnection network," *Proceedings of the Workshop on Parallel Computer Routing and Communication*, pp. 86–100, May 1994.

[348] L. D. Wittie, "Communication structures for large networks of microcomputers," *IEEE Transactions on Computers*, vol. C-30, no. 4, pp. 264–273, April 1981.

[349] P. H. Worley and I. T. Foster, "PSTSWM v4.0 (ParkBench MPI version)," December 1995. Available at *http://www.netlib.org/parkbench/compapps*.

[350] J. Wu, "Unicasting in faulty hypercubes using safety levels," *Proceedings of the 1995 International Conference on Parallel Processing*, vol. III, pp. 133–136, August 1995. Also available as Technical Report TR-CSE-95-2, Department of Computer Science and Engineering, Florida Atlantic University.

[351] C. L. Wu and T.-Y. Feng, "On a class of multistage interconnection networks," *IEEE Transactions on Computers*, vol. C-29, pp. 694–702, August 1980.

[352] H. Xu, Y. Gui and L. M. Ni, "Optimal software multicast in wormhole routed multistage networks," *Proceedings of Supercomputing*, pp. 703–712, 1994.

[353] Z. Xu and K. Hwang, "Modeling communication overhead: MPI and MPL performance on the IBM SP2," *IEEE Parallel & Distributed Technology*, pp. 9–23, Spring 1996.

[354] H. Xu, P. K. McKinley and L. M. Ni, "Efficient implementation of barrier synchronization in wormhole-routed hypercube multicomputers," *Journal of Parallel and Distributed Computing*, vol. 16, pp. 172–184, October 1992.

[355] W. Yost, *Cost Effective Fault Tolerance for Network Routing*, Master's Thesis, Department of Computer Science and Engineering, University of Washington, Seattle, WA., 1995.

[356] H. Zima, P. Brezany, B. Chapman, P. Mehrotra and A. Schwald, *Vienna Fortran: A Language Specification (Version 1.1)*, 1991.

Index

IEEE
COMPUTER
SOCIETY

Press Activities Board

IEEE Computer Society Publications

The world-renowned Computer Society publishes, promotes, and distributes a wide variety of authoritative computer science and engineering texts. These books are available in two formats: 100 percent original material by authors preeminent in their field who focus on relevant topics and cutting-edge research, and reprint collections consisting of carefully selected groups of previously published papers with accompanying original introductory and explanatory text.

Submission of proposals: For guidelines and information on Computer Society books, send e-mail to cs.books@computer.org or write to the Acquisitions Editor, IEEE Computer Society, P.O. Box 3014, 10662 Los Vaqueros Circle, Los Alamitos, CA 90720-1314. Telephone +1 714-821-8380. FAX +1 714-761-1784.

IEEE Computer Society Proceedings

The Computer Society also produces and actively promotes the proceedings of more than 130 acclaimed international conferences each year in multimedia formats that include hard and softcover books, CD-ROMs, videos, and on-line publications.

For information on Computer Society proceedings, send e-mail to cs.books@computer.org or write to Proceedings, IEEE Computer Society, P.O. Box 3014, 10662 Los Vaqueros Circle, Los Alamitos, CA 90720-1314. Telephone +1 714-821-8380. FAX +1 714-761-1784.

Additional information regarding the Computer Society, conferences and proceedings, CD-ROMs, videos, and books can also be accessed from our web site at http://computer.org/cspress

4/15/97